S0-AXI-927

Process Mining

Wil M.P. van der Aalst

Process Mining

Discovery, Conformance and Enhancement of Business Processes

Wil M.P. van der Aalst
Department Mathematics & Computer Science
Eindhoven University of Technology
Den Dolech 2
5612 AZ Eindhoven
The Netherlands
w.m.p.v.d.aalst@tue.nl

ISBN 978-3-642-19344-6 e-ISBN 978-3-642-19345-3
DOI 10.1007/978-3-642-19345-3
Springer Heidelberg Dordrecht London New York

Library of Congress Control Number: 2011926240

ACM Computing Classification (1998): H.4.1, H.2.8, I.2.6, F.3.2, D.2.2, J.1

Cover design: deblik

Printed on acid-free paper

Springer is part of Springer Science+Business Media (www.springer.com)

Thanks to Karin for understanding that science is more rewarding than running errands

Thanks to all people that contributed to ProM; the fruits of their efforts demonstrate that sharing a common goal is more meaningful than "cashing in the next publon"[1]

In remembrance of Gerry Straatman-Beelen (1932–2010)

[1] publon = smallest publishable unit

Preface

Process mining provides a new means to improve processes in a variety of application domains. There are two main drivers for this new technology. On the one hand, more and more events are being recorded thus providing detailed information about the history of processes. Despite the omnipresence of event data, most organizations diagnose problems based on fiction rather than facts. On the other hand, vendors of Business Process Management (BPM) and Business Intelligence (BI) software have been promising miracles. Although BPM and BI technologies received lots of attention, they did not live up to the expectations raised by academics, consultants, and software vendors.

Process mining is an emerging discipline providing comprehensive sets of tools to provide fact-based insights and to support process improvements. This new discipline builds on process model-driven approaches and data mining. However, process mining is much more than an amalgamation of existing approaches. For example, existing data mining techniques are too data-centric to provide a comprehensive understanding of the end-to-end processes in an organization. BI tools focus on simple dashboards and reporting rather than clear-cut business process insights. BPM suites heavily rely on experts modeling idealized to-be processes and do not help the stakeholders to understand the as-is processes.

This book presents a range of process mining techniques that help organizations to uncover their actual business processes. Process mining is not limited to process discovery. By tightly coupling event data and process models, it is possible to check conformance, detect deviations, predict delays, support decision making, and recommend process redesigns. Process mining breathes life into otherwise static process models and puts today's massive data volumes in a process context. Hence, managements trends related to process improvement (e.g., Six Sigma, TQM, CPI, and CPM) and compliance (SOX, BAM, etc.) can benefit from process mining.

Process mining, as described in this book, emerged in the last decade [102, 106]. However, the roots date back about half a century. For example, Anil Nerode presented an approach to synthesize finite-state machines from example traces in 1958 [71], Carl Adam Petri introduced the first modeling language adequately capturing concurrency in 1962 [73], and Mark Gold was the first to systematically explore different notions of learnability in 1967 [45]. When data mining started to flourish in the nineties, little attention was given to processes. Moreover, only recently event logs have become omnipresent thus enabling end-to-end process discovery. Since the first survey on process mining in 2003 [102], progress has been spectacular. Process mining techniques have become mature and supported by various tools. Moreover, whereas initially the primary focus was on process discovery, the process mining spectrum has broadened markedly. For instance, conformance checking, multi-perspective process mining, and operational support have become integral parts of ProM, one of the leading process mining tools.

This is the first book on process mining. Therefore, the intended audience is quite broad. The book provides a comprehensive overview of the state-of-the-art in process mining. It is intended as an introduction to the topic for practitioners, students, and academics. On the one hand, the book is accessible for people that are new to the topic. On the other hand, the book does not avoid explaining important concepts on a rigorous manner. The book aims to be self-contained while covering the entire process mining spectrum from process discovery to operational support. Therefore, it also serves as a reference handbook for people dealing with BPM or BI on a day-to-day basis.

The reader can immediately put process mining into practice due to the applicability of the techniques, the availability of (open-source) process mining software, and the abundance of event data in today's information systems. I sincerely hope that you enjoy reading this book and start using some of the amazing process mining techniques available today.

Schleiden, Germany
December 2010

Wil M.P. van der Aalst

Acknowledgements

Many individuals and organizations contributed to the techniques and tools described in this book. Therefore, it is important to acknowledge their support, efforts, and contributions.

All of this started in 1999 with a research project named "Process Design by Discovery: Harvesting Workflow Knowledge from Ad-hoc Executions" initiated by Ton Weijters and myself. At that time, I was still working as a visiting professor at the University of Colorado in Boulder. However, the research school BETA had encouraged me to start collaborating with existing staff in my new research group at TU/e (Eindhoven University of Technology). After talking to Ton it was clear that we could benefit from combining his knowledge of machine learning with my knowledge of workflow management and Petri nets. Process mining (at that time we called it workflow mining) was the obvious topic for which we could combine our expertise. This was the start of a very successful collaboration. Thanks Ton!

Since then many PhD students have been working on the topic: Laura Maruster, Ana Karla Alves de Medeiros, Boudewijn van Dongen, Minseok Song, Christian Günther, Anne Rozinat, Carmen Bratosin, R.P. Jagadeesh Chandra (JC) Bose, Ronny Mans, Maja Pesic, Joyce Nakatumba, Helen Schonenberg, Arya Adriansyah, and Joos Buijs. I'm extremely grateful for their efforts.

Ana Karla Alves de Medeiros was the first PhD student to work on the topic under my supervision (genetic process mining). She did a wonderful job; her thesis on genetic process mining was awarded with the prestigious ASML 2007 Promotion Prize and was selected as the best thesis by the KNAW research school BETA. Also Boudewijn van Dongen has been involved in the development of ProM right from the start. As a Master student he already developed the process mining tool EMiT, i.e., the predecessor of ProM. He turned out to be a brilliant PhD student and developed a variety of process mining techniques. Eric Verbeek did a PhD on workflow verification, but over time he got more and more involved in process mining research and the development of ProM. Many people underestimate the importance of a scientific programmer like Eric. Tool development and continuity are essential for scientific progress! Boudewijn and Eric have been the driving force behind

ProM and their contributions have been crucial for process mining research at TU/e. Moreover, they are always willing to help others. Thanks guys!

Christian Günther and Anne Rozinat joined the team in 2005. Their contributions have been of crucial importance for extending the scope of process mining and lifting the ambition level. Christian managed to make ProM look beautiful while significantly improving its performance. Moreover, his Fuzzy miner facilitated dealing with Spaghetti processes. Anne managed to widen the process mining spectrum by adding conformance checking and multi-perspective process mining to ProM. It is great that they succeeded in founding a process mining company (Fluxicon). Another person crucial for the development of ProM is Peter van den Brand. He set up the initial framework and played an important role in the development of the architecture of ProM 6. Based on his experiences with ProM, he set up a process mining company (Futura Process Intelligence). It is great to work with people like Peter, Christian, and Anne; they are essential for turning research results into commercial products. I sincerely hope that Fluxicon and Futura Process Intelligence continue to be successful (not only because of prospective sports cars ...).

Academics of various universities contributed to ProM and supported our process mining research. We are grateful to the Technical University of Lisbon, Katholieke Universiteit Leuven, Universitat Politècnica de Catalunya, Universität Paderborn, University of Rostock, Humboldt-Universität zu Berlin, University of Calabria, Queensland University of Technology, Tsinghua University, Universität Innsbruck, Ulsan National Institute of Science and Technology, Università di Bologna, Zhejiang University, Vienna University of Technology, Universität Ulm, Open University, Jilin University, University of Padua, and University of Nancy for their help. I would also like to thank the members of the IEEE Task Force on Process Mining for promoting the topic. We are grateful to all other organizations that supported process mining research at TU/e: NWO, STW, EU, IOP, LOIS, BETA, SIKS, Stichting EIT Informatica Onderwijs, Pallas Athena, IBM, LaQuSo, Philips Healthcare, ESI, Jacquard, Nuffic, BPM Usergroup, and WWTF. Special thanks go to Pallas Athena for promoting the topic of process mining and their collaboration in a variety of projects. More than 100 organizations provided event logs that helped us to improve our process mining techniques. Here, I would like to explicitly mention the AMC hospital, Philips Healthcare, ASML, Ricoh, Vestia, Catharina hospital, Thales, Océ, Rijkswaterstaat, Heusden, Harderwijk, Deloitte, and all organizations involved in the SUPER, ACSI, PoSecCo, and CoSeLoG projects. We are grateful for allowing us to use their data and for providing feedback.

It is impossible to name all of the individuals that contributed to ProM or helped to advance process mining. Nevertheless, I would like to make a modest attempt. Besides the people mentioned earlier, I would like to thank Piet Bakker, Huub de Beer, Tobias Blickle, Andrea Burattin, Riet van Buul, Toon Calders, Jorge Cardoso, Josep Carmona, Alina Chipaila, Francisco Curbera, Marlon Dumas, Schahram Dustdar, Paul Eertink, Dyon Egberts, Dirk Fahland, Diogo Ferreira, Walid Gaaloul, Stijn Goedertier, Adela Grando, Gianluigi Greco, Dolf Grünbauer, Antonella Guzzo, Kees van Hee, Joachim Herbst, Arthur ter Hofstede, John Hoogland, Ivo de Jong, Ivan Khodyrev, Thom Langerwerf, Massimiliano de Leoni, Jiafei Li, Ine van der

Ligt, Zheng Liu, Niels Lohmann, Peter Hornix, Fabrizio Maggi, Jan Mendling, Frits Minderhoud, Arnold Moleman, Marco Montali, Michael zur Muehlen, Jorge Munoz-Gama, Mariska Netjes, Andriy Nikolov, Mykola Pechenizkiy, Carlos Pedrinaci, Viara Popova, Silvana Quaglini, Manfred Reichert, Hajo Reijers, Remmert Remmerts de Vries, Stefanie Rinderle-Ma, Marcello La Rosa, Michael Rosemann, Vladimir Rubin, Stefania Rusu, Eduardo Portela Santos, Natalia Sidorova, Alessandro Sperduti, Christian Stahl, Keith Swenson, Nikola Trcka, Kenny van Uden, Irene Vanderfeesten, George Varvaressos, Marc Verdonk, Sicco Verwer, Jan Vogelaar, Hans Vrins, Jianmin Wang, Teun Wagemakers, Barbara Weber, Lijie Wen, Jan Martijn van der Werf, Mathias Weske, Michael Westergaard, Moe Wynn, Bart Ydo, and Marco Zapletal for their support. Thanks to all that read earlier drafts of this book (special thanks go to Christian, Eric, and Ton for their detailed comments).

Thanks to Springer-Verlag for publishing this book. Ralf Gerstner encouraged me to write this book and handled things in a truly excellent manner. Thanks Ralf!

More than 95% of book was written in beautiful Schleiden. Despite my sabbatical, there were many other tasks competing for attention. Thanks to my weekly visits to Schleiden (without Internet access!), it was possible to write this book in a three month period. The excellent coffee of Serafin helped when proofreading the individual chapters, the scenery did the rest.

As always, acknowledgements end with thanking the people most precious. Lion's share of credits should go to Karin, Anne, Willem, Sjaak, and Loes. They often had to manage without me under difficult circumstances. Without their continuing support, this book would have taken ages.

Schleiden, Germany Wil M.P. van der Aalst
December 2010

Contents

Chapter 1
Introduction

Information systems are becoming more and more intertwined with the operational processes they support. As a result, multitudes of events are recorded by today's information systems. Nevertheless, organizations have problems extracting value from these data. The goal of *process mining* is to use event data to extract process-related information, e.g., to automatically *discover* a process model by observing events recorded by some enterprise system. To show the importance of process mining, this chapter discusses the spectacular growth of event data and links this to the limitations of classical approaches to business process management. To explain the basic concepts, a small example is used. Finally, it is shown that process mining can play an important role in realizing the promises made by contemporary management trends such as SOX and Six Sigma.

1.1 Data Explosion

The expanding capabilities of information systems and other systems that depend on computing, are well characterized by Moore's law. Gordon Moore, the cofounder of Intel, predicted in 1965 that the number of components in integrated circuits would double every year. During the last fifty years, the growth has indeed been exponential, albeit at a slightly slower pace. For example, the number of transistors on integrated circuits has been doubling every two years. Disk capacity, performance of computers per unit cost, the number of pixels per dollar, etc. have been growing at a similar pace. Besides these incredible technological advances, people and organizations depend more and more on computerized devices and information sources on the Internet. The IDC Digital Universe Study of May 2010 illustrates the spectacular growth of data [56]. This study estimates that the amount of digital information (cf. personal computers, digital cameras, servers, sensors) stored exceeds 1 Zettabyte and predicts that the "digital universe" will to grow to 35 Zettabytes in 2010. The IDC study characterizes 35 Zettabytes as a "stack of DVDs reaching halfway to Mars". This is what we refer to as the *data explosion*.

W.M.P. van der Aalst, *Process Mining*,
DOI 10.1007/978-3-642-19345-3_1, © Springer-Verlag Berlin Heidelberg 2011

From Bits to Zettabytes

A "bit" is the smallest unit of information possible. One bit has two possible values: 1 (on) and 0 (off). A "byte" is composed of 8 bits and can represent $2^8 = 256$ values. To talk about larger amounts of data, multiples of 1000 are used: 1 Kilobyte (KB) equals 1000 bytes, 1 Megabyte (MB) equals 1000 KB, 1 Gigabyte (GB) equals 1000 MB, 1 Terabyte (TB) equals 1000 GB, 1 Petabyte (PB) equals 1000 TB, 1 Exabyte (EB) equals 1000 PB, and 1 Zettabyte (ZB) equals 1000 EB. Hence, 1 Zettabyte is 10^{21} = 1,000,000,000,000,000,000,000 bytes. Note that here we used the International System of Units (SI) set of unit prefixes, also known as SI prefixes, rather than binary prefixes. If we assume binary prefixes, then 1 Kilobyte is $2^{10} = 1024$ bytes, 1 Megabyte is $2^{20} = 1{,}048{,}576$ bytes, and 1 Zettabyte is $2^{70} \approx 1.18 \times 10^{21}$ bytes.

Most of the data stored in the digital universe is unstructured and organizations have problems dealing with such large quantities of data. One of the main challenges of today's organizations is to extract information and value from data stored in their information systems.

The importance of information systems is not only reflected by the spectacular growth of data, but also by the role that these systems play in today's business processes as the digital universe and the physical universe are becoming more and more aligned. For example, the "state of a bank" is mainly determined by the data stored in the bank's information system. Money has become a predominantly digital entity. When booking a flight over the Internet, the customer is interacting with many organizations (airline, travel agency, bank, and various brokers), often without actually realizing it. If the booking is successful, the customer receives an e-ticket. Note that an e-ticket is basically a number, thus illustrating the alignment between the digital and physical universe. When the SAP system of a large manufacturer indicates that a particular product is out of stock, it is impossible to sell or ship the product even when it is available in physical form. Technologies such as RFID (Radio Frequency Identification), GPS (Global Positioning System), and sensor networks will stimulate a further alignment of the digital universe and the physical universe. RFID tags make it possible to track and trace individual items. Also note that more and more devices are being monitored. For example, Philips Healthcare is monitoring its medical equipment (e.g., X-ray machines and CT scanners) all over the world. This helps Philips to understand the needs of customers, test their systems under realistic circumstances, anticipate problems, service systems remotely, and learn from recurring problems. The success of the "App Store" of Apple illustrates that location-awareness combined with a continuous Internet connection enables new ways to pervasively intertwine the digital universe and the physical universe.

The growth of a digital universe that is well-aligned with processes in organizations makes it possible to record and analyze *events*. Events may range from the withdrawal of cash from an ATM, a doctor setting the dosage of an X-ray machine, a citizen applying for a driver license, the submission of a tax declaration, and the receipt of an e-ticket number by a traveler. The challenge is to *exploit event data in a meaningful way*, for example, to provide insights, identify bottlenecks, anticipate problems, record policy violations, recommend countermeasures, and streamline processes. This is what process mining is all about!

1.2 Limitations of Modeling

Process mining, i.e., extracting valuable, process-related information from event logs, complements existing approaches to *Business Process Management* (BPM). BPM is the discipline that *combines knowledge from information technology and knowledge from management sciences and applies this to operational business processes* [93, 127]. It has received considerable attention in recent years due to its potential for significantly increasing productivity and saving cost. BPM can be seen as an extension of *Workflow Management* (WFM). WFM primarily focuses on the automation of business processes [57, 61, 98], whereas BPM has a broader scope: from process automation and process analysis to process management and the organization of work. On the one hand, BPM aims to improve operational business processes, possibly without the use of new technologies. For example, by modeling a business process and analyzing it using simulation, management may get ideas on how to reduce costs while improving service levels. On the other hand, BPM is often associated with software to manage, control, and support operational processes. This was the initial focus of WFM. Traditional WFM technology aims at the automation of business processes in a rather mechanistic manner without much attention for human factors and management support.

Process-Aware Information Systems (PAISs) include the traditional WFM systems, but also include systems that provide more flexibility or support specific tasks [37]. For example, larger ERP (Enterprise Resource Planning) systems (SAP, Oracle), CRM (Customer Relationship Management) systems, rule-based systems, call center software, high-end middleware (WebSphere), etc. can be seen as process-aware, although they do not necessarily control processes through some generic workflow engine. Instead, these systems have in common that there is an explicit process notion and that the information system is aware of the processes it supports. Also a database system or e-mail program may be used to execute steps in some business process. However, such software tools are not "aware" of the processes they are used in. Therefore, they are not actively involved in the management and orchestration of the processes they are used for. Some authors use the term BPMS (BPM system), or simply PMS (Process Management System), to refer systems that are "aware" of the processes they support. We use the term PAIS to stress that the scope is much broader than conventional workflow technology.

BPM and PAIS have in common that they heavily rely on *process models*. A plethora of notations exists to model operational business processes (e.g., Petri nets, BPMN, UML, and EPCs), some of which will be discussed in the next chapter. These notations have in common that processes are described in terms of activities

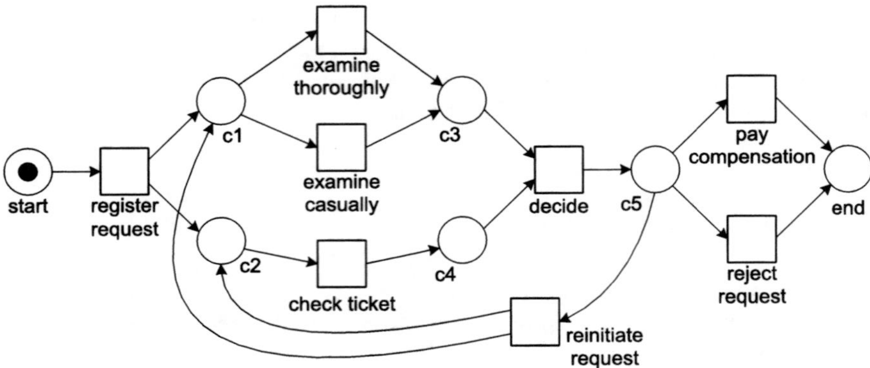

Fig. 1.1 A Petri net modeling the handling of compensation requests

(and possibly subprocesses). The ordering of these activities is modeled by describing casual dependencies. Moreover, the process model may also describe temporal properties, specify the creation and use of data, e.g., to model decisions, and stipulate the way that resources interact with the process (e.g., roles, allocation rules, and priorities).

Figure 1.1 shows a process model expressed in terms of a *Petri net* [35]. The model describes the handling of a request for compensation within an airline. Customers may request compensation for various reasons, e.g., a delayed or canceled flight. As Fig. 1.1 shows, the process starts by registering the request. This activity is modeled by transition *register request*. Each *transition* is represented by a square. Transitions are connected through *places* that model possible states of the process. Each place is represented by a circle. In a Petri net a transition is *enabled*, i.e., the corresponding activity can occur, if all input places hold a *token*. Transition *register request* has only one input place (*start*) and this place initially contains a token to represent the request for compensation. Hence, the corresponding activity is enabled and can occur. This is also referred to as *firing*. When firing, the transition consumes one token from each of its input places and produces one token for each of its output places. Hence, the firing of transition *register request* results in the removal of the token from input place *start* and the production of two tokens: one for output place $c1$ and one for output place $c2$. Tokens are shown as black dots. The configuration of tokens over places—in this case the state of the request—is referred to as *marking*. Figure 1.1 shows the initial marking consisting of one token in place *start*. The marking after firing transition *register request* has two tokens: one in place $c1$ and one in place $c2$. After firing transition *register request*, three transitions are enabled. The token in place $c2$ enables transition *check ticket*. This transition models an administrative check to see whether the customer is eligible to issue a request. For example, while executing *check ticket* it is verified whether the customer indeed has a ticket issued by the airline. In parallel, the token in $c1$ enables both *examine thoroughly* and *examine casually*. Firing *examine thoroughly* will remove the token from $c1$, thus disabling *examine casually*. Similarly, the oc-

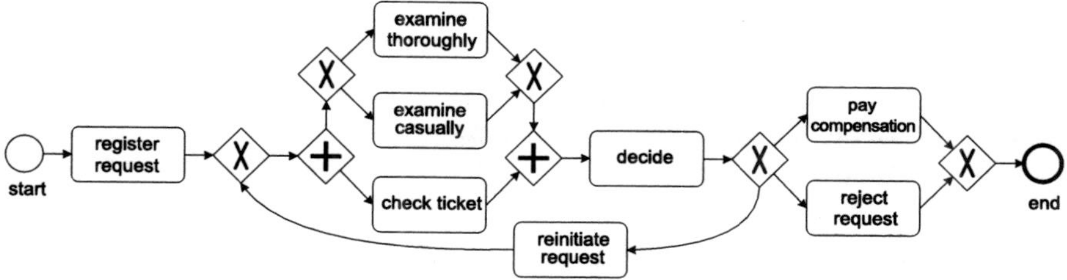

Fig. 1.2 The same process modeled in terms of BPMN

currence of *examine casually* will disable *examine thoroughly*. In other words, there is a choice between these two activities. Transition *examine thoroughly* is executed for requests that are suspicious or complex. Straightforward requests only need a casual examination. Firing *check ticket* does not disable any other transition, i.e., it can occur concurrently with *examine thoroughly* or *examine casually*. Transition *decide* is only enabled if both input places contain a token. The ticket needs to be checked (token in place $c4$) and the casual or thorough examination of the request has been conducted (token in place $c3$). Hence, the process synchronizes before making a decision. Transition *decide* consumes two tokens and produces one token for $c5$. Three transitions share $c5$ as an input place, thus modeling the three possible outcomes of the decision. The requested compensation is paid (transition *pay compensation* fires), the request is declined (transition *reject request* fires), or further processing is needed (transition *reinitiate request* fires). In the latter case, the process returns to the state marking places $c1$ and $c2$: transition *reinitiate request* consumes a token from $c5$ and produces a token for each of its output places. This was the marking directly following the occurrence of *register request*. In principle, several iterations are possible. The process ends after paying the compensation or rejecting the request.

Figure 1.1 models the process as a Petri net. There exist many different notations for process models. Figure 1.2 models the same process in terms of a so-called BPMN diagram [72, 127]. The *Business Process Modeling Notation* (BPMN) uses explicit *gateways* rather than places to model the control-flow logic. The diamonds with a "×" sign denote XOR split/join gateways, whereas diamonds with a "+" sign denote AND split/join gateways. The diamond directly following activity *register request* is an XOR-join gateway. This gateway is used to be able to "jump back" after making the decision to reinitiate the request. After this XOR-join gateway, there is an AND-split gateway to model that the checking of the ticket can be done in parallel with the selected examination type (thorough or casual). The remainder of the BPMN diagram is self explanatory as the behavior is identical to the Petri net described before.

Figures 1.1 and 1.2 show only the *control-flow*, i.e., the ordering of activities for the process described earlier. This is a rather limited view on business processes. Therefore, most modeling languages offer notations for modeling other perspectives such as the organizational or resource perspective ("The decision needs to be made by a manager"), the data perspective ("After four iteration always a decision is made unless more than 1 million Euro is claimed"), and the time perspective ("After two weeks the problem is escalated"). Although there are important differences between the various process modeling languages, we do not elaborate one these in this book. Instead, we refer to the systematic comparisons in the context of the *Workflow Patterns Initiative* [101, 130]. This allows us to focus on the role that process models play in BPM.

What Are Process Models Used for?

- *Insight*: while making a model, the modeler is triggered to view the process from various angles.
- *Discussion*: the stakeholders use models to structure discussions.
- *Documentation*: processes are documented for instructing people or certification purposes (cf. ISO 9000 quality management).
- *Verification*: process models are analyzed to find errors in systems or procedures (e.g., potential deadlocks).
- *Performance analysis*: techniques like simulation can be used to understand the factors influencing response times, service levels, etc.
- *Animation*: models enable end users to "play out" different scenarios and thus provide feedback to the designer.
- *Specification*: models can be used to describe a PAIS before it is implemented and can hence serve as a "contract" between the developer and the end user/management.
- *Configuration*: models can be used to configure a system.

Clearly, process models play an important role in larger organizations. When redesigning processes and introducing new information systems, process models are used for a variety of reasons. Typically, two types of models are used: (a) *informal models* and (b) *formal models* (also referred to as "executable" models). Informal models are used for discussion and documentation whereas formal models are used for analysis or enactment (i.e., the actual execution of process). On the one end of the spectrum there are "PowerPoint diagrams" showing high-level processes whereas on the other end of the spectrum there are process models captured in executable code. Whereas informal models are typically ambiguous and vague, formal models tend to have a rather narrow focus or are too detailed to be understandable by the stakeholders. The lack of alignment between both types of models has been discussed extensively in BPM literature [37, 53, 90, 93, 100, 127, 131]. Here, we would like to provide another view on the matter. Independent of the kind of model—informal or formal—one can reflect on the alignment between model and reality. A process model used to configure a workflow management system is probably well-aligned with reality as the model is used to force people to work in a particular way. Unfortunately, most hand-made models are disconnected from reality and provide only an idealized view on the processes at hand. Moreover, also formal models that allow for rigorous analysis techniques may have little to do with the actual process.

The value of models is limited if too little attention is paid to the alignment of model and reality. Process models become "paper tigers" when the people involved cannot trust them. For example, it makes no sense to conduct simulation experiments while using a model that assumes an idealized version of the real process. It is likely that—based on such an idealized model—incorrect redesign decisions are made. It is also precarious to start a new implementation project guided by process models that hide reality. A system implemented on the basis of idealized models is likely to be disruptive and unacceptable for end users. A nice illustration is the limited quality of most *reference models*. Reference models are used in the context of large enterprise systems such as SAP [25] but also to document processes for particular branches, cf. the NVVB (Nederlandse Vereniging Voor Burgerzaken) models describing the core processes in Dutch municipalities. The idea is that "best practices" are shared among different organizations. Unfortunately, the quality of such models leaves much to be desired. For example, the SAP reference model has very little to do with the processes actually supported by SAP. In fact, more than 20 percent of the SAP models contain serious flaws (deadlocks, livelocks, etc.) [66]. Such models are not aligned with reality and, thus, have little value for end users.

Given (a) the interest in process models, (b) the abundance of event data, and (c) the limited quality of hand-made models, it seems worthwhile to relate event data to process models. This way the actual processes can be discovered and existing process models can be evaluated and enhanced. This is precisely what process mining aims to achieve.

1.3 Process Mining

To position process mining, we first describe the so-called *BPM life-cycle* using Fig. 1.3. The life-cycle describes the different phases of managing a particular business process. In the *design* phase, a process is designed. This model is transformed into a running system in the *configuration/implementation* phase. If the model is already in executable form and a WFM or BPM system is already running, this phase may be very short. However, if the model is informal and needs to be hard-coded in conventional software, this phase may take substantial time. After the system supports the designed processes, the *enactment/monitoring* phase starts. In this phase, the processes are running while being monitored by management to see if any changes are needed. Some of these changes are handled in the *adjustment* phase shown in Fig. 1.3. In this phase, the process is not redesigned and no new software is created; only predefined controls are used to adapt or reconfigure the process. The *diagnosis/requirements* phase evaluates the process and monitors emerging requirements due to changes in the environment of the process (e.g., changing policies, laws, competition). Poor performance (e.g., inability to meet service levels) or new demands imposed by the environment may trigger a new iteration of the BPM life-cycle starting with the *redesign* phase.

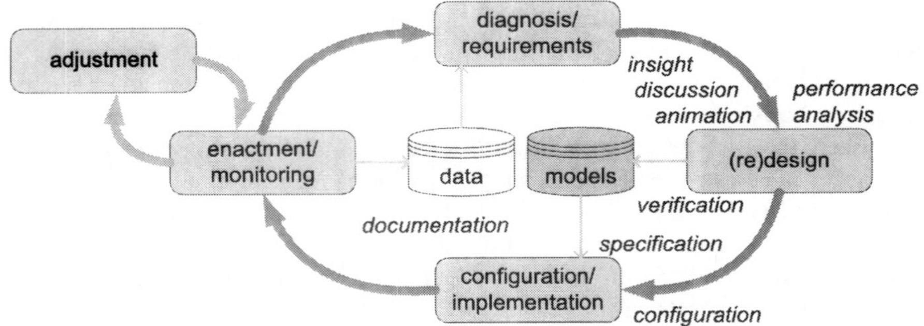

Fig. 1.3 The BPM life-cycle showing the different uses of process models

As Fig. 1.3 shows, process models play a dominant role in the (re)design and configuration/implementation phases, whereas data plays a dominant role in the enactment/monitoring and diagnosis/requirements phases. The figure also lists the different ways in which process models are used (as identified in Sect. 1.2). Until recently, there were few connections between the data produced while executing the process and the actual process design. In fact, in most organizations the diagnosis/requirements phase is not supported in a systematic and continuous manner. Only severe problems or major external changes will trigger another iteration of the life-cycle, and factual information about the current process is not actively used in redesign decisions. Process mining offers the possibility to truly "close" the BPM life-cycle. Data recorded by information systems can be used to provide a better view on the actual processes, i.e., deviations can be analyzed and the quality of models can be improved.

Process mining is a relative young research discipline that sits between machine learning and data mining on the one hand and process modeling and analysis on the other hand. The idea of process mining is to discover, monitor and improve real processes (i.e., not assumed processes) by extracting knowledge from event logs readily available in today's systems.

Figure 1.4 shows that process mining establishes links between the actual processes and their data on the one hand and process models on the other hand. As explained in Sect. 1.1, the digital universe and the physical universe become more and more aligned. Today's information systems log enormous amounts of events. Classical WFM systems (e.g., Staffware and COSA), BPM systems (e.g., BPM|one by Pallas Athena, SmartBPM by Pegasystems, FileNet, Global 360, and Teamwork by Lombardi Software), ERP systems (e.g., SAP Business Suite, Oracle E-Business Suite, and Microsoft Dynamics NAV), PDM systems (e.g., Windchill), CRM systems (e.g., Microsoft Dynamics CRM and SalesForce), middleware (e.g., IBM's WebSphere and Cordys Business Operations Platform), and hospital information systems (e.g., Chipsoft and Siemens Soarian) provide detailed information about the activities that have been executed. Figure 1.4 refers to such data as *event logs*. All of the PAISs just mentioned directly provide such event logs.

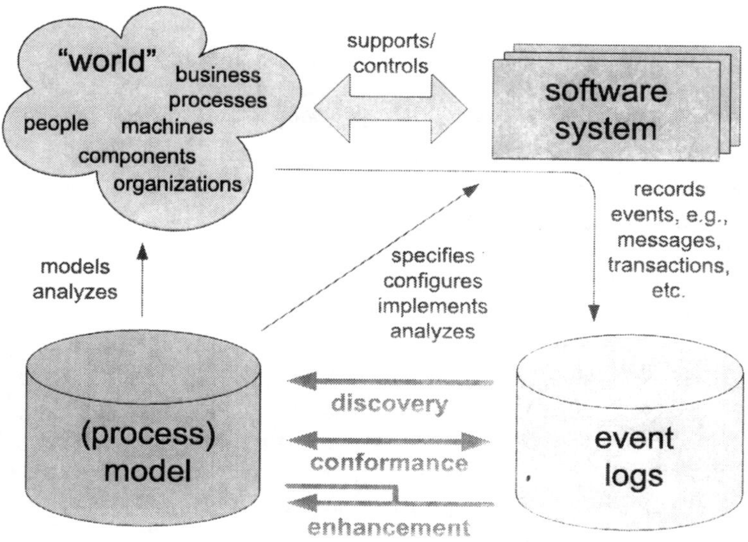

Fig. 1.4 Positioning of the three main types of process mining: *discovery*, *conformance*, and *enhancement*

However, most information systems store such information in unstructured form, e.g., event data is scattered over many tables or needs to be tapped off from subsystems exchanging messages. In such cases, event data exist but some efforts are needed to extract them. Data extraction is an integral part of any process mining effort.

Let us assume that it is possible to *sequentially record events* such that each event refers to an *activity* (i.e., a well-defined step in the process) and is related to a particular *case* (i.e., a process instance). Consider, for example, the handling of requests for compensation modeled in Fig. 1.1. The cases are individual requests and per case a *trace* of events can be recorded. An example of a possible trace is ⟨*register request*, *examine casually*, *check ticket*, *decide*, *reinitiate request*, *check ticket*, *examine thoroughly*, *decide*, *pay compensation*⟩. Here activity names are used to identify events. However, there are two *decide* events that occurred at different times (the fourth and eighth event of the trace), produced different results, and may have been conducted by different people. Obviously, it is important to distinguish these two decisions. Therefore, most event logs store additional information about events. In fact, whenever possible, process mining techniques use extra information such as the *resource* (i.e., person or device) executing or initiating the activity, the *timestamp* of the event, or *data elements* recorded with the event (e.g., the size of an order).

Event logs can be used to conduct three types of process mining as shown in Fig. 1.4.

The first type of process mining is *discovery*. A discovery technique takes an event log and produces a model without using any a-priori information. An example is the α-algorithm [103] that will be described in Chap. 5. This algorithm takes an event log and produces a Petri net explaining the behavior recorded in the log. For example, given sufficient example executions of the process shown in Fig. 1.1, the α-algorithm is able to automatically construct the Petri net without using any additional knowledge. If the event log contains information about resources, one can also discover resource-related models, e.g., a social network showing how people work together in an organization.

The second type of process mining is *conformance*. Here, an existing process model is compared with an event log of the same process. Conformance checking can be used to check if reality, as recorded in the log, conforms to the model and vice versa. For instance, there may be a process model indicating that purchase orders of more than one million Euro require two checks. Analysis of the event log will show whether this rule is followed or not. Another example is the checking of the so-called "four-eyes" principle stating that particular activities should not be executed by one and the same person. By scanning the event log using a model specifying these requirements, one can discover potential cases of fraud. Hence, conformance checking may be used to detect, locate and explain deviations, and to measure the severity of these deviations. An example is the conformance checking algorithm described in [80]. Given the model shown in Fig. 1.1 and a corresponding event log, this algorithm can quantify and diagnose deviations.

The third type of process mining is *enhancement*. Here, the idea is to extend or improve an existing process model using information about the actual process recorded in some event log. Whereas conformance checking measures the alignment between model and reality, this third type of process mining aims at changing or extending the a-priori model. One type of enhancement is *repair*, i.e., modifying the model to better reflect reality. For example, if two activities are modeled sequentially but in reality can happen in any order, then the model may be corrected to reflect this. Another type of enhancement is *extension*, i.e., adding a new perspective to the process model by cross-correlating it with the log. An example is the extension of a process model with performance data. For instance, by using timestamps in the event log of the "request for compensation" process, one can extend Fig. 1.1 to show bottlenecks, service levels, throughput times, and frequencies. Similarly, Fig. 1.1 can be extended with information about resources, decision rules, quality metrics, etc.

As indicated earlier, process models such as depicted in Figs. 1.1 and 1.2 show only the control-flow. However, when extending process models, additional perspectives are added. Moreover, discovery and conformance techniques are not limited to control-flow. For example, one can discover a social network and check the validity of some organizational model using an event log. Hence, orthogonal to the three types of mining (discovery, conformance, and enhancement), different perspectives can be identified.

In the remainder, we consider the following *perspectives*.

- The *control-flow perspective* focuses on the control-flow, i.e., the ordering of activities. The goal of mining this perspective is to find a good characterization of all possible paths, e.g., expressed in terms of a Petri net or some other notation (e.g., EPCs, BPMN, and UML ADs).
- The *organizational perspective* focuses on information about resources hidden in the log, i.e., which actors (e.g., people, systems, roles, and departments) are involved and how are they related. The goal is to either structure the organization by classifying people in terms of roles and organizational units or to show the social network.
- The *case perspective* focuses on properties of cases. Obviously, a case can be characterized by its path in the process or by the originators working on it. However, cases can also be characterized by the values of the corresponding data elements. For example, if a case represents a replenishment order, it may be interesting to know the supplier or the number of products ordered.
- The *time perspective* is concerned with the timing and frequency of events. When events bear timestamps it is possible to discover bottlenecks, measure service levels, monitor the utilization of resources, and predict the remaining processing time of running cases.

Note that the different perspectives are partially overlapping and non-exhaustive. Nevertheless, they provide a good characterization of the aspects that process mining aims to analyze.

In most examples given thus far it is assumed that process mining is done *off-line*, i.e., processes are analyzed afterward to see how they can be improved or better understood. However, more and more process mining techniques can also be used in an *online* setting. We refer to this as *operational support*. An example is the detection of nonconformance at the moment the deviation actually takes place. Another example is time prediction for running cases, i.e., given a partially executed case the remaining processing time is estimated based on historic information of similar cases. This illustrates that the "process mining spectrum" is broad and not limited to process discovery. In fact, today's process mining techniques are indeed able to support the whole BPM life-cycle shown in Fig. 1.3. Process mining is not only relevant for the design and diagnosis/requirements phases, but also for the enactment/monitoring and adjustment phases.

1.4 Analyzing an Example Log

After providing an overview of process mining and positioning it in the broader BPM discipline, we use the event log shown in Table 1.1 to clarify some of the foundational concepts. The table shows just a fragment of a possible log corresponding to the handling of requests for compensation. Each line presents one event. Note that events are already grouped per case. Case 1 has five associated events. The first event of Case 1 is the execution of activity *register request* by Pete on December 30th, 2010. Table 1.1 also shows a unique id for this event: 35654423. This is merely used for the identification of the event, e.g., to distinguish it from event 35654483 that also corresponds to the execution of activity *register request* (first event of second case). Table 1.1 shows a date and a timestamp for each event. In some event logs, this information is more coarse-grained and only a date or partial ordering of events is given. In other logs, there may be more elaborate timing information also showing when the activity was started, when it was completed, and sometimes even when it was offered to the resource. The times shown in Table 1.1 should be interpreted as completion times. In this particular event log, activities are considered to be atomic and the table does not reveal the duration of activities. In the table, each event is associated to a resource. In some event logs, this information will be missing. In other logs, more detailed information about resources may be stored, e.g., the role a resource has or elaborate authorization data. The table also shows the costs associated to events. This is an example of a data attribute. There may be many other data attributes. For example, in this particular example it would be interesting to record the outcome of the different types of examinations and checks. Another data element that could be useful for analysis is the amount of compensation requested. This could be an attribute of the whole case or stored as an attribute of the *register request* event.

Table 1.1 illustrates the typical information present in an event log. Depending on the process mining technique used and the questions at hand, only part of this information is used. The minimal requirements for process mining are that any event can be related to both a case and an activity and that events within a case are ordered. Hence, the "case id" and "activity" columns in Table 1.1 represent the bare minimum for process mining. By projecting the information in these two columns, we obtain the more compact representation shown in Table 1.2. In this table, each case is represented by a sequence of activities also referred to as *trace*. For clarity, the activity names have been transformed into single-letter labels, e.g., a denotes activity *register request*.

Process mining algorithms for process discovery can transform the information shown in Table 1.2 into process models. For instance, the basic α-algorithm [103] discovers the Petri net described earlier when providing it with the input data in Table 1.2. Figure 1.5 shows the resulting model with the compact labels just introduced. It is easy to check that all six traces in Table 1.2 are possible in the model. Let us replay the trace of the first case—$\langle a, b, d, e, h \rangle$—to show that the trace "fits" (i.e., conforms to) the model. In the initial marking shown in Fig. 1.5, a is indeed enabled because of the token in *start*. After firing a places $c1$ and $c2$ are marked, i.e., both places contain a token. b is enabled at this marking and its execution results in the marking with tokens in $c2$ and $c3$. Now we have executed $\langle a, b \rangle$ and the sequence $\langle d, e, h \rangle$ remains. The next event d is indeed enabled and its execution results in the marking enabling e (tokens in places $c3$ and $c4$). Firing e results in the marking with one token in $c5$. This marking enables the final event h in the trace.

Table 1.1 A fragment of some event log: each line corresponds to an event

Case id	Event id	Properties				
		Timestamp	Activity	Resource	Cost	...
1	35654423	30-12-2010:11.02	Register request	Pete	50	...
	35654424	31-12-2010:10.06	Examine thoroughly	Sue	400	...
	35654425	05-01-2011:15.12	Check ticket	Mike	100	...
	35654426	06-01-2011:11.18	Decide	Sara	200	...
	35654427	07-01-2011:14.24	Reject request	Pete	200	...
2	35654483	30-12-2010:11.32	Register request	Mike	50	...
	35654485	30-12-2010:12.12	Check ticket	Mike	100	...
	35654487	30-12-2010:14.16	Examine casually	Pete	400	...
	35654488	05-01-2011:11.22	Decide	Sara	200	...
	35654489	08-01-2011:12.05	Pay compensation	Ellen	200	...
3	35654521	30-12-2010:14.32	Register request	Pete	50	...
	35654522	30-12-2010:15.06	Examine casually	Mike	400	...
	35654524	30-12-2010:16.34	Check ticket	Ellen	100	...
	35654525	06-01-2011:09.18	Decide	Sara	200	...
	35654526	06-01-2011:12.18	Reinitiate request	Sara	200	...
	35654527	06-01-2011:13.06	Examine thoroughly	Sean	400	...
	35654530	08-01-2011:11.43	Check ticket	Pete	100	...
	35654531	09-01-2011:09.55	Decide	Sara	200	...
	35654533	15-01-2011:10.45	Pay compensation	Ellen	200	...
4	35654641	06-01-2011:15.02	Register request	Pete	50	...
	35654643	07-01-2011:12.06	Check ticket	Mike	100	...
	35654644	08-01-2011:14.43	Examine thoroughly	Sean	400	...
	35654645	09-01-2011:12.02	Decide	Sara	200	...
	35654647	12-01-2011:15.44	Reject request	Ellen	200	...
5	35654711	06-01-2011:09.02	Register request	Ellen	50	...
	35654712	07-01-2011:10.16	Examine casually	Mike	400	...
	35654714	08-01-2011:11.22	Check ticket	Pete	100	...
	35654715	10-01-2011:13.28	Decide	Sara	200	...
	35654716	11-01-2011:16.18	Reinitiate request	Sara	200	...
	35654718	14-01-2011:14.33	Check ticket	Ellen	100	...
	35654719	16-01-2011:15.50	Examine casually	Mike	400	...
	35654720	19-01-2011:11.18	Decide	Sara	200	...
	35654721	20-01-2011:12.48	Reinitiate request	Sara	200	...
	35654722	21-01-2011:09.06	Examine casually	Sue	400	...
	35654724	21-01-2011:11.34	Check ticket	Pete	100	...
	35654725	23-01-2011:13.12	Decide	Sara	200	...
	35654726	24-01-2011:14.56	Reject request	Mike	200	...

Table 1.1 (Continued)

Case id	Event id	Properties				
		Timestamp	Activity	Resource	Cost	...
6	35654871	06-01-2011:15.02	Register request	Mike	50	...
	35654873	06-01-2011:16.06	Examine casually	Ellen	400	...
	35654874	07-01-2011:16.22	Check ticket	Mike	100	...
	35654875	07-01-2011:16.52	Decide	Sara	200	...
	35654877	16-01-2011:11.47	Pay compensation	Mike	200	...
...	...	...	...	...	...	...

Table 1.2 A more compact representation of log shown in Table 1.1: a = *register request*, b = *examine thoroughly*, c = *examine casually*, d = *check ticket*, e = *decide*, f = *reinitiate request*, g = *pay compensation*, and h = *reject request*

Case id	Trace
1	$\langle a, b, d, e, h\rangle$
2	$\langle a, d, c, e, g\rangle$
3	$\langle a, c, d, e, f, b, d, e, g\rangle$
4	$\langle a, d, b, e, h\rangle$
5	$\langle a, c, d, e, f, d, c, e, f, c, d, e, h\rangle$
6	$\langle a, c, d, e, g\rangle$
...	...

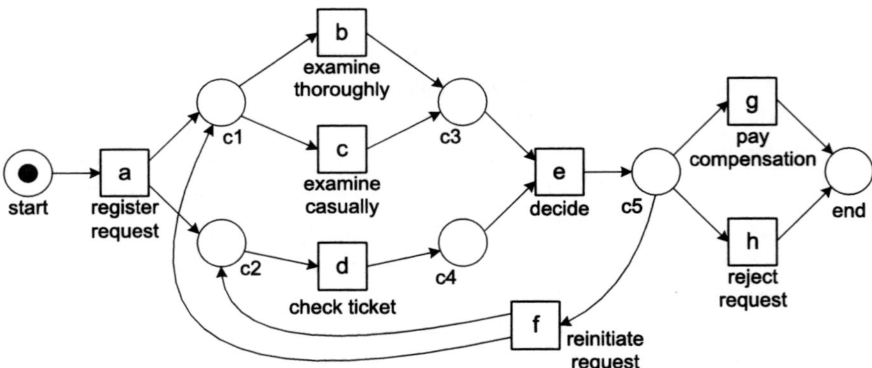

Fig. 1.5 The process model discovered by the α-algorithm [103] based on the set of traces $\{\langle a, b, d, e, h\rangle, \langle a, d, c, e, g\rangle, \langle a, c, d, e, f, b, d, e, g\rangle, \langle a, d, b, e, h\rangle, \langle a, c, d, e, f, d, c, e, f, c, d, e, h\rangle, \langle a, c, d, e, g\rangle\}$

After executing h, the case ends in the desired final marking with just a token in place *end*. Similarly, it can be checked that the other five traces shown in Table 1.2 are also possible in the model and that all of these traces result in the marking with just a token in place *end*.

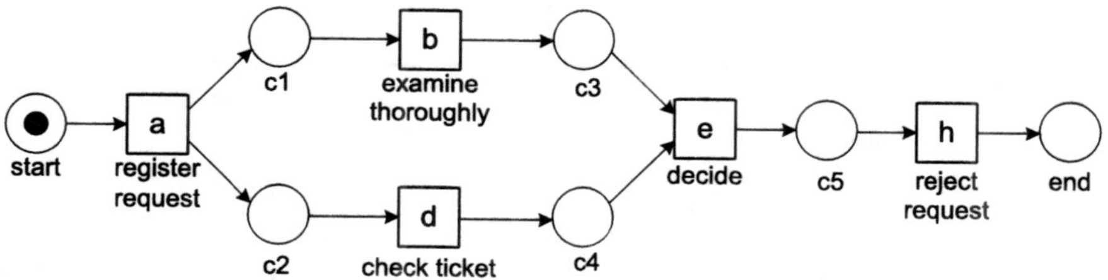

Fig. 1.6 The process model discovered by the α-algorithm based on Cases 1 and 4, i.e., the set of traces $\{\langle a, b, d, e, h\rangle, \langle a, d, b, e, h\rangle\}$

The Petri net shown in Fig. 1.5 also allows for traces not present in Table 1.2. For example, the traces $\langle a, d, c, e, f, b, d, e, g\rangle$ and $\langle a, c, d, e, f, c, d, e, f, c, d, e, f, c, d, e, f, b, d, e, g\rangle$ are also possible. This is a desired phenomenon as the goal is *not* to represent just the *particular set of example traces* in the event log. Process mining algorithms need to generalize the behavior contained in the log to show the most likely underlying model that is not invalidated by the next set of observations. One of the challenges of process mining is to balance between "overfitting" (the model is too specific and only allows for the "accidental behavior" observed) and "underfitting" (the model is too general and allows for behavior unrelated to the behavior observed).

When comparing the event log and the model, there seems to be a good balance between "overfitting" and "underfitting". All cases start with a and end with either g or h. Every e is preceded by d and one of the examination activities (b or c). Moreover, e is followed by f, g, or h. The repeated execution of b or c, d, and e suggests the presence of a loop. These characteristics are adequately captured by the net of Fig. 1.5.

Let us now consider an event log consisting of only two traces $\langle a, b, d, e, h\rangle$ and $\langle a, d, b, e, h\rangle$, i.e., Cases 1 and 4 of the original log. For this log, the α-algorithm constructs the Petri net shown in Fig. 1.6. This model only allows for two traces and these are exactly the ones in the small event log. b and d are modeled as being concurrent because they can be executed in any order. For larger and more complex models, it is important to discover concurrency. Not modeling concurrency typically results in large "Spaghetti-like" models in which the same activity needs to be duplicated.[1]

The α-algorithm is just one of many possible process discovery algorithms. For real-life logs, more advanced algorithms are needed to better balance between "overfitting" and "underfitting" and to deal with "incompleteness" (i.e., logs containing only a small fraction of the possible behavior due to the large number of alternatives) and "noise" (i.e., logs containing exceptional/infrequent behavior that should not automatically be incorporated in the model). This book will describe several of such algorithms and guide the reader in selecting one. In this section, we used Petri nets

[1] See, for example, Figs. 12.1 and 12.10 to understand why we use the term "Spaghetti" to refer to models that are difficult to comprehend.

Table 1.3 Another event log: Cases 7, 8, and 10 are not possible according to Fig. 1.5

Case id	Trace
1	$\langle a, b, d, e, h\rangle$
2	$\langle a, d, c, e, g\rangle$
3	$\langle a, c, d, e, f, b, d, e, g\rangle$
4	$\langle a, d, b, e, h\rangle$
5	$\langle a, c, d, e, f, d, c, e, f, c, d, e, h\rangle$
6	$\langle a, c, d, e, g\rangle$
7	$\langle \mathbf{a}, \mathbf{b}, \mathbf{e}, \mathbf{g}\rangle$
8	$\langle \mathbf{a}, \mathbf{b}, \mathbf{d}, \mathbf{e}\rangle$
9	$\langle a, d, c, e, f, d, c, e, f, b, d, e, h\rangle$
10	$\langle \mathbf{a}, \mathbf{c}, \mathbf{d}, \mathbf{e}, \mathbf{f}, \mathbf{b}, \mathbf{d}, \mathbf{g}\rangle$

to represent the discovered process models, because Petri nets are a succinct way of representing processes and have unambiguous and simple semantics. However, most mining techniques are independent of the desired representation. For instance, the discovered Petri net model shown in Fig. 1.5 can be (automatically) transformed into the BPMN model shown in Fig. 1.2.

As explained in Sect. 1.3, process mining is not limited to process discovery. Event logs can be used to check conformance and enhance existing models. Moreover, different perspectives may be taken into account. To illustrate this, let us first consider the event log shown in Table 1.3. The first six cases are as before. It is easy to see that Case 7 with trace $\langle a, b, e, g\rangle$ is not possible according to the model in Fig. 1.5. The model requires the execution of d before e, but d did not occur. This means that the ticket was not checked at all before making a decision and paying compensation. Conformance checking techniques aim at discovering such discrepancies [80]. When checking the conformance of the remainder of the event log, it can also be noted that Cases 8 and 10 do not conform either. Case 9 conforms although it is not identical to one of the earlier traces. Trace $\langle a, b, d, e\rangle$ (i.e., Case 8) has the problem that no concluding action was taken (rejection or payment). Trace $\langle a, c, d, e, f, b, d, g\rangle$ (Case 10) has the problem that the airline paid compensation without making a final decision. Note that conformance can be viewed from two angles: (a) the model does not capture the real behavior ("the model is wrong") and (b) reality deviates from the desired model ("the event log is wrong"). The first viewpoint is taken when the model is supposed to be *descriptive*, i.e., capture or predict reality. The second viewpoint is taken when the model is *normative*, i.e., used to influence or control reality.

The original event log shown in Table 1.1 also contains information about resources, timestamps and costs. Such information can be used to discover other perspectives, check the conformance of models that are not pure control-flow models, and to extend models with additional information. For example, one could derive a social network based on the interaction patterns between individuals. The social network can be based on the "handover of work" metric, i.e., the more frequent in-

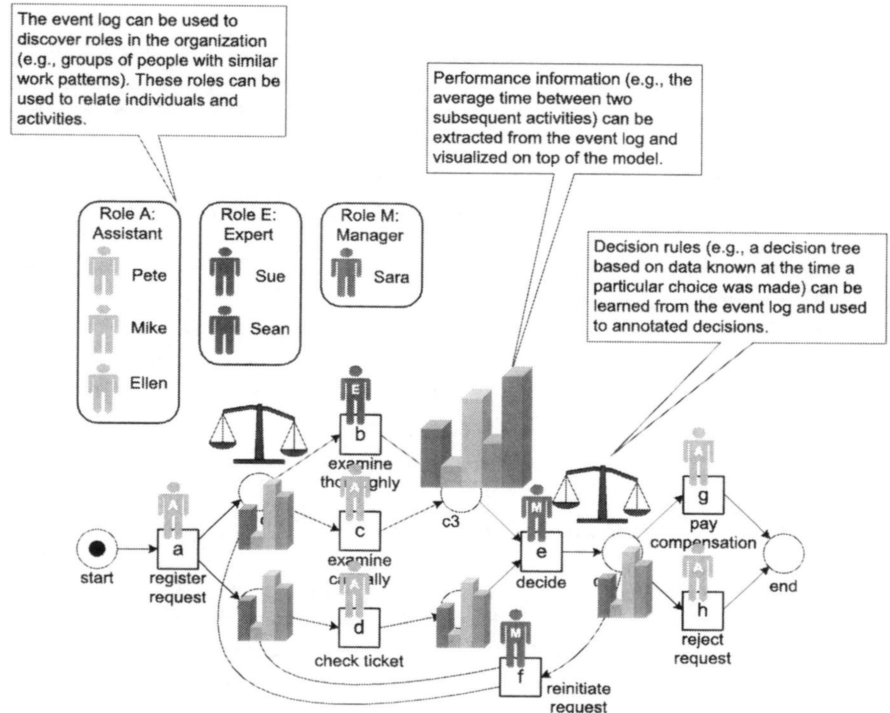

Fig. 1.7 The process model extended with additional perspectives: the organizational perspective ("What are the organizational roles and which resources are performing particular activities?"), the case perspective ("Which characteristics of a case influence a particular decision?"), and the time perspective ("Where are the bottlenecks in my process?")

dividual x performed an activity that is causally followed by an activity performed by individual y, the stronger the relation between x and y is [104].

Figure 1.7 illustrates the way in which a control-flow oriented model can be extended with the three other main perspectives mentioned in Sect. 1.3. Analysis of the event log shown in Table 1.1 may reveal that Sara is the only one performing the activities *decide* and *reinitiate* request. This suggests that there is a "manager role" and that Sara is the only one having this role. Activity *examine thoroughly* is performed only by Sue and Sean. This suggests some "expert role" associated to this activity. The remaining activities are performed by Pete, Mike and Ellen. This suggests some "assistant role" as shown in Fig. 1.7. Techniques for organizational process mining [88] will discover such organizational structures and relate activities to resources through roles. By exploiting resource information in the log, the organizational perspective can be added to the process model. Similarly, information on timestamps and frequencies can be used to add performance related information to the model. Figure 1.7 sketches that it is possible to measure the time that passes between an examination (activities b or c) and the actual decision (activity e). If this time is remarkably long, process mining can be used to identify the problem and discover possible causes. If the event log contains case-related information, this can be used to further analyze the decision points in the process. For instance, through decision point analysis it may be learned that requests for compensation of more than € 800 tend to be rejected.

Using process mining, the different perspectives can be cross-correlated to find surprising insights. Examples of such findings could be: "requests examined by Sean tend to be rejected more frequently", "requests for which the ticket is checked after examination tend to take much longer", "requests of less than € 500 tend to be completed without any additional iterations". Moreover, these perspectives can also be linked to conformance questions. For example, it may be shown that Pete is involved in relatively many incorrectly handled requests. These examples show that privacy issues need to be considered when analyzing event logs with information about individuals (see Sect. 8.3.3).

1.5 Play-in, Play-out, and Replay

One of the key elements of process mining is the emphasis on establishing a strong relation between a process model and "reality" captured in the form of an event log. Inspired by the terminology used by David Harel in the context of Live Sequence Charts [53], we use the terms *Play-in*, *Play-out*, and *Replay* to reflect on this relation. Figure 1.8 illustrates these three notions.

Play-out refers to the classical use of process models. Given a Petri net, it is possible to generate behavior. The traces in Table 1.2 could have been obtained by repeatedly "playing the token game" using the Petri net of Fig. 1.5. Play-out can be used both for the analysis and the enactment of business processes. A workflow engine can be seen as a "Play-out engine" that controls cases by only allowing the "moves" allowed according to the model. Hence, Play-out can be used to enact operational processes using some executable model. Simulation tools also use a Play-out engine to conduct experiments. The main idea of simulation is to repeatedly run a model and thus collect statistics and confidence intervals. Note that a simulation engine is similar to a workflow engine. The main difference is that the simulation engine interacts with a modeled environment whereas the workflow engine interacts with the real environment (workers, customers, etc.). Also classical verification approaches using exhaustive state-space analysis—often referred to as model checking [20]—can be seen as Play-out methods.

Play-in is the opposite of Play-out, i.e., example behavior is taken as input and the goal is to construct a model. Play-in is often referred to as *inference*. The α-algorithm and other process discovery approaches are examples of Play-in techniques. Note that the Petri net of Fig. 1.5 can be derived automatically given an event log like the one in Table 1.2. Most data mining techniques use Play-in, i.e., a model is learned on the basis of examples. However, traditionally, data mining has not been concerned with process models. Typical examples of models are decision trees ("people that drink more than five glasses of alcohol and smoke more

Play-In

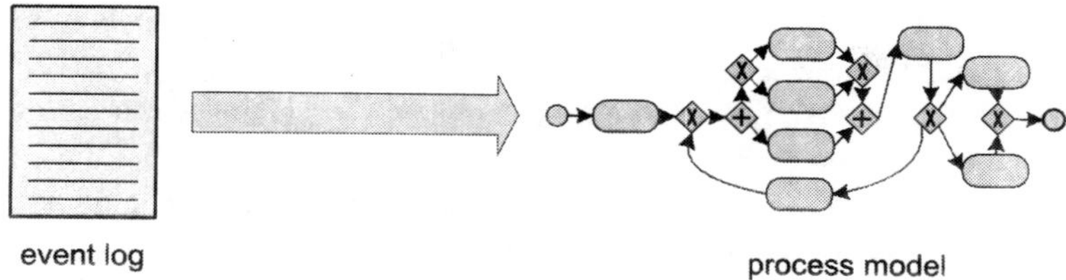

Play-Out

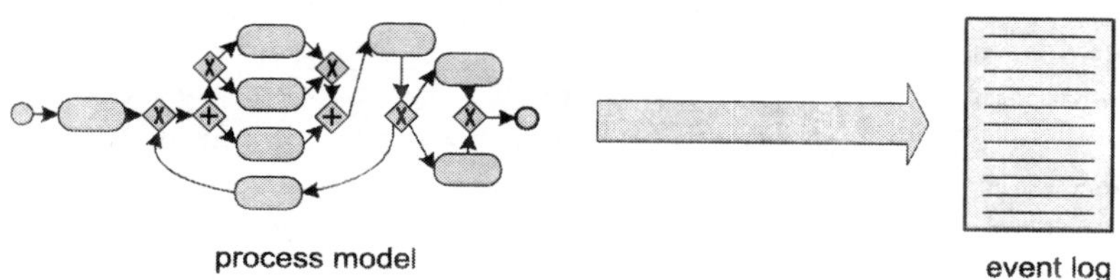

Replay

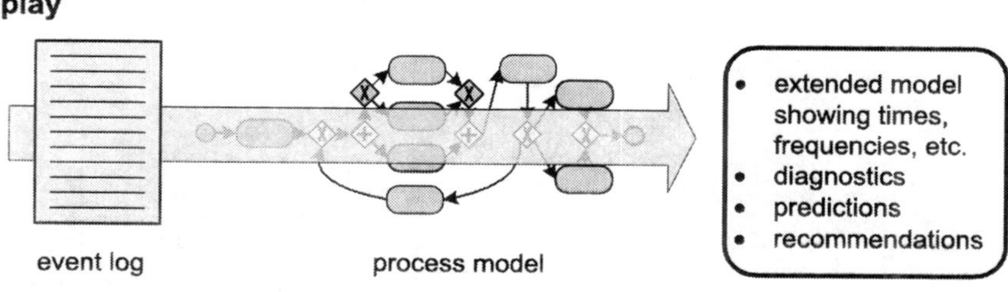

Fig. 1.8 Three ways of relating event logs (or other sources of information containing example behavior) and process models: *Play-in*, *Play-out*, and *Replay*

than 56 cigarettes tend to die young") and association rules ("people that buy diapers also buy beer"). Unfortunately, it is not possible to use conventional data mining techniques to Play-in process models. Only recently, process mining techniques have become readily available to discover process models based on event logs.

Replay uses an event log *and* a process model as input. The event log is "replayed" on top of the process model. As shown earlier it is possible to replay trace $\langle a, b, d, e, h\rangle$ on the Petri net in Fig. 1.5; simply "play the token game" by forcing the transitions to fire (if possible) in the order indicated. An event log may be replayed for different purposes:

- *Conformance checking*. Discrepancies between the log and the model can be detected and quantified by replaying the log. For instance, replaying trace $\langle a, b, e, h\rangle$ on the Petri net in Fig. 1.5 will show that d should have happened but did not.

- *Extending the model with frequencies and temporal information.* By replaying the log one can see which parts of the model are visited frequently. Replay can also be used to detect bottlenecks. Consider, for example, the trace $\langle a^8, b^9, d^{20}, e^{21}, h^{21}\rangle$ in which the superscripts denote timestamps. By replaying the trace on top of Fig. 1.5 one can see that e was enabled at time 20 and occurred at time 21. The enabling of e was delayed by the time it took to complete d; although d was enabled already at time 8, it occurred only at time 20.
- *Constructing predictive models.* By replaying event logs one can build predictive models, i.e., for the different states of the model particular predictions can be made. For example, a predictive model learned by replaying many cases could show that the expected time until completion after enabling e is eight hours.
- *Operational support.* Replay is not limited to historic event data. One can also replay partial traces of cases still running. This can be used for detecting deviations at run-time, e.g., the partial trace $\langle a^8, e^{11}\rangle$ of a case that is still running will never fit into Fig. 1.5. Hence, an alert can be generated before the case completes. Similarly, it is possible to predict the remaining processing time or the likelihood of being rejected of a case having a partial trace, e.g., a partial executed case $\langle a^8, b^9\rangle$ has an expected remaining processing time of 3.5 days and a 40 percent probability of being rejected. Such predictions can also be used to recommend suitable next steps to progress the case.

Desire Lines in Process Models

A desire line—also known as the social trail—is a path that emerges through erosion caused by footsteps of humans (or animals). The width and amount of erosion of the path indicates how frequently the path is used. Typically, the desire line follows the shortest or most convenient path between two points. Moreover, as the path emerges more people are encouraged to use it, thus stimulating further erosion. Dwight Eisenhower is often mentioned as one of the persons using this emerging group behavior. Before becoming the 34th president of the United States, he was the president of Columbia University. When he was asked how the university should arrange the sidewalks to best interconnect the campus buildings, he suggested letting the grass grow between buildings and delay the creation of sidewalks. After some time the desire lines revealed themselves. The places where the grass was most worn by people's footsteps were turned into sidewalks. In the same vein, replay can be used to show the *desire lines in processes*. The paths in the process model traveled most can be highlighted by using brighter colors or thicker arcs (cf. ProM's Fuzzy Miner [50]).

An interesting question is how desire lines can be used to better manage business processes. Operational support, e.g., predictions and recommendations derived from historic information, can be used to reinforce successful behavior and thus create suitable "sidewalks" in processes.

1.6 Trends

In this book, we position process mining as a powerful tool within a broader *Business Process Management* (BPM) context. As indicated before, the goal of BPM is to improve operational business processes by combining knowledge from information technology and knowledge from management sciences. It can also be positioned under the umbrella of *Business Intelligence* (BI). There is no clear definition for BI. On the one hand, it is a very broad term that includes anything that aims at providing actionable information that can be used to support decision making. On the other hand, vendors and consultants tend to conveniently skew the definition towards a particular tool or methodology. Clearly, process mining can be seen as a new collection of BI techniques. However, it is important to note that most BI tools are not really "intelligent" and do not provide any process mining capabilities. The focus is on querying and reporting combined with simple visualization techniques showing dashboards and scorecards. Some systems provide data mining capabilities or support *Online Analytical Processing* (OLAP). OLAP tools are used to view multidimensional data from different angles. On the one hand, it is possible to aggregate and consolidate data to create high-level reports. On the other hand, OLAP tools can drill down into the data to find detailed information. Typical data mining capabilities provided by more advanced tools are: *clustering* (discovering entities that are somewhat "similar"), *classification* (discovering rules that can be used to predict a particular property of an entity), *regression* (constructing a function that models the data with the least error), and *association rule learning* (searching for relationships between properties). Chapter 3 introduces these techniques and relates them to process mining.

Under the BI umbrella many fancy terms have been introduced to refer to rather simple reporting and dashboard tools. *Business Activity Monitoring* (BAM) refers to the real-time monitoring of business processes. BAM is often related to *Complex Event Processing* (CEP). CEP aims to react immediately if the stream of events shows a particular pattern, e.g., generate an alert when a combination of events occurs. *Corporate Performance Management* (CPM) is another buzzword for measuring the performance of a process or organization. Typically, CPM focuses on financial aspects. Recently, more and more software vendors started to use the term "analytics" to refer to advanced BI capabilities. *Visual analytics* focuses on the analysis of large amounts of data while exploiting the remarkable capabilities of humans to visually identify patterns and trends. *Predictive analytics* uses historic data to make forecasts. Clearly, process mining also aims at providing advanced analytics and some process mining techniques also heavily rely on advanced visualization and human interpretation. Moreover, as will be demonstrated in Chap. 9, process mining is not restricted to analyzing historic data and also includes operational support, i.e., providing predictions and recommendations in an online setting.

Also related are management approaches such as *Continuous Process Improvement* (CPI), *Total Quality Management* (TQM), and *Six Sigma*. These approaches have in common that processes are "put under a microscope" to see whether further improvements are possible. Clearly, process mining can help to analyze deviations and inefficiencies.

What Does "Six Sigma" Mean?

Today the term "Six Sigma" refers to a broad set of tools, techniques and methods to improve the quality of processes [75]. A typical process improvement project using the Six Sigma methodology follows the so-called *DMAIC* approach consisting of five steps: (a) *Define* the problem and set targets, (b) *Measure* key performance indicators and collect data, (c) *Analyze* the data to investigate and verify cause-and-effect relationships, (d) *Improve* the current process based on this analysis, and (e) *Control* the process to minimize deviations from the target. Six Sigma was originally developed by Motorola in the early 1980s and extended by many others. The term "Six Sigma" refers to the initial goal set by Motorola to minimize defects. In fact, the σ in "Six Sigma" refers to the standard deviation of a normal distribution. Given a normal distribution, 68.3% of the values lie within 1 standard deviation of the mean, i.e., a random draw from normal distribution with a mean value of μ and a standard deviation of σ has a probability of 0.683 to be in the interval $[\mu - \sigma, \mu + \sigma]$. Given the same normal distribution, 95.45% of randomly sampled values lie within two standard deviations of the mean, i.e., $[\mu - 2\sigma, \mu + 2\sigma]$, and 99.73% of the values lie within three standard deviations of the mean ($[\mu - 3\sigma, \mu + 3\sigma]$). The traditional quality paradigm in manufacturing defined a process as "capable" if the process's natural spread, plus and minus three σ, was less than the engineering tolerance. So, if deviations of up to three times the standard deviations are allowed, then on average 2700 out of one million cases will have a defect (i.e., samples outside the $[\mu - 3\sigma, \mu + 3\sigma]$ interval). Six Sigma aims to create processes were the standard deviation is so small that any value within 6 standard deviations of the mean can be considered as non-defective. In literature, often a 1.5 sigma shift (to accommodate for long term variations and decreasing quality) is taken into account [75]. This results in the following table:

Quality level	Defective Parts per Million Opportunities (DPMO)	Percentage passed
One Sigma	690,000 DPMO	31%
Two Sigma	308,000 DPMO	69.2%
Three Sigma	66,800 DPMO	93.32%
Four Sigma	6,210 DPMO	99.379%
Five Sigma	230 DPMO	99.977%
Six Sigma	3.4 DPMO	99.9997%

A process that "runs at One Sigma" has less than 690,000 defective cases per million cases, i.e., at least 31% of the cases is handled properly. A process that "runs at Six Sigma" has only 3.4 defective cases per million cases, i.e., on average 99.9997% of the cases is handled properly.

Whereas BI tools and management approaches such as Six Sigma mainly aim at improving operational performance, e.g., reducing flow time and defects, organizations are also putting more emphasis on *corporate governance*, *risk*, and *compliance*. Major corporate and accounting scandals including those affecting Enron, Tyco, Adelphia, Peregrine, and WorldCom have fueled interest in more rigorous auditing practices. Legislation such as the *Sarbanes-Oxley Act* (SOX) of 2002 and the *Basel II Accord* of 2004 was enacted in response to such scandals. The recent financial crisis also underscores the importance of verifying that organizations operate "within their boundaries". Process mining techniques offer a means to more rigorously check compliance and ascertain the validity and reliability of information about an organization's core processes.

The many acronyms in this section—BPM, BI, OLAP, BAM, CEP, CPM, CPI, TQM, SOX, etc.—are just a subset of the jargon used by business consultants and vendors. Additional terms like "(Business) Process Intelligence" are used as variations on the same theme. What can be distilled from the above is that there is a clear trend towards actually using the data available in today's systems. The data is used to *reason about the process* and for *decision making within the process*. Moreover, the acronyms express a clear desire to get more *insight* into the actual processes, to *improve* them, and to make sure that they are *compliant*. Unfortunately, most consultants and tool vendors are unable to provide the support needed and need hide behind a "thick layer of buzzwords". This book aims to provide a clear and refreshing view on the matter. Using recent breakthroughs in process mining, we will show that it is possible to simplify and unify the analysis of business processes based on facts. Moreover, the techniques and insights presented are directly applicable and are supported by process mining tools such as *ProM* (www.processmining.org).

1.7 Outlook

Process mining provides an important bridge between data mining and business process modeling and analysis. Process mining research at TU/e (Eindhoven University of Technology) started in 1999. At that time, there was little event data available and the initial process mining techniques were extremely naïve and hence unusable. Over the last decade, event data has become readily available and process mining techniques have matured. Moreover, process mining algorithms have been implemented in various academic and commercial systems. Today, there is an active group of researchers working on process mining and it has become one of the "hot topics" in BPM research. Moreover, there is a huge interest from industry in process mining. More and more software vendors started adding process mining functionality to their tools. Our open-source process mining tool ProM is widely used all over the globe and provides an easy starting point for practitioners, students, and academics. These developments are the main motivation for writing this book. Even though there are many books on data mining, business ~~un~~intelligence, process reengineering, and BPM, thus far, there was no book on process mining.

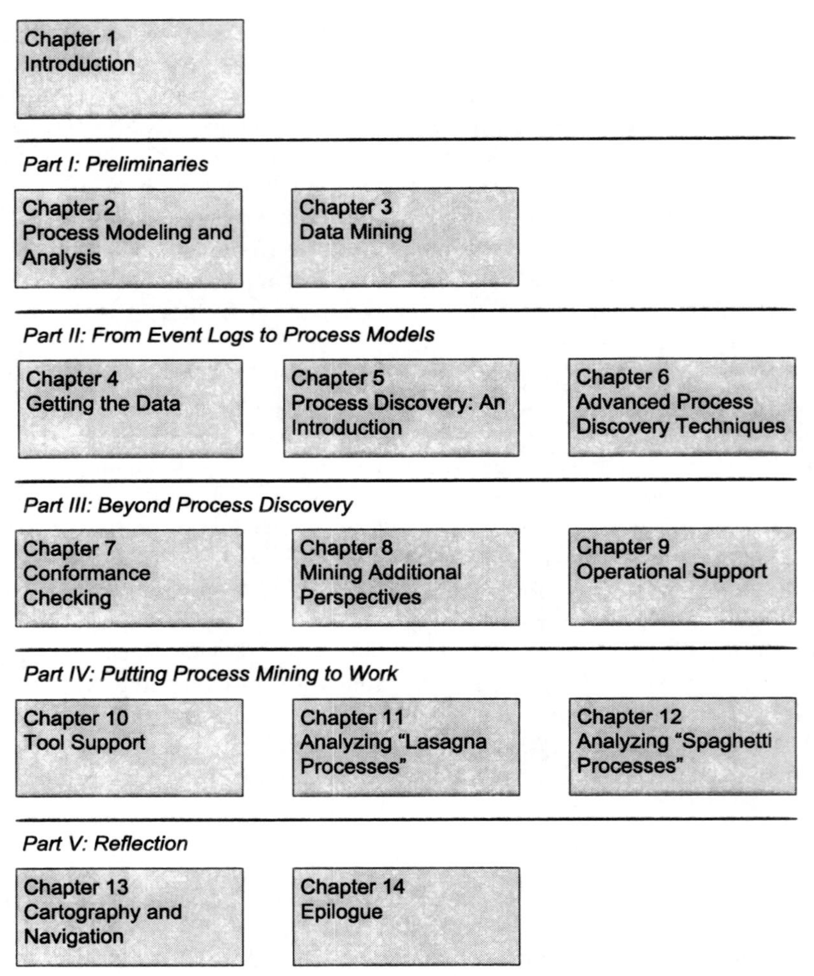

Fig. 1.9 Outline of the book

This book aims to provide a comprehensive overview of process mining. The book is intended for business process analysts, business consultants, process managers, graduate students, and BPM researchers. On the one hand, the book avoids delving into unnecessary details. On the other hand, the book does not shy away from formal definitions and technical issues needed to fully understand the essence of process mining. As Einstein said: "Everything should be made as simple as possible, but not one bit simpler".

Figure 1.9 shows an overview of the book. *Part* I provides the preliminaries necessary for reading the remainder of the book. *Chapter* 2 introduces different process modeling languages and provides an overview of model-based analysis techniques. *Chapter* 3 introduces standard data mining techniques such as decision tree learning and association rule learning. Process mining can be seen as a bridge between the preliminaries presented in both chapters.

Part II focuses on one particular process mining task: process discovery. *Chapter* 4 discusses the input needed for process mining. The chapter discusses different input formats and issues related to the extraction of event logs from heterogeneous data sources. *Chapter* 5 presents the α-algorithm step-by-step in such a way that the reader can understand how it works and see its limitations. This simple algorithm has problems dealing with less structured processes. Nevertheless, it provides a basic introduction into the topic and serves as a "hook" for discussing more advanced algorithms and general issues related to process mining. *Chapter* 6 introduces more advanced process discovery approaches. This way the reader gets a good understanding of the state-of-the-art and is guided in selecting suitable techniques.

Part III moves beyond process discovery, i.e., the focus is no longer on discovering the control-flow. *Chapter* 7 presents conformance checking approaches, i.e., techniques to compare and relate event logs and process models. It is shown that conformance can be quantified and that deviations can be diagnosed. *Chapter* 8 focuses on other perspectives: the organizational perspective, the case perspective, and the time perspective. *Chapter* 9 shows that process mining can also be used to support operational processes at runtime, i.e., while cases are running it is possible to detect violations, make predictions, and provide recommendations.

Part IV guides the reader in successfully applying process mining in practice. *Chapter* 10 provides an overview of the different process mining tools. The next two chapters are based on the observation that there are essentially two types of processes: "Lasagna processes" and "Spaghetti processes". Lasagna processes are well-structured and relatively simple. Therefore, process discovery is less interesting. The techniques presented in Part III are most relevant for Lasagna processes. The added value of process mining can be found in conformance checking, detailed performance analysis, and operational support. *Chapter* 11 explains how process mining can be applied in such circumstances and provides various real-life examples. Spaghetti processes are less structured. Therefore, the added value of process mining shifts to providing insights and generating ideas for better controlled processes. Advanced techniques such as prediction are less relevant for Spaghetti processes. *Chapter* 12 shows how to apply process mining in such less-structured environments.

Part V takes a step back and reflects on the material presented in the preceding parts. *Chapter* 13 provides a broader vision on the topic by comparing process modeling with cartography, and relating BPM systems to navigation systems provided by vendors such as TomTom, Garmin, and Navigon. The goal of this chapter is to provide a refreshing view on process management and reveal the limitations of existing information systems. *Chapter* 14 concludes the book by summarizing improvement opportunities provided by process mining. The chapter also discusses some of the key challenges and provides concrete pointers to start applying the material presented in this book.

Part I
Preliminaries

Chapter 1
Introduction

Part I: Preliminaries

Chapter 2
Process Modeling and Analysis

Chapter 3
Data Mining

Part II: From Event Logs to Process Models

Chapter 4
Getting the Data

Chapter 5
Process Discovery: An Introduction

Chapter 6
Advanced Process Discovery Techniques

Part III: Beyond Process Discovery

Chapter 7
Conformance Checking

Chapter 8
Mining Additional Perspectives

Chapter 9
Operational Support

Part IV: Putting Process Mining to Work

Chapter 10
Tool Support

Chapter 11
Analyzing "Lasagna Processes"

Chapter 12
Analyzing "Spaghetti Processes"

Part V: Reflection

Chapter 13
Cartography and Navigation

Chapter 14
Epilogue

Process mining provides a bridge between data mining and process modeling and analysis. Therefore, we provide an introduction to both fields. Chapter 2 reviews various process modeling notations and their analysis. Chapter 3 explains the main data mining techniques.

Chapter 2
Process Modeling and Analysis

The plethora of process modeling notations available today illustrates the relevance of process modeling. Some organizations may use only informal process models to structure discussions and to document procedures. However, organizations that operate at a higher BPM maturity level use models that can be analyzed and used to enact operational processes. Today, most process models are made by hand and are not based on a rigorous analysis of existing process data. This chapter serves two purposes. On the one hand, preliminaries are presented that will be used in later chapters. For example, various process modeling notations are introduced and some analysis techniques are reviewed. On the other hand, the chapter reveals the limitations of classical approaches, thus motivating the need for process mining.

2.1 The Art of Modeling

Since the industrial revolution, productivity has been increasing because of technical innovations, improvements in the organization of work, and the use of information technology. Adam Smith (1723–1790) showed the advantages of the division of labor. Frederick Taylor (1856–1915) introduced the initial principles of scientific management. Henry Ford (1863–1947) introduced the production line for the mass production of "black T-Fords". Around 1950 computers and digital communication infrastructures started to influence business processes. This resulted in dramatic changes in the organization of work and enabled new ways of doing business. Today, innovations in computing and communication are still the main drivers behind change in business processes. So, business processes have become more complex, heavily rely on information systems, and may span multiple organizations. Therefore, process modeling has become of the utmost importance. Process models assist in managing complexity by providing insight and documenting procedures. Information systems need to be configured and driven by precise instructions. Cross-organizational processes can only function properly if there is a common agreement on the required interactions. As a result, process models are widely used in today's organizations.

W.M.P. van der Aalst, *Process Mining*,

DOI 10.1007/978-3-642-19345-3_2,

Operations management, and in particular *operation research*, is a branch of management science heavily relying on modeling. Here a variety of mathematical models ranging from linear programming and project planning to queueing models, Markov chains, and simulation are used. For example, the location of a warehouse is determined using linear programming, server capacity is added on the basis of queueing models, and an optimal route in a container terminal is determined using integer programming. Models are used to reason *about processes* (redesign) and to make decisions *inside processes* (planning and control). The models used in operations management are typically tailored toward a particular analysis technique and only used for answering a specific question. In contrast, process models in BPM typically serve *multiple* purposes. A process model expressed in BPMN may be used to discuss responsibilities, analyze compliance, predict performance using simulation, and configure a WFM system. However, BPM and operations management have in common that making a good model is "an art rather than a science". Creating models is therefore a difficult and error-prone task. Typical errors include:

- *The model describes an idealized version of reality*. When modeling processes, the designer tends to concentrate on the "normal" or "desirable" behavior. For example, the model may only cover 80% of the cases assuming that these are representative. Typically this is not the case as the other 20% may cause 80% of the problems. The reasons for such oversimplifications are manifold. The designer and management may not be aware of the many deviations that take place. Moreover, the perception of people may be biased, depending on their role in the organization. Hand-made models tend to be subjective, and often there is a tendency to make things too simple just for the sake of understandability.
- *Inability to adequately capture human behavior*. Although simple mathematical models may suffice to model machines or people working in an assembly line, they are inadequate when modeling people involved in multiple processes and exposed to multiple priorities [95, 109]. A worker who is involved in multiple processes needs to distribute his attention over multiple processes. This makes it difficult to model one process in isolation. Workers also do not work at constant speed. A well-known illustration of this is the so-called *Yerkes–Dodson law* that describes the relation between workload and performance of people [95]. In most processes, one can easily observe that people will take more time to complete a task and effectively work fewer hours per day if there is hardly any work to do. Nevertheless, most simulation models sample service times from a fixed probability distribution and use fixed time windows for resource availability.
- *The model is at the wrong abstraction level*. Depending on the input data and the questions that need to be answered, a suitable abstraction level needs to be chosen. The model may be too abstract and thus unable to answer relevant questions. The model may also be too detailed, e.g., the required input cannot be obtained or the model becomes too complex to be fully understood. Consider, for example, a car manufacturer that has a warehouse containing thousands of spare parts. It may be tempting to model all of them in a simulation study to compare different inventory policies. However, if one is not aiming at making statements about a specific spare part, this is not wise. Typically it is very time consuming to change

the abstraction level of an existing model. Unfortunately, questions may emerge at different levels of granularity.

These are just some of the problems organizations face when making models by hand. Only experienced designers and analysts can make models that have a good predictive value and can be used as a starting point for a (re)implementation or redesign. An inadequate model can lead to wrong conclusions. Therefore, we advocate the use of event data. Process mining allows for the extraction of models based on *facts*. Moreover, process mining does not aim at creating a single model of the process. Instead, it provides *various views on the same reality at different abstraction levels*. For example, users can decide to look at the most frequent behavior to get a simple model ("80% model"). However, they can also inspect the full behavior by deriving the "100% model" covering all cases observed. Similarly, abstraction levels can be varied to create different views. Process mining can also reveal that people in organizations do not function as "machines". On the one hand, it may be shown that all kinds of inefficiencies take place. On the other hand, process mining can also visualize the remarkable flexibility of some workers to deal with problems and varying workloads.

2.2 Process Models

It is not easy to make good process models. Yet, they are important. Fortunately, process mining can facilitate the construction of better models in less time. Process discovery algorithms like the α-algorithm can automatically generate a process model. As indicated in Chap. 1, various process modeling notations exist. Sometimes the plethora of notations is referred to as the new "tower of Babel". Therefore, we describe only some basic notations. This section does not aim to provide a complete overview of existing process modeling notations. We just introduce the notations that we will use in the remainder. We would like to stress that it is relatively easy to automatically translate process mining results into the desired notation. For example, although the α-algorithm produces a Petri net, it is easy to convert the result into a BPMN model, BPEL model, or UML Activity Diagram. Again we refer to the systematic comparisons in the context of the Workflow Patterns Initiative [101, 130] for details.

In this section, we focus on the control-flow perspective of processes. We assume that there is a set of *activity labels* $\mathscr{A}$. The goal of a process model is to decide *which activities* need to be executed and in *what order*. Activities can be executed sequentially, activities can be optional or concurrent, and the repeated execution of the same activity may be possible.

2.2.1 Transition Systems

The most basic process modeling notation is a *transition system*. A transition system consists of *states* and *transitions*. Figure 2.1 shows a transition system consisting of

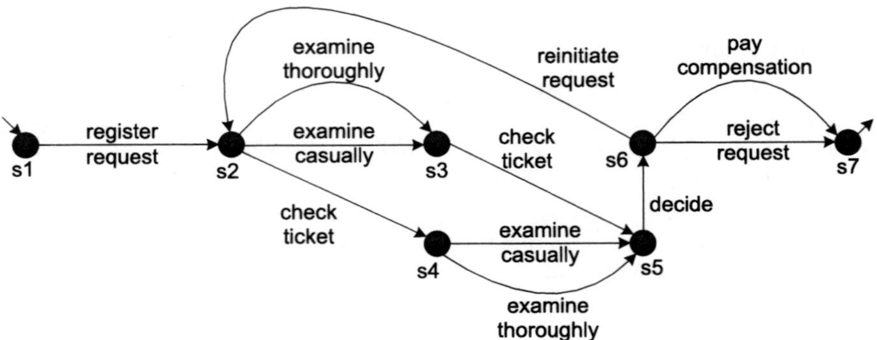

Fig. 2.1 A transition system having one initial state and one final state

seven states. It models the handling of a request for compensation within an airline as described in Sect. 1.2. The states are represented by black circles. There is one initial state labeled $s1$ and one final state labeled $s7$. Each state has a unique label. This label is merely an identifier and has no meaning. Transitions are represented by arcs. Each transition connects two states and is labeled with the name of an activity. Multiple arcs can bear the same label. For example, *check ticket* appears twice.

Definition 2.1 (Transition system) A *transition system* is a triplet $TS = (S, A, T)$ where S is the set of *states*, $A \subseteq \mathscr{A}$ is the set of *activities* (often referred to as *actions*), and $T \subseteq S \times A \times S$ is the set of *transitions*. $S^{start} \subseteq S$ is the set of *initial states* (sometimes referred to as "start" states), and $S^{end} \subseteq S$ is the set of *final states* (sometimes referred to as "accept" states).

The sets S^{start} and S^{end} are defined implicitly. In principle, S can be infinite. However, for most practical applications the state space is finite. In this case, the transition system is also referred to as a Finite-State Machine (FSM) or a finite-state automaton.

The transition system depicted in Fig. 2.1 can be formalized as follows: $S = \{s1, s2, s3, s4, s5, s6, s7\}$, $S^{start} = \{s1\}$, $S^{end} = \{s7\}$, $A = \{$*register request*, *examine thoroughly*, *examine casually*, *check ticket*, *decide*, *reinitiate request*, *reject request*, *pay compensation*$\}$, and $T = \{(s1,$ *register request*$, s2), (s2,$ *examine casually*$, s3), (s2,$ *examine thoroughly*$, s3), (s2,$ *check ticket*$, s4), (s3,$ *check ticket*$, s5), (s4,$ *examine casually*$, s5), (s4,$ *examine thoroughly*$, s5), (s5,$ *decide*$, s6), (s6,$ *reinitiate request*$, s2), (s6,$ *pay compensation*$, s7), (s6,$ *reject request*$, s7)\}$.

Given a transition system one can reason about its behavior. The transition starts in one of the initial states. Any path in the graph starting in such a state corresponds to a possible *execution sequence*. For example, the path *register request*, *examine casually*, *check ticket* in Fig. 2.1 is an example of an execution sequence starting in state $s1$ and ending in $s5$. There are infinitely many execution sequences for this transition system. A path *terminates successfully* if it ends in one of the final states. A path *deadlocks* if it reaches a nonfinal state without any outgoing transitions. Note that the absence of deadlocks does not guarantee successful termination. The transition system may *livelock*, i.e., some transitions are still enabled but it is impossible to reach one of the final states.

Any process model with executable semantics can be mapped onto a transition system. Therefore, many notions defined for transition systems can easily be translated to higher-level languages such as Petri nets, BPMN, and UML activity diagrams. Consider, for example, the seemingly simple question: "When are two processes the same from a behavioral point of view". As shown in [120], many equivalence notions can be defined. *Trace equivalence* considers two transition systems to be equivalent if their execution sequences are the same. More refined notions like *branching bisimilarity* also take the moment of choice into account. These notions defined for transition systems can be used for any pair of process models as long as the models are expressed in a language with executable semantics (see also Sect. 5.3).

Transition systems are simple but have problems expressing concurrency succinctly. Suppose that there are n parallel activities, i.e., all n activities need to be executed but any order is allowed. There are $n!$ possible execution sequences. The transition system requires 2^n states and $n \times 2^{n-1}$ transitions. This is an example of the well-known "state explosion" problem [91]. Consider for example 10 parallel activities. The number of possible execution sequences is $10! = 3,628,800$, the number of reachable states is $2^{10} = 1024$, and the number of transitions is $10 \times 2^{10-1} = 5120$. The corresponding Petri net is much more compact and needs only 10 transitions and 10 places to model the 10 parallel activities. Given the concurrent nature of business processes, more expressive models like Petri nets are needed to adequately represent process mining results.

2.2.2 Petri Nets

Petri nets are the oldest and best investigated process modeling language allowing for the modeling of concurrency. Although the graphical notation is intuitive and simple, Petri nets are executable and many analysis techniques can be used to analyze them [58, 77, 96]. In the Introduction, we already showed an example Petri net. Figure 2.2 shows the Petri net again with the various constructs highlighted. A Petri net is a bipartite graph consisting of *places* and *transitions*. The network structure is static, but, governed by the firing rule, *tokens* can flow through the network. The state of a Petri net is determined by the distribution of tokens over places and is referred to as its *marking*. In the initial marking shown in Fig. 2.2 there is only one token; *start* is the only marked place.

Definition 2.2 (Petri net) A *Petri net* is a triplet $N = (P, T, F)$ where P is a finite set of *places*, T is a finite set of *transitions* such that $P \cap T = \emptyset$, and $F \subseteq (P \times T) \cup (T \times P)$ is a set of directed arcs, called the *flow relation*. A *marked* Petri net is a pair (N, M), where $N = (P, T, F)$ is a Petri net and where $M \in \mathbb{B}(P)$ is a *multi-set* over P denoting the *marking* of the net. The set of all marked Petri nets is denoted $\mathcal{N}$.

The Petri net shown Fig. 2.2 can be formalized as follows: $P = \{start, c1, c2, c3, c4, c5, end\}$, $T = \{a, b, c, d, e, f, g, h\}$, and $F = \{(start, a), (a, c1), (a, c2), (c1, b), (c1, c), (c2, d), (b, c3), (c, c3), (d, c4), (c3, e), (c4, e), (e, c5), (c5, f), (f, c1), (f, c2), (c5, g), (c5, h), (g, end), (h, end)\}$.

Multi-sets

A marking corresponds to a multi-set of tokens. However, multi-sets are not only used to represent markings; later we will use multi-sets to model event logs where the same trace may appear multiple times. Therefore, we provide some basic notations used in the remainder.

A multi-set (also referred to as *bag*) is like a set in which each element may occur multiple times. For example, $[a, b^2, c^3, d^2, e]$ is the multi-set with nine elements: one a, two b's, three c's, two d's, and one e. The following three multi-set are identical: $[a, b, b, c^3, d, d, e]$, $[e, d^2, c^3, b^2, a]$, and $[a, b^2, c^3, d^2, e]$. Only the number of occurrences of each value matters, not the order. Formally, $\mathbb{B}(D) = D \to \mathbb{N}$ is the set of multi-sets (bags) over a finite domain D, i.e., $X \in \mathbb{B}(D)$ is a multi-set, where for each $d \in D$, $X(d)$ denotes the number of times d is included in the multi-set. For example, if $X = [a, b^2, c^3]$, then $X(b) = 2$ and $X(e) = 0$.

The sum of two multi-sets ($X \uplus Y$), the difference ($X \setminus Y$), the presence of an element in a multi-set ($x \in X$), and the notion of subset ($X \leq Y$) are defined in a straightforward way. For example, $[a, b^2, c^3, d] \uplus [c^3, d, e^2, f^3] = [a, b^2, c^6, d^2, e^2, f^3]$ and $[a, b] \leq [a, b^3, c]$. Moreover, we can also apply these operators to sets, where we assume that a set is a multi-set in which every element occurs exactly once. For example, $[a, b^2] \uplus \{b, c\} = [a, b^3, c]$. The operators are also robust with respect to the domains of the multi-sets, i.e., even if X and Y are defined on different domains, $X \uplus Y$, $X \setminus Y$, and $X \leq Y$ are defined properly by extending the domain whenever needed.

The marking shown in Fig. 2.2 is $[start]$, i.e., a multi-set containing only one token. The dynamic behavior of such a marked Petri net is defined by the so-called *firing rule*. A transition is *enabled* if each of its input places contains a token. An enabled transition can *fire* thereby consuming one token from each input place and producing one token for each output place. Hence, transition a is enabled at marking $[start]$. Firing a results in the marking $[c1, c2]$. Note that one token is consumed and two tokens are produced. At marking $[c1, c2]$, transition a is no longer enabled. However, transitions b, c, and d have become enabled. From marking $[c1, c2]$, firing b results in marking $[c2, c3]$. Here, d is still enabled, but b and c not anymore. Because of the loop construct involving f there are infinitely many firing sequences starting in $[start]$ and ending in $[end]$.

Assume now that the initial marking is $[start^5]$. Firing a now results in the marking $[start^4, c1, c2]$. At this marking, a is still enabled. Firing a again results in marking $[start^3, c1^2, c2^2]$. Transition a can fire five times in a row resulting in marking

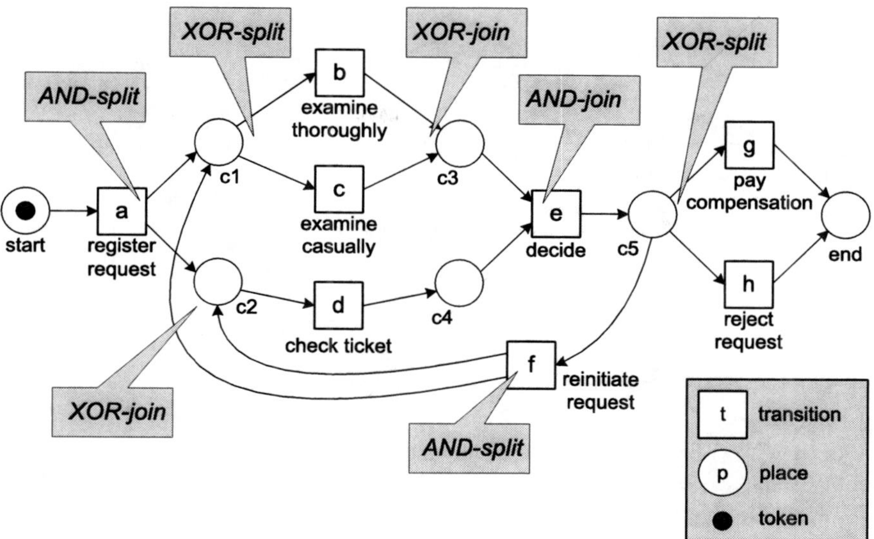

Fig. 2.2 A marked Petri net

$[c1^5, c2^5]$. Note that after the first occurrence of a, also b, c, and d are enabled and can fire concurrently.

To formalize the firing rule, we introduce a notation for input (output) places (transitions). Let $N = (P, T, F)$ be a Petri net. Elements of $P \cup T$ are called *nodes*. A node x is an *input node* of another node y if and only if there is a directed arc from x to y (i.e., $(x, y) \in F$). Node x is an *output node* of y if and only if $(y, x) \in F$. For any $x \in P \cup T$, $\bullet x = \{y \mid (y, x) \in F\}$ and $x \bullet = \{y \mid (x, y) \in F\}$. In Fig. 2.2, $\bullet c1 = \{a, f\}$ and $c1 \bullet = \{b, c\}$.

Definition 2.3 (Firing rule) Let (N, M) be a marked Petri net with $N = (P, T, F)$ and $M \in \mathbb{B}(P)$. Transition $t \in T$ is *enabled*, denoted $(N, M)[t\rangle$, if and only if $\bullet t \leq M$. The *firing rule* $\_[\_\rangle\_ \subseteq \mathcal{N} \times T \times \mathcal{N}$ is the smallest relation satisfying for any $(N, M) \in \mathcal{N}$ and any $t \in T$, $(N, M)[t\rangle \Rightarrow (N, M)[t\rangle(N, (M \setminus \bullet t) \uplus t\bullet)$.

$(N, M)[t\rangle$ denotes that t is enabled at marking M, e.g., $(N, [start])[a\rangle$ in Fig. 2.2. $(N, M)[t\rangle(N, M')$ denotes that firing this enabled transition results in marking M'. For example, $(N, [start])[a\rangle(N, [c1, c2])$ and $(N, [c3, c4])[e\rangle(N, [c5])$.

Let (N, M_0) with $N = (P, T, F)$ be a marked Petri net. A sequence $\sigma \in T^*$ is called a *firing sequence* of (N, M_0) if and only if, for some natural number $n \in \mathbb{N}$, there exist markings $M_1, \ldots, M_n$ and transitions $t_1, \ldots, t_n \in T$ such that $\sigma = \langle t_1, \ldots, t_n\rangle$ and, for all i with $0 \leq i < n$, $(N, M_i)[t_{i+1}\rangle$ and $(N, M_i)[t_{i+1}\rangle(N, M_{i+1})$.[1]

[1] X^* is the set of sequences containing elements of X, i.e., for any $n \in \mathbb{N}$ and $x_1, x_2, \ldots, x_n \in X$: $\langle x_1, x_2, \ldots, x_n\rangle \in X^*$. See also Sect. 4.2.

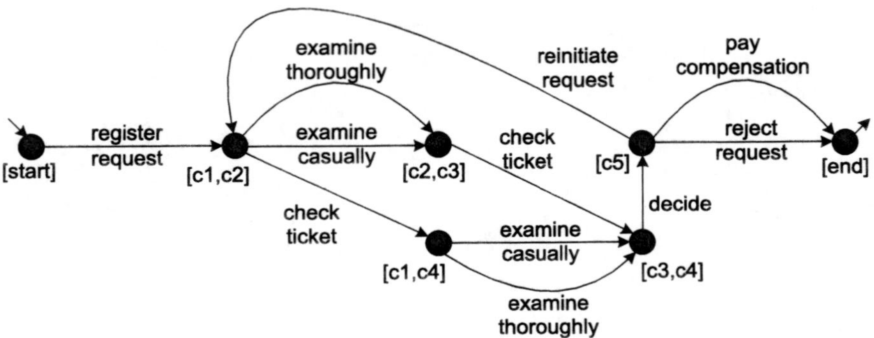

Fig. 2.3 The reachability graph of the marked Petri net shown in Fig. 2.2

Let (N, M_0) be the marked Petri net shown in Fig. 2.2, i.e., $M_0 = [start]$. The empty sequence $\sigma = \langle\ \rangle$ is enabled in (N, M_0), i.e., $\langle\ \rangle$ is a firing sequence of (N, M_0). The sequence $\sigma = \langle a, b\rangle$ is also enabled and firing σ results in marking $[c2, c3]$. Another possible firing sequence is $\sigma = \langle a, c, d, e, f, b, d, e, g\rangle$. A marking M is *reachable* from the initial marking M_0 if and only if there exists a sequence of enabled transitions whose firing leads from M_0 to M. The set of reachable markings of (N, M_0) is denoted $[N, M_0\rangle$. The marked Petri net shown in Fig. 2.2 has seven reachable markings.

In Fig. 2.2, transitions are identified by a single letter, but also have a longer label describing the corresponding activity. Thus far, we ignored these labels.

Definition 2.4 (Labeled Petri net) A *labeled Petri net* is a tuple $N = (P, T, F, A, l)$ where (P, T, F) is a Petri net as defined in Definition 2.2, $A \subseteq \mathscr{A}$ is a set of *activity labels*, and $l \in T \to A$ is a *labeling function*.

In principle, multiple transitions may bear the same label. One can think of the transition label as the *observable action*. Sometimes one wants to express that particular transitions are not observable. For this, we reserve the label τ. A transition t with $l(t) = \tau$ is unobservable. Such transitions are often referred to as *silent* or *invisible*. It is easy to convert any Petri net into a labeled Petri net; just take $A = T$ and $l(t) = t$ for any $t \in T$. The reverse is not always possible, e.g., when several transitions have the same label. It is also possible to convert a marked (labeled) Petri net into a transition system as is shown next.

Definition 2.5 (Reachability graph) Let (N, M_0) with $N = (P, T, F, A, l)$ be a marked labeled Petri net. (N, M_0) defines a transition system $TS = (S, A', T')$ with $S = [N, M_0\rangle$, $S^{start} = \{M_0\}$, $A' = A$, and $T' = \{(M, l(t), M') \in S \times A \times S \mid \exists_{t \in T} (N, M)[t\rangle(N, M')\}$. *TS* is often referred to as the *reachability graph* of (N, M_0).

Figure 2.3 shows the transition system generated from the labeled marked Petri net shown in Fig. 2.2. States correspond to reachable markings, i.e., multi-sets of

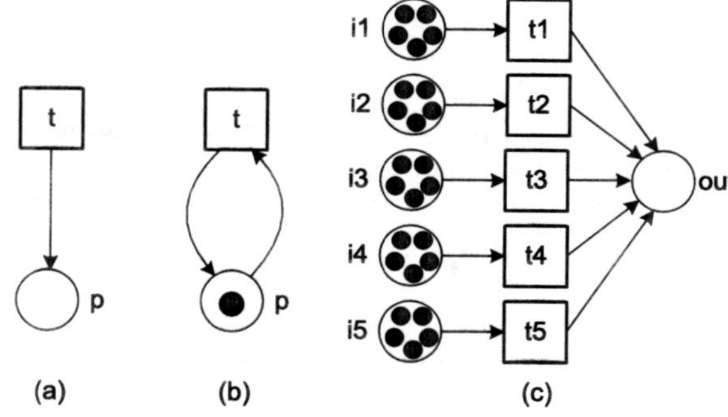

Fig. 2.4 Three Petri nets: (**a**) a Petri net with an infinite state space, (**b**) a Petri net with only one reachable marking, (**c**) a Petri net with 7776 reachable markings

tokens. Note that $S^{start} = \{[start]\}$ is a singleton containing the initial marking of the Petri net. The Petri net does not explicitly define a set of final markings S^{end}. However, in this case it is obvious to take $S^{end} = \{[end]\}$. Later, we will see that it is sometimes useful to distinguish deadlocks and livelocks from successful termination.

Note that we are overloading the term "transition"; the term may refer to a "box" in a Petri net or an "arc" in a transition system. In fact, one transition in a Petri net may correspond to many transitions in the corresponding transition system.

The Petri net in Fig. 2.2 and the transition system in Fig. 2.3 are of similar sizes. If the model contains a lot of concurrency or multiple tokens reside in the same place, then the transition system is much bigger than the Petri net. In fact, a marked Petri net may have infinitely many reachable states. The marked Petri net in Fig. 2.4(a) consists of only one place and one transition. Nevertheless, its corresponding transition system has infinitely many states: $S = \{[p^k] \mid k \in \mathbb{N}\}$. In this example, transition t is continuously enabled because it has no input place. Therefore, it can put any number of tokens in p. The Petri net in Fig. 2.4(b) has two arcs rather than one and now the only reachable state is $[p]$. The marked Petri net in Fig. 2.4(c) shows the effect of concurrency. The corresponding transition system has $6^5 = 7776$ states and 32,400 transitions.

Modern computers can easily compute reachability graphs with millions of states and analyze them. If the reachability graph is infinite, one can resort to the so-called *coverability graph* that presents a kind of over-approximation of the state space [77]. By constructing the reachability graph (if possible) or the coverability graph, one can answer a variety of questions regarding the behavior of the process modeled. Moreover, dedicated analysis techniques can also answer particular questions without constructing the state space, e.g., using the linear-algebraic representation of the Petri net. It is outside the scope of this book to elaborate on these. However, we list some generic properties typically investigated in the context of a marked Petri net.

- A marked Petri net (N, M_0) is *k-bounded* if no place ever holds more that k tokens. Formally, for any $p \in P$ and any $M \in [N, M_0\rangle$: $M(p) \leq k$. The marked Petri net in Fig. 2.4(c) is 25-bounded because in none of the 7776 reachable markings there is a place with more than 25 tokens. It is not 24-bounded, because in the final marking place *out* contains 25 tokens.

- A marked Petri net is *safe* if and only if it is 1-bounded. The marked Petri net shown in Fig. 2.2 is safe because in each of the seven reachable markings there is no place holding multiple tokens.
- A marked Petri net is *bounded* if and only if there exists a $k \in \mathbb{N}$ such that it is k-bounded. Figure 2.4(a) shows an unbounded net. The two other marked Petri nets in Fig. 2.4 (i.e., (b) and (c)) are bounded.
- A marked Petri net (N, M_0) is *deadlock free* if at every reachable marking at least one transition is enabled. Formally, for any $M \in [N, M_0\rangle$ there exists a transition $t \in T$ such that $(N, M)[t\rangle$. Figure 2.4(c) shows a net that is not deadlock free because at marking $[out^{25}]$ no transition is enabled. The two other marked Petri nets in Fig. 2.4 are deadlock free.
- A transition $t \in T$ in a marked Petri net (N, M_0) is *live* if from every reachable marking it is possible to enable t. Formally, for any $M \in [N, M_0\rangle$ there exists a marking $M' \in [N, M\rangle$ such that $(N, M')[t\rangle$. A marked Petri net is live if each of its transitions is live. Note that a deadlock-free Petri net does not need to be live. For example, merge the nets (b) and (c) in Fig. 2.4 into one marked Petri net. The resulting net is deadlock free, but not live.

Petri nets have a strong theoretical basis and can capture concurrency well. Moreover, a wide range of powerful analysis techniques and tools exists [77]. Obviously, this succinct model has problems capturing data-related and time-related aspects. Therefore, various types of high-level Petri nets have been proposed. *Colored Petri nets* (CPNs) are the most widely used Petri-net based formalism that can deal with data-related and time-related aspects [58, 96]. Tokens in a CPN carry a data value and have a timestamp. The data value, often referred to as "color", describes the properties of the object modeled by the token. The timestamp indicates the earliest time at which the token may be consumed. Transitions can assign a delay to produced tokens. This way waiting and service times can be modeled. A CPN may be hierarchical, i.e., transitions can be decomposed into subprocesses. This way large models can be structured. CPN Tools is a toolset providing support for the modeling and analysis of CPNs (www.cpntools.org).

2.2.3 *Workflow Nets*

When modeling business processes in terms of Petri nets, we often consider a subclass of Petri nets known as *WorkFlow nets* (WF-nets) [92, 114]. A WF-net is a Petri net with a dedicated source place where the process starts and a dedicated sink place where the process ends. Moreover, all nodes are on a path from source to sink.

Definition 2.6 (Workflow net) Let $N = (P, T, F, A, l)$ be a (labeled) Petri net and $\bar{t}$ a fresh identifier not in $P \cup T$. N is a *workflow net* (WF-net) if and only if (a) P contains an input place i (also called source place) such that $\bullet i = \emptyset$, (b) P contains an output place o (also called sink place) such that $o\bullet = \emptyset$, and (c) $\bar{N} = (P, T \cup \{\bar{t}\}, F \cup \{(o, \bar{t}), (\bar{t}, i)\}, A \cup \{\tau\}, l \cup \{(\bar{t}, \tau)\})$ is strongly connected, i.e., there is a directed path between any pair of nodes in $\bar{N}$.

$\bar{N}$ is referred to as the short-circuited net [92]. The unique sink place o is connected to the unique source place i in the resulting net.

Figure 2.2 shows an example of a WF-net with $i = start$ and $o = end$. None of the three Petri nets in Fig. 2.4 is a WF-net.

Why are WF-nets particularly relevant for business process modeling? The reason is that the process models used in the context of BPM describe the *life-cycle of cases* of a given kind. Examples of cases are insurance claims, job applications, customer orders, replenishment orders, patients, and credit applications. The process model is instantiated once for each case. Each of these process instances has a well-defined start ("case creation") and end ("case completion"). In-between these points, activities are conducted according to a predefined procedure. One model may be instantiated many times. For example, the process of handling insurance claims may be executed for thousands or even millions of claims. These instances can be seen as copies of the same WF-net, i.e., tokens of different cases are not mixed.

WF-nets are also a natural representation for process mining. There is an obvious relation between the firing sequences of a WF-net and the traces found in event logs. Note that one can only learn models based on examples. In the context of market basket analysis, i.e., finding patterns in what customers buy, one needs many examples of customers buying particular collections of products. Similarly, process discovery uses sequences of activities in which each sequence refers to a particular process instance. These can be seen as firing sequences of an unknown WF-net. Therefore, we will often focus on WF-nets. Recall that the α-algorithm discovered the WF-net in Fig. 1.5 using the set of traces shown in Table 1.2. Every trace corresponds to a case executed from begin to end.

Not every WF-net represents a correct process. For example, a process represented by a WF-net may exhibit errors such as deadlocks, activities that can never become active, livelocks, or garbage being left in the process after termination. Therefore, we define the following well-known correctness criterion [92, 114].

Definition 2.7 (Soundness) Let $N = (P, T, F, A, l)$ be a WF-net with input place i and output place o. N is *sound* if and only if:

- *Safeness*: $(N, [i])$ is safe, i.e., places cannot hold multiple tokens at the same time.
- *Proper completion*: for any marking $M \in [N, [i]\rangle$, $o \in M$ implies $M = [o]$.
- *Option to complete*: for any marking $M \in [N, [i]\rangle$, $[o] \in [N, M\rangle$.
- *Absence of dead parts*: $(N, [i])$ contains no dead transitions (i.e., for any $t \in T$, there is a firing sequence enabling t).

Note that the option to complete implies proper completion. The WF-net shown in Fig. 2.2 is sound. Soundness can be verified using standard Petri-net-based analysis techniques. In fact, soundness corresponds to liveness and safeness of the corresponding short-circuited net $\bar{N}$ introduced in Definition 2.6 [92]. This way efficient algorithms and tools can be applied. An example of a tool tailored toward the analysis of WF-nets is *Woflan* [121]. This functionality is also embedded in our process mining tool *ProM* described in Sect. 10.2.

2.2.4 YAWL

YAWL is both a workflow modeling *language* and an open-source workflow *system* [90]. The acronym YAWL stands for "Yet Another Workflow Language". The development of the YAWL language was heavily influenced by the *Workflow Patterns Initiative* [101, 130] mentioned earlier. Based on a systematic analysis of the constructs used by existing process modeling notations and workflow languages, a large collection of patterns was identified. These patterns cover all workflow perspectives, i.e., there are control-flow patterns, data patterns, resource patterns, change patterns, exception patterns, etc. The aim of YAWL is to offer direct support for many patterns while keeping the language simple. It can be seen as a reference implementation of the most important workflow patterns. Over time, the YAWL language and the YAWL system have increasingly become synonymous and have garnered widespread interest from both practitioners and the academic community alike. YAWL is currently one of the most widely used open-source workflow systems.

Here we restrict ourselves to the control-flow perspective. Figure 2.5 shows the main constructs. Each process has a dedicated start and end condition, like in WF-nets. Activities in YAWL are called *tasks*. *Conditions* in YAWL correspond to places in Petri nets. However, it is also possible to directly connect tasks without putting a condition in-between. Tasks have—depending on their type—a well-defined split and join semantics. An *AND-join/AND-split* task behaves like a transition, i.e., it needs to consume one token via each of the incoming arcs and produces a token along each of the outgoing arcs. An *XOR-split* selects precisely one of its outgoing arcs. The selection is based on evaluating data conditions. Only one token is produced and sent along the selected arc. An *XOR-join* is enabled once for every incoming token and does not need to synchronize. An *OR-split* selects one or more of its outgoing arcs. This selection is again based on evaluating data conditions. Note that an OR-split may select 2 out of three 3 outgoing arcs. The semantics of the *OR-join* are more involved. The OR-join requires at least one input token, but also synchronizes tokens that are "on their way" to the OR-join. As long as another token may arrive via one of the ingoing arcs, the OR-join waits. YAWL also supports *cancelation regions*. A task may have a cancelation region consisting of conditions, tasks, and arcs. Once the task completes all tokens are removed from this region. Note that tokens for the task's output conditions are produced after emptying the cancelation region. YAWL's cancelation regions provide a powerful mechanism to abort work in parallel branches and to reset parts of the workflow. Tasks in a YAWL model can be *atomic* or *composite*. A composite task refers to another YAWL model. This way models can be structured hierarchically. Atomic and composite tasks can

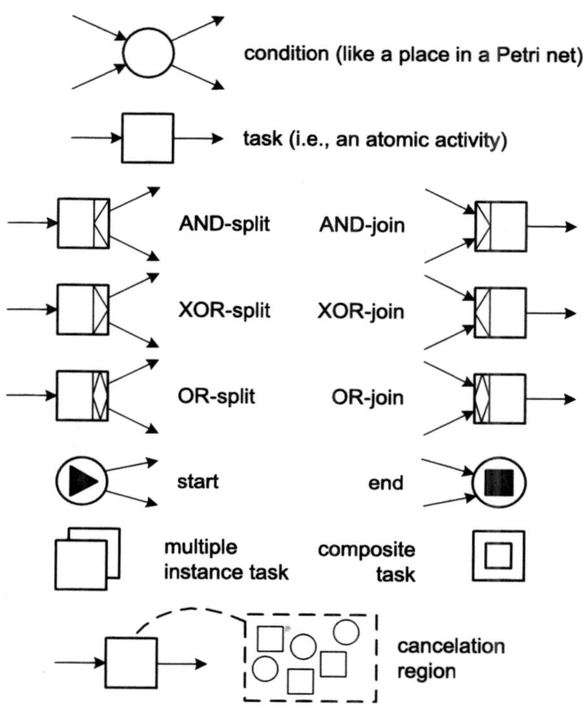

Fig. 2.5 YAWL notation

be instantiated multiple times in parallel. For example, when handling a customer order, some tasks needs to be executed for every order line. These order lines can be processed in any order. Therefore, a loop construct is less suitable. Figure 2.5 shows the icon for such a multiple instance task and all other constructs just mentioned.

Figure 2.6 shows an example YAWL model for the handling of a request for compensation within an airline. To show some of the features of YAWL, we extended the process described in Sect. 1.2 with some more complex behaviors. In the new model, it is possible that both examinations are executed. By using an OR-split and an OR-join, *examine causally* and/or *examine thoroughly* are executed. The model has also been extended with a cancelation region (see dotted box in Fig. 2.6). As long as there is a token in $c3$, task *new information* may be executed. When this happens, all tokens are removed from the region, i.e., checks and examinations are aborted. Task *new information* does not need to know where all tokens are and after the reset by this task the new state is $[c1, c2, c3]$. Explicit choices in YAWL (i.e., XOR/OR-splits) are driven by data conditions. In the Petri net in Fig. 2.2, all choices were nondeterministic. In the example YAWL model, the decision may be derived from the outcome of the check and the examination(s), i.e., the XOR-split *decide* may be based on data created in earlier tasks. As indicated, both the YAWL language and the YAWL system cover all relevant perspectives (resources, data, exceptions, etc.). For example, it is possible to model that decisions are taken by the

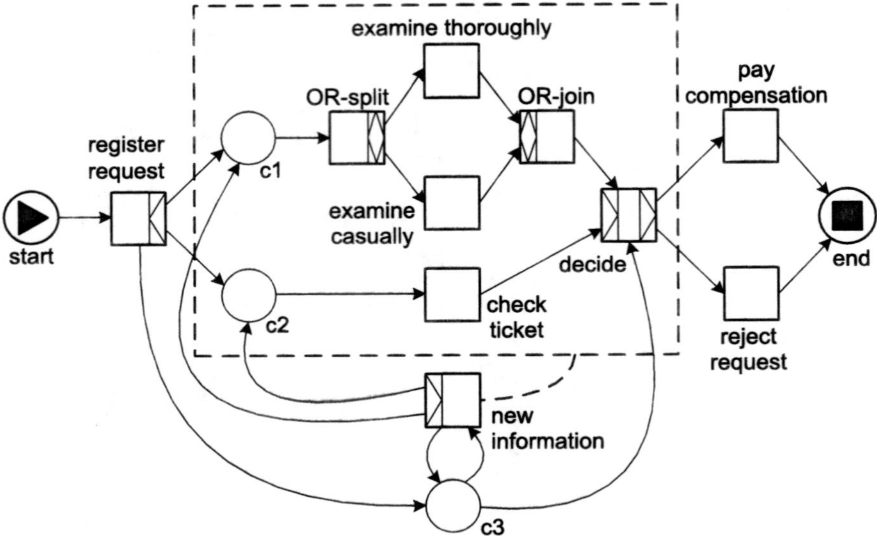

Fig. 2.6 Process model using the YAWL notation

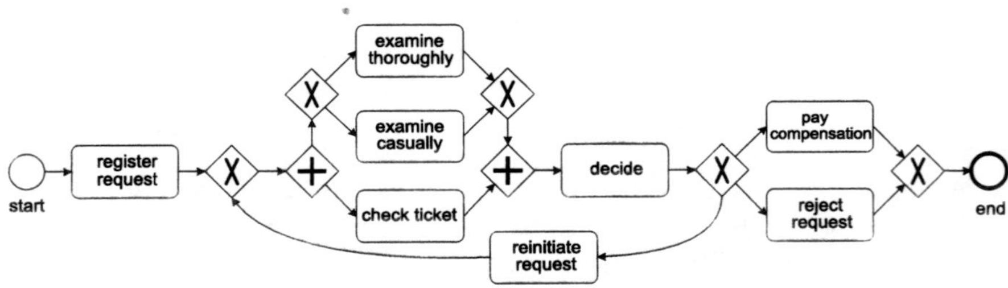

Fig. 2.7 Process model using the BPMN notation

manager and that it is not allowed that two examinations for the same request are done by the same person (4-eyes principle) [90].

2.2.5 Business Process Modeling Notation (BPMN)

Recently, the *Business Process Modeling Notation* (BPMN) has become one of the most widely used languages to model business processes. BPMN is supported by many tool vendors and has been standardized by the OMG [72]. Figure 2.7 shows the BPMN model already introduced in Sect. 1.2.

Figure 2.8 shows a small subset of all notational elements. Atomic activities are called *tasks*. Like in YAWL activities can be nested. Most of the constructs can be easily understood after the introduction to YAWL. A notable difference is that the

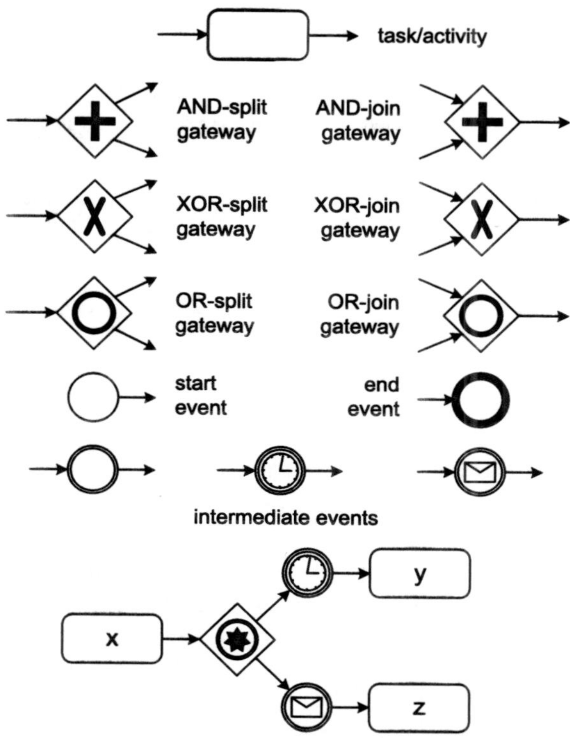

Fig. 2.8 BPMN notation

routing logic is not associated with tasks but with separate *gateways*. Figure 2.8 shows that there are split and join gateways of different types: AND, XOR, OR. The splits are based on data conditions. An *event* is comparable to a place in a Petri net. However, the semantics of places in Petri nets and events in BPMN are quite different. There is no need to insert events in-between activities and events cannot have multiple input or output arcs. *Start events* have one outgoing arc, *intermediate events* have one incoming and one outgoing arc, and *end events* have one incoming arc. Unlike in YAWL or a Petri net, one cannot have events with multiple incoming or outgoing arcs; splitting and joining needs to be done using gateways. To model the so-called *deferred choice* workflow pattern [101], one needs to use the event-based XOR gateway shown in Fig. 2.8. This illustrates the use of events. After executing task x, there is a race between two events. One of the events is triggered by a timeout. The other event is triggered by an external massage. The first event to occur determines the route taken. If the message arrives before the timer goes off, task z is executed. If the timer goes off before the massage arrives, task y is executed. Note that this construct can easily be modeled in YAWL using a condition with two output arcs.

Figure 2.8 shows just a tiny subset of all notations provided by BPMN. Most vendors support only a small subset of BPMN in their products. Moreover, users

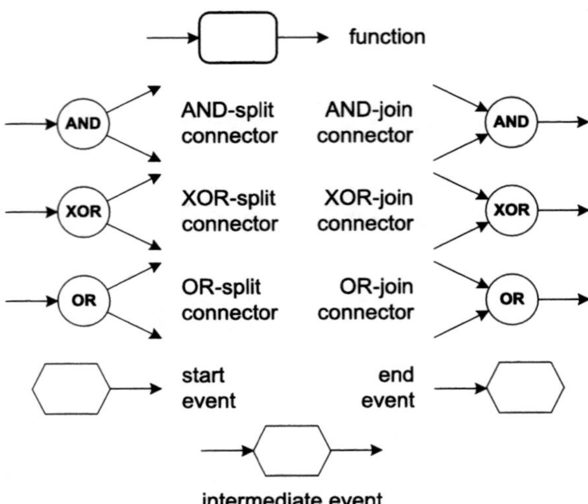

Fig. 2.9 EPC notation

typically use only few BPMN constructs. In [131] it was shown that the average subset of BPMN used in real-life models consists of less than 10 different symbols (despite the more than 50 distinct graphical elements offered to the modeler). For this reason, we will be rather pragmatic when it comes to process models and their notation.

2.2.6 Event-Driven Process Chains (EPCs)

Event-driven Process Chains (EPCs) provide a classical notation to model business processes [85]. The notation is supported by products such as ARIS and SAP R/3. Basically, EPCs cover a limited subset of BPMN and YAWL while using a dedicated graphical notation.

Figure 2.9 provides an overview of the different notational elements. *Functions* correspond to activities. A function has precisely one input arc and one output arc. Therefore, splitting and joining can only be modeled using *connectors*. These are comparable to the gateways in BPMN. Again splits and joins of type AND, XOR, and OR are supported. Like in BPMN, there are three types of *events* (start, intermediate, and end). Events and functions need to alternate along any path, i.e., it is not allowed to connect events to events or functions to functions.

Figure 2.10 shows another variation of the process for handling a request for compensation. Note that, because of the two OR connectors, it is possible to do both examinations or just one.

The EPC notation was one of the first notations allowing for OR splits and joins. However, the people who developed and evangelized EPCs did not provide clear semantics nor some reference implementation [100]. This triggered lively debates

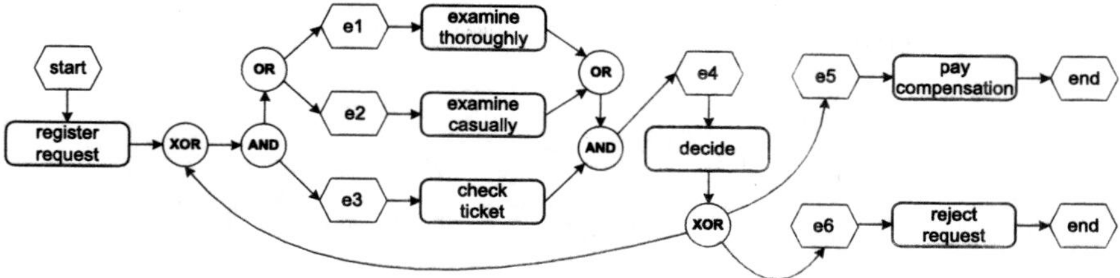

Fig. 2.10 Process model using the EPC notation

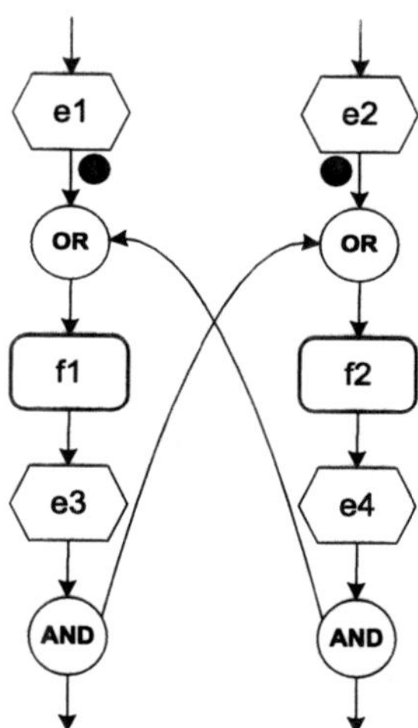

Fig. 2.11 The so-called "vicious circle" expressed using the EPC notation

resulting in various proposals and alternative implementations. Consider, for example, the so-called "vicious circle" shown in Fig. 2.11. The two tokens show the state of this process fragment; events $e1$ and $e2$ hold a token. It is unclear what could happen next, because both OR-joins depend on one another.

Should the OR-join below $e1$ block or not? Suppose that this OR-join blocks, then by symmetry also the other OR-join following $e2$ should block and the whole EPC deadlocks in the state shown Fig. 2.11. This seems to be wrong because if it deadlocks, the OR join will never receive an additional token, and hence should not have waited in the first place. Suppose that the OR-join following $e1$ does not block. By symmetry, the other OR-join should also not block and both $f1$ and $f2$ are executed and tokens flow toward both OR-joins via the two AND-splits. However, this implies that the OR-joins should both have blocked. Hence, there is a *paradox* because all possible decisions are wrong.

The vicious circle paradox shows that higher-level constructs may introduce all kinds of subtle semantic problems. Despite these problems and the different notations, the core concepts of the various languages are very similar.

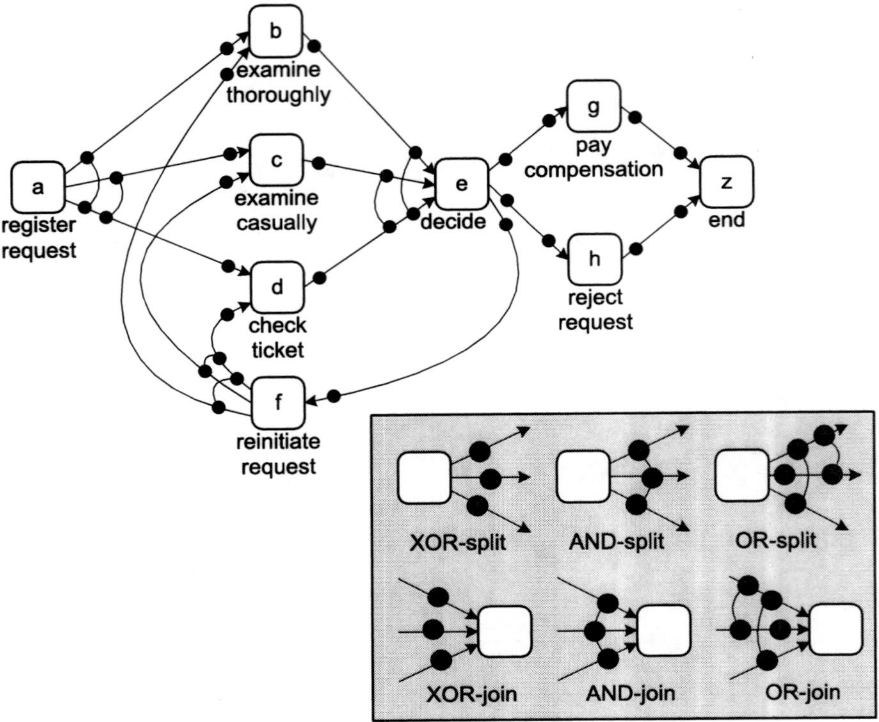

Fig. 2.12 Causal net C_1

2.2.7 Causal Nets

The notations discussed thus far connect activities (i.e., transitions, tasks, functions) through model elements like places (Petri nets), conditions (YAWL), connectors and events (EPC), gateways and events (BPMN). These elements interconnect activities but do not leave any "marks" in the event log, i.e., they need to be inferred by analyzing the behavior. Since the log does not provide concrete information about places, conditions, connectors, gateways and events, some mining algorithms use a representation consisting of just activities and no connecting elements [2, 31, 50, 123, 124].

Causal nets are a representation tailored toward process mining. A causal net is a graph where nodes represent activities and arcs represent causal dependencies. Each activity has a set of possible *input bindings* and a set of possible *output bindings*. Consider, for example, the causal net shown in Fig. 2.12. Activity a has only an empty input binding as this is the start activity. There are two possible output bindings: $\{b, d\}$ and $\{c, d\}$. This means that a is followed by either b and d, or c and d. Activity e has two possible input bindings ($\{b, d\}$ and $\{c, d\}$) and three possible output bindings ($\{g\}$, $\{h\}$, and $\{f\}$). Hence, e is preceded by either b and d, or c and d, and is succeeded by just g, h or f. Activity z is the end activity having two input bindings and one output binding (the empty binding). This activity has been added to create a unique end point. All executions commence with start activity a and finish with end activity z. As will be shown later, the causal net shown in Fig. 2.12 and the Petri net shown in Fig. 2.2 are trace equivalent, i.e., they both allow for the same set of traces. However, there are no places in the causal net; the routing logic is solely represented by the possible input and output bindings.

Definition 2.8 (Causal net) A *Causal net* (C-net) is a tuple $C = (A, a_i, a_o, D, I, O)$ where:

- $A \subseteq \mathscr{A}$ is a finite set of *activities*
- $a_i \in A$ is the *start activity*
- $a_o \in A$ is the *end activity*
- $D \subseteq A \times A$ is the *dependency relation*
- $AS = \{X \subseteq \mathscr{P}(A) \mid X = \{\emptyset\} \vee \emptyset \notin X\}$[2]
- $I \in A \to AS$ defines the set of possible *input bindings* per activity
- $O \in A \to AS$ defines the set of possible *output bindings* per activity

such that

- $D = \{(a_1, a_2) \in A \times A \mid a_1 \in \bigcup_{as \in I(a_2)} as\}$
- $D = \{(a_1, a_2) \in A \times A \mid a_2 \in \bigcup_{as \in O(a_1)} as\}$
- $\{a_i\} = \{a \in A \mid I(a) = \{\emptyset\}\}$
- $\{a_o\} = \{a \in A \mid O(a) = \{\emptyset\}\}$
- All activities in the graph (A, D) are on a path from a_i to a_o

The C-net of Fig. 2.12 can be described as follows. $A = \{a, b, c, d, e, f, g, h, z\}$ is the set of activities, $a = a_i$ is the unique start activity, and $z = a_o$ is the unique end activity. The arcs shown in Fig. 2.12 visualize the dependency relation $D = \{(a, b), (a, c), (a, d), (b, e), \ldots, (g, z), (h, z)\}$. Functions I and O describe the sets of possible input and output bindings. $I(a) = \{\emptyset\}$ is the set of possible input bindings of a, i.e., the only input binding is the empty set of activities. $O(a) = \{\{b, d\}, \{c, d\}\}$ is the set of possible output bindings of a, i.e., activity a is followed by d and either b or c. $I(b) = \{\{a\}, \{f\}\}$, $O(b) = \{\{e\}\}, \ldots, I(z) = \{\{g\}, \{h\}\}$, $O(z) = \{\emptyset\}$. Note that any element of AS is a set of sets of activities, e.g., $\{\{b, d\}, \{c, d\}\} \in AS$. If one of the elements is the empty set, then there cannot be any other elements, i.e., for any $X \in AS$: $X = \{\emptyset\}$ or $\emptyset \notin X$. This implies that only the unique start activity a_i has the empty binding as (only) possible input binding. Similarly, only the unique end activity a_o has the empty binding as (only) possible output binding.

An *activity binding* is a tuple (a, as^I, as^O) denoting the occurrence of activity a with input binding as^I and output binding as^O. For example, $(e, \{b, d\}, \{f\})$ denotes the occurrence of activity e in Fig. 2.12 while being preceded by b and d, and succeeded by f.

---

[2] $\mathscr{P}(A) = \{A' \mid A' \subseteq A\}$ is the powerset of A. Hence, elements of AS are *sets of sets* of activities.

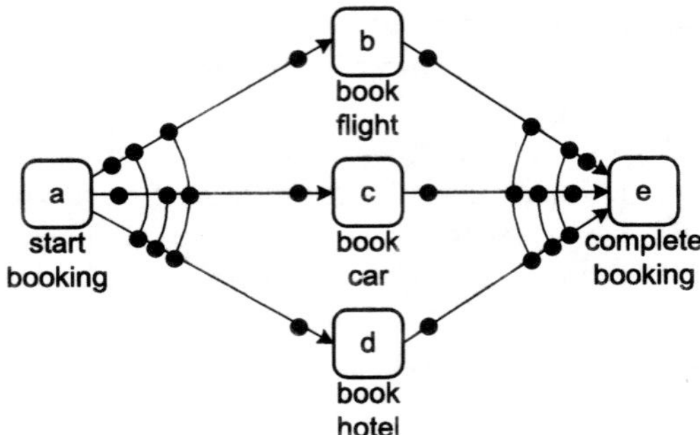

Fig. 2.13 Causal net C_2

Definition 2.9 (Binding) Let $C = (A, a_i, a_o, D, I, O)$ be a C-net. $B = \{(a, as^I, as^O) \in A \times \mathscr{P}(A) \times \mathscr{P}(A) \mid as^I \in I(a) \ \wedge \ as^O \in O(a)\}$ is the set of *activity bindings*. A *binding sequence* σ is a sequence of activity bindings, i.e., $\sigma \in B^*$.

A possible binding sequence for the C-net of Fig. 2.12 is $\langle(a, \emptyset, \{b, d\}), (b, \{a\}, \{e\}), (d, \{a\}, \{e\}), (e, \{b, d\}, \{g\}), (g, \{e\}, \{z\}), (z, \{g\}, \emptyset)\rangle$

Figure 2.13 shows another C-net modeling the booking of a trip. After activity a (*start booking*), there are three possible activities: b (*book flight*), c (*book car*), and d (*book hotel*). The process ends with activity e (*complete booking*). $O(a) = I(e) = \{\{b\}, \{c\}, \{b, d\}, \{c, d\}, \{b, c, d\}\}$, $I(a) = O(e) = \{\emptyset\}$, $I(b) = I(c) = I(d) = \{\{a\}\}$, and $O(b) = O(c) = O(d) = \{\{e\}\}$. A possible binding sequence for the C-net of Fig. 2.12 is $\langle(a, \emptyset, \{b, d\}), (d, \{a\}, \{e\}), (b, \{a\}, \{e\}), (e, \{b, d\}, \emptyset)\rangle$, i.e., the scenario in which a flight and a hotel are booked. Note that Fig. 2.13 does not allow for booking just a hotel nor is it possible to just book a flight and a car.

A binding sequence is *valid* if a predecessor activity and successor activity always "agree" on their bindings. For a predecessor activity x and successor activity y, we need to see the following "pattern": $\langle\ldots, (x, \{\ldots\}, \{y, \ldots\}), \ldots, (y, \{x, \ldots\}, \{\ldots\}), \ldots\rangle$, i.e., the occurrence of activity x with y in its output binding needs to be followed by the occurrence of activity y and the occurrence of activity y with x in its input binding needs to be preceded by the occurrence of activity x. To formalize the notion of a valid sequence, we first define the notion of *state*.

Definition 2.10 (State) Let $C = (A, a_i, a_o, D, I, O)$ be a C-net. $S = \mathbb{B}(A \times A)$ is the *state space* of C. $s \in S$ is a *state*, i.e., a multi-set of pending *obligations*. Function $\psi \in B^* \rightarrow S$ is defined inductively: $\psi(\langle\,\rangle) = [\,]$ and $\psi(\sigma \oplus (a, as^I, as^O)) = (\psi(\sigma) \setminus (as^I \times \{a\})) \uplus (\{a\} \times as^O)$ for any binding sequence $\sigma \oplus (a, as^I, as^O) \in B^*$.[3] $\psi(\sigma)$ is the state after executing binding sequence σ.

[3] $\sigma_1 \oplus \sigma_2$ is the concatenation of two sequences, e.g., $\langle a, b, c\rangle \oplus \langle d, e\rangle = \langle a, b, c, d, e\rangle$. It is also possible to concatenate a sequence and an element, e.g., $\langle a, b, c\rangle \oplus d = \langle a, b, c, d\rangle$. Recall that X^* is the set of all sequences containing elements of X and $\langle\,\rangle$ is the empty sequence. See also Sect. 4.2 for more notations for sequences.

Consider C-net C_1 shown in Fig. 2.12. Initially there are no pending "obligations", i.e., no output bindings have been enacted without having corresponding input bindings. If activity binding $(a, \emptyset, \{b, d\})$ occurs, then $\psi(\langle(a, \emptyset, \{b, d\})\rangle) = \psi(\langle\,\rangle) \setminus (\emptyset \times \{a\}) \uplus (\{a\} \times \{b, d\}) = [\,] \setminus [\,] \uplus [(a, b), (a, d)] = [(a, b), (a, d)]$. State $[(a, b), (a, d)]$ denotes the obligation to execute both b and d using input bindings involving a. Input bindings remove pending obligations whereas output bindings create new obligations.

A *valid sequence* is a binding sequence that (a) starts with start activity a_i, (b) ends with end activity a_o, (c) only removes obligations that are pending, and (d) ends without any pending obligations. Consider, for example, the valid sequence $\sigma = \langle(a, \emptyset, \{b, d\}), (d, \{a\}, \{e\}), (b, \{a\}, \{e\}), (e, \{b, d\}, \emptyset)\rangle$ for C-net C_2 in Fig. 2.13:

$$\begin{aligned}
\psi(\langle\,\rangle) &= [\,] \\
\psi(\langle(a, \emptyset, \{b, d\})\rangle) &= [(a, b), (a, d)] \\
\psi(\langle(a, \emptyset, \{b, d\}), (d, \{a\}, \{e\})\rangle) &= [(a, b), (d, e)] \\
\psi(\langle(a, \emptyset, \{b, d\}), (d, \{a\}, \{e\}), (b, \{a\}, \{e\})\rangle) &= [(b, e), (d, e)] \\
\psi(\langle(a, \emptyset, \{b, d\}), (d, \{a\}, \{e\}), (b, \{a\}, \{e\}), (e, \{b, d\}, \emptyset)\rangle) &= [\,]
\end{aligned}$$

Sequence σ indeed starts with start activity a, ends with end activity e, only removes obligations that are pending (i.e., for every input binding there was an earlier output binding), and ends without any pending obligations: $\psi(\sigma) = [\,]$.

Definition 2.11 (Valid) Let $C = (A, a_i, a_o, D, I, O)$ be a C-net and $\sigma = \langle(a_1, as_1^I, as_1^O), (a_2, as_2^I, as_2^O), \ldots, (a_n, as_n^I, as_n^O)\rangle \in B^*$ a binding sequence. σ is a *valid sequence* of C if and only if:

- $a_1 = a_i$, $a_n = a_o$, and $a_k \in A \setminus \{a_i, a_o\}$ for $1 < k < n$
- $\psi(\sigma) = [\,]$
- For any prefix $\langle(a_1, as_1^I, as_1^O), (a_2, as_2^I, as_2^O), \ldots, (a_k, as_k^I, as_k^O)\rangle = \sigma' \oplus (a_k, as_k^I, as_k^O) \in \mathit{pref}(\sigma)$: $(as_k^I \times \{a_k\}) \le \psi(\sigma')$

$V(C)$ is the set of all valid sequences of C.

The first requirement states that valid sequences start with a_i and end with a_o (a_i and a_o cannot appear in the middle of valid sequence). The second requirement states that at the end there should not be any pending obligations. (One can think of this as the constraint that no tokens left in the net.) The last requirement considers all nonempty prefixes of σ: $\langle(a_1, as_1^I, as_1^O), (a_2, as_2^I, as_2^O), \ldots, (a_k, as_k^I, as_k^O)\rangle$. The last activity binding of the prefix (i.e., (a_k, as_k^I, as_k^O)) should only remove pending obligations, i.e., $(as_k^I \times \{a_k\}) \le \psi(\sigma')$ where $as_k^I \times \{a_k\}$ are the obligations to be removed and $\psi(\sigma')$ are the pending obligations just before the occurrence of the kth binding. (One can think of this as the constraint that one cannot consume tokens that have not been produced.)

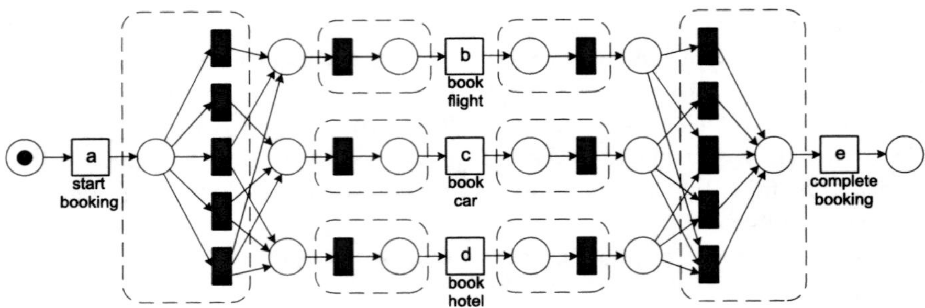

Fig. 2.14 A C-net transformed into a WF-net with silent transitions: every "sound run" of the WF-net corresponds to a valid sequence of the C-net C_2 shown in Fig. 2.13

Figure 2.13 has twelve valid sequences: only b is executed ($\langle(a, \emptyset, \{b\}), (b, \{a\}, \{e\}), (e, \{b\}, \emptyset)\rangle$), only c is executed (besides a and e), b and d are executed (two possibilities), c and d are executed (two possibilities), and b, c and d are executed ($3! = 6$ possibilities). The C-net in Fig. 2.12 has infinitely many valid sequences because of the loop construct involving f. For example, $\langle(a, \emptyset, \{c, d\}), (c, \{a\}, \{e\}), (d, \{a\}, \{e\}), (e, \{c, d\}, \{f\}), (f, \{e\}, \{c, d\}), (c, \{f\}, \{e\}), (d, \{f\}, \{e\}), (e, \{c, d\}, \{g\}), (g, \{e\}, \{z\}), (z, \{g\}, \emptyset)\rangle$.

For the semantics of a C-net we only consider valid sequences, i.e., *invalid sequences are not part of the behavior* described by the C-net. This means that C-nets do not use plain "token-game like semantics" as in BPMN, Petri nets, EPCs, and YAWL. The semantics of C-nets are more declarative as they are defined over complete sequences rather than a local firing rule. This is illustrated by the WF-net shown in Fig. 2.14. This WF-net aims to model the semantics of the C-net C_2 in Fig. 2.13. The input and output bindings are modeled by *silent transitions*. In Fig. 2.14 these are denoted by black rectangles without labels. Note that the WF-net also allows for many invalid sequences. For example, it is possible to enable b, c and d. After firing b, it is possible to fire e without firing c and d. This firing sequence does not correspond to a valid sequence because there are still pending commitments when executing the end activity e. However, if we only consider firing sequences of the WF-net that start with a token in the source place and end with a token in the sink place, then these match one-to-one with the valid sequences in $V(C_2)$.

The C-net shown in Fig. 2.12 and the WF-net shown in Fig. 2.2 are trace equivalent. Recall that in this comparison we consider all possible firing sequences of the WF-net and only valid sequences for the C-net.

We defined the notion of soundness for WF-nets (Definition 2.7) to avoid process models that have deadlocks, livelocks, and other anomalies, A similar notion can be defined for C-nets.

Definition 2.12 (Soundness of C-nets) A C-net $C = (A, a_i, a_o, D, I, O)$ is *sound* if (a) for all $a \in A$ and $as^I \in I(a)$ there exists a $\sigma \in V(C)$ and $as^O \subseteq A$ such that

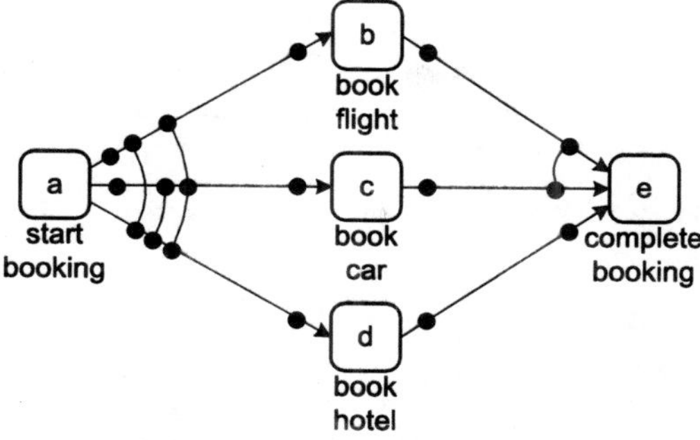

(a) unsound because there are no valid sequences

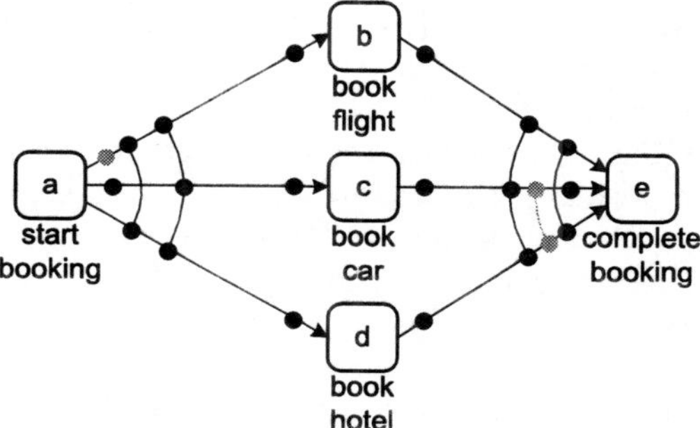

(b) unsound although there exist valid sequences

Fig. 2.15 Two C-nets that are not sound. The first net does not allow for any valid sequence, i.e., $V(C) = \emptyset$. The second net has valid sequences but also shows input/output bindings that are not realizable

$(a, as^I, as^O) \in \sigma$, and (b) for all $a \in A$ and $as^O \in O(a)$ there exists a $\sigma \in V(C)$ and $as^I \subseteq A$ such that $(a, as^I, as^O) \in \sigma$.

Since the semantics of C-nets already enforce "proper completion" and the "option to complete", we only need to make sure that there are valid sequences and that all parts of the C-net can potentially be activated by such a valid sequence. The C-nets C_1 and C_2 in Figs. 2.12 and 2.13 are sound. Figure 2.15 shows two C-nets that are not sound. In Fig. 2.15(a), there are no valid sequences because the output bindings of a and the input bindings of e do not match. For example, consider the binding sequence $\sigma = \langle(a, \emptyset, \{b\}), (b, \{a\}, \{e\})\rangle$. Sequence σ cannot be extended into a valid sequence because $\psi(\sigma) = [(b, e)]$ and $\{b\} \notin I(e)$, i.e., the input bindings of e do not allow for just booking a flight whereas the output bindings of a do. In Fig. 2.15(b), there are valid sequences, e.g., $\langle(a, \emptyset, \{c\}), (c, \{a\}, \{e\}), (e, \{c\}, \emptyset)\rangle$. However, not all bindings appear in one or more valid sequences. For example, the output binding $\{b\} \in O(a)$ does not appear in any valid sequence, i.e., after selecting just a flight the sequence cannot be completed properly. The input binding $\{c, d\} \in I(e)$ also does not appear in any valid sequence, i.e., the C-net suggests that only a car and hotel can be booked but there is no corresponding valid sequence.

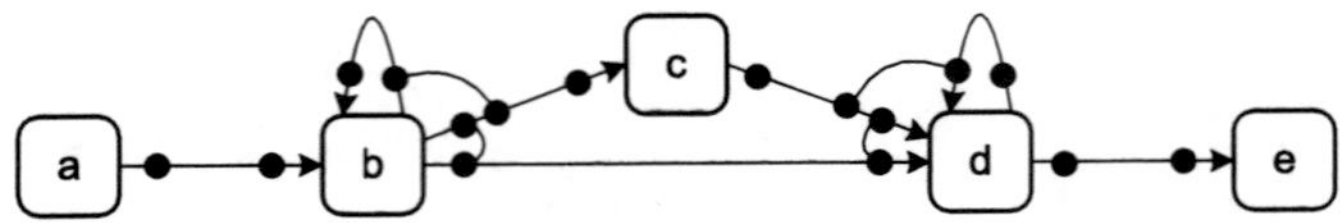

Fig. 2.16 A sound C-net that has no corresponding WF-net

Figure 2.16 shows an example of a sound C-net. One of the valid binding sequences for this C-net is $\langle(a,\emptyset,\{b\}),(b,\{a\},\{b,c\}),(b,\{b\},\{c,d\}),(c,\{b\},\{d\}),(c,\{b\},\{d\}),(d,\{b,c\},\{d\}),(d,\{c,d\},\{e\}),(e,\{d\},\emptyset)\rangle$, i.e., the sequence $\langle a,b,b,c,c,d,d,e\rangle$. This sequence covers all the bindings. Therefore, the C-net is sound. Examples of other valid sequences are $\langle a,b,c,d,e\rangle$, $\langle a,b,c,b,c,d,d,e\rangle$, and $\langle a,b,b,b,c,c,c,d,d,d,e\rangle$. Figure 2.16 illustrates the expressiveness of C-nets. Note that there is no sound WF-net that reproduces exactly the set of valid sequences of this C-net. If we use the construction shown in Fig. 2.14 for the C-net of Fig. 2.16, we get a WF-net that is able to simulate the valid sequences. However, the resulting WF-net also allows for invalid behavior and it is impossible modify the model such that the set of firing sequences coincides with the set of valid sequences.

Causal nets are particularly suitable for process mining given their declarative nature and expressiveness without introducing all kinds of additional model elements (places, conditions, events, gateways, etc.). Several process discovery and conformance checking approaches use a similar representation [2, 31, 50, 123, 124]. In Chap. 6, we elaborate on this when discussing some of the more advanced process mining algorithms.

2.3 Model-Based Process Analysis

In Sect. 1.2, we discussed the different reasons for making models. Figure 1.3 illustrated the use of these models in the BPM life-cycle. Subsequent analysis showed that existing approaches using process models ignore event data. In later chapters, we will show how to exploit event data when analyzing processes and their models. However, before doing so, we briefly summarize mainstream approaches for model-based analysis: *verification* and *performance analysis*. Verification is concerned with the correctness of a system or process. Performance analysis focuses on flow times, waiting times, utilization, and service levels.

2.3.1 Verification

In Sect. 2.2.3 we introduced the notion of soundness for WF-nets. This is a correctness criterion that can be checked using verification techniques. Consider, for example, the WF-net shown in Fig. 2.17. The model has been extended to model

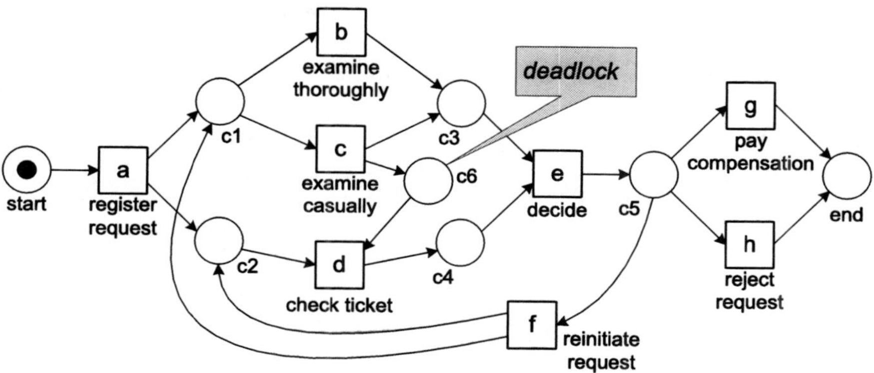

Fig. 2.17 A WF-net that is not sound

that *check ticket* should wait for the completion of *examine casually* but not for *examine thoroughly*. Therefore, place $c6$ was added to model this dependency. However, a modeling error was made. One of the requirements listed in Definition 2.7, i.e., the "option to complete" requirement, is not satisfied. The marking $[c2, c3]$ is reached by executing the firing sequence $\langle a, b \rangle$ and from this marking the desired end marking $[end]$ is no longer reachable. Note that $[c2, c3]$ is a dead marking, e.g., d is not enabled because $c6$ is empty.

Definition 2.12 defines a soundness notion for C-nets. The notion of soundness can easily be adapted for other languages such as YAWL, EPCs, and BPMN. When defining transition systems we already mentioned $S^{end} \subseteq S$ as the set of acceptable final states. Hence, we can define soundness as follows: a transition system is sound if and only if from any reachable state it is possible to reach a state in S^{end}. When introducing Petri nets we also defined generic properties such as liveness and boundedness. Some of these properties can be analyzed without constructing the state space. For example, for free-choice Petri nets, i.e., processes where choice and synchronization can be separated, liveness and boundedness can be checked by analyzing the rank of the corresponding incidence matrix [34]. Hence, soundness can be checked in polynomial time for free-choice WF-nets. Invariants can often be used to show boundedness or the unreachability of a particular marking. However, most of the more interesting verification questions require the exploration of (a part of) the state space.

Soundness is a generic property. Sometimes a more specific property needs to be investigated, e.g., "the ticket was checked for all rejected requests". Such properties can be expressed in *temporal logic* [20, 62]. *Linear Temporal Logic* (LTL) is an example of a temporal logic that, in addition to classical logical operators, uses temporal operators such as: always ($\Box$), eventually ($\Diamond$), until ($\sqcup$), weak until (W), and next time ($\bigcirc$). The expression $\Diamond h \Rightarrow \Diamond d$ means that for all cases in which h (*reject request*) is executed also d (*check ticket*) is executed. Another example is $\Box(f \Rightarrow \Diamond e)$ that states that any occurrence of f will be followed by e. *Model checking* techniques can be used to check such properties [20].

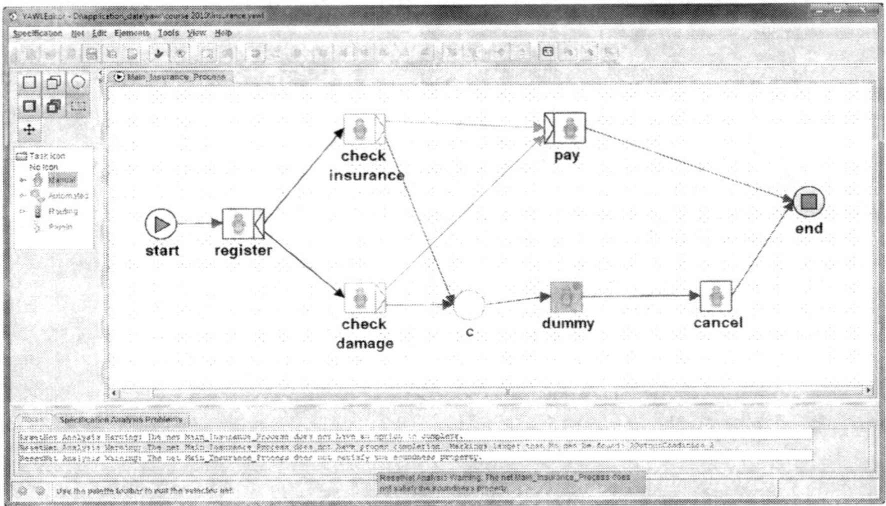

Fig. 2.18 An incorrect YAWL model: the cancelation region of *dummy* comprises of *check insurance*, *check damage*, condition *c* and the two implicit input conditions of *pay*. Hence, after cancelation, a token may be left on one of the output arcs of *register*

Another verification task is the comparison of two models. For example, the implementation of a process needs is compared to the high-level specification of the process. As indicated before, there exists different equivalence notions (trace equivalence, branching bisimilarity, etc.) [120]. Moreover, there are also various simulation notions demanding that one model can "follow all moves" of the other but not vice versa (see also Sect. 5.3).

There are various tools to verify process models. A classical example is Woflan that is tailored toward checking soundness [121]. Also workflow systems such as YAWL provide verification capabilities. Consider, for example, the screenshot shown in Fig. 2.18. The figure shows the editor of YAWL while analyzing the model depicted. The process starts with task *register*. After this task, two checks can be done in parallel: *check insurance* and *check damage*. These tasks are XOR-splits; depending on the result of the check, one of the output arcs is selected. If both checks are OK, task *pay* is executed. If one of the checks indicates a problem, then the *dummy* task is executed. This task has a cancelation region consisting of *check insurance*, *check damage*, condition *c* and the two implicit input conditions of *pay*. The goal of this region is to remove all tokens, cancel the claim, and then end. However, the verifier of YAWL reports a problem. The YAWL model is not correct, because there may a be token pending in one of the implicit output conditions of *register*, i.e., there may be still a token on the arc connecting *register* and *check insurance* or on the arc connecting *register* and *check damage*. As a result, the model may deadlock and "garbage" may be left behind. When these two implicit conditions are included in the cancelation region of the *dummy* task, then the verifier of YAWL will not find any problems and the model is indeed free of deadlocks and other anomalies.

2.3.2 Performance Analysis

The performance of a process or organization can be defined in different ways. Typically, three dimensions of performance are identified: *time*, *cost* and *quality*. For each of these performance dimensions, different *Key Performance Indicators* (KPIs) can be defined. When looking at the *time dimension* the following performance indicators can be identified:

- The *lead time* (also referred to as flow time) is the total time from the creation of the case to the completion of the case. In terms of a WF-net, this is the time it takes to go from source place i to sink place o. One can measure the average lead time over all cases. However, the degree of variance may also be important, i.e., it makes a difference whether all cases take more or less two weeks or if some take just a few hours whereas others take more than one month. The *service level* is the percentage of cases having a lead time lower than some threshold value, e.g., the percentage of cases handled within two weeks.
- The *service time* is the time actually worked on a case. One can measure the service time per activity, e.g., the average time needed to make a decision is 35 minutes, or for the entire case. Note that in case of concurrency the overall service time (i.e., summing up the times spent on the various activities) may be longer than the lead time. However, typically the service time is just a fraction of the lead time (minutes versus weeks).
- The *waiting time* is the time a case is waiting for a resource to become available. This time can be measured per activity or for the case as a whole. An example is the waiting time for a customer who wants to talk to a sales representative. Another example is the time a patient needs to wait before getting a knee operation. Again one may be interested in the average or variance of waiting times. It is also possible to focus on a service level, e.g., the percentage of patients that has a knee operation within three weeks after the initial diagnosis.
- The *synchronization time* is the time an activity is not yet fully enabled and waiting for an external trigger or another parallel branch. Unlike waiting time, the activity is not fully enabled yet, i.e., the case is waiting for synchronization rather than a resource. Consider, for example, a case at marking $[c2, c3]$ in the WF-net shown in Fig. 2.2. Activity e is waiting for *check ticket* to complete. The difference between the arrival time of the token in condition $c4$ and the arrival time of the token in condition $c3$ is the synchronization time.

Performance indicators can also be defined for the *cost dimension*. Different costing models can be used, e.g., Activity Based Costing (ABC), Time-Driven ABC, and Resource Consumption Accounting (RCA) [21]. The costs of executing an activity may be fixed or depend on the type of resource used, its utilization, or the duration of the activity. Resource costs may depend on the utilization of resources. A key performance indicator in most processes is the *average utilization* of resources over a given period, e.g., an operating room in a hospital has been used 85% of the time over the last two months. A detailed discussion of the various costing models is outside of the scope of this book.

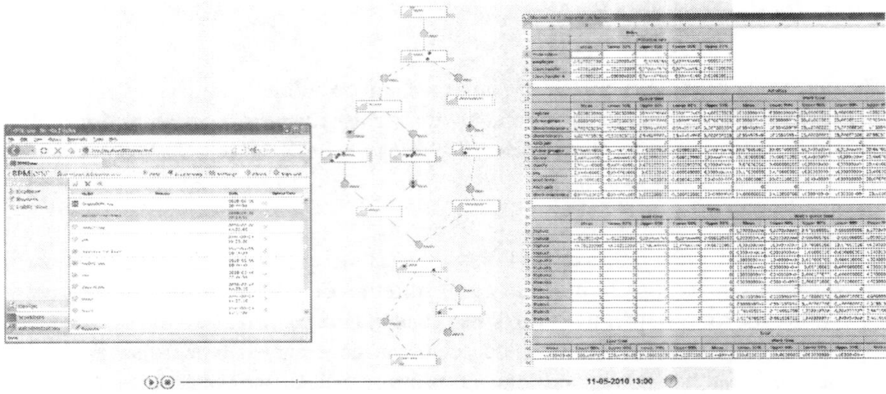

Fig. 2.19 Simulation using BPM|one of Pallas Athena: the modeled process can be animated and all kinds of KPIs of the simulated process are measured and stored in a spreadsheet

The *quality dimension* typically focuses on the "product" or "service" delivered to the customer. Like costs, this can be measured in different ways. One example is customer satisfaction measured through questionnaires. Another example is the average number of complaints per case or the number of product defects.

Whereas verification focuses on the (logical) correctness of the modeled process, performance analysis aims at improving processes with respect to time, cost, or quality. Within the context of operations management, many analysis techniques have been developed. Some of these techniques "optimize" the model given a particular performance indicator. For example, integer programming or Markov decision problems can be used to find optimal policies. For the types of process models described in this chapter "what if" analyses using simulation, queueing models, or Markov models are most appropriate. Analytical models typically require many assumptions and can only be used to answer particular questions. Therefore, one needs to resort to *simulation*. Most BPM tools provide simulation capabilities. Figure 2.19 shows a screenshot of BPM|one while simulating a process for handling insurance claims. BPM|one can animate the simulation run and calculate all kinds of KPIs related to time and cost (e.g., lead time, service time, waiting time, utilization, and activity costs).

Although many organizations have tried to use simulation to analyze their business processes at some stage, *few are using simulation in a structured and effective manner*. This may be caused by a lack of training and limitations of existing tools. However, there are also several additional and more fundamental problems. First of all, simulation models tend to *oversimplify* things. In particular, the behavior of resources is often modeled in a rather naïve manner. People do not work at constant speeds and need to distribute their attention over multiple processes. This can have dramatic effects on the performance of a process and, therefore, such aspects should not be "abstracted away" [95, 109]. Second, various *artifacts available are not used as input for simulation*. Modern organizations store events in logs and some may have accurate process models stored in their BPM/WFM systems. Also note that in many organizations, the state of the information system accurately reflects the state of the business processes supported by these systems. As discussed in Chap. 1, processes and information systems have become tightly coupled. Nevertheless, such information (i.e., event logs and status data) is rarely used for simulation or a lot of manual work is needed to feed this information into the model. Fortunately, as will be shown later in this book, process mining can assist in extracting such information and use this to realize performance improvements (see Sect. 8.6). Third, the focus of simulation is mainly on "design" whereas managers would also like to use simulation for "*operational decision making*", i.e., solving the concrete problem at hand rather than some abstract future problem. Fortunately, *short-term simulation* [95] can provide answers for questions related to "here and now". The key idea is to start all simulation runs from the current state and focus on the analysis of the transient behavior. This way a "fast forward button" into the future is provided.

2.3.3 Limitations of Model-Based Analysis

Verification and performance analysis heavily rely on the availability of high quality models. When the models and reality have little in common, model-based analysis does not make much sense. For example, the process model can be internally consistent and satisfy all kinds of desirable properties. However, if the model describes an idealized version of reality, this is quite useless as in reality all kinds of deviations may take place. Similar comments hold for simulation models. It may be that the model predicts a significant improvement whereas in reality this is not the case because the model is based on flawed assumptions. All of these problems stem from *a lack of alignment between hand-made models and reality*. Process mining aims to address these problems by establishing a direct connection between the models and actual low-level event data about the process. Moreover, the *discovery techniques discussed in this book allow for viewing the same reality from different angles and at different levels of abstraction*.

Chapter 3
Data Mining

Process mining builds on two pillars: (a) process modeling and analysis (as described in Chap. 2) and (b) data mining. This chapter introduces some basic data mining approaches and structures the field. The motivation for doing so is twofold. On the one hand, some process mining techniques build on classical data mining techniques, e.g., discovery and enhancement approaches focusing on data and resources. On the other hand, ideas originating from the data mining field will be used for the evaluation of process mining results. For example, one can adopt various data mining approaches to measure the quality of the discovered or enhanced process models. Existing data mining techniques are of little use for control-flow discovery, conformance checking, and other process mining tasks. Nevertheless, a basic understanding of data mining is most helpful for fully understanding the process mining techniques presented in subsequent chapters.

3.1 Classification of Data Mining Techniques

In [52], data mining is defined as "the analysis of (often large) data sets to find unsuspected relationships and to summarize the data in novel ways that are both understandable and useful to the data owner". The input data is typically given as a table and the output may be rules, clusters, tree structures, graphs, equations, patterns, etc. The growth of the "digital universe" described in Chap. 1 is the main driver for the popularity of data mining. Initially, the term "data mining" had a negative connotation especially among statisticians. Terms like "data snooping", "fishing", and "data dredging" refer to ad-hoc techniques to extract conclusions from data without a sound statistical basis. However, over time the data mining discipline has become mature as characterized by solid scientific methods and many practical applications [5, 15, 52, 67, 129].

W.M.P. van der Aalst, *Process Mining*,
DOI 10.1007/978-3-642-19345-3_3,

Table 3.1 Data set 1: Data about 860 recently deceased persons to study the effects of drinking, smoking, and body weight on the life expectancy

Drinker	Smoker	Weight	Age
Yes	Yes	120	44
No	No	70	96
Yes	No	72	88
Yes	Yes	55	52
No	Yes	94	56
No	No	62	93
...	...	...	...

Table 3.2 Data set 2: Data about 420 students to investigate relationships among course grades and the student's overall performance in the Bachelor program

Linear algebra	Logic	Programming	Operations research	Workflow systems	...	Duration	Result
9	8	8	9	9	...	36	Cum laude
7	6	–	8	8	...	42	Passed
–	–	5	4	6	...	54	Failed
8	6	6	6	5	...	38	Passed
6	7	6	–	8	...	39	Passed
9	9	9	9	8	...	38	Cum laude
5	5	–	6	6	...	52	Failed
...	...	...	...	...	...	...	...

3.1.1 Data Sets: Instances and Variables

Let us first look at three example data sets and possible questions. Table 3.1 shows part of a larger table containing information about 860 individuals that have recently deceased. For each person, the age of death is recorded (column *age*). Column *drinker* indicates whether the person was drinking alcohol. Column *smoker* indicates whether the person was smoking. Column *weight* indicates the bodyweight of the deceased person. Each row in Table 3.1 corresponds to a person. Questions may be:

- What is the effect of smoking and drinking on a person's bodyweight?
- Do people that smoke also drink?
- What factors influence a person's life expectancy the most?
- Can one identify groups of people having a similar lifestyle?

Table 3.2 shows another data set with information about 420 students that participated in a Bachelor program. Each row corresponds to a student. Students follow different courses. The table lists the highest mark for a particular course, e.g., the first student got a 9 for the course on linear algebra and an 8 for the course on logic. Table 3.2 uses the Dutch grading system, i.e., any mark is in-between 1 (lowest)

Table 3.3 Data set 3: Data on 240 customer orders in a coffee bar recorded by the cash register

Cappuccino	Latte	Espresso	Americano	Ristretto	Tea	Muffin	Bagel
1	0	0	0	0	0	1	0
0	2	0	0	0	0	1	1
0	0	1	0	0	0	0	0
1	0	0	0	0	0	0	0
0	0	0	0	0	1	2	0
0	0	0	1	1	0	0	0
...	...	...	...	...	...	...	...

and 10 (highest). Students who have a 5 or less, fail for the course. A "–" means that the course was not taken. The table shows only a selection of courses. Besides mandatory courses there are dozens of elective courses. The last two columns refer to the overall performance. The *duration* column indicates how long the student was enrolled before getting a degree or dropping out. The *result* column shows the final result: cum laude, passed, or failed. The university may be interested in the following questions:

- Are the marks of certain courses highly correlated?
- Which electives do excellent students (cum laude) take?
- Which courses significantly delay the moment of graduation?
- Why do students drop out?
- Can one identify groups of students having a similar study behavior?

The third data set, partly shown in Table 3.3, contains data about 240 orders in a café. Each row corresponds to one customer order. The columns refer to products. For instance, the first customer ordered a cappuccino and a muffin. This example is quite generic and analyzing such a data set is generally referred to as *market basket analysis*. For example, one can think of analyzing the product combinations purchased in a supermarket or in an electronic bookstore. Cafés, supermarkets, bookstores, etc. may be interested in the following questions:

- Which products are frequently purchased together?
- When do people buy a particular product?
- Is it possible to characterize typical customer groups?
- How to promote the sales of products with a higher margin?

Tables 3.1, 3.2, and 3.3 show three typical *data sets* used as input for data mining algorithms. Such a data set is often referred to as *sample* or *table*. The rows in the three tables are called *instances*. Alternative terms are: *individuals*, *entities*, *cases*, *objects*, and *records*. Instances may correspond to deceased persons, students, customers, orders, orderlines, messages, etc. The columns in the three tables are called *variables*. Variables are often referred to as *attributes*, *features*, or *data elements*. The first data set (Table 3.1) has four variables: *drinker*, *smoker*, *weight*, and *age*.

We distinguish between *categorical* variables and *numerical* variables. Categorical variables have a limited set of possible values and can easily be enumerated, e.g., a Boolean variable that is either true or false. Numerical variables have an ordering and cannot be enumerated easily. Examples are temperature (e.g., 39.7 degrees centigrade), age (44 years), weight (56.3 kilograms), number of items (3 coffees), and altitude (11 meters below sea level). Categorical variables are typically subdivided into *ordinal* variables and *nominal* variables. Nominal variables have no logical ordering. For example, Booleans (true and false), colors (Red, Yellow, Green), and EU countries (Germany, Italy, etc.) have no commonly agreed upon logical ordering. Ordinal variables have an ordering associated to it. For example, the *result* column in Table 3.2 refers to an ordinal variable that can have values "cum laude", "passed", and "failed". For most applications, it would make sense to consider the value "passed" in-between "cum laude" and "failed".

Before applying any data mining technique the data is typically preprocessed, e.g., rows and columns may be removed for various reasons. For instance, columns with less relevant information should be removed beforehand to reduce the dimensionality of the problem. Instances that are clearly corrupted should also be removed. Moreover, the value of a variable for a particular instance may be missing or have the wrong type. This may be due to an error while recording the data, but it may also have a particular reason. For example, in Table 3.2 some course grades are missing (denoted by "–"). These missing values are not errors but contain valuable information. For some kinds of analysis, the missing course grade can be treated as "zero", i.e., not taking the course is "lower" than the lowest grade. For other types of analysis, it may be that the values in such a column are mapped onto "yes" (participated in the course) and "no" (the entries that now have a "–").

When comparing Tables 3.1, 3.2, and 3.3 with the event log shown in Table 1.1 it becomes obvious that data mining techniques make less assumptions about the format of the input data than process mining techniques. For example, in Table 1.1 there are two notions, events and cases, rather than the single notion of an instance (i.e., row in table). Moreover, events are ordered in time whereas in Tables 3.1, 3.2, and 3.3 the ordering of the rows has no meaning. For particular questions, it is possible to convert an event log into a simple data set for data mining. We will refer to this as *feature extraction*. Later, we will use feature extraction for various proposes, e.g., analyzing decisions in a discovered process models and clustering cases before process discovery so that each cluster has a dedicated process model.

After showing the basic input format for data mining and discussing typical questions, we classify data mining techniques into two main categories: *supervised learning* and *unsupervised learning*.

3.1.2 Supervised Learning: Classification and Regression

Supervised learning assumes *labeled data*, i.e., there is a *response variable* that labels each instance. For instance, in Table 3.2 the *result* column could be selected as the response variable. Hence, each student is labeled as "cum laude", "passed", or "failed". The other variables are *predictor variables* and we are interested in explaining the response variable in terms of the predictor variables. Sometimes the response variable is called the *dependent variable* and the predictor variables are called *independent variables*. The goal is to explain the dependent variable in terms of the independent variables. For example, we would like to predict the final result of a student in terms of the student's course grades.

Techniques for supervised learning can be further subdivided into *classification* and *regression* depending on the type of response variable (categorical or numerical).

Classification techniques assume a *categorical* response variable and the goal is to classify instances based on the predictor variables. Consider, for example, Table 3.1. We would like to classify people into the class of smokers and the class of nonsmokers. Therefore, we select the categorical response variable *smoker*. Through classification we want to learn what the key differences between smokers and nonsmokers are. For instance, we could find that most smokers drink and die young. By applying classification to the second data set (Table 3.2) while using column *result* as a response variable, we could find the obvious fact that cum laude students have high grades. In Sect. 3.2, we will show how to construct a so-called *decision tree* using classification.

Regression techniques assume a *numerical* response variable. The goal is to find a function that fits the data with the least error. For example, we could select *age* as response variable for the data set in Table 3.1 and (hypothetically) find the function $age = 124 - 0.8 \times weight$, e.g., a person of 50 kilogram is expected to live until the age of 84 whereas a person of 100 kilogram is expected to live until the age of 44. For the second data set, we could find that the mark for the course on workflow systems heavily depends on the mark for linear algebra and logic, e.g., $\mathit{workflow\ systems} = 0.6 + 0.8 \times \mathit{linear\ algebra} + 0.2 \times \mathit{logic}$. For the third data set, we could (again hypothetically) find a function that predicts the number of bagels in terms of the numbers of different drinks.

The most frequently used regression technique is *linear regression*. Given a response variable y and predictor variables $x_1, x_2, \ldots, x_n$ a linear model $\hat{y} = f(x_1, x_2, \ldots, x_n) = a_0 + \sum_{i=1}^{n} a_i x_i$ is learned over the data set. For every instance in the data set, there is an error $|y - \hat{y}|$. A popular approach is to minimize the sum of squared errors, i.e., given m instances the goal is to find a function f such that $\sum_{j=1}^{m} (y_j - \hat{y}_j)^2$ is minimal. Other scoring functions are possible and more *general regression models* or even *neural networks* can be used. However, these techniques are out of the scope of this book and the interested reader is referred to [52].

Classification requires a categorical response variable. In some cases it makes sense to transform a numerical response variable into a categorical one. For example, for Table 3.1 one could decide to transform variable *age* into a categorical response variable by mapping values below 70 onto label "young" and values of 70 and above onto label "old". Now a decision tree can be constructed to classify instances into people that die(d) "young" and people that die(d) "old". Similarly, all values in Table 3.3 can be made categorical. For example, positive values are mapped onto "true" (the item was purchased) and value 0 is mapped onto "false" (the item was not purchased). After applying this mapping to Table 3.3, we can apply classification to the coffee shop data while using e.g., column *muffin* as a response variable. We could, for instance, find that customers who drink lots of tea tend to eat muffins.

3.1.3 Unsupervised Learning: Clustering and Pattern Discovery

Unsupervised learning assumes *unlabeled data*, i.e., the variables are *not* split into response and predictor variables. In this chapter, we consider two types of unsupervised learning: *clustering* and *pattern discovery*.

Clustering algorithms examine the data to find groups of instances that are similar. Unlike classification, the focus is not on some response variable but on the instance as a whole. For example, the goal could be to find homogeneous groups of students (Table 3.2) or customers (Table 3.3). Well-known techniques for clustering are *k-means clustering* and *agglomerative hierarchical clustering*. These will be briefly explained in Sect. 3.3.

There are many techniques to discover patterns in data. Often the goal is to find rules of the form *IF X THEN Y* where *X* and *Y* relate values of different variables. For example, *IF smoker* = *no AND age* $\geq$ 70 *THEN drinker* = *yes* for Table 3.1 or *IF logic* $\leq$ 6 *AND duration* > 50 *THEN result* = *failed* for Table 3.2. The most well-known technique is *association rule mining*. This technique will be explained in Sect. 3.4.

Note that decision trees can also be converted into rules. However, a decision tree is constructed for a particular response variable. Hence, rules extracted from a decision tree only say something about the response variable in terms of some of the predictor variables. Association rules are discovered using unsupervised learning, i.e., there is no need to select a response variable.

Data mining results may be both *descriptive* and *predictive*. Decision trees, association rules, regression functions say something about the data set used to learn the model. However, they can also be used to make predictions for new instances, e.g., predict the overall performance of students based on the course grades in the first semester.

In the remainder, we show some of the techniques mentioned in more detail. Moreover, at the end of this chapter we focus on measuring the quality of mining results.

3.2 Decision Tree Learning

Decision tree learning is a supervised learning technique aiming at the classification of instances based on predictor variables. There is one categorical response variable labeling the data and the result is arranged in the form of a tree. Figures 3.1, 3.2, and 3.3 show three decision trees computed for the data sets described earlier in this chapter. Leaf nodes correspond to possible values of the response variable. Non-leaf

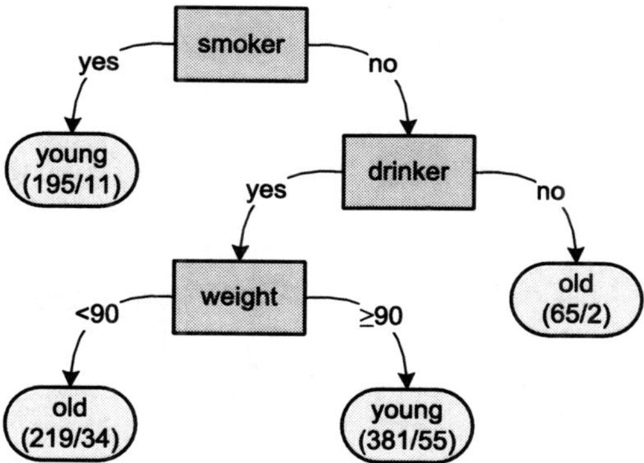

Fig. 3.1 A decision tree derived from Table 3.1. The 860 persons are classified into "young" (died before the age of 70) and "old" (died at 70 or later). People who smoke generally die young (195 persons of which 11 are misclassified). People who do not smoke and do no drink tend to live long (65 persons of which 2 are misclassified). People who only drink but are overweight (≥90) also die young (381 persons of which 55 are misclassified)

nodes correspond to predictor variables. In the context of decision tree learning, predictor variables are referred to as *attributes*. Every attribute node splits a set of instances into two or more subsets. The root node corresponds to all instances.

In Fig. 3.1, the root node represents all instances; in this case 860 persons. Based on the attribute *smoker* these instances are split into the ones that are smoking (195 persons) and the ones that not smoking ($860 - 195 = 665$ persons). The smokers are not further split. Based on this information instances are already labeled as "young", i.e., smokers are expected to die before the age of 70. The nonsmokers are split into drinkers and nondrinkers. The latter group of people is expected to live long and is thus labeled as "old". All leaf nodes have two numbers. The first number indicates the number of instances classified as such. The second number indicates the number of instances corresponding to the leaf node but wrongly classified. Of the 195 smokers who were classified as "young" 11 people were misclassified, i.e., did not die before 70 while smoking.

The other two decision trees can be read in the same manner. Based on an attribute, a set of instances may also be split into three (or even more) subsets. An attribute may appear multiple times in a tree but not twice on the same path. For example, in Fig. 3.2 there are two nodes referring to the course on linear algebra. However, these are not on the same path and thus refer to disjoint sets of students. As mentioned before, there are various ways to handle missing values depending on their assumed semantics. In Fig. 3.2, a missing course grade is treated as a kind of "zero" (see the left-most arc originating from the root node).

Decision trees such as the ones shown in Figs. 3.1, 3.2, and 3.3 can be obtained using a variety of techniques. Most of the techniques use a recursive top-down algorithm that works as follows:

1. Create the root node r and associate all instances to the root node. $X := \{r\}$ is the set of nodes to be traversed.

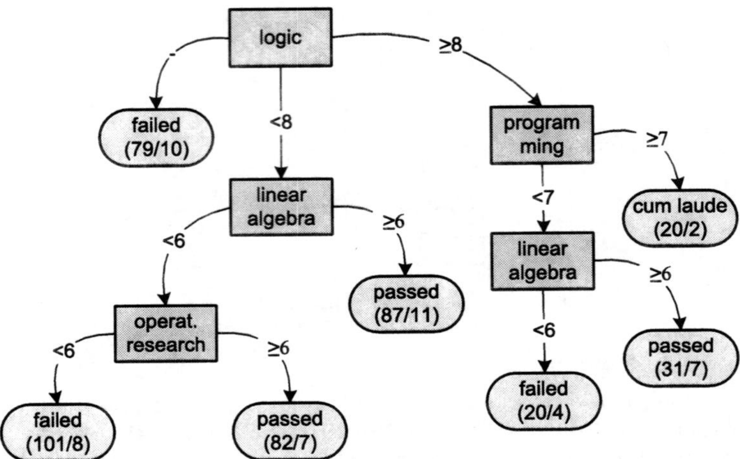

Fig. 3.2 A decision tree derived from Table 3.2. The 420 students are classified into "failed", "passed", and "cum laude" based on study results. Students that do not take the course on logic typically fail (79 students of which 10 are misclassified). Students that have a high mark for logic and programming, typically complete their degree cum laude (20 students of which 2 are misclassified)

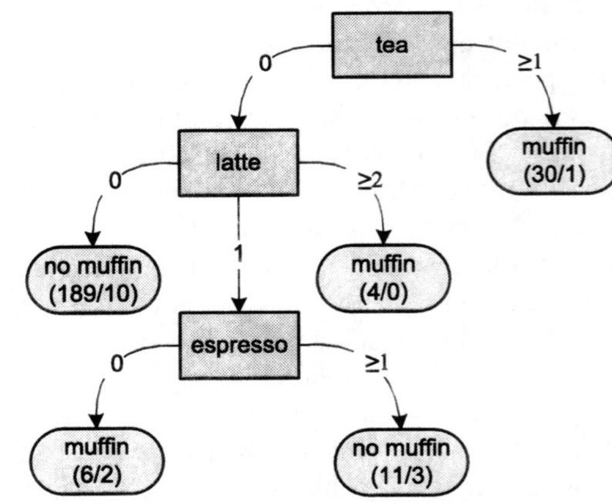

Fig. 3.3 A decision tree derived from Table 3.3 after converting response variable *muffin* into a Boolean. Customers who drink tea tend to eat muffins (30 customers of which 1 is misclassified). Customers who do not drink tea or latte typically do not eat muffins (189 customers of which 10 are misclassified)

2. If $X = \emptyset$, then return the tree with root r and end.
3. Select $x \in X$ and remove it from X, i.e., $X := X \setminus \{x\}$. Determine the "score" $s^{old}(x)$ of node x before splitting, e.g., based on entropy.
4. Determine if splitting is possible/needed. If not, go to step 2, otherwise continue with the next step.
5. For all possible attributes $a \in A$, evaluate the effects of splitting on the attribute. Select the attribute a providing the best improvement, i.e., maximize $s_a^{new}(x) - s^{old}(x)$. The same attribute should not appear multiple times on the same path

from the root. Also note that for numerical attributes, so-called "cut values" need to be determined (cf. <8 and ≥8 in Fig. 3.2).

6. If the improvement is substantial enough, create a set of child nodes Y, add Y to X (i.e., $X := X \cup Y$), and connect x to all child nodes in Y.
7. Associate each node in Y to its corresponding set of instances and go to step 2.

Here, we only provide a rough sketch of the generic algorithm. Many design decisions are needed to make a concrete decision tree learner. For example, one needs to decide when to stop adding nodes. This can be based on the improvement of the scoring function or because the tree is restricted to a certain depth. There are also many ways to select attributes. This can be based on entropy (see below), the Gini index of diversity, etc. When selecting a numeric attribute to split on, cut values need to be determined because it is unreasonable/impossible to have a child node for every possible value. For example, a customer can purchase any number of lattes and it would be undesirable to enumerate all possibilities when using this attribute to split. As shown in Fig. 3.2, node *latte* has only three child nodes based on two cut values partitioning the domain of natural numbers in $\{0\}$, $\{1\}$, and $\{2, 3, \ldots\}$.

These are just few of the many ingredients that determine a complete decision tree learning algorithm.

The crucial thing to see is that by *splitting the set of instances in subsets the variation within each subset becomes smaller*. This can be best illustrated using the notion of *entropy*.

Entropy: Encoding Uncertainty

Entropy is an information-theoretic measure for the uncertainly in a multi-set of elements. If the multi-set contains many different elements and each element is unique, then variation is maximal and it takes many "bits" to encode the individual elements. Hence, the entropy is "high". If all elements in the multi-set are the same, then actually no bits are needed to encode the individual elements. In this case the entropy is "low". For example, the entropy of the multi-set $[a, b, c, d, e]$ is much higher than the entropy of the multi-set $[a^5]$ even though both multi-sets have the same number of elements (5).

Assume that there is a multi-set X with n elements and there are k possible values, say $v_1, v_2, \ldots, v_k$, i.e., X is a multi-set over $V = \{v_1, v_2, \ldots, v_k\}$ with $|X| = n$. Each value v_i appears c_i times in X, i.e., $X = [(v_1)^{c_1}, (v_2)^{c_2}, \ldots, (v_k)^{c_k}]$. Without loss of generality, we can assume that $c_i \geq 1$ for all i, because values that do not appear in X can be removed from V upfront. The proportion of elements having value v_i is p_i, i.e., $p_i = c_i/n$. The entropy of X is measured in bits of information and is defined by the formula:

$$E = -\sum_{i=1}^{k} p_i \log_2 p_i$$

If all elements in X have the same value, i.e., $k = 1$ and $p_1 = 1$, then $E = -\log_2 1 = 0$. This means that no bits are needed to encode the value of an individual element; they are all the same anyway. If all elements in X are different, i.e., $k = n$ and $p_i = 1/k$, then $E = -\sum_{i=1}^{k}(1/k)\log_2(1/k) = \log_2 k$. For instance, if there are 4 possible values, then $E = \log_2 4 = 2$ bits are needed to encode each individual element. If there are 16 possible values, then $E = \log_2 16 = 4$ bits are needed to encode each individual element.
The proportion p_i can also been seen as a probability. Assume there is random stream of values such that there are four possible values $V = \{a, b, c, d\}$, e.g., a sequence like *bacaabadabaacada*... is generated. Value a has a probability of $p_1 = 0.5$, value b has a probability of $p_2 = 0.25$, value c has a probability of $p_3 = 0.125$, and value d has a probability of $p_4 = 0.125$. In this case $E = -((0.5\log_2 0.5) + (0.25\log_2 0.25) + (0.125\log_2 0.125) + (0.125\log_2 0.125)) = -((0.5\times -1)+(0.25\times -2)+(0.125\times -3)+(0.125\times -3)) = 0.5 + 0.5 + 0.375 + 0.375 = 1.75$ bits. This means that on average 1.75 bits are needed to encode one element. This is correct. Consider, for example, the following variable length binary encoding $a = 0$, $b = 11$, $c = 100$, and $d = 111$, i.e., a is encoded in one bit, b is encoded in two bits, and c and d are each encoded in three bits. Given the relative frequencies it is easy to see that this is (on average) the most compact encoding. Other encodings are either similar (e.g., $a = 1$, $b = 00$, $c = 011$, and $d = 000$) or require more bits on average. Suppose now that all four values have the same probability, i.e., $p_1 = p_2 = p_3 = p_4 = 0.25$. In this case $E = \log_2 4 = 2$. This is correct because there is no way to improve the encoding $a = 00$, $b = 01$, $c = 10$, and $d = 11$.
The example shows that by using information about the probability of each value, we can reduce the encoding from 2 bits to 1.75 bits on average. If the probabilities are more skewed, further reductions are possible. If value a has a probability of $p_1 = 0.9$, value b has a probability of $p_2 = 0.1$, value c has a probability of $p_3 = 0.05$, and value d has a probability of $p_4 = 0.05$, then $E = 0.901188$. This means that on average less than one bit is needed to encode each element.

Let us now apply the notion of entropy to decision tree learning. Figure 3.4 shows three steps in the construction of a decision tree for the data set shown in Table 3.1. We label the instances into "old" and "young". Moreover, for simplicity we abstract from the *weight* attribute. In the initial step, the tree consists only of a root. Since the majority of persons in our data set die before 70, we label this node as young. Since of the 860 persons in our data set only 546 actually die before 70, the remaining 314 persons are misclassified. Let us calculate the entropy for the root node: $E = -(((546/860)\log_2(546/860)) + ((314/860)\log_2(314/860))) = 0.946848$. This is a value close to the maximal value of one (in case both groups would have the same size).

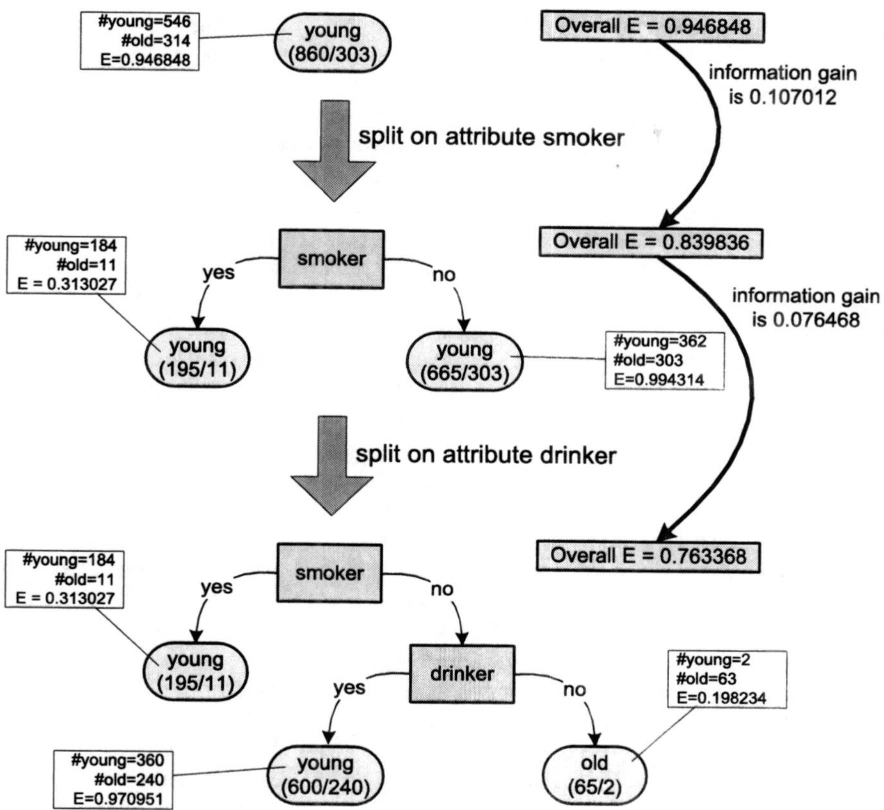

Fig. 3.4 Step-by-step construction of decision tree driven by information gain based on entropy

Next, Fig. 3.4 shows what happens if we split the data set based on attribute *smoker*. Now there are two leaf nodes both bearing the label young. Of the people that smoke (195), most die young (184). Hence, the entropy of this leaf node is very small: $E = -(((184/195)\log_2(184/195)) + ((11/195)\log_2(11/195))) = 0.313027$. This means that the variability is much smaller. The other leaf node is more heterogeneous: about half of the 665 non smokers (362 to be precise) die young. Indeed $E = -(((362/665)\log_2(362/665)) + ((303/665)\log_2(303/665))) = 0.994314$ is higher. However, the overall entropy is still lower. The overall entropy can be found by simply taking the weighted average, i.e., $E = (195/860) \times 0.313027 + (665/860) \times 0.994314 = 0.839836$.

As Fig. 3.4 shows the *information gain* is 0.107012. This is calculated by taking the old overall entropy (0.946848) minus the new overall entropy (0.839836). Note that still all persons are classified as young. However, we gained information by splitting on attribute *smoker*. The information gain, i.e., a reduction in entropy, was obtained because we were able to find a group of persons for which there is less variability; most smokers die young. The goal is to *maximize the information gain* by selecting a particular attribute to split on. Maximizing the information gain corresponds to minimizing the entropy and heterogeneity in leaf nodes. We could also have chosen the attribute *drinker* first. However, this would have resulted in a smaller information gain.

The lower part of Fig. 3.4 shows what happens if we split the set of nonsmokers based on attribute *drinker*. This results in two new leaf nodes. The node that corresponds to persons who do not smoke and do not drink has a low entropy value ($E = 0.198234$). This can be explained by the fact that indeed most of the people associated to this leaf node live long and there are only two exceptions to this rule. The entropy of the other new leaf node (people that drink but do not smoke) is again close two one. However, the overall entropy is clearly reduced. The information gain is 0.076468. Since we abstract from the *weight* attribute we cannot further split the leaf node corresponding to people that drink but do not smoke. Moreover, it makes no sense to split the leaf node with smokers because little can be gained as the entropy is already low.

Note that splitting nodes will always reduce the overall entropy. In the extreme case, all the leaf nodes corresponds to single individuals (or individuals having exactly the same attribute values). The overall entropy is then by definition zero. However, the resulting tree is not very useful and probably has little predictive value. It is vital to realize that the decision tree is learned based on *examples*. For instance, if in the data set no customer ever ordered six muffins, this does not imply that this is not possible. A decision tree is "overfitting" if it depends too much on the particularities of the data used to learn it (see also Sect. 3.6). An overfitting decision tree is overly complex and performs poorly on unseen instances. Therefore, it is important to select the right attributes and to stop splitting when little can be gained.

Entropy is just one of several measures that can be used to measure the diversity in a leaf node. Another measure is the *Gini index of diversity* that measures the "impurity" of a data set: $G = 1 - \sum_{i=1}^{k}(p_i)^2$. If all classifications are the same, then $G = 0$. G approaches 1 as there is more and more diversity. Hence, an approach can be to select the attribute that maximizes the reduction of the G value (rather than the E value).

See [5, 15, 52, 129] for more information (and pointers to the extensive literature) on the different strategies to build decision trees.

Decision tree learning is unrelated to process discovery, however it can be used in combination with process mining techniques. For example, process discovery techniques such as the α-algorithm help to locate all decision points in the process (e.g., the XOR/OR-splits discussed in Chap. 2). Subsequently, we can analyze each decision point using decision tree learning. The response variable is the path taken and the attributes are the data elements known at or before the decision point.

3.3 k-Means Clustering

Clustering is concerned with grouping instances into *clusters*. Instances in one cluster should be similar to each other and dissimilar to instances in other clusters. Clustering uses unlabeled data and, hence, requires an unsupervised learning technique.

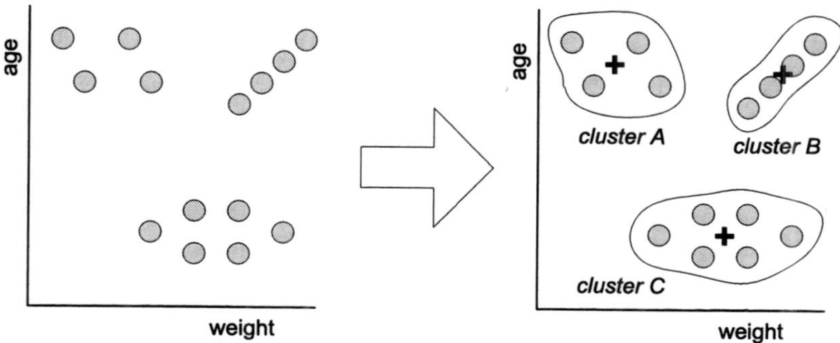

Fig. 3.5 Clustering instances in three clusters using k-means

Many clustering algorithms exist [5, 15, 52, 67, 129]. Here, we focus on *k-means clustering*.

Figure 3.5 illustrates the basic idea of clustering. Assume we have a data set with only two variables: *age* and *weight*. Such a data set could be obtained by projecting Table 3.1 onto the last two columns. The dots correspond to persons having a particular age and weight. Through a clustering technique like k-means, the three *clusters* shown on the right-hand side of Fig. 3.5 can be discovered. Ideally, the instances in one cluster are close to one another while being further away from instances in other clusters. Each of the clusters has a *centroid* denoted by a +. The centroid denotes the "center" of the cluster and can be computed by taking the average of the coordinates of the instances in the cluster. Note that Fig. 3.5 shows only two dimensions. This is a bit misleading as typically there will be many dimensions (e.g., the number of courses or products). However, the two dimensional view helps to understand the basic idea.

Distance-based clustering algorithms like k-means and agglomerative hierarchical clustering assume a *distance notion*. The most common approach is to consider each instance to be an n-dimensional vector where n is the number of variables and then simply take the Euclidian distance. For this purpose, ordinal values but also binary values need to be made numeric, e.g., *true* = 1, *false* = 0, *cum laude* = 2, *passed* = 1, *failed* = 0. Note that scaling is important when defining a distance metric. For example, if one variable represents the distance in meters ranging from 10 to 1,000,000 while another variable represents some utilization factor ranging from 0.2 to 0.8, then the distance variable will dominate the utilization variable. Hence, some normalization is needed.

Figure 3.6 shows the basic idea of k-means clustering. Here, we simplified things as much as possible, i.e., $k = 2$ and there are only 10 instances. The approach starts with a random initialization of two centroids denoted by the two + symbols. In Fig. 3.6(a), the centroids are randomly put onto the two dimensional space. Using the selected distance metric, all instances are assigned to the closest centroid. Here we use the standard Euclidian distance. All instances with an open dot are assigned to the centroid on the left whereas all the instances with a closed dot are assigned to the centroid on the right. Based on this assignment, we get two initial clusters. Now

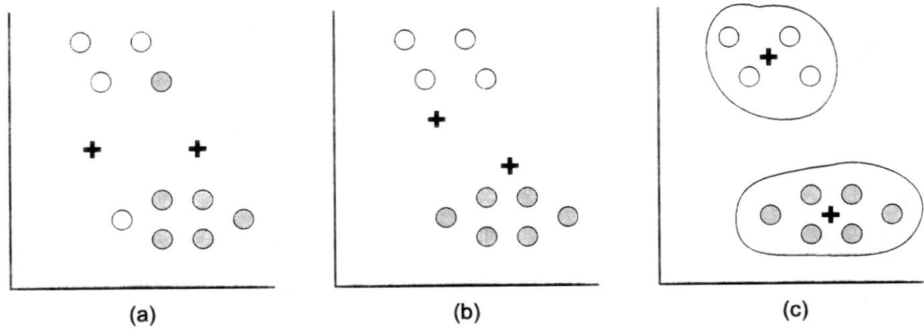

Fig. 3.6 Step-by-step evolution k-means

we compute the real center of each cluster. These form the new positions of the two centroids. The centroids in Fig. 3.6(b) are based on the clusters shown in Fig. 3.6(a). In Fig. 3.6(b), we again assign all instances to the centroid that is closest. This results in the two new clusters shown in Fig. 3.6(b). All instances with an open dot are assigned to one centroid whereas all the instances with a closed dot are assigned to the other one. Now we compute the real centers of these two new clusters. This results in a relocation of the centroids as shown in Fig. 3.6(c). Again we assign the instances to the centroid that is closest. However, now nothing changes and the location of the centroids remains the same. After converging the k-means algorithm outputs, the two clusters and related statistics.

The quality of a particular clustering can be defined as the average distance from an instance to its corresponding centroid. k-means clustering is only a heuristic and does not guarantee that it finds the k clusters that minimize the average distance from an instance to its corresponding centroid. In fact, the result depends on the initialization. Therefore, it is good to repeatedly execute the algorithm with different initializations and select the best one.

There are many variants of the algorithm just described. However, we refer to standard literature for details [5, 15, 52, 67, 129]. One of the problems when using the k-means algorithm is determining the number of clusters k. For k-means this is fixed from the beginning. Note that the average distance from an instance to its corresponding centroid decreases as k is increased. In the extreme case every instance has its own cluster and the average distance from an instance to its corresponding centroid is zero. This is not very useful. Therefore, a frequently used approach is to start with a small number of clusters and then gradually increase k as long as there are significant improvements.

Another popular clustering technique is *Agglomerative Hierarchical Clustering* (AHC). Here, a variable number of clusters is generated. Figure 3.7 illustrates the idea. The approach works as follows. Assign each instance to a dedicated singleton cluster. Now search for the two clusters that are closest to one another. Merge these two clusters into a new cluster. For example, the initial clusters consisting of just a and just b are merged into a new cluster ab. Now search again for the two clusters

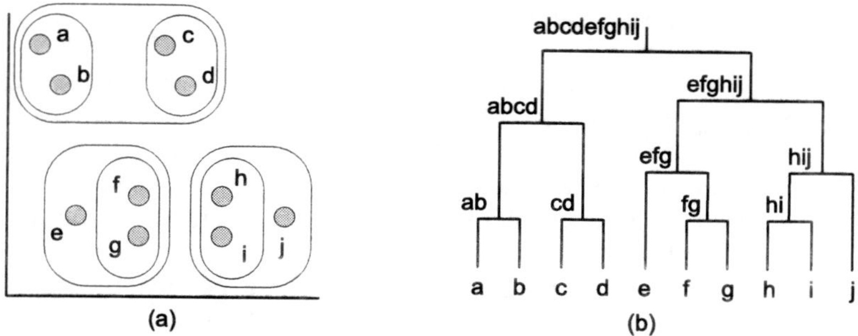

Fig. 3.7 Agglomerative hierarchical clustering: (**a**) clusters and (**b**) dendrogram

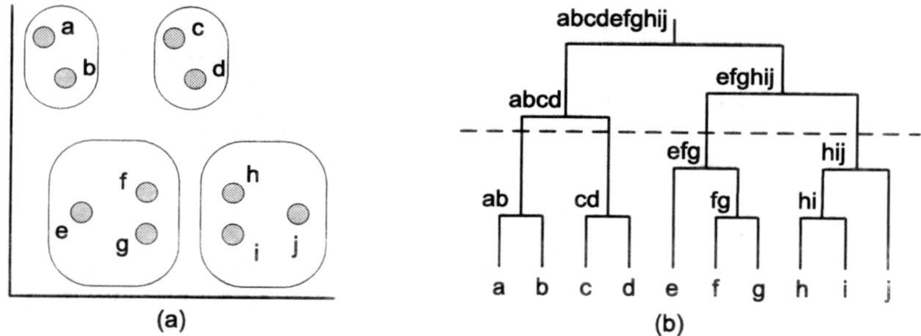

Fig. 3.8 *Any horizontal line in dendrogram* corresponds to a concrete clustering at a particular level of abstraction

that are closest to one another and merge them. This is repeated until all instances are in the same cluster. Figure 3.7(a) shows all intermediate clusters, i.e., all except the initial singleton clusters and the final overall cluster. Because of the hierarchical nature of the agglomerative hierarchical clustering, we can visualize the clusters using a so-called *dendrogram* as shown in Fig. 3.7(b).

Any horizontal line cutting through the dendrogram corresponds to a concrete clustering. For example, Fig. 3.8(b) shows such a horizontal line. The clusters resulting from this are shown in Fig. 3.8(a). Moving the line to the bottom of the dendrogram results in many singleton clusters. Moving the line all the way up results in a single cluster containing all instances. By moving the horizontal line, the user can vary the abstraction level.

Clustering is only indirectly related to process discovery as described in Chap. 1. Nevertheless, clustering can be used as a preprocessing step for process mining [12, 32, 46]. By grouping similar cases together it may be possible to construct partial process models that are easier to understand. If the process model discovered for all cases is too complex to comprehend, then it may be useful to first identify clusters and then discover simpler models per cluster.

3.4 Association Rule Learning

Decision trees can be used to predict the value of some response variable that has been identified as being important. Driven by the response variable, rules like "people who drink and smoke die before 70" can be found. *Association rule learning* aims at finding similar rules but now *without* focusing on a particular response variable. The goal is to find rules of the form *IF X THEN Y* where X is often called the *antecedent* and Y the *consequent*. Such rules are also denoted as $X \Rightarrow Y$. X and Y can be any conjunction of "*variable* = *value*" terms. The only requirement is that X and Y are nonempty and any variable appears at most once in X and Y. Examples are *IF smoker = no AND age* ≥ 70 *THEN drinker = yes* for Table 3.1 or *IF logic* ≤ 6 *AND duration* > 50 *THEN result = failed* for Table 3.2. Typically, only categorical variables are considered. However, there are various techniques to transform numerical variables in categorical ones.

When learning association rules of the form $X \Rightarrow Y$, three metrics are frequently used: *support*, *confidence*, and *lift*. Let N_X be the number of instances for which X holds. N_Y is the number of instances for which Y holds. $N_{X \wedge Y}$ is the number of instances for which both X and Y hold. N is the total number of instances. The support of a rule $X \Rightarrow Y$ is defined as

$$support(X \Rightarrow Y) = N_{X \wedge Y}/N$$

The support indicates the applicability of the approach, i.e., the fraction of instances for which with both antecedent and consequent hold. Typically a rule with high support is more useful than a rule with low support.

The confidence of a rule $X \Rightarrow Y$ is defined as

$$confidence(X \Rightarrow Y) = N_{X \wedge Y}/N_X$$

A rule with high confidence, i.e., a value close to 1, indicates that the rule is very reliable, i.e., if X holds, then Y will also hold. A rule with high confidence is definitely more useful than a rule with low confidence.

The lift of a rule $X \Rightarrow Y$ is defined as

$$lift(X \Rightarrow Y) = \frac{N_{X \wedge Y}/N}{(N_X/N)\,(N_Y/N)} = \frac{N_{X \wedge Y}\, N}{N_X\, N_Y}$$

If X and Y are independent, then the lift will be close to 1. If $lift(X \Rightarrow Y) > 1$, then X and Y correlate positively. For example $lift(X \Rightarrow Y) = 5$ means that X and Y happen five times more together than what would be the case if they were independent. If $lift(X \Rightarrow Y) < 1$, then X and Y correlate negatively (i.e., the occurrence of X makes Y less likely and vice versa). Rules with a higher lift value are generally considered to be more interesting. However, typically lift values are only considered if certain thresholds with respect to support and confidence are met.

In the remainder of this section, we restrict ourselves to a special form of association rule learning known as *market basket analysis*. Here we only consider binary variables that should be interpreted as present or not. For example, let us consider the first two columns in Table 3.1. This data set can be rewritten to so called *item-sets*: $[\{drinker, smoker\}, \{\ \}, \{drinker\}, \{drinker, smoker\}, \{smoker\}, \{\ \}, \ldots]$. If we ignore the number of items ordered in Table 3.3, then it is also straightforward to rewrite this data set in terms of item-sets: [{*cappuccino*, *muffin*}, {*latte*, *muffin*, *bagel*}, {*espresso*}, {*cappuccino*}, {*tea*, *muffin*}, {*americano*, *ristretto*}, ...]. The latter illustrates why the term "market basket" analysis is used for systematically analyzing such input. Based on item-sets, the goal is to generate rules of the form $X \Rightarrow Y$ where X and Y refer to disjoint non-empty sets of items. For example, $smoker \Rightarrow drinker$, $tea \wedge latte \Rightarrow muffin$, and $tea \Rightarrow muffin \wedge bagel$. Recall that there are $N = 240$ customer orders in Table 3.3. Assume that $N_{tea} = 50$ (i.e., 50 orders included at least one cup of tea), $N_{latte} = 40$, $N_{muffin} = 40$, $N_{tea \wedge latte} = 20$, and $N_{tea \wedge latte \wedge muffin} = 15$ (i.e., 15 orders included at least one tea, at least one latte, and at least one muffin). Let us consider the rule $tea \wedge latte \Rightarrow muffin$, i.e., $X = tea \wedge latte$ and $Y = muffin$. Given the numbers indicated we can easily compute the three metrics defined earlier:

$$support(X \Rightarrow Y) = N_{X \wedge Y}/N = N_{tea \wedge latte \wedge muffin}/N = 15/240 = 0.0625$$

$$confidence(X \Rightarrow Y) = N_{X \wedge Y}/N_X = N_{tea \wedge latte \wedge muffin}/N_{tea \wedge latte} = 15/20 = 0.75$$

$$lift(X \Rightarrow Y) = \frac{N_{X \wedge Y}\ N}{N_X\ N_Y} = \frac{N_{tea \wedge latte \wedge muffin}\ N}{N_{tea \wedge latte}\ N_{muffin}} = \frac{15 \times 240}{20 \times 40} = 4.5$$

Hence the $tea \wedge latte \Rightarrow muffin$ has a support of 0.0625, a confidence of 0.75, and a lift of 4.5.

If we also assume that $N_{tea \wedge muffin} = 25$, then we can deduce that the rule $tea \Rightarrow muffin$ has a support of 0.104167, a confidence of 0.5, and a lift of 3. Hence, this more compact rule has a better support but lower confidence and lift.

Let us also assume that $N_{latte \wedge muffin} = 35$. This implies that the rule $tea \Rightarrow latte \wedge muffin$ has a support of 0.0625, a confidence of 0.3, and a lift of 2.057. This rule has a rather poor performance compared to the original rule $tea \wedge latte \Rightarrow muffin$: the support is the same, but the confidence and lift are much lower.

To systematically *generate* association rules, one typically defines two parameters: *minsup* and *minconf*. The support of any rule $X \Rightarrow Y$ should be above the threshold *minsup*, i.e., $support(X \Rightarrow Y) \geq minsup$. Similarly, the confidence of any rule $X \Rightarrow Y$ should be above the threshold *minconf*, i.e., $confidence(X \Rightarrow Y) \geq minconf$. Association rules can now be generated as follows:

1. Generate all *frequent item-sets*, i.e., all sets Z such that $N_Z/N \geq minsup$ and $|Z| \geq 2$.
2. For each frequent item-set Z, consider all partitionings of Z into two nonempty subsets X and Y. If $confidence(X \Rightarrow Y) \geq minconf$, then keep the rule $X \Rightarrow Y$. If $confidence(X \Rightarrow Y) < minconf$, then discard the rule.
3. Output the rules found.

This simple algorithm has two problems. First of all, there is a computational problem related to the first step. If there are m variables, then there are $2^m - m - 1$ possible item-sets. Hence, for 100 products ($m = 100$) there are

1267650600228229401496703205275

candidate frequent item-sets. The second problem is that many uninteresting rules are generated. For example, after presenting the rule $tea \wedge latte \Rightarrow muffin$, there is no point in also showing $tea \Rightarrow latte \wedge muffin$ even when it meets the *minsup* and *minconf* thresholds. Many techniques have been developed to speed-up the generation of association rules and to select the most interesting rules. Here we only sketch the seminal *Apriori algorithm*.

Apriori: Efficiently Generating Frequent Item-Sets

The Apriori algorithm is one of the best known algorithms in computer science. The algorithm, initially developed by Agrawal and Srikant [3], is able to speed up the generation of association rules by exploiting the following two observations:

1. If an item-set is *frequent* (i.e., an item-set with a support above the threshold), then all of its non-empty subsets are also frequent. Formally, for any pair of non-empty item-sets X, Y: if $Y \subseteq X$ and $N_X/N \geq minsup$, then $N_Y/N \geq minsup$.
2. If, for any k, I_k is the set of all frequent item-sets with cardinality k and $I_l = \emptyset$ for some l, then $I_k = \emptyset$ for all $k \geq l$.

These two properties can be used to dramatically reduce the search-space when constructing the set of frequent item-sets. For example, if item-set $\{a, b\}$ is infrequent, then it does not make any sense to look at item-sets containing both a and b. The Apriori algorithm works as follows:

1. Create I_1. This is the set of singleton frequent item-sets, i.e., item-sets with a support above the threshold *minsup* containing just one element.
2. $k := 1$.
3. If $I_k = \emptyset$, then output $\bigcup_{i=1}^{k} I_i$ and end. If $I_k \neq \emptyset$, continue with the next step.
4. Create C_{k+1} from I_k. C_{k+1} is the candidate set containing item-sets of cardinality $k+1$. Note that one only needs to consider elements that are the union of two item-sets A and B in I_k such that $|A \cap B| = k$ and $|A \cup B| = k+1$.
5. For each candidate frequent item-set $c \in C_{k+1}$: examine all subsets of c with k elements; delete c from C_{k+1} if any of the subsets is not a member of I_k.
6. For each item-set c in the pruned candidate frequent item-set C_{k+1}, check whether c is indeed frequent. If so, add c to I_{k+1}. Otherwise, discard c.
7. $k := k+1$ and return to Step 3.

The algorithm only considers candidates for I_{k+1} that are not ruled out by evidence in I_k. This way the number of traversals through the data set is reduced dramatically.

Association rules are related to process discovery. Recall that the α-algorithm also traverses the event log looking for patterns. However, association rules do not consider the ordering of activities and do not aim to build an overall process model.

3.5 Sequence and Episode Mining

The Apriori algorithm uses the monotonicity property that all subsets of a frequent item-set are also frequent. Many other pattern or rule discovery problems have similar monotonicity properties, thus enabling efficient implementations. A well-known example is the *mining of sequential patterns*. After introducing sequence mining, we also describe an approach to *discover frequent episodes* and mention some other data mining techniques relevant for process mining.

3.5.1 Sequence Mining

The Apriori algorithm does not consider the ordering of events. Sequence mining overcomes this problem by analyzing sequences of item-sets. One of the early approaches was developed by Srikant and Agrawal [89]. Here, we sketch the essence of this approach. To explain the problem addressed by sequence mining, we consider the data set shown in Table 3.4. Each line corresponds to a customer ordering a set of items, e.g., at 9.02 on January 2nd 2011, Wil ordered a cappuccino, one day later he orders an espresso and a muffin. Per customer there is a sequence of orders. Orders have a sequence number, a timestamp, and an item-set. A more compact representation of the first customer sequence is $\langle\{cappuccino\}, \{espresso, muffin\}, \{americano, cappuccino\}, \{espresso, muffin\}, \{cappuccino\}, \{americano, cappuccino\}\rangle$. The goal is to find frequent sequences defined by a pattern like $\langle\{cappuccino\}, \{espresso, muffin\}, \{cappuccino\}\rangle$. A sequence is frequent if the pattern is contained in a predefined proportion of the customer sequences in the data set.

A sequence $\langle a_1, a_2, \ldots, a_n\rangle$ is a *subsequence* of another sequence $\langle b_1, b_2, \ldots, b_m\rangle$ if there exist integers $i_1 < i_2 < \cdots < i_n$ such that $a_1 \subseteq b_{i_1}, a_2 \subseteq b_{i_2}, \ldots, a_n \subseteq b_{i_n}$. For example, the sequence $\langle\{x\}, \{x, y\}, \{y\}\rangle$ is a subsequence of $\langle\{z\}, \{x\}, \{z\}, \{x, y, z\}, \{y, z\}, \{z\}\rangle$ because $\{x\} \subseteq \{x\}$, $\{x, y\} \subseteq \{x, y, z\}$, and $\{y\} \subseteq \{y, z\}$. However, $\langle\{x\}, \{y\}\rangle$ is not a subsequence of $\langle\{x, y\}\rangle$ and vice versa. The *support* of a sequence s is the fraction of sequences in the data set that has s as a subsequence. A sequence is *frequent* if its support meets some threshold *minsup*. Consider, for example, the data sets consisting of just the three visible customer sequences in Table 3.4. Pattern $\langle\{tea\}, \{bagel, tea\}\rangle$ has a support of $1/3$ as it is only a subsequence of Mary's sequence. Pattern $\langle\{espresso\}, \{cappuccino\}\rangle$ has a support of $2/3$ as it is a subsequence of both Wil's and Bill's subsequences, but not a subsequence of Mary's sequence. Pattern $\langle\{cappuccino\}, \{espresso, muffin\}\rangle$ has a support of $3/3 = 1$.

Table 3.4 A fragment of a data set used for sequence mining: each line corresponds to an order

Customer	Seq. number	Timestamp	Items
Wil	1	02-01-2011:09.02	{*cappuccino*}
	2	03-01-2011:10.06	{*espresso*, *muffin*}
	3	05-01-2011:15.12	{*americano*, *cappuccino*}
	4	06-01-2011:11.18	{*espresso*, *muffin*}
	5	07-01-2011:14.24	{*cappuccino*}
	6	07-01-2011:14.24	{*americano*, *cappuccino*}
Mary	1	30-12-2010:11.32	{*tea*}
	2	30-12-2010:12.12	{*cappuccino*}
	3	30-12-2010:14.16	{*espresso*, *muffin*}
	4	05-01-2011:11.22	{*bagel*, *tea*}
Bill	1	30-12-2010:14.32	{*cappuccino*}
	2	30-12-2010:15.06	{*cappuccino*}
	3	30-12-2010:16.34	{*bagel*, *espresso*, *muffin*}
	4	06-01-2011:09.18	{*ristretto*}
	5	06-01-2011:12.18	{*cappuccino*}
...	...	...	...

In principle, there is an infinite number of potential patterns. However, just like in the Apriori algorithm a monotonicity property can be exploited: if a sequence is frequent, then its subsequences are also frequent. Therefore, it is possible to efficiently generate patterns. Frequent sequences can also be used to create rules of the form $X \Rightarrow Y$ where X is a pattern and Y is an extension or continuation of the pattern. Consider, for example, $X = \langle\{cappuccino\}, \{espresso\}\rangle$ and $Y = \langle\{cappuccino\}, \{espresso\}, \{latte, muffin\}\rangle$. Suppose that X has a support of 0.05 and Y has a support of 0.04. Then the confidence of $X \Rightarrow Y$ is $0.04/0.05 = 0.8$, i.e., 80% of the customer that ordered a cappuccino followed by an espresso later also order a muffin and latte.

In [89], several extensions of the above approach have been proposed. For example, it is possible to add taxonomies, sliding windows, and time constraints. For practical applications, it is important to relax the strict subsequence requirement such that a one-to-one matching of item-sets is no longer needed.

3.5.2 Episode Mining

Another problem that can be solved using an Apriori-like approach is the *discovery of frequent episodes* [63]. Here a sliding window is used to analyze how frequent

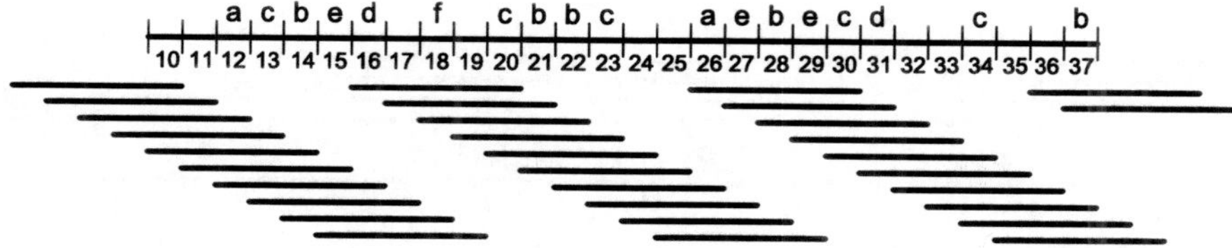

Fig. 3.9 A timed sequence of events and the corresponding time windows

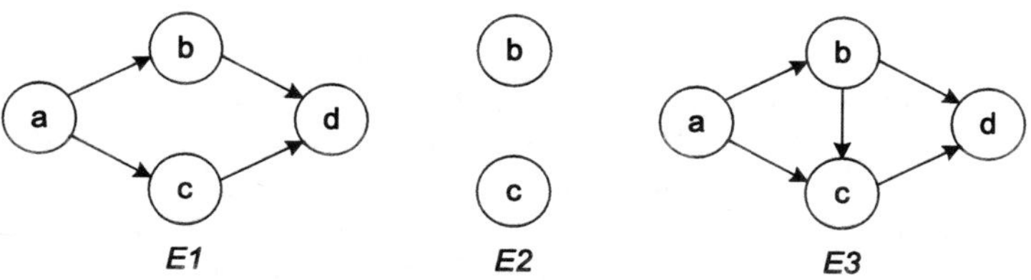

Fig. 3.10 Three episodes

an *episode* is appearing. An episode defines a partial order. The goal is to discover frequent episodes.

Input for episode mining is a time sequence as shown in Fig. 3.9. The timed sequence starts at time 10 and ends at time 37. The sequence consists of discrete time points, and, as shown in Fig. 3.9, at some points in time an event occurs. An event has a type (e.g., the activity that happened) and a timestamp. For example, an event of type *a* occurs at time *12*, an event of type *c* occurs at time *13*, etc. Figure 3.9 also shows 32 *time windows* of length 5. These are all the windows (partially) overlapping with the timed sequence. The length 5 is a predefined parameter of the algorithm used to discover frequent patterns. An episode *occurs* in a time window if the partial order is "embedded" in it.

Figure 3.10 shows three episodes. An episode is described by a directed acyclic graph. The nodes refer to event types and the arcs define a partial order. For example, episode $E1$ defines that *a* should be followed by *b* and *c*, *b* should be followed by *d*, and *c* should be followed by *d*. Episode $E2$ merely states that *b* and *c* should both happen at least once. Episode $E3$ states that *a* should be followed by *b* and *c*, *b* should be followed by *c*, *b* should be followed by *d*, and *c* should be followed by *d*. This episode contains two redundant arcs: the arc from *a* to *c* and the arc from *b* to *d* can be removed without changing the requirements. An episode *occurs* in a time window if it is possible to assign events to nodes in the episode such that the ordering relations are satisfied. Note that the episode only defines the minimal set of events, i.e., there may be all kinds of additional events. The key requirement is that the episode is embedded.

To illustrate the notion of "occurring in a time window", we use Fig. 3.11. Consider episode $E1$ and slide a window of length 5 from left to right. There are 32 possible positions. However, just one of the 32 windows embeds episode $E1$. This is the window starting at time 12 shown below the timed sequence in Fig. 3.11. Here

Fig. 3.11 Occurrences of episodes $E1$ and $E2$

we find the sequence $\langle a, c, b, e, d \rangle$. Clearly all the requirements are met in the sequence: a is followed by b and this b is followed by d, the same a is also followed by c and this c is followed by the same d.

Now consider episode $E2$ and again slide a window of length 5 from left to right. This pattern is much more frequent. Figure 3.11 shows all time windows in which the pattern occurs. In total there are 16 windows where $E2$ is embedded. Note that the only requirement is that both b and c occur: no ordering relation is defined.

Episode $E3$ does not occur in the time sequence if we use a window length of 5. There is no window of length of 5 where the sequence $\langle a, b, c, d \rangle$ is embedded. If the window length is extended to 6, $E3$ occurs once. The corresponding window starts at time 26. Here we find the sequence $\langle a, e, b, e, c, d \rangle$.

The *support* of an episode is the fraction of windows in which the episode occurs. For a window size of 5 time units, the support of $E1$ is $1/32$, the support of $E2$ is $16/32 = 0.5$, and the support of $E3$ is $0/32 = 0$. Like for sequence mining and association rule learning, we define a threshold for the support. All episodes having a support of at least this threshold are *frequent*. For example, if the threshold is 0.2 then $E2$ is frequent whereas $E1$ and $E3$ are not.

The goal is to generate all frequent episodes. Note that there are typically many potential candidates (all partial orders over the set of event types). Fortunately, like in the Apriori algorithm, we can exploit a monotonicity property to quickly rule out bad candidates. To explain this property, we need to define the notion of a *subepisode*. $E1$ is a subepisode of $E3$ because $E1$ is a subgraph of $E3$, i.e., the nodes and arcs of $E1$ are contained in $E3$. $E2$ is a subepisode of both $E1$ and $E3$. It is easy to see that, if an episode E is frequent, then also all of its subepisodes are frequent. This monotonicity property can be used to speed-up the search process.

Frequent episodes can also be used to create rules of the form $X \Rightarrow Y$ where X is a subepisode of Y. As before the confidence of such a rule can be computed. In our example, rule $E1 \Rightarrow E3$ has a confidence of $0/1 = 0$, i.e., a very poor rule. Rule $E2 \Rightarrow E1$ has a confidence of $1/16$.

Episode mining and sequence mining can be seen as variants of association rule learning. Because they take into account the ordering of events, they are related to process discovery. However, there are many differences with process mining algorithms. First of all, *only local patterns* are considered, i.e., no overall process model is created. Second, the focus is on frequent behavior without trying to generate models that also *exclude* behavior. Consider, for example, episode $E1$ in Fig. 3.10. Also the time window $\langle a, b, d, c, d \rangle$ contains the episode despite the two occurrences of d. Therefore, episodes cannot be read as if they are process models. Moreover, episodes *cannot model choices*, *loops*, etc. Finally, episode mining and sequence mining *cannot handle concurrency* well. Sequence mining searches for sequential patterns only. Episode mining runs into problems if there are concurrent episodes, because it is unclear what time window to select to get meaningful episodes.

3.5.3 Other Approaches

In the data mining and machine learning communities, several other techniques have been developed to analyze sequences of events. Applications are in text mining (sequences of letters and words), bio-informatics (analysis of DNA sequences), speech recognition, web analytics, etc. Examples of techniques that are used for this purpose are *neural networks* and *hidden Markov models* [5, 67].

Artificial neural networks try to mimic the human brain in order to learn complex tasks. An artificial neural network is an interconnected group of nodes, akin to the vast network of neurons in the human brain. Different learning paradigms can be used to train the neural network: supervised learning, unsupervised learning, and reinforcement learning [5, 67]. Advantages are that neural networks can exploit parallel computing and that they can be used to solve ill-defined tasks, e.g., image and speech recognition. The main drawback is that the resulting model (e.g., a multi-layer perceptron), is typically not human readable. Hence there is no resulting process model in the sense of Chap. 2 (e.g., a WF-net or BPMN model).

Hidden Markov models are an extension of ordinary Markov processes. A hidden Markov model has a set of states and transition probabilities. Moreover, unlike standard Markov models, in each state an observation is possible, but the state itself remains hidden. Observations have probabilities per state as shown in Fig. 3.12. Three fundamental problems have been investigated for hidden Markov models [5]:

- Given an observation sequence, how to compute the probability of the sequence given a hidden Markov model?
- Given an observation sequence and a hidden Markov model, how to compute the most likely "hidden path" in the model?
- Given a set of observation sequences, how to derive the hidden Markov model that maximizes the probability of producing these sequences?

The last problem is most related to process mining but also the most difficult problem. The well-known Baum–Welch algorithm [5] is a so-called Expectation-Maximization (EM) algorithm that solves this problem iteratively for a fixed number of states. Although hidden Markov models are versatile and relevant for process mining, there are several complications. First of all, there are many computational challenges due to the time consuming iterative procedures. Second, one needs to guess an appropriate number of states as this is input to the algorithm. Third, the resulting hidden Markov model is typically not very accessible for the end user, i.e.,

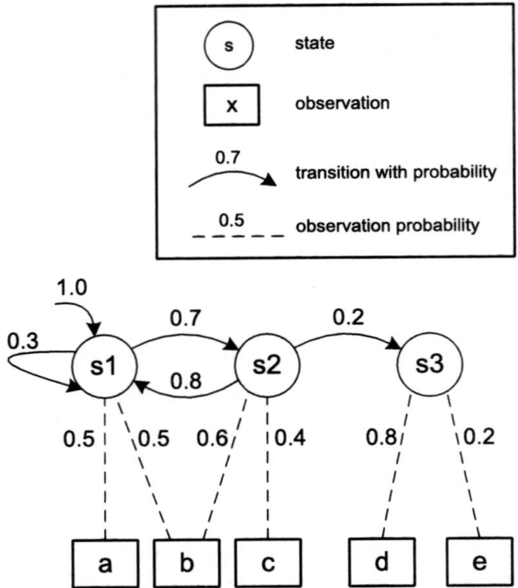

Fig. 3.12 A hidden Markov model with three states: $s1$, $s2$, and $s3$. *The arcs* have state transition probabilities as shown, e.g., in state $s2$ the probability of moving to state $s3$ is 0.2 and the probability of moving to state $s1$ is 0.8. Each visit to a state generates an observation. The observation probabilities are also given. When visiting $s2$ the probability of observing b is 0.6 and the probability of observing c is 0.4. Possible observation sequences are $\langle a, b, c, d\rangle$, $\langle a, b, b, c\rangle$, and $\langle a, b, c, b, b, a, c, e\rangle$. For the observation sequence $\langle a, b, c, d\rangle$, it is clear what the hidden sequence is: $\langle s1, s2, s2, s3\rangle$. For the other two observation sequences, multiple hidden sequences are possible

accurate models are typically large and even for small examples the interpretation of the states is difficult. Clearly, hidden Markov models are at a lower abstraction level than the notations discussed in Chap. 2.

3.6 Quality of Resulting Models

This chapter provided an overview of the mainstream data mining techniques most relevant for process mining. Although some of these techniques can be exploited for process mining, they cannot be used for important process mining tasks such as process discovery, conformance checking, and process enhancement. However, there is an additional reason for showing a variety of data mining techniques. Like in data mining it is non-trivial to analyze the quality of process mining results. Here one can benefit from experiences in the data mining field. Therefore, we discuss some of the validation and evaluation techniques developed for the algorithms presented in this chapter. First, we focus on the quality of classification results, e.g., obtained through a decision tree. Second, we describe general techniques for cross-validation. Here,

		predicted class		
		failed	passed	cum laude
actual class	failed	178	22	0
	passed	21	175	2
	cum laude	1	3	18

Fig. 3.13 Confusion matrix for the decision tree shown in Fig. 3.2. Of the 200 students who failed, 178 are classified as failed and 22 are classified as passed. None of the failing students was classified as cum laude. Of the 198 students who passed, 175 are classified correctly, 21 were classified as failed, and 2 as cum laude

we concentrate on k-fold cross-validation. Finally, we conclude with a more general discussion on Occam's razor.

3.6.1 Measuring the Performance of a Classifier

In Sect. 3.2, we showed how to construct a decision tree. As discussed, there are many design decisions when developing a decision tree learner (e.g., selection of attributes to split on, when to stop splitting, and determining cut values). The question is how to evaluate the performance of a decision tree learner. This is relevant for judging the trustworthiness of the resulting decision tree and for comparing different approaches. A complication is that one can only judge the performance based on *seen* instances although the goal is also to predict good classifications for *unseen* instances. However, for simplicity, let us first assume that we first want to judge the result of a classifier (like a decision tree) on a given data set.

Given a data set consisting of N instances we know for each instance what the actual class is and what the predicted class is. For example, for a particular person that smokes, we may predict that the person will die young (predicted class is "young"), even though the person dies at age 104 (actual class is "old"). This can be visualized using a so-called *confusion matrix*. Figure 3.13 shows the confusion matrix for the data set shown in Table 3.2 and the decision tree shown in Fig. 3.2. The decision tree classifies each of the 420 students into an actual class and a predicted class. All elements on the diagonal are predicted correctly, i.e., $178 + 175 + 18 = 371$ of the 420 students are classified correctly (approximately 88%).

There are several performance measures based on the confusion matrix. To define these let us consider a data set with only two classes: "positive" (+) and "negative" (−). Figure 3.14(a) shows the corresponding 2×2 confusion matrix. The following entries are shown:

- *tp* is the number of *true positives*, i.e., instances that are correctly classified as positive.
- *fn* is the number of *false negatives*, i.e., instances that are predicted to be negative but should have been classified as positive.

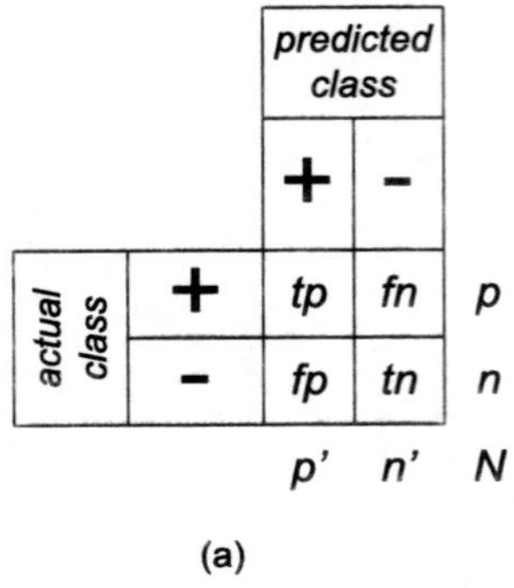

(a)

name	formula
error	(fp+fn)/N
accuracy	(tp+tn)/N
tp-rate	tp/p
fp-rate	fp/n
precision	tp/p'
recall	tp/p

(b)

Fig. 3.14 Confusion matrix for two classes and some performance measures for classifiers

- *fp* is the number of *false positives*, i.e., instances that are predicted to be positive but should have been classified as negative.
- *tn* is the number of *true negatives*, i.e., instances that are correctly classified as negative.

Figure 3.14(a) also shows the sums of rows and columns, e.g., $p = tp + fn$ is the number of instances that are actually positive, $n' = fn + tn$ is the number of instances that are classified as negative by the classifier. $N = tp + fn + fp + tn$ is the total number of instances in the data set. Based on this it is easy to define the measures shown in Fig. 3.14(b). The *error* is defined as the proportion of instances misclassified: $(fp + fn)/N$. The *accuracy* measures the fraction of instances on the diagonal of the confusion matrix. The "true positive rate", *tp-rate*, also known as "hit rate", measures the proportion of positive instances indeed classified as positive. The "false positive rate", *fp-rate*, also known as "false alarm rate", measures the proportion of negative instances wrongly classified as positive. The terms *precision* and *recall* originate from information retrieval. Precision is defined as tp/p'. Here, one can think of p' as the number of documents that have been retrieved based on some search query and *tp* as the number of documents that have been retrieved and also should have been retrieved. Recall is defined as tp/p where p can be interpreted as the number of documents that should have been retrieved based on some search query. It is possible to have high precision and low recall; few of the documents searched for are returned by the query, but those that are returned are indeed relevant. It is also possible to have high recall and low precision; many documents are returned (including the ones relevant), but also many irrelevant documents are returned. Note that recall is the same as *tp*-rate. There is another frequently used metric not shown in Fig. 3.14(b): the so-called *F*1 *score*. The F1 score takes the harmonic mean of precision and recall: $(2 \times precision \times recall)/(precision + recall)$. If either the precision or recall is really poor (i.e., close to 0), then the F1 score is also close to 0. Only if both precision and recall are really good, the F1 score is close to 1.

To illustrate the different metrics let us consider the three decision trees depicted in Fig. 3.4. In the first two decision trees, all instances are classified as young. Note

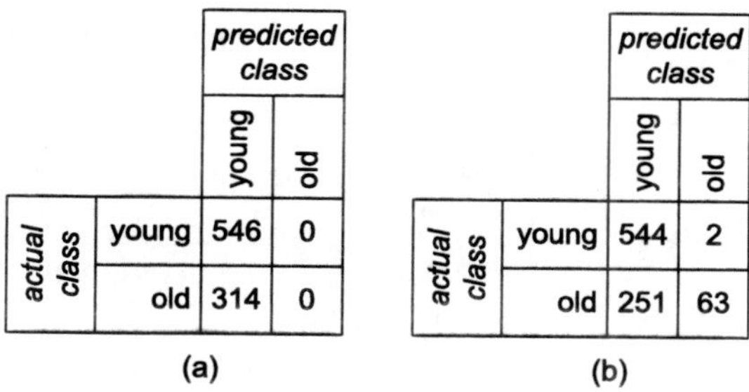

Fig. 3.15 Two confusion matrices for the decision trees in Fig. 3.4

that even after splitting the root node based on the attribute *smoker*, still all instances are predicted to die before 70. Figure 3.15(a) shows the corresponding confusion matrix assuming "*young* = *positive*" and "*old* = *negative*". $N = 860$, $tp = p = 546$, and $fp = n = 314$. Note that $n' = 0$ because all are classified as young. The error is $(314 + 0)/860 = 0.365$, the *tp*-rate is $546/546 = 1$, the *fp*-rate is $314/314 = 1$, precision is $546/860 = 0.635$, recall is $546/546 = 1$, and the F1 score is 0.777. Figure 3.15(b) shows the confusion matrix for the third decision tree in Fig. 3.4. The error is $(251 + 2)/860 = 0.292$, the *tp*-rate is $544/546 = 0.996$, the *fp*-rate is $251/314 = 0.799$, precision is $544/795 = 0.684$, recall is $544/546 = 0.996$, and the F1 score is 0.811. Hence, as expected, the classification improved: the error and *fp*-rate decreased considerably and the *tp*-rate, precision and F1 score increased. Note that the recall went down slightly because of the two persons that are now predicted to live long but do not (despite not smoking nor drinking).

3.6.2 Cross-Validation

The various performance metrics computed using the confusion matrix in Fig. 3.15(b) are based on the same data set as the data set used to learn the third decision tree in Fig. 3.4. Therefore, the confusion matrix is only telling something about *seen* instances, i.e., instances used to learn the classifier. In general, it is trivial to provide classifiers that score perfectly (i.e., precision, recall and F1 score are all 1) on seen instances. (Here, we assume that instances are unique or instances with identical attributes belong to the same class.) For example, if students have a unique registration number, then the decision tree could have a leaf node per student thus perfectly encoding the data set. However, this does not say anything about *unseen* instances, e.g., the registration number of a new student carries no information about expected performance of this student.

The most obvious criterion to estimate the performance of a classifier is its predictive accuracy on unseen instances. The number of unseen instances is potentially very large (if not infinite), therefore an estimate needs to be computed on a test set. This is commonly referred to as *cross-validation*. The data set is split into a *training set* and a *test set*. The training set is used to learn a model whereas the test set is used to evaluate this model based on unseen examples.

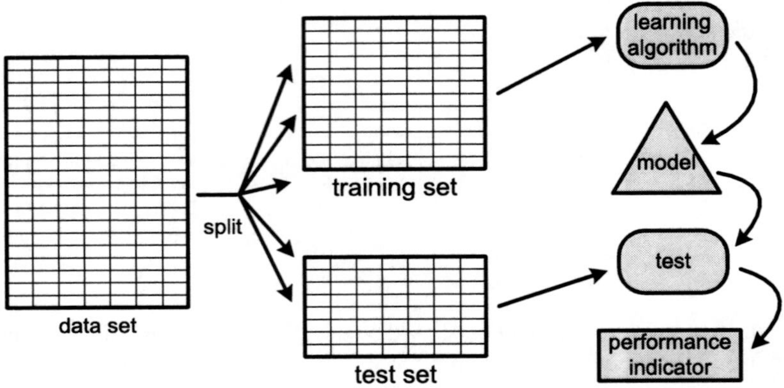

Fig. 3.16 Cross-validation using a test and training set

It is important to realize that cross-validation is not limited to classification but can be used for any data mining technique. The only requirement for cross-validation is that the performance of the result can be measured in some way. For classification, we defined measures such as *precision*, *recall*, *F* 1 *score*, and *error*.

For regression, also various measures can be defined. In the context of linear regression, the *mean square error* is a standard indicator of quality. If $y_1, y_2, \ldots, y_n$ are the actual values and $\hat{y}_1, \hat{y}_2, \ldots, \hat{y}_n$ the predicted values according to the linear regression model, then $(\sum_{i=1}^{n}(y_i - \hat{y}_i)^2)/n$ is the mean square error.

Clustering is typically used in a more descriptive or explanatory manner, and rarely used to make direct predictions about unseen instances. Nevertheless, the clusters derived for a training set could also be tested on a test set. Assign all instances in the test set to the closest centroid. After doing this, the *average distance* of each instance to its centroid can be used as a performance measure.

In the context of association rule mining, we defined metrics such as *support*, *confidence*, and *lift*. One can learn association rules using a training set and then test the discovered rules using the test set. The confidence metric then indicates the proportion of instances for which the rule holds while being applicable. Later, we will also define such metrics for process mining. For example, given an event log that serves as a test set and a Petri net model, one can look at the proportion of instances that can be replayed by the model.

Figure 3.16 shows the basic setting for cross-validation. The data set is split into a test and training set. Based on the training set, a model is generated (e.g., a decision tree or regression model). Then the performance is analyzed using the test set. If just one number is generated for the performance indicator, then this does not give an indication of the reliability of the result. For example, based on some test set the F1 score is 0.811. However, based on another test set the F1 score could be completely different even if the circumstances did not change. Therefore, one often wants to calculate a *confidence interval* for such a performance indicator. Confidence intervals can only be computed over multiple measurements. Here, we discuss two possibilities.

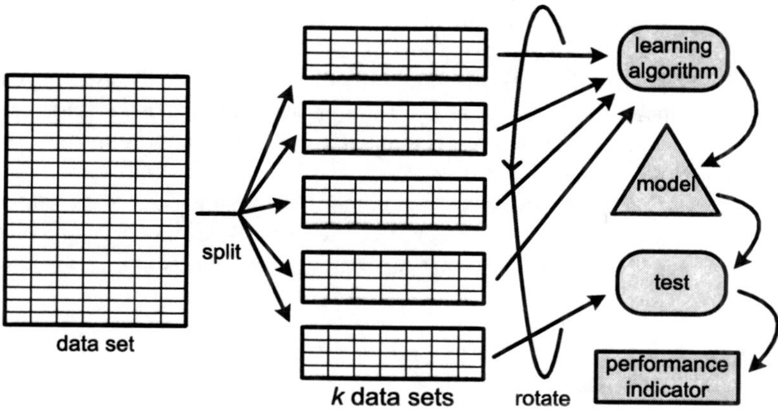

Fig. 3.17 k-fold cross-validation

The first possibility is that one is measuring a performance indicator that is the average over of a large set of independent measurements. Consider for example classification. The test set consists of N instances that are mutually independent. Hence, each classification $1 \leq i \leq N$ can be seen as a separate test x_i where $x_i = 1$ means that the classification is wrong and $x_i = 0$ means that the classification is good. These tests can be seen as samples from a Bernoulli distribution with parameter p (p is the probability of a wrong classification). This distribution has an expected value p and variance $p(1-p)$. If we assume that N is large, then the average error $(\sum_{i=1}^{n} x_i)/N$ is approximately normal distributed. This is due to the central limit theorem, also known as the "law of large numbers". Using this assumption, we find the *95% confidence interval* which is $[p - \alpha_{0.95}\sqrt{p(1-p)/N}, p + \alpha_{0.95}\sqrt{p(1-p)/N}]$, i.e., with 95% certainty the real average error will lie within $p - \alpha_{0.95}\sqrt{p(1-p)/N}$ and $p + \alpha_{0.95}\sqrt{p(1-p)/N}$. $\alpha_{0.95} = 1.96$ is a standard value that can be found in any statistics textbook, p is the measured average error rate, and N is the number of tests. For calculating the 90% or 99% confidence interval, one can use $\alpha_{0.90} = 1.64$ and $\alpha_{0.99} = 2.58$, respectively. Note that it is only possible to calculate such an interval if there are many independent measurements possible based on a single test run.

The second possibility is *k-fold cross-validation*. This approach is used when there are relatively few instances in the data set or when the performance indicator is defined on a set of instances rather than a single instance. For example, the F1 score cannot be defined for one instance in isolation. Figure 3.17 illustrates the idea behind k-fold cross-validation. The data set is split into k equal parts, e.g., $k = 10$. Then k tests are done. In each test, one of the subsets serves as a test set whereas the other $k-1$ subsets serve together as the training set. If subset $i \in \{1, 2, \ldots, k\}$ is used as a test set, then the union of subsets $\{1, 2, \ldots, i-1, i+1, \ldots, k\}$ is used as the training set. One can inspect the individual tests or take the average of the k folds.

There are two advantages associated to k-fold cross-validation. First of all, all data is used both as training data and test data. Second, if desired, one gets k tests of the desired performance indicator rather than just one. Formally, the tests cannot be considered to be independent as the training sets used in the k folds overlap considerably. Nevertheless, the k folds make it possible to get more insight into the reliability.

An extreme variant of k-fold cross-validation is "leave-one-out" cross-validation, also known as jack-knifing. Here $k = N$, i.e., the test sets contain only one element at a time. See [5, 67] for more information on the various forms of cross-validation.

3.6.3 Occam's Razor

Evaluating the quality of data mining results is far from trivial. In this subsection, we discuss some additional complications that are also relevant for process mining.

Learning is typically an "ill posed problem", i.e., only examples are given. Some examples may rule out certain solutions, however, typically many possible models remain. Moreover, there is typically a *bias* in both the target representation and the learning algorithm. Consider, for example, the sequence $2, 3, 5, 7, 11, \ldots$. What is the next element in this sequence? Most readers will guess that it is 13, i.e., the next prime number, but there are infinitely many sequences that start with $2, 3, 5, 7, 11$. Yet, there seems to be preference for hypothesizing about some solutions. The term *inductive bias* refers to a preference for one solution rather than another which cannot be determined by the data itself but which is driven by external factors.

A *representational bias* refers to choices that are implicitly made by selecting a particular representation. For example, in Sect. 3.2, we assumed that in a decision tree the same attribute may appear only once on a path. This representational bias rules out certain solutions, e.g., a decision tree where closer to the root a numerical attribute is used in a coarse-grained manner and in some subtrees it is used in a fine-grained manner. Linear regression also makes assumptions about the function used to best fit the data. The function is assumed to be linear although there may be other non-linear functions that fit the data much better. Note that a representational bias is not necessarily bad, e.g., linear regression has been successfully used in many application domains. However, it is important to realize that the search space is limited by the representation used. The limitations can guide the search process, but also exclude good solutions.

A *learning bias* refers to strategies used by the algorithm that give preference to particular solutions. For example, in Fig. 3.4, we used the criterion of information gain (reduction of entropy) to select attributes. However, we could also have used the Gini index of diversity G rather than entropy E to select attributes, thus resulting in different decision trees.

Both factors also play a role in process mining. Consider, for example, Fig. 1.5 in the first chapter. This process model was discovered using the α-algorithm [103] based on the set of traces $\{\langle a, b, d, e, h\rangle, \langle a, d, c, e, g\rangle, \langle a, c, d, e, f, b, d, e, g\rangle,$

$\langle a, d, b, e, h\rangle$, $\langle a, c, d, e, f, d, c, e, f, b, d, e, h\rangle$, $\langle a, c, d, e, g\rangle\}$. Clearly, there is a representational bias. The assumption is that the process can be presented by a Petri net where every transition bears a unique and visible label. Many processes cannot be represented by such a Petri net. The α-algorithm also has a learning bias as it is focusing on "direct succession". If a is directly followed by b in the event log, then this information is used. However, an observation such as "a is eventually followed by b in the event log" is not exploited by the α-algorithm.

An inductive bias is not necessarily bad. In fact it is often needed to come to a solution. However, the analyst should be aware of this and reflect on the implicit choices made.

Curse of Dimensionality

Some data sets have many variables. However, for most data mining problems the amount of data needed to maintain a specific level of accuracy is exponential in the number of parameters [52]. High-dimensional problems, i.e., analyzing a data set with many variables, may be computationally intractable or lead to incorrect conclusions. This is the "*curse of dimensionality*" that many real-life applications of data mining are confronted with. Consider, for example, a supermarket selling 1000 products. In this case, there are $2^{1000} - 1$ potential item-sets. Although the Apriori algorithm can quickly rule out many irrelevant candidates, the generation of association rules in such a setting is likely to encounter performance problems. Moreover, the interpretation of the results is typically difficult due to an excessive number of potential rules. In a supermarket having hundreds or thousands of products, there are many customers that purchase a unique combination of products. If there are 1000 different products, then there are $2^{1000} - 1 \approx 1.07 \times 10^{301}$ possible shopping lists (ignoring quantities). Although the probability that two customers purchase the same is small, the number of potential rules is very large. This problem is not restricted to association rule learning. Clustering or regression in a 1000 dimensional space will suffer from similar problems. Typical approaches to address this problem are *variable selection* and *transformation* [52]. The goal of variable selection is to simply remove irrelevant of redundant variables. For example, the student's registration number and address are irrelevant when predicting study progress. Sometimes the data set can be transformed to reduce dimensionality, e.g., taking the average mark rather than individual marks per course.

Another problem is the delicate balance between *overfitting* and *underfitting*. A learned model is overfitting if it is too specific and too much driven by accidental information in the data set. For example, when constructing a decision tree for a training set without conflicting input (i.e., instances with identical attributes belong to the same class), it is easy to construct a decision tree with a perfect F1 score. This tree can be obtained by continuing to split nodes until each leaf node corresponds to instances belonging to the same class. However, it is obvious that such a decision tree is too specific and has little predictive value.

A learned model is underfitting if it is too general and allows for things not "supported by evidence" in the data set. Whereas overfitting can be characterized by a lack of generalization, underfitting has the opposite problem: too much generalization. Consider, for example, the generation of association rules. Generating many detailed rules due to very low settings of *minsup* and *minconf*, corresponds to overfitting. Many rules are found, but these are probably rather specific for the training set. Generating very few rules due to very high settings of *minsup* and *minconf*, corresponds to underfitting. In the extreme case, no association rules are found. Note that the model with no rules fits any data set and, hence, carries no information.

Underfitting is particularly problematic if the data set contains *no negative examples*. Consider, for example, the confusion matrix in Fig. 3.14(a). Suppose that we have a training set with only positive examples, i.e., $n = 0$ in the training set. How to construct a decision tree without negative examples? Most algorithms will simply classify everything as positive. This shows that classification assumes both positive and negative examples. This is not the case for association rule learning. Consider, for example, the data set shown in Table 3.3. Suppose that the item-set $\{latte, tea, bagel\}$ does not appear in the data set. This implies that no customer ordered these three items together in the training set. Can we conclude from this that it is not possible to order these three items together? Of course not! Therefore, association rule learning focuses on positive examples that are somehow frequent. Nevertheless, for some applications it would be useful to be able to discover "negative rules" such as the rule that customers are not allowed to order latte's, teas, and bagels in a single order.

A good balance between overfitting and underfitting is of the utmost importance for process discovery. Consider again the Petri net model shown in Fig. 1.5. The model allows for the behavior seen in the event log. It also generalizes as it allows for more sequences than present in the training set. In the event log there is no trace $\langle a, h \rangle$, i.e., the scenario in which a request is registered and immediately rejected does not appear in the log. This does not necessarily imply that this is not possible. However, constructing a model that allows for $\langle a, h \rangle$ although it is not in the log would result in a model that is clearly underfitting. This dilemma is caused by the lack of negative examples in the event log. The traces in the event log show what has happened and not what could not happen. This problem will be addressed in later chapters.

We conclude this chapter with *Occam's Razor*, a principle attributed to the 14th-century English logician William of Ockham. The principle states that "one should not increase, beyond what is necessary, the number of entities required to explain anything", i.e., one should look for the "simplest model" that can explain what is observed in the data set. This principle is related to finding a natural balance between overfitting and underfitting. The *Minimal Description Length* (MDL) principle tries to operationalize Occam's Razor [47, 129]. According to the MDL paradigm, model quality is no longer only based on predicting performance (e.g., F1 score), but also on the simplicity of the model. Moreover, it does not aim at cross-validation in the sense of Sect. 3.6.2. In MDL, performance is judged on the training data alone and not measured against new, unseen instances. The basic idea is that the "best" model is the one that *minimizes the encoding of both model and data set*. Here the insight is used that any regularity in the data can be used to compress the data, i.e., to describe it using fewer symbols than the number of symbols needed to describe the data literally. The more regularities there are, the more the data can be *compressed*. Equating "learning" with "finding regularity", implies that the more we are able to compress the data, the more we have learned about the data [47]. Obviously, a data set can be encoded more compactly if valuable knowledge about the data set is captured in the model. However, encoding such knowledge also requires space. A complex and overfitting model helps to reduce the encoding of the data set. A simple and underfitting model can be stored compactly, but does not help in reducing the encoding of the data set. Note that this idea is related to the notion of entropy in decision tree learning. When building the decision tree, the goal is to find homogeneous leaf nodes that can be encoded compactly. However, when discussing algorithms for decision tree learning in Sect. 3.2 there was no penalty for the complexity of the decision tree itself. The goal of MDL is to minimize the entropy of (a) the data set encoded using the learned model and (b) the encoding of the model itself. To balance between overfitting and underfitting, variable weights may be associated to both encodings.

Applying Occam's Razor is not easy. Extracting reliable and meaningful insights from complex data is far from trivial. In fact, it is much easier to transform complex data sets into "impressive looking garbage" by abusing the techniques presented in this chapter. However, when used wisely, data mining can add tremendous value. Moreover, process mining adds the "process dimension" to data and can be used to dissect event data from a more holistic perspective. As will be shown in the remainder, process mining creates a solid bridge between process modeling and analysis on the one hand and data mining on the other.

Part II
From Event Logs to Process Models

Chapter 1
Introduction

Part I: Preliminaries

Chapter 2
Process Modeling and Analysis

Chapter 3
Data Mining

Part II: From Event Logs to Process Models

Chapter 4
Getting the Data

Chapter 5
Process Discovery: An Introduction

Chapter 6
Advanced Process Discovery Techniques

Part III: Beyond Process Discovery

Chapter 7
Conformance Checking

Chapter 8
Mining Additional Perspectives

Chapter 9
Operational Support

Part IV: Putting Process Mining to Work

Chapter 10
Tool Support

Chapter 11
Analyzing "Lasagna Processes"

Chapter 12
Analyzing "Spaghetti Processes"

Part V: Reflection

Chapter 13
Cartography and Navigation

Chapter 14
Epilogue

After providing preliminaries needed for a good understanding of the "roots" of process mining, we focus on the most challenging process mining task: discovering a process model from an event log. First, in Chap. 4 we describe the input required for process discovery. Then, Chap. 5 describes the α-algorithm in detail. This rather naïve algorithm helps to understand the basics and also sets the scene for discussing the challenges related to process mining. Finally, Chap. 6 gives an overview of state-of-the-art process discovery algorithms and shows how they address the challenges identified.

Chapter 4
Getting the Data

Process mining is impossible without proper event logs. This chapter describes the information that should be present in such event logs. Depending on the process mining technique used, these requirements may vary. The challenge is to extract such data from a variety of data sources, e.g., databases, flat files, message logs, transaction logs, ERP systems, and document management systems. When merging and extracting data, both syntax and semantics play an important role. Moreover, depending on the questions one seeks to answer, different views on the available data are needed.

4.1 Data Sources

In Chap. 1, we introduced the concept of process mining. The idea is to analyze event data from a process-oriented perspective. The goal of process mining is to answer questions about operational processes. Examples are:

- What *really* happened in the past?
- Why did it happen?
- What is likely to happen in the future?
- When and why do organizations and people deviate?
- How to control a process better?
- How to redesign a process to improve its performance?

In subsequent chapters, we will discuss various techniques to answer the preceding questions. However, first we focus on the event data needed.

Figure 4.1 shows the overall "process mining workflow" emphasizing the role of event data. Starting point is the "raw" data hidden in all kinds of data sources. A data source may be a simple flat file, an Excel spreadsheet, a transaction log, or a database table. However, one should not expect all the data to be in a single well-structured data source. The reality is that event data is typically scattered over different data sources and often quite some efforts are needed to collect the relevant

W.M.P. van der Aalst, *Process Mining*,
DOI 10.1007/978-3-642-19345-3_4,

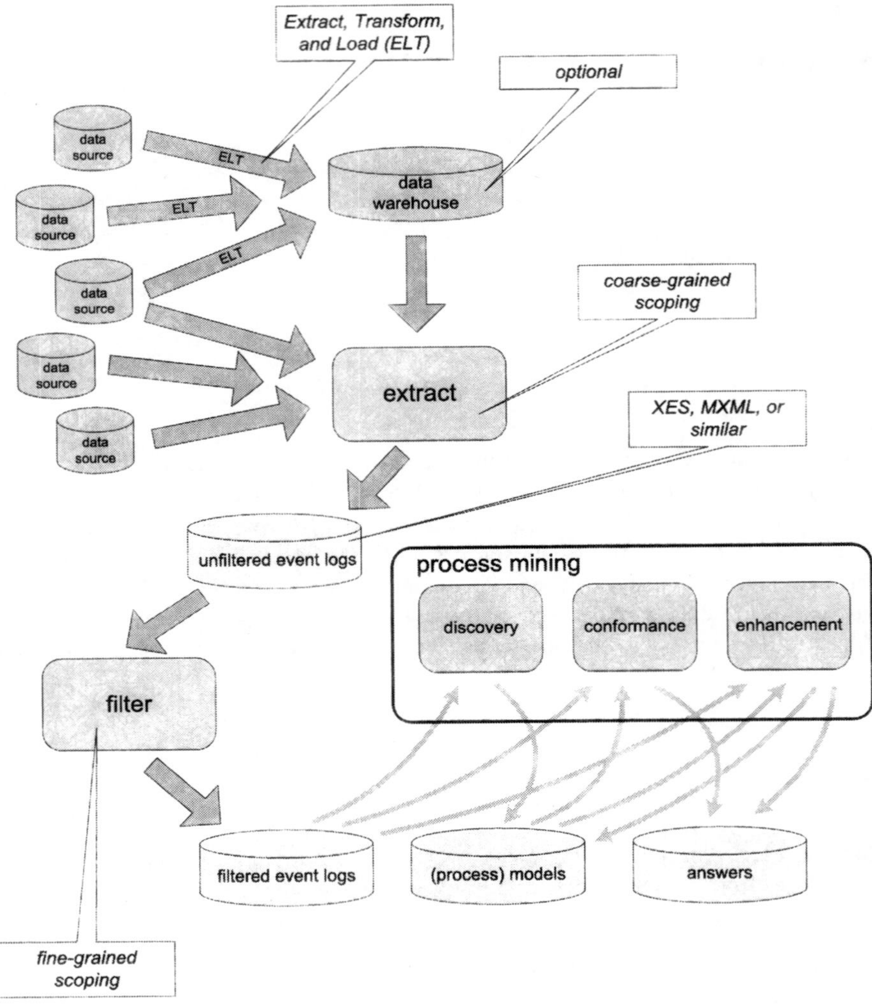

Fig. 4.1 Overview describing the workflow of getting from heterogeneous data sources to process mining results

data. Consider, for example, a full SAP implementation that typically has more than 10,000 tables. Data may be scattered due to technical or organizational reasons. For example, there may be legacy systems holding crucial data or information systems used only at the departmental level. For cross-organizational process mining, e.g., to analyze supply chains, data may even be scattered over multiple organizations. Events can also be captured by tapping of message exchanges [107] (e.g., SOAP messages) and recording read and write actions [36]. Data sources may be structured and well-described by meta data. Unfortunately, in many situations, the data is unstructured or important meta data is missing. Data may originate from web pages, emails, PDF documents, scanned text, screen scraping, etc. Even if data is structured and described by meta data, the sheer complexity of enterprise information systems may be overwhelming, There is no point in trying to exhaustively extract events logs from thousands of tables and other data sources. Data extraction should be driven by questions rather than the availability of lots of data.

In the context of BI and data mining, the phrase "*Extract, Transform, and Load*" (ETL) is used to describe the process that involves: (a) *extracting* data from outside sources, (b) *transforming* it to fit operational needs (dealing with syntactical and semantical issues while ensuring predefined quality levels), and (c) *loading* it into the target system, e.g., a data warehouse or relational database. A *data warehouse* is a single logical repository of an organization's transactional and operational data. The data warehouse does not produce data but simply taps off data from operational systems. The goal is to unify information such that it can be used for reporting, analysis, forecasting, etc. Figure 4.1 shows that ETL activities can be used to populate a data warehouse. It may require quite some efforts to create the common view required for a data warehouse. Different data sources may use different keys, formatting conventions, etc. For example, one data source may identify a patient by her last name and birth date while another data source uses her social security number. One data source may use the date format "31-12-2010" whereas another uses the format "2010/12/31".

If a data warehouse already exists, it most likely holds valuable input for process mining. However, many organizations do not have a good data warehouse. The warehouse may contain only a subset of the information needed for end-to-end process mining, e.g., only data related to customers is stored. Moreover, if a data warehouse is present, it does not need to be process oriented. For example, the typical warehouse data used for *Online Analytical Processing* (OLAP) does not provide much process-related information. OLAP tools are excellent for viewing multidimensional data from different angles, drilling down, and for creating all kinds of reports. However, OLAP tools do not require the storage of business events and their ordering. The data sets used by the mainstream data mining approaches described in Chap. 3 also do not store such information. For example, a decision tree learner can be applied to any table consisting of rows (instances) and columns (variables). As will be shown in the next section, process mining requires information on relevant events and their order.

Whether there is a data warehouse or not, data needs to be extracted and converted into event logs. Here, *scoping* is of the utmost importance. Often the problem is not the syntactical conversion but the selection of suitable data. Questions like "Which of the more than 10,000 SAP tables to convert?" need to be answered first. Typical formats to store event logs are *XES* (eXtensible Event Stream) and *MXML* (Mining eXtensible Markup Language). These will be discussed in Sect. 4.3. For the moment, we assume that *one event log corresponds to one process*, i.e., when scoping the data in the extraction step, only events relevant for the process to be analyzed should be included. In Sect. 4.4, we discuss the problem of converting "3-D data" into "2-D event logs", i.e., events are projected onto the desired process model.

Depending on the questions and viewpoint chosen, different event logs may be extracted from the same data set. Consider for example the data in a hospital. One may be interested in the discovery of patient flows, i.e., typical diagnosis and treatment paths. However, one may also be interested in optimizing the workflow within the radiology department. Both questions require different event logs, although some events may be shared among the two required event logs. Once an event log is created, it is typically *filtered*. Filtering is an iterative process. *Coarse-grained scoping* was done when extracting the data into an event log. Filtering corresponds to *fine-grained scoping* based on initial analysis results. For example, for process discovery one can decide to focus on the 10 most frequent activities to keep the model manageable.

Based on the filtered log, the different types of process mining described in Sect. 1.3 can be applied: *discovery*, *conformance*, and *enhancement*.

Although Fig. 4.1 does not reflect the iterative nature of the whole process well, it should be noted that process mining results most likely trigger new questions and these questions may lead to the exploration of new data sources and more detailed data extractions. Typically, several iterations of the extraction, filtering, and mining phases are needed.

4.2 Event Logs

Table 4.1 shows a fragment of the event log already discussed in Chap. 1. This table illustrates the typical information present in an event log used for process mining. The table shows events related to the handling of requests for compensation. We assume that an event log contains data related to a *single process*, i.e., the first coarse-grained scoping step in Fig. 4.1 should make sure that all events can be related to this process. Moreover, each event in the log needs to refer to a *single process instance*, often referred to as *case*. In Table 4.1, each request corresponds to a case, e.g., Case 1. We also assume that events can be related to some *activity*. In Table 4.1, events refer to activities like *register request*, *check ticket*, and *reject*. These assumptions are quite natural in the context of process mining. All mainstream process modeling notations, including the ones discussed in Chap. 2, specify a process as a collection of activities such that the life-cycle of a single instance is described. Hence, the "case id" and "activity" columns in Table 4.1 represent the bare minimum for process mining. Moreover, events within a case need to be ordered. For example, event 35654423 (the execution of activity *register request* for Case 1) occurs before event 35654424 (the execution of activity *examine thoroughly* for the same case). Without ordering information, it is of course impossible to discover causal dependencies in process models.

Table 4.1 also shows additional information per event. For example, all events have a *timestamp* (i.e., date and time information such as "30-12-2010:11.02"). This information is useful when analyzing performance related properties, e.g., the waiting time between two activities. The events in Table 4.1 also refer to *resources*, i.e., the persons executing the activities. Also *costs* are associated to events. In the context of process mining, these properties are referred to as *attributes*. These attributes are similar to the notion of variables in Chap. 3.

Table 4.1 A fragment of some event log: each line corresponds to an event

Case id	Event id	Properties				
		Timestamp	Activity	Resource	Cost	...
1	35654423	30-12-2010:11.02	Register request	Pete	50	...
	35654424	31-12-2010:10.06	Examine thoroughly	Sue	400	...
	35654425	05-01-2011:15.12	Check ticket	Mike	100	...
	35654426	06-01-2011:11.18	Decide	Sara	200	...
	35654427	07-01-2011:14.24	Reject request	Pete	200	...
2	35654483	30-12-2010:11.32	Register request	Mike	50	...
	35654485	30-12-2010:12.12	Check ticket	Mike	100	...
	35654487	30-12-2010:14.16	Examine casually	Pete	400	...
	35654488	05-01-2011:11.22	Decide	Sara	200	...
	35654489	08-01-2011:12.05	Pay compensation	Ellen	200	...
3	35654521	30-12-2010:14.32	Register request	Pete	50	...
	35654522	30-12-2010:15.06	Examine casually	Mike	400	...
	35654524	30-12-2010:16.34	Check ticket	Ellen	100	...
	35654525	06-01-2011:09.18	Decide	Sara	200	...
	35654526	06-01-2011:12.18	Reinitiate request	Sara	200	...
	35654527	06-01-2011:13.06	Examine thoroughly	Sean	400	...
	35654530	08-01-2011:11.43	Check ticket	Pete	100	...
	35654531	09-01-2011:09.55	Decide	Sara	200	...
	35654533	15-01-2011:10.45	Pay compensation	Ellen	200	...
4	35654641	06-01-2011:15.02	Register request	Pete	50	...
	35654643	07-01-2011:12.06	Check ticket	Mike	100	...
	35654644	08-01-2011:14.43	Examine thoroughly	Sean	400	...
	35654645	09-01-2011:12.02	Decide	Sara	200	...
	35654647	12-01-2011:15.44	Reject request	Ellen	200	...
...	...	...	...	...	...	...

Figure 4.2 shows the tree structure of an event log. Using this figure, we can list our assumptions about event logs.

- A *process* consists of *cases*.
- A case consists of *events* such that each event relates to precisely one case.
- Events within a case are *ordered*.
- Events can have *attributes*. Examples of typical attribute names are activity, time, costs, and resource.

Not all events need to have the same set of attributes, However, typically, events referring to the same activity have the same set of attributes.

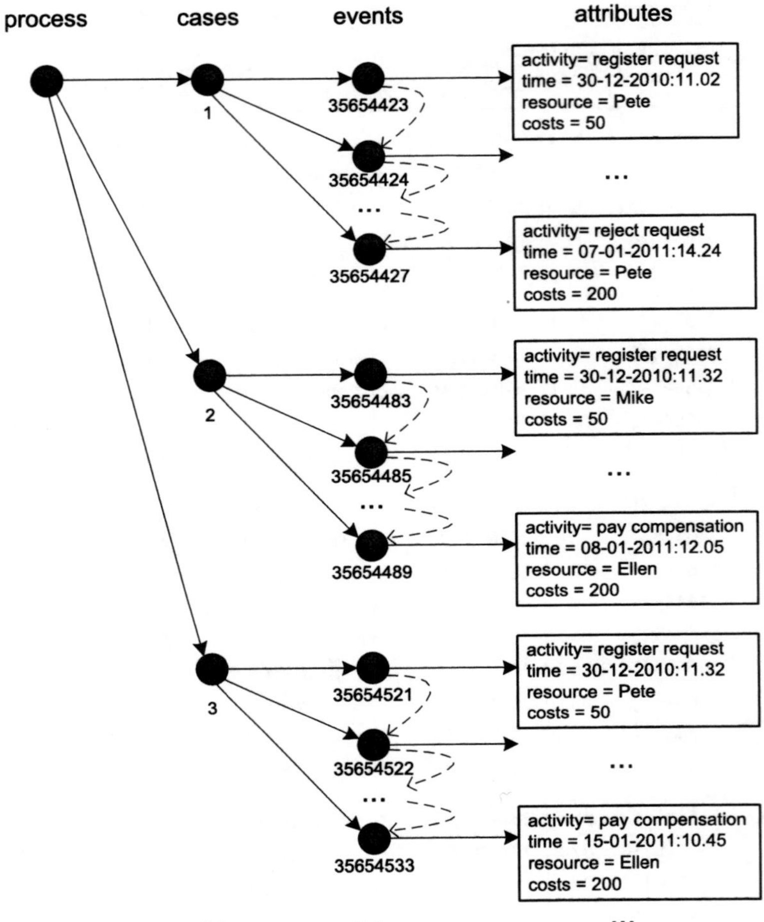

Fig. 4.2 Structure of event logs

To be able to reason about logs and to precisely specify the requirements for event logs, we formalize the various notions.

Definition 4.1 (Event, attribute) Let $\mathscr{E}$ be the *event universe*, i.e., the set of all possible event identifiers. Events may be characterized by various *attributes*, e.g., an event may have a timestamp, correspond to an activity, is executed by a particular person, has associated costs, etc. Let AN be a set of attribute names. For any event $e \in \mathscr{E}$ and name $n \in AN$: $\#_n(e)$ is the value of attribute n for event e. If event e does not have an attribute named n, then $\#_n(e) = \perp$ (null value).

For convenience we assume the following standard attributes:

- $\#_{activity}(e)$ is the *activity* associated to event e.

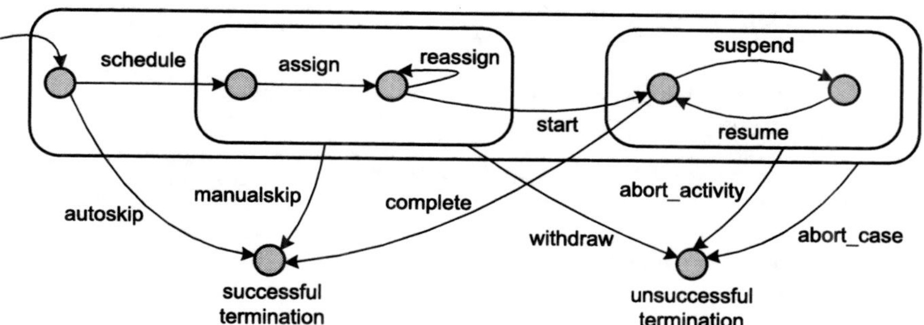

Fig. 4.3 Standard transactional life-cycle model

- $\#_{time}(e)$ is the *timestamp* of event e.
- $\#_{resource}(e)$ is the *resource* associated to event e.
- $\#_{trans}(e)$ is the *transaction type* associated to event e, examples are schedule, start, complete, and suspend.

These are just examples. None of these attributes is mandatory. However, for these standard attributes we will assume some conventions. For example, timestamps should be nondescending in the event log. Moreover, we assume a time domain $\mathcal{T}$, i.e., $\#_{time}(e) \in \mathcal{T}$ for any $e \in \mathcal{E}$. The transaction type attribute $\#_{trans}(e)$ refers to the life-cycle of activities. In most situations, activities take time. Therefore, events may point out for example the start or completion of activities. In this book, we assume the *transactional life-cycle model* shown in Fig. 4.3.

Figure 4.4 shows some examples to explain the life-cycle model. The life-cycles of five activity instances are shown: a, b, c, d, and e. a is first scheduled for execution (i.e., an event e_1 with $\#_{trans}(e_1) = schedule$ and $\#_{activity}(e_1) = a$ occurs), then the activity is assigned to a resource (i.e., an event e_2 with $\#_{trans}(e_2) = assign$ and $\#_{activity}(e_2) = a$ occurs). Later the activity is started by this resource, and finally the activity completes. Note that four events were recorded for this activity instance. Activity instance b has seven events associated to it. Compared to a the activity is reassigned (i.e., the resource that is supposed to execute the activity is changed), suspended (temporarily halted), and resumed. Of course it is possible to skip stages in the transactional life-cycle model, because events are not recorded or because certain steps are not necessary. Activity instance d in Fig. 4.4 has just two events; e just one, i.e., for e only the completion of the activity instance is recorded. Transaction type "autoskip" refers to an action by the system bypassing the activity. Transaction type "manualskip" refers to resource initiated skipping. Transaction types "abort_activity" and "abort_case" correspond to aborting the activity or the whole case. A "withdraw" event signals the situation in which the activity is canceled before it was started. Figure 4.3 shows all transaction types, their enabling, and their effect. For example, according to the transactional life-cycle model, "abort_activity" is only possible when the activity instance is running (i.e., started, suspended, or resumed).

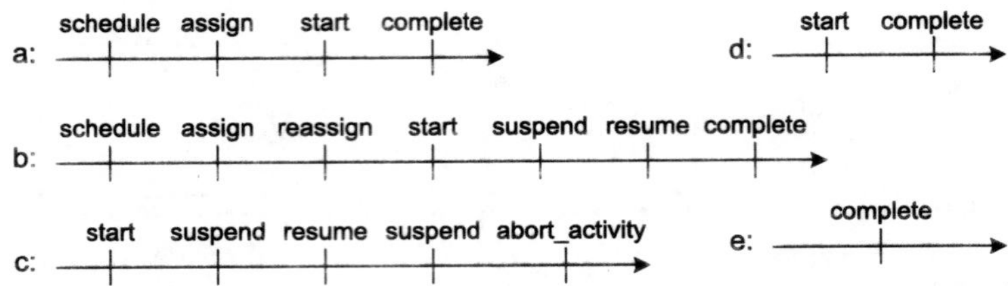

Fig. 4.4 Transactional events for five activity instances

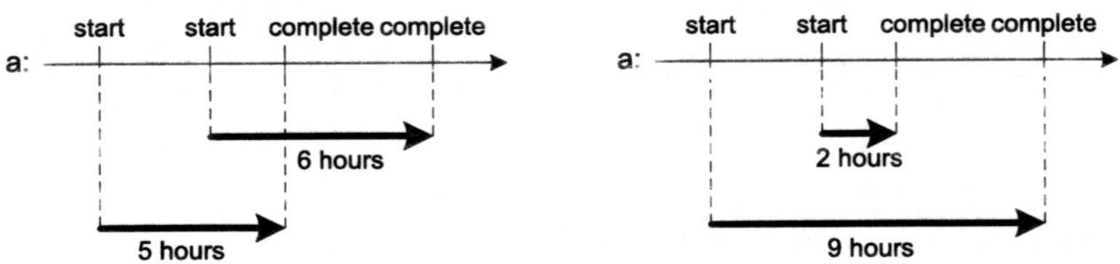

Fig. 4.5 Two scenarios involving two activity instance leaving the same footprint in the log

Events can have many attributes. We often refer to the event by its activity name. Technically this is not correct. There may be many events that refer to the same activity name. Within a case, these events may refer to the same activity instance (e.g., start and complete events) or different activity instances (e.g., in a loop). This distinction is particularly important when measuring service times, waiting times, etc. Consider, for example, the scenario in which the same activity is started twice for the same case, i.e., two activity instances are running in parallel, and then one of them completes. Did the activity that was started first complete or the second one? Figure 4.5 illustrates the dilemma. Given the footprint of two starts followed by two completes of the same activity, there are two possible scenarios. In one scenario, the durations of the two activity instances are 5 and 6. In the other scenario, the durations of the activity instances are 9 and 2. Yet they leave the same footprint in the event log.

This problem can be addressed by adding information to the log or by using heuristics. This can be seen as a "secondary correlation problem", i.e., relating two events within the same case. The primary correlation problem is to relate events to cases, i.e., process instances [39]. Figure 4.5 shows that even within one case there may be the need to correlate events because they belong to the same activity instance. When implementing systems, such information can easily be added to the logs; just provide an activity instance attribute to keep track of this. When dealing with existing systems this is not as simple as it seems. For example, when correlating messages between organizations there may be the need to scan the content of the message to find a suitable identifier (e.g., address or name). It is also possible to use heuristics to resolve most problems, e.g., in Fig. 4.5 one could just assume a first-in-first-out order and pick the first scenario. Moreover, one may introduce timeouts when the time between a start event and complete event is too long. For example, start events that are not followed by a corresponding complete event within 45 minutes are removed from the log.

Process mining techniques can be used to automatically discover process models. In these process models, activities play a central role. These correspond to transitions in Petri nets, tasks in YAWL, functions in EPCs, state transitions in transition systems, and tasks in BPMN. However, the transactional life-cycle model in Fig. 4.3 shows that there may be multiple events referring to the same activity. Some process mining techniques take into account the transactional model whereas others just consider atomic events. Moreover, sometimes we just want to focus on complete events whereas at other times the focus may be on withdrawals. This can be supported by filtering (e.g., removing events of a particular type) and by the concept of a *classifier*. A *classifier is a function that maps the attributes of an event onto a label* used in the resulting process model. This can be seen as the "name" of the event. In principle, there can be many classifiers. However, only one is used at a time. Therefore, we can use the notation $\underline{e}$ to refer to the name used in the process model.

Definition 4.2 (Classifier) For any event $e \in \mathcal{E}$, $\underline{e}$ is the *name* of the event.

If events are simply identified by their activity name, then $\underline{e} = \#_{activity}(e)$. This means that activity instance a in Fig. 4.4 would be mapped onto $\langle a, a, a, a \rangle$. In this case the basic α-algorithm (not using transactional information) would create just one a transition. If events are identified by their activity name and transaction type, then $\underline{e} = (\#_{activity}(e), \#_{trans}(e))$. Now activity instance a would be mapped onto $\langle (a, \mathit{schedule}), (a, \mathit{assign}), (a, \mathit{start}), (a, \mathit{complete}) \rangle$ and the basic α-algorithm would create four transitions referring to a's life-cycle. As shown in Sect. 5.2.4, transaction type attributes such as start, complete, etc. can be exploited to create a two-level process model that hides the transactional life-cycles of individual activities in subprocesses. It is also possible to use a completely different classifier, e.g., $\underline{e} = \#_{resource}(e)$. In this case events are named after the resources executing them. In this book, we assume the classifier $\underline{e} = \#_{activity}(e)$ as the *default classifier*. This is why we considered the activity attribute to be mandatory in our initial examples. From now on, we only require a classifier.

Sequences

Sequences are the most natural way to present traces in an event log. When describing the operational semantics of Petri nets and transition systems, we also modeled behavior in terms of sequences. Given their importance, we introduce some useful operators on sequences.

For a given set A, A^* is the set of all finite sequences over A. A finite sequence over A of length n is a mapping $\sigma \in \{1, \dots, n\} \to A$. Such a sequence is represented by a string, i.e., $\sigma = \langle a_1, a_2, \dots, a_n \rangle$ where $a_i = \sigma(i)$ for $1 \le i \le n$. $|\sigma|$ denotes the length of the sequence, i.e. $|\sigma| = n$. $\sigma \oplus a' = \langle a_1, \dots, a_n, a' \rangle$ is the sequence with element a' appended at the end. Similarly, $\sigma_1 \oplus \sigma_2$ appends sequence σ_2 to σ_1 resulting a sequence of length $|\sigma_1| + |\sigma_2|$.
$hd^k(\sigma) = \langle a_1, a_2, \dots, a_{k\ min\ n} \rangle$, i.e., the "head" of the sequence consisting of the first k elements (if possible). Note that $hd^0(\sigma)$ is the empty sequence and for $k \ge n$: $hd^k(\sigma) = \sigma$. $pref(\sigma) = \{hd^k(\sigma) \mid 0 \le k \le n\}$ is the set of prefixes of σ.
$tl^k(\sigma) = \langle a_{(n-k+1)\ max\ 1}, a_{k+2}, \dots, a_n \rangle$, i.e., the "tail" of the sequence composed of the last k elements (if possible). Note that $tl^0(\sigma)$ is the empty sequence and for $k \ge n$: $tl^k(\sigma) = \sigma$.
$\sigma \uparrow X$ is the projection of σ onto some subset $X \subseteq A$, e.g., $\langle a, b, c, a, b, c, d \rangle \uparrow \{a, b\} = \langle a, b, a, b \rangle$ and $\langle d, a, a, a, a, a, a, d \rangle \uparrow \{d\} = \langle d, d \rangle$.
For any sequence $\sigma = \langle a_1, a_2, \dots, a_n \rangle$ over A, $\partial_{set}(\sigma) = \{a_1, a_2, \dots, a_n\}$ and $\partial_{multiset}(\sigma) = [a_1, a_2, \dots, a_n]$. ∂_{set} converts a sequence into a set, e.g., $\partial_{set}(\langle d, a, a, a, a, a, a, d \rangle) = \{a, d\}$. a is an element of σ, denoted as $a \in \sigma$, if and only if $a \in \partial_{set}(\sigma)$. $\partial_{multiset}$ converts a sequence into a multi-set, e.g., $\partial_{multiset}(\langle d, a, a, a, a, a, a, d \rangle) = [a^6, d^2]$. $\partial_{multiset}(\sigma)$ is also known as the *Parikh vector* of σ. These conversions allow us to treat sequences as sets or bags when needed.

An event log consists of cases and cases consist of events. The events for a case are represented in the form of a *trace*, i.e., a sequence of unique events. Moreover, cases, like events, can have attributes.

Definition 4.3 (Case, trace, event log) Let $\mathscr{C}$ be the *case universe*, i.e., the set of all possible case identifiers. Cases, like events, have attributes. For any case $c \in \mathscr{C}$ and name $n \in AN$: $\#_n(c)$ is the value of attribute n for case c ($\#_n(c) = \perp$ if case c has no attribute named n). Each case has a special mandatory attribute *trace*: $\#_{trace}(c) \in \mathscr{E}^*$.[1] $\hat{c} = \#_{trace}(c)$ is a shorthand for referring to the trace of a case.

A *trace* is a finite sequence of events $\sigma \in \mathscr{E}^*$ such that each event appears only once, i.e., for $1 \le i < j \le |\sigma|$: $\sigma(i) \ne \sigma(j)$.

An *event log* is a set of cases $L \subseteq \mathscr{C}$ such that each event appears at most once in the entire log, i.e., for any $c_1, c_2 \in L$ such that $c_1 \ne c_2$: $\partial_{set}(\hat{c_1}) \cap \partial_{set}(\hat{c_2}) = \emptyset$.

If an event log contains timestamps, then the ordering in a trace should respect these timestamps, i.e., for any $c \in L$, i and j such that $1 \le i < j \le |\hat{c}|$: $\#_{time}(\hat{c}(i)) \le \#_{time}(\hat{c}(j))$.

Events and cases are represented using *unique* identifiers. An identifier $e \in \mathscr{E}$ refers to an event and an identifier $c \in \mathscr{C}$ refers to a case. This mechanism allows us

[1] In the remainder, we assume $\#_{trace}(c) \ne \langle\ \rangle$, i.e., traces in a log contain at least one event.

to point to a specific event or a specific case. This is important as there may be many events having identical attributes, e.g., start events of some activity a may have been recorded for different cases and even within a case there may be multiple of such events. Similarly, there may be different cases that followed the same path in the process. These identifiers are just a technicality that helps us to point to particular events and cases. Therefore, they do not need to exist in the original data source and may be generated when extracting the data from different data sources.

Events and cases may have any number of attributes. Using the classifier mechanism, each event gets a name. Therefore, we often require events to have an activity attribute. Cases always have a trace attribute; $\hat{c} = \#_{trace}(c)$ is the sequence of events that have been recorded for c.

By formalizing event logs in this way, we *precisely* formulate the *requirements* we impose on event logs *without* discussing a concrete *syntax*. Moreover, we can use this formal representation to query the event log and use it as a starting point for analysis and reasoning. Some examples:

- $\{\#_{activity}(e) \mid c \in L \ \wedge \ e \in \hat{c}\}$ is the set of all activities appearing in log L.
- $\{\#_{resource}(e) \mid c \in L \ \wedge \ e \in \hat{c} \ \wedge \ \#_{trans}(e) = manualskip\}$ is the set of all resources that skipped an activity.
- $\{a \in \mathscr{A} \mid c \in L \ \wedge \ a = \#_{activity}(\hat{c}(1)) \ \wedge \ a = \#_{activity}(\hat{c}(|\hat{c}|))\}$ is the set of all activities that served as start and end activity for the same case.

Table 4.1 defines an event log in the sense of Definition 4.3. $L = \{1, 2, 3, 4, \ldots\}$ is the set of cases shown in Table 4.1. $\hat{1} = \#_{trace}(1) = \langle 35654423, 35654424, 35654425, 35654426, 35654427\rangle$ is the trace of Case 1. $\#_{activity}(35654423) =$ *register request* is the activity associated to event 35654423. $\#_{time}(35654423) =$ 30-12-2010:11.02 is the timestamp associated to this event. $\#_{resource}(35654423) =$ *Pete* is the resource doing the registration. $\#_{costs}(35654423) = 50$ are the costs associated to event 35654423. $\#_{activity}(35654424) =$ *examine thoroughly* is the activity associated to second event of Case 1. Etc.

Depending on the attributes in the log, different types of analysis are possible. Figure 4.6 sketches possible results. The Petri net can be discovered by just using the activity attribute ($\#_{activity}(e)$). To measure durations of activities, one needs to have a transactional attribute ($\#_{trans}(e)$) to distinguish start from completion, and timestamps ($\#_{time}(e)$). To measure costs, the costs attribute is used ($\#_{costs}(e)$). Figure 4.6 also shows a *role* per activity and a *social network*. These have been discovered using the resource attribute ($\#_{resource}(e)$). For example, activities *decide* and *reinitiate request* require the role *manager* and Sara is the only one having this role. The social network in Fig. 4.6 shows how work is flowing through the organization, e.g., activities done by Sara are often followed by activities of Ellen. The thicker the connecting arc is, the more work is handed over from one person to another.

Table 4.1 happens to show unique id's for both events and cases, i.e., elements of the sets $\mathscr{E} = \{35654423, 35654424, 35654425, 35654426, 35654427, \ldots\}$ (event universe) and $\mathscr{C} = \{1, 2, 3, 4, \ldots\}$ (case universe) are shown *explicitly* in the table. This is not mandatory; these identities are just used for mathematical convenience and have no further meaning. One can think of them as a symbolic key in a table

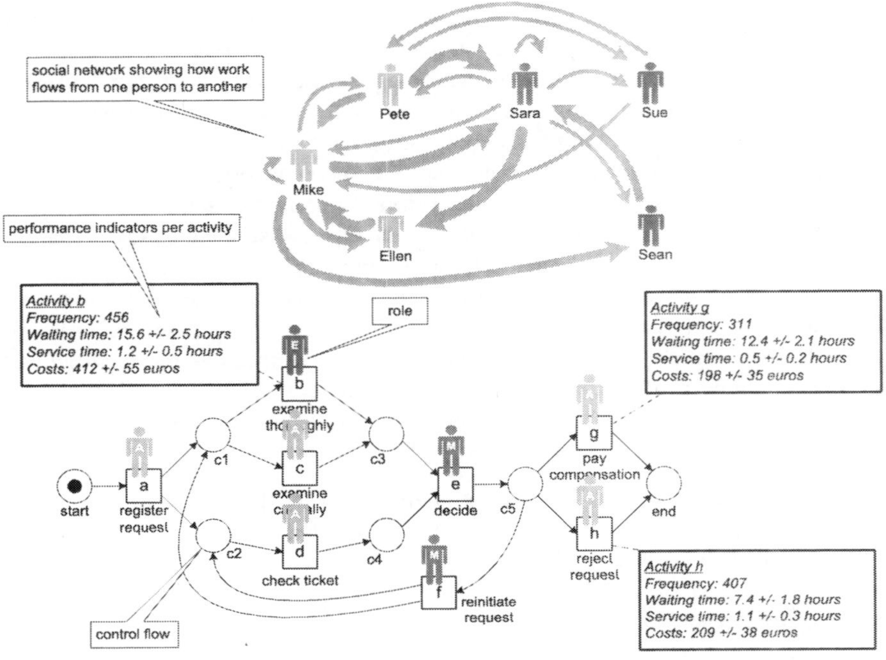

Fig. 4.6 Various types of process mining results based on the attributes in the event log

or a position in an XML document. The reason for adding them is that this way it becomes easy to refer to a particular case or event. In fact, for simple algorithms like the α-algorithm, Definition 4.3 is a bit of overkill. See for example Table 1.2 in Sect. 1.4 showing the essential information used to construct a Petri net. If one is just interested in activity names (or some other classifier), the definition can be simplified drastically as is shown next.

Definition 4.4 (Simple event log) Let $\mathscr{A}$ be a set of activity names. A *simple* trace σ is a sequence of activities, i.e., $\sigma \in \mathscr{A}^*$. A *simple* event log L is a multi-set of traces over $\mathscr{A}$, i.e., $L \in \mathbb{B}(\mathscr{A}^*)$.[2]

A simple event log is just a multi-set of traces over some set $\mathscr{A}$. For example $[\langle a,b,c,d\rangle^3, \langle a,c,b,d\rangle^2, \langle a,e,d\rangle]$ defines a log containing 6 cases. In total there are $3 \times 4 + 2 \times 4 + 1 \times 3 = 23$ events. All cases start with a and end with d. In a simple log there are no attributes, e.g., timestamps and resource information are abstracted from. Moreover, cases and events are no longer uniquely identifiable. For example, the three cases following the sequence $\langle a,b,c,d\rangle$ in the simple event log $[\langle a,b,c,d\rangle^3, \langle a,c,b,d\rangle^2, \langle a,e,d\rangle]$ cannot be distinguished.

[2]Note that we still assume that each trace contains at least one element, i.e., $\sigma \in L$ implies $\sigma \neq \langle\,\rangle$.

Definition 4.5 (Transforming an event log into a simple event log) Let $L \subseteq \mathscr{C}$ be an event log as defined in Definition 4.3. Assume that a classifier has been defined: $\underline{e}$ is the name of event $e \in \mathscr{E}$. This classifier can also be applied to sequences, i.e., $\underline{\langle e_1, e_2, \ldots, e_n \rangle} = \langle \underline{e_1}, \underline{e_2}, \ldots, \underline{e_n} \rangle$. $\underline{L} = [\ \underline{(\hat{c})} \mid c \in L\ ]$ is the simple event log corresponding to L.

All cases in L are converted into sequences of (activity) names using the classifier. A case $c \in L$ is an identifier from the case universe $\mathscr{C}$. $\hat{c} = \#_{trace}(c) = \langle e_1, e_2, \ldots, e_n \rangle \in \mathscr{E}^*$ is the sequence of events executed for c. $\underline{(\hat{c})} = \langle \underline{e_1}, \underline{e_2}, \ldots, \underline{e_n} \rangle$ maps these events onto (activity) names using the classifier.

If we apply this transformation to the event log shown in Table 4.1 while assuming the default classifier ($\underline{e} = \#_{activity}(e)$), then we obtain the event log:

$$\begin{aligned}\underline{L} = [&\langle \textit{register request}, \textit{examine thoroughly}, \textit{check ticket}, \textit{decide}, \textit{reject request} \rangle,\\ &\langle \textit{register request}, \textit{check ticket}, \textit{examine casually}, \textit{decide}, \textit{pay compensation} \rangle,\\ &\langle \textit{register request}, \textit{examine casually}, \textit{check ticket}, \textit{decide}, \textit{reinitiate request},\\ &\ \textit{examine thoroughly}, \textit{check ticket}, \textit{decide}, \textit{pay compensation} \rangle,\\ &\langle \textit{register request}, \textit{check ticket}, \textit{examine thoroughly}, \textit{decide}, \textit{reject request} \rangle,\\ &\ldots]\end{aligned}$$

Another classifier could have been used to create a simple log. For example, when using the classifier $\underline{e} = \#_{resource}(e)$, the following log is obtained:

$$\begin{aligned}\underline{L} = [&\langle \textit{Pete}, \textit{Sue}, \textit{Mike}, \textit{Sara}, \textit{Pete} \rangle, \langle \textit{Mike}, \textit{Mike}, \textit{Pete}, \textit{Sara}, \textit{Ellen} \rangle,\\ &\langle \textit{Pete}, \textit{Mike}, \textit{Ellen}, \textit{Sara}, \textit{Sara}, \textit{Sean}, \textit{Pete}, \textit{Sara}, \textit{Ellen} \rangle,\\ &\langle \textit{Pete}, \textit{Mike}, \textit{Sean}, \textit{Sara}, \textit{Ellen} \rangle, \ldots]\end{aligned}$$

In this event log, the activity names have been replaced by the names of the people executing the activities. Such projections are used when constructing a social network.

In the remainder, we will use whatever notation is most suitable. Definition 4.3 specifies a precise but very generic description of an event log that can be used for various purposes. Definition 4.4 describes a very simple format without any attributes. This format is useful for explaining simple process discovery algorithms that are not using the information stored in additional attributes. For simple event logs, we focus on a single attribute (typically the activity name). As shown, any event log L can be easily converted into a simple event log $\underline{L}$.

4.3 XES

Until recently, the de facto standard for storing and exchanging events logs was *MXML* (Mining eXtensible Markup Language). MXML emerged in 2003 and was later adopted by the process mining tool ProM. Using MXML, it is possible to store event logs such as the one shown in Table 4.1 using an XML-based syntax. *ProMimport* is a tool supporting the conversion of different data sources to MXML, e.g., MS Access, Aris PPM, CSV, Apache, Adept, PeopleSoft, Subversion, SAP R/3, Protos, CPN Tools, Cognos, and Staffware. MXML has a standard notation for storing timestamps, resources, and transaction types. Moreover, one can add arbitrary data elements to events and cases. The latter resulted in ad-hoc extensions of MXML where certain data attributes were interpreted in a specific manner. For example, *SA-MXML* (Semantically Annotated Mining eXtensible Markup Language) is a semantic annotated version of the MXML format used by the ProM framework. SA-MXML incorporates references between elements in logs and concepts in ontologies. For example, a resource can have a reference to a concept in an ontology describing a hierarchy of roles, organizational entities, and positions. To realize these semantic annotations, existing XML elements were interpreted in a new manner. Other extensions were realized in a similar manner. Although this approach worked quite well in practice, the various ad-hoc extensions also revealed shortcomings of the MXML format. This triggered the development of *XES* (eXtensible Event Stream) [48].

XES is the successor of MXML. Based on many practical experiences with MXML, the XES format has been made less restrictive and truly extendible. In September 2010, the format was adopted by the *IEEE Task Force on Process Mining*. The format is supported by tools such as ProM (as of version 6), Nitro, XESame, and OpenXES. See www.xes-standard.org for detailed information about the standard.

Figure 4.7 shows the XES meta model expressed in terms of a UML class diagram. An XES document (i.e., XML file) contains one log consisting of any number of traces. Each trace describes a sequential list of events corresponding to a particular case. The log, its traces, and its events may have any number of attributes. Attributes may be nested. There are five core types: *String*, *Date*, *Int*, *Float*, and *Boolean*. These correspond to the standard XML types: *xs:string*, *xs:dateTime*, *xs:long*, *xs:double*, and *xs:boolean*. For example, 2011-12-17T21:00:00.000+02:00 is a value of type *xs:dateTime* representing nine o'clock in the evening of December 17th 2011 in timezone GMT+2.

XES does not prescribe a fixed set of mandatory attributes for each element (log, trace, and event); an event can have any number of attributes. However, to provide semantics for such attributes, the log refers to so-called *extensions*. An extension gives semantics to particular attributes. For example, the *Time extension* defines a timestamp attribute of type *xs:dateTime*. This corresponds to the $\#_{time}(e)$ attribute used in Sect. 4.2. The *Organizational extension* defines a resource attribute of type *xs:string*. This corresponds to the $\#_{resource}(e)$ attribute used in Sect. 4.2. Users can define their own extensions. For example, it is possible to develop domain specific or even organization specific extensions. Figure 4.7 shows that a log declares the set of extensions to be used. Each extension may define attributes that are considered to be standard when the extension is used.

In Sect. 4.2, we used $\mathcal{C}$ and $\mathcal{E}$ to denote the case respectively event universe. This was used to be able to refer to a case and event. In XES, such unique identifiers are not necessary. In fact, one can think of the position in the log as the identifier of an event or case.

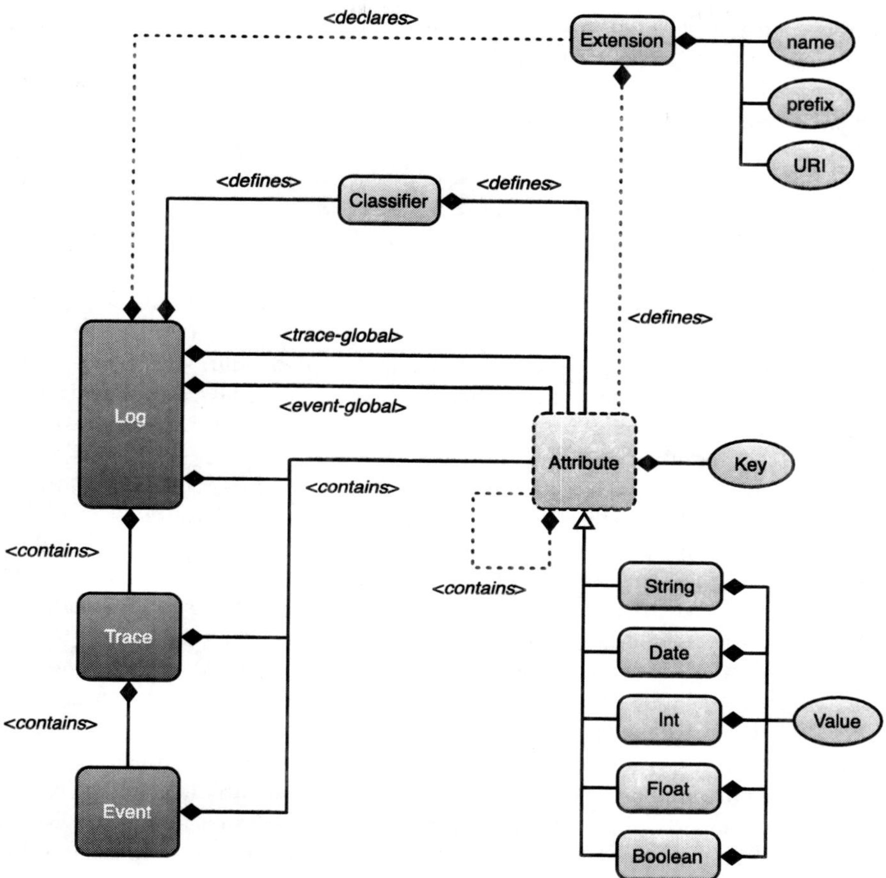

Fig. 4.7 Meta model of XES [48]. A log contains traces and each trace contains events. Logs, traces, and events have attributes. Extensions may define new attributes and a log should declare the extensions used in it. Global attributes are attributes that are declared to be mandatory. Such attributes reside at the trace or event level. Attributes may be nested. Event classifiers are defined for the log and assign a "label" (e.g., activity name) to each event. There may be multiple classifiers

XES may declare particular attributes to be *mandatory*. For example, it may be stated that any trace should have a name or that any event should have a timestamp. For this purpose, a log holds two lists of *global attributes*: one for the traces and one for the events.

XES supports the *classifier* concept described earlier (Definition 4.2). An XES log defines an arbitrary number of classifiers. Each classifier is specified by a list of attributes. Any two events that have the identical values with respect to these attributes are considered to be equal for that classifier. These attributes should be mandatory event attributes. For example, if a classifier is specified by both a name attribute and a resource attribute, then two events are mapped onto the same class if their name and resource attributes coincide.

The XES meta model shown in Fig. 4.7 does not prescribe a concrete syntax. In principle many serializations are possible. However, to exchange XES documents, a standard XML serialization is used. Figure 4.8 shows a fragment of the XES XML serialization of the event log of Table 4.1. In the example XES log, three extensions are declared: *Concept*, *Time*, and *Organizational*. For each of these extensions a shorter prefix is given. These prefixes are used in the attribute names. For example, the *Time* extension defines an attribute *timestamp*. As shown in Fig. 4.8, this extension uses prefix *time*, therefore the timestamp of an event is stored using the key *time:timestamp*.

The example log in Fig. 4.8 specifies two lists of global attributes. Traces have one global attribute: attribute *concept:name* is mandatory for all traces. Events have three global attributes: attributes *time:timestamp*, *concept:name* and *org:resource* are mandatory for all events.

Three classifiers are defined in the XES log shown in Fig. 4.8. Classifier *Activity* classifies events based on the *concept:name* attribute. Classifier *Resource* classifies events based on the *org:resource* attribute. Classifier *Both* classifies events based on two attributes: *concept:name* and *org:resource*. Recall that Definition 4.2 already introduced the concept of a classifier: an event $e \in \mathcal{E}$ is classified as $\underline{e}$. For example, $\underline{e} = \#_{resource}(e)$ classifies events based on the resource executing the event.

For more information about the concrete syntax of XES we refer to www.xes-standard.org. However, the fragment shown in Fig. 4.8 already demonstrates that XES indeed operationalizes the concept of an event log as described in Definition 4.3. Moreover, the extension mechanism makes the format extendible while at the same time providing semantics for commonly used attributes. In the context of XES, five *standard extensions* have been defined. These extensions are described in the so-called *XESEXT* XML format [48]. Here, we only mention a subset of standard attributes defined by these extensions.

- The *concept extension* defines the *name* attribute for traces and events. Note that the example XES file indeed uses *concept:name* attributes for traces and events. For traces, the attribute typically represents some identifier for the case. For events, the attribute typically represents the activity name. The concept extension also defines the *instance* attribute for events. This is used to distinguish different activity instances in the same trace. This extension can be used to resolve the dilemma shown in Fig. 4.5.
- The *life-cycle extension* defines the *transition* attribute for events. When using the standard *transactional life-cycle model* shown in Fig. 4.3, possible values of this attribute are "schedule", "start", "complete", "autoskip", etc.
- The *organizational extension* defines three standard attributes for events: *resource*, *role*, and *group*. The resource attribute refers to the resource that triggered or executed the event. The role and group attributes characterize the (required) capabilities of the resource and the resource's position in the organization. For example, an event executed by a sales manager may have role "manager" and group "sales department" associated to it.

```
<?xml version="1.0" encoding="UTF-8" ?>
   <extension name="Concept" prefix="concept" uri="http://.../concept.xesext"/>
   <extension name="Time" prefix="time" uri="http://.../time.xesext"/>
   <extension name="Organizational" prefix="org" uri="http://.../org.xesext"/>
   <global scope="trace">
      <string key="concept:name" value="name"/>
   </global>
   <global scope="event">
      <date key="time:timestamp" value="2010-12-17T20:01:02.229+02:00"/>
      <string key="concept:name" value="name"/>
      <string key="org:resource" value="resource"/>
   </global>
   <classifier name="Activity" keys="concept:name"/>
   <classifier name="Resource" keys="org:resource"/>
   <classifier name="Both" keys="concept:name org:resource"/>
   <trace>
      <string key="concept:name" value="1"/>
      <event>
         <string key="concept:name" value="register request"/>
         <string key="org:resource" value="Pete"/>
         <date key="time:timestamp" value="2010-12-30T11:02:00.000+01:00"/>
         <string key="Event_ID" value="35654423"/>
         <string key="Costs" value="50"/>
      </event>
      <event>
         <string key="concept:name" value="examine thoroughly"/>
         <string key="org:resource" value="Sue"/>
         <date key="time:timestamp" value="2010-12-31T10:06:00.000+01:00"/>
         <string key="Event_ID" value="35654424"/>
         <string key="Costs" value="400"/>
      </event>
      <event>
         <string key="concept:name" value="check ticket"/>
         <string key="org:resource" value="Mike"/>
         <date key="time:timestamp" value="2011-01-05T15:12:00.000+01:00"/>
         <string key="Event_ID" value="35654425"/>
         <string key="Costs" value="100"/>
      </event>
      <event>
         <string key="concept:name" value="decide"/>
         <string key="org:resource" value="Sara"/>
         <date key="time:timestamp" value="2011-01-06T11:18:00.000+01:00"/>
         <string key="Event_ID" value="35654426"/>
         <string key="Costs" value="200"/>
      </event>
      <event>
         <string key="concept:name" value="reject request"/>
         <string key="org:resource" value="Pete"/>
         <date key="time:timestamp" value="2011-01-07T14:24:00.000+01:00"/>
         <string key="Event_ID" value="35654427"/>
         <string key="Costs" value="200"/>
      </event>
   </trace>
```

Fig. 4.8 Fragment of an XES file

```
  <trace>
    <string key="concept:name" value="2"/>
    <event>
      <string key="concept:name" value="register request"/>
      <string key="org:resource" value="Mike"/>
      <date key="time:timestamp" value="2010-12-30T11:32:00.000+01:00"/>
      <string key="Event_ID" value="35654483"/>
      <string key="Costs" value="50"/>
    </event>
    ...
  </trace>
  ...
</log>
```

Fig. 4.8 (Continued)

- The *time extension* defines the *timestamp* attribute for events. Since such a timestamp is of type *xs:dateTime*, both a date and time are recorded.
- The *semantic extension* defines the *modelReference* attribute for all elements in the log. This extension is inspired by *SA-MXML*. The references in the log point to concepts in an ontology. For example, there may be an ontology describing different kinds of customers, e.g., Silver, Gold, and Platinum customers. Using the *modelReference* attribute, a trace can point to this ontology thus classifying the customer.

Users and organizations can add new extensions and share these with others. For example, general extensions referring to costs, risks, context, etc. can be added. However, extensions may also be domain specific (e.g., healthcare, customs, or retail) or organization specific.

Currently, XES is supported by tools such as ProM, Nitro, XESame, and OpenXES. ProM is probably the most widely used process mining tool (see Sect. 10.2) providing a wide variety of process mining techniques. ProM 6 can load both MXML and XES files. Nitro (www.fluxicon.com) is an easy-to-use tool to quickly convert event logs into the XES format. XESame (www.processmining.org) generates XES files from collections of database tables. Here, the idea is that given a set of tables there may be different views possible (see also Sect. 4.4). Therefore, XES files serve as a view on the event data. OpenXES (www.openxes.org) is the XES reference implementation, an open source java library for reading, storing, and writing XES logs. OpenXES can easily be embedded in other tools and is able to efficiently (de)serialize large event logs into/from XML files. This frees software developers from developing tedious code to import and export event data.

Challenges when Extracting Event Logs
Definition 4.3 provides a succinct formal definition of the requirements an event log needs to satisfy. XES operationalizes these requirements and provides a concrete syntax. Hence, the target format is well-defined. Nonetheless, extracting events logs may be very challenging. Here, we list the five most important challenges.

- *Challenge* 1: *correlation*
  Events in an event log are grouped per case. This simple requirement can be quite challenging as it requires *event correlation*, i.e., events need to be related to each other. Consider, for example, event data scattered over multiple tables or even multiple systems. How to identify events and their corresponding cases? Also consider messages exchanged with other organizations. How to relate responses to the original requests? When designing logging functionality from scratch, it is quite easy to address this problem. However, when dealing with legacy and a variety or interconnected systems, additional efforts are needed to correlate events; see [39] for an example of an approach to correlate events without any a-priori information.
- *Challenge* 2: *timestamps*
  Events need to be ordered per case. In principle, such ordering does not require timestamps. However, when merging data from different sources, one typically needs to depend on timestamps to sort events (in order of occurrence). This may be problematic because of multiple clocks and delayed recording. For example, in an X-ray machine the different components have local clocks and events are often queueing before being recorded. Therefore, there may be significant differences between the actual time an event takes place and its timestamp in the log. As a result the ordering of events is unreliable, e.g., cause and effect may be reversed. In other applications, timestamps may be too coarse. In fact, many information systems only record a date and not a timestamp. For example, most events in a hospital are recorded in the hospital information system based on a patient id and a date, without storing the actual time of the test or visit. As a result, it is impossible to reconstruct the order of events on a given day. One way to address this problem is to assume only a partial ordering of events (i.e., not a total order) and subsequently use dedicated process mining algorithms for this. Another way to (partially) address the problem is to "guess" the order based on domain knowledge or frequent patterns across days.
- *Challenge* 3: *snapshots*
  Cases may have a lifetime extending beyond the recorded period, e.g., a case was started before the beginning of the event log or was still running when the recording stopped. Therefore, it is important to realize that event logs typically just provide a *snapshot* of a longer running process. When the average duration of a case is short compared to the length of the recording, it is best to solve this problem by removing incomplete cases. In many cases, the initial and final activities are known, thus making it easy to filter the event log: simply remove all cases with a missing "head" or "tail". However, when the average duration of a case is of the same order of magnitude as the length of the recording, it becomes difficult to discover end-to-end processes.

- *Challenge* 4: *scoping*
  The fourth problem is the scoping of the event log. Enterprise information systems may have thousands of tables with business-relevant data (cf. a typical SAP installation). How to decide which tables to incorporate? Domain knowledge is needed to locate the required data and to scope it. Obviously, the desired scope depends on both the available data and the questions that need to be answered.
- *Challenge* 5: *granularity*
  In many applications, the events in the event log are at a different level of granularity than the activities relevant for end users. Some systems produce low-level events that are too detailed to be presented to stakeholders interested in managing or improving the process. Fortunately, there are several approaches to preprocess low-level event logs. For example, in [13] it is shown that frequently appearing low-level patterns can be abstracted into events representing activities.

The availability of high-quality event logs is essential for process mining. Moreover, good events logs can serve many other purposes. Sometimes the term *business process provenance* is used to refer to the systematic collection of the information needed to reconstruct what has actually happened in the business process. From an auditing point of view the systematic, reliable, and trustworthy recording of events is essential. The term "provenance" originates from scientific computing [27]. Here, provenance information is recorded to ensure that scientific experiments are reproducible. High-quality event logs that cannot be tampered with make sure that "history cannot be rewritten or obscured" and serve as a solid basis for process improvement and auditing. Therefore, XES should be seen in a provenance context that extends beyond process discovery and includes topics such as conformance checking. We will elaborate on this topic in Part III.

4.4 Flattening Reality into Event Logs

In order to do process mining, events need to be related to cases. As indicated before, this is natural as a process model describes the life-cycle of a case of a particular type. All activities in a conventional process model (independent of the notation used) correspond to status changes of such a case. We will refer to such process models as *flat models*. In this book, we adopt this (often hidden) assumption associated to all mainstream process modeling notations. However, it is important to realize that *real-life processes are not flat*. We use a simple example to illustrate this.

Consider the class diagram shown in Fig. 4.9 describing a database consisting of four tables. Table *Order* contains information about orders. For example, each record in the *Order* table has a unique order number, refers to a customer, and has

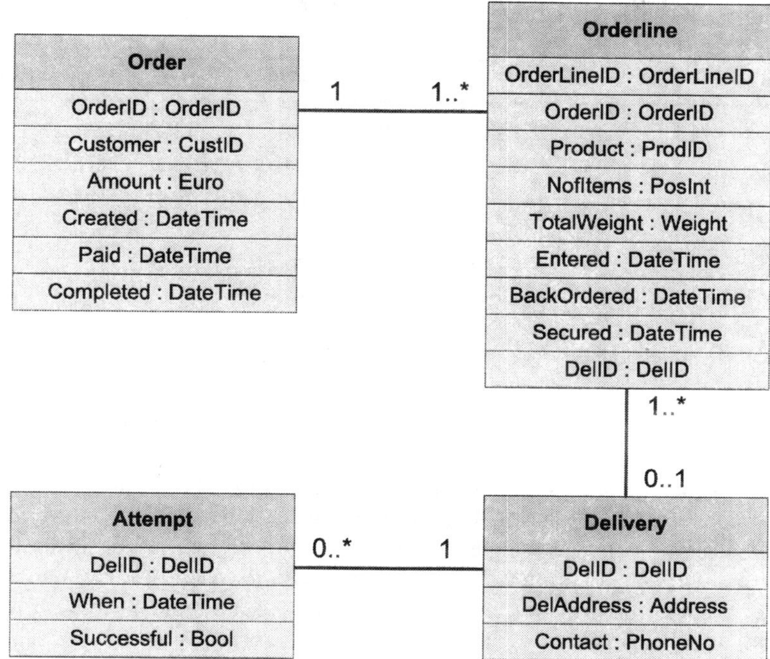

Fig. 4.9 Class diagram showing the relations between orders, order lines, deliveries, and delivery attempts

an associated amount. Multiple products can be ordered in one order. Therefore, Table *Orderline* holds information about individual order lines. Records in the *Orderline* table refer to orders in the *Order* table. Figure 4.9 shows that each order line corresponds to one order and each order corresponds to one or more order lines. One order line describes which type of product is ordered, the quantity, and weight. Table *Delivery* holds information about deliveries. Each delivery corresponds to a collection of order lines. These order lines are delivered to a particular address. To deliver the corresponding collection of products, multiple attempts may be needed. Table *Attempts* stores information about these attempted deliveries. An attempt may be successful or not. If not, another attempt is made at a later point in time. Figure 4.9 shows that each delivery corresponds to zero or more attempts and one or more order lines. Each order line corresponds to at most one delivery.

Table 4.2 shows a small fragment of a larger *Order* table. For each order, up to three timestamps are recorded. The timestamp in the *Created* column denotes the time at which the order was created. The *Paid* column denotes the time at which the order was paid and the *Completed* column denotes the time at which the order was completed. Table 4.2 shows several *null* timestamps. This indicates that the corresponding events did not take place yet.

Table 4.3 shows some example records of the *Orderline* table. Each line refers to a particular product. For example, order line 112346 corresponds to two iPod nanos

Table 4.2 Some records of the *Order* table

Order					
OrderID	Customer	Amount	Created	Paid	Completed
91245	John	100	28-11-2011:08.12	02-12-2011:13.45	05-12-2011:11.33
91561	Mike	530	28-11-2011:12.22	03-12-2011:14.34	05-12-2011:09.32
91812	Mary	234	29-11-2011:09.45	02-12-2011:09.44	04-12-2011:13.33
92233	Sue	110	29-11-2011:10.12	Null	Null
92345	Kirsten	195	29-11-2011:14.45	02-12-2011:13.45	Null
92355	Pete	320	29-11-2011:16.32	Null	Null
...	...	...	...	...	...

that are part of order 91245. Each order line refers to an order and to a delivery (if already created). For each order line, up to three timestamps are recorded: the time of entering the order line (column *Entered*), the time of back ordering (column *BackOrdered*), and the time of securing the item (column *Secured*). A *null* value indicates that the corresponding event did not take place (yet). Typically, only few order lines will be back-ordered (i.e., most rows will have a null value in the *BackOrdered* column). A backorder is an order line that cannot be delivered because of a lack of sufficient inventory. Therefore, the inventory needs to be replenished before the backorder can be delivered. Since only few order lines become backorders, column *BackOrdered* has many null values. Once the products are available and reserved for a particular order line, the corresponding timestamp is added in column *Secured*.

Information about deliveries is stored in the *Delivery* table shown in Table 4.4. For each delivery, an address and a phone number are recorded. Each delivery refers to a collection of order lines and may require multiple attempts.

Attempts to deliver products are recorded in the *Attempt* table. Table 4.5 shows some example attempts. An attempt has a timestamp and refers to a delivery (column *DellID*). Delivery 882345 required three attempts before the corresponding set of order lines could be delivered successfully. Delivery 882346 required only one attempt.

The four tables show only a snapshot of the available data. Orders that have not yet been fully handled may have many null values.

The database consisting of tables *Order*, *Orderline*, *Delivery*, and *Attempts* is a bit artificial and its design could be improved. For example, the tables with multiple timestamps could have been split into multiple tables. Moreover, in an ERP system like SAP much more detailed information is stored. Hence, the four tables are an oversimplification of reality and only serve as a means to explain the problem of *flattening reality for process mining*.

Clearly the timestamps in the four tables correspond to events related to the "overall ordering and delivery" process. However, when creating an event log, each event needs to be associated to a particular case. Therefore, we need to flatten the four tables into one table with a "case id" column. However, one can choose from

Table 4.3 Part of the *Orderline* table: each record corresponds to an order line. An order line refers to an order (column *OrderID*) and a delivery (column *DellID*)

Orderline								
OrderLineID	OrderID	Product	NofItems	TotalWeight	Entered	BackOrdered	Secured	DellID
112345	91245	iPhone 4G	1	0.250	28-11-2011:08.13	Null	28-11-2011:08.55	882345
112346	91245	iPod nano	2	0.300	28-11-2011:08.14	28-11-2011:08.55	30-11-2011:09.06	882346
112347	91245	iPod classic	1	0.200	28-11-2011:08.15	Null	29-11-2011:10.06	882345
112448	91561	iPhone 4G	1	0.250	28-11-2011:12.23	Null	28-11-2011:12.59	882345
112449	91561	iPod classic	1	0.200	28-11-2011:12.24	28-11-2011:16.22	Null	Null
112452	91812	iPhone 4G	5	1.250	29-11-2011:09.46	Null	29-11-2011:10.58	882346
...	...	...	...	...	...	...	...	...

Table 4.4 Some records of the *Delivery* table

Delivery		
DellID	DelAddress	Contact
882345	5513VJ-22a	0497-2553660
882346	5513XG-45	040-2298761
...	...	...

Table 4.5 Part of the *Attempt* table

Attempt		
DellID	When	Successful
882345	05-12-2011:08.55	False
882345	06-12-2011:09.12	False
882345	07-12-2011:08.56	True
882346	05-12-2011:08.43	True
...	...	...

four types of cases: orders, order lines, deliveries, and attempts. Any record in one of the four tables potentially corresponds to a case. Which one to choose?

Let us assume that we are mainly interested in orders. Therefore, we let each case correspond to a record in table *Order*. Table *Order* has up to three timestamps per record. Hence, only three events per case can be found if only the *Order* table is considered and information about order lines and deliveries related to an order remains unused. When using only records from the *Order* table, control-flow discovery will most likely return a sequential process consisting of three steps: *create*, *pay*, and *complete*. To obtain a process model containing more activities, we need to consider the other tables. By using the references in the tables, orders can be related to order lines. In turn, order lines can be related to deliveries and the corresponding attempts. For example, order lines 112345, 112346 and 112347 refer to order 91245. Figure 4.10 shows all events that can be found by searching for all records that can be related to order 91245. The rectangles refer to concrete records in the four tables. The rounded rectangles refer to possible events and their attributes. All events in the figure refer to case 91245. As Fig. 4.10 shows, order 91245 is related to order lines 112345, 112346 and 112347, and deliveries 882345 and 882346. For delivery 882345 there are three corresponding attempt records, and for delivery 882346 only one.

The top three events in Fig. 4.10 (the events directly connected to the root node) would have been the only events if only the *Order* table would have been considered. There are also various intermediate selections possible, resulting in subsets of the events shown in Fig. 4.10. For example, only the top ten events remain if only the *Order* and *Orderline* tables are considered, thus abstracting from deliveries.

Table 4.6 shows an event log using the selection illustrated by Fig. 4.10. As before, each line corresponds to an event. The *case id* column shows how events are correlated, i.e., each event refers to an order. The *activity* column names events as

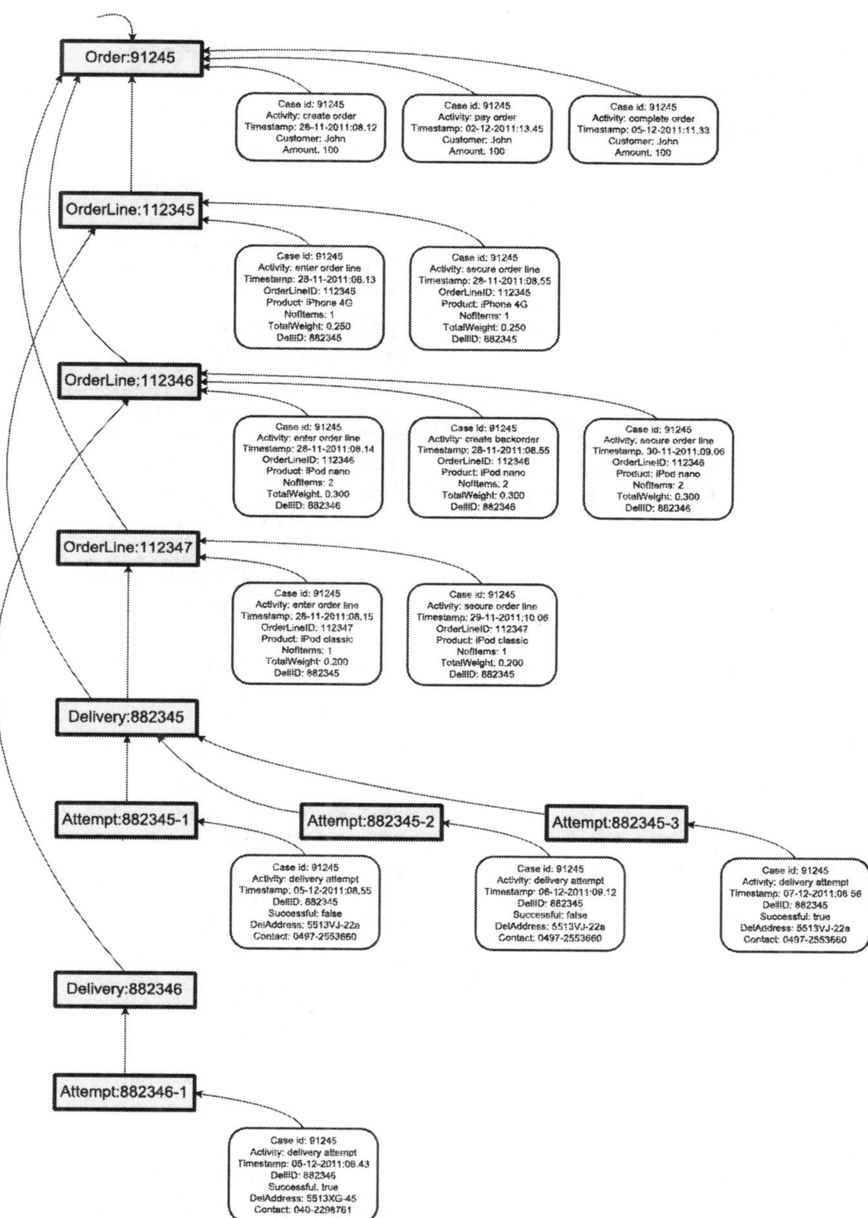

Fig. 4.10 All events that can be related to order 91245. *The 14 rounded rectangles* correspond to events associated to case 91245. *The squared rectangles* represent records in one of the four tables

Table 4.6 Events extracted from all four tables using order records from the *Order* table as a starting point

Attempt			
Case id	Activity	Timestamp	Other attributes
91245	Create order	28-11-2011:08.12	Customer: John, Amount: 100
91245	Enter order line	28-11-2011:08.13	OrderLineID: 112345, Product: iPhone 4G, NofItems: 1, TotalWeight: 0.250, DelIID: 882345
91245	Enter order line	28-11-2011:08.14	OrderLineID: 112346, Product: iPod nano, NofItems: 2, TotalWeight: 0.300, DelIID: 882346
91245	Enter order line	28-11-2011:08.15	OrderLineID: 112347, Product: iPod classic, NofItems: 1, TotalWeight: 0.200, DelIID: 882345
91245	Secure order line	28-11-2011:08.55	OrderLineID: 112345, Product: iPhone 4G, NofItems: 1, TotalWeight: 0.250, DelIID: 882345
91245	Create backorder	28-11-2011:08.55	OrderLineID: 112346, Product: iPod nano, NofItems: 2, TotalWeight: 0.300, DelIID: 882346
91245	Secure order line	29-11-2011:10.06	OrderLineID: 112347, Product: iPod classic, NofItems: 1, TotalWeight: 0.200, DelIID: 882345
91245	Secure order line	30-11-2011:09.06	OrderLineID: 112346, Product: iPod nano, NofItems: 2, TotalWeight: 0.300, DelIID: 882346
91245	Pay order	02-12-2011:13.45	Customer: John, Amount: 100
91245	Delivery attempt	05-12-2011:08.43	DelIID: 882346, Successful: true, DelAddress: 5513XG-45, Contact: 040-2298761
91245	Delivery attempt	05-12-2011:08.55	DelIID: 882345, Successful: false, DelAddress: 5513VJ-22a, Contact: 0497-2553660
91245	Complete order	05-12-2011:11.33	Customer: John, Amount: 100
91245	Delivery attempt	06-12-2011:09.12	DelIID: 882345, Successful: false, DelAddress: 5513VJ-22a, Contact: 0497-2553660
91245	Delivery attempt	07-12-2011:08.56	DelIID: 882345, Successful: true, DelAddress: 5513VJ-22a, Contact: 0497-2553660
91561	Create order	28-11-2011:12.22	Customer: Mike, Amount: 530
91561	Enter order line	28-11-2011:12.23	OrderLineID: 112448, Product: iPhone 4G, NofItems: 1, TotalWeight: 0.250, DelIID: 882345
...	...	...	...
...	...	...	...

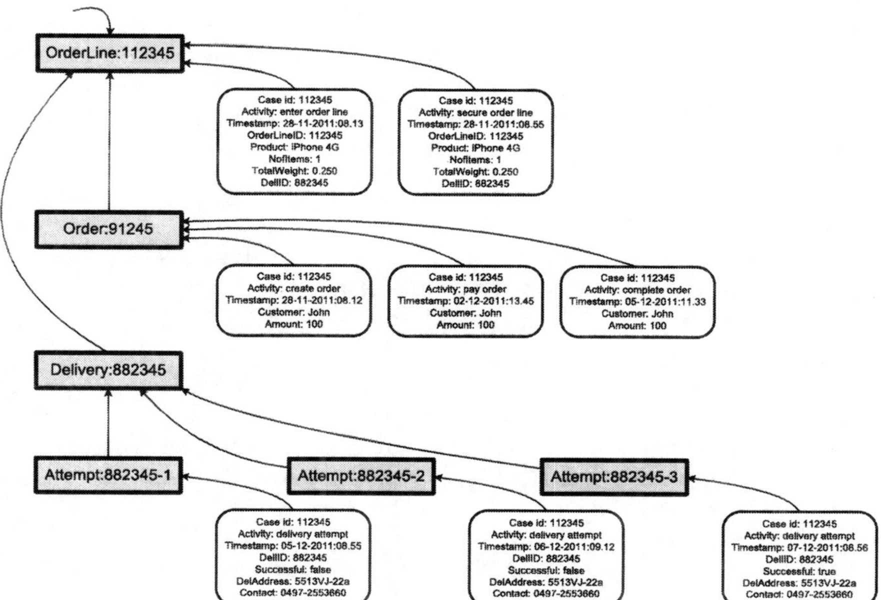

Fig. 4.11 All events that can be related to order line 112345

already shown Fig. 4.10. The *timestamp* column shows the date and time associated to the event. The *other attributes* column shows additional attributes. Depending on the type of activity, different attributes are recorded. Table 4.6 shows that there is quite some redundancy in the event log. This is partly unavoidable due to the structure that logs should have. However, the case attributes *Customer* and *John* do not need to be repeated for each event; one could have used case attributes rather than event attributes.

Table 4.6 *flattens* the original database consisting of four tables. The flattened event log is like a *view* on the complete data set. Alternative views are possible. For example, Fig. 4.11 shows another way to flatten the original database. Now cases correspond to order lines rather than orders. Hence, the root node is order line 112345. This is an order line of order 91245 and three attempts were needed to deliver the iPhone 4G. The timestamps in the *Order* table have been used to create events associated to order line cases rather than orders. Based on the view sketched in Fig. 4.11, one can generate another event log.

In Fig. 4.10, the root node is an order. In Fig. 4.11, the root node is an order line. Similarly, it is possible to take a delivery or delivery attempts as root node. Moreover, various selections of events can be used, e.g., the three order-related events or the three delivery-related events in Fig. 4.11 could have been left out from the selection. This shows that many views on the original data set are possible, i.e., there are many ways to flatten reality as recorded into a single event log.

Flattening a data set into an event log can be compared to aggregating multidimensional data in Online Analytical Processing (OLAP). For example, using a typical OLAP tool, sales data can be viewed by product categories, by region, and/or by quarter. Depending on the type of question, a different view on the data can be chosen. One important difference is that in process mining we analyze processes rather than a simple OLAP cube. Therefore, we need to correlate events and order them, thus making the extraction process more complex.

Proclets: Seeing in 3-D

Process mining shows that the assumptions made by classical process modeling languages such as BPMN, UML ADs, Statecharts, BPEL, YAWL, WF-nets, and EPCs are somewhat artificial. They only provide *one monolithic view* on the real process of interest. The process is flattened to allow for a diagram that describes the life-cycle of one case in isolation. The application of process mining to real-life processes shows that squeezing a process into such a single monolithic flat model is problematic. Like in physics, where experiments help to (in)validate models, process discovery also helps to reveal the limitations of oversimplified models. The empirical nature of process mining helps managers, consultants, and process analysts to better understand the "fabric of real business processes" and, thus, also see the limitations of conventional process modeling languages.

Proclets [99] are one of the few business process modeling languages allowing for *3-D process models*. Rather than describing the whole process in terms of one monolithic 2-D process model, the process is modeled as a collection of interacting Proclets. For example, when modeling orders and deliveries, the class diagram of Fig. 4.9 can be used as a starting point. Based on this class diagram four classes of Proclets are identified: orders, order lines, deliveries, and delivery attempts. Each Proclet class is modeled separately. The Proclets interact and are related by following the real anatomy of the process.

See [99] for more examples illustrating that classical notations force the modeler to *straightjacket* processes into one monolithic model. Unfortunately, hierarchy concepts in conventional languages do not support one-to-many or many-to-many relationships. In Fig. 4.9, orders and deliveries are in a many-to-many relationship: one order may result in multiple deliveries and one delivery many involve order lines of different orders. This cannot be handled by the refinement of activities; order and delivery Proclets need to coexist independent of one another.

Object-oriented modeling and artifact-centric modeling use ideas related to Proclets. However, mainstream process modeling notations and BPM systems still use conventional 2-D notations. The ACSI project [1] aims to promote the use of Proclets and develop new process mining techniques for non-monolithic processes.

Although it is important to view business processes in 3-D, we often need to resort to 2-D models for a variety of reasons. Here, we mention three of them. First of all, the data sources provided may only allow for a 2-D view, e.g., only one table is provided as input. Second, users expect process models in terms of classical 2-D process modeling languages such as BPMN, UML ADs, Statecharts, BPEL, YAWL, WF-nets, and EPCs. Last but not least, most process mining techniques require flattening the data. Therefore, we advocate the following approach.

- Create a *process-oriented data warehouse* containing information about relevant events. The data warehouse should avoid storing aggregated data, and gather the raw business events instead. In traditional data warehouses, events are aggregated into quantitative data, thus hampering process analysis.
- Depending on the questions, define an appropriate *view*. Based on the chosen view, *flatten* the required data to produce an event log (e.g., in XES format). This corresponds to taking a *2-D slice* from the 3-D data.
- Use the 2-D slice to apply a variety of *process mining* techniques. If needed, *filter* the event log further (e.g., removing infrequent activities). Continue extracting, filtering, and mining until the questions are answered.

Depending on the questions, it may be the case that multiple 2-D slices need to be taken to create a 3-D view on the overall process. This view is consistent with Fig. 4.1; by extracting the event data the scope of the process is determined.

Chapter 5
Process Discovery: An Introduction

Process discovery is one of the most challenging process mining tasks. Based on an event log, a process model is constructed thus capturing the behavior seen in the log. This chapter introduces the topic using the rather naïve α-algorithm. This algorithm nicely illustrates some of the general ideas used by many process mining algorithms and helps to understand the notion of process discovery. Moreover, the α-algorithm serves as a stepping stone for discussing challenges related to process discovery.

5.1 Problem Statement

As discussed in Chap. 1, there are three types of process mining: discovery, conformance, and enhancement. Moreover, we identified various perspectives, e.g., the control-flow perspective, the organizational or resource perspective, the data perspective, and the time perspective. In this chapter, we focus on the *discovery* task and the *control-flow* perspective. This combination is often referred to as *process discovery*. The general process discovery problem can be formulated as follows.

Definition 5.1 (General process discovery problem) Let L be an event log as defined in Definition 4.3 or as specified by the XES standard (cf. Sect. 4.3). A *process discovery algorithm* is a function that maps L onto a process model such that the model is "representative" for the behavior seen in the event log. The challenge is to find such an algorithm.

This definition does not specify what kind of process model should be generated, e.g., a BPMN, EPC, YAWL, or Petri net model. Moreover, event logs with potentially many attributes may be used as input. Recall that the XES format allows for storing information related to all perspectives whereas here the focus is on the control-flow perspective. The only requirement is that the behavior is "representative", but it is unclear what this means.

Definition 5.1 is rather broad and vague. The target format is not specified and a potentially "rich" event log is used as input without specifying tangible require-

W.M.P. van der Aalst, *Process Mining*,

DOI 10.1007/978-3-642-19345-3_5,

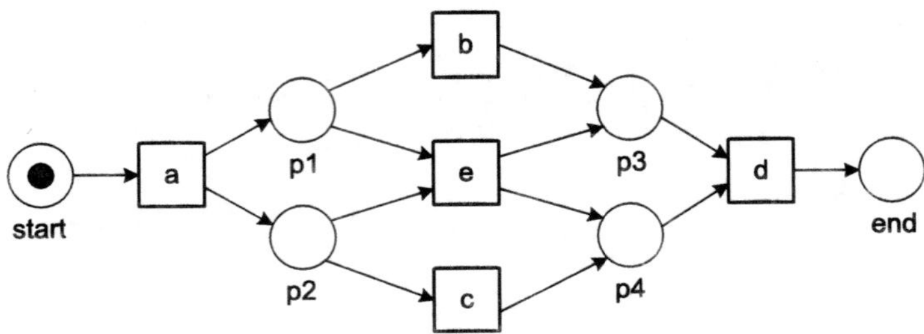

Fig. 5.1 WF-net N_1 discovered for $L_1 = [\langle a,b,c,d\rangle^3, \langle a,c,b,d\rangle^2, \langle a,e,d\rangle]$

ments. To make things more concrete, we define the target to be a Petri net model. Moreover, we use a *simple event log* as input (cf. Definition 4.4). A simple event log L is a multi-set of traces over some set of activities $\mathscr{A}$, i.e., $L \in \mathbb{B}(\mathscr{A}^*)$. For example,

$$L_1 = \big[\langle a,b,c,d\rangle^3, \langle a,c,b,d\rangle^2, \langle a,e,d\rangle\big]$$

L_1 is a simple log describing the history of six cases. The goal is now to discover a Petri net that can "replay" event log L_1. Ideally, the Petri net is a sound WF-net as defined in Sect. 2.2.3. Based on these choices, we reformulate the process discovery problem and make it more concrete.

Definition 5.2 (Specific process discovery problem) A *process discovery algorithm* is a function γ that maps a log $L \in \mathbb{B}(\mathscr{A}^*)$ onto a marked Petri net $\gamma(L) = (N, M)$. Ideally, N is a *sound WF-net* and all traces in L correspond to possible firing sequences of (N, M).

Function γ defines a so-called "Play-in" technique as described in Chap. 1. Based on L_1, a process discovery algorithm γ could discover the WF-net shown in Fig. 5.1, i.e., $\gamma(L_1) = (N_1, [start])$. Each trace in L_1 corresponds to a possible firing sequence of WF-net N_1 shown in Fig. 5.1. Therefore, it is easy to see that the WF-net can indeed replay all traces in the event log. In fact, each of the three possible firing sequences of WF-net N_1 appears in L_1.

Let us now consider another event log:

$$L_2 = \big[\langle a,b,c,d\rangle^3, \langle a,c,b,d\rangle^4, \langle a,b,c,e,f,b,c,d\rangle^2, \langle a,b,c,e,f,c,b,d\rangle, \\ \langle a,c,b,e,f,b,c,d\rangle^2, \langle a,c,b,e,f,b,c,e,f,c,b,d\rangle\big]$$

L_2 is a simple event log consisting of 13 cases represented by 6 different traces. Based on event log L_2, some γ could discover WF-net N_2 shown in Fig. 5.2. This WF-net can indeed replay all traces in the log. However, not all firing sequences of N_2 correspond to traces in L_2. For example, the firing sequence $\langle a,c,b,e,f,c,b,d\rangle$ does not appear in L_2. In fact, there are infinitely many firing sequences because of the loop construct in N_2. Clearly, these cannot all appear in the event log. Therefore, Definition 5.2 does not require all firing sequences of (N, M) to be traces in L.

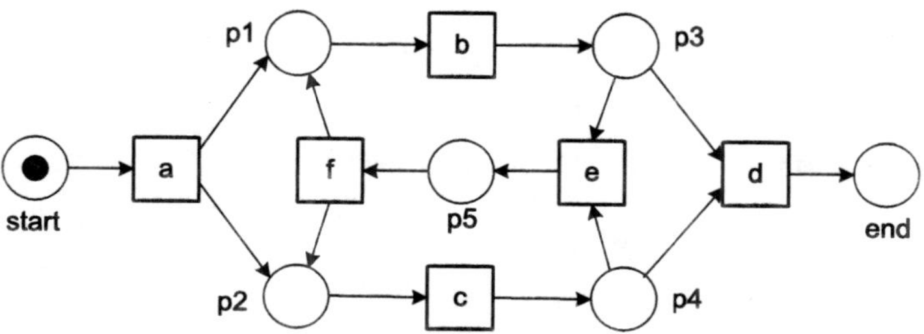

Fig. 5.2 WF-net N_2 discovered for $L_2 = [\langle a,b,c,d\rangle^3, \langle a,c,b,d\rangle^4, \langle a,b,c,e,f,b,c,d\rangle^2, \langle a,b,c,e,f,c,b,d\rangle, \langle a,c,b,e,f,b,c,d\rangle^2, \langle a,c,b,e,f,b,c,e,f,c,b,d\rangle]$

In this chapter, we focus on the discovery of Petri nets. The reason is that Petri nets are simple and graphical while still allowing for the modeling of concurrency, choices, and iteration. This is illustrated by Figs. 5.1 and 5.2. In both models, activities b and c are concurrent. In N_1, there is choice following a. In N_2, there is choice between d and e each time both b and c complete. Both N_1 and N_2 are sound WF-nets. As explained in Chap. 2, WF-nets are a natural subclass of Petri nets tailored toward the modeling and analysis of operational processes. A process model describes the life-cycle of one case. Therefore, WF-nets explicitly model the creation and the completion of the cases. The creation is modeled by putting a token in the unique source place i (place *start* in Figs. 5.1 and 5.2). The completion is modeled by reaching the state marking the unique sink place o (place *end* in Figs. 5.1 and 5.2). Given a unique source place i and a unique sink place o, the soundness requirement described in Definition 2.7 follows naturally. Recall that a WF-net N is *sound* if and only if

- $(N, [i])$ is *safe*, i.e., places cannot hold multiple tokens at the same time.
- For any marking $M \in [N, [i]\rangle$, $o \in M$ implies $M = [o]$, i.e., if the sink place is marked, all other places should be empty (*proper completion*).
- For any marking $M \in [N, [i]\rangle$, $[o] \in [N, M\rangle$, i.e., it is always possible to mark the sink place (*option to complete*).
- $(N, [i])$ contains *no dead transitions*, i.e., all parts of the model are potentially reachable.

Most process modeling notations use or assume correctness criteria similar to soundness. For instance, deadlocks and livelocks are symptoms of a process that cannot complete (properly). These phenomena are undesired, independent of the notation used.

Although we use WF-nets in this chapter, this does not imply that discovered process models cannot be presented using other notations. As discussed in Chap. 2, there exist many translations from Petri nets into other notations and vice versa. Compact formalisms with formal semantics like Petri nets are most suitable to develop and explain process mining algorithms. The representation used to show results to end users is less relevant for the actual process discovery task. For example, the WF-nets depicted in Figs. 5.1 and 5.2 can also be presented in terms of the

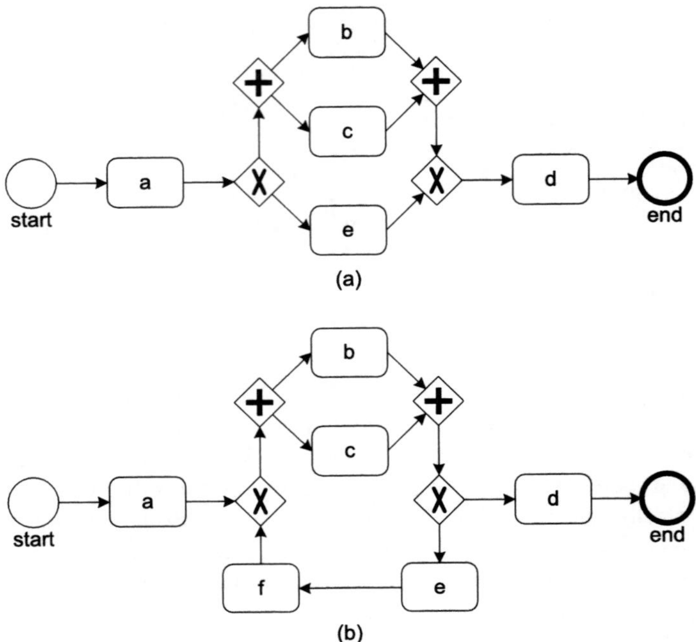

Fig. 5.3 Two BPMN models: (**a**) the model corresponding to WF-net N_1 discovered for L_1, and (**b**) the model corresponding to WF-net N_2 discovered for L_2

two trace equivalent BPMN models shown in Fig. 5.3. Similarly, the discovered models could have been translated into equivalent EPCs, UML activity diagrams, statecharts, YAWL models, BPEL specifications, etc.

In the general problem formulation (Definition 5.1), we stated that the discovered model should be "representative" for the behavior seen in the event log. In Definition 5.2, this was operationalized by requiring that the model is able to replay all behavior in this log, i.e., any trace in the event log is a possible firing sequence of the WF-net. This is the so-called "fitness" requirement. In general, there is a trade-off between the following four quality criteria:

- *Fitness*: the discovered model should allow for the behavior seen in the event log.
- *Precision*: the discovered model should not allow for behavior completely unrelated to what was seen in the event log.
- *Generalization*: the discovered model should generalize the example behavior seen in the event log.
- *Simplicity*: the discovered model should be as simple as possible.

A model having a good fitness is able to replay most of the traces in the log. Precision is related to the notion of *underfitting* presented in the context of data mining (see Sect. 3.6.3). A model having a poor precision is underfitting, i.e., it allows for behavior that is very different from what was seen in the event log. Generalization is related to the notion of *overfitting*. An overfitting model does not generalize enough, i.e., it is too specific and too much driven by examples in the event log. The fourth quality criterion is related to Occam's Razor which states that "one should not increase, beyond what is necessary, the number of entities required to explain anything" (see Sect. 3.6.3). Following this principle, we look for the "simplest process model" that can explain what is observed in the event log.

It turns out to be challenging to balance the four quality criteria. For instance, an oversimplified model is likely to have a low fitness or lack of precision. Moreover, there is an obvious trade-off between underfitting and overfitting. We discuss these four quality criteria later in this chapter. However, we first introduce a concrete process discovery algorithm.

5.2 A Simple Algorithm for Process Discovery

This section introduces the α-algorithm [103]. This algorithm is an example of a γ function as mentioned in Definition 5.2, i.e., given a simple event log it produces a Petri net that (hopefully) can replay the log. The α-algorithm was one of the first process discovery algorithms that could adequately deal with concurrency (see Sect. 6.5). However, the α-algorithm should not be seen as a very practical mining technique as it has problems with noise, infrequent/incomplete behavior, and complex routing constructs. Nevertheless, it provides a good introduction into the topic. The α-algorithm is simple and many of its ideas have been embedded in more complex and robust techniques. We will use the algorithm as a baseline for discussing the challenges related to process discovery and for introducing more practical algorithms.

5.2.1 Basic Idea

Input for the α-algorithm is a simple event log L over $\mathscr{A}$, i.e., $L \in \mathbb{B}(\mathscr{A}^*)$. In the remainder, we will simply refer to L as the event log. We refer to the elements of $\mathscr{A}$ as *activities*, see Sect. 2.2. These activities will correspond to transitions in the discovered Petri net. In this chapter, we will use the convention that capital letters refer to sets of activities (e.g., $A, B \subseteq \mathscr{A}$), whereas for individual activities no capitalization is used (e.g., $a, b, c, \ldots \in \mathscr{A}$). The output of the α-algorithm is a marked Petri net, i.e., $\alpha(L) = (N, M)$. We aim at the discovery of WF-nets. Therefore, we can omit the initial marking and write $\alpha(L) = N$ (the initial marking is implied; $M = [i]$).

The α-algorithm *scans the event log for particular patterns*. For example, if activity a is followed by b but b is never followed by a, then it is assumed that there is a causal dependency between a and b. To reflect this dependency, the corresponding Petri net should have a place connecting a to b. We distinguish four *log-based ordering relations* that aim to capture relevant patterns in the log.

Table 5.1 Footprint of L_1: $a \#_{L_1} a$, $a \rightarrow_{L_1} b$, $a \rightarrow_{L_1} c$, etc.

	a	b	c	d	e
a	$\#_{L_1}$	$\rightarrow_{L_1}$	$\rightarrow_{L_1}$	$\#_{L_1}$	$\rightarrow_{L_1}$
b	$\leftarrow_{L_1}$	$\#_{L_1}$	$\Vert_{L_1}$	$\rightarrow_{L_1}$	$\#_{L_1}$
c	$\leftarrow_{L_1}$	$\Vert_{L_1}$	$\#_{L_1}$	$\rightarrow_{L_1}$	$\#_{L_1}$
d	$\#_{L_1}$	$\leftarrow_{L_1}$	$\leftarrow_{L_1}$	$\#_{L_1}$	$\leftarrow_{L_1}$
e	$\leftarrow_{L_1}$	$\#_{L_1}$	$\#_{L_1}$	$\rightarrow_{L_1}$	$\#_{L_1}$

Definition 5.3 (Log-based ordering relations) Let L be an event log over $\mathscr{A}$, i.e., $L \in \mathbb{B}(\mathscr{A}^*)$. Let $a, b \in \mathscr{A}$:

- $a >_L b$ if and only if there is a trace $\sigma = \langle t_1, t_2, t_3, \ldots, t_n\rangle$ and $i \in \{1, \ldots, n-1\}$ such that $\sigma \in L$ and $t_i = a$ and $t_{i+1} = b$
- $a \rightarrow_L b$ if and only if $a >_L b$ and $b \not>_L a$
- $a \#_L b$ if and only if $a \not>_L b$ and $b \not>_L a$
- $a \Vert_L b$ if and only if $a >_L b$ and $b >_L a$

Consider for instance $L_1 = [\langle a, b, c, d\rangle^3, \langle a, c, b, d\rangle^2, \langle a, e, d\rangle]$ again. For this event log, the following log-based ordering relations can be found

$$>_{L_1} = \{(a, b), (a, c), (a, e), (b, c), (c, b), (b, d), (c, d), (e, d)\}$$
$$\rightarrow_{L_1} = \{(a, b), (a, c), (a, e), (b, d), (c, d), (e, d)\}$$
$$\#_{L_1} = \{(a, a), (a, d), (b, b), (b, e), (c, c), (c, e), (d, a), (d, d), (e, b), (e, c), (e, e)\}$$
$$\Vert_{L_1} = \{(b, c), (c, b)\}$$

Relation $>_{L_1}$ contains all pairs of activities in a "directly follows" relation. $c >_{L_1} d$ because d directly follows c in trace $\langle a, b, c, d\rangle$. However, $d \not>_{L_1} c$ because c never directly follows d in any trace in the log. $\rightarrow_{L_1}$ contains all pairs of activities in a "causality" relation, e.g., $c \rightarrow_{L_1} d$ because sometimes d directly follows c and never the other way around ($c >_{L_1} d$ and $d \not>_{L_1} c$). $b \Vert_{L_1} c$ because $b >_{L_1} c$ and $c >_{L_1} b$, i.e., sometimes c follows b and sometimes the other way around. $b \#_{L_1} e$ because $b \not>_{L_1} e$ and $e \not>_{L_1} b$.

For any log L over $\mathscr{A}$ and $x, y \in \mathscr{A}$: $x \rightarrow_L y$, $y \rightarrow_L x$, $x \#_L y$, or $x \Vert_L y$, i.e., precisely one of these relations holds for any pair of activities. Therefore, the *footprint* of a log can be captured in a matrix as shown in Table 5.1.

The footprint of event log L_2 is shown in Table 5.2. The subscripts have been removed to not clutter the table. When comparing the footprints of L_1 and L_2, one can see that only the e and f columns and rows differ.

The log-based ordering relations can be used to *discover patterns* in the corresponding process model as is illustrated in Fig. 5.4. If a and b are in sequence, the log will show $a \rightarrow_L b$. If after a there is a choice between b and c, the log will show $a \rightarrow_L b$, $a \rightarrow_L c$, and $b \#_L c$ because a can be followed by b and c, but b will not be followed by c and vice versa. The logical counterpart of this so-called XOR-split

Table 5.2 Footprint of $L_2 = [\langle a,b,c,d\rangle^3, \langle a,c,b,d\rangle^4, \langle a,b,c,e,f,b,c,d\rangle^2, \langle a,b,c,e,f,c,b,d\rangle, \langle a,c,b,e,f,b,c,d\rangle^2, \langle a,c,b,e,f,b,c,e,f,c,b,d\rangle]$

	a	b	c	d	e	f
a	$\#$	$\rightarrow$	$\rightarrow$	$\#$	$\#$	$\#$
b	$\leftarrow$	$\#$	$\parallel$	$\rightarrow$	$\rightarrow$	$\leftarrow$
c	$\leftarrow$	$\parallel$	$\#$	$\rightarrow$	$\rightarrow$	$\leftarrow$
d	$\#$	$\leftarrow$	$\leftarrow$	$\#$	$\#$	$\#$
e	$\#$	$\leftarrow$	$\leftarrow$	$\#$	$\#$	$\rightarrow$
f	$\#$	$\rightarrow$	$\rightarrow$	$\#$	$\leftarrow$	$\#$

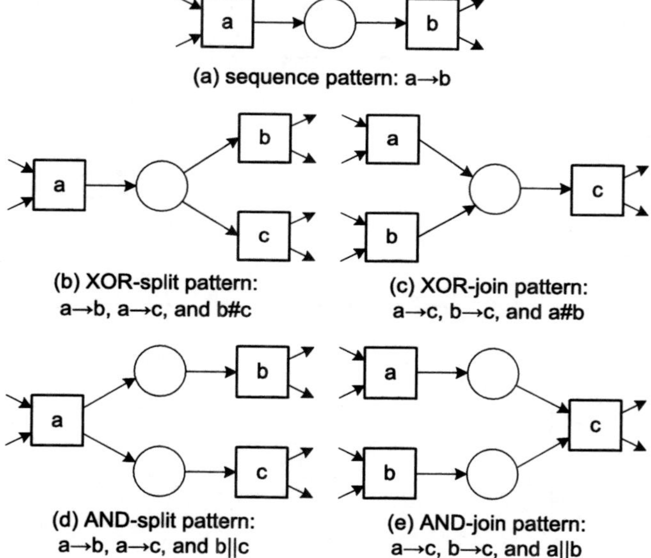

Fig. 5.4 Typical process patterns and the footprints they leave in the event log

pattern is the XOR-join pattern as shown in Fig. 5.4(b–c). If $a \rightarrow_L c$, $b \rightarrow_L c$, and $a \#_L b$, then this suggests that after the occurrence of either a or b, c should happen. Figure 5.4(d–e) shows the so-called AND-split and AND-join patterns. If $a \rightarrow_L b$, $a \rightarrow_L c$, and $b \parallel_L c$, then it appears that after a both b and c can be executed in parallel (AND-split pattern). If $a \rightarrow_L c$, $b \rightarrow_L c$, and $a \parallel_L b$, then the log suggests that c needs to synchronize a and b (AND-join pattern).

Figure 5.4 only shows simple patterns and does not present the additional conditions needed to extract the patterns. However, the figure nicely illustrates the basic idea.

Consider, for example, WF-net N_3 depicted in Fig. 5.5 and the event log L_3 describing four cases

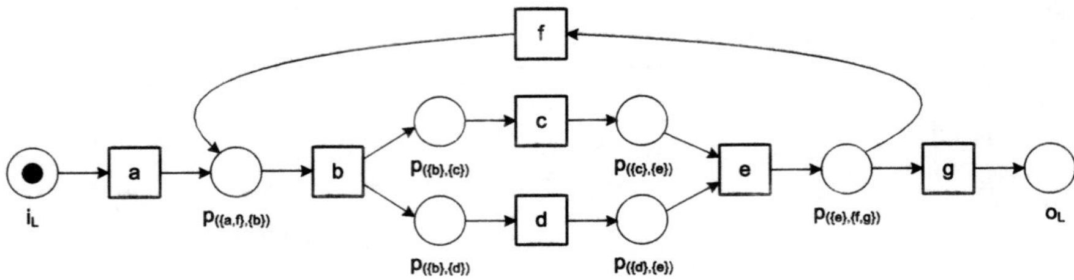

Fig. 5.5 WF-net N_3 derived from $L_3 = [\langle a,b,c,d,e,f,b,d,c,e,g\rangle, \langle a,b,d,c,e,g\rangle^2, \langle a,b,c,d,e,f,b,c,d,e,f,b,d,c,e,g\rangle]$

Table 5.3 Footprint of L_3

	a	b	c	d	e	f	g
a	$\#$	$\rightarrow$	$\#$	$\#$	$\#$	$\#$	$\#$
b	$\leftarrow$	$\#$	$\rightarrow$	$\rightarrow$	$\#$	$\leftarrow$	$\#$
c	$\#$	$\leftarrow$	$\#$	$\parallel$	$\rightarrow$	$\#$	$\#$
d	$\#$	$\leftarrow$	$\parallel$	$\#$	$\rightarrow$	$\#$	$\#$
e	$\#$	$\#$	$\leftarrow$	$\leftarrow$	$\#$	$\rightarrow$	$\rightarrow$
f	$\#$	$\rightarrow$	$\#$	$\#$	$\leftarrow$	$\#$	$\#$
g	$\#$	$\#$	$\#$	$\#$	$\leftarrow$	$\#$	$\#$

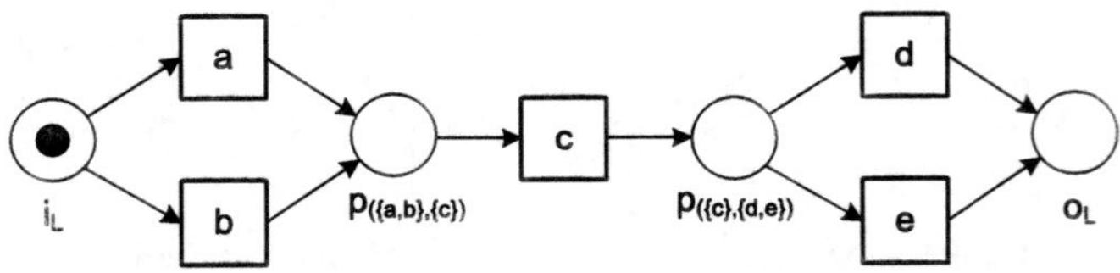

Fig. 5.6 WF-net N_4 derived from $L_4 = [\langle a,c,d\rangle^{45}, \langle b,c,d\rangle^{42}, \langle a,c,e\rangle^{38}, \langle b,c,e\rangle^{22}]$

$$L_3 = \bigl[\langle a,b,c,d,e,f,b,d,c,e,g\rangle, \langle a,b,d,c,e,g\rangle^2, \langle a,b,c,d,e,f,b,c,d,e,f,b,d,c,e,g\rangle\bigr]$$

The α-algorithm constructs WF-net N_3 based on L_3 (see Fig. 5.5).

Table 5.3 shows the footprint of L_3. Note that the patterns in the model indeed match the log-based ordering relations extracted from the event log. Consider, for example, the process fragment involving b, c, d, and e. Obviously, this fragment can be constructed based on $b \rightarrow_{L_3} c$, $b \rightarrow_{L_3} d$, $c \parallel_{L_3} d$, $c \rightarrow_{L_3} e$, and $d \rightarrow_{L_3} e$. The choice following e is revealed by $e \rightarrow_{L_3} f$, $e \rightarrow_{L_3} g$, and $f \#_{L_3} g$. Etc.

Another example is shown in Fig. 5.6. WF-net N_4 can be derived from L_4

$$L_4 = \bigl[\langle a,c,d\rangle^{45}, \langle b,c,d\rangle^{42}, \langle a,c,e\rangle^{38}, \langle b,c,e\rangle^{22}\bigr]$$

L_4 contains information about 147 cases that follow one of the four possible traces. There are two start and two end activities. These can be detected easily by looking for the first and last activities in traces.

5.2.2 Algorithm

After showing the basic idea and some examples, we describe the α-algorithm [103].

Definition 5.4 (α-algorithm) Let L be an event log over $T \subseteq \mathscr{A}$. $\alpha(L)$ is defined as follows.

(1) $T_L = \{t \in T \mid \exists_{\sigma \in L}\ t \in \sigma\}$
(2) $T_I = \{t \in T \mid \exists_{\sigma \in L}\ t = \mathit{first}(\sigma)\}$
(3) $T_O = \{t \in T \mid \exists_{\sigma \in L}\ t = \mathit{last}(\sigma)\}$
(4) $X_L = \{(A, B) \mid A \subseteq T_L\ \wedge\ A \neq \emptyset\ \wedge\ B \subseteq T_L\ \wedge\ B \neq \emptyset\ \wedge\ \forall_{a \in A} \forall_{b \in B}\ a \rightarrow_L b\ \wedge\ \forall_{a_1, a_2 \in A}\ a_1 \#_L a_2\ \wedge\ \forall_{b_1, b_2 \in B}\ b_1 \#_L b_2\}$
(5) $Y_L = \{(A, B) \in X_L \mid \forall_{(A', B') \in X_L} A \subseteq A'\ \wedge B \subseteq B' \Longrightarrow (A, B) = (A', B')\}$
(6) $P_L = \{p_{(A,B)} \mid (A, B) \in Y_L\} \cup \{i_L, o_L\}$
(7) $F_L = \{(a, p_{(A,B)}) \mid (A, B) \in Y_L\ \wedge\ a \in A\} \cup \{(p_{(A,B)}, b) \mid (A, B) \in Y_L\ \wedge\ b \in B\} \cup \{(i_L, t) \mid t \in T_I\} \cup \{(t, o_L) \mid t \in T_O\}$
(8) $\alpha(L) = (P_L, T_L, F_L)$

L is an event log over some set T of activities. In Step 1, it is checked which activities do appear in the log (T_L). These will correspond to the transitions of the generated WF-net. T_I is the set of start activities, i.e., all activities that appear first in some trace (Step 2). T_O is the set of end activities, i.e., all activities that appear last in some trace (Step 3). Steps 4 and 5 form the core of the α-algorithm. The challenge is to determine the places of the WF-net and their connections. We aim at constructing places named $p_{(A,B)}$ such that A is the set of input transitions ($\bullet p_{(A,B)} = A$) and B is the set of output transitions ($p_{(A,B)}\bullet = B$) of $p_{(A,B)}$.

The basic motivation for finding $p_{(A,B)}$ is illustrated by Fig. 5.7. All elements of A should have causal dependencies with all elements of B, i.e., for all $(a, b) \in A \times B$: $a \rightarrow_L b$. Moreover, the elements of A should never follow one another, i.e., for all $a_1, a_2 \in A$: $a_1 \#_L a_2$. A similar requirement holds for B.

Table 5.4 shows the structure in terms of the footprint matrix introduced earlier. If we *only* consider the columns and rows related to $A \cup B$ and group the rows and columns belonging to A and B, respectively, we get the pattern shown in Table 5.4. There are four quadrants. Two quadrants only contain the symbol #. This shows that the elements of A should never follow another (upper-left quadrant) and that the elements of B should never follow another (lower-right quadrant). The upper-right quadrant only contains the symbol $\rightarrow$, any of the elements in A can be followed by any of the elements in B but never the other way around. By symmetry, the lower-left quadrant only contains the symbol $\leftarrow$.

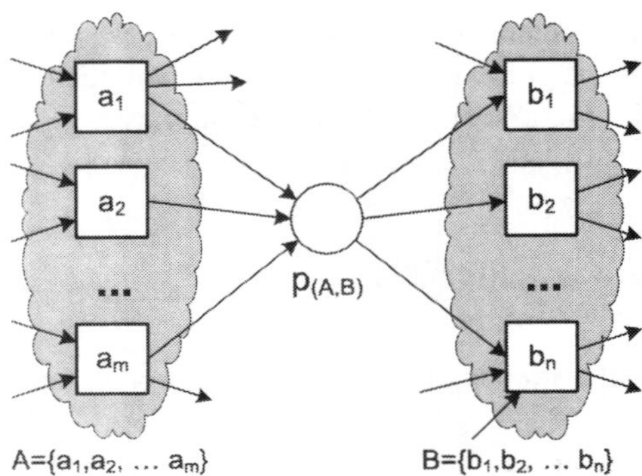

Fig. 5.7 Place $p_{(A,B)}$ connects the transitions in set A to the transitions in set B

Table 5.4 How to identify $(A, B) \in X_L$? Rearrange the rows and columns corresponding to $A = \{a_1, a_2, \dots, a_m\}$ and $B = \{b_1, b_2, \dots, b_n\}$ and remove the other rows and columns from the footprint

	a_1	a_2	...	a_m	b_1	b_2	...	b_n
a_1	#	#	...	#	$\rightarrow$	$\rightarrow$	...	$\rightarrow$
a_2	#	#	...	#	$\rightarrow$	$\rightarrow$	...	$\rightarrow$
...	...	...	...	...	...	...	...	...
a_m	#	#	...	#	$\rightarrow$	$\rightarrow$	...	$\rightarrow$
b_1	$\leftarrow$	$\leftarrow$	...	$\leftarrow$	#	#	...	#
b_2	$\leftarrow$	$\leftarrow$	...	$\leftarrow$	#	#	...	#
...	...	...	...	...	...	...	...	...
b_n	$\leftarrow$	$\leftarrow$	...	$\leftarrow$	#	#	...	#

Let us consider L_1 again. Clearly, $A = \{a\}$ and $B = \{b, e\}$ meet the requirements stated in Step 4. Also $A' = \{a\}$ and $B' = \{b\}$ meet the same requirements. X_L is the set of all such pairs that meet the requirements just mentioned. In this case:

$$X_{L_1} = \big\{\big(\{a\}, \{b\}\big), \big(\{a\}, \{c\}\big), \big(\{a\}, \{e\}\big), \big(\{a\}, \{b, e\}\big), \big(\{a\}, \{c, e\}\big), \\ \big(\{b\}, \{d\}\big), \big(\{c\}, \{d\}\big), \big(\{e\}, \{d\}\big), \big(\{b, e\}, \{d\}\big), \big(\{c, e\}, \{d\}\big)\big\}$$

If one would insert a place for any element in X_{L_1}, there would be too many places. Therefore, only the "maximal pairs" (A, B) should be included. Note that for any pair $(A, B) \in X_L$, nonempty set $A' \subseteq A$, and nonempty set $B' \subseteq B$, it is implied that $(A', B') \in X_L$. In Step 5, all nonmaximal pairs are removed, thus yielding:

$$Y_{L_1} = \big\{\big(\{a\}, \{b, e\}\big), \big(\{a\}, \{c, e\}\big), \big(\{b, e\}, \{d\}\big), \big(\{c, e\}, \{d\}\big)\big\}$$

Step 5 can also be understood in terms the footprint matrix. Consider Table 5.4 and let A' and B' be such that $\emptyset \subset A' \subseteq A$ and $\emptyset \subset B' \subseteq B$. Removing rows and columns $A \cup B \setminus (A' \cup B')$ results in a matrix still having the pattern shown in Table 5.4. Therefore, we only consider maximal matrices for constructing Y_L.

Table 5.5 Footprint of L_5

	a	b	c	d	e	f
a	#	→	#	#	→	#
b	←	#	→	←	‖	→
c	#	←	#	→	‖	#
d	#	→	←	#	‖	#
e	←	‖	‖	‖	#	→
f	#	←	#	#	←	#

Every element of $(A, B) \in Y_L$ corresponds to a place $p_{(A,B)}$ connecting transitions A to transitions B. In addition, P_L also contains a unique source place i_L and a unique sink place o_L (cf. Step 6). Remember that the goal is to create a WF-net.[1]

In Step 7, the arcs of the WF-net are generated. All start transitions in T_I have i_L as an input place and all end transitions T_O have o_L as output place. All places $p_{(A,B)}$ have A as input nodes and B as output nodes. The result is a Petri net $\alpha(L) = (P_L, T_L, F_L)$ that describes the behavior seen in event log L.

Thus far, we presented four logs and four WF-nets. Application of the α-algorithm shows that indeed $\alpha(L_3) = N_3$ and $\alpha(L_4) = N_4$. In Figs. 5.5 and 5.6, the places are named based on the sets Y_{L_3} and Y_{L_4}. Moreover, $\alpha(L_1) = N_1$ and $\alpha(L_2) = N_2$ modulo renaming of places (because different place names are used in Figs. 5.1 and 5.2). These examples show that the α-algorithm is indeed able to discover WF-nets based on event logs.

Let us now consider event log L_5:

$$L_5 = [\langle a, b, e, f\rangle^2, \langle a, b, e, c, d, b, f\rangle^3, \langle a, b, c, e, d, b, f\rangle^2, \langle a, b, c, d, e, b, f\rangle^4, \langle a, e, b, c, d, b, f\rangle^3]$$

Table 5.5 shows the footprint of the log.

Let us now apply the 8 steps of the algorithm for $L = L_5$:

$$T_L = \{a, b, c, d, e, f\}$$

$$T_I = \{a\}$$

$$T_I = \{f\}$$

$$X_L = \{(\{a\}, \{b\}), (\{a\}, \{e\}), (\{b\}, \{c\}), (\{b\}, \{f\}), (\{c\}, \{d\}), (\{d\}, \{b\}), (\{e\}, \{f\}), (\{a, d\}, \{b\}), (\{b\}, \{c, f\})\}$$

$$Y_L = \{(\{a\}, \{e\}), (\{c\}, \{d\}), (\{e\}, \{f\}), (\{a, d\}, \{b\}), (\{b\}, \{c, f\})\}$$

$$P_L = \{p_{(\{a\},\{e\})}, p_{(\{c\},\{d\})}, p_{(\{e\},\{f\})}, p_{(\{a,d\},\{b\})}, p_{(\{b\},\{c,f\})}, i_L, o_L\}$$

[1]Nevertheless, the α-algorithm may construct a Petri net that is not a WF-net (see, for instance, Fig. 5.12). Later, we will discuss such problems in detail.

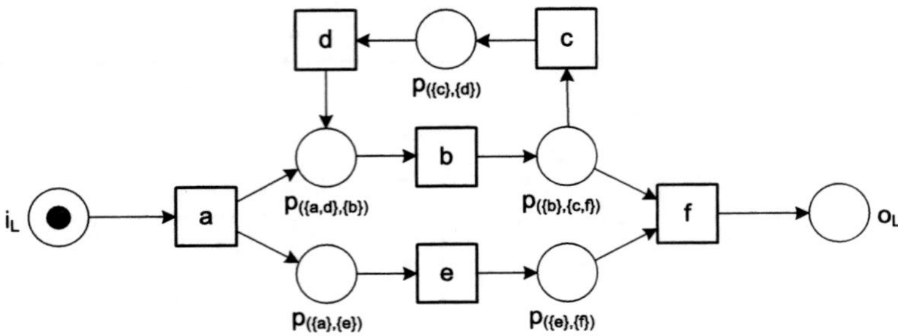

Fig. 5.8 WF-net N_5 derived from $L_5 = [\langle a,b,e,f\rangle^2, \langle a,b,e,c,d,b,f\rangle^3, \langle a,b,c,e,d,b,f\rangle^2, \langle a,b,c,d,e,b,f\rangle^4, \langle a,e,b,c,d,b,f\rangle^3]$

$$\begin{aligned}F_L = \big\{&(a, p_{(\{a\},\{e\})}), (p_{(\{a\},\{e\})}, e), (c, p_{(\{c\},\{d\})}), (p_{(\{c\},\{d\})}, d),\\ &(e, p_{(\{e\},\{f\})}), (p_{(\{e\},\{f\})}, f), (a, p_{(\{a,d\},\{b\})}), (d, p_{(\{a,d\},\{b\})}),\\ &(p_{(\{a,d\},\{b\})}, b), (b, p_{(\{b\},\{c,f\})}), (p_{(\{b\},\{c,f\})}, c), (p_{(\{b\},\{c,f\})}, f),\\ &(i_L, a), (f, o_L)\big\}\\ \alpha(L) = &(P_L, T_L, F_L)\end{aligned}$$

Figure 5.8 shows $N_5 = \alpha(L_5)$, i.e., the model just computed. N_5 can indeed replay the traces in L_5. Place names are not shown in Fig. 5.8, and we will also not show them in later WF-nets, because they can be derived from the surrounding transition names and just clutter the diagram.

5.2.3 Limitations of the α-Algorithm

In [103], it was shown that the α-algorithm can discover a large class of WF-nets if one assumes that the log is *complete* with respect to the log-based ordering relation $>_L$. This assumption implies that, for any complete event log L, $a >_L b$ if a can be directly followed by b. Consequently, a footprint like the one shown in Table 5.5 is assumed to be valid. We revisit the notion of completeness later in this chapter.

Even if we assume that the log is complete, the α-algorithm has some problems. There are many different WF-nets that have the same possible behavior, i.e., two models can be structurally different but trace equivalent. Consider, for instance, the following event log:

$$L_6 = \big[\langle a,c,e,g\rangle^2, \langle a,e,c,g\rangle^3, \langle b,d,f,g\rangle^2, \langle b,f,d,g\rangle^4\big]$$

$\alpha(L_6)$ is shown in Fig. 5.9. Although the model is able to generate the observed behavior, the resulting WF-net is needlessly complex. Two of the input places of g are redundant, i.e., they can be removed without changing the behavior. The places denoted as p_1 and p_2 are so-called *implicit places* and can be removed without

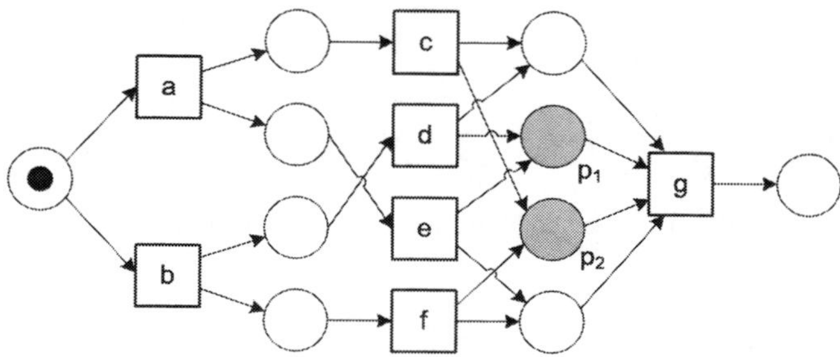

Fig. 5.9 WF-net N_6 derived from $L_6 = [\langle a, c, e, g\rangle^2, \langle a, e, c, g\rangle^3, \langle b, d, f, g\rangle^2, \langle b, f, d, g\rangle^4]$. The two highlighted places are redundant, i.e., removing them will simplify the model without changing its behavior

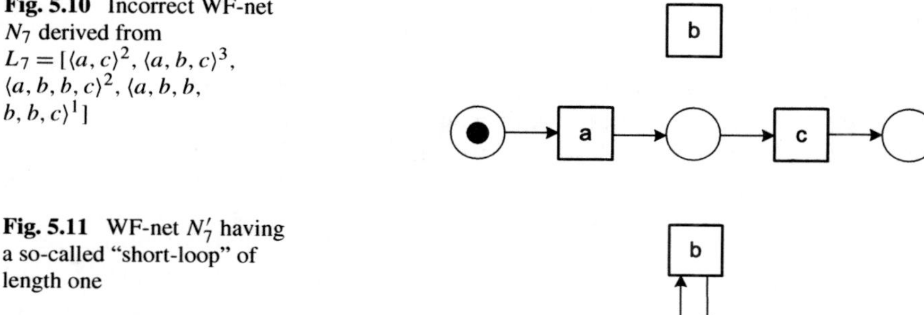

Fig. 5.10 Incorrect WF-net N_7 derived from $L_7 = [\langle a, c\rangle^2, \langle a, b, c\rangle^3, \langle a, b, b, c\rangle^2, \langle a, b, b, b, b, c\rangle^1]$

Fig. 5.11 WF-net N_7' having a so-called "short-loop" of length one

affecting the set of possible firing sequences. In fact, Fig. 5.9 shows only one of many possible trace equivalent WF-nets.

The original α-algorithm (as presented in Sect. 5.2.2) has problems dealing with short loops, i.e., loops of length one or two. For a loop of length one, this is illustrated by WF-net N_7 in Fig. 5.10, which shows the result of applying the basic algorithm to L_7.

$$L_7 = [\langle a, c\rangle^2, \langle a, b, c\rangle^3, \langle a, b, b, c\rangle^2, \langle a, b, b, b, b, c\rangle^1]$$

The resulting model is not a WF-net as transition b is disconnected from the rest of the model. The models allows for the execution of b before a and after c. This is not consistent with the event log. This problem can be addressed easily as shown in [30]. Using an improved version of the α-algorithm, one can discover the WF-net shown in Fig. 5.11.

The problem with loops of length two is illustrated by Petri net N_8 in Fig. 5.12 which shows the result of applying the basic algorithm to L_8.

$$L_8 = [\langle a, b, d\rangle^3, \langle a, b, c, b, d\rangle^2, \langle a, b, c, b, c, b, d\rangle]$$

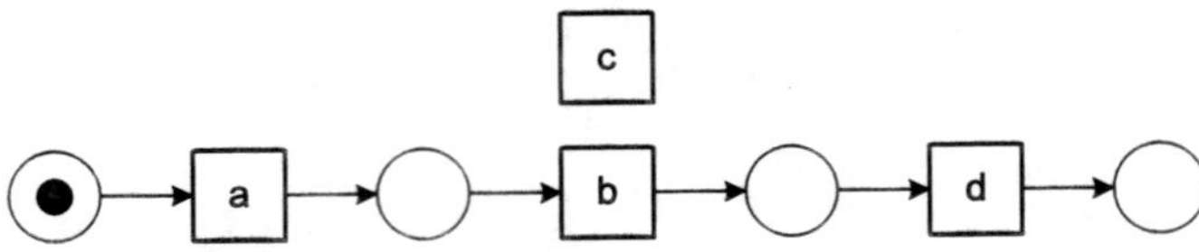

Fig. 5.12 Incorrect WF-net N_8 derived from $L_8 = [\langle a,b,d\rangle^3, \langle a,b,c,b,d\rangle^2, \langle a,b,c,b,c,b,d\rangle]$

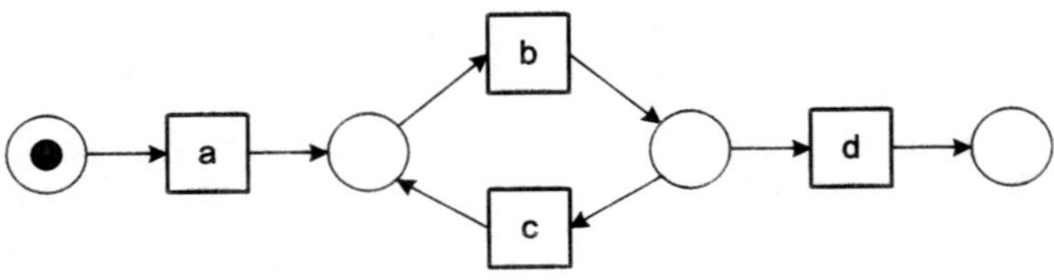

Fig. 5.13 Corrected WF-net N_8' having a so-called "short-loop" of length two

The following log-based ordering relations are derived from this event log: $a \rightarrow_{L_8} b$, $b \rightarrow_{L_8} d$, and $b \parallel_{L_8} c$. Hence, the basic algorithm incorrectly assumes that b and c are in parallel because they follow one another. The model shown in Fig. 5.12 is not even a WF-net, because c is not on a path from source to sink. Using the extension described in [30], the improved α-algorithm correctly discovers the WF-net shown in Fig. 5.13.

There are various ways to improve the basic α-algorithm to be able to deal with loops. The α^+-algorithm described in [30] is one of several alternatives to address problems related to the original algorithm presented in Sect. 5.2.2. The α^+-algorithm uses a pre and postprocessing phase. The preprocessing phase deals with loops of length two whereas the preprocessing phase inserts loops of length one.

The basic algorithm has no problems mining loops of length three or more. For a loop of involving at least three activities (say a, b, and c), concurrency can be distinguished from loops using relation $>_L$. For a loop, we find only $a >_L b$, $b >_L c$, and $c >_L a$. If the three activities are concurrent, we find $a >_L b$, $a >_L c$, $b >_L a$, $b >_L c$, $c >_L a$, and $c >_L b$. Hence, it is easy to detect the difference. Note that for a loop of length two this is not the case. For a loop involving a and b, we find $a >_L b$ and $b >_L a$. If a and b are concurrent, we find the same relations. Hence, both constructs leave the same footprint in the event log.

A more difficult problem is the discovery of so-called *nonlocal dependencies* resulting from non-free choice process constructs. An example is shown in Fig. 5.14. This net would be a good candidate after observing the following event log:

$$L_9 = \left[\langle a,c,d\rangle^{45}, \langle b,c,e\rangle^{42}\right]$$

However, the α-algorithm will derive the WF-net without the places labeled p_1 and p_2. Hence, $\alpha(L_9) = N_4$, as shown in Fig. 5.6, although the traces $\langle a,c,e\rangle$ and $\langle b,c,d\rangle$ do not appear in L_9. Such problems can be (partially) resolved using refined versions of the α-algorithm such as the one presented in [125].

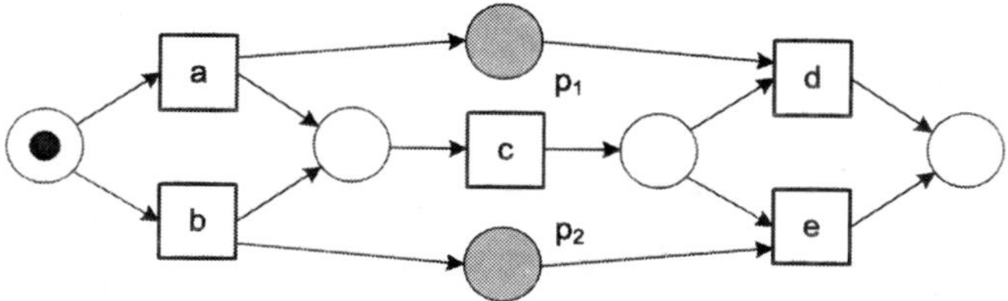

Fig. 5.14 WF-net N_9 having a non-local dependency

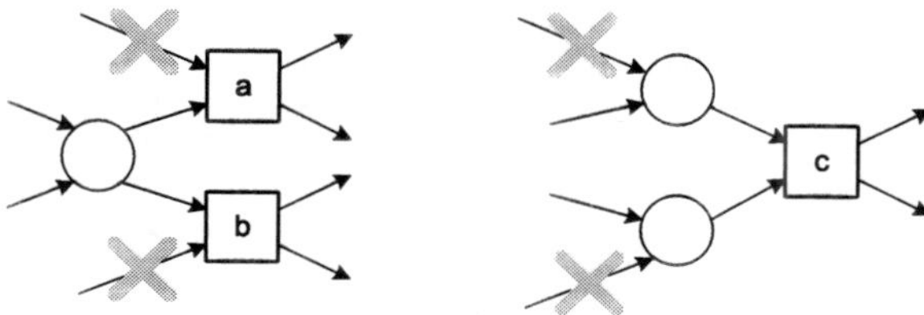

Fig. 5.15 Two constructs that may jeopardize the correctness of the discovered WF-net

Another limitation of the α-algorithm is that *frequencies are not taken into account*. Therefore, the algorithm is very sensitive to noise and incompleteness (see Sect. 5.4.2).

The α-algorithm is able to discover a large class of models. The basic 8-line algorithm has some limitations when it comes to particular process patterns (e.g., short-loops and non-local dependencies). Some of these problems can be solved using various refinements. As shown in [30, 103], the α-algorithm guarantees to produce a correct process model provided that the underlying process can be described by a WF-net that does not contain duplicate activities (two transitions with the same activity label) and silent transitions (activities that are not recorded in the event log), and does not use the two constructs shown in Fig. 5.15. See [30, 103] for the precise requirements.

Even if the underlying process is using constructs as shown in Fig. 5.15, the α-algorithm may still produce a useful process model. For instance, the α-algorithm is unable to discover the highlighted places (p_1 and p_2) in Fig. 5.14, but still produces a sound process model that is able to replay the log.

5.2.4 Taking the Transactional Life-Cycle into Account

When describing the typical information in event logs in Chap. 4, we discussed the *transactional life-cycle model* of an *activity instance*. Figure 4.3 shows examples of transaction types, e.g., schedule, start, complete, and suspend. Events often have such a transaction type attribute, e.g., $\#_{trans}(e) = complete$. The standard life-cycle extension of XES also provides such an attribute. The α-algorithm can be easily adapted to take this information into account. First of all, the log could be projected

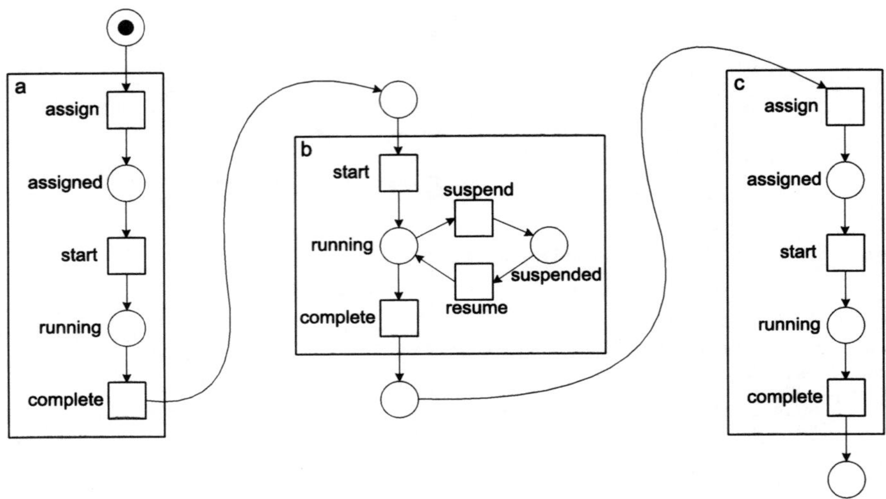

Fig. 5.16 Mining event logs with transactional information; the life-cycle of each activity is represented as a subprocess

onto smaller event logs in which each of the smaller logs contains all events related to a specific activity. This information can be used to discover the transactional life-cycle for each activity. Second, when mining the overall process, information about the general transactional life-cycle (e.g., Fig. 4.3) or information about an activity-specific transactional life-cycle can be exploited. Figure 5.16 illustrates the latter. All events related to an activity are mapped onto transitions embedded in a subprocess. The relations between the transitions for each subprocess are either discovered separately or modeled using domain knowledge. Figure 5.16 shows a sequence of three activities. Activities a and c share a common transactional life-cycle involving the event types *assign*, *start*, and *complete*. Activity b has a transactional life-cycle involving the event types *start*, *suspend*, *resume*, and *complete*.

5.3 Rediscovering Process Models

In Chap. 7, we will describe *conformance checking* techniques for measuring the quality of a process model *with respect to an event log*. However, when discussing the results of the α-algorithm, we already concluded that some WF-nets "could not be discovered" based on an event log. This assumes that we aim to discover a particular, known, model. In reality, we often do not know the "real" model. In fact, in practice, there is no such thing as *the* model describing a process. There may be many models (i.e., views on the same reality) and the process being studied may change while being discovered. However, as sketched in Fig. 5.17, we can create the experimental setting for testing process discovery algorithms in which we assume the original model to be known.

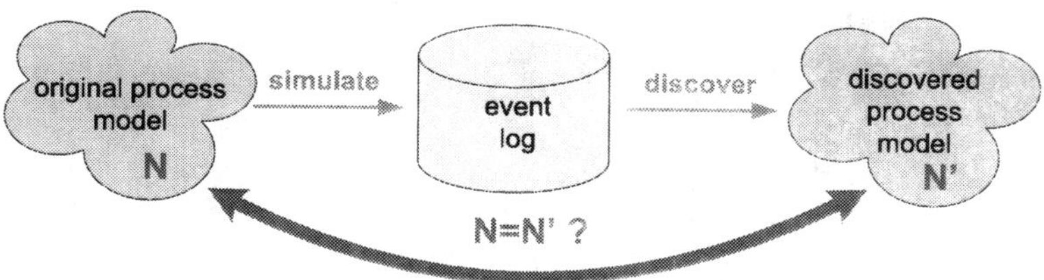

Fig. 5.17 The rediscovery problem: is the discovered model N' equivalent to the original model N

Starting point in Fig. 5.17 is a process model, e.g., a WF-net N. Based on this model we can run many simulation experiments and record the simulated events in an event log. Let us assume that the event log is complete with respect to some criterion, e.g., if x can be followed by y in N it happened at least once according to log. Using the complete event log as input for a process discovery algorithm (e.g., the α-algorithm), we can construct a new model. Now the question is: "What do the discovered model N' and the original model N have in common? Are they equivalent?" Equivalence can be viewed at different levels. For example, it is unreasonable to expect that a discovery algorithm is able to reconstruct the original layout as this information is not in the log; layout information is irrelevant for the behavior of a process. For the same reason, it is unreasonable to expect that the original place names of the WF-net can be reconstructed. The α-algorithm generates places named $p_{(A,B)}$. These are of course not intended to match original place names. Therefore, we need to focus on *behavior* (and not on layout and syntax) when comparing the discovered model N' and the original model N.

Three Notions of Behavioral Equivalence
As shown in [120], many equivalence notions can be defined. Here, we informally describe three well-known notions: *trace equivalence*, *bisimilarity*, and *branching bisimilarity*. These notions are defined for a pair of transition systems TS_1 and TS_2 (Sect. 2.2.1) and not for higher-level languages such as WF-nets, BPMN, EPCs, and YAWL. However, any model with executable semantics can be transformed into a transition system. Therefore, we can assume that the original process model N and the discovered process model N' mentioned in Fig. 5.17 define two transition systems that can be used as a basis for comparison.
Trace equivalence considers two transition systems to be equivalent if their sets of execution sequences are identical. Let TS_2 be the transition system corresponding to WF-net $N_6 = \alpha(L_6)$ shown in Fig. 5.9 and let TS_1 be the transition system corresponding to the same WF-net but now without places p_1 and p_2. Although both WF-nets are syntactically different, the sets of execution sequences of TS_1 and TS_2 are the same. However, two transition systems that allow for the same set of execution sequences may also be quite different as illustrated by Fig. 5.18.

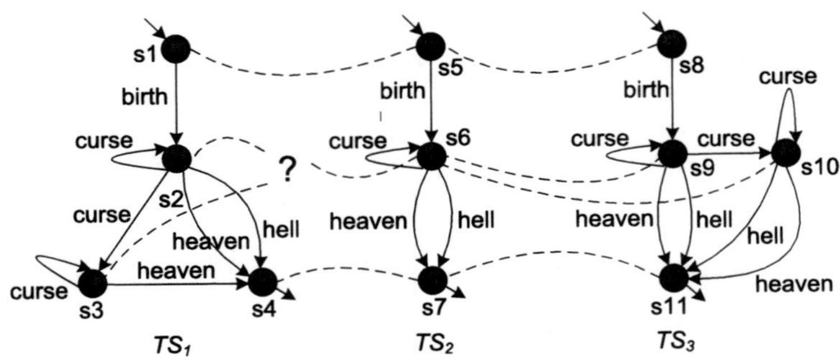

Fig. 5.18 Three trace equivalent transition systems: TS_1 and TS_2 are not bisimilar, but TS_2 and TS_3 are bisimilar

The three transition systems in Fig. 5.18 are trace equivalent: any trace in one transition system is also possible in any of the other transition systems. For instance, the trace $\langle birth, curse, curse, curse, heaven \rangle$ is possible in all three transition systems. However, there is a relevant difference between TS_1 and TS_2. In TS_1, one can end up in state $s3$ where one will always go to heaven despite the cursing. Such a state does not exist in TS_2; while cursing in state $s6$ one can still go to hell. When moving from state $s2$ to state $s3$ in TS_1, a choice was made which cannot be seen in the set of traces but that is highly relevant for understanding the process.

Bisimulation equivalence, or bisimilarity for short, is a more refined notion taking into account the moment of choice. Two transition systems are bisimilar if the first system can "mimic any move" of the second, and vice versa (using the same relation). Consider, for example, TS_2 and TS_3 in Fig. 5.18. TS_2 can simulate TS_3 and vice versa. The states of both transition systems are related by dashed lines; $s5$ is related to $s8$, $s6$ is related to both $s9$ and $s10$, and $s7$ is related to $s11$. In two related states, the same set of actions needs to be possible and taking any of these actions on one side should lead to a related state when taking the same action on the other side. Because TS_2 can move from $s5$ to $s6$ via action *birth*, TS_3 should also be able to take a *birth* action in $s8$ resulting in a related state ($s9$). TS_2 and TS_3 are bisimilar because any action by one can be mimicked by the other. Now consider TS_1 and TS_2. Here, it is impossible to relate $s3$ in TS_1 to a corresponding state in TS_2. If $s3$ is related to $s6$, then in $s3$ it should be possible to do a *hell* action, but this is not the case. Hence, TS_2 can simulate TS_1, i.e., any action in TS_1 can be mimicked by TS_2, but TS_1 *cannot* simulate TS_2. Therefore, TS_1 and TS_2 are not bisimilar. Bisimulation equivalence is a stronger equivalence relation than trace equivalence, i.e., if two transition systems are bisimilar, then they are also trace equivalent.

Branching bisimulation equivalence, or branching bisimilarity for short, takes *silent actions* into account. In Chap. 2, we introduced already the label τ for this purpose. A τ action is "invisible", i.e., cannot be observed. In terms of process mining, this means that the corresponding activity is not recorded in the event log. As before, two transition systems are branching bisimilar if the first system can "follow any move" of the second and vice versa, but now taking τ actions into account. (Here, we do not address subtle differences between weak bisimulation, also known as observational equivalence, and branching bisimulation equivalence [120].) If one system takes a τ action, then the second system may also take a τ action or do nothing (as long as the states between both systems remain related). If one system takes a non-τ action, then the second system should also be able to take the same non-τ action possibly preceded by sequence of τ actions. The states before and after the non-τ action, need to be related. Figure 5.19 shows two YAWL models and their corresponding transition systems TS_1 and TS_2. The two transition systems are *not* branching bisimilar. The reason is that in the YAWL model on the left, a choice is made after task *check*, whereas in the other model the choice is postponed until either *reject* or *accept* happens. Therefore, the YAWL model on the left cannot simulate the model on the right. Technically, states $s3$ and $s4$ in TS_1 do not have a corresponding state in TS_2. It is impossible to relate $s3$ and $s4$ to $s7$ since $s7$ allows for both actions whereas $s3$ and $s4$ allow for only one action. The YAWL model on the right models the so-called *deferred choice* workflow pattern whereas the YAWL model on the left models the more common *exclusive choice* pattern [101].

Branching bisimulation equivalence is highly relevant for process mining since typically not all actions are recorded in the event log. For example, if the choice made in task *check* is not recorded in the event log, then one discovers the YAWL model on the right, i.e., the right moment of choice cannot be captured.

Although both models in Fig. 5.19 are not branching bisimilar, they are trace equivalent. In both models, there are only two possible (visible) traces: $\langle check, reject \rangle$ and $\langle check, accept \rangle$.

We refer to [120] for formal definitions of the preceding concepts. Here, we discuss these concepts because they are quite important when judging process mining results.

The different notions of equivalence show that the comparison of the original model and the discovered model in Fig. 5.17 is not a simple syntactical check. Instead a choice must be made with respect to the type of behavioral equivalence that is appropriate.

As mentioned before, the experimental setting shown in Fig. 5.17 can only be used in the situation in which the model is known beforehand. In most applications, such a model is not known. Moreover, classical notions such as trace equivalence, bisimilarity, and branching bisimilarity provide only true/false answers. As

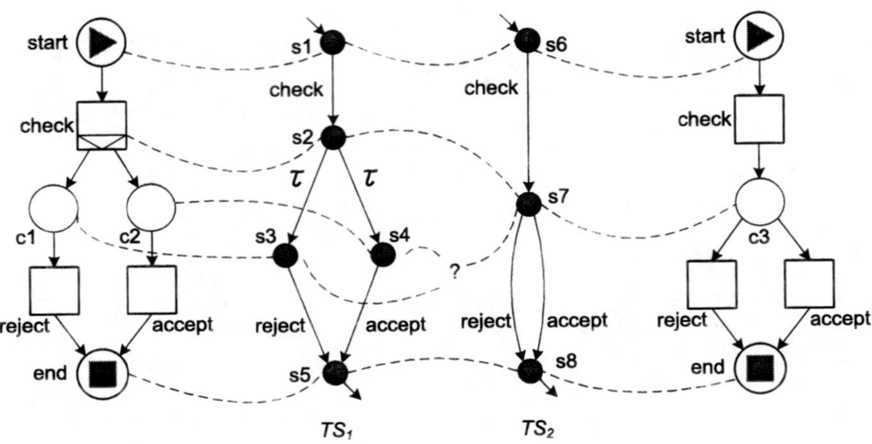

Fig. 5.19 Two YAWL models and the corresponding transition systems

discussed in [33], a binary equivalence is not very useful in the context of process mining. If two processes are very similar (identical except for some exceptional paths), classical equivalence checks will simply conclude that the processes are not equivalent rather than stating that the processes are e.g., 95% similar. Therefore, this book will focus on the comparison of a model and an event log rather than comparing two models. For instance, in Chap. 7 we will show techniques that can conclude that 95% of the event log "fits" the model.

5.4 Challenges

The α-algorithm was one of the first process discovery algorithms to adequately capture concurrency (see also Sect. 6.5). Today there are much better algorithms that overcome the weaknesses of the α-algorithm. These are either variants of the α-algorithm or algorithms that use a completely different approach, e.g., genetic mining or synthesis based on regions. In Chap. 6, we review some of these alternative approaches. However, before presenting new process discovery techniques, we first elaborate on the main challenges. For this purpose, we show the effect that a representational bias can have (Sect. 5.4.1). Then we discuss problems related to the input event log that may be noisy or incomplete (Sect. 5.4.2). In Sect. 5.4.3, we discuss the four quality criteria mentioned earlier: fitness, precision, generalization, and simplicity. Finally, Sect. 5.4.4 again emphasizes that discovered models are just a view on reality. Hence, the usefulness of the model strongly depends on the questions one seeks to answer.

Fig. 5.20 A WF-net having two transitions with the same label describing event log $L_{10} = [\langle a, a\rangle^{55}]$

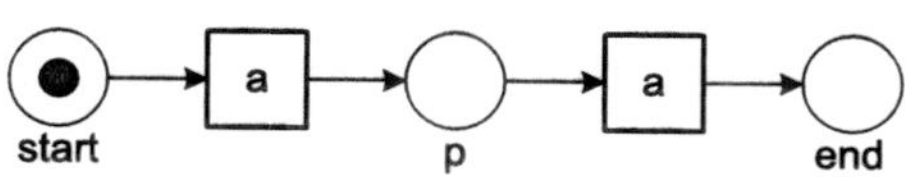

5.4.1 Representational Bias

At the beginning of the chapter we decided to focus on a mining algorithm that produces a WF-net, i.e., we assumed that the underlying process can be adequately described by a WF-net. Any discovery technique requires such a *representational bias*. For example, algorithms for learning decision trees (see Sect. 3.2) make similar assumptions about the structure of the resulting tree. For instance, most decision tree learners can only split once on an attribute on every path in the tree.

When discussing the α-algorithm we assumed that the process to be discovered is a sound WF-net. More specifically, we assumed that the underlying process can be described by a WF-net where each transition bears a unique and visible label. In such a WF-net it is not possible to have two transitions with the same label (i.e., $l(t_1) = l(t_2)$ implies $t_1 = t_2$) or transitions whose occurrences remain invisible (i.e., it is not possible to have a so-called silent transition, so for all transitions t: $l(t) \neq \tau$). (See Sect. 2.2.2 and the earlier discussion on branching bisimulation equivalence.) These assumptions may seem harmless, but have a noticeable effect on the class of process models that can be discovered. We show two examples illustrating the impact of such a representational bias.

For an event log like $L_{10} = [\langle a, a\rangle^{55}]$, i.e., for all cases precisely two a's are executed, ideally one would like to discover the WF-net shown in Fig. 5.20. Unfortunately, this process model will not be discovered due to the representational bias of the α-algorithm. There is no WF-net without duplicate and τ labels that has the desired behavior and the α-algorithm can only discover such WF-nets (i.e., each transition needs to have unique visible label).

Let us now consider event log $L_{11} = [\langle a, b, c\rangle^{20}, \langle a, c\rangle^{30}]$. Figure 5.21(a) describes the underlying process well: activity b can be skipped by executing the τ transition. Figure 5.21(b) shows an alternative WF-net using two a transitions and no τ transition. These two models are trace equivalent. (They are not branching bisimilar because the moment of choice is different.) However, it is not possible to construct a WF-net without duplicate and τ labels that is trace equivalent to these two models. Figure 5.21(c) shows the model produced by the α-algorithm; because of the representational bias the algorithm is destined to fail for this log. The WF-net in Fig. 5.21(c) can only reproduce trace $\langle a, b, c\rangle$ and not $\langle a, c\rangle$.

Event logs L_{10} and L_{11} illustrate the effect a representational bias can have. However, from the viewpoint of the α-algorithm, the choice to not consider duplicate labels and τ transitions is sensible. τ transitions are not recorded in the log and hence any algorithm will have problems reconstructing their behavior. Multiple transitions with the same label are undistinguishable in the event log. Therefore, any algorithm will have problems associating the corresponding events to one of these transitions.

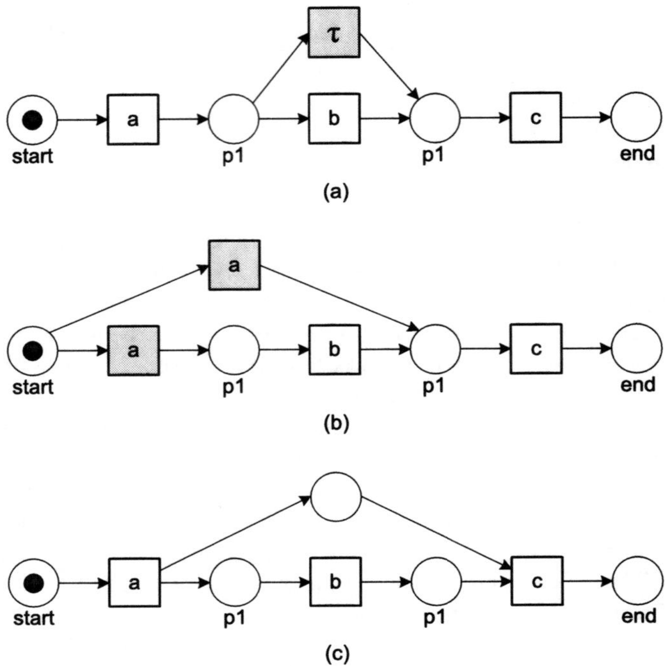

Fig. 5.21 Three WF-nets for the event log $L_{11} = [\langle a, b, c\rangle^{20}, \langle a, c\rangle^{30}]$

The problems sketched previously apply to many process discovery algorithms. For example, the choice between the concurrent execution of b and c or the execution of just e shown in Fig. 5.1 cannot be handled by many algorithms. Most algorithms do *not* allow for so-called "non-free-choice constructs" where concurrency and choice meet. The concept of *free-choice nets* is well-defined in the Petri net domain [34]. A Petri net is free choice if any two transitions sharing an input place have identical input sets, i.e., $\bullet t_1 \cap \bullet t_2 \neq \emptyset$ implies $\bullet t_1 = \bullet t_2$ for any $t_1, t_2 \in T$. Most analysis questions (e.g., soundness) can be answered in polynomial time for free-choice nets [92, 114]. Moreover, many process modeling languages are inherently free-choice, thus making this an interesting subclass. Unfortunately, in reality processes tend to be non-free-choice. The example of Fig. 5.1 shows that sometimes the α-algorithm is able to deal with non-free-choice constructs. However, there are many non-free-choice processes that cannot be discovered by the α-algorithm (see, for example, N_9 in Fig. 5.14). The non-free-choice construct is just one of many constructs that existing process mining algorithms have problems with. Other examples are arbitrary nested loops, cancelation, unbalanced splits and joins, and partial synchronization. In this context, it is important to observe *process discovery is, by definition, restricted by the expressive power of the target language*, i.e., the representational bias.

For the reader interested in the topic, we refer to the *workflow patterns* [101, 130] mentioned earlier. These patterns help to discuss and identify the representational bias of a language.

The representational bias helps limiting the search space of possible candidate models. This can make discovery algorithms more efficient. However, it can also be used to give preference to particular types of models. It seems that existing approaches can benefit from selecting a more suitable representational bias. For instance, the α-algorithm may yield models that have deadlocks or livelocks. Here it would be nice to have a representational bias to limit the search space to only sound models (i.e., free of deadlocks and other anomalies). Unfortunately, currently, this can typically only be achieved by severely limiting the expressiveness of the modeling language or by using more time-consuming analysis techniques. Consider, for example, the so-called *block-structured* process models. A model is block-structured if it satisfies a number of syntactical requirements such that soundness is guaranteed by these requirements. Different definitions exist [37, 90, 127]. Most of these definitions require a one-to-one correspondence between splits and joins, e.g., concurrent paths created by an AND-split need to be synchronized by the corresponding AND-join. Since many real-life processes are not block structured (see, for example, Figs. 12.1 and 12.10), one should be careful to not limit the expressiveness too much. Note that techniques that turn unstructured models into block-structured process models tend to introduce many duplicate or silent activities. Therefore, such transformations do not alleviate the core problems.

5.4.2 Noise and Incompleteness

To discover a suitable process model, it is assumed that the event log contains a *representative sample of behavior*. Besides the issues mentioned in Chap. 4 (e.g., correlating events and scoping the log), there are two related phenomena that may make an event log less representative for the process being studied:

- *Noise*: the event log contains rare and infrequent behavior not representative for the typical behavior of the process.[2]
- *Incompleteness*: the event log contains too few events to be able to discover some of the underlying control-flow structures.

---

[2]Note that the definition of noise may be a bit counter-intuitive. Sometimes the term "noise" is used to refer to incorrectly logged events, i.e., errors that occurred while recording the events. Such a definition is not very meaningful as no event log will explicitly reveal such errors. Hence, we consider "outliers" as noise. Moreover, we assume that such outliers correspond to exceptional behavior rather than logging errors.

5.4.2.1 Noise

Noise, as defined in this book, does not refer to incorrect logging. When extracting event logs from various data sources one needs to try to locate data problems as early as possible. However, at some stage one needs to assume that the event log contains information on what really happened. It is impossible for a discovery algorithm do distinguish incorrect logging from exceptional events. This requires human judgment and pre- and postprocessing of the log. Therefore, we use the term "noise" to refer to rare and infrequent behavior ("outliers") rather than errors related to event logging. For process mining, it is important to filter out noise and several process discovery approaches specialize in doing so, e.g., heuristic mining, genetic mining, and fuzzy mining.

Recall the *support* and *confidence* metrics defined in the context of learning association rules. The support of a rule $X \Rightarrow Y$ indicates the applicability of the rule, i.e., the fraction of instances for which with both antecedent and consequent hold. The confidence of a rule $X \Rightarrow Y$ indicates the reliability of the rule. If rule $tea \wedge latte \Rightarrow muffin$ has a support of 0.2 and a confidence of 0.9, then 20% of the customers actually order tea, latte and muffins at the same time and 90% of the customers that order tea and latte also order a muffin. For learning association rules, we defined a threshold for both confidence and support, i.e., rules with low confidence or support are considered to be noise.

Let us informally apply the idea of confidence and support to the basic α-algorithm. Starting point for the α-algorithm is the $>_L$ relation. Recall that $a >_L b$ if and only if there is a trace in L in which a is directly followed by b. Now we can define the support of $a >_L b$ based on number of times the pattern $\langle \ldots, a, b, \ldots \rangle$ appears in the log, e.g., the fraction of cases in which the pattern occurs. Subsequently, we can use a threshold for cleaning the $>_L$ relation. The confidence of $a >_L b$ can be defined by comparing the number of times the pattern $\langle \ldots, a, b, \ldots \rangle$ appears in the log divided by the frequency of a and b. For example, suppose that $a >_L b$ has a reasonable support, e.g., the pattern $\langle \ldots, a, b, \ldots \rangle$ occurs 1000 times in the log. Moreover, a occurs 1500 times and b occurs 1200 times. Clearly, $a >_L b$ has a good confidence. However, if the pattern $\langle \ldots, a, b, \ldots \rangle$ occurs 1000 times and a and b are very frequent and occur each more than 100,000 times , then the confidence in $a >_L b$ is much lower. The $>_L$ relation is the basis for the footprint matrices as shown in Tables 5.1, 5.2, 5.3, and 5.5. Hence, by removing "noisy $a >_L b$ rules", we obtain a more representative footprint, and a better starting point for the α-algorithm. (There are several complications when doing this, however, the basic idea should be clear.) This simplified discussion shows how "noise" can be quantified and addressed when discovering process models. When presenting heuristic mining in Sect. 6.2, we return to this topic.

In the context of noise, we also talk about the 80/20 *model*. Often we are interested in the process model that can describe 80% of the behavior seen in the log. This model is typically relatively simple because the remaining 20% of the log account for 80% of the variability in the process.

5.4.2.2 Incompleteness

When it comes to process mining the notion of *completeness* is also very important. It is related to noise. However, whereas noise refers to the problem of having "too much data" (describing rare behavior), completeness refers to the problem of having "too little data".

Like in any data mining or machine learning context one cannot assume to have seen all possibilities in the "training material" (i.e., the event log at hand). For WF-net N_1 in Fig. 5.1 and event log $L_1 = [\langle a,b,c,d\rangle^3, \langle a,c,b,d\rangle^2, \langle a,e,d\rangle]$, the set of possible traces found in the log is exactly the same as the set of possible traces in the model. In general, this is not the case. For instance, the trace $\langle a,b,e,c,d\rangle$ may be possible but did not (yet) occur in the log. Process models typically allow for an exponential or even infinite number of different traces (in case of loops). Moreover, some traces may have a much lower probability than others. Therefore, it is unrealistic to assume that every possible trace is present in the event log.

The α-algorithm assumes a relatively weak notion of completeness to avoid this problem. Although N_3 has infinitely many possible firing sequences, a small log like $L_3 = [\langle a,b,c,d,e,f,b,d,c,e,g\rangle, \langle a,b,d,c,e,g\rangle^2, \langle a,b,c,d,e,f,b,c,d,e,f,b,d,c,e,g\rangle]$ can be used to construct N_3. The α-algorithm uses a local completeness notion based on $>_L$, i.e., if there are two activities a and b, and a can be directly followed by b, then this should be observed at least once in the log.

To illustrate the relevance of completeness, consider a process consisting of 10 activities that can be executed in parallel and a corresponding log that contains information about 10,000 cases. The total number of possible interleavings in the model with 10 concurrent activities is $10! = 3{,}628{,}800$. Hence, it is impossible that each interleaving is present in the log as there are fewer cases (10,000) than potential traces (3,628,800). Even if there are 3,628,800 cases in the log, it is extremely unlikely that all possible variations are present. To motivate this consider the following analogy. In a group of 365 people it is very unlikely that everyone has a different birthdate. The probability is $365!/365^{365} \approx 1.454955 \times 10^{-157} \approx 0$, i.e., incredibly small. The number of atoms in the universe is often estimated to be approximately 10^{79} [128]. Hence, the probability of picking a particular atom from the entire universe is much higher than covering all 365 days. Similarly, it is unlikely that all possible traces will occur for any process of some complexity because most processes have much more than 365 possible execution paths. In fact, because typically some sequences are less probable than others, the probability of finding all traces is even smaller. Therefore, weaker completeness notions are needed. For the process in which 10 activities can be executed in parallel, local completeness can reduce the required number of observations dramatically. For example, for the α-algorithm only $10 \times (10-1) = 90$ rather than 3,628,800 different observations are needed to construct the model.

5.4.2.3 Cross-Validation

The preceding discussion on completeness and noise shows the need for *cross-validation* as discussed in Sect. 3.6.2. The event log can be split into a *training log* and a *test log*. The training log is used to learn a process model whereas the test log is used to evaluate this model based on unseen cases. Chapter 7 will present concrete techniques for evaluating the quality of a model with respect to an event log. For example, if many traces of the test log do not correspond to possible firing sequences of the WF-net discovered based on the training log, then one can conclude that the quality of the model is low.

Also *k-fold cross-validation* can be used, i.e., the event log is split into k equal parts, e.g., $k = 10$. Then k tests are done. In each test, one of the subsets serves as a test log whereas the other $k - 1$ subsets serve together as the training log.

One of the problems for cross validation is the lack of negative examples, i.e., the log only provides examples of possible behavior and does not provide explicit examples describing scenarios that are impossible (see discussion in Sect. 3.6.3). This is complicating cross-validation. One possibility is to insert artificially generated negative events [43, 44, 81]. The basic idea is to compare the quality of the discovered model with respect to the test log containing *actual behavior* with the quality of the discovered model with respect to a test log containing *random behavior*. Ideally, the model scores much better on the log containing actual behavior than on the log containing random behavior.

Cross-validation can also be applied at the level of the footprint matrix. Simply split the event log in k parts and construct the footprint matrix for each of the k parts. If the k footprint matrices are very different (even for smaller values of k), then one can be sure that the event log does not meet the completeness requirement imposed by the α-algorithm. Such a validation can be done before constructing the process model. If there are strong indications that $>_L$ is far from complete, more advanced process mining techniques need to be applied and the results need to be interpreted with care (see also Chap. 6).

5.4.3 Four Competing Quality Criteria

Completeness and noise refer to qualities of the event log and do not say much about the quality of the discovered model. Determining the quality of a process mining result is difficult and is characterized by many dimensions. In this book, we refer to four main quality dimensions: *fitness*, *simplicity*, *precision*, and *generalization*. In this section, we review these four dimensions without providing concrete metrics. Some of the dimensions will be discussed in later chapters in more detail. However, after reading this section it should already be clear that they can indeed be quantified.

Figure 5.22 gives a high-level characterization of the four quality dimensions. A model with good *fitness* allows for the behavior seen in the event log. A model has a perfect fitness if all traces in the log can be replayed by the model from beginning to end. There are various ways of defining fitness. It can be defined at the case level, e.g., the fraction of traces in the log that can be fully replayed. It can also be defined at the event level, e.g., the fraction of events in the log that are indeed possible according to the model. When defining fitness, many design decisions need to be

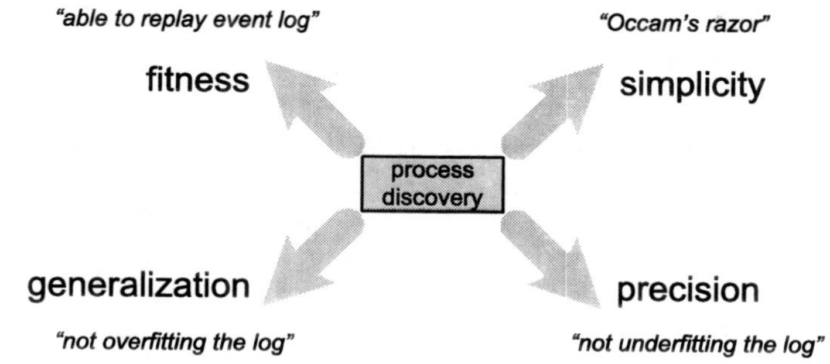

Fig. 5.22 Balancing the four quality dimensions: *fitness*, *simplicity*, *precision*, and *generalization*

made. For example: What is the penalty if a step needs to be skipped and what is the penalty if tokens remain in the WF-net after replay? Later, we will give concrete definitions for fitness.

In Sect. 3.6.1, we defined performance measures like error, accuracy, *tp*-rate, *fp*-rate, precision, recall, and F1 score. Recall, also known as the *tp*-rate, measures the proportion of positive instances indeed classified as positive (tp/p). The traces in the log are positive instances. When such an instance can be replayed by the model, then the instance is indeed classified as positive. Hence, the various notions of fitness can be seen as variants of the recall measure. Most of the notions defined in Sect. 3.6.1 cannot be used because there are *no negative examples*, i.e., *fp* and *tn* are unknown (see Fig. 3.14). Since the event log does not contain information about events that could *not* happen at a particular point in time, other notations are needed.

The *simplicity* dimension refers to *Occam's Razor*. This principle was already discussed in Sect. 3.6.3. In the context of process discovery, this means that the simplest model that can explain the behavior seen in the log, is the best model. The complexity of the model could be defined by the number of nodes and arcs in the underlying graph. Also more sophisticated metrics can be used, e.g., metrics that take the "structuredness" or "entropy" of the model into account. See [66] for an empirical evaluation of the *model complexity metrics* defined in literature. In Sect. 3.6.3, we also mentioned that this principle can be operationalized using the *Minimal Description Length* (MDL) principle [47, 129].

Fitness and simplicity alone are not adequate. This is illustrated by the so-called "flower model" shown in Fig. 5.23. The "flower Petri net" allows for any sequence starting with *start* and ending with *end* and containing any ordering of activities in between. Clearly, this model allows for all event logs used to introduce the α-algorithm. The added *start* and *end* activities in Fig. 5.23 are just a technicality to turn the "flower model" into a WF-net. Surprisingly, all event logs shown thus far ($L_1, L_2, \ldots, L_{11}$) can be replayed by this single model. This shows that the model is not very useful. In fact, the "flower model" does not contain any knowledge other than the activities in the event log. The "flower model" can be constructed based on the occurrences of activities only. The resulting model is simple and has a perfect fitness. Based on the first two quality dimensions, this model is acceptable. This shows that the fitness and simplicity criteria are necessary, but not sufficient.

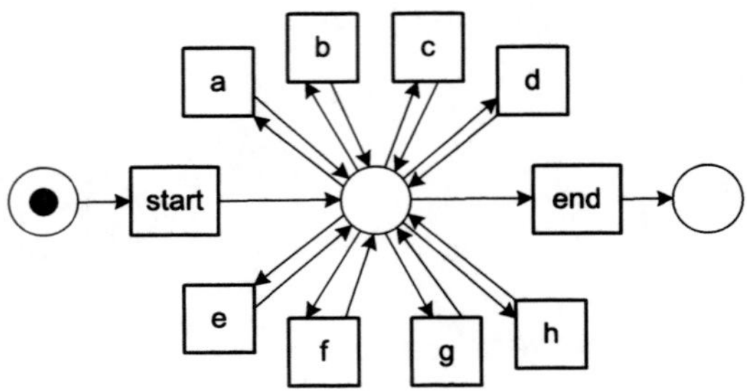

Fig. 5.23 The so-called "flower Petri net" allowing for any log containing activities $\{a, b, \dots, h\}$

If the "flower model" is on one end of the spectrum, then the "enumerating model" is on the other end of the spectrum. The enumerating model of a log simply lists all the sequences possible, i.e., there is a separate sequential process fragment for each trace in the model. At the start there is one big XOR split selecting one of the sequences and at the end these sequences are joined using one big XOR join. If such a model is represented by a Petri net and all traces are unique, then the number of transitions is equal to the number of events in the log. The "enumerating model" is simply an encoding of the log. Such a model is complex but, like the "flower model", has a perfect fitness.

Extreme models such as the "flower model" (anything is possible) and the "enumerating model" (only the log is possible) show the need for two additional dimensions. A model is *precise* if it does not allow for "too much" behavior. Clearly, the "flower model" lacks precision. A model that is not precise is "underfitting". Underfitting is the problem that the model over-generalizes the example behavior in the log, i.e., the model allows for behaviors very different from what was seen in the log.

A model should *generalize* and not restrict behavior to the examples seen in the log (like the "enumerating model"). A model that does not generalize is "overfitting". Overfitting is the problem that a very specific model is generated whereas it is obvious that the log only holds example behavior, i.e., the model explains the particular sample log, but a next sample log of the same process may produce a completely different process model.

Process mining algorithms need to strike a balance between "overfitting" and "underfitting". A model is overfitting if it does not generalize and only allows for the exact behavior recorded in the log. This means that the corresponding mining technique assumes a very strong notion of completeness: "If the sequence is not in the event log, it is not possible!". An underfitting model over-generalizes the things seen in the log, i.e., it allows for more behavior even when there are no indications in the log that suggest this additional behavior (like in Fig. 5.23).

Let us now consider some examples showing that it is difficult to balance between being too general and too specific. Consider, for example, WF-net N_4 shown in Fig. 5.6 and N_9 shown in Fig. 5.14. Both nets can produce the log $L_9 = [\langle a, c, d\rangle^{45}, \langle b, c, e\rangle^{42}]$, but only N_4 can produce $L_4 = [\langle a, c, d\rangle^{45}, \langle b, c, d\rangle^{42}, \langle a, c, e\rangle^{38}, \langle b, c, e\rangle^{22}]$. Clearly, N_4 is the logical choice for L_4. Moreover, although both nets can produce L_9, it is obvious that N_9 is a better model for L_9 as none of the 87 cases follows one of the two additional paths ($\langle b,c,d\rangle$ and $\langle a,c,e\rangle$). However, now consider $L_{12} = [\langle a,c,d\rangle^{99}, \langle b,c,d\rangle^{1}, \langle a,c,e\rangle^{2}, \langle b,c,e\rangle^{98}]$. One can argue that N_4 is a better model for L_{12} as all traces can be reproduced. However, 197 out of 200 traces can be explained by the more precise model N_9. If the three traces are seen as noise, the main behavior is captured by N_9 and not N_4. Such considerations show that there is a delicate balance between "overfitting" and "underfitting". Hence, it is difficult, if not impossible, to select "the best" model.

Figure 5.24 illustrates the preceding discussion using the example from Chap. 1. Assume that the four models that are shown are discovered based on the event log also depicted in the figure. There are 1391 cases. Of these 1391 cases, 455 followed the trace $\langle a,c,d,e,h\rangle$. The second most frequent trace is $\langle a,b,d,e,g\rangle$ which was followed by 191 cases.

If we apply the α-algorithm to this event log, we obtain model N_1 shown in Fig. 5.24. A comparison of the WF-net N_1 and the log shows that this model is quite good; it is simple and has a good fitness. Moreover, it balances between overfitting and underfitting.

The other three models in Fig. 5.24 have problems with respect to one or more quality dimensions. WF-net N_2 models only the most frequent trace, i.e., it only allows for the sequence $\langle a,c,d,e,h\rangle$. Hence, none of the other $1391 - 455 = 936$ traces fits. Moreover, the model does not generalize, i.e., N_2 is also overfitting.

WF-net N_3 is a variant of the "flower model". Only the start and end transitions are captured well. The fitness is good, the model is simple, and not overfitting. However, N_3 lacks precision, i.e., is underfitting, as for example the trace $\langle a,b,b,b,b,b,b,f,f,f,f,f,g\rangle$ is possible. This behavior seems to be very different from any of the traces in the log.

Figure 5.24 shows only a part of WF-net N_4. This model simply enumerates the 21 different traces seen in the event log. This model is precise and has a good fitness. However, WF-net N_4 is overly complex and is overfitting.

The four models in Fig. 5.24 illustrate the four quality dimensions. Each of these dimensions can be quantified as shown in [80]. In [80], a replay technique is described to quantify fitness resulting in a value between 0 (very poor fitness) to 1 (perfect fitness). A notion called "structural appropriateness" considers the simplicity dimension; the model is analyzed to see whether it is "minimal in structure". Another notion called "behavioral appropriateness" analyzes the balance between overfitting and underfitting. There are different ways to operationalize the four quality dimensions shown in Fig. 5.22. Depending on the representational bias and goals of the analyst, different metrics can be quantified.

5.4.4 Taking the Right 2-D Slice of a 3-D Reality

The simple examples shown in this chapter already illustrate that process discovery is a nontrivial problem that requires sophisticated analysis techniques. Why is pro-

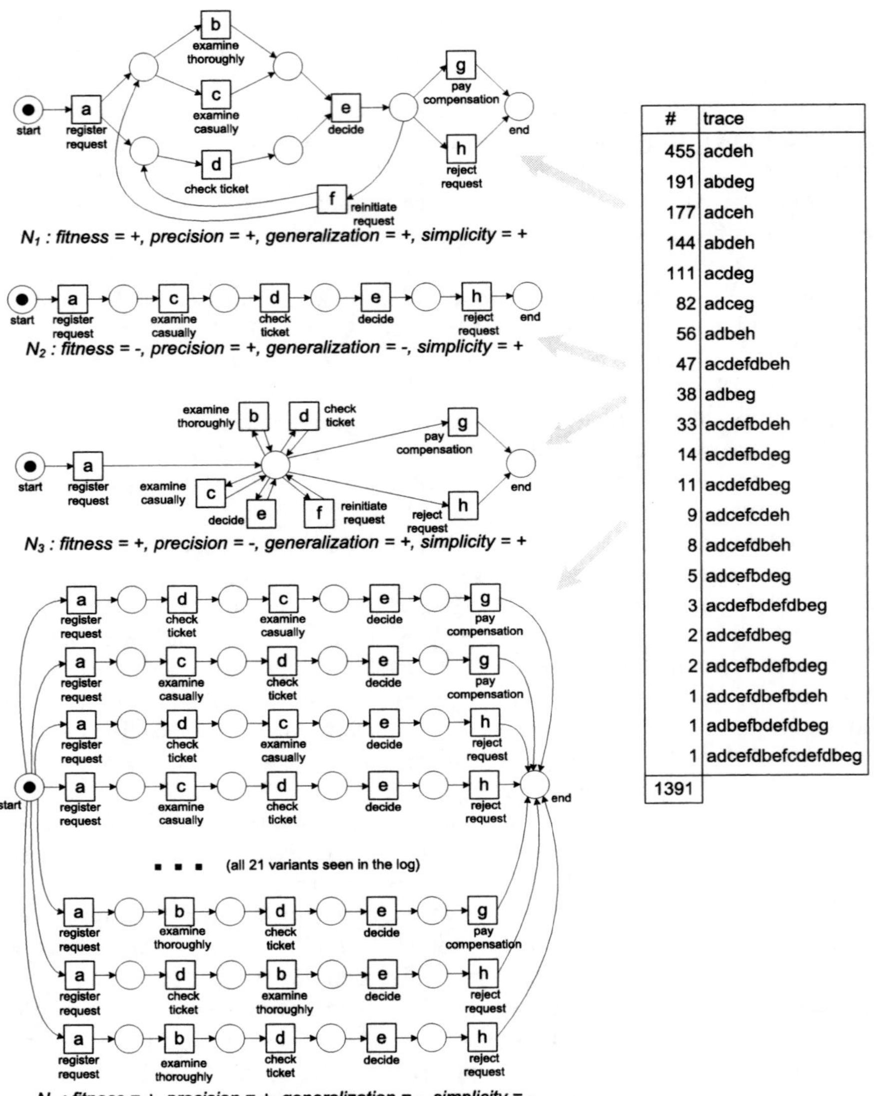

#	trace
455	acdeh
191	abdeg
177	adceh
144	abdeh
111	acdeg
82	adceg
56	adbeh
47	acdefdbeh
38	adbeg
33	acdefbdeh
14	acdefbdeg
11	acdefdbeg
9	adcefcdeh
8	adcefdbeh
5	adcefbdeg
3	acdefbdefdbeg
2	adcefdbeg
2	adcefbdefbdeg
1	adcefdbefbdeh
1	adbefbdefdbeg
1	adcefdbefcdefdbeg
1391	

Fig. 5.24 Four alternative models for the same log

cess mining such a difficult problem? There are obvious reasons that also apply to many other data mining and machine learning problems, e.g., dealing with noise and a complex and large search space. However, there are also some specific problems:

- There are *no negative examples* (i.e., a log shows what has happened but does not show what could not happen).

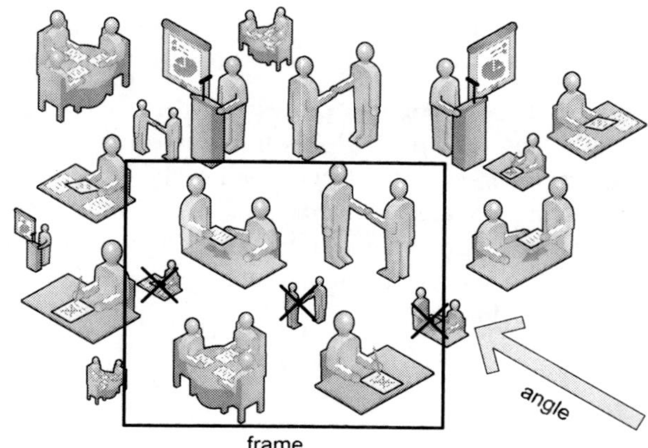

Fig. 5.25 Creating a 2-D slice of a 3-D reality: the process is *viewed* from a specific angle, the process is scoped using a *frame*, and the *resolution* determines the granularity of the resulting model

- Due to concurrency, loops, and choices the *search space has a complex structure* and the log typically contains only a *fraction* of all possible behaviors.
- There is *no clear relation between the size of a model and its behavior* (i.e., a smaller model may generate more or less behavior although classical analysis and evaluation methods typically assume some monotonicity property).

The next chapter will show several process discovery techniques that adequately address these problems.

As we will see in Part III, the discovered process model is *just the starting point* for analysis. By relating events in the log to the discovered model, all kinds of analysis are possible, e.g., checking conformance, finding bottlenecks, optimizing resource allocation, reducing undesired variability, time prediction, and generating recommendations.

One should not seek to discover *the* process model. Process models are just a *view on reality*. Whether a process model is suitable or not, ultimately depends on the questions one would like to answer. Real-life processes are complex and may have many dimensions; models only provide a view on this reality. As discussed in Sect. 4.4, this means that the "3-D reality needs to be flattened into a 2-D process model" in order to apply process mining techniques. For instance, there are many "2-D slices" that one could take of a data set involving customer orders, order lines, deliveries, payments, replenishment orders, etc. Obviously, the different slices result in the discovery of different process models. Using the metaphor of a "process view", a discovered process model views reality from a particular "angle", is "framed", and is shown using a particular "resolution":

- A discovered model views reality from a particular *angle*. For example, the same process may be analyzed from the viewpoint of a complete order, a delivery, a customer, or an order line.
- A discovered model *frames* reality. The frame determines the boundaries of the process and selects the perspectives of interest (control-flow, information, resources, etc.).

- A discovered model provides a view at a specific *resolution*. The same process can be viewed using a coarser or finer granularity showing less or more details.

Figure 5.25 illustrates the "process view" metaphor. Given a data set it is possible to *zoom in*, i.e., selecting a smaller frame and increasing resolution, resulting in a more fine-grained model of a selected part of the process. It is also possible to *zoom out*, i.e., selecting a larger frame and decreasing resolution, resulting in a more coarse-grained model covering a larger part of the end-to-end process. Both the data set used as input and the questions that need to be answered determine which 2-D slices are most useful.

Chapter 6
Advanced Process Discovery Techniques

The α-algorithm nicely illustrates some of the main ideas behind process discovery. However, this simple algorithm is unable to manage the trade-offs involving the four quality dimensions described in Chap. 5 (fitness, simplicity, precision, and generalization). To successfully apply process mining in practice, one needs to deal with noise and incompleteness. This chapter focuses on more advanced process discovery techniques. The goal is not to present one particular technique in detail, but to provide an overview of the most relevant approaches. This will assist the reader in selecting the appropriate process discovery technique. Moreover, insights into the strengths and weaknesses of the various approaches support the correct interpretation and effective use of the discovered models.

6.1 Overview

Figure 6.1 summarizes the problems mentioned in the context of the α-algorithm. Each back dot represents a trace (i.e., a sequence of activities) corresponding to one or more cases in the event log. (Recall that multiple cases may have the same corresponding trace.) An event log typically contains only a fraction of the possible behavior, i.e., the dots should only be seen as *samples* of a much larger set of possible behaviors. Moreover, one is typically primarily interested in frequent behavior and not in all possible behavior, i.e., one wants to abstract from noise and therefore not all dots need to be relevant for the process model to be constructed.

Recall that we defined noise as infrequent or exceptional behavior. It is interesting to analyze such noisy behaviors, however, when constructing the overall process model, the inclusion of infrequent or exceptional behavior leads to complex diagrams. Moreover, it is typically impossible to make reliable statements about noisy behavior given the small set of observations. Figure 6.1 distinguishes between frequent behavior (solid rectangle with rounded corners) and all behavior (dashed rectangle), i.e., normal and noisy behavior. The difference between normal and noisy behavior is a matter of definition, e.g., normal behavior could be defined as the 80%

W.M.P. van der Aalst, *Process Mining*,
DOI 10.1007/978-3-642-19345-3_6,

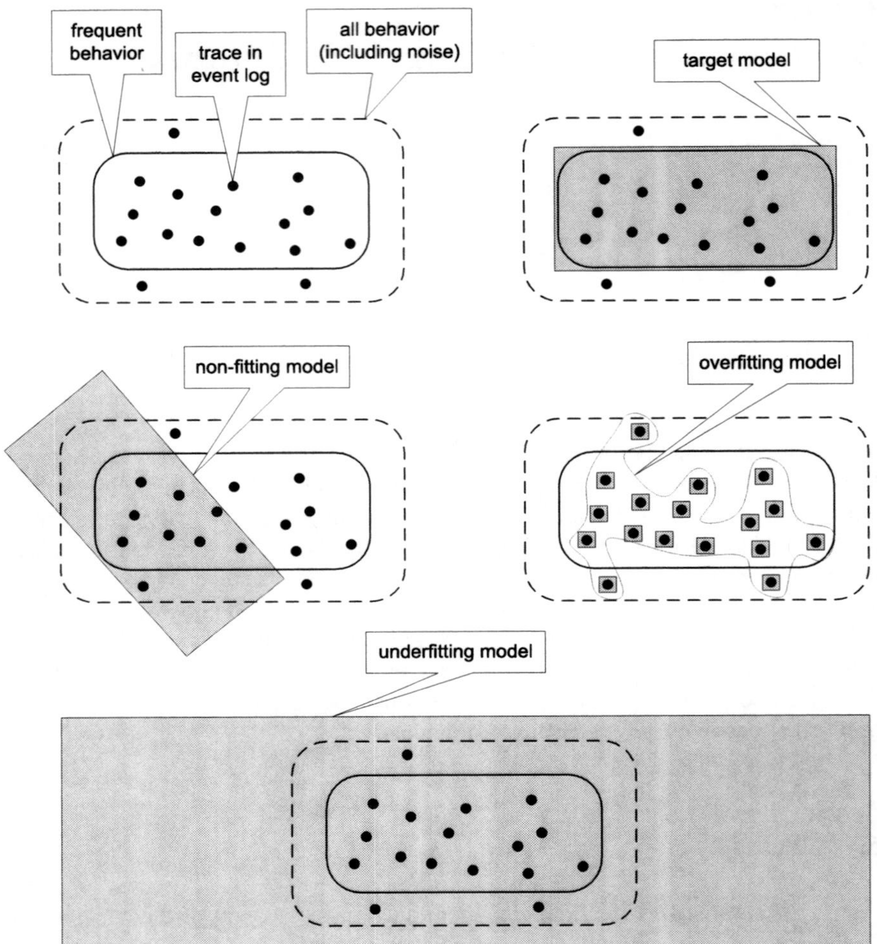

Fig. 6.1 Overview of the challenges that process discovery techniques need to address

most frequently occurring traces. Earlier we mentioned the 80/20 *model*, i.e., the process model that is able to describe 80% of the behavior seen in the log. This model is typically relatively simple because the remaining 20% of the log may easily account for 80% of the variability in the process.

Let us assume that the two rectangles with rounded corners can be determined by observing the process infinitely long and that the process does not change (i.e., no concept drift). Based on these assumptions, Fig. 6.1 sketches four discovered models depicted by shaded rectangles. These discovered models are based on the example traces in the log, i.e., the black dots. The "ideal process model" allows for the behavior coinciding with the frequent behavior seen when the process would be observed ad infinitum while being in steady state. The "non-fitting model" in

Fig. 6.1 is unable to characterize the process well as it is not even able to capture the examples in the event log used to learn the model. The "overfitting model" does not generalize and only says something about the examples in the current event log. New examples will most likely not fit into this model. The "underfitting model" lacks precision and allows for behavior that would never be seen if the process would be observed ad infinitum.

Figure 6.1 illustrates the challenges process discovery techniques need to address: How to extract a simple target model that is not underfitting, overfitting, nor non-fitting? Clearly, the α-algorithm is unable to do so. Therefore, we present more advanced approaches. However, before doing so, we describe typical characteristics of process discovery algorithms.

6.1.1 Characteristic 1: Representational Bias

The first, and probably most important, characteristic of a process discovery algorithm is its *representational bias*, i.e., the class of process models that can be discovered. For instance, the α-algorithm is only able to discover Petri nets in which each transition has a unique and visible label. Instead of Petri nets, some other representation can be used, e.g., a subclass of BPMN, EPCs, YAWL, hidden Markov models, transition systems, and causal nets. The representational bias determines the search space and potentially limits the expressiveness of the discovered model. Consider, for example, the three process models for event log $L_{11} = [\langle a,b,c\rangle^{20}, \langle a,c\rangle^{30}]$ in Fig. 5.21. If the representational bias allows for duplicate labels (two transitions with the same label) or silent (τ) transitions, a suitable WF-net can be discovered. However, if the representational bias does not allow for this, the discovery algorithm is destined to fail and will not find a suitable WF-net. The *workflow patterns* [101, 130] are a tool to discuss and identify the representational bias of a language. Here, we do not discuss the more than 40 control-flow patterns. Instead, we mention some typical representational limitations imposed by process discovery algorithms:

- *Inability to represent concurrency*. Low-level models, such as Markov models, flow charts, and transition systems, do not allow for the modeling of concurrency other than enumerating all possible interleavings. Recall that such a low-level model will need to show $2^{10} = 1024$ states and $10 \times 2^{10-1} = 5120$ transitions to model a process with 10 parallel activities. Higher level models (like Petri nets and BPMN) only need to depict 10 activities and $2 \times 10 = 20$ "local" states (states before and after each activity).
- *Inability to deal with (arbitrary) loops*. Many process discovery algorithms impose some limitations on loops, e.g., the α-algorithm needs a pre- and postprocessing step to deal with shorts loops (see Figs. 5.11 and 5.13). The "Arbitrary Cycles" pattern [101, 130] is typically not supported by algorithms that assume the underlying model to be block structured.

- *Inability to represent silent actions.* In some notations, it is impossible to model silent actions like the skipping of an activity. Although such events are not explicitly recorded in the event log, they need to be reflected in the model. This limits the expressive power as illustrated by Fig. 5.21.
- *Inability to represent duplicate actions.* In many notations, there cannot be two activities having the same label. If the same activity appears in different parts of the process, but these different instances of the same activity cannot be distinguished in the event log, then most algorithms will assume a single activity thus creating causal dependencies (e.g., nonexisting loops) that do not exist in the actual process.
- *Inability to model OR-splits/joins.* As shown in Chap. 2, YAWL, BPMN, EPCs, causal nets, etc. allow for the modeling of OR-splits and OR-joins; see for example the models depicted in Figs. 2.6, 2.10 and 2.13 using such constructs. If the representational bias of a discovery algorithm does not allow for OR-splits and OR-joins, then the discovered model may be more complex or the algorithm is unable to find a suitable model.
- *Inability to represent non-free-choice behavior.* Most algorithms do not allow for non-free-choice constructs, i.e., constructs where concurrency and choice meet. Figure 5.1 uses a non-free-choice construct, because places $p1$ and $p2$ serve both as an XOR-split (to choose between doing just e or both b and c) and as an AND-split (to start the concurrent activities b and c). This WF-net can be discovered by the α-algorithm. However, non-free-choice constructs can also represent non-local dependencies as is illustrated by the WF-net in Fig. 5.14. Such WF-nets cannot be discovered by the basic α-algorithm. Whereas WF-nets can express non-free-choice behavior, many discovery algorithms use a representation that cannot do so.
- *Inability to represent hierarchy.* Most process discovery algorithms work on "flat" models. A notable exception is the Fuzzy Miner [50] that extracts hierarchical models. Activities that have a lower frequency but that are closely related to other low frequent activities are grouped into subprocesses. The representational bias determines whether, in principle, hierarchical models can be discovered or not.

6.1.2 Characteristic 2: Ability to Deal with Noise

Noisy behavior, i.e., exceptional/infrequent behavior, should not be included in the discovered model (see Sect. 5.4.2). First of all, users typically want to see the mainstream behavior. Second, it is impossible to infer meaningful information on activities or patterns that are extremely rare. Therefore, the more mature algorithms address this issue by abstracting from exceptional/infrequent behavior. Noise can be removed by preprocessing the log, or the discovery algorithm can abstract from noise while constructing the model. The ability or inability to deal with noise is an important characteristic of a process discovery algorithm.

6.1.3 Characteristic 3: Completeness Notion Assumed

Related to noise is the issue of *completeness*. Most process discovery algorithms make an implicit or explicit completeness assumption. For example, the α-algorithm assumes that the relation $>_L$ is complete, i.e., if one activity can be directly followed by another activity, then this should be seen at least once in the log. Other algorithms make other completeness assumptions. Some algorithms assume that the event log contains all possible traces, i.e., a very strong completeness assumption. This is very unrealistic and results in overfitting models. Algorithms that are characterized by a strong completeness assumption tend to overfit the log. A completeness assumption that is too weak tends to result in underfitting models.

6.1.4 Characteristic 4: Approach Used

There are many different approaches to do the actual discovery. It is impossible to give a complete overview. Moreover, several approaches are partially overlapping in terms of the techniques used. Nevertheless, we briefly discuss four characteristic families of approaches.

6.1.4.1 Direct Algorithmic Approaches

The first family of process discovery approaches extracts some *footprint* from the event log and uses this footprint to *directly* construct a process model. The α-algorithm [103] is an example of such an approach: relation $>_L$ is extracted from the log and based on this relation a Petri net is constructed. There are several variants of the α-algorithm [30, 125, 126] using a similar approach. Approaches using so-called "language-based regions" [8, 18, 115] infer places by converting the event log into a system of inequations. In this case, the system of inequations can be seen as the footprint used to construct the Petri net. See [119] for a survey of process mining approaches producing a Petri net. The approaches described in [50, 123, 124] also extract footprints from event logs. However, these approaches take frequencies into account to address issues related to noise and incompleteness.

6.1.4.2 Two-Phase Approaches

The second family of process discovery approaches uses a two-step approach in which first a "low-level model" (e.g., a transition system or Markov model) is constructed. In the second step, the low-level model is converted into a "high-level model" that can express concurrency and other (more advanced) control-flow patterns. An example of such an approach is described in [111]. Here a transition system is extracted from the log using a customizable abstraction mechanism. Subsequently, the transition system is converted into a Petri net using so-called "state-based regions" [23]. The resulting model can be visualized as a Petri net, but can also be converted into other notations (e.g., BPMN and EPCs). Similar approaches can be envisioned using hidden Markov models [5]. Using an Expectation-Maximization (EM) algorithm such as the Baum–Welch algorithm, the "most likely" Markov model can be derived from a log. Subsequently this model is converted into high-level model. A drawback of such approaches is that the representational bias cannot be exploited during discovery. Moreover, some of the mappings are "lossy", i.e., the process model needs to be slightly modified to fit the target language. These algorithms also tend to be rather slow compared to more direct algorithmic approaches.

6.1.4.3 Computational Intelligence Approaches

Techniques originating from the field of *computational intelligence* form the basis for the third family of process discovery approaches. Examples of techniques are ant colony optimization, genetic programming, genetic algorithms, simulated annealing, reinforcement learning, machine learning, neural networks, fuzzy sets, rough sets, and swarm intelligence. These techniques have in common that they use an evolutionary approach, i.e., the log is not directly converted into a model but uses an iterative procedure to mimic the process of natural evaluation. It is impossible to provide an overview of computational intelligence techniques here. Instead we refer to [5, 67] and use the *genetic process mining* approach described in [31] as an example. This approach starts with an initial population of individuals. Each individual corresponds to a randomly generated process model. For each individual a fitness value is computed describing how well the model fits with the log. Populations evolve by selecting the fittest individuals and generating new individuals using genetic operators such as crossover (combining parts of two individuals) and mutation (random modification of an individual). The fitness gradually increases from generation to generation. The process stops once an individual (i.e., model) of acceptable quality is found.

6.1.4.4 Partial Approaches

The approaches described thus far produce a complete end-to-end process model. It is also possible to focus on rules or frequent patterns. In Sect. 3.5.1, an approach for *mining of sequential patterns* was described [89]. This approach is similar to the discovery of association rules, however, now the order of events is taken into account. Another technique using an Apriori-like approach is the *discovery of frequent episodes* [63] described in Sect. 3.5.2. Here a sliding window is used to analyze how frequent an "episode" (i.e., a partial order) is appearing. Similar approaches exist to learn declarative (LTL-based) languages like *Declare* [108].

In the remainder, we discuss three approaches in more detail: heuristic mining (Sect. 6.2), genetic process mining (Sect. 6.3), and region-based mining (Sect. 6.4). The chapter concludes with a historical perspective on process discovery going back to the classical work of Marc Gold, Anil Nerode, Alan Biermann, and others.

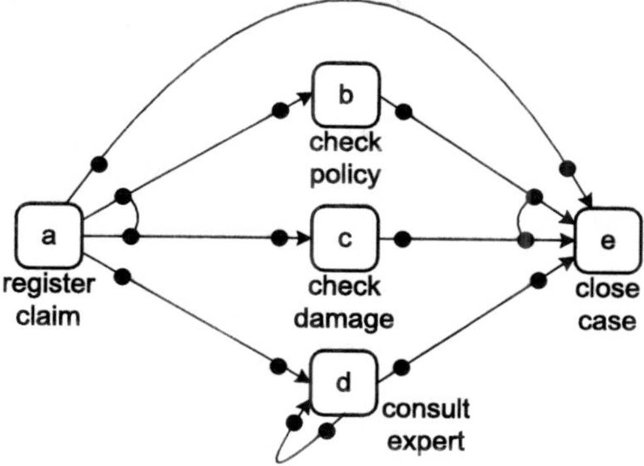

Fig. 6.2 Causal net modeling the handling of insurance claims

6.2 Heuristic Mining

Heuristic mining algorithms as described in [123, 124] use a representation similar to causal nets (see Sect. 2.2.7). Moreover, these algorithms take frequencies of events and sequences into account when constructing a process model. The basic idea is that infrequent paths should not be incorporated into the model. Both the representational bias provided by causal nets and the usage of frequencies makes the approach much more robust than most other approaches.

6.2.1 Causal Nets Revisited

In Sect. 2.2.7, we introduced the notion of causal nets, also referred to as C-nets. Figure 6.2 shows another example of a C-net. There is one start activity a representing the registration of an insurance claim. There is one end activity e that closes the case. Activity a has three output bindings: $\{b, c\}$, $\{d\}$ and $\{e\}$, indicating that after completing a, activities b and c are activated, d is activated, or e is activated. Recall that only valid sequences are considered (see Definition 2.11) when reasoning about the behavior of a C-net. A binding sequence is valid if the sequence (a) starts with start activity $a_i = a$, (b) ends with end activity $a_o = e$, (c) only removes obligations that are pending, and (d) ends without any pending obligations. Suppose that a occurs with output binding $\{b, c\}$. After executing $\langle(a, \emptyset, \{b, c\})\rangle$, there are two pending obligations: (a, b) and (a, c). This indicates that in the future b should occur with a in its input binding. Similarly, c should occur with a in its input binding. Executing b removes the obligation (a, b), but creates a new obligation (b, e), etc. An example of a valid sequence is $\langle(a, \emptyset, \{b, c\}), (b, \{a\}, \{e\}), (c, \{a\}, \{e\}), (e, \{b, c\}, \emptyset)\rangle$. At the end, there are no pending obligations. $\langle(a, \emptyset, \{d\}), (d, \{a\}, \{d\}), (d, \{d\}, \{e\}), (e, \{d\}, \emptyset)\rangle$ is another valid sequence. Because of the loop involving d, there are infinitely many valid sequences.

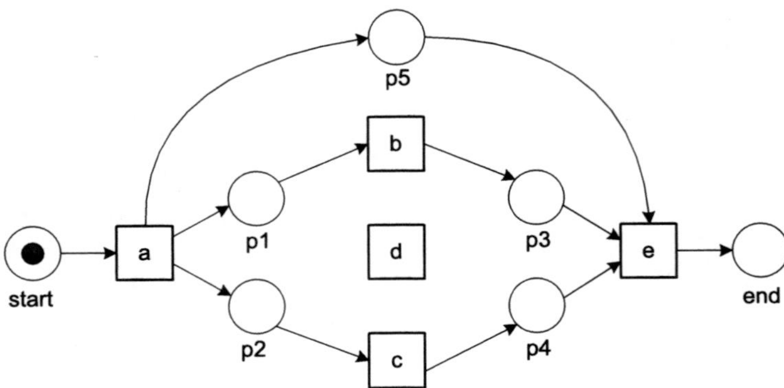

Fig. 6.3 WF-net constructed by the α-algorithm. The resulting model does not allow for $\langle a, e\rangle$, $\langle a, b, e\rangle$, $\langle a, c, e\rangle$, $\langle a, d, e\rangle$, $\langle a, d, d, e\rangle$, and $\langle a, d, d, d, e\rangle$

The process modeled by Fig. 6.2 cannot be expressed as a WF-net (assuming that each transition has a unique visible label). This illustrates that C-nets are a more suitable representation for process discovery.

There are subtle differences between the notation used in [123, 124] and the C-nets used in this book. Whereas C-nets are very similar to the notation used in [123], there are relevant differences with [124]. In the original heuristic mining algorithm, input and output bindings are a conjunction of mutually exclusive disjunctions, e.g., $O(t) = \{\{a, b\}, \{b, c\}, \{b, d\}\}$ means that t will activate a or b, and b or c, and b or d. These are exclusive or's. Hence, using the C-net semantics provided in Sect. 2.2.7 this corresponds to $O(t) = \{\{a, c, d\}, \{b\}\}$, i.e., either just b is activated or a, c and d are activated. C-nets are more intuitive and also more expressive (in a practical sense) than the original heuristic nets. Therefore, we use C-nets in the remainder.

6.2.2 Learning the Dependency Graph

To illustrate the basic concepts used by heuristic mining algorithms, we use the following event log:

$$L = \left[\langle a, e\rangle^5, \langle a, b, c, e\rangle^{10}, \langle a, c, b, e\rangle^{10}, \langle a, b, e\rangle^1, \langle a, c, e\rangle^1, \langle a, d, e\rangle^{10}, \langle a, d, d, e\rangle^2, \langle a, d, d, d, e\rangle^1\right]$$

If we assume the three traces with frequency one to be noise, then the remaining 37 traces in the log correspond to valid sequences of the C-net in Fig. 6.2. Before explaining how to derive such a C-net, we first apply the α-algorithm to event log L. The result is shown in Fig. 6.3.

As expected, the α-algorithm does not infer a suitable model. The model does not allow for frequent traces, such as $\langle a, e\rangle$ and $\langle a, d, e\rangle$. By accident, the model also does not allow for infrequent traces such as $\langle a, b, e\rangle$, $\langle a, c, e\rangle$, and $\langle a, d, d, d, e\rangle$.

Table 6.1 Frequency of the "directly follows" relation in event log L: $|x >_L y|$ is the number of times x is directly followed by y in L

$\|>_L\|$	a	b	c	d	e
a	0	11	11	13	5
b	0	0	10	0	11
c	0	10	0	0	11
d	0	0	0	4	13
e	0	0	0	0	0

There are two main problems. One problem is that the α-algorithm has a representational bias that does not allow for skipping activities (e.g., jumping from a to e) and cannot handle the requirement that d should be executed at least once when selected. The other problem is that the α-algorithm does not consider frequencies. Therefore, we use C-nets and take frequencies into account for heuristic mining.

Table 6.1 shows the number of times one activity is directly followed by another activity. For instance, $|d >_L d| = 4$, i.e., in the entire log d is followed four times by another d (two times in $\langle a, d, d, e\rangle^2$ and two times in $\langle a, d, d, d, e\rangle^1$). Using Table 6.1, we can calculate the value of the *dependency relation* between any pair of activities.

Definition 6.1 (Dependency measure) Let L be an event log[1] over $\mathscr{A}$ and $a, b \in \mathscr{A}$. $|a >_L b|$ is the number of times a is directly followed by b in L, i.e.,

$$|a >_L b| = \sum_{\sigma \in L} L(\sigma) \times \left|\left\{1 \leq i < |\sigma| \mid \sigma(i) = a \wedge \sigma(i+1) = b\right\}\right|$$

$|a \Rightarrow_L b|$ is the value of the dependency relation between a and b:

$$|a \Rightarrow_L b| = \begin{cases} \frac{|a>_L b| - |b>_L a|}{|a>_L b| + |b>_L a| + 1} & \text{if } a \neq b \\ \frac{|a>_L a|}{|a>_L a| + 1} & \text{if } a = b \end{cases}$$

$|a \Rightarrow_L b|$ produces a value between -1 and 1. If $|a \Rightarrow_L b|$ is close to 1, then there is a strong positive dependency between a and b, i.e., a is often the cause of b. A value close to 1 can only be reached if a is often directly followed by b but b is hardly ever directly followed by a. If $|a \Rightarrow_L b|$ is close to -1, then there is a strong negative dependency between a and b, i.e., b is often the cause of a. There is a special case for $|a \Rightarrow_L a|$. If a is often followed by a this suggests a loop and a strong reflexive dependency. However, $\frac{|a>_L a| - |a>_L a|}{|a>_L a| + |a>_L a| + 1} = 0$ by definition. Therefore, the following formula is used: $|a \Rightarrow_L a| = \frac{|a>_L a|}{|a>_L a|+1}$. Table 6.2 shows the dependency measures for event log L.

Using the information in Tables 6.1 and 6.2, we can derive the so-called *dependency graph*. The dependency graph corresponds to the dependency relation

[1]Note that in this chapter we again assume that the event log is simple (like in Chap. 5), because at this stage we still abstract from the other perspectives.

Table 6.2 Dependency measures between the five activities based on event log L

$\|\Rightarrow_L\|$	a	b	c	d	e
a	$\frac{0}{0+1}=0$	$\frac{11-0}{11+0+1}=0.92$	$\frac{11-0}{11+0+1}=0.92$	$\frac{13-0}{13+0+1}=0.93$	$\frac{5-0}{5+0+1}=0.83$
b	$\frac{0-11}{0+11+1}=-0.92$	$\frac{0}{0+1}=0$	$\frac{10-10}{10+10+1}=0$	$\frac{0-0}{0+0+1}=0$	$\frac{11-0}{11+0+1}=0.92$
c	$\frac{0-11}{0+11+1}=-0.92$	$\frac{10-10}{10+10+1}=0$	$\frac{0}{0+1}=0$	$\frac{0-0}{0+0+1}=0$	$\frac{11-0}{11+0+1}=0.92$
d	$\frac{0-13}{0+13+1}=-0.93$	$\frac{0-0}{0+0+1}=0$	$\frac{0-0}{0+0+1}=0$	$\frac{4}{4+1}=0.80$	$\frac{13-0}{13+0+1}=0.93$
e	$\frac{0-5}{0+5+1}=-0.83$	$\frac{0-11}{0+11+1}=-0.92$	$\frac{0-11}{0+11+1}=-0.92$	$\frac{0-13}{0+13+1}=-0.93$	$\frac{0}{0+1}=0$

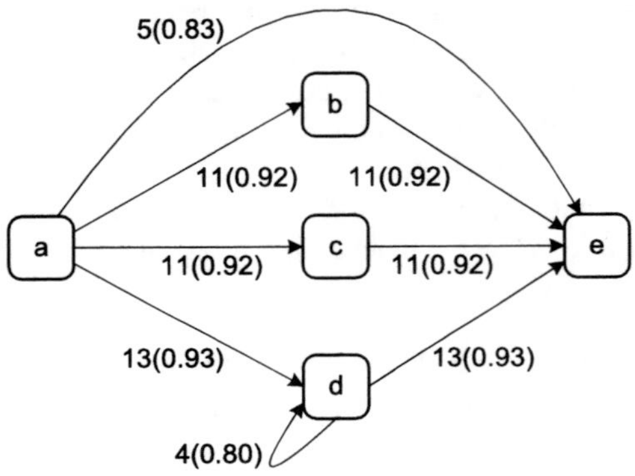

Fig. 6.4 Dependency graph using a threshold of 2 for $|>_L|$ and 0.7 for $|\Rightarrow_L|$: *each arc* shows the $|>_L|$ value and the $|\Rightarrow_L|$ value between brackets. For example, $|a >_L d| = 13$ and $|a \Rightarrow_L d| = 0.93$

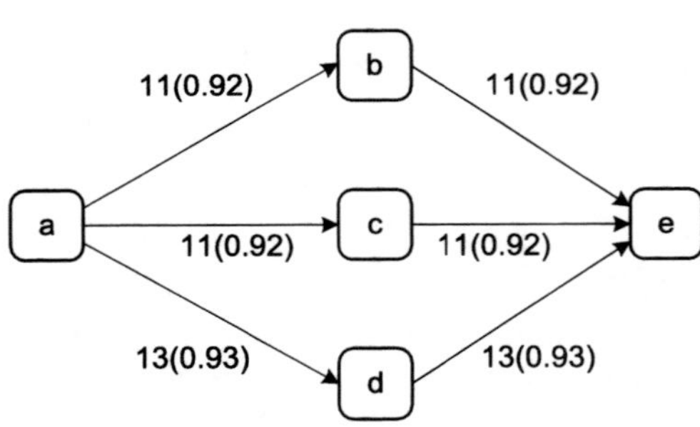

Fig. 6.5 Dependency graph using a threshold of 5 for $|>_L|$ and 0.9 for $|\Rightarrow_L|$. The self loop involving d disappeared because $|d >_L d| = 4 < 5$ and $|d \Rightarrow_L d| = 0.80 < 0.9$. The connection between a and e disappeared because $|a \Rightarrow_L e| = 0.83 < 0.9$

$D \subseteq A \times A$ in Definition 2.8. In a dependency graph, only arcs are shown that meet certain *thresholds*. The dependency graph shown in Fig. 6.4 uses a threshold of 2 for $| >_L |$ and 0.7 for $| \Rightarrow_L |$, i.e., an arc between x and y is only included if $|x >_L y| \geq 2$ and $|x \Rightarrow_L y| \geq 0.7$.

Figure 6.5 shows another dependency graph based on Tables 6.1 and 6.2 using higher thresholds. As a result, two arcs disappear. Obviously, the dependency graph does not show the routing logic, e.g., one cannot see that after a, both b and c can be executed concurrently. Nevertheless, the dependency graph reveals the "backbone" of the process model.

The two dependency graphs show that, for a given event log, different models can be generated by adjusting the thresholds. This way the user can decide to focus on the mainstream behavior or to also include low frequent (i.e., noisy) behavior. In Figs. 6.4 and 6.5 the set of activities is the same. The two thresholds cannot be used to remove low frequent activities. This should be done by preprocessing the event log. For example, one could decide to concentrate on the most frequent activities and simply remove all other activities from the event log before calculating the dependency measures. Other techniques such as the one used by the Fuzzy Miner [50] remove such activities while realizing the dependency graph.

As shown in [123, 124], various refinements can be used to improve the dependency graph. For instance, it is possible to better deal with loops of length two and long distance dependencies. (See discussion in context of the processes shown in Figs. 5.13 and 5.14.)

6.2.3 Learning Splits and Joins

The goal of heuristic mining is to extract a C-net $C = (A, a_i, a_o, D, I, O)$ from the event log. The nodes of the dependency graph correspond to the set of activities A. The arcs of the dependency graph correspond to the dependency relation D. In a C-net, there is a unique start activity a_i and a unique end activity a_o. This is just a technicality. One can preprocess the log and insert artificial start and end events to each trace. Hence the assumption that there is a unique start activity a_i and a unique end activity a_o imposes no practical limitations. In fact, it is convenient to have a clear start and end. We also assume that in the dependency graph all activities are on a path from a_i to a_o. Activities that are not on such a path should be removed or the thresholds need to be adjusted locally such that a minimal set of connections is established. It makes no sense to include activities that are not on a path from a_i to a_o: such an activity would be dead or could be active before the case starts, and does not contribute to the completion of the case. Therefore, we can assume that, by constructing the dependency graph, we already have the core structure of the C-net: (A, a_i, a_o, D). Hence, only the functions $I \in A \rightarrow AS$ and $O \in A \rightarrow AS$ need to be derived to complete the C-net.

Given a dependency graph (A, a_i, a_o, D), we define $\circ a = \{a' \in A \mid (a', a) \in D\}$ and $a\circ = \{a' \in A \mid (a, a') \in D\}$ for any $a \in A$. Clearly, $I(a_i) = O(a_o) = \{\emptyset\}$. There are $2^{|\circ a|} - 1$ potential elements for $I(a)$ for any $a \neq a_i$ and $2^{|a\circ|} - 1$ potential elements for $O(a)$ for any $a \neq a_o$. Consider, for example, the dependency graph shown in Fig. 6.4. $a\circ = \{b, c, d, e\}$. Hence, $O(a)$ has $2^4 - 1 = 15$ potential output bindings: $\{b\}$, $\{c\}$, $\{d\}$, $\{e\}$, $\{b, c\}$, $\{b, d\}, \ldots, \{b, c, d, e\}$. $O(b)$ has only $2^1 - 1 = 1$ possible element: $\{e\}$. $I(b)$ also has just one possible element: $\{a\}$. $O(d)$ has $2^2 - 1 = 3$ potential output bindings: $\{d\}$, $\{e\}$, and $\{d, e\}$. $I(d)$ also has $2^2 - 1 = 3$ potential input bindings: $\{a\}$, $\{d\}$, and $\{a, d\}$.

If there is just one potential binding element, then this element should be taken. Hence, $I(b) = \{\{a\}\}$, $I(c) = \{\{a\}\}$, $O(b) = \{\{e\}\}$, and $O(c) = \{\{e\}\}$. For the other

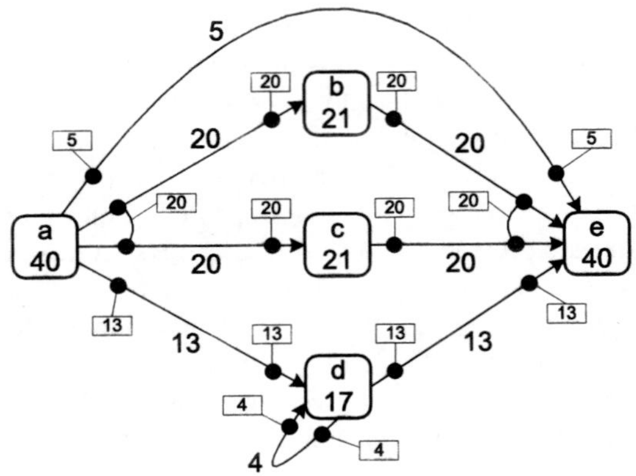

Fig. 6.6 C-net derived from the event log L. *Each node* shows the frequency of the corresponding activity. *Every arc* has a frequency showing how often both activities agreed on a common binding. The frequencies of input and output bindings are also depicted, e.g., 20 of the 40 occurrences of a were followed by the concurrent execution of b and c

input and output bindings, subsets need to be selected based on the event log. To do this, the event log is replayed on the dependency graph to see how frequent output sets are triggered.

Consider for example $O(d)$. In event log L, activity d is four times followed by just d and 13 times by just e; d is never followed by both d and e. Therefore, $\{e\}$ is definitely included in $O(d)$ because it is the most frequent output binding. $\{d\}$ may be included depending on the threshold for including bindings. If we assume that both possible bindings are included, then $O(d) = \{\{d\}, \{e\}\}$. Similarly, we find $I(d) = \{\{a\}, \{d\}\}$. Let us now consider $O(a)$. As indicated earlier, there are $2^4 - 1 = 15$ possible output bindings. Replaying the event log on the dependency graph shows that a is 5 times followed by e (in traces $\langle a, e\rangle^5$), a is 20 times followed by both b and c (in traces $\langle a, b, c, e\rangle^{10}$ and $\langle a, c, b, e\rangle^{10}$), and a is 13 times followed by d (in traces $\langle a, d, e\rangle^{10}$, $\langle a, d, d, e\rangle^2$, and $\langle a, d, d, d, e\rangle^1$). Activity a is once followed by just b (in trace $\langle a, b, e\rangle$) and is once followed by just c (in trace $\langle a, c, e\rangle$). Let us assume that the latter two output bindings are below a preset threshold. Then $O(a) = \{\{b, c\}, \{d\}, \{e\}\}$, i.e., of the 15 possible output bindings only three are frequent enough to be included.

Many replay strategies are possible to determine the frequency of a binding. In [78, 123, 124] heuristics are used to select the bindings to be included. In [2], a variant of the A^* algorithm is used to find an "optimal" replay of traces on the dependency graph. The semantics of a C-net are global, i.e., the validity of a binding sequence cannot be determined locally (like in a Petri net). We refer to [2, 78, 123, 124] for example replay strategies.

By replaying the event log on the dependency graph, we can estimate the frequencies of input and output bindings. Using thresholds, it is possible to exclude bindings based on their frequencies. This results in functions I and O, thus completing the C-net. Figure 6.6 shows the C-net based on the dependency graph in Fig. 6.4. As shown $O(a) = \{\{b, c\}, \{d\}, \{e\}\}$ and $I(e) = \{\{a\}, \{b, c\}, \{d\}\}$. Bindings $\{b\}$ and $\{c\}$ are not included in $O(a)$ and $I(e)$ because they occur only once (below threshold). Figure 6.6 also shows the frequencies of activities, dependencies, and bindings. For example, activity a occurred 40 times. The output binding $\{b, c\}$ of a

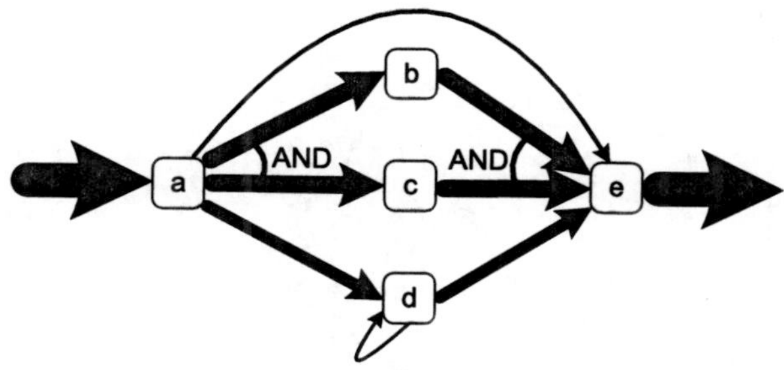

Fig. 6.7 Alternative visualization of the C-net clearly showing the "highways" in the process model

occurred 20 times. Activity d occurred 17 times: 13 times triggered by a and 4 times by d itself. Activity b occurred 21 times. The frequency of the only input binding $\{a\}$ is only 20. This difference is caused by the exclusion of the infrequent output binding $\{b\}$ of a (this binding occurs only in trace $\langle a, b, e \rangle$). A similar difference can be found for activity c.

Figure 6.7 provides a more intuitive visualization of the C-net of Fig. 6.6. Now the thickness of the arcs corresponds to the frequencies of the corresponding paths. Such visualizations are important to get insight into the main process flows. In Chap. 13, we will adopt the metaphor of a roadmap to visualize process models. A roadmap highlights highways using thick lines and bright colors. At the same time insignificant roads are not shown. Figure 6.7 illustrates that the same can be done using heuristic mining.

The approach presented in this section is quite generic and can be applied to other representations. A notable example is the *fuzzy mining* approach described in [49, 50]. This approach provides an extensible set of parameters to determine which activities and arcs need to be included. Moreover, the approach can construct hierarchical models, i.e., less frequent activities may be moved to subprocesses. Also the metaphor of a roadmap is exploited to create process models that can be understood easily while providing information on the frequency and importance of activities and paths (cf. Sect. 13.1.3).

6.3 Genetic Process Mining

The α-algorithm and techniques for heuristic and fuzzy mining provide process models in a direct and deterministic manner. *Evolutionary approaches* use an iterative procedure to mimic the process of natural evolution. Such approaches are not deterministic and depend on randomization to find new alternatives. This section describes *genetic process mining* [31] as an example of a process discovery approach using a technique from the field of computational intelligence.

Figure 6.8 shows an overview of the approach used in [31]. Like in any genetic algorithm there are four main steps: (a) initialization, (b) selection, (c) reproduction, and (d) termination.

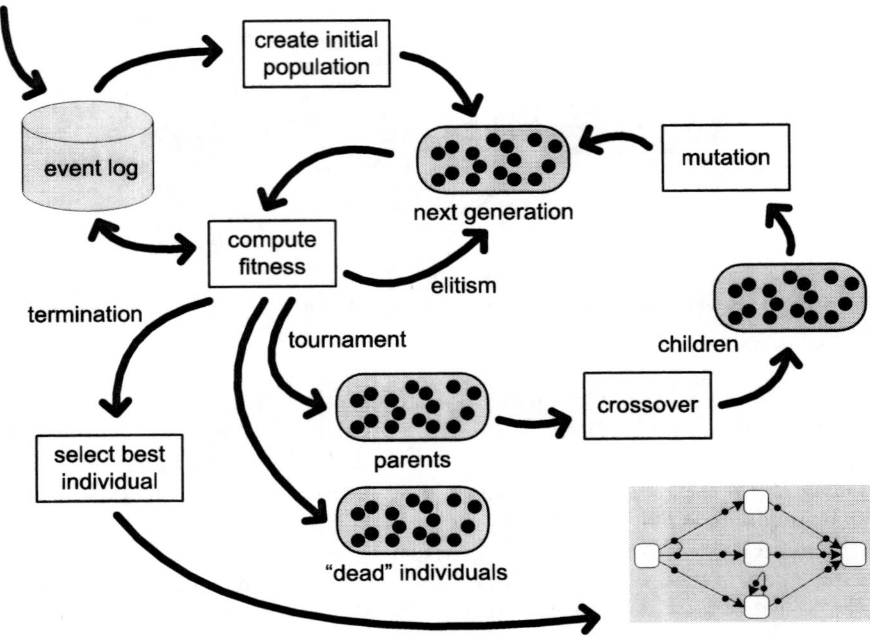

Fig. 6.8 Overview of the approach used for genetic process mining

In the *initialization* step, the initial population is created. This is the first generation of individuals to be used. Here an individual is a process model. Using the activity names appearing in the log, process models are created *randomly*. There may be hundreds or even thousands individuals in each generation. The process models (i.e., individuals) in the initial population may have little to do with the event log; the activity names are the same but the behaviors of the initial models are likely to be very different from the behavior seen in the event log. However, "by accident" the generated models may have parts that fit parts of the event log due random effects and the large number of individuals.

In the *selection* step, the fitness of each individual is computed. A fitness function determines the quality of the individual in relation to the log.[2] In Sect. 5.4.3, we discussed different ways of measuring the quality of a model. A simple criterion is the proportion of traces in the log that can be replayed by the model. This is not a good fitness function, because it is very likely that none of the models in the initial population can replay any of the traces in the event log. Moreover, using this criterion an over-general model like the "flower model" would have a high fitness.

[2]Note that we overload the term "fitness" in this book. On the one hand, we use it to refer to the ability to replay the event log (see Sects. 5.4.3 and 7.2). On the other hand, we use it for the selection of individuals in genetic process mining. Note that the latter interpretation includes the former, but also adds other elements of the four criteria mentioned in Sect. 5.4.3.

Therefore, a more refined fitness function needs to be used that also rewards the partial correctness of the model and takes into account all four competing quality criteria described in Sect. 5.4.3. The best individuals, i.e., the process models having the highest fitness value are moved to the next generation. This is called *elitism*. For instance, the best 1% of the current generation is passed on to the next generation without any modifications. Through *tournaments*, "parents" are selected for creating new individuals. Tournaments among individuals and elitism should make sure that the "genetic material of the best process models" has the highest probability of being used for the next generation: *survival of the fittest*. As a result, individuals with a poor fitness are unlikely to survive. Figure 6.8 refers to such models as "dead" individuals.

In the *reproduction* phase, the selected parent individuals are used to create new offspring. Here two genetic operators are used: *crossover* and *mutation*. For crossover two individuals are taken and used to create two new models; these end up in the pool with "child models" shown in Fig. 6.8. These child models share parts of the genetic material of their parents. The resulting children are then modified using mutation, e.g., randomly adding or deleting a causal dependency. Mutation is used to insert new generic material in the next generation. Without mutation, evolution beyond the genetic material in the initial population is impossible.

Through reproduction (i.e., crossover and mutation) and elitism, a new generation is created. For the models in this generation the fitness is computed. Again the best individuals move on to the next round (elitism) or are used to produce new offspring. This is repeated and the expectation is that the "quality" of each generation gets better and better. The evolution process *terminates* when a satisfactory solution is found, i.e., a model having at least the desired fitness. Depending on the event log it may take a very long time to converge. In fact, due to the representational bias and noise in the event log there may not be a model that has the desired level of fitness. Therefore, other termination criteria may be added (e.g., a maximum number of generations or stopping when 10 successive generations do not produce better individuals). When terminating, a model with the best fitness is returned.

The approach described in Fig. 6.8 is very general. When actually implementing a genetic process mining algorithm the following design choices need to made:

- *Representation of individuals*. Each individual corresponds to a process model described in a particular language, e.g., Petri nets, C-nets, BPMN, or EPCs. This choice is important as it determines the class of processes that can be discovered (representational bias). Moreover, it should be possible to define suitable genetic operators for the representation chosen. In [31], a variant of C-nets is used.
- *Initialization*. For the initial population, models need to be generated randomly. In [31], two approaches are proposed: (a) an approach where with a certain probability a causal dependency between two activities is inserted to create C-nets and (b) an approach in which a randomized variant of heuristic mining is used to create an initial population with a higher average fitness than purely randomly generated C-nets.
- *Fitness function*. Here, the challenge is to define a function that balances the four competing quality criteria described in Sect. 5.4.3. Many fitness functions can be

defined. The fitness function drives the evolution process and can be used to favor particular models. In [31], the proportion of events in the log that can be parsed by the model is computed. This is combined with penalties for having many enabled activities (cf. the flower model in Fig. 5.23).

- *Selection strategy* (*tournament and elitism*). The genetic algorithm needs to determine the fraction of individuals that go to the next round without any changes. Through elitism, it is ensured that good models do not get lost due to crossover or mutation. There are different approaches to select parents for crossover. In [31], parents are selected by randomly taking five individuals and then selecting the best one, i.e., a tournament among five randomly selected models is used.
- *Crossover*. The goal of crossover is to recombine existing genetic material. The basic idea is to create a new process model that uses parts of its two parent models. In [29, 31], both parents are C-nets having the same set of activities. One of these common activities is selected randomly, say a. Let $I_1(a)$ and $O_1(a)$ be the possible bindings of one parent, and let $I_2(a)$ and $O_2(a)$ be the potential bindings of the other parent. Now parts of $I_1(a)$ are swapped with parts of $I_2(a)$ and parts of $O_1(a)$ are swapped with parts of $O_2(a)$. Subsequently, both C-nets are repaired as bindings need to be consistent among activities. The crossover of two parent models results in two new child models. These child models may be mutated before being added to the next generation.
- *Mutation*. The goal of mutation is to randomly insert new genetic material. In [29, 31], each activity in each child resulting from crossover has a small probability of being selected for mutation. If this is the case, say a is selected for mutation, then $I(a)$ or $O(a)$ is randomly modified by adding or removing potential bindings.

The above list shows that many design decisions need to be taken when developing a genetic process mining algorithm. We refer to [29, 31] for concrete examples. An essential choice is the representation of individuals. The approach described in [29, 31] uses a variant of C-nets similar to the notation used for the initial heuristic mining algorithm [124]. However, many other representations are possible.

To illustrate the genetic operators, we show a crossover example and a mutation example. For clarity we use Petri nets to describe the individuals before and after modification. Figure 6.9 shows two "parent" models and two "child" models resulting from crossover. In this example, the crossover point is the line through activities e and f. Figure 6.10 shows an example of mutation: one place is removed and one arc is added.

Figures 6.9 and 6.10 nicely illustrate the idea behind the two genetic operators: crossover and mutation. However, the realization of such operators is not as simple as these examples suggest. Typically repair actions are needed after crossover and mutation. For instance, the resulting model may no longer be a WF-net or C-net. Again we refer to [29, 31] for concrete examples.

Genetic process mining is *flexible* and *robust*. Like heuristic mining techniques, it can deal with noise and incompleteness. The approach can also be adapted and extended easily. By changing the fitness function, it is possible to give preference to particular constructs. Unfortunately, like most evolutionary approaches, genetic process mining is *not very efficient* for larger models and logs. It may take a very long

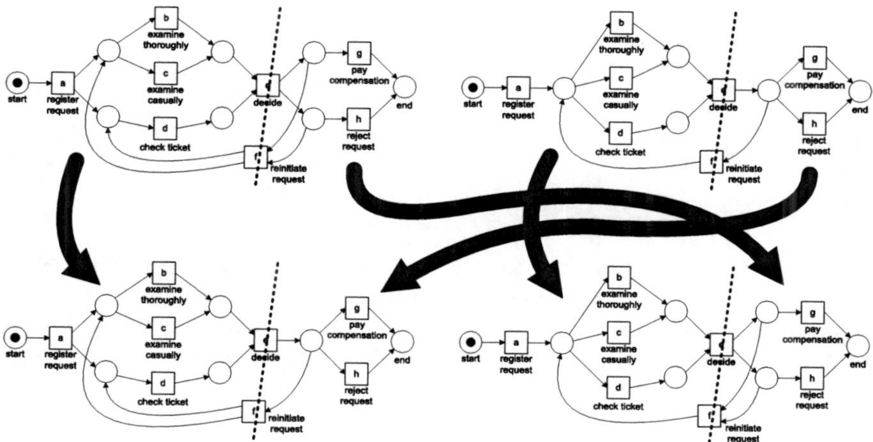

Fig. 6.9 Two parent models (*top*) and two child models resulting from a crossover. The crossover points are indicated by the *dashed lines*

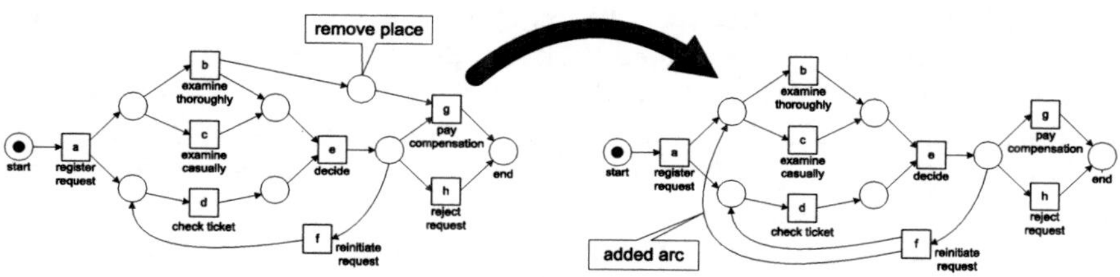

Fig. 6.10 Mutation: a place is removed and *an arc* is added

time to discover a model having an acceptable fitness. In theory, it can be shown that suitably chosen genetic operators guarantee that eventually a model with optimal fitness will be produced. However, in practice this argument is not useful given the potentially excessive computation times. One advantage is that it is easy to provide parallel implementations of genetic process mining. It is possible to partition the individuals or the event log over multiple computation nodes (e.g., nodes in a computational computer grid) [16]. It is also useful to combine heuristics with genetic process mining. In this case, genetic process mining is used to improve a process model obtained using heuristic mining. This saves computation time and may result in models that could never have been obtained through conventional algorithms searching only for local dependencies.

6.4 Region-Based Mining

In the context of Petri nets, researchers have been looking at the so-called *synthesis problem*, i.e., constructing a system model from a description of its behavior.

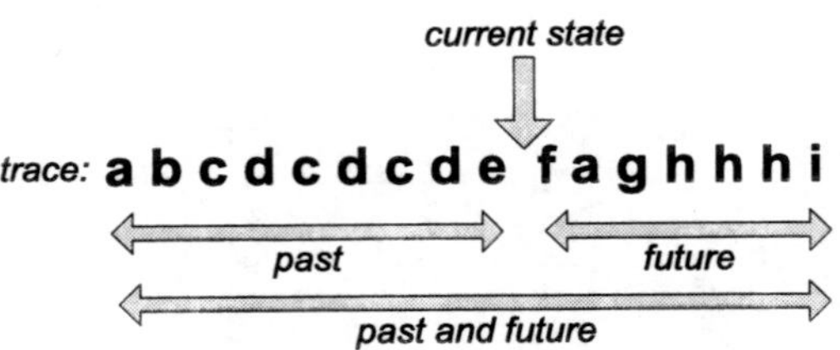

Fig. 6.11 Every position in a trace corresponds to a state, e.g., the state after executing the first nine events of a trace consisting of 16 events. To characterize the state, the past and/or future can be used as "ingredients"

State-based regions can be used to construct a Petri net from a transition system. Language-based regions can be used to construct a Petri net from a prefix-closed language. Synthesis approaches using language-based regions can be applied directly to event logs. To apply state-based regions, one first needs to create a transition system.

6.4.1 Learning Transition Systems

To construct a Petri net using state-based regions, we first need to discover a transition system based on the traces in the event log. Recall that a transition system can be described by a triplet $TS = (S, A, T)$ where S is the set of *states*, $A \subseteq \mathscr{A}$ is the set of *activities*, and $T \subseteq S \times A \times S$ is the set of *transitions*. $S^{start} \subseteq S$ is the set of *initial states*. $S^{end} \subseteq S$ is the set of *final states*. (See Sect. 2.2.1 for an introduction to transition systems.)

How to construct $TS = (S, A, T)$ *based on some simple event log* L *over* $\mathscr{A}$*, i.e.,* $L \in \mathbb{B}(\mathscr{A}^*)$? An obvious choice is to take A to be the set of activities in the simple event log. In order to determine the set of states, each "position" in each trace in the log needs to be mapped onto a corresponding state. This is illustrated by Fig. 6.11.

Let $\sigma' = \langle a, b, c, d, c, d, c, d, e, f, a, g, h, h, h, i \rangle \in L$ be a trace in the event log. Every position in this trace, i.e., before the first event, in-between two events, or after the last event should correspond to a state in the transition system. Consider, for example, the state shown in Fig. 6.11. The partial trace $\sigma'_{past} = \langle a, b, c, d, c, d, c, d, e \rangle$ describes the past of the corresponding case. $\sigma'_{future} = \langle f, a, g, h, h, h, i \rangle$ describes the future of this case. A *state representation* function $l^{state}()$ is a function that, given some sequence σ and a number k indicating the number of events of σ that have occurred, produces some state, e.g., the set of activities that have occurred in the first k events.

Let $\sigma = \langle a_1, a_2, \ldots, a_n \rangle \in L$ be a trace of length n. $l_1^{state}(\sigma, k) = hd^k(\sigma) = \langle a_1, a_2, \ldots, a_k \rangle$ is an example of a state representation function. Recall that $hd^k(\sigma)$ was defined in Sect. 4.2; the function returns the "head" of the sequence σ consisting of the first k elements. $l_1^{state}(\sigma, k)$ describes the current state by the *full history* of the case after k events. For instance, $l_1^{state}(\sigma', 9) = \langle a, b, c, d, c, d, c, d, e \rangle$.

$l_2^{state}(\sigma, k) = tl^{n-k}(\sigma) = \langle a_{k+1}, a_{k+2}, \ldots, a_n \rangle$ is another example of a state representation function. $l_2^{state}(\sigma, k)$ describes the current state by the *full future* of the case after k events. $l_2^{state}(\sigma', 9) = \langle f, a, g, h, h, h, i \rangle$.

Fig. 6.12 Transition system $TS_{L_1, l_1^{state}()}$ derived from $L_1 = [\langle a,b,c,d\rangle^3, \langle a,c,b,d\rangle^2, \langle a,e,d\rangle]$ using $l_1^{state}(\sigma,k) = hd^k(\sigma)$

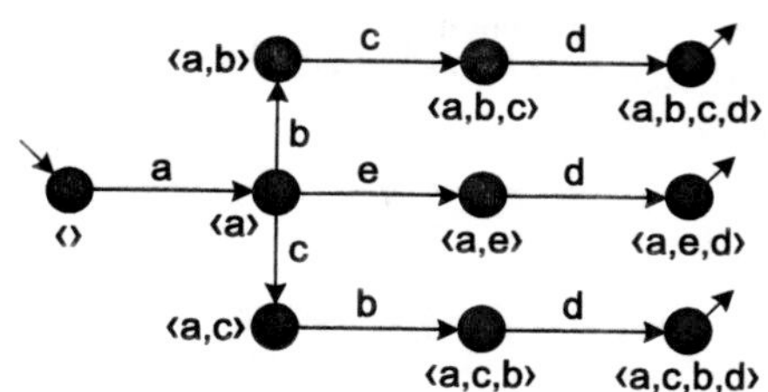

$l_3^{state}(\sigma,k) = \partial_{multiset}(hd^k(\sigma)) = [a_1, a_2, \ldots, a_k]$ is a state representation function converting the full history into a multi-set. This function assumes that for the current state the order of events is not important, only the frequency of activities matters. $l_3^{state}(\sigma', 9) = [a^1, b^1, c^3, d^3, e^1]$, i.e., in the state shown in Fig. 6.11 a, b, and e have been executed once and both c and d have been executed three times.

$l_4^{state}(\sigma,k) = \partial_{set}(hd^k(\sigma)) = \{a_1, a_2, \ldots, a_k\}$ is a state representation function taking a set representation of the full history. For this state representation function the order and frequency of activities do not matter. For the current state, it only matters which activities have been executed at least once. $l_4^{state}(\sigma', 9) = \{a,b,c,d,e\}$.

Functions $l_1^{state}()$, $l_3^{state}()$, and $l_4^{state}()$ all consider the full history of the case after k events: $l_1^{state}()$ does not abstract from the order and frequency of past activities, $l_3^{state}()$ abstracts from the order, and $l_4^{state}()$ abstracts from both order and frequency. Hence, $l_4^{state}()$ provides a coarser abstraction than $l_1^{state}()$. By definition $l_4^{state}(\sigma_1,k) = l_4^{state}(\sigma_2,k)$ if $l_1^{state}(\sigma_1,k) = l_1^{state}(\sigma_2,k)$ (but not the other way around). Function $l_2^{state}()$ is based on the future rather than the past.

Using some state representation function $l^{state}()$, we can automatically construct a transition system based on some event log L.

Definition 6.2 (Transition system based on event log) Let $L \in \mathbb{B}(\mathscr{A}^*)$ be an event log and $l^{state}()$ a state representation function. $TS_{L,l^{state}()} = (S, A, T)$ is a transition system based on L and $l^{state}()$ with:

- $S = \{l^{state}(\sigma,k) \mid \sigma \in L \wedge 0 \le k \le |\sigma|\}$ is the state space.
- $A = \{\sigma(k) \mid \sigma \in L \wedge 1 \le k \le |\sigma|\}$ is the set of activities.
- $T = \{(l^{state}(\sigma,k), \sigma(k+1), l^{state}(\sigma,k+1)) \mid \sigma \in L \wedge 0 \le k < |\sigma|\}$ is the set of transitions.
- $S^{start} = \{l^{state}(\sigma,0) \mid \sigma \in L\}$ is the set of initial states.
- $S^{end} = \{l^{state}(\sigma,|\sigma|) \mid \sigma \in L\}$ is the set of final states.

Let us consider event log $L_1 = [\langle a,b,c,d\rangle^3, \langle a,c,b,d\rangle^2, \langle a,e,d\rangle]$. Figure 6.12 shows transition system $TS_{L_1,l_1^{state}()}$. Consider, for example, a case with trace $\sigma = \langle a,b,c,d\rangle$. Initially, the case is in state $l_1^{state}(\sigma,0) = \langle\,\rangle$. After executing a the case is in state $l_1^{state}(\sigma,1) = \langle a\rangle$. After executing b state $l_1^{state}(\sigma,2) = \langle a,b\rangle$ is reached. Executing c results in state $l_1^{state}(\sigma,3) = \langle a,b,c\rangle$. Executing the last event d results in state $l_1^{state}(\sigma,4) = \langle a,b,c,d\rangle$. The five states visited by this case are added to the transition system. The corresponding transitions are also added. The same is done for $\langle a,c,b,d\rangle$ and $\langle a,e,d\rangle$, thus resulting in the transition system of Fig. 6.12.

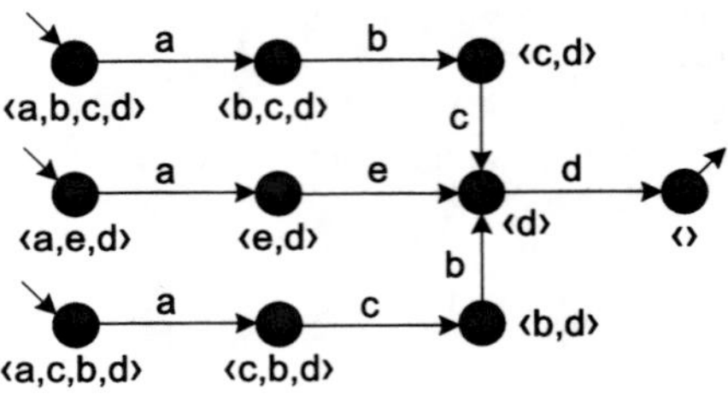

Fig. 6.13 Transition system $TS_{L_1,l_2^{state}()}$ derived from L_1 using $l_2^{state}(\sigma,k) = tl^{|\sigma|-k}(\sigma)$

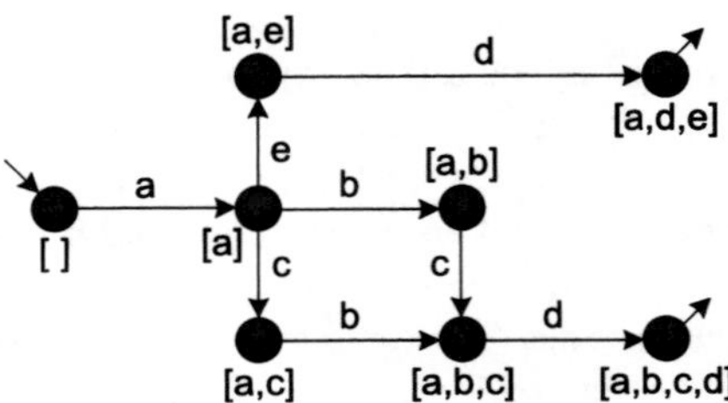

Fig. 6.14 Transition system $TS_{L_1,l_3^{state}()}$ derived from L_1 using $l_3^{state}(\sigma,k) = \partial_{multiset}(hd^k(\sigma))$

Using state representation function $l_2^{state}()$, we obtain transition system $TS_{L_1,l_2^{state}()}$ shown in Fig. 6.13. In this transition system, there are three initial states and only one final state, because this abstraction uses the future rather than the past. Consider, for example, a case with trace $\sigma = \langle a,e,d\rangle$. Initially, the case is in state $l_2^{state}(\sigma,0) = \langle a,e,d\rangle$, i.e., all three activities still need to occur. After executing a, the case is in state $l_2^{state}(\sigma,1) = \langle e,d\rangle$. After executing e state $l_2^{state}(\sigma,2) = \langle d\rangle$ is reached. Executing the last event d results in state $l_2^{state}(\sigma,3) = \langle\,\rangle$.

Transition system $TS_{L_1,l_3^{state}()}$ is shown in Fig. 6.14. Here, the states are represented by the multi-sets of activities that have been executed before. For instance, $l_3^{state}(\langle a,b,c,d\rangle,3) = [a,b,c]$. Because there are no repeated activities $TS_{L_1,l_4^{state}()}$ is identical to $TS_{L_1,l_3^{state}()}$ apart from the naming of states, e.g., $l_4^{state}(\langle a,b,c,d\rangle,3) = \{a,b,c\}$ rather than $[a,b,c]$.

The sets of traces allowed by the three transition systems shown in Figs. 6.12, 6.13, and 6.14 are the same: $\langle a,b,c,d\rangle$, $\langle a,c,b,d\rangle$, $\langle a,e,d\rangle$. This is not always the case. Add, for example, the trace $\langle a,c,b,f,f\rangle$ to L_1. In this case, $TS_{L_1,l_4^{state}()}$ allows for traces $\langle a,b,c,f,f\rangle$ and $\langle a,c,b,f,f,f,f,f\rangle$, i.e., b and c may be swapped and any number of f events is allowed at the end. $TS_{L_1,l_3^{state}()}$ allows for traces $\langle a,b,c,f,f\rangle$ and $\langle a,c,b,f,f\rangle$, but not $\langle a,c,b,f,f,f,f,f\rangle$. $TS_{L_1,l_1^{state}()}$ allows for trace $\langle a,c,b,f,f\rangle$, but not $\langle a,b,c,f,f\rangle$. Since $l_4^{state}()$ provides a coarser abstraction than $l_1^{state}()$, it generalizes more.

The state representation functions mentioned thus far are just examples. Depending on the desired abstraction, another state representation function can be defined. The essential question is whether partially executed cases are considered to be in the same state or not. For instance, if we assume that only the last activity matters, we can use state representation function $l_5^{state}(\sigma,k) = tl^1(hd^k(\sigma))$. This results in transition system $TS_{L_1,l_5^{state}()}$ shown in Fig. 6.15. Now, states in the transition system are

Fig. 6.15 Transition system $TS_{L_1, l_5^{state}()}$ derived from L_1 using $l_5^{state}(\sigma, k) = tl^1(hd^k(\sigma))$

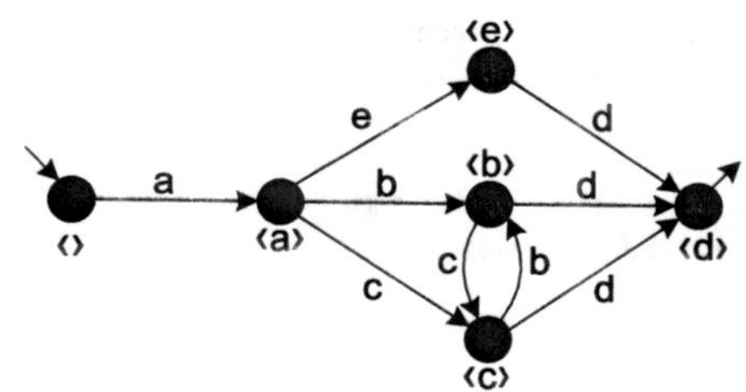

labeled with the last activity executed. For the initial state, this results in the empty sequence. $TS_{L_1, l_5^{state}()}$ allows for the traces in the event log, but also traces such as $\langle a, b, c, b, c, d \rangle$. Another example is $l_6^{state}(\sigma, k) = hd^3(tl^{|\sigma|-k}(\sigma))$, i.e., the state is determined by the next three events.

Thus far, we only considered a simple event log as input. Real-life event logs contain much more information as was shown in Chap. 4 (cf. Definition 4.3 and the XES format). Information about resources and data can also be taken into account when constructing a transition system. This information can be used to identify states and to label transitions. For example, states may encode whether the customer being served is a gold or silver customer. Transitions can be labeled with resource names rather than activity names. See [111] for a systematic treatment of the topic.

A transition system defines a "low-level" process model. Unfortunately, such models cannot express higher level constructs and suffer from the "state explosion" problem. As indicated before, a simple process with 10 parallel activities already results in a transition system with $2^{10} = 1024$ states and $10 \times 2^{10-1} = 5120$ transitions. Fortunately, state-based regions can be used to synthesize a more compact model from such transition systems.

6.4.2 Process Discovery Using State-Based Regions

After transforming an event log into a low-level transition system, we can synthesize a Petri net from it. In turn, this Petri net can be used to construct a process model in some other high-level notation (e.g., BPMN, UML activity diagrams, YAWL, and EPCs). The challenge is to fold a large transition system into a smaller Petri net by detecting concurrency. The core idea is to discover *regions* that correspond to *places*. A region is a set of states such that all activities in the transition system "agree" on the region.

Definition 6.3 (State-based region) Let $TS = (S, A, T)$ be a transition system and $R \subseteq S$ be a subset of states. R is a *region* if for each activity $a \in A$ one of the following conditions hold:

1. All transitions $(s_1, a, s_2) \in T$ *enter* R, i.e., $s_1 \notin R$ and $s_2 \in R$.
2. All transitions $(s_1, a, s_2) \in T$ *exit* R, i.e., $s_1 \in R$ and $s_2 \notin R$.
3. All transitions $(s_1, a, s_2) \in T$ *do not cross* R, i.e., $s_1, s_2 \in R$ or $s_1, s_2 \notin R$.

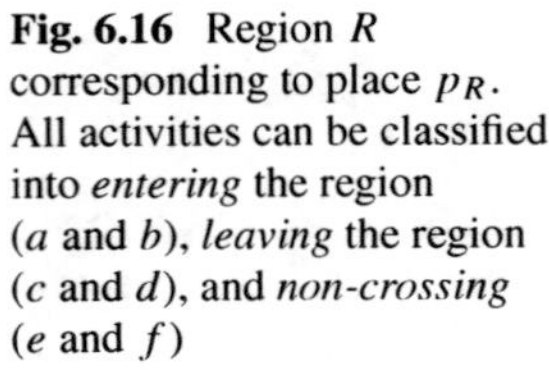

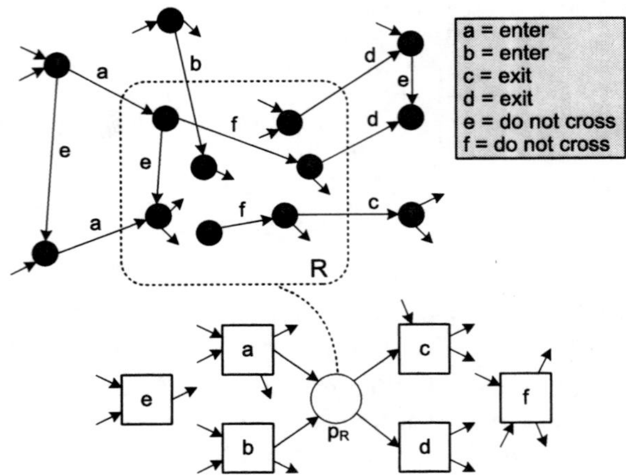

Fig. 6.16 Region R corresponding to place p_R. All activities can be classified into *entering* the region (a and b), *leaving* the region (c and d), and *non-crossing* (e and f)

Let R be a region. In this case all activities can be classified into *entering* the region, *leaving* the region, and *non-crossing*. An activity cannot be entering the region in one part of the transition system and exiting the region in some other part. Figure 6.16 illustrates the concept. The dashed rectangle describes a region R, i.e., a set of states in the transition system. All activities need to take a position with respect to this region. All a-labeled transitions enter region R. If there would be a transition with an a label not connecting a state outside the region to a state inside the region, then R would not be a region. All b-labeled transitions enter the region, all c and d labeled transitions exit the region. All e and f labeled transitions do not cross R, i.e., they always connect two states outside the region or two states inside the region.

By definition, the union of two regions is again a region. Therefore, we are only interested in *minimal* regions. The basic idea is that each minimal region R corresponds to a place p_R in a Petri net as shown in Fig. 6.16. The activities entering the region become Petri-net transitions having p_R as output place, activities leaving the region become output transitions of p_R, and activities that do not cross the region correspond to Petri-net transitions not connected to p_R. Hence, the minimal regions fully encode a Petri net.

Figure 6.17 illustrates the concept of state-based regions using a concrete example. By applying Definition 6.3, we find six minimal regions. Consider for example $R_1 = \{[a], [a, c]\}$. All a labeled transitions in the transition system enter R_1 (there is only one), all b labeled transitions exit R_1 (there are two such transitions), all e labeled transitions exit R_1 (there is only one), and all other transitions in the transition system do not cross R_1. Hence, R_1 is a region corresponding to place $p1$ with input transition a and output transitions b and e. $R_2 = \{[a], [a, b]\}$ is another region: a enters R_2, c and e exit R_2, and all other transitions in the transition system do not cross R_2. R_2 is the region corresponding to place $p2$ in Fig. 6.17. In the Petri net constructed based on the six minimal regions, b and c are concurrent.

Figure 6.17 shows a small process with very little concurrency. Therefore, the transition system and Petri net have similar sizes. However, for larger processes

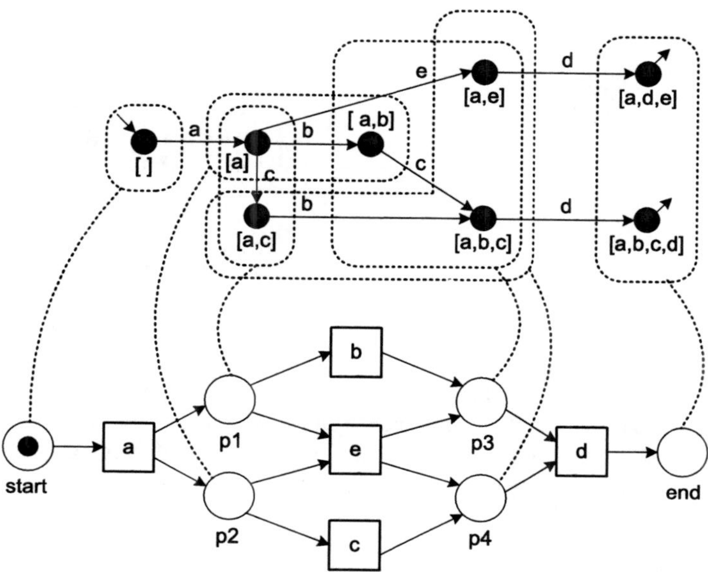

Fig. 6.17 Transition system $TS_{L,l_3^{state}()}$ derived from $L_1 = [\langle a,b,c,d\rangle^3, \langle a,c,b,d\rangle^2, \langle a,e,d\rangle]$ is converted into a Petri net using state-based regions

with lots of concurrency the reduction can be spectacular. The transition system modeling 10 parallel activities having $2^{10} = 1024$ states and $10 \times 2^{10-1} = 5120$ transitions, can be reduced into a Petri net with only 20 places and 10 transitions.

The transition system in Fig. 6.17 was obtained from log L_1 using state representation function $l_3^{state}()$. In fact, in this example, the discovered process model using this two-step approach is identical to the model discovered by the α-algorithm. This demonstrates that a two-step approach can be used to convert an event log into a Petri net. Therefore, process discovery using transition system construction and state-based regions is an alternative to the approaches presented thus far.

Figure 6.17 only conveys the basic idea behind regions [38]. The synthesis of Petri nets using state-based regions is actually more involved and can be customized to favor particular process patterns. As shown in [23], any finite transition system can be converted into a bisimilar Petri net, i.e., the behaviors of the transition system and Petri net are equivalent even if we consider the moment of choice (see Sect. 5.3). However, for some Petri nets it may be necessary to perform "label splitting". As a result, the Petri net may have multiple transitions referring to the same activity. This way the WF-net shown in Fig. 5.20 can be discovered. Moreover, it is also possible to enforce the resulting Petri net to have particular properties, e.g., free-choice [34]. See [111] for more information about the two-step approach.

Classical state-based regions aim at producing a Petri net that is bisimilar to the transition system. This means that while constructing the Petri net the behavior is not generalized. Therefore, it is important to select a coarser state representation function when constructing the transition system. For larger processes, a state repre-

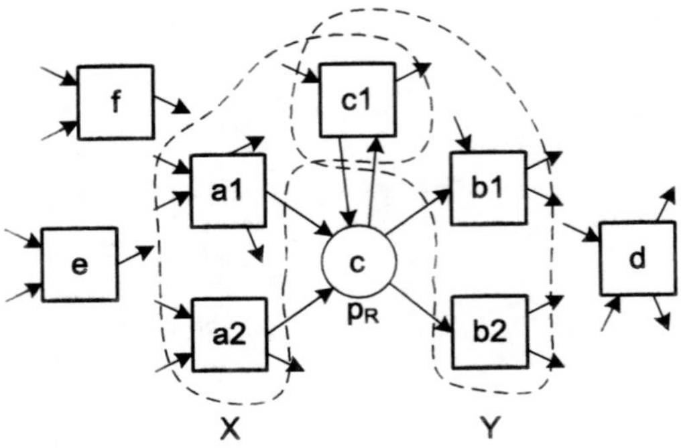

Fig. 6.18 Region $R = (X, Y, c)$ corresponding to place p_R: $X = \{a1, a2, c1\} = \bullet p_R$, $Y = \{b1, b2, c1\} = p_R\bullet$, and c is the initial marking of p_R

sentation function like $l_1^{state}()$ definitely results in an overfitting model that can only replay the log without any form of generalization. Many abstractions (i.e., state representation functions) are possible to balance between overfitting and underfitting. In [111], these are described systematically.

6.4.3 Process Discovery Using Language-Based Regions

As illustrated by Fig. 6.16, the goal of state-based regions is to determine the places in a Petri net. Language-based regions also aim at finding such places but do not use a transition system as input; instead some "language" is used as input. Several techniques and variants of the problem have been defined. In this section we only present the basic idea and refer to literature for details [7, 8, 18, 115].

Suppose, we have an event log in which the events refer to a set of activities A. For this log one could construct a Petri net $N_\emptyset$ with the set of transitions being A and no places. Since a transition without any input places is continuously enabled, this Petri net is able to reproduce the log. In fact, the Petri net $N_\emptyset$ can reproduce any log over A. In Sect. 5.4.3 we referred to such a model as the "flower model". There we added places and transitions to model this behavior in terms of a WF-net. However, the idea is the same. Adding places to the Petri net $N_\emptyset$ can only limit the behavior.

Consider for example place p_R in Fig. 6.18. Removing place p_R will not remove any behavior. However, adding p_R may remove behavior possible in the Petri net without this place. The behavior gets restricted when a place is empty while one of its output transitions wants to consume a token from it. For example, $b1$ is blocked if p_R is unmarked while all other input places of $b1$ are marked. Suppose now that we have a set of traces L. If these traces are possible in the net with place p_R, then they are also possible in the net without p_R. The reverse does not always hold. This triggers the question whether p_R can be added without disabling any of the traces in L. This is what regions are all about.

Definition 6.4 (Language-based region) Let $L \in \mathbb{B}(\mathscr{A}^*)$ be a simple event log. $R = (X, Y, c)$ is a *region* of L if and only if:

- $X \subseteq \mathscr{A}$ is the set of input transitions of R.
- $Y \subseteq \mathscr{A}$ is the set of output transitions of R.
- $c \in \{0, 1\}$ is the initial marking of R.
- For any $\sigma \in L$, $k \in \{1, \dots, |\sigma|\}$, $\sigma_1 = hd^{k-1}(\sigma)$, $a = \sigma(k)$, $\sigma_2 = hd^k(\sigma) = \sigma_1 \oplus a$:

$$c + \sum_{t \in X} \partial_{multiset}(\sigma_1)(t) - \sum_{t \in Y} \partial_{multiset}(\sigma_2)(t) \geq 0$$

$R = (X, Y, c)$ is a region of L if and only if inserting a place p_R with $\bullet p_R = A$, $p_R \bullet = B$, and initially c tokens does not disable the execution of any of the traces in L. To check this, Definition 6.4 inspects all events in the event log. Let $\sigma \in L$ be a trace in the log. $a = \sigma(k)$ is the kth event in this trace. This event should not be disabled by place p_R. Therefore, we calculate the number of tokens $M(p_R)$ that are in this place just before the occurrence of the kth event.

$$M(p_R) = c + \sum_{t \in X} \partial_{multiset}(\sigma_1)(t) - \sum_{t \in Y} \partial_{multiset}(\sigma_1)(t)$$

$\sigma_1 = hd^{k-1}(\sigma)$ is the partial trace of events that occurred before the occurrence of the kth event. $\partial_{multiset}(\sigma_1)$ converts this partial trace into a multi-set. $\partial_{multiset}(\sigma_1)$ is also known as the *Parikh vector* of σ_1. $\sum_{t \in X} \partial_{multiset}(\sigma_1)(t)$ counts the number of tokens produced for place p_R, $\sum_{t \in Y} \partial_{multiset}(\sigma_1)(t)$ counts the number of tokens consumed from this place, and c is the initial number of tokens in p_R. Therefore, $M(p_R)$ is indeed the number of tokens in p_R just before the occurrence of the kth event. This number should be positive. In fact, there should be at least one token in p_R if $a \in Y$. In other words, $M(p_R)$ minus the number of tokens consumed from p_R by the kth event should be nonnegative. Hence,

$$\begin{aligned} M(p_R) &- \sum_{t \in Y} \partial_{multiset}\big(\langle a \rangle\big)(t) \\ &= c + \sum_{t \in X} \partial_{multiset}(\sigma_1)(t) - \sum_{t \in Y} \partial_{multiset}(\sigma_2)(t) \geq 0 \end{aligned}$$

This shows that a region R, according to Definition 6.4, indeed corresponds to a so-called *feasible place* p_R, i.e., a place that can be added without disabling any of the traces in the event log.

The requirement stated in Definition 6.4 can also be formulated in terms of an inequation system. To illustrate this, we use an example log from Chap. 5:

$$L_9 = \big[\langle a, c, d \rangle^{45}, \langle b, c, e \rangle^{42}\big]$$

There are five activities. For each activity t, we introduce two variables: x_t and y_t. $x_t = 1$ if transition t produces a token for p_R and $x_t = 0$ if not. $y_t = 1$ if transition t consumes a token from p_R and $y_t = 0$ if not. A potential region $R = (X, Y, c)$ corresponds to an assignment for all of these variables: $x_t = 1$ if $t \in X$, $x_t = 0$ if

$t \notin X$, $y_t = 1$ if $t \in Y$, $y_t = 0$ if $t \notin Y$. The requirement stated in Definition 6.4 can now be reformulated in terms of the variables x_a, x_b, x_c, x_d, x_e, y_a, y_b, y_c, y_d, y_e, and c:

$$\begin{aligned} c - y_a &\geq 0 \\ c + x_a - (y_a + y_c) &\geq 0 \\ c + x_a + x_c - (y_a + y_c + y_d) &\geq 0 \\ c - y_b &\geq 0 \\ c + x_b - (y_b + y_c) &\geq 0 \\ c + x_b + x_c - (y_b + y_c + y_e) &\geq 0 \\ c, x_a, \ldots, x_e, y_a, \ldots, y_e &\in \{0, 1\} \end{aligned}$$

Note that these inequations are based on all nonempty prefixes of $\langle a, c, d\rangle$ and $\langle b, c, e\rangle$. Any solution of this linear inequation system corresponds to a region. Some example solutions are:

$$\begin{aligned} & R_1 = (\emptyset, \{a, b\}, 1) \\ & c = y_a = y_b = 1, \qquad x_a = x_b = x_c = x_d = x_e = y_c = y_d = y_e = 0 \\ & R_2 = (\{a, b\}, \{c\}, 0) \\ & x_a = x_b = y_c = 1, \qquad c = x_c = x_d = x_e = y_a = y_b = y_d = y_e = 0 \\ & R_3 = (\{c\}, \{d, e\}, 0) \\ & x_c = y_d = y_e = 1, \qquad c = x_a = x_b = x_d = x_e = y_a = y_b = y_c = 0 \\ & R_4 = (\{d, e\}, \emptyset, 0) \\ & x_d = x_e = 1, \qquad c = x_a = x_b = x_c = y_a = y_b = y_c = y_d = y_e = 0 \\ & R_5 = (\{a\}, \{d\}, 0) \\ & x_a = y_d = 1, \qquad c = x_b = x_c = x_d = x_e = y_a = y_b = y_c = y_e = 0 \\ & R_6 = (\{b\}, \{e\}, 0) \\ & x_b = y_e = 1, \qquad c = x_a = x_c = x_d = x_e = y_a = y_b = y_c = y_d = 0 \end{aligned}$$

Consider for example $R_6 = (\{b\}, \{e\}, 0)$. This corresponds to the solution $x_b = y_e = 1$ and $c = x_a = x_c = x_d = x_e = y_a = y_b = y_c = y_d = 0$. If we fill out the values in the inequation system, we can see that this is indeed a solution. If we construct a Petri net based on these six regions, we obtain the WF-net shown in Fig. 6.19.

Suppose that the trace $\langle a, c, e\rangle$ is added to event log L_9. This results in three additional inequations:

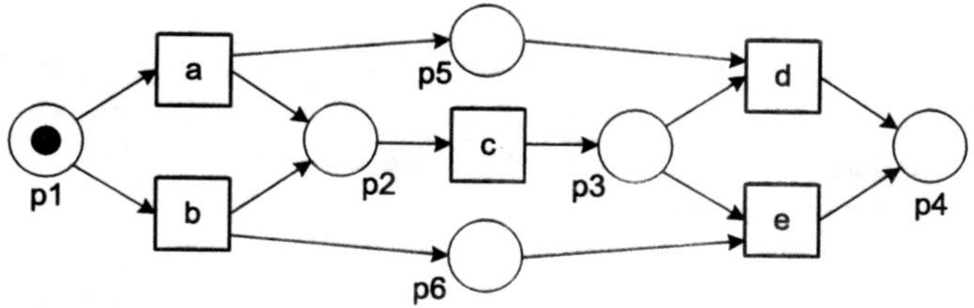

Fig. 6.19 WF-net constructed using regions $R_1, \ldots, R_6$: $p1$ corresponds to $R_1 = (\emptyset, \{a,b\}, 1)$, $p2$ corresponds to $R_2 = (\{a,b\}, \{c\}, 0)$, etc.

$$c - y_a \geq 0$$

$$c + x_a - (y_a + y_c) \geq 0$$

$$c + x_a + x_c - (y_a + y_c + y_e) \geq 0$$

Only the last inequation is new. Because of this inequation, $x_b = y_e = 1$ and $c = x_a = x_c = x_d = x_e = y_a = y_b = y_c = y_d = 0$ is no longer a solution. Hence, $R_6 = (\{b\}, \{e\}, 0)$ is not a region anymore and place $p6$ needs to be removed from the WF-net shown in Fig. 6.19. After removing this place, the resulting WF-net indeed allows for $\langle a, c, e \rangle$.

One of the problems of directly applying language-based regions is that the linear inequation system has many solutions. Few of these solutions correspond to sensible places. For example, $x_a = x_b = y_d = y_e = 1$ and $c = x_c = x_d = x_e = y_a = y_b = y_c = 0$ also defines a region: $R_7 = (\{a,b\}, \{d,e\}, 0)$. However, adding this place to Fig. 6.19 would only clutter the diagram. Another example is $c = x_a = x_b = y_c = 1$ and $x_c = x_d = x_e = y_a = y_b = y_d = y_e = 0$ i.e., region $R_8 = (\{a,b\}, \{c\}, 1)$. This region is a weaker variant R_2 as the place is initially marked.

Another problem is that classical techniques for language-based regions aim at a Petri net that does not allow for any behavior not seen in the log [8]. This means that the log is considered to be complete. As shown before, this is very unrealistic and results in models that are complex and overfitting. To address these problems, dedicated techniques have been proposed. For instance, in [115] it is shown how to avoid overfitting and how to ensure that the resulting model has desirable properties (WF-net, free-choice, etc.). Nevertheless, pure region-based techniques tend to have problems handling noise and incompleteness. Therefore, combinations of heuristic mining and region-based techniques seem more suitable for practical applications.

6.5 Historical Perspective

On the one hand, process mining is a relatively young field. All the process discovery techniques described in this chapter were developed in the last decade. Moreover, it is only recently that mature process discovery techniques and effective implementations have become available. On the other hand, process discovery has its roots in various established scientific disciplines ranging from concurrency theory, inductive inference and stochastics to data mining, machine learning and computational intelligence. It is impossible to do justice to the numerous contributions to process mining originating from different scientific domains. Hence, this section should be seen as a modest attempt to provide a historical perspective on the origins of process discovery.

In 1967, Mark Gold showed in his seminal paper "Language identification in limit" [45] that even regular languages cannot be exactly identified from positive examples only. In [45], Gold describes several inductive inference problems. The challenge is to guess a "rule" (e.g., a regular expression) based on an infinite stream of examples. An inductive inference method is able to "learn the rule in the limit" if after a finite number of examples the method is always able to guess the correct rule and does not need to revise its guess anymore based on new examples. A regular language is a language that can be accepted by a finite transition system (also referred to as a finite state machine). Regular languages can also be described in terms of regular expressions. For example, the regular expression $ab^*(c \mid d)$ denotes the set of traces starting with a, then zero or more b's and finally a c or d. Regular expressions were introduced by Stephen Cole Kleene [59] in 1956. In the Chomsky hierarchy of formal grammars, regular languages are the least expressive (i.e., Type-3 grammar). For example, it is impossible to express the language $\{a^n b^n \mid n \in \mathbb{N}\}$, i.e., the language containing traces that start with any number of a's followed by the same number of b's. Despite the limited expressiveness of regular expressions, Gold showed in [45] that they *cannot* be learned in the limit from positive examples only.

Many inductive inference problems have been studied since Gold's paper (see the survey in [6]). For instance, subclasses of the class of regular languages have been identified that can be learned in the limit (e.g., the so-called k-reversible languages [6]). Moreover, if an "oracle" is used that can indicate whether particular examples are possible or not, a larger class of languages can be learned. This illustrates the importance of negative examples when learning. However, as indicated before, one will not find negative examples in an event log; *the fact that something did not happen provides no guarantee that it cannot happen*. Inductive inference focuses on learning a language perfectly. This is not the aim of process mining. Real-life event logs will contain noise and are far from complete. Therefore, the theoretical considerations in the context of inductive inference are less relevant for process mining.

Before the paper of Gold, there were already techniques to construct a finite state machine from a finite set of example traces. A naïve approach is to use the state representation function $l_1^{state}(\sigma, k) = hd^k(\sigma)$ described in Sect. 6.4.1 to construct a finite state machine. Such a finite state machine can be made smaller by using the classical Myhill–Nerode theorem [71]. Let L be a language over some alphabet $\mathscr{A}$ and consider $\sigma_x, \sigma_y \in \mathscr{A}^*$. σ_x and σ_y are *equivalent* if there is no $\sigma_z \in \mathscr{A}^*$ such that $\sigma_x \oplus \sigma_z \in L$ while $\sigma_y \oplus \sigma_z \notin L$ or $\sigma_y \oplus \sigma_z \in L$ while $\sigma_x \oplus \sigma_z \notin L$. Hence, two traces are equivalent if their "sets of possible futures" coincide. This equivalence notion divides the elements of L into equivalence classes. If L is a regular language, then there are finitely many equivalence classes. The Myhill–Nerode theorem states that if there are k such equivalence classes, then the smallest finite state machine accepting L has k states. Several approaches have been proposed to minimize finite state machines using these insights (basically folding equivalent states). In [10], a modification of the Myhill–Nerode equivalence relation is proposed for constructing a finite state machine based on a set of sample traces L with a parameter to balance precision and complexity. Here two states are considered equivalent if their k-tails are the same. In 1972, Alan Biermann also proposed an approach to "learn" a Turing machine from a set of sample computations [9].

In the mid 1990s, people like Rakesh Agrawal and others developed various data mining algorithms to find frequent patterns in large datasets. In [3], the Apriori algorithm for finding association rules was presented. These techniques were extended to sequences and episodes [52, 63, 89]. However, none of these techniques aimed at discovering end-to-end processes. More related is the work on hidden Markov models [5]. Here end-to-end processes can be considered. However, these models are sequential and cannot be easily converted into readable business process models.

In the second half of the 1990s, Cook and Wolf developed process discovery techniques in the context of software engineering processes. In [22], they described three methods for process discovery: one using neural networks, one using a purely algorithmic approach, and one Markovian approach. The authors considered the latter two to be the most promising approaches. The purely algorithmic approach builds a finite state machine in which states are fused if their futures (in terms of possible behavior in the next k steps) are identical. (Note that this is essentially the approach proposed by Biermann and Feldmann in [10].) The Markovian approach uses a mixture of algorithmic and statistical methods and is able to deal with noise. All approaches described in [22] are limited to sequential processes, i.e., no concurrency is discovered.

In 1998, two papers [4, 26] appeared that, independently of one another, proposed to apply process discovery in the context of business process management.

In [4], Agrawal, Gunopulos, and Leymann presented an approach to discover the so-called "conformal process graph" from event logs. This work was inspired by the process notation used by Flowmark and the presence of event logs in WFM systems. The approach discovers causal dependencies between activities, but is not able to find AND/XOR/OR-splits and joins, i.e., the process logic is implicit. Moreover, the approach has problems dealing with loops: a trace $\langle a, a, a\rangle$ is simply relabeled into $\langle a_1, a_2, a_3\rangle$ to make the conformal process graph acyclic.

In the same year, Anindya Datta [26] proposed a technique to discover business process models by adapting the Biermann–Feldmann algorithm [10] for constructing finite state machines based on example traces. Datta added probabilistic elements to the original approach and embedded the work in the context of workflow management and business process redesign. The approach assumes that case identifiers are unknown, i.e., the setting is similar to the work in [39] where the challenge is to correlate events and discover cases. The resulting process model is again a sequential model.

Joachim Herbst [54, 55] was one of the first aiming at the discovery of more complicated process models. He proposed stochastic task graphs as an intermediate representation before constructing a workflow model in terms of the ADONIS modeling language. In the induction step, task nodes are merged and split in order to discover the underlying process. A notable difference with most approaches is that the same activity can appear multiple times in the process model, i.e., the approach allows for duplicate labels. The graph generation technique is similar to the approach of [4]. The nature of splits and joins (i.e., AND or OR) is discovered in the transformation step, i.e., the step in which the stochastic task graph is transformed into an ADONIS workflow model with block-structured splits and joins.

Most of the classical approaches have problems dealing with concurrency, i.e., either sequential models are assumed (e.g., transition systems, finite state machines, Markov chains, and hidden Markov models) or there is a post-processing step to discover concurrency. The first model to adequately capture concurrency was already introduced by Carl Adam Petri in 1962 [73]. (Note that the graphical notation as we know it today was introduced later.) However, classical process discovery techniques do not take concurrency into account. The α-algorithm [103] described in Sect. 5.2 and a predecessor of the heuristic miner [124] described in Sect. 6.2 were developed concurrently and share the same ideas when it comes to handling concurrency. These were the first process discovery techniques taking concurrency as a starting point (and not as an afterthought or post-optimization). The α-algorithm was used to explore the theoretical limits of process discovery [103]. Several variants of the α-algorithm have been proposed to lift some of its limitations [29, 30, 116, 119, 125]. The focus of heuristic mining was (and still is) on dealing with noise and incompleteness [123, 124].

Techniques such as the α-algorithm and heuristic mining do not guarantee that the model can replay all cases in the event log. In [116, 117] an approach is presented that guarantees a fitness of 1, i.e., all traces in the event log can be replayed in the discovered model. This is achieved by creatively using OR-splits and joins. As a result, the discovered model is typically underfitting. In [43, 44], artificially generated "negative events" are inserted to transform process discovery into a classification problem. The insertion of negative events corresponds to the completeness assumptions made by algorithms like the α-algorithm, e.g., "if a is never directly followed by b, then this is not possible".

Region-based approaches are able to express more complex control-flow structures without underfitting. State-based regions were introduced by Ehrenfeucht and Rozenberg [38] in 1989 and generalized by Cortadella et al. [23]. In [111, 118] it is shown how these state-based regions can be applied to process mining. In parallel, several authors applied language-based regions to process mining [8, 115]. In [18], Joseph Carmona and Jordi Cortadella present an approach based on convex polyhedra. Here, the Parikh vector of each prefix in the log is seen as a polyhedron. By taking the convex hull of these convex polyhedra one obtains an over-approximation of the possible behavior. The resulting polyhedron can be converted into places using a construction similar to language-based regions. The synthesis/region-based approaches typically guarantee a fitness of 1. Unfortunately, these approaches also have problems dealing with noise.

For practical applications of process discovery, it is essential that noise and incompleteness are handled well. Surprisingly, only few discovery algorithms focus on addressing these issues. Notable exceptions are heuristic mining [123, 124], fuzzy mining [50], and genetic process mining [31]. Therefore, we put emphasis on these techniques in this chapter. Also see [102, 106, 119] for additional pointers to related work.

Part III
Beyond Process Discovery

Chapter 1
Introduction

Part I: Preliminaries

Chapter 2
Process Modeling and Analysis

Chapter 3
Data Mining

Part II: From Event Logs to Process Models

Chapter 4
Getting the Data

Chapter 5
Process Discovery: An Introduction

Chapter 6
Advanced Process Discovery Techniques

Part III: Beyond Process Discovery

Chapter 7
Conformance Checking

Chapter 8
Mining Additional Perspectives

Chapter 9
Operational Support

Part IV: Putting Process Mining to Work

Chapter 10
Tool Support

Chapter 11
Analyzing "Lasagna Processes"

Chapter 12
Analyzing "Spaghetti Processes"

Part V: Reflection

Chapter 13
Cartography and Navigation

Chapter 14
Epilogue

In the previous part, the focus was on process discovery. However, in many situations, there is already a (partial) process model. Chapter 7 presents techniques for checking the quality of such models. Moreover, process models (discovered or made by hand) should not only describe control-flow: the other perspectives also need to be addressed. Chapter 8 exhibits techniques for mining additional perspectives involving resources, time, and data. Chapter 9 extends the scope even further and shows how process mining can be used to directly influence cases that are still running.

Chapter 7
Conformance Checking

After covering control-flow discovery in depth in Part II, this chapter looks at the situation in which both a process model and an event log are given. The model may have been constructed by hand or may have been discovered. Moreover, the model may be normative or descriptive. Conformance checking relates events in the event log to activities in the process model and compares both. The goal is to find commonalities and discrepancies between the modeled behavior and the observed behavior. Conformance checking is relevant for business alignment and auditing. For example, the event log can be replayed on top of the process model to find undesirable deviations suggesting fraud or inefficiencies. Moreover, conformance checking techniques can also be used for measuring the performance of process discovery algorithms and to repair models that are not aligned well with reality.

7.1 Business Alignment and Auditing

In Sect. 1.5, we introduced the terms Play-in, Play-out, and Replay. *Play-out* is the classical use of process models; the model generates behavior. For instance, by playing the "token game" in a WF-net, example behaviors can be generated. Simulation and workflow engines use Play-out to analyze and enact process models. *Play-in* is the opposite of Play-out, i.e., example behavior is taken as input and the goal is to construct a model. The discovery techniques presented in Chaps. 5 and 6 can be used for Play-in. *Replay* uses both an event log and a process model as input, i.e., history is replayed using the model to analyze various phenomena. For example, in Chap. 8 we will show that replay can be used for analyzing bottlenecks and decision analysis. In Chap. 9, replay will be used to predict the behavior of running cases and to recommend suitable actions. In this chapter, we focus on *conformance checking* using replay.

Figure 7.1 illustrates the main idea of conformance checking. The behavior of a process model and the behavior recorded in an event log are compared to find commonalities and discrepancies. Such analysis results in *global conformance measures*

W.M.P. van der Aalst, *Process Mining*,
DOI 10.1007/978-3-642-19345-3_7,

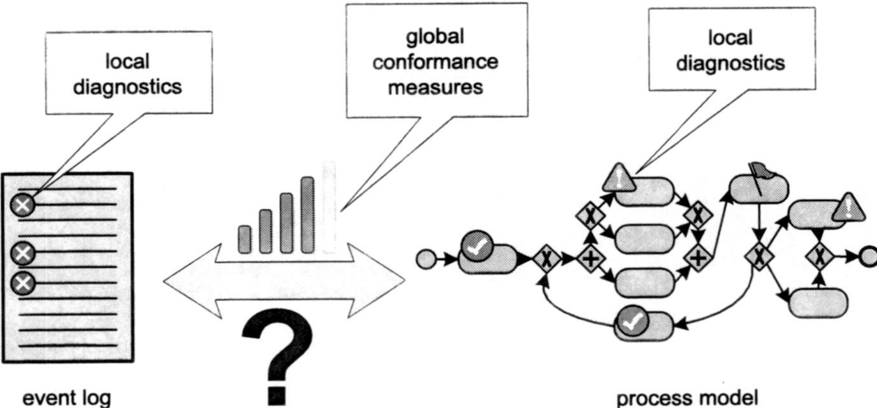

Fig. 7.1 Conformance checking: comparing observed behavior with modeled behavior. Global conformance measures quantify the overall conformance of the model and log. Local diagnostics are given by highlighting the nodes in the model where model and log disagree. Cases that do not fit are highlighted in the visualization of the log

(e.g., 85% of the cases in the event log can be replayed by the model) and *local diagnostics* (e.g., activity x was executed 15 times although this was not allowed according to the model). The interpretation of non-conformance depends on the purpose of the model. If the model is intended to be *descriptive*, then discrepancies between model and log indicate that the model needs to be improved to capture reality better. If the model is *normative*, then such discrepancies may be interpreted in two ways. Some of the discrepancies found may expose *undesirable deviations*, i.e., conformance checking signals the need for a better control of the process. Other discrepancies may reveal *desirable deviations*. For instance, workers may deviate to serve the customers better or to handle circumstances not foreseen by the process model. In fact, flexibility and non-conformance often correlate positively. For example, in some hospitals the phrase "breaking the glass" is used to refer to deviations that are recorded but that actually save lives. Nevertheless, even if most deviations are desired, it is important that stakeholders have insight into such discrepancies.

When checking conformance, it is important to view deviations from two angles: (a) the model is "wrong" and does not reflect reality ("How to improve the model?"), and (b) cases deviate from the model and corrective actions are needed ("How to improve control to enforce a better conformance?"). Conformance checking techniques should support both viewpoints. Therefore, Fig. 7.1 shows deviations on both sides.

In Chap. 1, we related process mining to corporate governance, risk, compliance, and legislation such as the Sarbanes-Oxley Act (SOX) and the Basel II Accord. Corporate accounting scandals have triggered a series of new regulations. Although country-specific, there is a large degree of commonality between Sarbanes-Oxley (US), Basel II/III (EU), J-SOX (Japan), C-SOX (Canada), 8th EU Directive (EURO-SOX), BilMoG (Germany), MiFID (EU), Law 262/05 (Italy), Code Lippens (Belgium), Code Tabaksblat (Netherlands), and others. These regulations require companies to identify the financial and operational risks inherent to their business processes, and establish the appropriate controls to address them. Although the focus of these regulations is on financial aspects, they illustrate the desire to make processes transparent and auditable. The ISO 9000 family of standards is another illustration of this trend. For instance, *ISO 9001:2008* requires organizations to model their operational processes. Currently, these standards do not force organizations to check conformance at the event level. For example, the real production process may be very different from the modeled production process. Nevertheless, the relation to conformance checking is evident. In this chapter, we take a more technological perspective and show concrete techniques for quantifying conformance and diagnosing non-conformance. However, before doing so, we briefly reflect on the relation between conformance checking, business alignment, and auditing.

The goal of *business alignment* is to make sure that the information systems and the real business processes are well aligned. People should be supported by the information system rather than work behind its back to get things done. Unfortunately, there is often a mismatch between the information system on the one hand and the actual processes and needs of workers and management on the other hand. There are various reasons for this. First of all, most organization use product software, i.e., generic software that was not developed for a specific organization. A typical example is the SAP system which is based on so-called "best practices", i.e., typical processes and scenarios are implemented. Although such systems are configurable, the particular needs of an organization may be different from what was envisioned by the product software developer. Second, processes may change faster than the information system, because of external influences. Finally, there may be different stakeholders in the organization having conflicting requirements, e.g., a manager may want to enforce a fixed working procedure whereas an experienced worker prefers to have more flexibility to serve customers better.

Process mining can assist in improving the alignment of information systems, business processes, and the organization. By analyzing the real processes and diagnosing discrepancies, new insights can be gathered showing how to improve the support by information systems.

The term *auditing* refers to the evaluation of organizations and their processes. Audits are performed to ascertain the validity and reliability of information about these organizations and associated processes. This is done *to check whether business processes are executed within certain boundaries set by managers, governments, and other stakeholders*. For instance, specific rules may be enforced by law or company policies and the auditor should check whether these rules are followed or not. Violations of these rules may indicate fraud, malpractice, risks, and inefficiencies. Traditionally, auditors can only provide *reasonable assurance* that business processes are executed within the given set of boundaries. They check the operating effectiveness of controls that are designed to ensure reliable processing. When these controls are not in place, or otherwise not functioning as expected, they typically *only check samples of factual data*, often in the "paper world".

However, today detailed information about processes is being recorded in the form of event logs, audit trails, transaction logs, databases, data warehouses, etc.

Therefore, it should no longer be acceptable to only check a small set of samples off-line. Instead, *all events in a business process can be evaluated and this can be done while the process is still running*. The availability of log data and advanced process mining techniques enables new forms of auditing (also see the work done in the PoSecCo project [74]). Process mining in general, and conformance checking in particular, provide the means to do so.

7.2 Token Replay

In Sect. 5.4.3, we discussed four quality criteria: fitness, precision, generalization, and simplicity. These were illustrated using Fig. 5.24. In this figure, one event log is given and four process models are shown. For each of these models, a subjective judgment is given with respect to the four quality criteria. As the models are rather extreme, the scores for the various quality criteria are evident. However, in a more realistic setting it is much more difficult to judge the quality of a model. This section shows how the notion of *fitness* can be quantified. Fitness measures "the proportion of behavior in the event log possible according to the model". Of the four quality criteria, fitness is most related to conformance.

To explain the various fitness notions, we use the event log L_{full} described in Table 7.1. This is the same event log as the one used in Fig. 5.24. There are 1391 cases in L_{full} distributed over 21 different traces. For example, there are 455 cases following trace $\sigma_1 = \langle a, c, d, e, h \rangle$, 191 cases following trace $\sigma_2 = \langle a, b, d, e, g \rangle$, etc.

Figure 7.2 shows four models related to event log L_{full}. WF-net N_1 is the process model discovered when applying the α-algorithm to L_{full}. WF-net N_2 is a sequential model that, compared to N_1, requires the examination (activity b or c) to take place before checking the ticket (activity d). Clearly, N_2 does not allow for all traces in Table 7.1. For example, $\sigma_3 = \langle a, d, c, e, h \rangle$ is not possible according to WF-net N_2. WF-net N_3 has no choices, e.g., the request is always rejected. Many traces in Table 7.1 cannot be replayed by this model, e.g., $\sigma_2 = \langle a, b, d, e, g \rangle$ is not possible according to WF-net N_3. WF-net N_4 is a variant of the "flower model": the only requirement is that traces need to start with a and end with g or h. Clearly, all traces in Table 7.1 can be replayed by N_4.

A naïve approach toward conformance checking would be to simply count the fraction of cases that can be "parsed completely" (i.e., the proportion of cases corresponding to firing sequences leading from $[start]$ to $[end]$). Using this approach the fitness of N_1 is $\frac{1391}{1391} = 1$, i.e., all 1391 cases in L_{full} correspond to a firing sequence of N_1 ("can be replayed"). The fitness of N_2 is $\frac{948}{1391} = 0.6815$ because 948 cases can be replayed correctly whereas 443 cases do not correspond to a firing sequence of N_2. The fitness of N_3 is $\frac{632}{1391} = 0.4543$: only 632 cases have a trace corresponding to a firing sequence of N_2. The fitness of N_4 is $\frac{1391}{1391} = 1$ because the "flower model" is able to replay all traces in Table 7.1. This naïve fitness metric is less suitable for more realistic processes. Consider for instance a variant of WF-net N_1 in

Table 7.1 Event log L_{full}: a = *register request*, b = *examine thoroughly*, c = *examine casually*, d = *check ticket*, e = *decide*, f = *reinitiate request*, g = *pay compensation*, and h = *reject request*

Frequency	Reference	Trace
455	σ_1	$\langle a, c, d, e, h\rangle$
191	σ_2	$\langle a, b, d, e, g\rangle$
177	σ_3	$\langle a, d, c, e, h\rangle$
144	σ_4	$\langle a, b, d, e, h\rangle$
111	σ_5	$\langle a, c, d, e, g\rangle$
82	σ_6	$\langle a, d, c, e, g\rangle$
56	σ_7	$\langle a, d, b, e, h\rangle$
47	σ_8	$\langle a, c, d, e, f, d, b, e, h\rangle$
38	σ_9	$\langle a, d, b, e, g\rangle$
33	σ_{10}	$\langle a, c, d, e, f, b, d, e, h\rangle$
14	σ_{11}	$\langle a, c, d, e, f, b, d, e, g\rangle$
11	σ_{12}	$\langle a, c, d, e, f, d, b, e, g\rangle$
9	σ_{13}	$\langle a, d, c, e, f, c, d, e, h\rangle$
8	σ_{14}	$\langle a, d, c, e, f, d, b, e, h\rangle$
5	σ_{15}	$\langle a, d, c, e, f, b, d, e, g\rangle$
3	σ_{16}	$\langle a, c, d, e, f, b, d, e, f, d, b, e, g\rangle$
2	σ_{17}	$\langle a, d, c, e, f, d, b, e, g\rangle$
2	σ_{18}	$\langle a, d, c, e, f, b, d, e, f, b, d, e, g\rangle$
1	σ_{19}	$\langle a, d, c, e, f, d, b, e, f, b, d, e, h\rangle$
1	σ_{20}	$\langle a, d, b, e, f, b, d, e, f, d, b, e, g\rangle$
1	σ_{21}	$\langle a, d, c, e, f, d, b, e, f, c, d, e, f, d, b, e, g\rangle$

which places $p1$ and $p2$ are merged into a single place. Such a model will have a fitness of $\frac{0}{1391} = 0$, because none of the traces can be replayed. This fitness notion seems to be too strict as most of the model seems to be consistent with the event log. This is especially the case for larger process models. Consider, for example, a trace $\sigma = \langle a_1, a_2, \ldots, a_{100}\rangle$ in some log L. Now consider a model that cannot replay σ, but that can replay 99 of the 100 events in σ (i.e., the trace is "almost" fitting). Also consider another model that can only replay 10 of the 100 events in σ (i.e., the trace is not fitting at all). Using the naïve fitness metric, the trace would simply be classified as nonfitting for both models without acknowledging that σ was almost fitting in one model and in complete disagreement with the other model. Therefore, we use a fitness notion defined *at the level of events* rather than full traces.

In the naïve fitness computation just described, we stopped replaying a trace once we encounter a problem and mark it as nonfitting. Let us now just continue replaying the trace on the model but record is all situations where a transition is forced to fire without being enabled, i.e., we count all missing tokens. Moreover, we record the tokens that remain at the end. To explain the idea, we first replay σ_1 on top of WF-net N_1. Note that σ_1 can be replayed completely. However, we

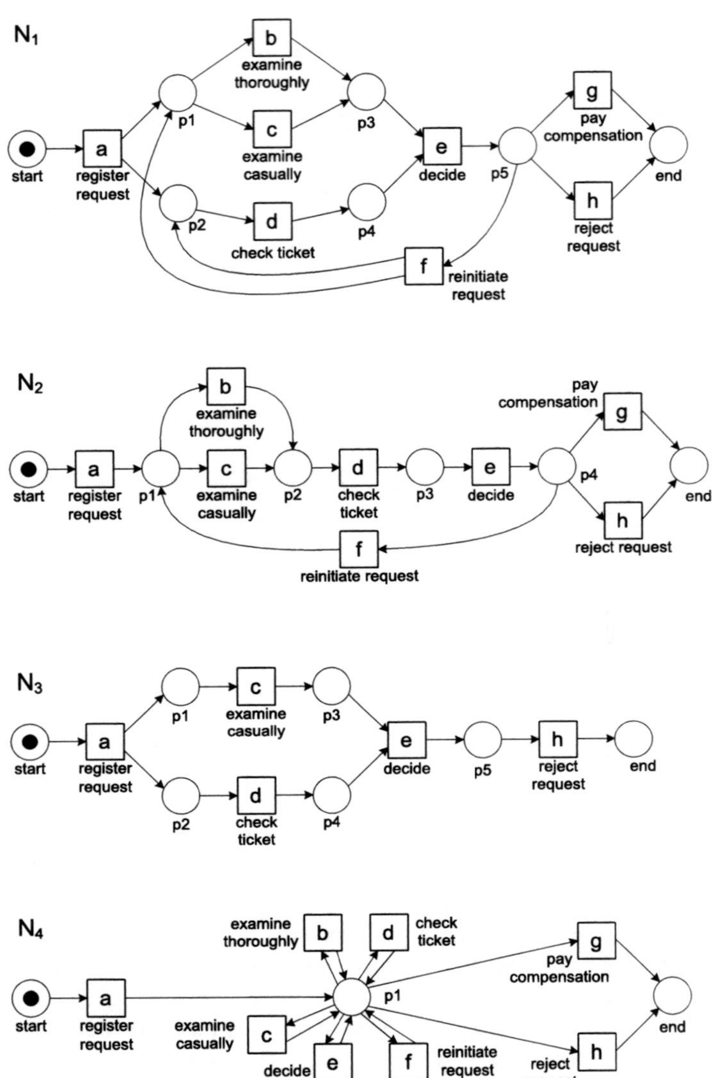

Fig. 7.2 Four WF-nets: N_1, N_2, N_3 and N_4

use this example to introduce the notation. Figure 7.3 shows the various stages of replay. Four counters are shown at each stage: p (produced tokens), c (consumed tokens), m (missing tokens), and r (remaining tokens). Let us first focus on p and c. Initially, $p = c = 0$ and all places are empty. Then the environment produces a token for place *start*. Therefore, the p counter is incremented: $p = 1$. Now we need to replay $\sigma_1 = \langle a, c, d, e, h \rangle$, i.e., we first fire transition a. This is possible. Since a consumes one token and produces two tokens, the c counter is incremented by

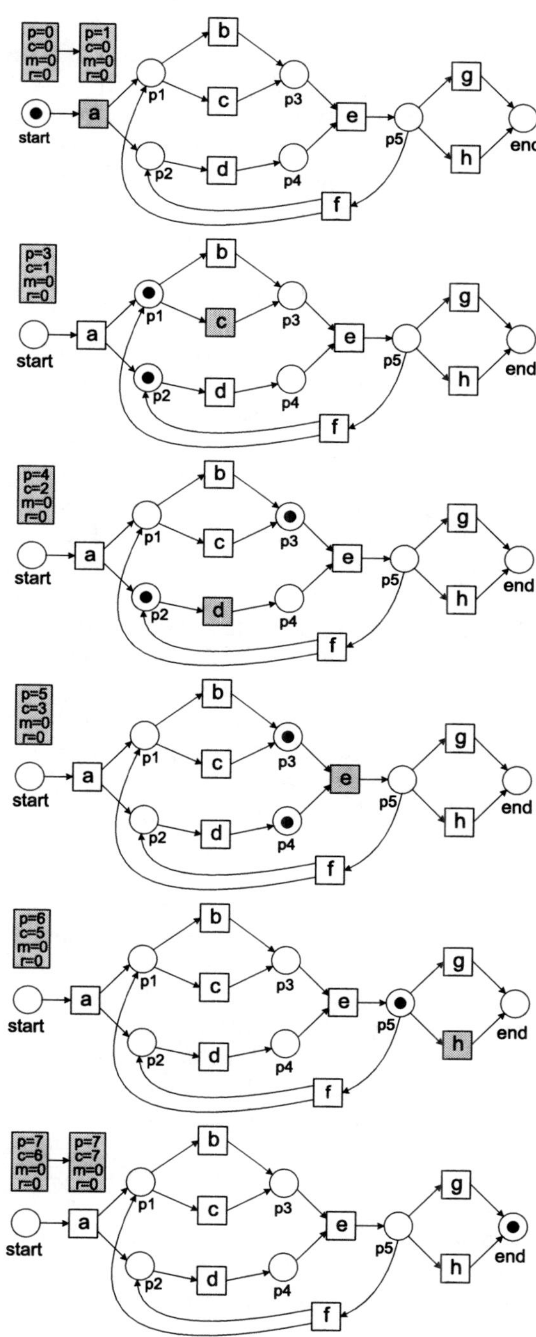

Fig. 7.3 Replaying $\sigma_1 = \langle a, c, d, e, h \rangle$ on top of WF-net N_1. There are four counters: p (produced tokens), c (consumed tokens), m (missing tokens), and r (remaining tokens)

1 and the p counter is incremented by 2. Therefore, $p = 3$ and $c = 1$ after firing transition a. Then we replay the second event (c). Firing transition c results in $p = 4$ and $c = 2$. After replaying the third event (i.e. d) $p = 5$ and $c = 3$. They we replay e. Since e consumes two tokens and produces one, the result is $p = 6$ and $c = 5$. Then we replay the last event (h). Firing h results in $p = 7$ and $c = 6$. At the end, the environment consumes a token from place *end*. Hence the final result is $p = c = 7$ and $m = r = 0$. Clearly, there are no problems when replaying the σ_1, i.e., there are no missing or remaining tokens ($m = r = 0$).

The fitness of a case with trace σ on WF-net N is defined as follows:

$$\mathit{fitness}(\sigma, N) = \frac{1}{2}\left(1 - \frac{m}{c}\right) + \frac{1}{2}\left(1 - \frac{r}{p}\right)$$

The first parts computes the fraction of missing tokens relative to the number of consumed tokens. $1 - \frac{m}{c} = 1$ if there are no missing tokens ($m = 0$) and $1 - \frac{m}{c} = 0$ if all tokens to be consumed were missing ($m = c$). Similarly, $1 - \frac{r}{p} = 1$ if there are no remaining tokens and $1 - \frac{r}{p} = 0$ if none of the produced tokens was actually consumed. We use an equal penalty for missing and remaining tokens. By definition: $0 \leq \mathit{fitness}(\sigma, N) \leq 1$. In our example, $\mathit{fitness}(\sigma_1, N_1) = \frac{1}{2}(1 - \frac{0}{7}) + \frac{1}{2}(1 - \frac{0}{7}) = 1$ because there are no missing or remaining tokens.

Let us now consider a trace that cannot be replayed properly. Figure 7.4 shows the process of replaying $\sigma_3 = \langle a, d, c, e, h\rangle$ on WF-net N_2. Initially, $p = c = 0$ and all places are empty. Then the environment produces a token for place *start* and the p counter is updated: $p = 1$. The first event (a) can be replayed. After firing a, we have $p = 2$, $c = 1$, $m = 0$, and $r = 0$. Now we try to replay the second event. This is not possible, because transition d is not enabled. To fire d, we need to add a token to place $p2$ and record the missing token, i.e., the m counter is incremented. The p and c counter are updated as usual. Therefore, after firing d, we have $p = 3$, $c = 2$, $m = 1$, and $r = 0$. We also tag place $p2$ to remember that a token was missing. Then we replay the next three events (c, e, h). The corresponding transitions are enabled. Therefore, we only need to update p and c counters. After replaying the last event, we have $p = 6$, $c = 5$, $m = 1$, and $r = 0$. In the final state $[p2, \mathit{end}]$, the environment consumes the token from place *end*. A token remains in place $p2$. Therefore, place $p2$ is tagged and the r counter is incremented. Hence, the final result is $p = c = 6$ and $m = r = 1$. Figure 7.4 shows diagnostic information that helps to understand the nature of non-conformance. There was a situation in which d occurred but could not happen according to the model (m-tag) and there was a situation in which d was supposed to happen but did not occur according to the log (r-tag). Moreover, we can compute the fitness of trace σ_3 on WF-net N_2 based on the values of p, c, m, and r:

$$\mathit{fitness}(\sigma_3, N_2) = \frac{1}{2}\left(1 - \frac{1}{6}\right) + \frac{1}{2}\left(1 - \frac{1}{6}\right) = 0.8333$$

As a third example, we replay $\sigma_2 = \langle a, b, d, e, g\rangle$ on top of WF-net N_3. Now the situation is slightly different because N_3 does not contain all activities appearing in the event log. In such a situation it seems reasonable to abstract from these events. Hence, we effectively replay $\sigma_2' = \langle a, d, e\rangle$. Figure 7.5 shows the process of replaying these three events. The first problem surfaces when replaying e. Since c did not

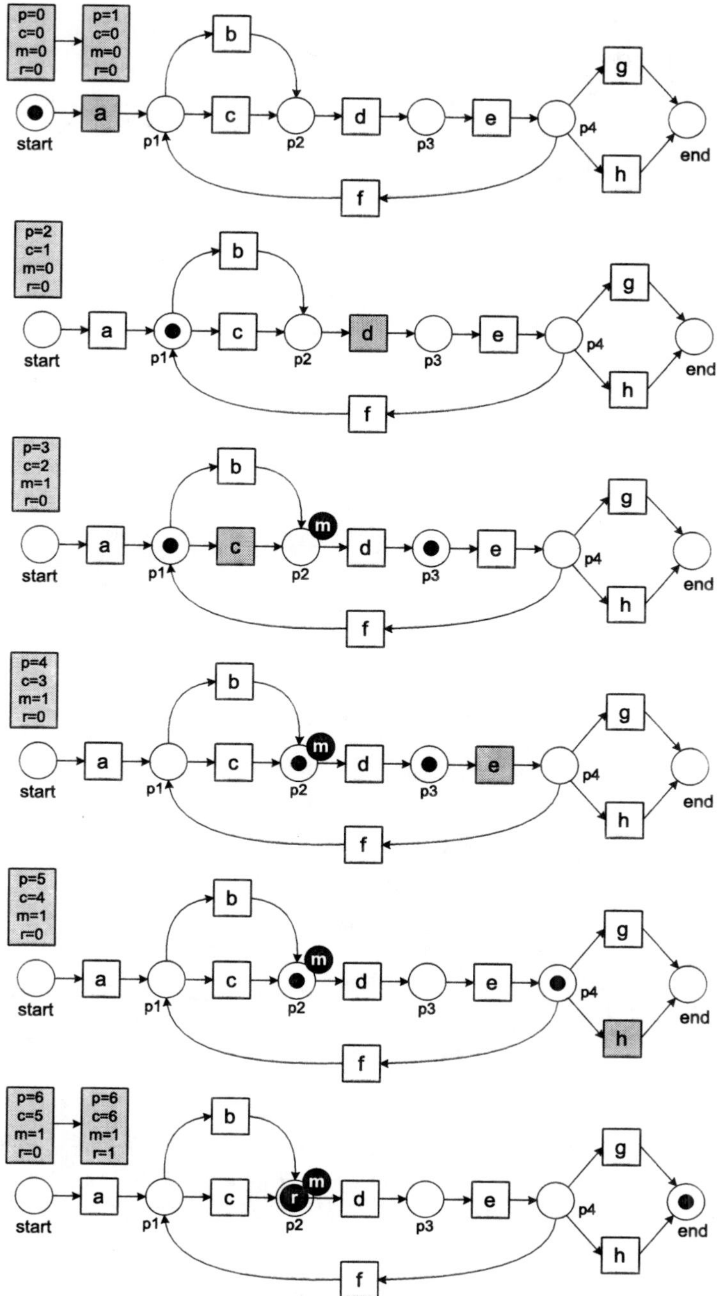

Fig. 7.4 Replaying $\sigma_3 = \langle a, d, c, e, h \rangle$ on top of WF-net N_2: one token is missing ($m = 1$) and one token is remaining ($r = 1$). The r-tag and m-tag highlight the place where σ_3 and the model diverge

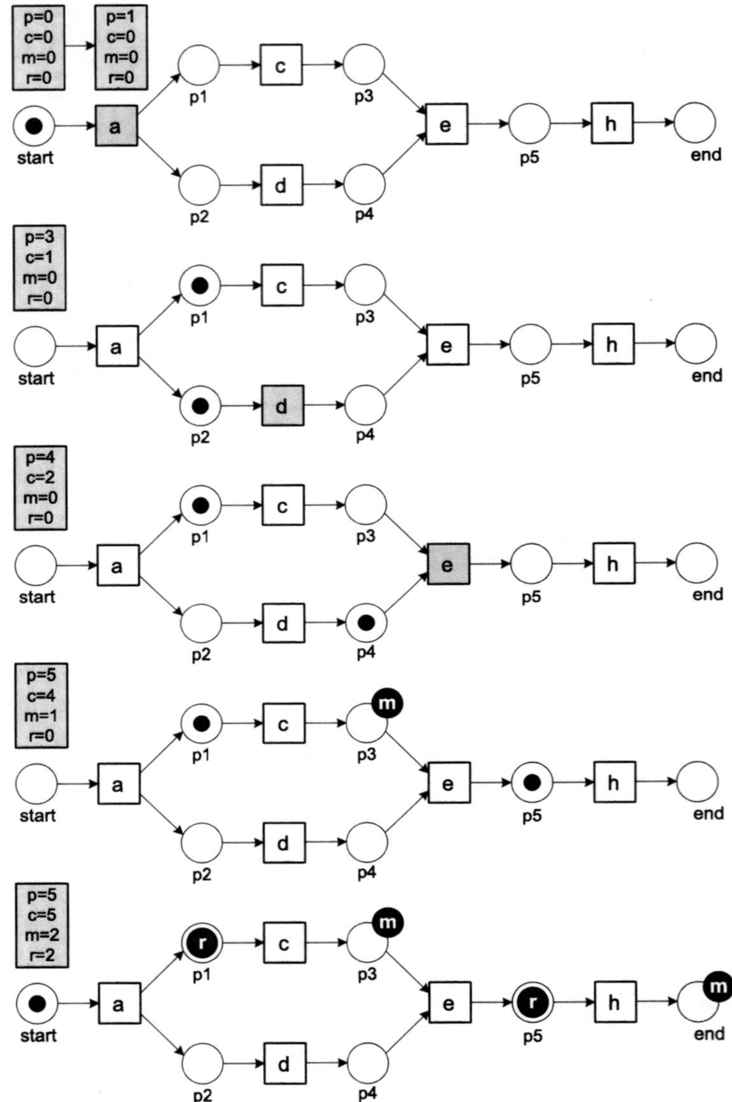

Fig. 7.5 To replay $\sigma_2 = \langle a, b, d, e, g \rangle$ on top of WF-net N_3, all events not corresponding to activities in the model are removed first. Replaying $\sigma_2' = \langle a, d, e \rangle$ shows that two tokens are missing ($m = 2$) and two tokens are remaining ($r = 2$) thus resulting in a fitness of 0.6

fire, place $p3$ is still empty and e is not enabled. The missing token is recorded ($m = 1$) and place $p3$ gets an m-tag. After replaying σ_2', the resulting marking is $[p1, p5]$. Now the environment needs to consume the token from place *end*. However, place *end* is not marked. Therefore, another missing token is recorded ($m = 2$)

and also place *end* gets an m-tag. Moreover, two tokens are remaining: one in place $p1$ and one in place $p5$. The places are tagged with an r-tag, and the two remaining tokens are recorded $r = 2$. This way we find a fitness of 0.6 for trace σ_2 and WF-net N_3 based on the values $p = 5$, $c = 5$, $m = 2$, and $r = 2$:

$$\mathit{fitness}(\sigma_2, N_3) = \frac{1}{2}\left(1 - \frac{2}{5}\right) + \frac{1}{2}\left(1 - \frac{2}{5}\right) = 0.6$$

Moreover, Fig. 7.5 clearly shows the cause of this poor conformance: c was supposed to happen according to the model but did not happen, e happened but was not possible according to the model, and h was supposed to happen but did not happen.

Figures 7.3, 7.4, 7.5 illustrate how to analyze the fitness of a single case. The same approach can be used to analyze the fitness of a log consisting of many cases. Simply take the sums of all produced, consumed, missing, and remaining tokens, and apply the same formula. Let $p_{N,\sigma}$ denote the number of produced tokens when replaying σ on N. $c_{N,\sigma}$, $m_{N,\sigma}$, $r_{N,\sigma}$ are defined in a similar fashion, e.g., $m_{N,\sigma}$ is the number of missing tokens when replaying σ on N. Now we can define the fitness of an event log L on WF-net N:

$$\mathit{fitness}(L, N) = \frac{1}{2}\left(1 - \frac{\sum_{\sigma \in L} L(\sigma) \times m_{N,\sigma}}{\sum_{\sigma \in L} L(\sigma) \times c_{N,\sigma}}\right) + \frac{1}{2}\left(1 - \frac{\sum_{\sigma \in L} L(\sigma) \times r_{N,\sigma}}{\sum_{\sigma \in L} L(\sigma) \times p_{N,\sigma}}\right)$$

Note that $\sum_{\sigma \in L} L(\sigma) \times m_{N,\sigma}$ is total number of missing tokens when replaying the entire event log, because $L(\sigma)$ is the frequency of trace σ and $m_{N,\sigma}$ is the number of missing tokens for a single instance of σ. The value of $\mathit{fitness}(L, N)$ is between 0 (very poor fitness; none of the produced tokens is consumed and all of the consumed tokens are missing) and 1 (perfect fitness; all cases can be replayed without any problems). Although $\mathit{fitness}(L, N)$ is a measure focusing on tokens in places, we will interpret it as a measure on events. The intuition of $\mathit{fitness}(L, N) = 0.9$ is that about 90% of the *events* can be replayed correctly.[1] This is only an informal characterization as fitness depends on missing and remaining tokens rather than events. For instance, a transition that is forced to fire during replay may have multiple empty input places. Note that if two subsequent events are swapped in a sequential process, this results in one missing and one remaining token. This seems reasonable, but also shows that the relation between the proportion of events that cannot be replayed correctly and the proportion of tokens that are missing or remaining is rather indirect.

By replaying the entire event log, we can now compute the fitness of event log L_{full} for the four models in Fig. 7.2

$$\mathit{fitness}(L_{\mathit{full}}, N_1) = 1$$
$$\mathit{fitness}(L_{\mathit{full}}, N_2) = 0.9504$$
$$\mathit{fitness}(L_{\mathit{full}}, N_3) = 0.8797$$
$$\mathit{fitness}(L_{\mathit{full}}, N_4) = 1$$

[1] In the remainder of this book, we often use this intuitive characterization of fitness, although from a technical point of view this is incorrect as $\mathit{fitness}(L, N)$ is only an indication of the fraction of events that can be replayed correctly.

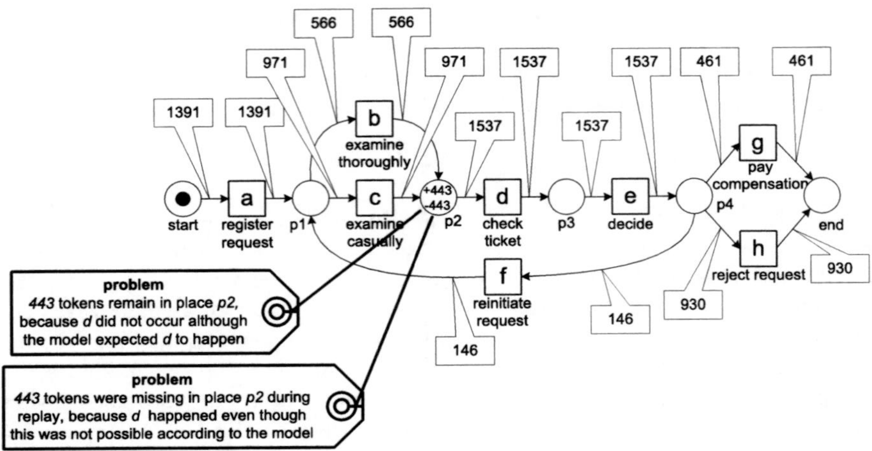

Fig. 7.6 Diagnostic information showing the deviations ($fitness(L_{full}, N_2) = 0.9504$)

This shows that, as expected, N_1 and N_4 can replay event log L_{full} without any problems (i.e., fitness 1). $fitness(L_{full}, N_2) = 0.9504$. Intuitively, this means that about 95% of the events in L_{full} can be replayed correctly on N_2. As indicated earlier, this can be viewed in two ways:

- Event log L_{full} has a fitness of 0.9504, i.e., about 5% of the events deviate.
- Process model N_2 has a fitness of 0.9504, i.e., the model is unable to explain 5% of the observed behavior.

The first view is used when the model is considered to be normative and correct ("the event log, i.e. reality, does not conform to the model"). The second view is used when the model should be descriptive ("the process model does not conform to reality"). $fitness(L_{full}, N_3) = 0.8797$, i.e., about 88% of the events in L_{full} can be replayed on N_3. Hence, process model N_3 has the lowest fitness of the four models.

Typically, the event-based fitness is higher than the naïve case-based fitness. This is also the case here. WF-net N_2 can only replay 68% of the cases from start to end. However, about 95% of the individual events can be replayed.

Figure 7.6 shows some the diagnostics than can be generated based on replaying event log L_{full} on process model N_2. The numbers on arcs indicate the flow of produced and consumed tokens. These show how cases flowed through the model, e.g., 146 times a request was reinitiated, 930 requests were rejected and 461 requests resulted in a payment. The places tagged during replay (i.e., the m and r-tags in Figs. 7.3, 7.4, and 7.5) can be aggregated to diagnose conformance problems and reveal their severity. As Fig. 7.6 shows, 443 times activity d happend although it was not supposed to happen and 443 times activity d was supposed to happen but did not. The reason is that d was executed before b or c, which is not possible according to this sequential model.

Similarly, diagnostic information is shown for N_3 in Fig. 7.7. There the problems are more severe. For example, 566 times a decision was made (activity e) without

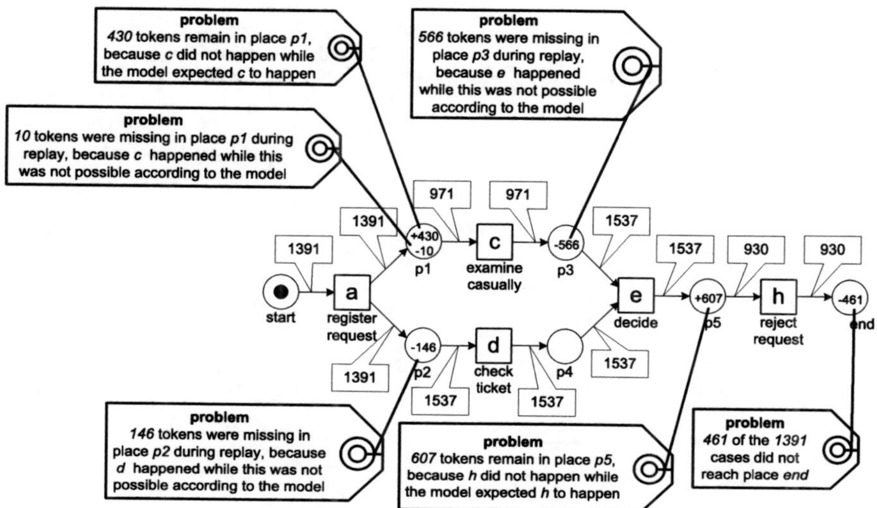

Fig. 7.7 Diagnostic information showing the deviations ($fitness(L_{full}, N_3) = 0.8797$)

being examined casually (activity c), and 461 cases did not reach the end because the request was not rejected.

As Fig. 7.8 shows, an event log can be split into two sublogs: *one event log containing only fitting cases and one event log containing only non-fitting cases*. Each of the event logs can be used for further analysis. For example, one could construct a process model for the event log containing only deviating cases. Also other data and process mining techniques can be used. For instance, it is interesting to know which people handled the deviating cases and whether these cases took longer or were more costly. In case fraud is suspected, one may create a social network based on the event log with deviating cases (see Sect. 8.3).

One could also use classification techniques to further investigate non-conformance. Recall that a decision tree can be learned from a table with one response variable and multiple predictor variables. Whether a case fits or not can be seen as the value of a response variable whereas characteristics of the case (e.g., case and event attributes) serve a predictor variables. The resulting decision tree attempts to explain conformance in terms of characteristics of the case. For example, one could find out that cases from gold customers handled by Pete tend to deviate. We will elaborate on this in Sect. 8.5.

The idea to replay event logs on process models is not limited to Petri nets. Any process modeling notation with executable semantics allows for replay. See also the replay techniques used in [31, 50, 123, 124]. However, having explicit places and a clear start and end place in WF-nets facilitates the generation of meaningful diagnostics. Replay becomes more complicated when there are duplicate and silent activities, e.g., transitions with a τ label or two transitions with the same label. In general, there can be a many-to-many relationship between event names in the event

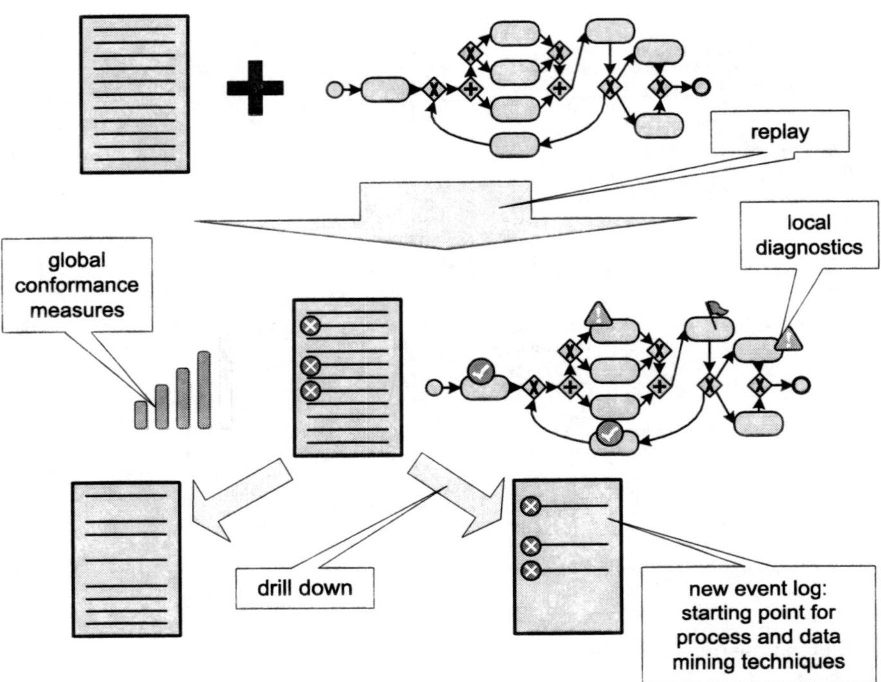

Fig. 7.8 Conformance checking provides global conformance measures like *fitness*(L, N) and local diagnostics (e.g., showing activities that were executed although not allowed according to the process model). Moreover, the event log is partitioned into fitting and non-fitting cases. Both sublogs can be used for further analysis, e.g., discovering a process model for the deviating cases

log and activity names in the process model. Activities that appear in the event log but that have no counterpart in the model are easy to handle; as illustrated when computing *fitness*(σ_2, N_3) one can simply discard these events. For handling duplicate and silent activities, local state-space explorations can be used to find the corresponding (most likely) path in the process model [80]. For instance, τ-labeled transitions in the model that do not correspond to events in the log are only executed if they can enable transitions that correspond to subsequent events in the event log. The drawback is that such local state-space explorations can be time-consuming for larger event logs. Moreover, local state-space exploration provides only a heuristic. For example, if two transitions with the same label are enabled, then randomly taking one of them can have effects on the fitness of the model at a later stage in the trace; see [80] for details. Also see the more advanced replay technique described in [2]. Here, a variant of the A^* algorithm is used to find an "optimal" replay of cases.

The techniques described in [2, 80] can deal with the situation that the set of activities in the model A_M differs from the set of activities in the event log A_L. The activities in the log but not in the model $(A_L \setminus A_M)$ are simply ignored and the activities in the model but not in the log $(A_M \setminus A_L)$ are considered to be silent. This may lead to rather optimistic conformance values. Alternatively, one can also preprocess the model and log such that both agree on the set of activities. After this preprocessing step, events referring to activities that do not appear in the model and the skipping of activities that do not appear in the log are considered to be deviations.

In this section, we focused exclusively on fitness (i.e., the proportion of events in the log that can be explained by the process model). This is only one of the four quality criteria discussed in Sect. 5.4.3. For conformance checking, the other three quality criteria are less relevant. However, replay techniques can also be used to analyze *precision* (avoiding underfitting models) and *generalization* (avoiding overfitting models). This can be done by keeping track of the number of enabled transitions during replay. If, on average, many transitions are enabled during replay, the model is likely to be underfitting. If, on average, very few transitions are enabled during replay, the model is likely to be overfitting. For example, in the "flower model" N_4 in Fig. 7.2, activities b, c, d, e, and f are all continuously enabled in-between start and end. The relatively high mean number of enabled transitions when replaying the log using N_4, suggests that the model is underfitting. See [33, 78, 80] for more information.

7.3 Comparing Footprints

In Sect. 5.2, we defined the notion of a *footprint*, i.e., a matrix showing causal dependencies. Such a matrix characterizes the event log. For instance, Table 7.2 shows the footprint matrix of L_{full}. This matrix is derived from the "directly follows" relation $>_{L_{full}}$. Clearly, process models also have a footprint: simply generate a complete event log, i.e., Play-out the model and record execution sequences. From the viewpoint of a footprint matrix, an event log is complete if and only if all activities that can follow one another do so at least once in the log. Applying this to N_1 in Fig. 7.2 results in the same footprint matrix (i.e., Table 7.2). This suggests that the event log and the model "conform".

Table 7.3 shows the footprint matrix generated for WF-net N_2, i.e., Play-out N_2 to record a complete log and derived its footprint. Comparing both footprint matrices (Tables 7.2 and 7.3) reveals several differences as shown in Table 7.4. For example, the relation between a and d changed from $\rightarrow$ to #. When comparing event log L_{full} with WF-net N_2 it can indeed be seen that in L_{full} activity a is directly followed by d whereas this is not possible in N_2. The relation between b and d changed from $\|$ to $\rightarrow$. This reflects that in WF-net N_2 both activities are no longer parallel. Besides providing detailed diagnostics, Table 7.4 can also be used to quantify conformance. For instance, 12 of the 64 cells differ. Hence, one could say that the conformance based on the footprints is $1 - \frac{12}{64} = 0.8125$.

Conformance analysis based on footprints is only meaningful if the log is complete with respect to the "directly follows" relation $>_L$. This can be verified using k-fold cross-validation (see Sect. 3.6.2).

Interestingly, both models and event logs have footprints. This allows for *log-to-model* comparisons as just described, i.e., it can be checked whether and model

Table 7.2 Footprint of L_{full} and N_1

	a	*b*	*c*	*d*	*e*	*f*	*g*	*h*
a	#	→	→	→	#	#	#	#
b	←	#	#	∥	→	←	#	#
c	←	#	#	∥	→	←	#	#
d	←	∥	∥	#	→	←	#	#
e	#	←	←	←	#	→	→	→
f	#	→	→	→	←	#	#	#
g	#	#	#	#	←	#	#	#
h	#	#	#	#	←	#	#	#

Table 7.3 Footprint of N_2 shown in Fig. 7.2

	a	*b*	*c*	*d*	*e*	*f*	*g*	*h*
a	#	→	→	#	#	#	#	#
b	←	#	#	→	#	←	#	#
c	←	#	#	→	#	←	#	#
d	#	←	←	#	→	#	#	#
e	#	#	#	←	#	→	→	→
f	#	→	→	#	←	#	#	#
g	#	#	#	#	←	#	#	#
h	#	#	#	#	←	#	#	#

Table 7.4 Differences between the footprints of L_{full} and N_2. The event log and the model "disagree" on 12 of the 64 cells of the footprint matrix

	a	*b*	*c*	*d*	*e*	*f*	*g*	*h*
a				→:#				
b				∥:→	→:#			
c				∥:→	→:#			
d	←:#	∥:←	∥:←			←:#		
e		←:#	←:#					
f				→:#				
g								
h								

and log "agree" on the ordering of activities. However, the same approach can be used for *log-to-log* and *model-to-model* comparisons. Comparing the footprints of two process models (model-to-model comparison) allows for the quantification of their similarity. Comparing the footprints of two event logs (log-to-log comparison) can, for example, be used for detecting *concept drift*. The term concept drift refers to the situation in which the process is changing while being analyzed. For instance, in the beginning of the event log two activities may be concurrent whereas later in the log these activities become sequential. This can be discovered by splitting the log into smaller logs and analyzing the footprints of the smaller logs. A log-to-log comparison of a sequence of event logs may reveal concept drift. Such a "second order process mining" requires lots of data because all the smaller logs are assumed to be complete with respect to $>_L$.

A topic typically neglected in literature and tools is the *cross-validation of conformance*. The event log is just a sample of behavior. This sample may be too small to make a reliable statement about conformance. Moreover, there may be additional complications like concept drift. For example, the average conformance over 2011 is 0.80, however, in the beginning of the year it was 0.90, but during the last two months conformance has been below 0.60. Most techniques provide a single conformance metric without stating anything about the reliability of the measure or concept drift. For instance, suppose we have a large event log L_1 and a small event log L_2 such that $L_2 \subset L_1$ and $|L_2| = 0.01 \times |L_1|$, i.e., L_2 contains 1% of the cases in L_1. Suppose that $\mathit{fitness}(L_1, N) = 0.9$ and $\mathit{fitness}(L_2, N) = 0.6$. Clearly, the first value is much more reliable (as it is based on a log 100 times larger) but this is not expressed in the metric. If there is enough data to do cross-validation, the event log could be split randomly into k parts (see also Sect. 3.6.2). Then the fitness could be computed for all k parts. These k independent measures could then be used to create a confidence interval for the conformance of the underlying process, e.g., the fitness is, with 90% confidence, between 0.86 and 0.94. Some of the conformance measures have a tendency to go up or down when the event log is larger or smaller. Whereas token replay is insensitive to the size of the log, other measures like the ones based on the footprint matrix depend on the size and completeness of the event log. Consider, for example, an event log L split into two smaller logs L_1 and L_2. Assuming that the process is in steady state, the expected value for $\mathit{fitness}(L, N)$ is identical to the expected value for $\mathit{fitness}(L_1, N)$ and $\mathit{fitness}(L_2, N)$. This does not hold for measures like the footprint matrix: relation $>_L$ can only grow if the log gets larger. Relative thresholds, as used for heuristic mining, may be used to reduce this effect.

The footprint is just one of many possible characterizations of event logs and models. In principle, any temporal property can be used. Instead of the "directly follows" relation also an "eventually follows" relation $\gg_L$ can be used. $a \gg_L b$ means that there is at least one case for which a was eventually followed by b. This can also be combined with some time window, e.g., a was followed by b within four steps or a was followed by b within four hours. It is also possible to take frequencies into account (see for example measures such as $|a >_L b|$ and $|a \Rightarrow_L b|$ defined in the context of heuristic mining) and use thresholds. Clearly, the characterizations used to compare logs and models should match the notion of conformance one is interested in.

The token-based replay technique described in Sect. 7.2 and the comparison of footprint matrices can be used to check the conformance of an event log and a *whole* process model. It is of course also possible to directly check specific *constraints*, sometimes referred to as "business rules". An example of a constraint is that activity a should always be followed by activity b. Another example is the so-called *4-eyes principle*: activities a and b should never be executed by the same person, e.g., to avoid fraud. In [105] it is shown how an LTL-based language can be used in the context of process mining. *Linear Temporal Logic* (LTL) is an example of a temporal logic that, in addition to classical logical operators, uses temporal operators such as: always ($\Box$), eventually ($\Diamond$), until ($\sqcup$), weak until (W), and next time ($\bigcirc$) [20]. For instance, one could formulate the rule $\Box(a \Rightarrow \Diamond(g \vee h))$, i.e., if a occurs, it should eventually be followed by g or h. Another example is the rule $\Diamond g \Leftrightarrow !(\Diamond h)$ stating that eventually either g should happen or h should happen, but not both. The directly follows relation $a >_L b$ used earlier can be expressed in LTL: "$\Diamond(a \ \wedge \ \bigcirc(b))$" (for at least one case). This illustrates that behavioral characterizations such as footprints can often be expressed in terms of LTL. LTL-based constraints as defined in [105] may also include explicit time and data. For example, it is possible to state that within two days after the occurrence of activity e, one of the activities g or h should have happened. Another example is that for gold customers the request should be handled in one week and for silver customers in two weeks.

Constraints may be used to split the log into two parts as described in Fig. 7.8. This way it is possible to further investigate cases that violate some business rule.

Declare: A Constraint-Based Workflow Language

In this book, we focus on mainstream process modeling languages like Petri nets, BPMN, EPCs, and YAWL. These languages are procedural and aim to describe end-to-end processes. In the context of conformance checking it is interesting to also consider declarative process modeling languages. *Declare* is such a language (in fact a family of languages) and a fully functional WFM system [68, 108]. Declare uses a graphical notation and semantics based on LTL. Figure 7.9 shows a Declare specification consisting of four constraints. The construct connecting activities g and h is a so-called *non-coexistence constraint*. In terms of LTL, this constraint means "$!((\Diamond g) \wedge (\Diamond h))$"; $\Diamond g$ and $\Diamond h$ cannot both be true, i.e., it cannot be the case that both g and h happen for the same case. There are two *precedence constraints*. The semantics of the precedence constraint connecting e to g can also be expressed in terms of LTL: "$(!g)\ W\ e$", i.e., g should not happen before e has happened. Since the weak until (W) is used in "$(!g)\ W\ e$", traces without any g and e events also satisfy the constraint. Similarly, h should not happen before e has happened: "$(!h)\ W\ e$". The constraint connecting a to g and h is a so-called branched constraint involving three activities. This *response constraint* states that every occurrence of a should eventually be followed by g or h: "$\Box(a \Rightarrow (\Diamond(g \vee h)))$". The latter constraint allows for $\langle a, a, a, g, h, a, a, h \rangle$ but not $\langle a, g, h, a \rangle$. Example traces that satisfy all four constraints are $\langle a, a, e, e, g \rangle$ and $\langle a, e, h, e \rangle$.

Procedural languages only allow for activities that are explicitly triggered through control-flow (token semantics). In a declarative language like Declare "*everything is possible unless explicitly forbidden*".

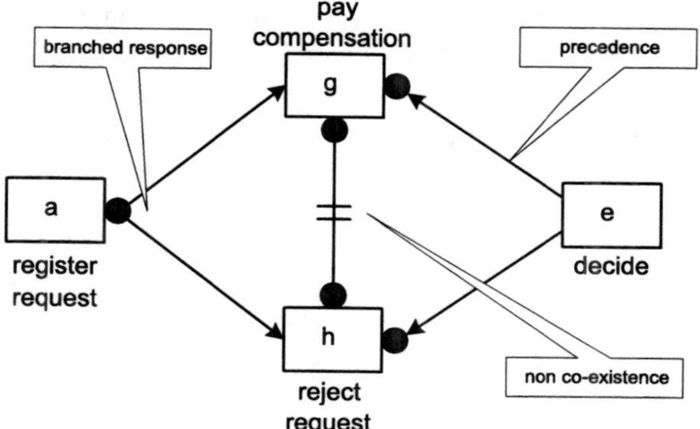

Fig. 7.9 *Declare* specification consisting of four constraints: two precedence constraints, one non-coexistence constraint, and one branched response constraint

The Declare language is supported by a WFM system that is much more flexible than traditional procedural WFM/BPM systems [108]. Moreover, it is possible to learn Declare models by analyzing event logs [60, 68]. The graphical constraint language is also suitable for conformance checking. Given an event log, it is possible to check all the constraints. Consider, for instance, Fig. 7.9. Given an event log one can show for each constraint the proportion of cases that respects this constraint [68, 108]. In case of conformance checking, complex time-based constraints may be used (e.g., after every occurrence of activity a for a gold customer, activity g or h should happen within 24 hours).

7.4 Other Applications of Conformance Checking

Conformance checking can be used for improving the alignment of business processes, organizations, and information systems. As shown, replay techniques and footprint analysis help to identify differences between a process model and the real process as recorded in the event log. The differences identified may lead to changes of the model or process. For example, exposing deviations between the model and process may lead to better work instructions or changes in management. Conformance checking is also a useful tool for auditors that need to make sure that processes are executed within the boundaries set by various stakeholders.

In this section, we show that conformance checking can be used for other purposes such as repairing models and evaluating process discovery algorithms. Moreover, through conformance checking event logs get connected to process models and thus provide a basis for all kinds of analysis.

7.4.1 Repairing Models

When a process model and an event log "disagree" on the process, this should lead to adaptations of the model or the process itself. Let us assume that we want to use conformance checking to *repair the model*, i.e., to align it with reality. The diagnostics provided in Figs. 7.6 and 7.7 can be used to (semi-)automatically repair the model. For instance, paths that are never taken can be removed from the model. Note that Figs. 7.6 and 7.7 show the frequency of activities and their causal dependencies. This may lead to the removal of activities that are never (or seldom) executed or the removal of choices. Token replay does not help to remove concurrency that is never used (e.g., activities modeled in parallel but executed in sequence). However, this can be seen in the footprint matrix. After removing unused parts of the model, the m and r-tags pointing to missing and remaining tokens can be used to repair the model. An m-tag points out activities that happened in the process but that were not possible according to the model. An r-tag points out activities that did not happen but that were supposed to happen according to the model. Comparing the footprint matrices of the log and model will show similar problems. Such information can be used by a designer to repair the model. In principle, it is possible to do this automatically. For example, given a set of edit operations on the model one could look for the model that is "closest" to the original model but that has a fitness of, say, more than 0.9. It is fairly straightforward to develop a genetic algorithm that minimizes the edit distance while ensuring a minimal fitness level: edit operations to repair a model are closely related to the genetic operations (mutation and crossover) described in Sect. 6.3.

7.4.2 Evaluating Process Discovery Algorithms

In Sect. 5.4, we discussed the challenges that process discovery algorithms are facing: incompleteness, noise, etc. Process discovery is a complex task and many algorithms have been proposed in literature. As discussed in [81], it is not easy to compare the different algorithms. Compared to classical data mining challenges there seem to be much more dimensions both in terms of *representation* (see, for instance, the more than 40 control-flow patterns gathered in the context of the Workflow Patterns Initiative [101, 130]) and *quality criteria*. In Sect. 5.4.3, we described four quality dimensions: *fitness*, *simplicity*, *precision*, and *generalization*. Obviously, conformance checking is closely related to measuring the fitness of a discovered model. Whether the model used for conformance checking is made by hand or discovered using some process mining algorithm is irrelevant for the techniques presented in this chapter. Hence, conformance checking, as described in this chapter, can also be used to evaluate and compare process discovery algorithms. Although the focus of token replay in Sect. 7.2 was on the fitness dimension, replay can also be used to say something about the precision and generalization dimensions. A model with a severe lack of precision, will, on average, have many enabled transitions during replay. If, on average, very few transitions are enabled during replay, the model is likely to be overfitting and thus not general enough. Also the footprint matrix can be used to analyze precision and generalization [80]. Conformance checking is unrelated to the simplicity dimension. Obviously, a process discovery

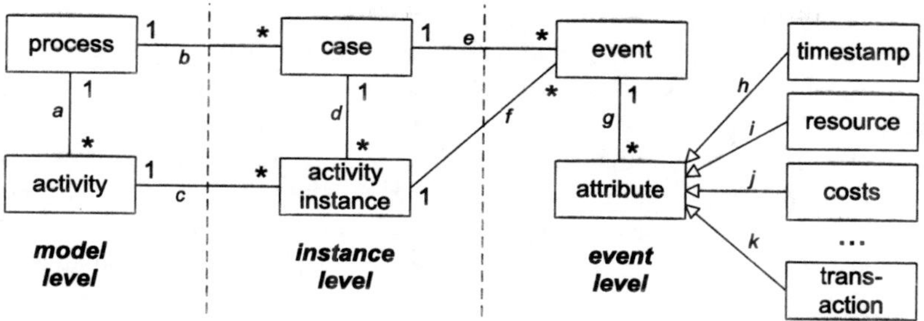

Fig. 7.10 The instance level—established during conformance checking—connects the model level and the event level

algorithm should generate the simplest model possible that is able to explain the behavior. See [66] for an overview of 19 metrics used to quantify the complexity and understandability of a process model. The metrics consider aspects such as the size of the model (e.g., the number of nodes and/or arcs) and the "structuredness" or "homogeneity" of the model [66].

7.4.3 Connecting Event Log and Process Model

While replaying the model, events in the log are related to activities in the model, i.e., the event log is *connected* to the process model. This may seem insignificant at first sight. However, this is of crucial importance for the subsequent chapters. *By relating events to activities, information extracted from the log can be used to enrich the process.* For example, timestamps in the event log can be used to make statements about the duration of some modeled activity.

Figure 7.10 shows the connection between the process model and event log established during replay. Three levels are identified: model level, instance level, and event level. The model level and the event level typically *exist independent of one another*; people make process models without relating them to (raw) data in the information system and processes generate data while being unaware of the process models that may exist. Notable exceptions are WFM and BPM systems for which such a connection already exists. This is why such systems are not just important for process automation, but also serve as a powerful enabler for business intelligence solutions. However, for the majority of processes, there is no supporting WFM or BPM system. As a result, process models (if they exist) and event data are at best loosely coupled. Fortunately, *token replay can be used to establish a tight coupling between the model and event levels*.

The instance level shown in Fig. 7.10 consists of *cases* and *activity instances* that connect *processes* and *activities* in the model to *events* in the event log. When modeling, cases and activity instances only exist in abstract form. It is clear that a WF-net or BPMN model can be instantiated, thus creating a case. However, only when observing a real process one can talk about concrete instances of the process (i.e., a case). The same holds for activities and activity instances. In a WF-net or BPMN model, an activity is just a square. Only when the process is executed, such an activity is instantiated for a particular case. Within the same case (i.e., process instance) there may be multiple instances of the same activity. For instance, some check activity may be performed multiple times for the same customer request (cf. loops). When modeling a process such activity instances only exist in abstract form.

Typical event data exist in the form of collections of records possibly distributed over multiple tables. A record in such a table may correspond to one or more events and lists a number of properties (attributes), e.g., date information, some amount, and credit rating. As discussed in Chap. 4, one of the main challenges is to locate these events and to correlate them. Each event needs to be related to a particular case. When replaying the event log on a model, each event that "fits into the model" is connected to an activity instance. Note that there can be multiple instances of the same activity for each case. Moreover, a single activity instance may correspond to multiple events. Consider a case c with a loop involving activity a. Two instances of a are executed for c: $a_{c,1}$ and $a_{c,2}$. For each of these two activity instances, there may be multiple events. For example, the first activity is offered, started, and aborted (three events corresponding to $a_{c,1}$) whereas the second activity is assigned, started, suspended, resumed, and completed (five events corresponding to $a_{c,2}$). See also Sect. 4.2 where the transactional life-cycle is discussed in detail. When describing replay, we did not elaborate on the different events types (start, complete, abort, etc.). However, such transactional information can be taken into account when replaying the event log.

During replay events are connected to activity instances. *This way the event log "breathes life" into otherwise static process models.* As a result, all kinds of information extracted from the event log can be projected onto the model, e.g., showing bottlenecks and highlighting frequent paths.

The class diagram shown in Fig. 7.10 shows the following associations and cardinalities:

- *a* Every process may have an arbitrary number of activities, but each activity belongs to precisely one process.
- *b* Every case belongs to precisely one process.
- *c* Every activity instance refers to precisely one activity.
- *d* Every activity instance belongs to precisely one case; there may be several activity instances for each activity/case combination.
- *e* Every event refers to precisely one case.
- *f* Every event corresponds to one activity instance; for the same activity instance there may be multiple events.
- *g* Every attribute refers to one event; each attribute has a name and a value, e.g., "(*birthdate*, *29-01-1966*)".
- *h–k* There are different types of attributes, e.g., time, resource, cost and transactional information.

It is easy to imagine situations in which the same event refers to multiple cases and activity instances (see also Sect. 4.4). In Fig. 7.10, we assume that in such cases the event is replicated for the various instances, e.g., create a dedicated viewpoint for each view one would like to consider.

The attributes provide valuable information when being connected to activities. For instance, timestamps can be used to visualize bottlenecks, waiting times, etc. Resource data attached to events can be used to learn working patterns and allocation rules. Cost information can be projected onto process models to see inefficiencies. The next chapter will elaborate on this.

Chapter 8
Mining Additional Perspectives

Whereas the main focus of process discovery is on the control-flow perspective, event logs may contain a wealth of information relating to other perspectives such as the organizational perspective, the case perspective, and the time perspective. Therefore, we now shift our attention to these other perspectives. Organizational mining can be used to get insight into typical work patterns, organizational structures, and social networks. Timestamps and frequencies of activities can be used to identify bottlenecks and diagnose other performance related problems. Case data can be used to better understand decision-making and analyze differences among cases. Moreover, the different perspectives can be merged into a single model providing an integrated view on the process. Such an integrated model can be used for "what if" analysis using simulation.

8.1 Perspectives

Thus far, the focus of this book was on control-flow, i.e., the ordering of activities. The chapters on process discovery and conformance checking often used a so-called "simple event log" as a starting point (see Definition 4.4). However, as discussed in Chap. 4, event logs typically contain much more information. Events and cases can have any number of attributes (see Definitions 4.1 and 4.3). The extension mechanism of XES illustrates how such attributes can be structured and stored. Moreover, as stressed in Sect. 1.3, process mining is not limited to the control-flow perspective. Therefore, we now focus on adding some of the other perspectives.

Figure 8.1 shows a typical scenario. The starting point is an event log and some initial process model. Note that the process model may have been constructed manually or discovered through process mining. Important is that the process model and event log are connected. In Sect. 7.4.3, we showed that the replay approaches used in the context of conformance checking can be used to tightly couple model and log. As discussed using Fig. 7.10, activity instances discovered during replay connect modeled activities to recorded events. This way attributes of events (resources,

W.M.P. van der Aalst, *Process Mining*,
DOI 10.1007/978-3-642-19345-3_8, © Springer-Verlag Berlin Heidelberg 2011

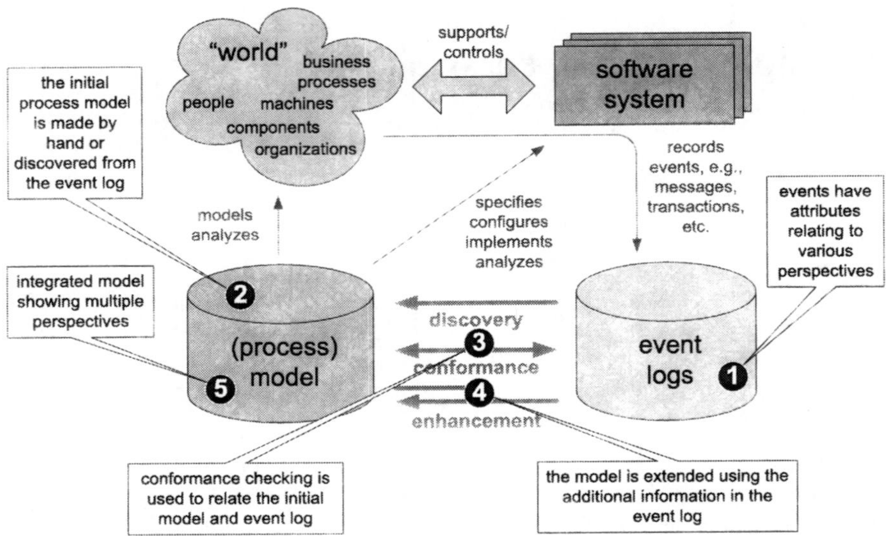

Fig. 8.1 The organizational, case, and time perspectives can be added to the original control-flow model using attributes from the event log

timestamps, costs, etc.) can be used to extend the initial model. For example, information about service or waiting times extracted from the event log can be added to the model. After adding the different perspectives, an *integrated* process model is obtained.

Figure 8.1 lists the three main types of process mining: *discovery*, *conformance*, and *enhancement*. Let us focus on the third type of process mining. Enhancement aims to extend or improve an existing process model using information about the actual process recorded in some event log. One type of enhancement is *repair* as discussed in Sect. 7.4.1. Here, we devote our attention to other type of enhancement: *extension*. Through extension we add a new perspective to the process model by cross-correlating it with the log.

In the remainder, we show some examples of log-based model extension. Section 8.3 discusses various process mining techniques related to the organizational perspective. Here, information about resources is used to analyze working patterns and to see how work "flows" through an organization. Extensions based on the time perspective are discussed in Sect. 8.4. When events bear timestamps it is possible to discover bottlenecks, measure service levels, monitor the utilization of resources, and predict the remaining processing time of running cases. Section 8.5 focuses on other attributes and their effects on decision making. This section illustrates that classical data mining techniques such as decision tree learning can be used to extend a process model with the case perspective. The different perspectives can be merged into a single integrated process model. Section 8.6 shows how such an integrated model can be constructed and used. For instance, a complete simulation model can be mined and subsequently used for "what if" analysis.

Table 8.1 A fragment of some event log: each line corresponds to an event

Case id	Event id	Properties				
		Time	Activity	Trans	Resource	Cost
1	35654423	30-12-2010:11.02	Register request	Start	Pete	
	35654424	30-12-2010:11.08	Register request	Complete	Pete	50
	35654425	31-12-2010:10.06	Examine thoroughly	Start	Sue	
	35654427	31-12-2010:10.08	Check ticket	Start	Mike	
	35654428	31-12-2010:10.12	Examine thoroughly	Complete	Sue	400
	35654429	31-12-2010:10.20	Check ticket	Complete	Mike	100
	35654430	06-01-2011:11.18	Decide	Start	Sara	
	35654431	06-01-2011:11.22	Decide	Complete	Sara	200
	35654432	07-01-2011:14.24	Reject request	Start	Pete	
	35654433	07-01-2011:14.32	Reject request	Complete	Pete	200
2	35654483	30-12-2010:11.32	Register request	Start	Mike	
	35654484	30-12-2010:11.40	Register request	Complete	Mike	50
	35654485	30-12-2010:12.12	Check ticket	Start	Mike	
	35654486	30-12-2010:12.24	Check ticket	Complete	Mike	100
	35654487	30-12-2010:14.16	Examine casually	Start	Pete	
	35654488	30-12-2010:14.22	Examine casually	Complete	Pete	400
	35654489	05-01-2011:11.22	Decide	Start	Sara	
	35654490	05-01-2011:11.29	Decide	Complete	Sara	200
	35654491	08-01-2011:12.05	Pay compensation	Start	Ellen	
	35654492	08-01-2011:12.15	Pay compensation	Complete	Ellen	200
...	...	...	...	...	...	...

8.2 Attributes: A Helicopter View

Before discussing approaches to discover the resource, time, and case perspectives, we provide another example showing the kind of information one can find in a typical event log. Table 8.1 shows a small fragment of a larger event log. Compared to earlier examples, each event now also has a *transaction type*. Consider, for example, the first two events in Table 8.1. The first event refers to the *start* of an activity instance, whereas the second event refers to the *completion* of this instance. By taking the difference between the timestamps of both events, it can be derived that Pete worked for six minutes on Case 1 when registering the request of the customer. Only events with transaction type *complete* have a cost attribute. Note that Sue and Mike are both working on the same case at the same time, because activities *examine thoroughly* and *check ticket* for Case 1 are overlapping.

Table 8.2 shows the *case attributes* stored in the event log. These are attributes that refer to the case as a whole rather than an individual event (see Definition 4.3). Case 1 is a request initiated by customer *Smith*. This customer has an identification

Table 8.2 Attributes of cases

Case id	Custid	Name	Type	Region	Amount
1	9911	Smith	Gold	South	989.50
2	9915	Jones	Silver	West	546.00
3	9912	Anderson	Silver	North	763.20
4	9904	Thompson	Silver	West	911.70
5	9911	Smith	Gold	South	812.10
6	9944	Baker	Silver	East	788.00
7	9944	Baker	Silver	East	792.80
8	9911	Smith	Gold	South	544.70
...	...	...	...	...	...

number *9911*. Customer Smith is a *gold* customer in region *south*. The amount of compensation requested is € 989.50. Cases 5 and 8 are also initiated by the same customer. Case 2 is initiated by silver customer *Jones* from region *west*. This customer claimed an amount of € 546.00.

Each of the events implicitly refers to attributes of the corresponding case. For instance, event 35654483 implicitly refers to silver customer Jones because the event is executed for Case 2. In Chap. 4, we formalized the notion of an event log and event attributes. Consider for example $e = 35654431$ and some of its attributes: $\#_{case}(e) = 1$, $\#_{activity}(e) = decide$, $\#_{time}(e) = $ 06-01-2011:11.22, $\#_{resource}(e) = Sara$, $\#_{trans}(e) = complete$, $\#_{cost}(e) = 200$, $\#_{custid}(e) = 9911$, $\#_{name}(e) = Smith$, $\#_{type}(e) = gold$, $\#_{region}(e) = south$, and $\#_{amount}(e) = 989.50$. For process discovery, we ignored most of these attributes. This chapter will show how to use these attributes to create an integrated model covering different perspectives.

A first step in any process mining project is to get a feeling for the process and the data in the event log. The so-called *dotted chart* provides a helicopter view of the process [87]. In a dotted chart, each event is depicted as a dot in a two dimensional plane as shown in Fig. 8.2. The horizontal axis represents the *time* of the event. The vertical axis represents the *class* of the event. To determine the class of an event, we use a *classifier* as described in Definition 4.2. A classifier is a function that maps the attributes of an event onto a label, $\underline{e}$ is the *class* of the event. An example of a classifier is $\underline{e} = \#_{case}(e)$, i.e., the case id of the event. Other examples are $\underline{e} = \#_{activity}(e)$ (the name of the activity being executed) and $\underline{e} = \#_{resource}(e)$ (the resource triggering the event). In this particular example, $\underline{e} = \#_{region}(e)$ would be a classifier mapping the event onto the region of the customer.

Every line in the dotted chart shown in Fig. 8.2 refers to a class, e.g., if the classifier $\underline{e} = \#_{resource}(e)$ is used, then every line corresponds to a resource. The dots on such a line describe the events belonging to this class, e.g., all events executed by a particular resource. The time dimension can be *absolute* or *relative*. If time is relative, the first event of each case takes place at time zero. Hence, the horizontal position of the dot depends on the time passed since the first event for the same case. The time dimension can be *real* or *logical*. For real time, the actual timestamp is used. For logical time, events are simply enumerated without considering the actual

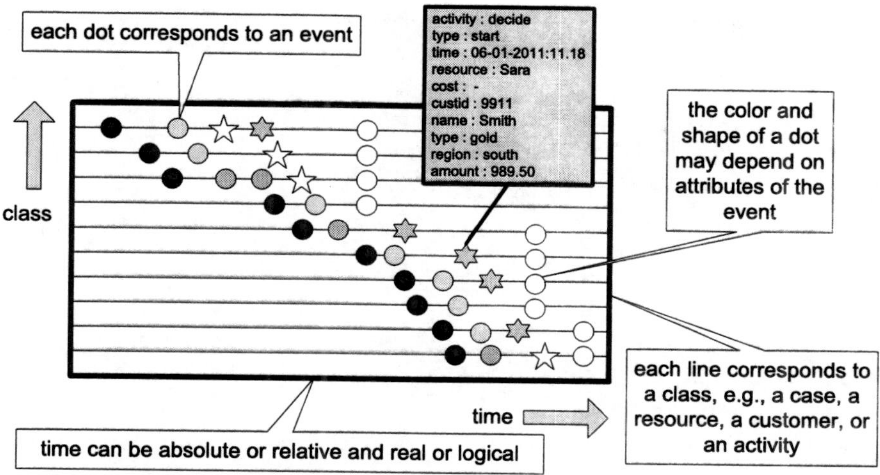

Fig. 8.2 Dotted chart: events are visualized as *dots*. Their position, color, and shape depend on the attributes of the corresponding event

timestamps: only their ordering is taken into account. The first event has time 0, the second event has time 1, etc. Also logical time can be absolute (global numbering) or relative (each case starts at time 0).

As Fig. 8.2 shows, the shape and color of a dot may depend on other attributes, i.e., there is also a classifier for the shape of the dot and a classifier for the color of the dot. For instance, if the classifier $\underline{e} = \#_{case}(e)$ is used, then every line corresponds to a case. The shape of the dot may depend on the resource triggering the corresponding event and the color of the dot may depend on the name of the corresponding activity. In our example, the shape of the dot can also depend on the type of customer (silver or gold) and the color of the dot may depend on the region (north, east, south, or west).

Figure 8.2 shows only a schematic view of the dotted chart. Figures 8.3 and 8.4 show two dotted charts based on a real event log. The event log was extracted from the database of a large Dutch housing agency. The event log contains 5987 events relating to 208 cases and 74 activity names. Each case refers to a housing unit (e.g., an apartment). The case starts when the tenant wants to terminate the current lease and ends when the new tenant has moved into the unit. Both figures show 5987 dots. The classifier $\underline{e} = \#_{case}(e)$ is used, i.e., every line corresponds to a unit. The color of the dot depends on the name of the corresponding activity. There are 74 colors: one for each of the possible activities. Figure 8.3 uses absolute/real times for the horizontal dimension. Cases are sorted by the time of the first event. These initial events do not form a straight line. If the arrival rate of new cases would be constant, the frontier formed by initial events would resemble a straight line rather than the curve shown in Fig. 8.3. The curved frontier line shows that the arrival process increases in intensity toward the middle of the time window visualized in Fig. 8.3. Moreover, it seems that events are not evenly spread over the time window. There

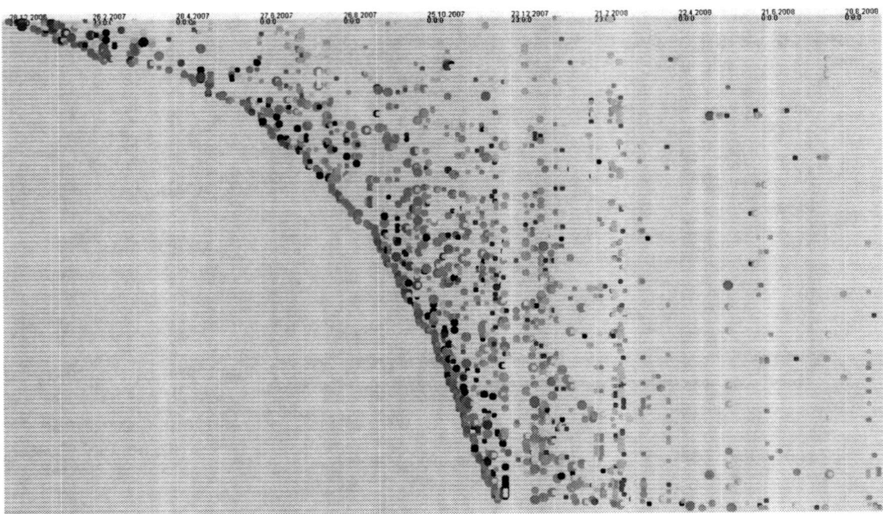

Fig. 8.3 Dotted chart for a process of a housing agency using absolute time. The influx of new cases increases over time. Moreover, several periods with little activity can be identified

are periods with little activity. Figure 8.4 uses relative/real times. This figure shows that there is a huge variation in flow time. About 45% of the cases are handled in less than 150 days whereas about 10% of the cases take more than one year.

The dotted chart is a very powerful tool to view a process from different angles. One can see all events in one glance while potentially showing different perspectives at the same time (class, color, shape, and time). Moreover, by zooming in one can investigate particular patterns. For example, when classifier $\underline{e} = \#_{resource}(e)$ is used one can immediately see when a resource has been inactive for a longer period.

In the dotted charts shown in this section, timestamps are used to align events in the horizontal dimension. As shown in [14], it is also possible to align events based on their context rather than time. As a result, repeating patterns in the event log are aligned so that it becomes easy to see common behavior and deviations without constructing a process model. The identification of such patterns helps understanding the "raw" behavior captured in the event log. As indicated in Chap. 4, event logs often contain low-level events that are of little interest to management. The challenge is to aggregate low-level events into events that are meaningful for stakeholders. Therefore, the event log is often preprocessed after a visual inspection of the log using dotted charts. There are several approaches to preprocess low-level event logs. For example, frequently appearing low-level patterns can be abstracted into events representing activities at the business level [13]. Also activity-based filtering can be used to preprocess the log. We elaborate on this in Chaps. 12 and 13.

The dotted chart can be seen as an example of a *visual analytics* technique. Visual analytics leverages on the remarkable capabilities of humans to visually identify patterns and trends in large datasets. Even though Fig. 8.3 shows almost six thousand

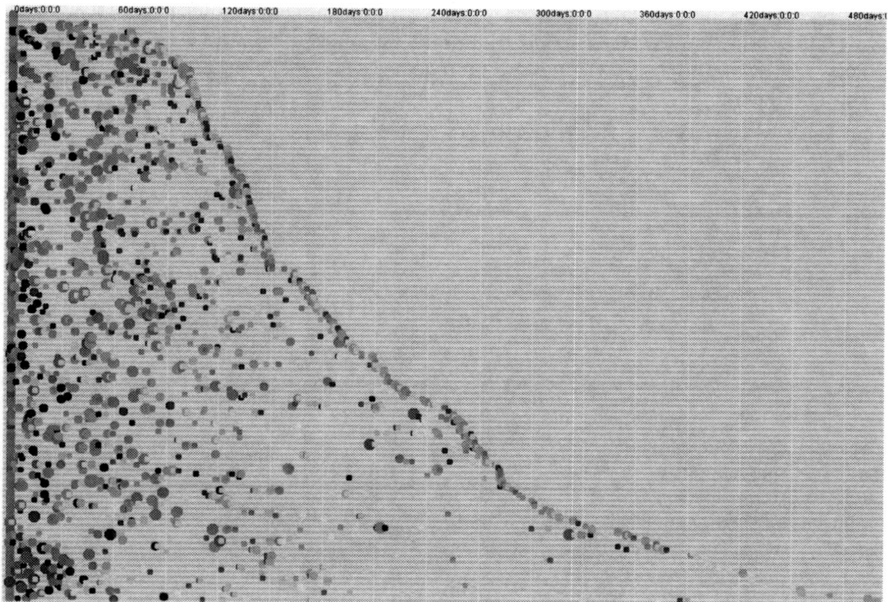

Fig. 8.4 Dotted chart for the process of the housing agency using relative time, i.e., all cases start at time zero. The chart reveals a large variation in flow times: some cases are handled in a few days whereas others take more than a year

events, people involved in this process can see patterns, trends, and irregularities in one glance.

8.3 Organizational Mining

Organizational mining focuses on the *organizational perspective* [88, 104]. Starting point for organizational mining is typically the $\#_{resource}(e)$ attribute present in most event logs. Table 8.3 shows a fragment of a larger event log in which each event has a resource attribute; all complete events have been projected onto their resource and activity attributes. This event log is based on the process model from Chap. 1. Using such information, there are techniques to learn more about people, machines, organizational structures (roles and departments), work distribution, and work patterns.

By analyzing an event log as shown in Table 8.3, it is possible to analyze the relation between resources and activities. Table 8.4 shows the mean number of times a resource performs an activity per case. For instance, activity a is executed exactly once for each case (take the sum of the first column). Pete, Mike, and Ellen are the only ones executing this activity. In 30% of the cases, a is executed by Pete, 50% is executed by Pete, and 20% is executed by Ellen. Activities e and f are always

Table 8.3 Compact representation of the event log highlighting the resource attribute of each event (a = *register request*, b = *examine thoroughly*, c = *examine casually*, d = *check ticket*, e = *decide*, f = *reinitiate request*, g = *pay compensation*, and h = *reject request*)

Case id	Trace
1	$\langle a^{Pete}, b^{Sue}, d^{Mike}, e^{Sara}, h^{Pete}\rangle$
2	$\langle a^{Mike}, d^{Mike}, c^{Pete}, e^{Sara}, g^{Ellen}\rangle$
3	$\langle a^{Pete}, c^{Mike}, d^{Ellen}, e^{Sara}, f^{Sara}, b^{Sean}, d^{Pete}, e^{Sara}, g^{Ellen}\rangle$
4	$\langle a^{Pete}, d^{Mike}, b^{Sean}, e^{Sara}, h^{Ellen}\rangle$
5	$\langle a^{Ellen}, c^{Mike}, d^{Pete}, e^{Sara}, f^{Sara}, d^{Ellen}, c^{Mike}, e^{Sara}, f^{Sara}, b^{Sue}, d^{Pete}, e^{Sara}, h^{Mike}\rangle$
6	$\langle a^{Mike}, c^{Ellen}, d^{Mike}, e^{Sara}, g^{Mike}\rangle$
...	...

Table 8.4 Resource-activity matrix showing the mean number of times a person performed an activity per case

	a	b	c	d	e	f	g	h
Pete	0.3	0	0.345	0.69	0	0	0.135	0.165
Mike	0.5	0	0.575	1.15	0	0	0.225	0.275
Ellen	0.2	0	0.23	0.46	0	0	0.09	0.11
Sue	0	0.46	0	0	0	0	0	0
Sean	0	0.69	0	0	0	0	0	0
Sara	0	0	0	0	2.3	1.3	0	0

executed by Sara. Activity e is executed, on average, 2.3 times per case. The event log conforms to the process model shown in Fig. 1.1. Hence, for some cases e is executed only once whereas for other cases e is executed repeatedly (2.3 times on average). On average, activity f is executed 1.3 times. This suggests that the middle part of the process (composed of activities b, c, d, e, and f) needs to be redone for the majority of cases. Consider for example Case 5 in Table 8.3; e is executed three times and f is executed twice for this case.

8.3.1 Social Network Analysis

Sociometry, also referred to as sociography, refers to methods that present data on interpersonal relationships in graph or matrix form [122]. The term sociometry was coined by Jacob Levy Moreno who already used such techniques in the 1930s to better assign students to residential cottages in a training facility. Until recently, the input data for sociometry consisted mainly of interviews and questionnaires. However, with the availability of vast amounts of electronic data, new ways of gathering input data are possible.

Here we restrict ourselves to *social networks* as shown in Fig. 8.5. The nodes in a social network correspond to organizational entities. Often, but not always, there

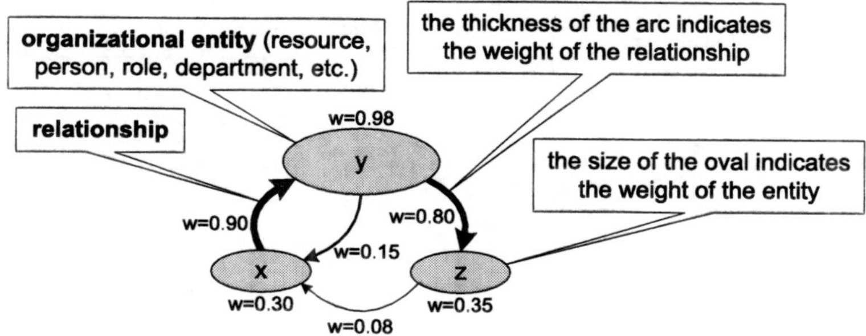

Fig. 8.5 A social network consists of *nodes* representing organizational entities and *arcs* representing relationships. *Both nodes and arcs* can have weights indicated by "$w = \ldots$" and the size of the shape

is a one-to-one correspondence between the resources found in the log and organizational entities (i.e., nodes). In Fig. 8.5, nodes x, y, and z could refer to persons. The nodes in a social network may also correspond to aggregate organizational entities such as roles, groups, and departments. The arcs in a social network correspond to relationships between such organizational entities. Arcs and nodes may have *weights*. The weight of an arc or node indicates its *importance*. For instance, node y is more important than x and z as is indicated by its size. The relationship between x and y is much stronger than the relationship between z and x as shown by the thickness of the arc. The interpretation of "importance" depends on the social network. Later, we will give some examples to illustrate the concept.

Sometimes the term *distance* is used to refer to the inverse of the weight of an arc. An arc connecting two organizational entities has a high weight if the distance between both entities is small. If the distance from node x to node y is large, then the weight of the corresponding arc is small (or the arc is not present in the social network).

A wide variety of metrics have been defined to analyze social networks and to characterize the role of individual nodes in such a diagram [122]. For example, if all other nodes are in short distance to a given node and all geodesic paths (i.e., shortest paths in the graph) visit this node, then clearly the node is very central (like a spider in the web). There are different metrics for this intuitive notion of *centrality*. The Bavelas–Leavitt index of centrality is a well-known example that is based on the geodesic paths in the graph. Let i be an node and let $D_{j,k}$ be the geodesic distance from node j to node k. The Bavelas–Leavitt index of centrality is defined as $BL(i) = (\sum_{j,k} D_{j,k})/(\sum_{j,k} D_{j,i} + D_{i,k})$. The index divides the sum of all geodesic distances by the sum of all geodesic distances from and to node i. Other related metrics are *closeness* (1 divided by the sum of all geodesic distances to a given node) and *betweenness* (a ratio based on the number of geodesic paths visiting a given node) [104, 122]. Recall that distance can be seen as the inverse of arc weight.

Notions such as centrality analyze the position of one organizational entity, say a person, in the whole social network. There are also metrics making statements about the network as a whole, e.g., the degree of connectedness. Moreover, there are also

Table 8.5 Handover of work matrix showing the mean number of handovers from one person to another per case

	Pete	Mike	Ellen	Sue	Sean	Sara
Pete	0.135	0.225	0.09	0.06	0.09	1.035
Mike	0.225	0.375	0.15	0.1	0.15	1.725
Ellen	0.09	0.15	0.06	0.04	0.06	0.69
Sue	0	0	0	0	0	0.46
Sean	0	0	0	0	0	0.69
Sara	0.885	1.475	0.59	0.26	0.39	1.3

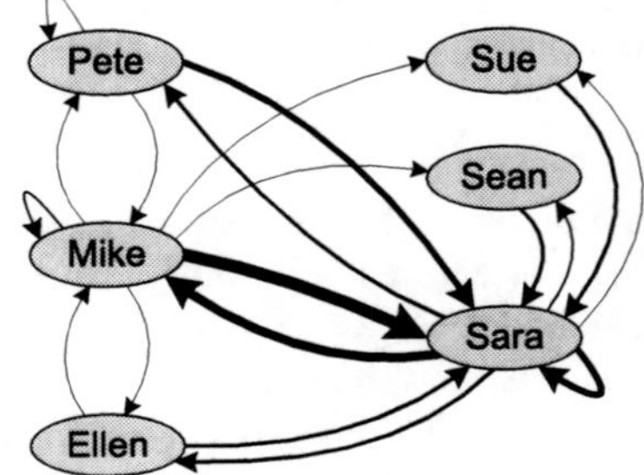

Fig. 8.6 Social network based on handover of work at the level of individual resources using a threshold of 0.1. *The thickness of the arcs* is based on the frequency of handovers from one person to another

techniques to identify *cliques* (groups of entities that are strongly connected to each other while having fewer connections to entities outside the clique).

Clearly, event logs with $\#_{resource}(e)$ attributes provide an excellent source of information for social network analysis. For instance, based on the event log one can count the number of times *work is handed over from one resource to another*. Consider for example Case 1 having the following trace: $\langle a^{Pete}, b^{Sue}, d^{Mike}, e^{Sara}, h^{Pete} \rangle$. Clearly, there is a handover of work from Pete to Sue and Mike after the completion of a. Note that Sue does not hand over work to Mike, because b and d are concurrent. However, both Sue and Mike hand over work to Sara, because activity e requires input from both b and d. Finally, Sara hands over work to Pete. Hence, in total there are five handovers: (a^{Pete}, b^{Sue}), (a^{Pete}, d^{Mike}), (b^{Sue}, e^{Sara}), (d^{Mike}, e^{Sara}), and (e^{Sara}, h^{Pete}). Table 8.5 shows the average number of handovers from one resource to another. For instance, Mike frequently hands over work to Sara: on average 1.725 times per case. Sue and Sean only hand over work to Sara as they only execute activity b. It is important to note that the discovered process model is exploited when constructing the social network. The causal dependencies in the process model are used to count handovers in the event log. This way only "real" handovers of work are counted, e.g., concurrent activities may follow one another but do not contribute the number of handovers.

Table 8.5 encodes a social network. All nonzero cells represent "handover of work" relationships. When visualizing a social network, typically a threshold is used. If we set the threshold to 0.1, we obtain the social network shown in Fig. 8.6. All cells with a value of at least 0.1 are turned into arcs in the social network. To keep the diagram simple, we only assigned weights to arcs and not to nodes. As Fig. 8.6

Table 8.6 Handover of work matrix at the role level

	Assistant	Expert	Manager
Assistant	1.5	0.5	3.45
Expert	0	0	1.15
Manager	2.95	0.65	1.3

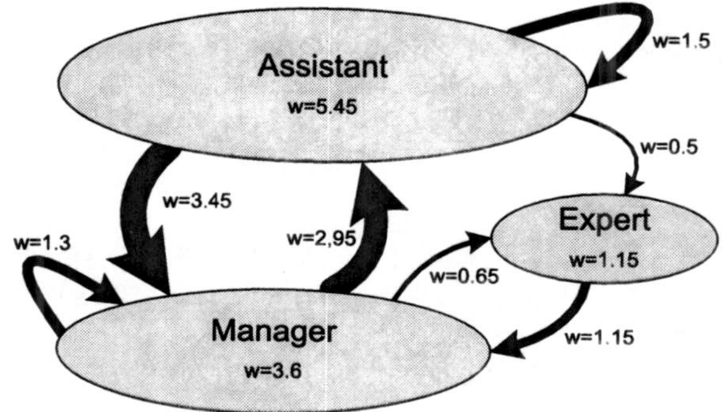

Fig. 8.7 Social network based on handover of work at the level of roles. *The weights of nodes* are based on the number of times a resource having the role performs an activity. *The weights of the arcs* are based of the average number of times a handover takes place from one role to another per case

shows, there is a strong connection between Mike and Sara. On average, there are 1.725 handovers from Mike to Sara and 1.475 handovers from Sara to Mike. The social network clearly shows the flow of work in the organization and can be used to compute metrics such as the Bavelas–Leavitt index of centrality. Such analysis shows that Sara and Mike are most central in the social network.

The nodes in a social network correspond to organizational entities. In Fig. 8.6, the entities are individual resources. However, it is also possible to construct social networks at the level of departments, teams, or roles. Assume, for example, that there are three roles: *Assistant*, *Expert*, and *Manager*. Pete, Mike, and Ellen have the role *Assistant*, Sue and Sean have the role *Expert*, and Sara is the only one having the role *Manager*. Later, we will show that such roles can be discovered from frequent patterns in the event log. Moreover, such information is typically available in the information system. Now we can count the number of handovers at the role level. Consider again Case 1: $\langle a^{Pete}, b^{Sue}, d^{Mike}, e^{Sara}, h^{Pete}\rangle$. Using the information about roles, we can rewrite this trace to $\langle a^{Assistant}, b^{Expert}, d^{Assistant}, e^{Manager}, h^{Assistant}\rangle$. Again we find five handovers: one from role *Assistant* to role *Expert* $(a^{Assistant}, b^{Expert})$, one from role *Assistant* to role *Assistant* $(a^{Assistant}, d^{Assistant})$, one from role *Expert* to role *Manager* $(b^{Expert}, e^{Manager})$, one from role *Assistant* to role *Manager* $(d^{Assistant}, e^{Manager})$, and one from role *Manager* to role *Assistant* $(e^{Manager}, h^{Assistant})$. Table 8.6 shows the average frequency of such handovers per case. This matrix containing sociometric information can be converted into a social network as shown in Fig. 8.7.

The social network in Fig. 8.7 has weighted nodes and arcs. The weights are visualized graphically. For instance, the biggest node is role *Assistant* with a weight of 5.45. This weight indicates the average number of activities executed by this role.

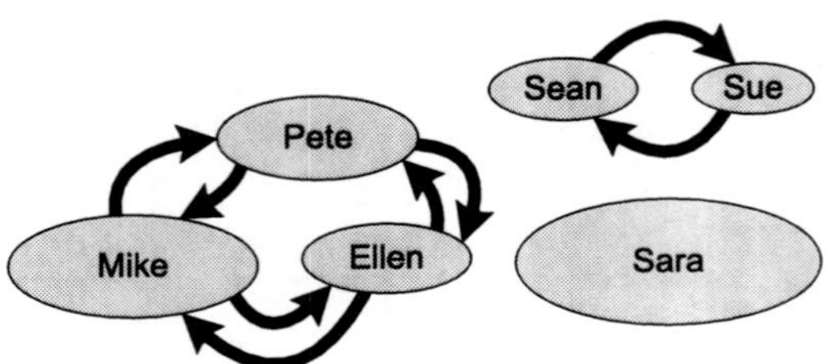

Fig. 8.8 Social network based on similarity of profiles. Resources that execute similar collections of activities are related. Sara is the only resource executing e and f. Therefore, she is not connected to other resources. Self-loops are suppressed as they contain no information (self-similarity)

The weight of role *Expert* is only 1.15, because the two experts (Sue and Sean) only execute activity b which, on average, is executed 1.15 times per case. The weights of the arcs are directly taken from Table 8.6. Clearly, handovers among the roles *Assistant* and *Manager* are most frequent.

Counting handovers of work is just one of many ways of constructing a social network from an event log. In [104] various types of social networks are presented. For example, one can simply count how many times two resources have worked on the same case, i.e., two nodes have a strong relationship when they frequently work together on common cases. One can also use Table 8.4 to quantify the *similarity* of two resources. Every row in the resource-activity matrix can be seen as the *profile* of a resource. Such a vector describes the relevant features of a resource. For example, Pete has profile $P_{Pete} = (0.30, 0.0, 0.345, 0.69, 0.0, 0.0, 0.135, 0.165)$, Mike has profile $P_{Mike} = (0.5, 0.0, 0.575, 1.15, 0.0, 0.0, 0.225, 0.275)$, and Sara has profile $P_{Sara} = (0.0, 0.0, 0.0, 0.0, 2.3, 1.3, 0.0, 0.0)$. Clearly, P_{Pete} and P_{Mike} are very similar whereas P_{Pete} and P_{Sara} are not. The distance between two profiles can be quantified using well-known distance measures such as the *Minkowski distance*, *Hamming distance*, and *Pearson's correlation coefficient*. Moreover, clustering techniques such as *k-means clustering* and *agglomerative hierarchical clustering* can be used to group similar resources together based on their profile (see Sect. 3.3). Two resources in the same cluster (or in close proximity according to the distance metric) are strongly related whereas resources in different clusters (or far away from each other) have no significant relationship in the social network.

For the resource-activity matrix shown in Table 8.4, it does not matter which distance metric or clustering technique is used. All will come to the conclusion that Pete, Mike, and Ellen are very similar and thus have a strong relationship in the social network based on similarity. Similarly, Sue and Sean have a strong relationship in the social network based on similarity. Sara is clearly different from the resources in the two other groups. Figure 8.8 shows the social network based on similarity. Here one can clearly see the roles *Assistant*, *Expert*, and *Manager* mentioned before. However, now the roles are discovered based on the profiles of the resources.

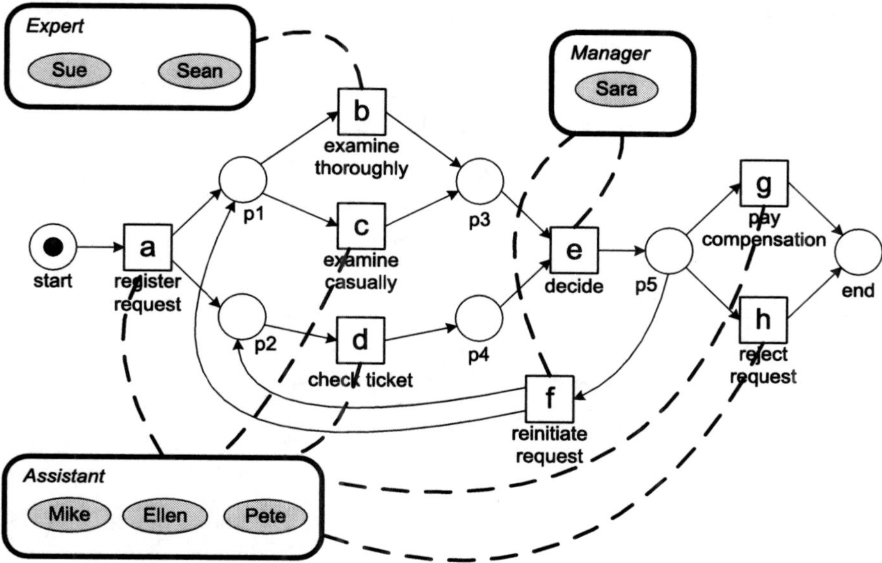

Fig. 8.9 Organizational model discovered based on the event log

8.3.2 Discovering Organizational Structures

The behavior of a resource can be characterized by a *profile*, i.e., a vector indicating how frequent each activity has been executed by the resource. By using such profiles, various clustering techniques can be used to discover similar resources. Figure 8.8 showed an example in which three roles are discovered based on similarities of the profiles of the six resources. In Sect. 3.3, we introduced k-means clustering and agglomerative hierarchical clustering. For k-means clustering the number of clusters is decided upfront. Agglomerative hierarchical clustering produces a dendrogram allowing for a variable number of clusters depending on the desired granularity. Additional relevant features of resources (authorizations, salary, age, etc.) can be added to the profile before clustering. This all depends on the information available. After clustering the resources into groups, these groups can be related to activities in the process. Figure 8.9 shows the end result using the roles discovered earlier.

The three roles *Assistant*, *Expert*, and *Manager* in Fig. 8.9 have the property that they partition the set of resources. In general this will not be the case, e.g., a resource can have multiple roles (e.g., a consultant that is also team leader). Moreover, each activity corresponds to precisely one role. Also this does not always need to be the case. Figure 8.10 sketches a more general situation.

The hypothetical organizational model in Fig. 8.10 connects the process model and the resources seen in the event log. There are eighth organizational entities: $oe1, \dots, oe8$. The model is hierarchical, e.g., $oe4$ contains resource $r5$ and all resources of $oe6$, $oe7$, and $oe8$. Hence five resources belong to organizational entity

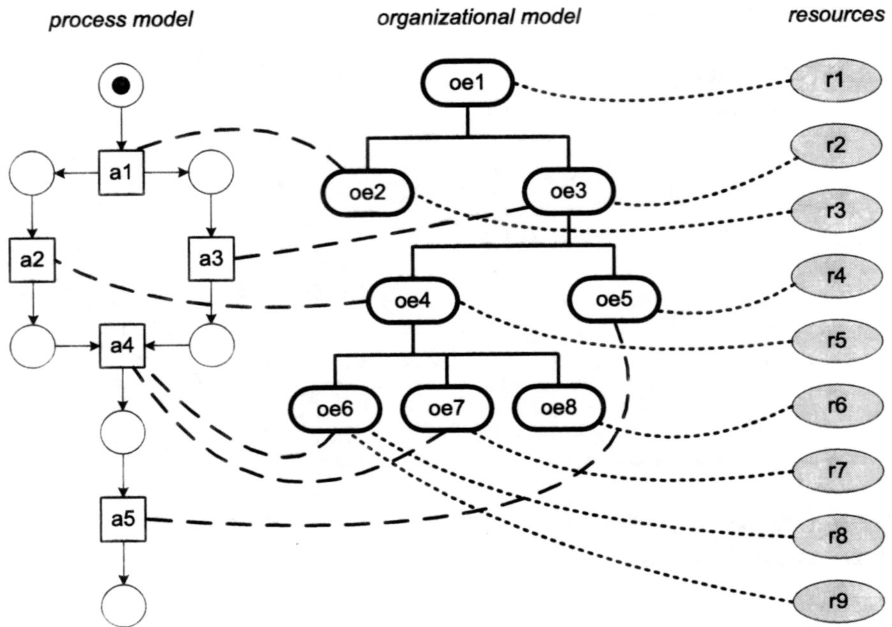

Fig. 8.10 The organizational entities discovered connect activities in the process model to sets resources

*oe*4: *r*5, *r*6, *r*7, *r*8, and *r*9. Organizational entity *oe*1, i.e., the root node, contains all nine resources. If agglomerative hierarchical clustering is used to cluster resources, one automatically gets such a hierarchical structure. Figure 3.7 in Sect. 3.3 shows how agglomerative hierarchical clustering creates a *dendrogram* and Fig. 3.8 shows how any horizontal line defines a level in the hierarchy. The translation from a dendrogram to a hierarchical structure as shown in Fig. 8.10 is straightforward.

Activity *a*1 in Fig. 8.10 can only be performed by resource *r*3 whereas activity *a*2 can be executed by *r*5, *r*6, *r*7, *r*8, or *r*9. For more information about organizational mining, we refer to [88].

8.3.3 Analyzing Resource Behavior

Figure 8.10 shows how activities, organizational entities, and resources can be related. Since events in the log refer to activities and resources (and indirectly also to organizational entities), performance measures extracted from the event log can be projected onto such models. For instance, frequencies can be projected onto activities, organizational entities, and resources. It could be shown that resource *r*5 performed 150 activities in the last month: 100 times *a*2 and 50 times *a*3. By aggregating such information, it could be deduced that organizational entity *oe*4 was used 300 times in the same period.

In Table 8.3, we abstracted from transaction types, i.e., we did not consider the start and completion of an activity instance. Most logs will contain such information. For example, Table 8.1 shows the start and completion of each activity instance. Some logs will even show when a workitem is offered to a resource or when it is assigned. If such events are recorded, then a diagram such as Fig. 8.10 can also show detailed time related information. For example, the utilization and response times of resources can be shown.

Assuming that the event log contains high quality information including precise timestamps and transaction types, the behavior of resources can be analyzed in detail [95]. Of course privacy issues play an important role here. However, the event log can be anonymized prior to analysis. Moreover, in most organizations one would like to do such analysis at an aggregate level rather than at the level of individuals. For instance, in Sect. 2.1, we mentioned the Yerkes–Dodson law of arousal which describes the relation between workload and performance of people. This law hypothesizes that people work faster when the workload increases. If the event log contains precise timestamps and transaction types, then it is easy to empirically investigate this phenomenon. For any activity instance, one knows its duration and by scanning the log it is also easy to see what the workload was when the activity instance was being performed by some resource. Using supervised learning (e.g., regression analysis or decision tree analysis), the effects of different workloads on service and response times can be measured. See [95] for more examples.

Privacy and Anonymization

Event logs may contain sensitive or private data. Events refer to actions and properties of customers, employees, etc. For instance, when applying process mining in a hospital it is important to ensure data privacy. It would be unacceptable that data about patients would be used by unauthorized persons or that event data about treatments would be used in a way not intended when releasing the data. The challenge in process mining is to use event logs to improve processes and information systems while protecting personally identifiable information and not revealing sensitive data. Therefore, most event logs contain *anonymized* attribute values. For example, the name of the customer or employee is often irrelevant for questions that need to be answered. To make an attribute anonymous, the original value is mapped onto a new value in a deterministic manner. This ensures that one can correlate attributes in one event to attributes in another event without knowing the actual values. For instance, all occurrences of the name "Wil van der Aalst" are mapped onto "Q2T4R5R7X1Y9Z". The mapping of the original value onto the anonymized value should be such that it is not easy (or even impossible) to compute the inverse of the mapping. Anonymous data can sometimes be de-anonymized by combining different data sources. For example, it is often possible to trace back an individual based on her birth date and the birth dates of her children. Therefore, even "anonymous data" should be handled carefully.

Note that process mining techniques do not create *new* data. The information stored in event logs originates from other databases and audit trails. Therefore, privacy and security issues already exist before applying process mining. Nevertheless, the active use of data and process mining techniques increases the risk of data misuse. Organizations should therefore continuously balance the benefits of creating and using event data against potential privacy and security problems.

8.4 Time and Probabilities

The *time perspective* is concerned with the timing and frequency of events. In most event logs, events have a timestamp ($\#_{time}(e)$). The granularity of these timestamps may vary. In some logs only date information is given, e.g., "30-12-2010". Other event logs have timestamps with millisecond precision. The presence of timestamps enables the discovery of bottlenecks, the analysis of service levels, the monitoring of resource utilization, and the prediction of remaining processing times of running cases. In this section we focus on *replaying event logs with timestamps*. A small modification of the replay approach presented in Sect. 7.2 suffices to include the time perspective in process models.

Table 8.7 shows a fragment of some larger event log highlighting the role of timestamps. To simplify the presentation, we use fictive two-digit timestamps rather than verbose timestamps like "30-12-2010:11.02". Moreover, we assume that each event has a start event and a complete event. Obviously, the replay approach does not depend on these simplifying assumptions.

Figure 8.11 shows some raw diagnostic information after replaying the three cases shown in Table 8.7. Activity a has three activity instances; one for each case. The first instance of a runs from time 12 to time 19. Hence, the duration of this activity instance is 7 time units. Activity d has four activity instances. For Case 3, there are two instances of d; one running from time 35 to time 40 and one running from time 62 to time 67. The durations of all activity instances are shown. Also places are annotated to indicate how long tokens remained there. For example, there were four periods in which a token resided in place $p1$: one token corresponding to Case 1 resided in $p1$ for 6 time units (from time 19 until time 25), one token corresponding to Case 2 resided in $p1$ for 7 time units (from time 23 until time 30), and two tokens corresponding to Case 3 resided in this place (one for $32 - 30 = 2$ time units and one for $60 - 55 = 5$ time units). These times can be found using the approach presented in Sect. 7.2. The only modifications are that now tokens bear timestamps and statistics are collected during replay. In this example, all three cases fit perfectly (i.e., no missing or remaining tokens). One needs to ignore non-fitting events or cases to deal with logs that do not have a conformance of 100%. Heuristics are needed to deal with such situations, but here we assume perfect fitness.

Figure 8.12 shows another view on the information gathered while replaying the three cases. Consider for instance Case 3. For this case, an instance of activity a was

Table 8.7 Compact representation of the event log highlighting timestamps; artificial timestamps are used to simplify the presentation of the time-based replay approach

Case id	Trace
1	$\langle a^{12}_{start}, a^{19}_{complete}, b^{25}_{start}, d^{26}_{start}, b^{32}_{complete}, d^{33}_{complete}, e^{35}_{start}, e^{40}_{complete}, h^{50}_{start}, h^{54}_{complete} \rangle$
2	$\langle a^{17}_{start}, a^{23}_{complete}, d^{28}_{start}, c^{30}_{start}, d^{32}_{complete}, c^{38}_{complete}, e^{50}_{start}, e^{59}_{complete}, g^{70}_{start}, g^{73}_{complete} \rangle$
3	$\langle a^{25}_{start}, a^{30}_{complete}, c^{32}_{start}, c^{35}_{complete}, d^{35}_{start}, d^{40}_{complete}, e^{45}_{start}, e^{50}_{complete}, f^{50}_{start}, f^{55}_{complete}, b^{60}_{start}, d^{62}_{start}, b^{65}_{complete}, d^{67}_{complete}, e^{80}_{start}, e^{87}_{complete}, g^{90}_{start}, g^{98}_{complete} \rangle$
...	...

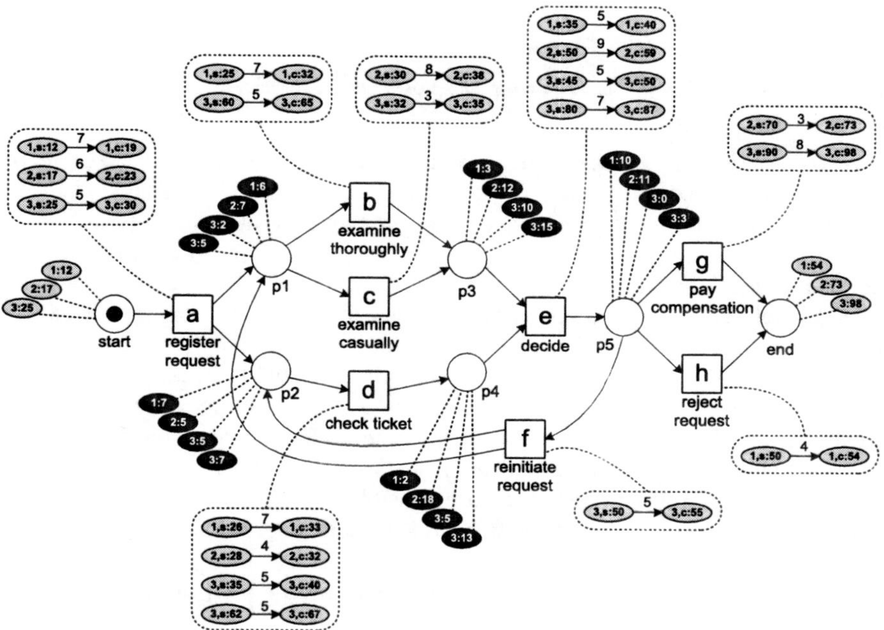

Fig. 8.11 Timed replay of the first three cases in the event log: Case 1 starts at time 12 and ends at time 54, Case 2 starts at time 17 and ends at time 73, Case 3 starts at time 25 and ends at time 98

running from time 25 until time 30. At time 30, c and d became enabled. However, as shown, c started at time 32 and d started at time 35. This implies that there was a waiting time of 2 before c started and a waiting time of 5 before d started. After completing c and d, i.e., at time 40, the first instance of e became enabled. Since the first instance of activity e ran from time 45 until 50, the waiting time for this instance of e was $45 - 40 = 5$ time units. Note that from time 35 until time 45 there was a token in place $p3$ (because c completed at time 35 and e started at time 45). However, only half of this period should be considered as waiting time for e, because e only got enabled at time 40 when d completed. As discussed in Sect. 7.4.3, such

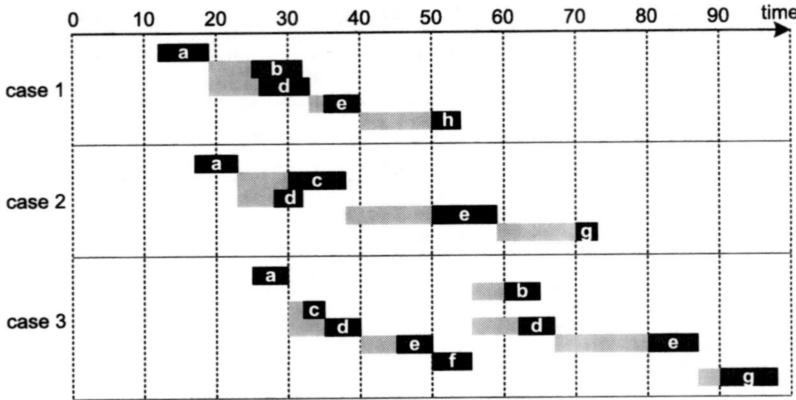

Fig. 8.12 Timeline showing the activity instances of the first three activities

diagnostics are *only possible because events in the log have been coupled to model elements through replay*.

After replay, for each place a collection of "token visits" has been recorded. Each token visit has a start and end time. Hence, a multi-set of durations can be derived. In the example, place $p1$ has the multi-set $[6, 7, 2, 5, \ldots]$ of durations. For a large event log such a multi-set will contain thousands of elements. Hence, it is possible to fit a distribution and to compute standard statistics such as mean, standard deviation, minimum, and maximum. The same holds for activity instances. Every activity instance has a start and end time. Hence, a multi-set of service times can be derived. For example, activity e in the example has the multi-set $[5, 9, 5, 7 \ldots]$ of activity durations. Also here standard statistics can be computed. These can also be computed for waiting times. It is also possible to compute confidence intervals to derive statements such as "the 90% confidence interval for the mean waiting time for activity x is between 40 and 50 minutes".

Figures 8.11 and 8.12 demonstrate that replay can be used to provide various kinds of performance related information:

- *Visualization of waiting and service times*. Statistics such as the average waiting time for an activity can be projected onto the process model. Activities with a high variation in service time could be highlighted in the model, etc.
- *Bottleneck detection and analysis*. The multi-set of durations attached to each place can be used to discover and analyze bottlenecks. The places where most time is spent can be highlighted. Moreover, cases that spend a long time in a particular place can be further investigated. This is similar to the selection of non-conforming cases described earlier (cf. Fig. 7.8), i.e., the sublog of delayed cases can be analyzed separately to find root causes for the delays.
- *Flow time and SLA analysis*. Figure 8.11 also shows that the overall flow time can be computed. (In fact, no process model is needed for this.) One can also point to two arbitrary points in the process, say x and y, and compute how many times a case flows from x to y. The multi-set of durations to go from x to y can

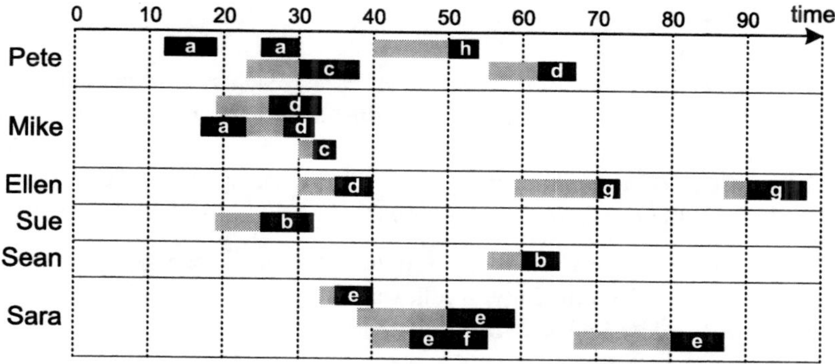

Fig. 8.13 Timeline showing the activity instances projected onto resources. Such projections of the event log allow for the analysis of resource behavior and their utilization

be used to compute all kinds of statistics, e.g., the average flow time between x and y or the fraction of cases taking more than some preset norm. This can be used to monitor Service Level Agreements (SLAs). For instance, it could be that there is a contractual agreement that for 90% of the cases y should be executed within 48 hours after the completion of x. Non-conformance with respect to such an SLA can be highlighted in the model.

- *Analysis of frequencies and utilization.* While replaying the model, times and frequencies are collected. These can be used to show routing probabilities in the model. For example, after e there is a choice to do f, g or h. By analyzing frequencies, one can indicate in the model that in 56% of choices, e is followed by f, in 20% g is chosen, and in 24% h is chosen. By combining frequencies and average service times, one can also compute the utilization of resources. Figure 8.13 shows all activity instances and their waiting times *projected onto the resources* executing them. This illustrates that replay can be used to analyze resource behavior.

The event log shown in Table 8.7 only contains *start* and *complete* events. In Chap. 4, we identified additional event types such as *assign*, *schedule*, *suspend*, *resume*, *manualskip*, *abort_case*, and *withdraw*. If an event log contains such events, more statistics can be collected during replay. For instance, if *start* events are preceded by *assign* events, it is possible to analyze how long it takes to start executing the activity instance after being assigned to a specific resource. The transactional life-cycle shown in Fig. 4.3 can be used when replaying the event log.

It can also be the case that the event log does not contain transactional information, i.e., the $\#_{trans}(e)$ attribute is missing in the log. In this case activities are assumed to be atomic. Nevertheless, it is still possible to analyze the time that passes in-between such atomic activities. In addition, heuristics can be applied to "guess" the duration of activity instances.

8.5 Decision Mining

The *case perspective* focuses on properties of cases. Each case is characterized by its case attributes, the attributes of its events, the path taken, and performance information (e.g., flow times).

First, we focus on the influence of case and event attributes on the routing of cases. In Fig. 8.9 there are two *decision points*:

- After registering the request (activity a) either a thorough examination (activity b) or a casual examination (activity c) follows.
- After making a decision (activity e), activity g (pay compensation), activity h (reject request), or activity f (reinitiate request) follows.

Both decision points are of type XOR-split: precisely one of several alternatives is chosen. *Decision mining* aims to find rules explaining such choices in terms of characteristics of the case [79]. For example, by analyzing the event log used to discover Fig. 8.9 one could find that customers from the southern region are always checked thoroughly and that requests by silver customers always get rejected. Clearly, *a classification technique like decision tree learning can be used to find such rules* (see Sect. 3.2). Recall that the input for decision tree learning is a table where every row lists one categorical response variable (e.g., the chosen activity) and multiple predictor variables (e.g., properties of the customer). The decision tree aims to explain the response variable in terms of the predictor variables.

Consider, for example, the situation shown in Fig. 8.14. Using three different notations (YAWL, BPMN, and Petri nets) a choice is depicted: activity x is followed by either activity y or activity z. The table in Fig. 8.14 shows different cases for which this choice needs to be made. There are three predictor variables (*type*, *region*, and *amount*) and one response variable (*activity*). Variables *type*, *region*, and *activity* are categorical and variable *amount* is numerical. The predictor variables correspond to knowledge known about the case at the point in time when the decision was made. The response variable *activity* is determined based on a scan of the event log. The event log will reveal whether x was followed by y or z. The table in Fig. 8.14 serves as input for some decision tree learning algorithm as explained in Sect. 3.2. The resulting decision tree can be rewritten into a rule. Based on the example table, classification will show that the value of the response variable is y if the customer is a gold customer and the amount is lower than € 500. Otherwise, the value of the response variable is z as shown in Fig. 8.14.

Petri nets cannot express OR-splits and joins directly. However, in higher-level languages like BPMN and YAWL one can express such behavior. Figure 8.15 shows an OR-split using the YAWL and BPMN notation: activity x is followed by y, or z, or y and z. Note that the response variable *activity* is still categorical and can be determined by scanning the log. The table in Fig. 8.15 can be analyzed using a decision tree learner and the result can be transformed into one rule for each of the output arcs. The response variable is "just y" if the customer is a gold customer and the amount is less than € 500, the response variable is "just z" if the customer is a silver customer and the amount is at least € 500, and the response variable is

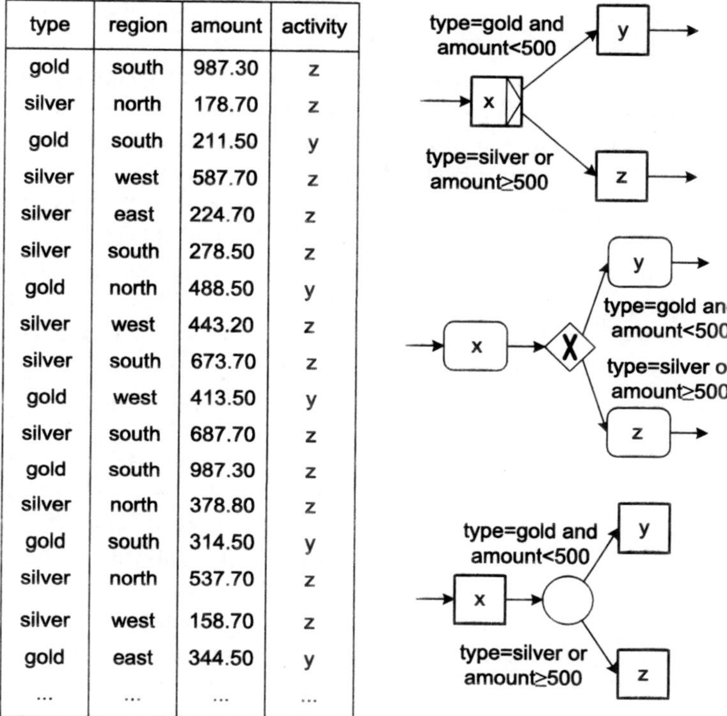

type	region	amount	activity
gold	south	987.30	z
silver	north	178.70	z
gold	south	211.50	y
silver	west	587.70	z
silver	east	224.70	z
silver	south	278.50	z
gold	north	488.50	y
silver	west	443.20	z
silver	south	673.70	z
gold	west	413.50	y
silver	south	687.70	z
gold	south	987.30	z
silver	north	378.80	z
gold	south	314.50	y
silver	north	537.70	z
silver	west	158.70	z
gold	east	344.50	y
...	...	...	...

Fig. 8.14 Decision mining: using case and event attributes, a rule is learned for the XOR-split. The result is shown using different notations: YAWL (*top*), BPMN (*middle*), and Petri nets (*bottom*)

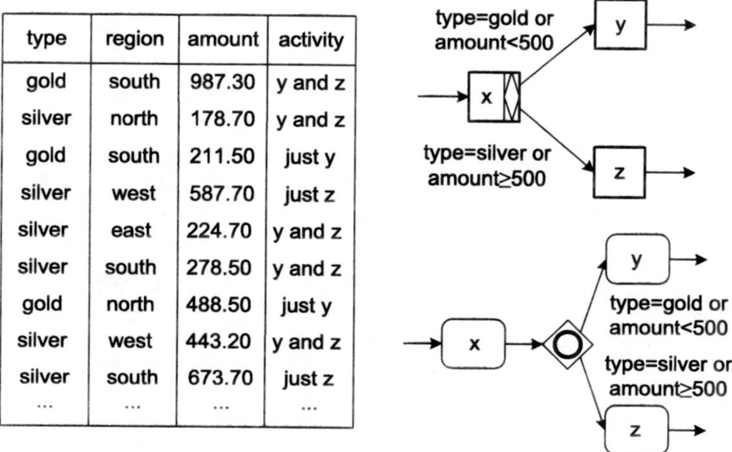

type	region	amount	activity
gold	south	987.30	y and z
silver	north	178.70	y and z
gold	south	211.50	just y
silver	west	587.70	just z
silver	east	224.70	y and z
silver	south	278.50	y and z
gold	north	488.50	just y
silver	west	443.20	y and z
silver	south	673.70	just z
...	...	...	...

Fig. 8.15 Decision mining: using case and event attributes, a rule is learned for the OR-split. The response variable has three possible values: just y, just z, and both y and z

"y and z" in all other cases. Based on this classification, the conditions shown in the YAWL and BPMN models can be derived.

For the predictor variables, all case and event attributes can be used. Consider for instance the decision point following activity e and event 35654431 in Table 8.1. The case and event attributes of this event are shown in Tables 8.1 and 8.2. Hence, predictor variables for event 35654431 are: $case = 1$, $activity = decide$, $time =$ 06-01-2011:11.22, $resource = Sara$, $trans = complete$, $cost = 200$, $custid = 9911$, $name = Smith$, $type = gold$, $region = south$, and $amount = 989.50$. As described in [79] also the attributes of earlier and later events can be taken into account. For example, all attributes of all events in the trace up to the decision moment can be used. In the process shown in Fig. 8.9 one could find the rule that all cases that involve Sean get rejected in the decision point following activity e.

There may be loops in the model. Hence, the same decision point may be visited multiple times for the same case. Each visit corresponds to a new row in the table used by the decision tree algorithm. For example, in the process shown in Fig. 8.9, there may be cases for which e is executed four times. The first three times e is be followed by f and the fourth time e is followed by g or h. Each of the four decisions corresponds to a row in the table used for classification. Using replay, the outcome of the decision (i.e., the response variable) can be identified for each row. Also note that the values of the predictor variables for these four rows may be different.

In some cases, it may be impossible to derive a reasonable decision rule. The reason may be that there is too little data or that decisions are seemingly random or based on considerations not in the event log. In such cases, replay can be used to provide a probability for each branch. Hence, such a decision point is characterized by probabilities rather than data dependent decision rules.

The procedure can be repeated for all decision points in a process model. The results can be used to extend the process model, thus incorporating the case perspective.

Classification in Process Mining

The application of classification techniques like decision tree learning is *not limited to decision mining* as illustrated by Figs. 8.14 and 8.15: *additional predictor variables* may be used and *alternative response variables* can be analyzed.

In Figs. 8.14 and 8.15, only attributes of events and cases are used as predictor variables. However, also behavioral information can be used. For instance, in Fig. 8.9 it would be interesting to count the number of times that f has been executed. This may influence the decision point following activity e. For example, it could be the case that a request is never initiated more than two times. It may also be that timing information is used as a predictor variable. For instance, if the time taken to check the ticket is less than five minutes, then it is more likely that the request is rejected. It is also possible to use *contextual* information as a predictor variable. Contextual information is information that is not in the event log and that is not necessarily related to a particular case. For example, the weather may influence a decision. This can only be discovered if the weather condition is taken into account as a predictor variable. Decisions may also depend on the volume of work in the pipeline. One can imagine that the choice between b and c in Fig. 8.9 depends on the workload of the two experts Sue and Sean. When they are overloaded, it may be less likely that b is selected. These examples illustrate that predictor variables are not limited to case and event attributes. However, note the "curse of dimensionality" discussed in Sect. 3.6.3. Analyzing decision points with many predictor variables may be computationally intractable.

In Figs. 8.14 and 8.15, we used classification to learn decision rules. The predictor variables can also be used to learn *other properties of the process*. For instance, one may be interested in characterizing cases for which a particular activity is executed. Classification can also be used to uncover reasons for non-conformance. As shown in Fig. 7.8, the event log can be split into two sublogs: one event log containing only fitting cases and one event log containing only non-fitting cases. The observation whether a case fits or not, can be seen as a response variable. Hence, classification techniques like decision tree learning can be used to characterize cases that deviate. For example, one could learn the rule that cases of gold customers from the southern region tend to deviate from the normative model. Similarly, one could learn rules related to the lateness of cases. For instance, one could find out that cases involving Ellen tend to be delayed.

These examples show that established classification techniques can be combined with process mining once the process model and the event log are connected through replay techniques.

8.6 Bringing It All Together

In this chapter, we showed that a control-flow model can be extended with additional perspectives extracted from the event log. Figure 8.16 sketches the approach to obtain a fully integrated model covering all relevant aspects of the process at hand. The approach consists of five steps. For each step, we provide pointers to chapters and sections in this book:

- *Step 1: obtain an event log.* Chapter 4 showed how to extract event data from a variety of systems. As explained using Fig. 4.1, this is an iterative process. The dotted chart described in Sect. 8.2 helps to explore the event log and guide the filtering process.
- *Step 2: create or discover a process model.* Chapters 5 and 6 focus on techniques for process discovery. Techniques such as heuristic mining and genetic mining

can be used to obtain a process model. However, also existing hand-made models can be used.
- *Step 3: connect events in the log to activities in the model.* As discussed in Sect. 7.4.3, this step is essential for projecting information onto models and to add perspectives. Using the replay technique described in Sect. 7.2, events in the log and activities in the model get connected.
- *Step 4: extend the model.* This is the topic of the current chapter.
  - *Step 4a: add the organizational perspective.* As shown in Sect. 8.3, it is possible to analyze the social network and subsequently identify organizational entities that connect activities to groups of resources.
  - *Step 4b: add the time perspective.* Timestamps and frequencies can be used to learn probability distributions that adequately describe waiting and service times and routing probabilities. Section 8.4 demonstrates that the replay techniques used for conformance checking can be modified to add the time perspective to process models.
  - *Step 4c: add the case perspective.* Section 8.5 showed how to use attributes in the log for decision mining. This shows which data is relevant and should be included in the model.
  - *Step 4d: add other perspectives.* Depending on the information in the log other perspectives may be added to model. For example, information on risks and costs can be added to the model. Existing risk analysis techniques and costing approaches such as Activity Based Costing (ABC) and Resource Consumption Accounting (RCA) can be used to extend the model [21].
- *Step 5: return the integrated model.*

In Chaps. 11 and 12, we provide an overall life-cycle describing a process mining project (L^* life-cycle model). This more elaborate life-cycle incorporates Fig. 8.16.

The integrated model resulting from the steps in Fig. 8.16, can be used for various purposes. First of all, it provides a *holistic view* on the process. This provides new insights and may generate various ideas for process improvement. Moreover, the integrated model can be used as input for other tools and approaches. For instance, it can be used as a starting point for configuring a WFM or BPM system. During the configuration of such a system for a specific process, one needs to provide a model for the control-flow and the other perspectives. The integrated model can also be used to generate a simulation model covering all perspectives. For example, in [83] it is shown that the techniques described in this chapter can be used to generate a simulation model in *CPN Tools*. CPN Tools is a powerful simulation environment based on *colored Petri nets* [58, 96] (see www.cpntools.org).

The resulting simulation model closely follows reality as it is based on event logs rather than human modeling. The colored Petri net models control-flow, data flow, decisions, resources, allocation rules, service times, routing probabilities, arrival processes, etc., thus capturing all aspects relevant for simulation. The integrated simulation model can be used for "what if" analysis to explore different redesigns and control strategies.

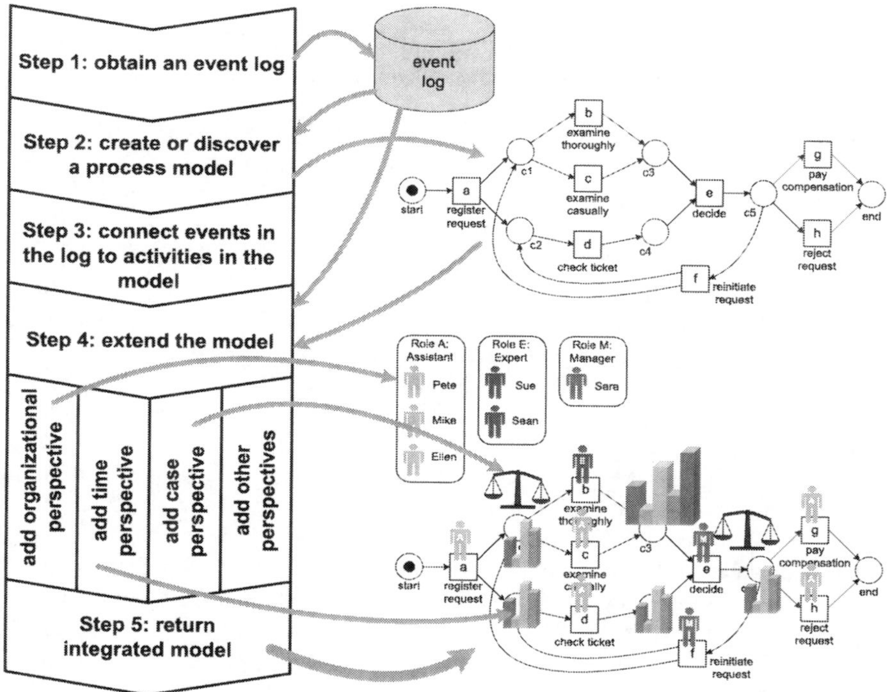

Fig. 8.16 Approach to come to a fully integrated model covering the organizational, time, and case perspectives

Short-Term Simulation

As stressed earlier, it is essential that events in the log are connected to model elements. This allows for the projection of dynamic information onto models: the event log "breathes life" into otherwise static process models. Moreover, the merging of the various perspectives into a single model depends on this. Establishing a good connection between an event log and model may be difficult and require several iterations. However, when using a BPM system, this connection already exists; BPM systems are driven by explicit workflow models and provide excellent event logs. Moreover, internally such systems also have an explicit representation of the state of each running case. This enables a new type of simulation called *short-term simulation* [84, 95]. The key idea is to start all simulation runs from the current state and focus the analysis of the transient behavior. This way a "*fast forward button*" into the future is provided.

Figure 8.16 sketches how a simulation model could be obtained that closely matches reality. The current state obtained from the BPM system, i.e., the markings of all cases and related data elements, can be loaded into the simulation as a realistic initial state.

To understand the importance of short-term simulation, we elaborate on the difference between *transient analysis* and *steady-state analysis*. The key idea of simulation is to execute a model repeatedly. The reason for doing the experiments repeatedly, is to not come up with just a single value (e.g., "the average response time is 10.36 minutes") but to provide confidence intervals (e.g., "the average response time is with 90 percent certainty between 10 and 11 minutes"). For transient analysis, the focus is on the initial part of future behavior, i.e., starting from the initial state the "near future" is explored. For transient analysis, the initial state is very important. If the simulation starts in a state with long queues of work, then in the near future flow times will be long and it may take some time to get rid of the backlog. For steady-state analysis, the initial state is irrelevant. Typically, the simulation is started "empty" (i.e., without any cases in progress) and only when the system is filled with cases the measurements start.

Steady-state analysis is most relevant for answering strategic and tactical questions. Transient analysis is most relevant for operational decision making. Lion's share of contemporary simulation support aims at steady-state analysis and, hence, is limited to strategic and tactical decision making. Short-term simulation focuses on operational decision making; starting from the current state—loaded from the BPM system—the "near future" is explored repeatedly [95]. This shows what will happen if no corrective actions are taken. Moreover, "what if" analysis can be used to explore the effects of different actions (e.g., adding resources and reconfiguring the process).

In [84], it is shown how this approach can be realized using the BPM system *YAWL*, the process mining tool *ProM*, and the simulation tool *CPN Tools*. This illustrates the potentially spectacular synergetic effects that can be achieved by combining workflow automation, process mining, and simulation.

Chapter 9
Operational Support

Most process-mining techniques work on "post mortem" event data, i.e., they analyze events that belong to cases that have already completed. Obviously, it is not possible to influence the execution of "post mortem" cases. Moreover, cases that are still in the pipeline cannot be guided on the basis of "post mortem" event data only. Today, however, many data sources are updated in (near) real-time and sufficient computing power is available to analyze events when they occur. Therefore, process mining should not be restricted to off-line analysis and can also be used for online operational support. This chapter broadens the scope of process mining to include online decision support. For example, for a running case the remaining flow time can be predicted and suitable actions can be recommended to minimize costs.

9.1 Refined Process Mining Framework

Thus far, we identified three main types of process mining: *discovery*, *conformance*, and *enhancement* (cf. Figs. 1.4 and 8.1). Orthogonal to these types of process mining we identified several perspectives including: the *control-flow perspective* ("How?"), the *organizational perspective* ("Who?"), and the *case/data perspective* ("What?"). The classification of process mining techniques into discovery, conformance, and enhancement does reflect that analysis can be done *online* or *off-line*. Moreover, Figs. 1.4 and 8.1 do not acknowledge that there are essentially two types of models ("de jure models" and "de facto models") and two types of data ("pre mortem" and "post mortem" event data) [95].

Figure 9.1 shows our *refined process mining framework*. As before, we assume some external "world" consisting of business processes, people, organizations, etc. and supported by some information system. The information system records information about this "world" in such a way that events logs can be extracted as described in Chap. 4.

Figure 9.1 emphasizes the systematic, reliable, and trustworthy recording of events by using the term *provenance*. This term originates from scientific comput-

W.M.P. van der Aalst, *Process Mining*,
DOI 10.1007/978-3-642-19345-3_9, © Springer-Verlag Berlin Heidelberg 2011

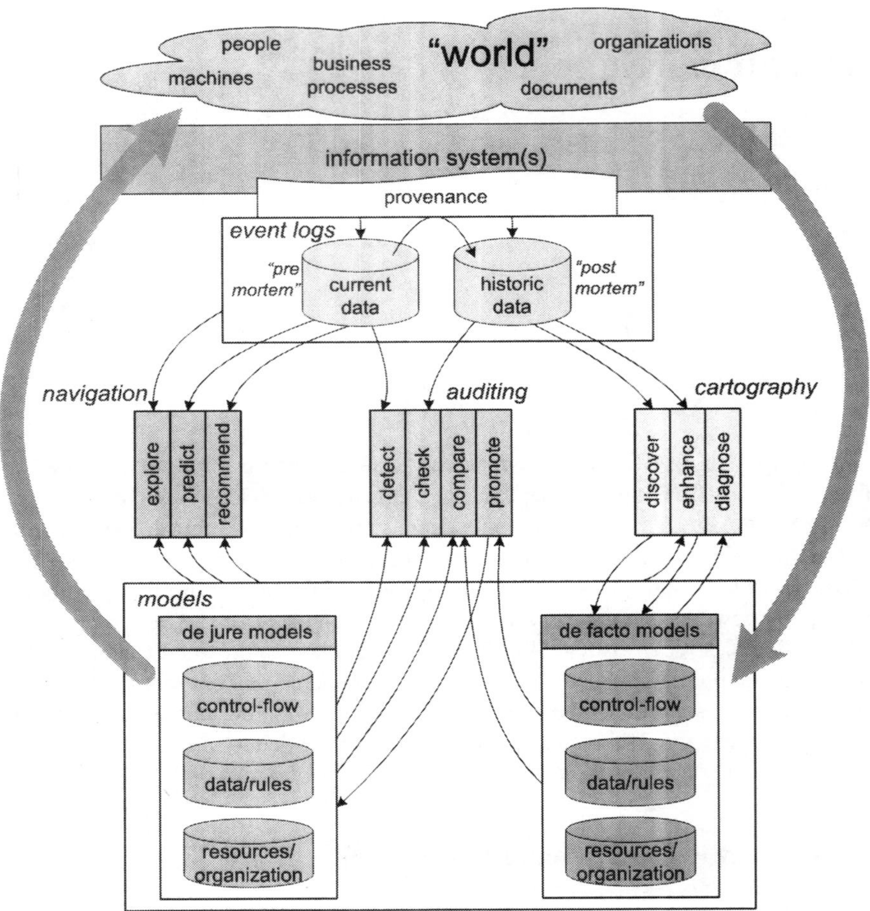

Fig. 9.1 Refined process mining framework

ing, where it refers to the data that is needed to be able to reproduce an experiment [27]. *Business process provenance* aims to systematically collect the information needed to reconstruct what has actually happened in a process or organization. When organizations base their decisions on event data, it is essential to make sure that these describe history well. Moreover, from an auditing point of view it is necessary to ensure that event logs cannot be tampered with. Business process provenance refers to the set of activities needed to ensure that history, as captured in event logs, "cannot be rewritten or obscured" such that it can serve as a reliable basis for process improvement and auditing.

Data in event logs are partitioned into "*pre mortem*" and "*post mortem*" *event data* in the refined process mining framework depicted in Fig. 9.1. "Post mortem" event data refer to information about cases that have completed, i.e., these data can be used for process improvement and auditing, but not for influencing the cases they refer to. Most event logs considered thus far contained only historic, i.e., "post mortem", event data. "Pre mortem" event data refer to cases that have not yet completed. If a case is still running, i.e., the case is still "alive" (pre mortem), then it may be possible that information in the event log about this case (i.e., current data) can be exploited to ensure the correct or efficient handling of this case.

"Post mortem" event data is most relevant for *off-line process mining*, e.g., discovering the control-flow of a process based on one year of event data. For *online process mining*, a mixture of "pre mortem" (current) and "post mortem" (historic) data is needed. For example, historic information can be used to learn a predictive model. Subsequently, information about a running case is combined with the predictive model to provide an estimate for the remaining flow time of the case.

The refined process mining framework also distinguishes between two types of models: "*de jure models*" and "*de facto models*". *A de jure model is normative*, i.e., it specifies how things should be done or handled. For example, a process model used to configure a BPM system is normative and forces people to work in a particular way. *A de facto model is descriptive* and its goal is not to steer or control reality. Instead, de facto models aim to capture reality. The techniques presented in Chaps. 5 and 6 aim to produce de facto models. Figure 9.1 also highlights that models can cover different perspectives, i.e., process mining is not limited to control-flow and is also concerned with resources, data, organizational entities, decision points, costs, etc. The two large arrows in Fig. 9.1 illustrate that de facto models are derived from reality (right downward arrow) and that de jure models aim to influence reality (left upward arrow).

After refining event logs into "pre mortem" and "post mortem" and partitioning models into "de jure" and "de facto", we can identify ten process mining related activities as shown in Fig. 9.1. These ten activities are grouped into three categories: *cartography*, *auditing*, and *navigation*.

9.1.1 Cartography

Process models can be seen as the "maps" describing the operational processes of organizations, i.e., just like geographic maps, process models aim to describe reality. In order to do this, *abstractions* are needed. For example, on a roadmap a highway may be denoted by an orange line having a thickness of four millimeters. In reality the highway will not be orange; the orange coloring is just used to emphasize the importance of highways. If the scale of the map is 1 : 500,000, then the thickness of the line corresponds to a highway of 2 kilometers wide. In reality, the highway will not be so broad. If the thickness of the line would correspond to reality (assuming the same scale), it would be approximately 0.05 millimeter (for a highway of 25 meters wide). Hence, the highway would be (close to) invisible. Therefore, the scale is modified to make the map more readable and useful. When making process models, we need to use similar abstractions. In Chap. 13, we will elaborate on the relationships between process maps and geographic maps. Also note that in Sect. 5.4.4 we already used the metaphor of a "process view" to argue that a discovered process model views reality from a particular "angle", is "framed", and shown using a particular "resolution". Metaphors such as "maps" and "views" help in understanding the role of process models in BPM.

Figure 9.1 shows that three activities are grouped under cartography: *discover*, *enhance*, and *diagnose*.

- *Discover*. This activity is concerned with the extraction of (process) models as discussed in Chaps. 5 and 6.
- *Enhance*. When existing process models (either discovered or hand-made) can be related to events logs, it is possible to enhance these models. The connection can be used to repair models or to extend them. In Sect. 7.4.1, we showed that models can be made more faithful using the diagnostics provided by conformance checking techniques. Chapter 8 illustrated how attributes in event logs can be used to add additional perspectives to a model.
- *Diagnose*. This activity does not directly use event logs and focuses on classical model-based process analysis as discussed in Sect. 2.3, e.g., process models can be checked for the absence of deadlocks or alternative models can be simulated to estimate the effect of various redesigns on average cycle times.

9.1.2 Auditing

In Sect. 7.1, we defined *auditing* as the set of activities used to check whether business processes are executed within certain boundaries set by managers, governments, and other stakeholders [112]. In Fig. 9.1, the auditing category groups all activities that are concerned with the comparison of behaviors, e.g., two process models or a process model and an event log are put side by side.

- *Detect*. This activity compares de jure models with current "pre mortem" data (events of running process instances) with the goal to detect deviations at run-time. The moment a predefined rule is violated, an alert is generated.
- *Check*. As demonstrated in Chap. 7, historic "post mortem" data can be cross-checked with de jure models. The goal of this activity is to pinpoint deviations and quantify the level of compliance.
- *Compare*. De facto models can be compared with de jure models to see in what way reality deviates from what was planned or expected. Unlike for the previous two activities, no event log is used directly. However, the de facto model may have been discovered using historic data; this way event data are used indirectly for the comparison. In Sect. 7.3, we showed that footprints can be used for model-to-model (and log-to-model) comparisons.
- *Promote*. Based on an analysis of the differences between a de facto model and a de jure model, it is possible to promote parts of the de facto model to a new de jure model. By promoting proven "best practices" to the de jure model, existing processes can be improved.

Note that the *detect* and *check* activities are similar except for the event data used. The former activity uses "pre mortem" data and aims at online analysis to be able to react immediately when a discrepancy is detected. The latter activity uses "post mortem" data and is done off-line.

9.1.3 Navigation

The last category of process mining activities aim at business process *navigation*. Unlike the cartography and auditing activities, navigation activities are forward-looking. For example, process mining techniques can be used to make predictions about the future of a particular case and guide the user in selecting suitable actions. When comparing this with a car navigation system from TomTom or Garmin, this corresponds to functionalities such predicting the arrival time and guiding the driver using spoken instructions. In Chap. 13, we elaborate on the similarities between car navigation and process mining.

Figure 9.1 lists three navigation activities: *explore*, *predict*, and *recommend*.

- *Explore*. The combination of event data and models can be used to explore business processes at run-time. Running cases can be visualized and compared with similar cases that were handled earlier.
- *Predict*. By combining information about running cases with models (discovered or hand-made), it is possible to make predictions about the future, e.g., the remaining flow time and the probability of success.
- *Recommend*. The information used for predicting the future can also be used to recommend suitable actions (e.g., to minimize costs or time). The goal is to enable functionality similar to the guidance given by car navigation systems.

In earlier chapters, we focused on activities using historic ("post mortem") data only, i.e., activities *discover*, *enhance*, and *check* in Fig. 9.1. In the remainder of this chapter, we shift our attention to online analysis also using "pre mortem" data.

9.2 Online Process Mining

Traditionally, process mining has been used in an off-line fashion using only "post mortem" data. This means that only completed cases are being considered, i.e., the traces in the event log are *complete* traces corresponding to cases that were fully handled in the past. For *operational support* we also consider "pre mortem" event data and respond to such data in an online fashion. Now only running cases are considered as these can, potentially, still be influenced. A running case may still generate events. Therefore, it is described by a *partial* trace.

Figure 9.2 shows the essence of operational support. Consider a case for which activities a and b have been executed. Partial trace $\sigma_p = \langle a, b \rangle$ describes the known past of the case. Note that the two events may have all kinds of attributes (e.g.,

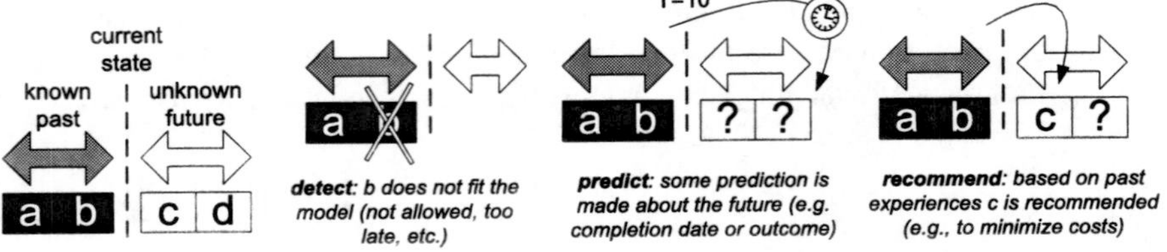

Fig. 9.2 Three process mining activities related to operational support: *detect*, *predict*, and *recommend*

Table 9.1 Fragment of event log with timestamps and transactional information. For instance, event a^{12}_{start} denotes the start of activity a at time 12

Case id	Trace
1	$\langle a^{12}_{start}, a^{19}_{complete}, b^{25}_{start}, d^{26}_{start}, b^{32}_{complete}, d^{33}_{complete}, e^{35}_{start}, e^{40}_{complete}, h^{50}_{start}, h^{54}_{complete}\rangle$
2	$\langle a^{17}_{start}, a^{23}_{complete}, d^{28}_{start}, c^{30}_{start}, d^{32}_{complete}, c^{38}_{complete}, e^{50}_{start}, e^{59}_{complete}, g^{70}_{start}, g^{73}_{complete}\rangle$
3	$\langle a^{25}_{start}, a^{30}_{complete}, c^{32}_{start}, c^{35}_{complete}, d^{35}_{start}, d^{40}_{complete}, e^{45}_{start}, e^{50}_{complete}, f^{50}_{start}, f^{55}_{complete}, b^{60}_{start}, d^{62}_{start}, b^{65}_{complete}, d^{67}_{complete}, e^{80}_{start}, e^{87}_{complete}, g^{90}_{start}, g^{98}_{complete}\rangle$
...	...

timestamps and associated resources), but these are not shown here. In the state after observing σ_p, the future of the case is not known yet. One possible future could be that c and d will be executed resulting in a complete trace $\sigma_c = \langle a, b, c, d\rangle$. Figure 9.2 shows three operational support activities: *detect*, *predict*, and *recommend*. These correspond to the activities already mentioned in the context of Fig. 9.1.

- *Detect*. This activity compares the partial trace σ_p with some normative model, e.g., a process model or an LTL constraint. Such a check could reveal a violation as shown in Fig. 9.2. If b was not allowed after a, an alert would be generated.
- *Predict*. This activity makes statements about the events following σ_p. For example, the expected completion time could be predicted by comparing the current case to similar cases that were handled in the past.
- *Recommend*. Recommendations guide the user in selecting the next activity after σ_p. For example, it could be that, based on historic information, it is recommended to execute activity c next (e.g., to minimize costs or flow time).

Note that all three activities assume some model, e.g., predictions and recommendations could be based on a regression model or obtained using simulation. Besides the three operational support activities illustrated by Fig. 9.2, it is also possible to simply explore partial traces. For example, dotted chart visualization and other visual analytics techniques can also be applied to running cases.

In the remainder, we show how some of the process mining techniques presented earlier can be modified to provide operational support. In order to do this, we use the event log shown in Table 9.1. This log was also used in earlier chapters and is based on the running example introduced in Chap. 1. The WF-net shown in Fig. 1.1 models

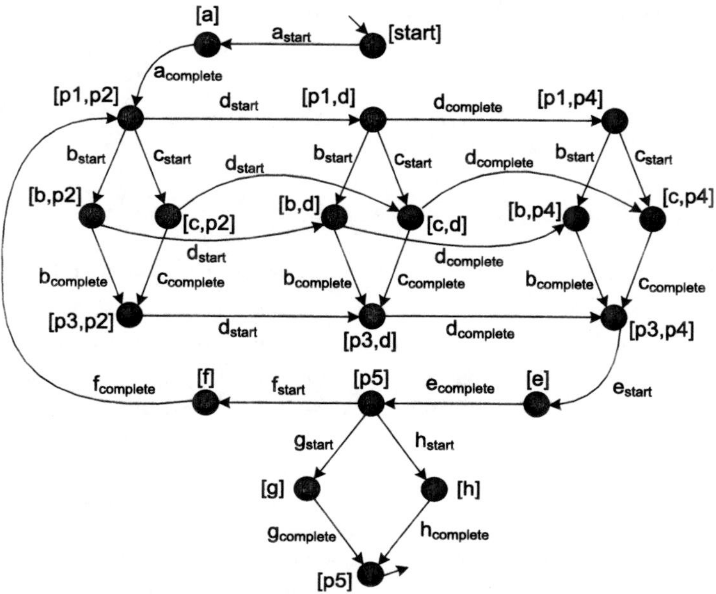

Fig. 9.3 Transition system modeling the process that generated the event log shown in Table 9.1. This process was already modeled in terms of a WF-net (Fig. 1.1) and in terms of BPMN (Fig. 1.2). However, in this transition system we model the start and completion of an activity explicitly. In terms of the WF-net in Fig. 1.1, this means that transition a is split into transitions a_{start} and $a_{complete}$ connected by a place named a. Etc.

the process for which events have been recorded in Table 9.1. Figure 1.2 models the same process in terms of BPMN. Independent of the notation used, we can also derive a transition system modeling the same process as is shown in Fig. 9.3. The transition system labels the nodes with markings of the corresponding Petri net in which each activity is modeled by a start and complete transition. Transition a_{start} consumes a token from place *start* and produces a token for place a. The token in place a models that activity a is being executed. Transition $a_{complete}$ consumes a token from place a and produces a token for each of the places $p1$ and $p2$ (state $[p1, p2]$ in Fig. 9.3). The state labeled $[b, d]$ in Fig. 9.3 corresponds to the marking with tokens in b and d, i.e., activities b and d are being executed in parallel. The state space of the BPMN model shown in Fig. 1.2 is isomorphic to the transition system shown in Fig. 9.3.

9.3 Detect

The first operational support activity we elaborate on is *detecting* deviations at runtime. This can be seen as conformance checking "on-the-fly". Compared to conformance checking as described in Chap. 7 there are two important differences: (a) we

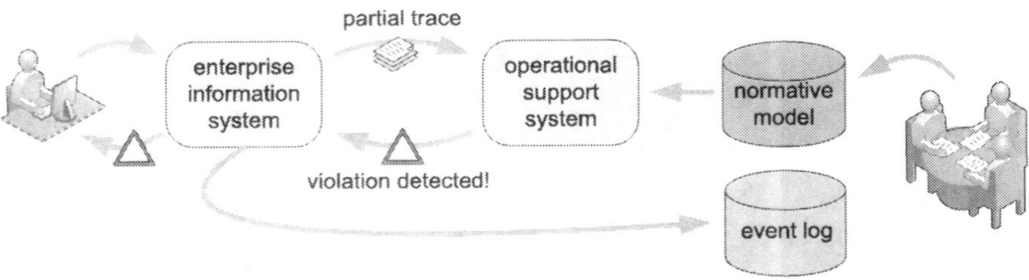

Fig. 9.4 Detecting violations at run-time: the moment a deviation is detected, an alert is generated

do no consider the log as a whole but focus on the *partial trace of a particular case*, and (b) in case of a deviation there should be an *immediate response* when the deviation occurs. Figure 9.4 illustrates this type of operational support. Users are interacting with some enterprise information system. Based on their actions, events are recorded. The partial trace of each case is continuously checked by the operational support system, i.e., each time an event occurs, the partial trace of the corresponding case is sent to the operational support system. The operational support system immediately generates an alert if a deviation is detected. The enterprise information system and its users can take appropriate actions based on this alert, e.g., a manager is notified such that corrective actions can be taken.

All cases in the event log shown in Table 9.1 conform to the transition system of Fig. 9.3, the WF-net shown in Fig. 1.1, and the BPMN model shown in Fig. 1.2. Therefore, when these cases were executing, no deviations could be detected with respect to these models. Assume now that the more restrictive WF-net shown in Fig. 9.5 describes the desired normative behavior. Compared to the original model activity d (i.e., checking the ticket) should occur after b or c (i.e., one of the examinations).[1]

Let us now consider the first case: $\sigma_1 = \langle a^{12}_{start}, a^{19}_{complete}, b^{25}_{start}, d^{26}_{start}, b^{32}_{complete}, d^{33}_{complete}, e^{35}_{start}, e^{40}_{complete}, h^{50}_{start}, h^{54}_{complete}\rangle$. After each event it is checked whether there is a deviation or not. At time 12, after executing the first event a^{12}_{start} no deviation is found, because trace $\langle a^{12}_{start}\rangle$ can be replayed in Fig. 9.5 without missing tokens.[2] The next two events can also be replayed, i.e., $\langle a^{12}_{start}, a^{19}_{complete}, b^{25}_{start}\rangle$ is a possible firing sequence of the WF-net in which each activity is refined into a start and complete transition. The state after replaying the three events is $[c2, b]$. The next event, i.e., d^{26}_{start} is not possible in this state. Hence, an *alert* is generated at time

[1] Note that this diagram can be simplified by removing place $c2$, the arc from $c3$ to e, and the arc from d to $c3$ (i.e., N_2 in Fig. 7.2). The simplified model has the same behavior, i.e., both are bisimilar.

[2] The WF-net Fig. 9.5 has only one transition per activity while the log contains start and complete events. As described in Sect. 5.2.4, each activity can be described by a small subprocess. Assume that all transitions in Fig. 9.5 are split into a start transition and complete transition connected through a place named after the activity. For example, transition a is refined into transitions a_{start} and $a_{complete}$ connected by a place a. Note that the transition system in Fig. 9.3 used the same naming convention.

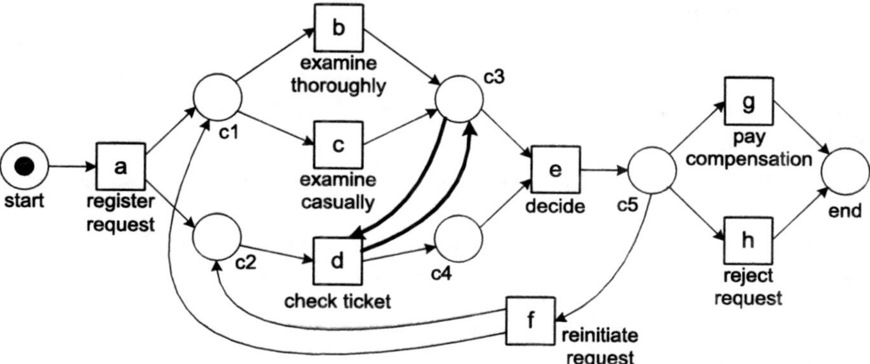

Fig. 9.5 WF-net modeling an additional constraint: d can only be started once b or c has completed

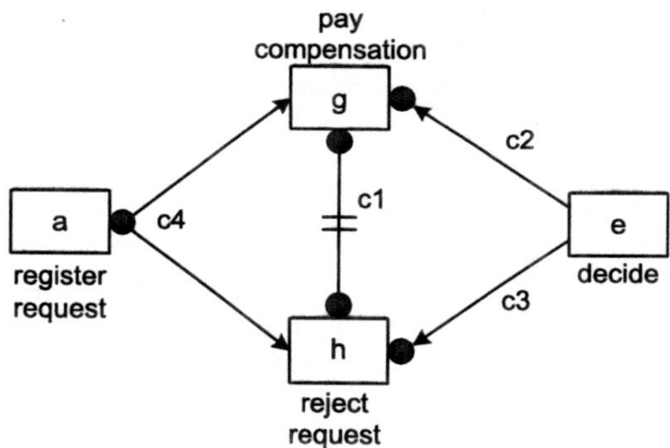

Fig. 9.6 Declare specification composed of four constraints: $c1$, $c2$, $c3$, and $c4$

26 based on partial trace $\langle a^{12}_{start}, a^{19}_{complete}, b^{25}_{start}, d^{26}_{start}\rangle$. The alert signals that activity d was started without being enabled. For the second case a deviation is detected at time 28; based on the partial trace $\langle a^{17}_{start}, a^{23}_{complete}, d^{28}_{start}\rangle$ an alert is generated stating that d was started before it was enabled. For the third case a deviation is detected at time 62. The prefix $\langle a^{25}_{start}, a^{30}_{complete}, c^{32}_{start}, c^{35}_{complete}, d^{35}_{start}, d^{40}_{complete}, e^{45}_{start}, e^{50}_{complete}, f^{50}_{start}, f^{55}_{complete}, b^{60}_{start}, d^{62}_{start}\rangle$ cannot be replayed properly because the second instance of d is started without being enabled. These examples show that the replay approach from Chap. 7 can also be used at run-time for detecting deviations the moment they happen.

In Chap. 7 we introduced *Declare* as an example of a constraint-based language. We used the Declare model shown in Fig. 9.6 to explain some of basic concepts. Each of the four constraints shown can be specified in terms of LTL. Constraint $c1$ is a non-coexistence constraint stating that g and h should not both happen. The LTL expression for this constraint is $!((\Diamond g) \wedge (\Diamond h))$. Constraint $c2$ is a precedence constraint $((!g)\ W\ e)$ modeling the requirement that g should not happen before e has happened. Constraint $c3$ is a similar precedence constraint, but now referring to

h rather than g. Constraint $c4$ is a branched response constraint stating that every occurrence of a should eventually be followed by g or h, i.e., $\Box(a \Rightarrow (\Diamond(g \vee h)))$.

Consider some case having a partial trace σ_p listing the events that have happened thus far. Each constraint c in Fig. 9.6 is in one of the following states for partial trace σ_p:

- *Satisfied*: the LTL formula corresponding to c evaluates to true for the partial trace σ_p.
- *Temporarily violated*: the LTL formula corresponding to c evaluates to false for σ_p, however, there is a longer trace σ'_p that has σ_p as a prefix and for which the LTL formula corresponding to c evaluates to true.
- *Permanently violated*: the LTL formula corresponding to c evaluates to false for σ_p and all its extensions, i.e., there is no σ'_p that has σ_p as a prefix and for which the LTL formula evaluates to true.

These three notions can be lifted from the level of a *single constraint* to the level of a *complete Declare specification*. A Declare specification is *satisfied* for a case if all of its constraints are satisfied. A Declare specification is *temporarily violated* by a case if for the current partial trace at least one of the constraints is violated, however, there is a possible future in which all constraints are satisfied. A Declare specification is *permanently violated* by a case if no such future exists.

None of the cases shown in Table 9.1 violates any of the constraints shown in Fig. 9.6, i.e., for each trace, at the *end*, all constraints are satisfied. Let us now consider a scenario in which for a case the trace $\sigma = \langle a, b, d, g \rangle$ is executed. For simplicity, we removed timestamps and transactional information. Initially, i.e., for trace $\sigma_0 = \langle \, \rangle$, all constraints are satisfied. After executing a, i.e., for prefix $\sigma_1 = \langle a \rangle$, constraint $c4$ is temporarily violated. Because there is a possible future in which all constraints are satisfied, there is no need to generate an alert. However, diagnostic information stating that constraint $c4$ is temporarily violated could be provided. Executing b and d does not change the situation, i.e., both partial traces $\sigma_2 = \langle a, b \rangle$ and $\sigma_3 = \langle a, b, d \rangle$ temporarily violate $c4$. However, after executing g the situation changes. Partial trace $\sigma_4 = \langle a, b, d, g \rangle$ satisfies constraint $c4$. However, constraint $c2$ is permanently violated by σ_4 as there is no "possible future" in which e occurs before g. Therefore, a deviation is detected and reported.

Figure 9.7 shows another Declare model. Constraint $c1$ is the same non-coexistence constraint as before. Constraint $c2$ is a response constraint stating that every occurrence of activity e should eventually be followed by g, i.e., $\Box(e \Rightarrow (\Diamond g))$ in LTL terms. Constraint $c3$ is a similar response constraint (every occurrence of activity e should eventually be followed by h). Constraint $c4$ is a precedence constraint $((!g)\ W\ a)$ modeling the requirement that g should not happen before a has happened. Constraint $c5$ is also a precedence constraint $((!h)\ W\ a)$. Assume that Fig. 9.7 is the normative model. Let us first consider a scenario in which for a case the trace $\sigma = \langle a, b, d, g \rangle$ is executed. For all prefixes, all of the constraints are satisfied, i.e., no alerts need to be executed during the lifetime of this case. Let us now consider the scenario $\sigma = \langle a, b, d, e, g \rangle$. No alerts need to be generated for the first three events. In fact at any stage all five constraints are satisfied. However, after executing e constraints $c2$ and $c3$ are temporarily violated. To remove these temporary violations,

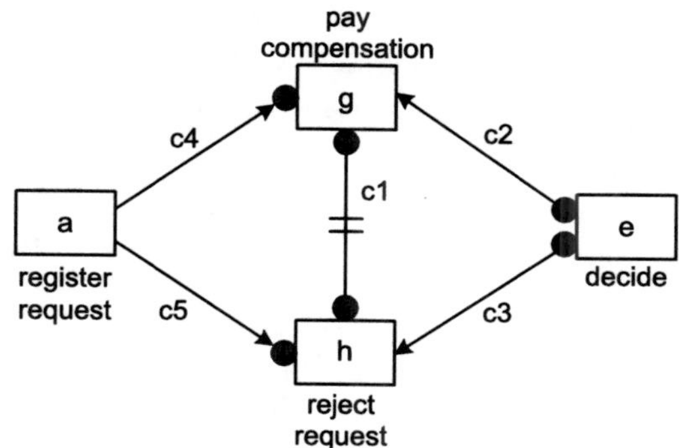

Fig. 9.7 Another Declare specification. Note that $c1$, $c2$, and $c3$ imply that e cannot be executed without permanently violating the specification

both g and h need to be executed after $\langle a, b, d, e \rangle$. However, the execution of both g and h results in a permanent violation of $c1$. Because there is no possible future in which *all* constraints are satisfied, the Declare specification is permanently violated by prefix $\langle a, b, d, e \rangle$ and an alert is generated directly after e occurs. Note that in the latter scenario, there are only temporarily violated constraints whereas the whole specification is permanently violated. Therefore, advanced reasoning is required to determine whether an event signifies a deviation or not. As shown in [68, 108], one can use model checking or abductive logic programming to detect such deviations and provide informative alerts.

9.4 Predict

The second operational support activity we consider is *prediction*. As shown in Fig. 9.8, we again consider the setting in which users are interacting with some enterprise information system. The events recorded for cases can be sent to the operational support system in the form of partial traces. Based on such a partial trace and some predictive model, a prediction is generated. Examples of predictions are:

- The predicted remaining flow time is 14 days.
- The predicted probability of meeting the legal deadline is 0.72.
- The predicted total cost of this case is € 4500.
- The predicted probability that activity a will occur is 0.34.
- The predicted probability that person r will work on this case is 0.57.
- The predicted probability that a case will be rejected is 0.67.
- The predicted total service time is 98 minutes.

In the fictive example shown in Fig. 9.8, the operational support system predicts that the completion date will be April 25, 2011.

Various techniques can be used to generate predictions. For example, the supervised learning techniques discussed in Sect. 3.1.2 can be used to answer some of these questions. Using feature extraction, relevant properties of the partial trace need to be mapped onto predictor variables. Moreover, the feature we would like to

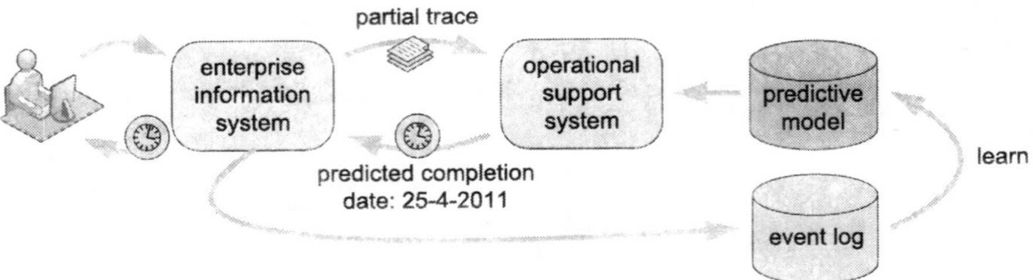

Fig. 9.8 Both the partial trace of a running case and some predictive model are used to provide a prediction (e.g., remaining flow time, expected total costs, or probability of success)

predict is mapped onto a response variable. The response variable is often a performance indicator, e.g., remaining flow time or total costs. If the response variable is numeric, typically regression analysis is used. For a categorical response variable, classification techniques such as decision tree learning can be used. The predictive model is based on historic "post mortem" event data, but can be used to make predictions for the cases that are still running.

Given the variety of approaches and the broad spectrum of possible questions, we cannot provide a comprehensive overview of prediction techniques. Therefore, as an example, we select one particular technique answering a specific question. In the remainder, we show how to *predict the remaining flow time using an annotated transition system* [110, 113]. Starting point for this approach is an event log with timestamps as shown in Table 9.1 and a transition system such as the one shown in Fig. 9.3. The transition system can be obtained by computing the state-space of a process model expressed in another language (WF-nets, BPMN, YAWL, EPCs, etc.). For example, the transition system in Fig. 9.3 can be obtained from the WF-net in Fig. 1.1 or the BPMN model in Fig. 1.2. The transition system can also be obtained using the technique described in Sect. 6.4.1, i.e., using an event log L and a state representation function $l^{state}()$, one can automatically generate a transition system able to replay the event log.

Assuming that the event log fits the transition system, one can replay the events on the model and collect timing information. Non-fitting events and/or cases can be simply ignored or handled as described in Sect. 7.2. Figure 9.9 shows the timed replay of the first two traces in Table 9.1.

Let us consider the first case: $\langle a^{12}_{start}, a^{19}_{complete}, b^{25}_{start}, d^{26}_{start}, b^{32}_{complete}, d^{33}_{complete}, e^{35}_{start}, e^{40}_{complete}, h^{50}_{start}, h^{54}_{complete}\rangle$. This case started at time 12 and ended at time 54. Hence, its flow time was 42 time units. States visited by this case are annotated with a tag (t, e, r, s) where t is the *time* the state is visited, e is the *elapsed time* since the start when visiting the state, r is the *remaining flow time*, and s is the *sojourn time*. State $[a]$ is tagged with the annotation $(t = 12, e = 0, r = 42, s = 7)$ because this state was visited by the case directly after the first event a^{12}_{start} occurred. $t = 12$ because event a^{12}_{start} occurred at time 12. $e = 12 - 12 = 0$ because no time elapsed after executing just one event. $r = 54 - 12 = 42$ is the remaining time until the end of the case after a was started at time 12. $s = 19 - 12 = 7$ because

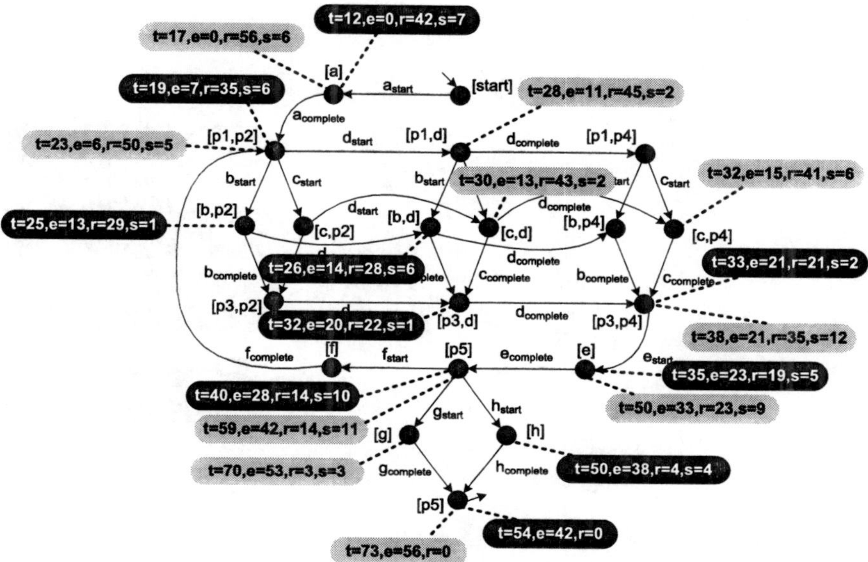

Fig. 9.9 Statistics collected while replaying the first two cases: t is the time the state is visited, e is the elapsed time since the start when visiting the state, r is the remaining flow time, and s is the sojourn time

the next event occurred 7 time units later. State $[p1, p2]$ is tagged with annotation $(t = 19, e = 7, r = 35, s = 6)$ because a completed at time $t = 19$. $e = 19 - 12 = 7$ because a completed 7 time units after the case started. $r = 54 - 19 = 35$ because the case ended at time 54. $s = 25 - 19 = 6$ because the next event occurred 6 time units later. Figure 9.9 shows all annotations related to the first two cases. For example, state $[p3, p4]$ was visited once by each of the two cases resulting in annotations $(t = 33, e = 21, r = 21, s = 2)$ and $(t = 38, e = 21, r = 35, s = 12)$. The initial state $[start]$ has no annotations since no events have occurred when visiting this state. The final state $[p5]$ has no sojourn time because there is no next event when visiting this state.

Table 9.1 shows only a fragment of the whole event log. However, it is obvious that the other cases in the log can be replayed in a similar fashion to gather more annotations. For example, the third case visited state $[p3, p4]$ twice: after event $d^{40}_{complete}$ and after event $d^{67}_{complete}$. The first visit resulted in annotation $(t = 40, e = 15, r = 58, s = 5)$ and the second visit resulted in annotation $(t = 67, e = 42, r = 31, s = 13)$. Assuming a large event log, there may be hundreds or even thousands of annotations per state. For each state, x it is possible to create a multi-set $Q^{remaining}_x$ of remaining flow times based on these annotations. For state $[p3, p4]$ this multi-set is $Q^{remaining}_{[p3,p4]} = [21, 35, 58, 31, \ldots]$: the first case visited state $[p3, p4]$ once (21 time units before completion), the second case visited $[p3, p4]$ once (35 time units before completion), the third case visited $[p3, p4]$ twice (58 and 31 time units before completion), etc. Similar multi-sets exist for elapsed times

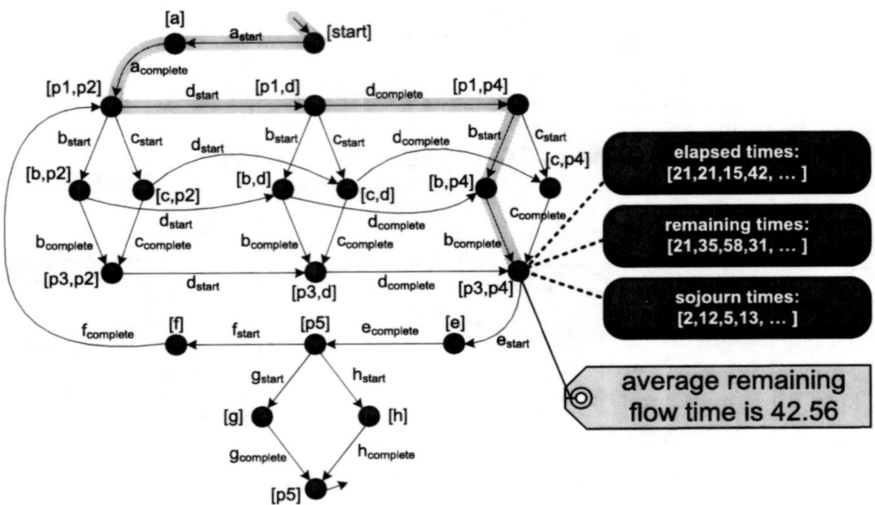

Fig. 9.10 Each state has a multi-set of remaining flow times (one element for each visit). This is the basis for predicting the remaining flow time of future cases. For a case with partial trace $\langle a^{512}_{start}, a^{518}_{complete}, d^{525}_{start}, d^{526}_{complete}, b^{532}_{start}, b^{533}_{complete}\rangle$, the predicted remaining flow time is 42.56. This is the mean remaining flow time of cases in state $[p3, p4]$

($Q^{elapsed}_{[p3,p4]} = [21, 21, 15, 42, \ldots]$) and sojourn times ($Q^{sojourn}_{[p3,p4]} = [2, 12, 5, 13, \ldots]$). Based on these multi-sets all kinds of statistics can be computed. For example, the *mean remaining flow time* in state $[p3, p4]$ is $\sum_{q \in Q} \frac{Q(q) \times q}{|Q|}$ with $Q = Q^{remaining}_{[p3,p4]}$. Like in Sect. 8.4, it is possible to compute other standard statistics such as standard deviation, minimum, and maximum. One can also fit a distribution on the sample data using standard statistical software. For example, based on the samples $Q^{remaining}_{[p3,p4]} = [21, 35, 58, 31, \ldots]$ one could find that these remaining flow times are best described by a Gamma distribution with parameters $r = 8.0502$ and $\lambda = 0.18915$. This distribution has a mean of 42.56 and a standard deviation of 15.0. As shown in Chap. 8, such insights can be used to extend models with the time information. Moreover, the annotated transition system can also be used actively, and predict the remaining time for a running case.

Figure 9.10 shows the transition system with annotations for state $[p3, p4]$. Moreover, the path of a partial trace of a case that is still running is highlighted in the figure. The partial trace of this case is: $\langle a^{512}_{start}, a^{518}_{complete}, d^{525}_{start}, d^{526}_{complete}, b^{532}_{start}, b^{533}_{complete}\rangle$. At time 533, we are interested in the remaining flow time of this case. An obvious predictor for the remaining flow time of the running case is the mean remaining flow time of all earlier cases in the same state, i.e., 42.56. Hence, the case is expected to complete around time 575.56. This illustrates that for any running case, at any point in time, one can predict the remaining flow time.

The annotated transition system can be used to make more refined statements about the predicted remaining flow time. For example, it is clear that the size of multi-set $Q^{remaining}_{[p3,p4]}$ and the standard deviation of the historic samples in this multi-set have impact on the reliability of the prediction. Rather than giving a single prediction value, it is also possible to produce predictions like "With 90% confidence the remaining flow time is predicted to be between 40 and 45 days" or "78% of similar cases were handled within 50 days". Moreover, as shown in [113] it is possible to use cross-validation to determine the quality of predictions.

The approach based on an annotated transition system is not restricted to predicting the remaining flow time. Obviously, one could predict the sojourn time in a similar fashion. Moreover, also non-time-related predictions can be made using the same approach. For example, suppose that we are interested in whether the request is accepted (activity g occurs) or rejected (activity h occurs). To make such predictions, we annotate states with information about known outcomes for "post mortem" cases. For example, $Q^{accepted}_{[p3,p4]} = [0, 1, 1, 1, \ldots]$. For state $[p3, p4]$, a "0" is added to this multi-set for each visit of a case that will be rejected and "1" is added for each visit of a case that will be accepted. The average value of $Q^{accepted}_{[p3,p4]}$ is a predictor for the probability that a case visiting state $[p3, p4]$ will be accepted. This example shows that a *wide variety of predictions* can be generated using a suitable annotated transition system. It is important to note that process-related information is taken into account, i.e., the prediction is based on the *state* of the running case rather than some static attribute. Classical data mining approaches (e.g., based on regression or decision trees) typically use static attributes of a case rather than state information.

The transition system shown in Fig. 9.10 happens to coincide with the states of the WF-net and BPMN model provided earlier. However, as discussed in Sect. 6.4.1, different transition systems can be constructed based on an event log. The event log L and the state representation function $l^{state}(\,)$ determine the level of detail and the aspects considered. For example, it is possible to abstract from irrelevant activities resulting in a more coarse-grained transition system. However, it is also possible to include information about resources and data in the state, thus resulting in a more fine-grained transition system. There should be sufficient visits to all states to make reliable predictions. The transition system is too fine-grained if many states are rarely visited when replaying log L. The level of abstraction should be consistent with the size of the log and the response variable that needs to be predicted. For supervised learning, this is generally referred to as the problem of feature extraction, i.e., determining the predictor variables that are most relevant for predicting the response variable. See [113] for more details and examples.

The approach based on annotated transition systems is just one of many approaches that could be used for prediction. For example, *short-term simulation* could be used to explore the possible futures of a particular case in a particular state (see Sect. 8.6). The simulation model learned based on historic data is initialized with the current state of the running case. Subsequently, the remaining lifetime of the case is simulated repeatedly to obtain sample measurements for the performance indicator to be predicted.

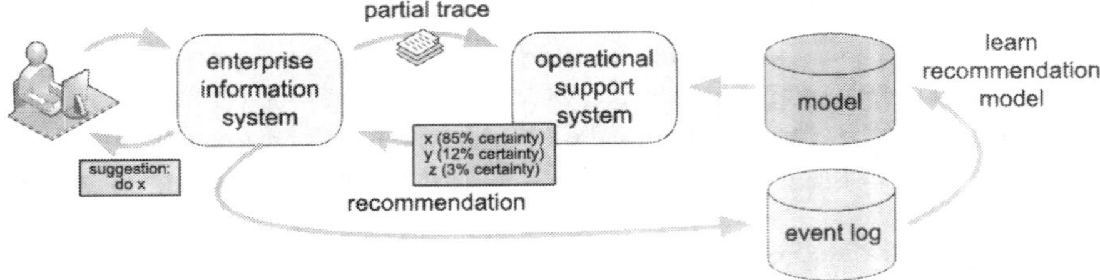

Fig. 9.11 A model based on historic data is used to provide recommendations for running cases. Recommendations are not enforced and may have quality attributes attached, e.g., in 85% of similar cases, x is the activity that minimizes flow time

9.5 Recommend

The third operational support activity we consider in this chapter is *recommendation*. As Fig. 9.11 shows, the setting is similar to prediction, i.e., a partial trace is sent to the operational support system followed by a response. However, the response is not a prediction but a recommendation about what to do next. To provide such a recommendation, a model is learned from "post mortem" event data. Moreover, the operational support system should know what the *decision space* is, i.e., what are the possible actions from which to choose one. Based on the recommendation model, these actions are ordered. For example, in Fig. 9.11 the operational support system recommends to do action x with 85% certainty. The other two possible actions have a "lower" recommendation: y is recommended with 12% certainty and z is recommended with 3% certainty. In most cases it is impossible to give a recommendation that is guaranteed to be optimal; the best choice for the next step may depend on the occurrence of unknown external events in the future. For example, in Fig. 9.11 there may be cases for which z turns out to be the best choice.

A recommendation is always given *with respect to a specific goal*. Examples of goals are:

- Minimize the remaining flow time
- Minimize the total costs
- Maximize the fraction of cases handled within 4 weeks
- Maximize the fraction of cases that is accepted
- Minimize resource usage

These goals can also be aggregated and combined, e.g., to balance between cost reduction and flow time reduction. To operationalize such a goal, a performance indicator needs to be defined, e.g., remaining flow time or total costs. This performance indicator corresponds to the response variable in supervised learning.

A recommendation makes statements about a set of possible actions, i.e., the decision space. The decision space may be a set of activities, e.g., $\{f, g, h\}$. This means that in the current state activities f, g, and h are possible candidates and the question to be answered by the operational support system is "Which candidate is

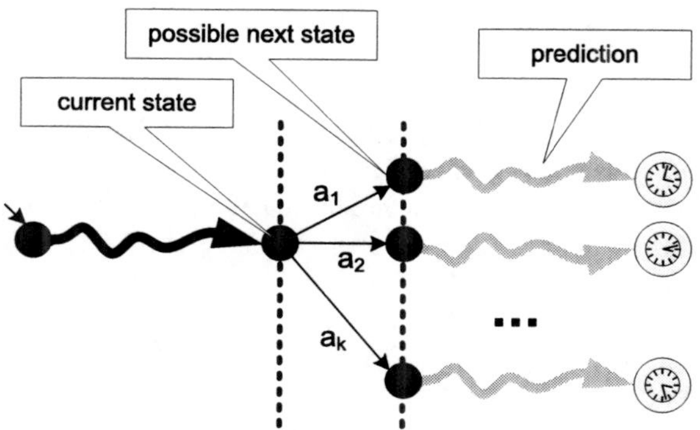

Fig. 9.12 Recommendations can be based on predictions. For every possible choice, simply predict the performance indicator of interest. Then, recommend the best one(s)

best given the goal selected?". However, the decision space may also consist of a set of resources and the goal is then to recommend the best resource to execute a given activity. For example, the operational support system could recommend allocating activity h to Mike to minimize the flow time. This example shows that recommendations are not limited to control-flow and can also refer to other perspectives. Therefore, we use the term "action" rather than activity. The decision space for a running case may be part of the message sent from the enterprise information system to the operational support system. Otherwise, the recommendation model should be able to derive the decision space based on the partial trace.

As shown in Fig. 9.12, recommending an action to achieve a goal is closely related to predicting the corresponding performance indicator. Suppose that for a case having a partial trace σ_p we need to recommend some action from a set of possible actions $\{a_1, a_2, \ldots, a_k\}$. The existing partial trace can be extended by assuming that action a_1 is selected (although it did not happen yet). σ_1 is the resulting extended partial trace, i.e., $\sigma_1 = \sigma_p \oplus a_1$. (Here we assume that a_1 is an activity and we use simple traces.) The same can be done for all other actions resulting in a set of partial traces $D = \{\sigma_1, \sigma_2, \ldots, \sigma_k\}$. Now a prediction is made for the selected performance indicator and each element of D. The resulting predictions are compared and ranked. If σ_2 has the best predicted value (e.g., shortest remaining flow time), then a_2 is recommended first.

Depending on the prediction technique used, the recommendation can also include information about its reliability/quality, e.g., the confidence or certainty that a particular selection is optimal with respect to the goal. For example, in Fig. 9.11 the recommendation attaches a confidence to each of the three possible actions. How to interpret such confidence values depends on the underlying prediction method. For example, if short-term simulation is used, then the 85% certainty of x mentioned in Fig. 9.11 (i.e., the confidence attached to recommendation x) would mean that in 85% of the simulation experiments action x resulted in the shortest remaining flow time.

9.6 Process Mining Spectrum

The refined process mining framework shown in Fig. 9.1 illustrates the broadness of the *process mining spectrum*. We identified 10 process mining activities ranging from discovery and conformance checking to the three operational support activities described in this chapter. These activities may be concerned with "de jure" or "de facto" models, "pre mortem" or "post mortem" event data, and one or more perspectives (control-flow perspective, organizational perspective, case/data perspective, etc.). In this chapter, we showed that process mining techniques originally intended for off-line analysis can be adapted for operational support. For example, replay techniques originally developed for conformance checking can be used to *detect* policy violations, *predict* remaining flow times, and *recommend* activities in an online setting.

Part IV
Putting Process Mining to Work

Chapter 1
Introduction

Part I: Preliminaries

Chapter 2
Process Modeling and Analysis

Chapter 3
Data Mining

Part II: From Event Logs to Process Models

Chapter 4
Getting the Data

Chapter 5
Process Discovery: An Introduction

Chapter 6
Advanced Process Discovery Techniques

Part III: Beyond Process Discovery

Chapter 7
Conformance Checking

Chapter 8
Mining Additional Perspectives

Chapter 9
Operational Support

Part IV: Putting Process Mining to Work

Chapter 10
Tool Support

Chapter 11
Analyzing "Lasagna Processes"

Chapter 12
Analyzing "Spaghetti Processes"

Part V: Reflection

Chapter 13
Cartography and Navigation

Chapter 14
Epilogue

This part reviews available tool support for process mining and presents a methodology for process mining. The methodology identifies two types of processes (Lasagna and Spaghetti processes) and discusses use cases for process mining in various domains. Using the L^* life-cycle model, guidelines for analyzing Lasagna and Spaghetti processes are given. Moreover, examples of analysis results based on real-life event logs are provided.

Chapter 10
Tool Support

Many vendors offer Business Intelligence (BI) software products. Unfortunately, most of these products are data-centric and focus on rather simplistic forms of analysis. As shown in the preceding chapters, process-centric, truly "intelligent" BI is possible due to advances in process mining. For example, ProM is an open-source process mining tool supporting all of the techniques mentioned in this book. Process discovery, conformance checking, social network analysis, organizational mining, decision mining, history-based prediction and recommendation, etc. are all supported by ProM. Recently, several software vendors started adding process mining capabilities to their products. This chapter provides an overview of the market for BI products. Moreover, ProM and other tools supporting process mining are described in more detail.

10.1 Business Intelligence?

Forrester defines *Business Intelligence* (BI) in two ways. The broad definition provided by Forrester is "BI is a set of methodologies, processes, architectures, and technologies that transform raw data into meaningful and useful information used to enable more effective strategic, tactical, and operational insights and decision-making" [40]. Forrester also provides a second, more narrow, definition: "BI is a set of methodologies, processes, architectures, and technologies that leverage the output of information management processes for analysis, reporting, performance management, and information delivery" [40]. As indicated in Sect. 1.6, many overlapping terms are used when describing BI technologies, e.g., Business Activity Monitoring (BAM), Corporate Performance Management (CPM), and Business Process Intelligence (BPI). Clear definitions of these terms are missing. It seems that some BI vendors are deliberately using confusing terminology to verbally distinguish themselves from their competitors and to suggest more functionality than actually implemented. Nevertheless, the market for BI products is steadily growing and maturing. Some of the most widely used BI products are [41]: *IBM Cognos Business Intelligence* (IBM), *Oracle Business Intelligence* (Oracle), *SAP BusinessObjects* (SAP), *WebFOCUS* (Information Builders), *MS SQL Server* (Microsoft), *MicroStrategy*

W.M.P. van der Aalst, *Process Mining*,
DOI 10.1007/978-3-642-19345-3_10,

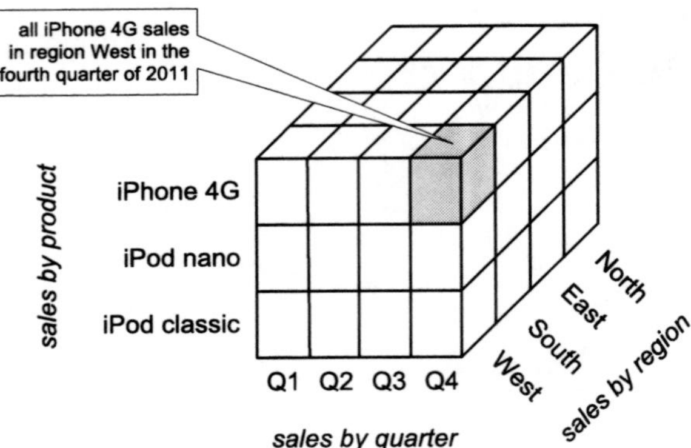

Fig. 10.1 Three dimensional OLAP cube containing sales data. *Each cell* refers to all sales of a particular product in a particular region and in a particular period. *For each cell*, the BI product can compute metrics such as the number of items sold or the total value

(MicroStrategy), *NovaView* (Panorama Software), *QlikView* (QlikTech), *SAS Enterprise Business Intelligence* (SAS), *TIBCO Spotfire Analytics* (TIBCO), *Jaspersoft* (Jaspersoft), and *Pentaho BI Suite* (Pentaho). The typical functionality provided by these products includes:

- *ETL* (Extract, Transform, and Load). All products support the extraction of data from various sources. The extracted data is then transformed into a standard data format (typically a multidimensional table) and loaded into the BI system.
- *Ad-hoc querying*. Users can explore the data in an ad-hoc manner (e.g., drilling down and "slicing and dicing").
- *Reporting*. All BI products allow for the definition of standard reports. Users without any knowledge of the underlying data structures can simply generate such predefined reports. A report may contain various tables, graphs, and scorecards.
- *Interactive dashboards*. All BI products allow for the definition of dashboards consisting of tabular data and a variety of graphs. These dashboards are interactive, e.g., the user can change, refine, aggregate, and filter the current view using predefined controls.
- *Alert generation*. It is possible to define events and conditions that need to trigger an alert, e.g., when sales drop below a predefined threshold an e-mail is sent to the sales manager.

The BI tools mentioned before do *not* take an event log as a starting point. The input is relational data (i.e., one or more tables) or multidimensional data. The core of most BI tools is an OLAP (Online Analytical Processing) engine driven by tabular data organized in a so-called OLAP cube. Consider, for example, an OLAP cube containing sales data. As shown in Fig. 10.1, the dimensions of such a cube may include product type, region, and quarter. Assume we are interested in the number of items sold. In this case, the BI product can show the number of products sold for each cell in the OLAP cube. Suppose that in the fourth quarter (Q4) very few iPhones were sold in region West. Then one can drill down into this cell. For instance, one can look at individual sales, view the sales per month (refinement of Q4 into October, November, and December), or view the sales per shop (refinement of the region dimension). When drilling down, the information is refined. Pivoting the data, often referred to as "slicing and dicing", helps to see particular patterns. By "slicing" the OLAP cube, the analyst can zoom into a selected slice of the overall data, e.g., only looking at sales of the iPod nano. The term "dicing" refers to the reordering of dimensions, e.g., one can look at the sales of different products within a given region or, alternatively, view the sales per region for a given product. One can look at an OLAP cube as a dice. Using this metaphor, dicing corresponds to "throwing the dice" to look at the data from another angle. The results can be viewed in tabular form or visualized using various charts. BI products support a broad range of charts, e.g., pie charts, bar charts, radar plots, scatter plots, speedometers, Pareto charts, box plots, and scorecards. Any of these charts can be part of some predefined dashboard or report.

The mainstream BI products from vendors such as IBM, Oracle, SAP, and Microsoft do *not* support process mining. All of the systems mentioned earlier are *data-centric* and are *unaware* of the processes the data refers to. For example, BI products can analyze an OLAP cube with sales data as shown in Fig. 10.1, but do this without considering the underlying process. The sales events are immediately aggregated without trying to distill the underlying process. BI products do *not* show the *end-to-end process* and *cannot zoom into selected parts* of this process.

Another problem of mainstream BI products is that the focus is on fancy-looking dashboards and rather simple reports, rather than a deeper analysis of the data collected. This is surprising as the "I" in BI refers to "intelligence". Unfortunately, the business ~~un~~intelligence market is dominated by large vendors that focus on monitoring and reporting rather than analytics. Gartner [41] and Forrester [40] report a shift from "measurement" to "analysis, forecasting, predictive analytics, optimization". However, no clear definitions of such capabilities are provided and most vendors tend to interpret these terms in a rather deceptive manner. *Data mining or statistical analysis are often added as an afterthought.* For instance, IBM acquired SPSS to add some "intelligence" to their IBM Cognos Business Intelligence offering. TIBCO Spotfire Analytics uses the statistical programming environment called *S+* (a close relative of the well-known *R* open-source language for statistical computing and visualization). The open-source BI products of Jaspersoft and Pentaho can connect to open-source data mining tools such as *WEKA* (Waikato Environment for Knowledge Analysis, weka.wikispaces.com) and *R* (www.r-project.org).

Pentaho: An Open-Source BI Suite

To illustrate the functionality of mainstream BI products, we briefly discuss one of the leading open-source BI products. The Pentaho BI Suite can be downloaded from www.pentaho.com and consists of software to:

- Extract, transform, and load data from different sources (CSV files, databases, Google Analytics, RSS, etc.)
- Design reports and dashboards
- Generate reports
- Visualize dashboards showing tabular data and a variety of charts
- View OLAP cubes in an interactive manner

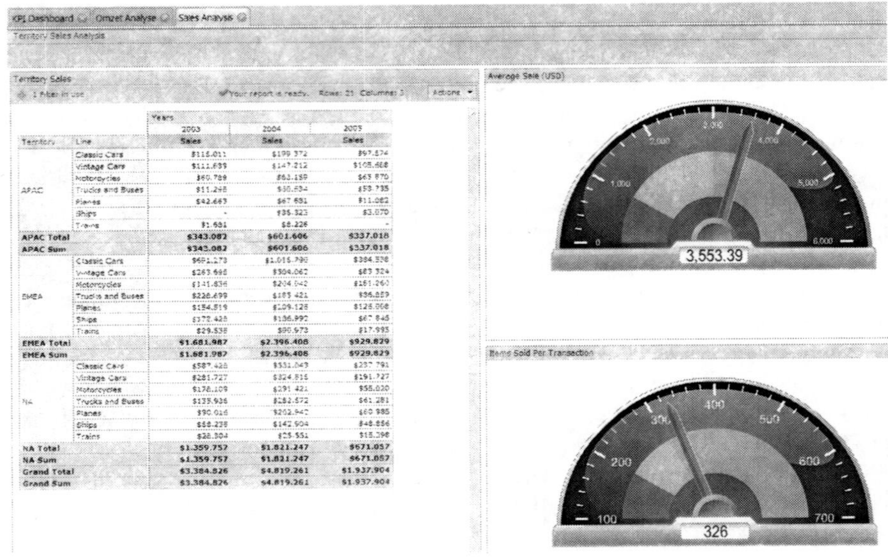

Fig. 10.2 Screenshot of Pentaho 3.7.0 showing *a dashboard*. The table displays multidimensional sales data per territory, per product line, and per year. It is possible to drill down into each of these dimensions. One speedometer shows the average selling price of all products sold. The other speedometer shows the average number of items sold per transaction

Figure 10.2 shows a dashboard consisting of one table and two speedometers. The Pentaho BI Suite itself does not provide any data mining capabilities. However, it is possible to plug-in external data mining software. Pentaho is one of the main sponsors of the WEKA project [129] and it is possible to use the data mining algorithms of WEKA (clustering, decision trees, classification, association rule mining, etc.) on data extracted using the Pentaho BI Suite [129]. Pentaho is easy to use and has intuitive design tools to create dashboards, reports, and extractions. Unfortunately, none of the process mining techniques discussed in the this book are supported.

Data mining tools such as WEKA are also data-centric. However, unlike mainstream BI tools they provide some form of "intelligence", e.g., WEKA supports classification (e.g., decision tree learning), clustering (e.g., k-means clustering), and association rule learning (e.g., the Apriori algorithm). WEKA expects so-called "arff" files as input. Such a file stores tabular data such as shown in Tables 3.1, 3.2, and 3.3. It is impossible to directly load an event log into WEKA. However, it is possible to convert XES or MXML data into tabular data that can be analyzed by WEKA. After conversion, each row either corresponds to an event or a case. For example, it is possible to extract variables like flow time, the frequency of some activity, etc. for each case. Similarly, it is possible to create a table where each row lists the attributes of some event. However, either way, the ordering of events is lost. This illustrates that data mining tools, like the mainstream BI products, are data-centric rather than process-centric.

10.2 ProM

As discussed, existing BI products are data-centric and limited when it comes to more advanced forms of analysis. Data mining tools offer more "intelligence", but are also data-centric. Systems that are process-centric, e.g., BPM/WFM systems, simulation tools, and process modeling tools, focus on *Play-out* rather than *Play-in* or *Replay* (cf. Sect. 1.5). Therefore, the traditional software platforms are not useable for process mining. This triggered the development of various stand-alone process mining tools. In 2002, there were several, rather simple, process mining tools available, e.g., *MiMo* (α-miner based on ExSpect), *EMiT* (α-miner taking transactional information into account), *Little Thumb* (predecessor of the heuristic miner), *InWolvE* (miner based on stochastic activity graphs), and *Process Miner* (miner assuming structured models) [102]. At this time, several researchers were building simple prototypes to experiment with process discovery techniques. However, these tools were based on rather naïve assumptions (simple process models and small but complete data sets) and provided hardly any support for real-life process mining projects (scalability, intuitive user interface, etc.). Clearly, it did not make any sense to build a dedicated process mining tool for every newly conceived process discovery technique. This observation triggered the development of the *ProM framework*, a "plug-able" environment for process mining using MXML as input format. The goal of the first version of this framework was to provide a common basis for all kinds of process mining techniques, e.g., supporting the loading and filtering of event logs and the visualization of results. This way people developing new process discovery algorithms did not have to worry about extracting, converting, and loading event data. Moreover, for standard model types such as Petri nets, EPCs, and social networks default visualizations were provided by the framework.

In 2004, the first fully functional version of ProM framework (*ProM 1.1*) was released. This version contained 29 plug-ins: 6 mining plug-ins (the classic α miner, the Tshinghua α miner, the genetic miner, the multi-phase miner, the social network miner, and the case data extraction miner), 7 analysis plug-ins (e.g., the LTL checker), 4 import plug-ins (e.g., plug-ins to load Petri nets and EPCs), 9 export plug-ins, and 3 conversion plug-ins (e.g., a plug-in to convert EPCs into Petri nets). Over time more plug-ins were added. For instance, *ProM 4.0* (released in 2006) contained already 142 plug-ins. The 27 mining plug-ins of ProM 4.0 included also the heuristic miner and a region-based miner using Petrify. Moreover, ProM 4.0 contained a first version of the conformance checker described in [80]. *ProM 5.2* was released in 2009. This version contained 286 plug-ins: 47 mining plug-ins, 96 analysis plug-ins, 22 import plug-ins, 45 export plug-ins, 44 conversion plug-ins, and 32 filter plug-ins. Figure 10.3 shows two plug-ins of ProM 5.2. This version *supports all of the process mining techniques presented in this book*. For example, each of the

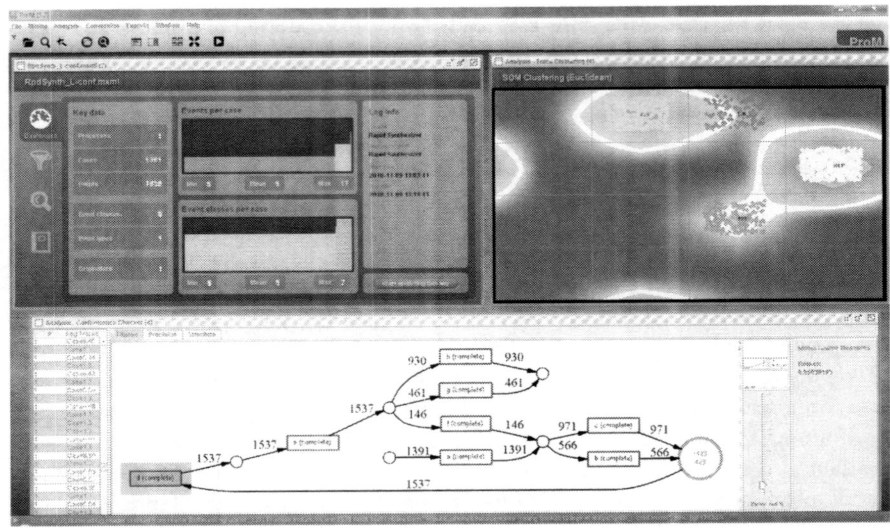

Fig. 10.3 Screenshot of ProM 5.2 showing two of the 286 plug-ins. *The bottom window* shows the *conformance checker* plug-in while checking the fitness of event log L_{full} described in Table 7.1 and WF-net N_2 depicted in Fig. 7.2. The plug-in identifies the conformance problem (the log and model disagree on the position of d) and returns a fitness value computed using the approach presented in Sect. 7.2: $fitness(L_{full}, N_2) = 0.95039195$. *The left window* shows the trace clustering plug-in using Self Organizing Maps (SOM) to find homogeneous groups of cases. The largest cluster contains 641 cases. These are the cases that were rejected without a thorough examination (i.e., traces σ_1, σ_3, σ_{13} in Table 7.1)

discovery algorithms presented in Chap. 6 (genetic mining, heuristic mining, fuzzy mining, etc.) corresponds to one of the 47 mining plug-in of ProM 5.2. The replay approach presented in Sect. 7.2 describes only one of the conformance checking techniques supported by ProM's conformance checker plug-in [80]. This illustrates that this book can only cover a fraction of the functionality provided by ProM.

The spectacular growth of the number of plug-ins in the period from 2004 to 2009 illustrates that ProM realized its initial goal to provide a platform for the development of new process mining techniques. ProM has become the de facto standard for process mining. Research groups from all over the globe contributed to the development of ProM and thousands of organizations downloaded ProM. In the same period we applied ProM in more than 100 organizations, e.g., in the context of joint research projects, Master projects, and consultancy projects. The large number of plug-ins and the many practical applications also revealed some problems. For example, ProM 5.2 can be quite confusing for the inexperienced user who is confronted with almost 300 plug-ins. Moreover, in ProM 5.2 (and earlier versions) the user interface and the underlying analysis techniques are tightly coupled, i.e., most plug-ins require user interaction. To be able to run ProM remotely and to embed process mining functionality in other systems, we decided to completely re-implement ProM from scratch. This allowed us to learn from earlier experiences and to develop a completely new architecture based an improved plug-in infrastructure.

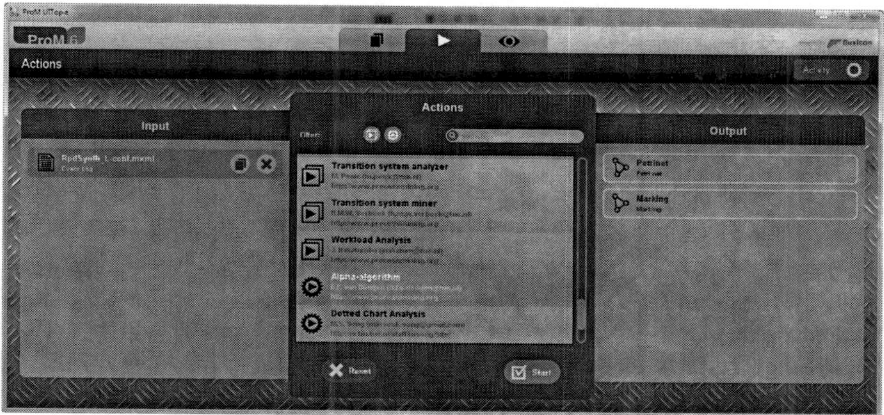

Fig. 10.4 Screenshot of ProM 6. After loading the event log described in Table 7.1, a list of applicable plug-ins is shown and the plug-in implementing the α-algorithm is selected

ProM 6 (released in November 2010) is based on XES rather than MXML. XES is the new process mining standard adopted by the IEEE Task Force on Process Mining (cf. Sect. 4.3). Although ProM 5.2 was already able to load enormous event logs, scalability and efficiency were further improved by using OpenXES [48, 49]. ProM 6 can distribute the execution of plug-ins over multiple computers. This can be used to improve performance (e.g., using grid computing) and to offer ProM as a service. For instance, at TU/e (Eindhoven University of Technology) we use a dedicated process mining grid to handle huge data sets and to conduct large-scale experiments [16]. The user interface has been re-implemented to be able to deal with many plug-ins, logs, and models at the same time. Plug-ins are now distributed over so-called packages and can be chained into composite plug-ins. Packages contain related sets of plug-ins. ProM 6 provides a so-called package manager to add, remove, and update packages. Users should only load packages that are relevant for the tasks they want to perform. This way it is possible to avoid overloading the user with irrelevant functionality. Moreover, ProM 6 can be customized for domain specific or even organization specific applications.

Figures 10.4 and 10.5 show the selection of the Alpha miner plug-in and the resulting process model discovered by ProM 6. Figure 10.6 shows a screenshot of the social network miner of ProM 6 while analyzing interactions between individuals in a Dutch municipality.

Not all plug-ins of ProM 5.2 have been reimplemented in ProM 6. Nevertheless, most of the process mining techniques described in this book are supported by new plug-ins developed for ProM 6. Table 10.1 shows some of these plug-ins. These are all related to process mining. However, it should be noted that ProM (both version 5.2 and 6) supports process analysis in the broadest sense, e.g., also the analysis techniques mentioned in Sect. 2.3 are supported by ProM or the tools that ProM interfaces with (e.g., CPN Tools). For example, the plug-in "Analyze structural properties of a Petri net" computes transition invariants, place invariants,

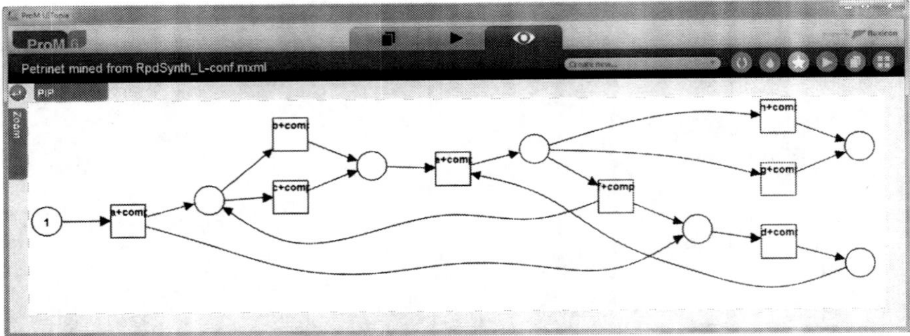

Fig. 10.5 Screenshot of ProM 6 showing the WF-net discovered by the α-algorithm after selecting the corresponding plug-in in Fig. 10.4

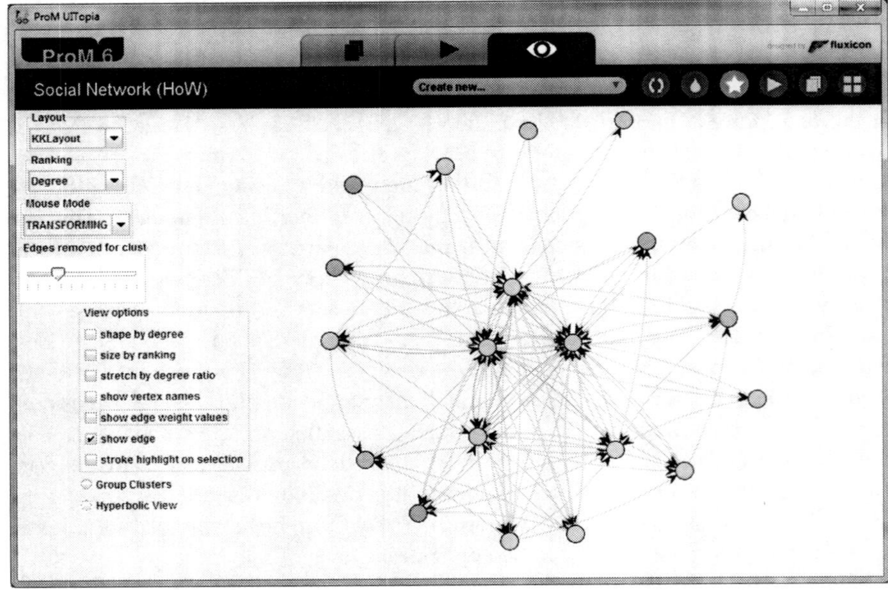

Fig. 10.6 Social network miner (based on handover of work) in ProM 6 (see Sect. 8.3.1)

S-components, T-components, traps, siphons, TP- and PT-handles, etc. The plug-in "Analyze behavioral properties of a Petri net" computes unbounded places, dead transitions, dead markings, home markings, coverability graphs, etc. The "Woflan" plug-in checks the soundness of WF-nets (cf. Sect. 2.2.3) [121]. Moreover, powerful Petri-net-based analysis tools such as *LoLa*, *Wendy*, *Uma*, and *Petrify* are embedded in ProM as plug-ins. For example, Wendy can be used to generate an operating guideline for a service expressed in terms of a Petri net, and Uma can be used to unfold a Petri net. Nevertheless, there are still several advanced plug-ins supported

Table 10.1 Some of the process mining plug-ins present in ProM 6

Plug-in	Description
Alpha miner	Discovers a Petri net using the α-algorithm, see Sect. 5.2
Heuristic miner	Discovers a C-net using heuristic mining, see Sect. 6.2
Genetic miner	Discovers a C-net using genetic mining, see Sect. 6.3
Fuzzy miner	Discovers a fuzzy model using fuzzy mining, see Sect. 13.1.3 and [50]
Transition system miner	Discovers a transition system based on a state representation function and a log, see Sect. 6.4.1
Transition system to Petri net	Uses state-based regions to create a Petri net based on a transition system, see Sect. 6.4.2
Declare miner	Discovers a Declare model, see Sect. 7.3
ILP miner	Discovers a Petri net using language-based regions, see Sect. 6.4.3
Simple log filter	Filtering a log by answering simple questions, see Fig. 12.6(b)
Dotted chart analysis	Creates a dotted chart showing all events at a glance, see Sect. 8.2
Trace alignment	Similar to dotted chart, but now events are aligned based on their context rather than time [14]
Guide tree miner	Clusters cases in a tree based on similarities [12]
Social network miner	Creates a social network based on a selected criterion, see Fig. 10.6
LTL checker	Checks a property expressed in terms of LTL [105]
Fitness	Computes fitness of Petri net based on event log
ETConformance	Checks conformance by counting "escaping edges" from the state space of the log to the state space of the model [70]
Replay log on flexible model	Conformance checker based on A^* algorithm [2]; can also be applied to Petri nets, C-nets and YAWL models
PomPom	Automatically abstracts from infrequently visited parts of a Petri net, see also Sect. 13.1.3 showing the same idea using fuzzy models
Transition system analyzer	Creates a model to predict the remaining flow time, see Sect. 9.4 and [110, 113]

by ProM 5.2 that are not yet available for ProM 6. See, for example, the plug-ins related to constructing a complete simulation model covering all perspectives, cf. Sect. 8.6. Other examples are the organizational miners using (amongst others) the approach of Sect. 8.3.2, and the decision miner using the technique described in Sect. 8.5. These are some of the 286 plug-ins provided by ProM 5.2 but not yet re-implemented for ProM 6. New plug-ins will be added to future versions of ProM 6. For instance, a whole range of new plug-ins based on replay will be added [2]. These plug-ins will provide improved conformance checking and performance analysis techniques.

It is impossible to provide a complete overview of the functionality of ProM. The reader is encouraged to visit www.processmining.org to learn more about ProM's functionality. ProM is open-source software[1] and can be freely downloaded from www.processmining.org or prom.sf.net. To extract files from different data sources, tools such as XESame, ProMimport, and Nitro can be used (cf. Sect. 4.3).

In Sect. 10.1, we criticized mainstream BI products for being data-centric and not very intelligent. The hundreds of ProM plug-ins implementing all of the techniques described in this book illustrate that it is possible to support BI efforts using tools that are process-centric and truly intelligent. Fortunately, more and more analysts and vendors see the need to support process mining as is shown in the next section.

10.3 Other Process Mining Tools

The functionality of ProM is unprecedented, i.e., there is no product offering a comparable set of process mining algorithms. However, the tool requires process mining expertise and is not supported by a commercial organization. Hence, it has the advantages and disadvantages common for open-source software. Fortunately, there is a growing number of commercially available software products offering process mining capabilities. Some of these products embed process mining functionality in a larger system, e.g., Pallas Athena embeds process mining in their BPM suite BPM|one. Other products aim at simplifying process mining using an intuitive user interface. As mentioned before, the large number of plug-ins of ProM can be rather overwhelming. Besides these commercial initiatives, there are also several research groups developing stand-alone process discovery tools. Table 10.2 shows some of the process mining tools currently available. We would like to stress that there are huge differences in terms of maturity and capabilities.

In the previous section, we described ProM in detail. Before discussing some of the other tools, it is important to stress that many organizations (other than TU/e) contributed to ProM. For example, people from the following organizations (co-)developed ProM plug-ins (version 5.2 or 6): Technical University of Lisbon, Katholieke Universiteit Leuven, Universitat Politècnica de Catalunya, Universität Paderborn, University of Rostock, Humboldt-Universität zu Berlin, University of Calabria, Queensland University of Technology, Tsinghua University, Universität Innsbruck, Ulsan National Institute of Science and Technology, Università di Bologna, Zhejiang University, Vienna University of Technology, Universität Ulm, Open University, Jilin University, University of Padua, University of Nancy, etc. The reason for mentioning these organizations is that some the more substantial ProM plug-ins developed by these parties provide more functionality than some of the less mature tools mentioned in Table 10.2.

Reflect|one by Pallas Athena and *Reflect* by Futura Process Intelligence are essentially the same product. Reflect is one of the more mature products and can be used as a stand-alone tool or as a component of the BPM|one suite. Discovered

[1] ProM framework is released under the GNU Lesser General Public License (L-GPL).

Table 10.2 Examples of process mining products: commercial tools C, academic tools A, and open-source tools O

Product name	Type	Organization
ARIS Process Performance Manager	C	Software AG (www.softwareag.com)
Enterprise Visualization Suite	C	Businesscape (www.businesscape.no)
Disco	C	Fluxicon (www.fluxicon.com)
Genet/Petrify	A	Universitat Politècnica de Catalunya (www.lsi.upc.edu)
Interstage BPME	C	Fujitsu (www.fujitsu.com)
OKT Process Mining suite	O	Exeura s.r.l. (www.exeura.com)
Process Discovery Focus	C	Iontas (Verint Systems) (www.iontas.com)
ProcessAnalyzer	C	QPR (www.qpr.com)
ProM	O	process mining group (managed by the AIS group at TU/e) (www.processmining.org)
Rbminer/Dbminer	A	Universitat Politècnica de Catalunya (www.lsi.upc.edu)
Reflect|one	C	Pallas Athena (www.pallas-athena.com)
Reflect	C	Futura Process Intelligence (www.futuratech.nl)
ServiceMosaic	A	University of New South Wales (soc.cse.unsw.edu.au)

models can be uploaded into the BPM system of Pallas Athena and it is also possible to apply process mining techniques to predefined models (e.g., workflow or simulation models). This way the whole BPM life-cycle can be supported. Reflect aims at user-friendliness and scalability. It uses two different discovery algorithms; one is based on the genetic mining approach described in Sect. 6.3 and the other one assumes a sequential model (just XOR-splits/joins) to facilitate the filtering of infrequent behavior. Reflect also supports organizational mining by creating social networks based on handovers of work (cf. Sect. 8.3.1). Discovered models can be turned into simulation models to support what-if analysis. Reflect does not support conformance checking and prediction.

Both Pallas Athena and Futura Process Intelligence were selected as "Cool Vendor" by Gartner in 2009 because of their process mining capabilities. Besides Pallas Athena and Futura Process Intelligence, also ProcessGold is providing process mining services based on Reflect. Examples of organizations using Reflect are ING-DiBa (banking), Herold Business Data (media), Coney (accountancy), and E.Novation (healthcare integration). Figures 10.7 and 10.8 show two screenshots of Reflect illustrating some of the functionality.

Disco by Fluxicon is a stand-alone tool for process mining analysis, with a focus on high performance (i.e., handling large and complex data sets) and ease of use. The process mining algorithm of this tool is based on the fuzzy mining approach described in [49, 50]. Disco supports seamless abstraction and generalization using the cartography metaphor mentioned in Sect. 9.1.1. This way the tool is able to deal also

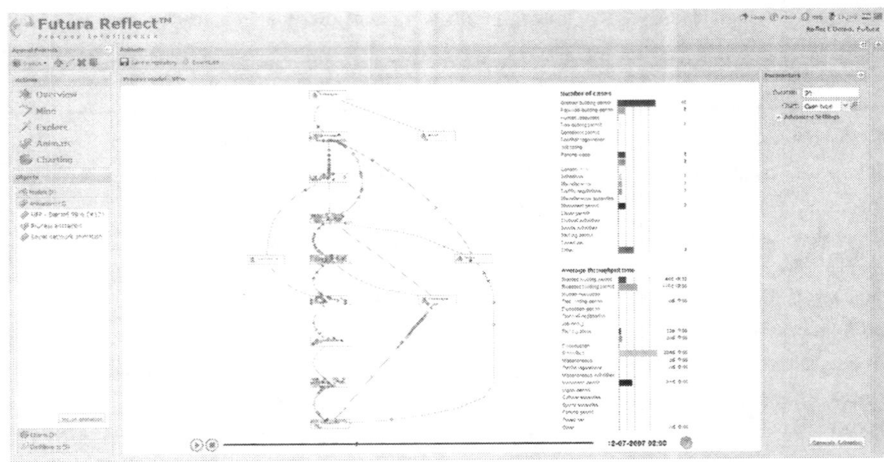

Fig. 10.7 (Color online) Screenshot of Reflect while animating a discovered process model. The event log used to discover the process model is replayed to analyze bottlenecks in a municipality. There are 21 kinds of cases (e.g., building permits, tree cutting permits, and demolition permits) that are identified by *different colors*. For example, the flow of granted building permits is animated using *blue tokens*. Also statistics such as throughput time are collected, e.g., granted building permits have a mean throughput time of 46 days

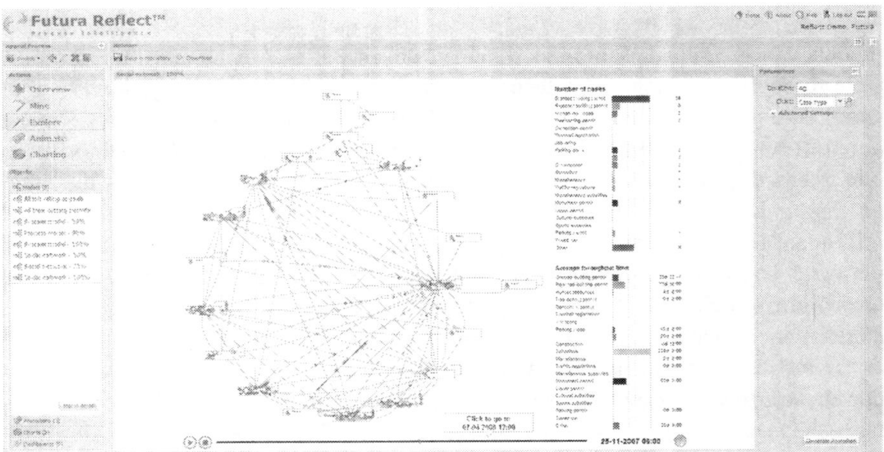

Fig. 10.8 Screenshot of Reflect while analyzing the social network of a municipality. The social network was discovered using the same event log as in Fig. 10.7. By replaying the event log on the social network, it is possible to see the flow of work through the organization and identify bottlenecks

with complex, Spaghetti-like processes. (We further elaborate on this metaphor in Sect. 13.1.) Other dimensions like performance can be analyzed through advanced visualizations of the mined process models. Disco is currently in private beta, and

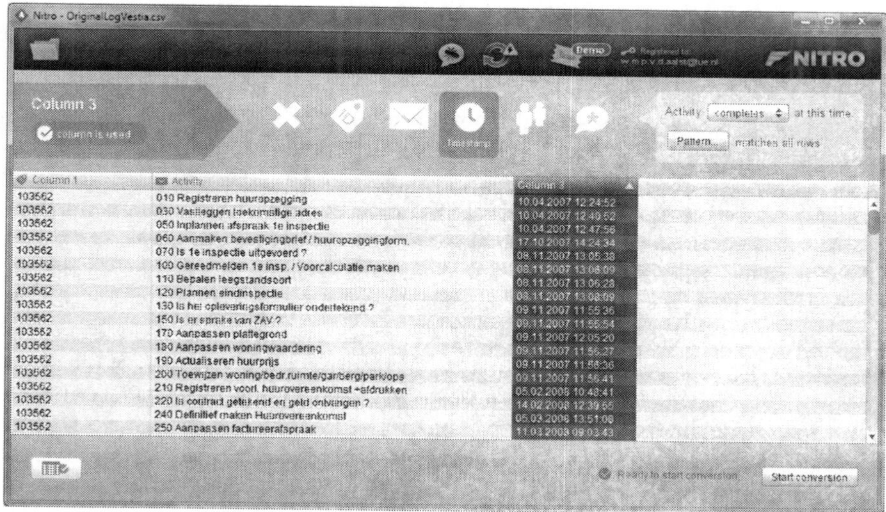

Fig. 10.9 Screenshot of Nitro while converting a CSV file into an XES file. The tool suggest a mapping based on the content *in each column*, e.g., Nitro is able to recognize different time formats and automatically maps these onto the appropriate XES or MXML notation

is scheduled to be publicly released in late 2011. Disco is complemented by Nitro shown in Fig. 10.9. Nitro is an ETL tool tailored toward the extraction of event logs (fluxicon.com/nitro).

Interstage BPME (Business Process Management through Evidence), also known as Interstage Automated Process Discovery, is offered by Fujitsu as a service, i.e., organizations do not need to install a software product. The discovered process can be uploaded in Interstage BPM Studio (or other systems that support XPDL). The focus is on process discovery, i.e., providing insights into what is actually happening. The tool is unable to discover concurrency, but is able to seamlessly abstract from infrequent behavior. Interstage BPME is able to analyze performance using indicators such flow time. Additional perspectives are not discovered (other than time) and advanced features like prediction, recommendation, and conformance checking are not supported.

The *ARIS Process Performance Manager* (PPM) by Software AG (initially developed by IDS Scheer) supports some of the process mining techniques described in this book. The focus is mainly on performance analysis (drilling down to the instance level, benchmarking, and dashboards) [11]. Models of instances can be merged into process models (like in [117]) thus supporting "slicing and dicing" at the process level. Recent versions of ARIS PPM also support organizational mining as described in Sect. 8.3 (also see [88]). ARIS PPM does not support conformance checking, prediction, and recommendation.

The *Enterprise Visualization Suite* by Businesscape focuses on the analysis of SAP supported business processes. *Process Discovery Focus* by Iontas supports process discovery. Iontas was recently acquired by Verint Systems, making the future of this process mining product less clear. The *OKT Process Mining suite* by Exeura uses the process discovery approach presented in [46]. *QPR ProcessAnalyzer* uses a process discovery algorithm inspired by the α-algorithm and heuristic mining. The product has been applied in several Finish hospitals.

Genet, *Petrify*, *Rbminer*, and *Dbminer* are all synthesis tools using state-based regions [23]. As shown in Sect. 6.4, an event log can be converted into a transition system and subsequently synthesized into a Petri net. Classical region theory needs to be extended/relaxed to make it more applicable for process discovery, e.g., Rbminer adapts the classical theory to provide more compact and readable process models [86]. These tools only support control-flow discovery and rely on ProM for conformance checking [70]. *ServiceMosaic* is tailored toward the analysis of service interaction logs, e.g., the logs of HP SOA Manager. The tool discovers transition systems, but is unable to discover concurrency; instead the focus is on dealing with noise and protocol refinement [69].

It is impossible to give a complete overview of all products supporting process mining. Table 10.2 only list products that offer process discovery capabilities. For instance, we did not list IBM's WebSphere suite which includes a component called the *WebSphere Business Monitor*. IBM aims to support the whole life-cycle using WebSphere, e.g., when designing a process to be implemented, it is possible to specify what should be monitored. At run-time KPIs are mapped on the process model used to configure WebSphere. Note that WebSphere does not support process discovery. As a result there is also no support for the more advanced process mining techniques. Most of the larger BPM suites, e.g., Global 360, FileNet BPM, Metastorm BPM, Oracle BPM Suite, Pegasystems, Savvion BusinessManager, WebMethods, and Tibco iProcess Suite, still lack mature process mining support. However, most vendors are currently integrating process discovery capabilities [42] thus following the strategy of Pallas Athena.

Table 10.2 also does not list (a) tools for converting various data sources into event logs, e.g., ProMimport (promimport.sourceforge.net), Nitro (Fig. 10.9), and XESame (processmining.org), (b) tools for generating, managing, and comparing process models, e.g., PLG [17], Apromore (apromore.org), and BeehiveZ (sourceforge.net/projects/beehivez/), and (c) process verification/synthesis tools such as LoLa and Wendy (service-technology.org).

10.4 Outlook

As shown in this chapter, traditional BI products leave much to be desired as they are not process-centric and focus on simple dashboards and reports rather than more advanced, i.e. truly "intelligent", analysis capabilities. Fortunately, there are already several process mining tools available. ProM supports all of the process mining techniques discussed in this book. Moreover, there are several commercial tools that aim at supporting less experienced users or that embed process mining capabilities in larger systems (cf. BPM|one of Pallas Athena). It seems that most of the larger BPM vendors are currently embedding process discovery in their products. Few commercial vendors are supporting conformance checking. Also the more advanced features discussed in Part III (e.g., operational support and short-term simulation) are rarely supported. Given the increased emphasis on compliance, corporate governance, risk management, and performance management, it can be expected that also conformance checking and operational support will be added to the next generation of BPM systems.

Chapter 11
Analyzing "Lasagna Processes"

Lasagna processes are relatively structured and the cases flowing through such processes are handled in a controlled manner. Therefore, it is possible to apply all of the process mining techniques presented in the preceding chapters. This chapter characterizes Lasagna processes and discusses typical use cases for process mining. Moreover, the different stages of a process mining project for improving a Lasagna process are described. The resulting life-cycle model guides users of process mining tools like ProM. Moreover, different application scenarios are discussed.

11.1 Characterization of "Lasagna Processes"

Unlike Spaghetti processes, Lasagna processes have a clear structure and most cases are handled in a prearranged manner. There are relatively few exceptions and stakeholders have a reasonable understanding of the flow of work. It is impossible to define a formal requirement characterizing Lasagna processes. As a rule of thumb we use the following informal criterion: *a process is a Lasagna process if with limited efforts it is possible to create an agreed-upon process model that has a fitness of at least 0.8*, i.e., more than 80% of the events happen as planned and stakeholders confirm the validity of the model. This implies (assuming that a suitable event log can be extracted) that all of the process mining techniques presented in this book can be applied.

The spectrum ranging from Lasagna processes to Spaghetti processes is a *continuum*. Sometimes the terms "structured", "semi-structured", and "unstructured" are used to refer to the same continuum. In a *structured process* (i.e., Lasagna process) all activities are repeatable and have a well defined input and output. In highly structured processes most activities can, in principle, be automated. In *semistructured processes* the information requirements of activities are known and it is possible to sketch the procedures followed. However, some activities require human judgment and people can deviate depending on taste or the characteristics of the case being handled. In *unstructured processes* (i.e., Spaghetti process) it is difficult to define pre- and post-conditions for activities. These processes are driven by

W.M.P. van der Aalst, *Process Mining*,
DOI 10.1007/978-3-642-19345-3_11, © Springer-Verlag Berlin Heidelberg 2011

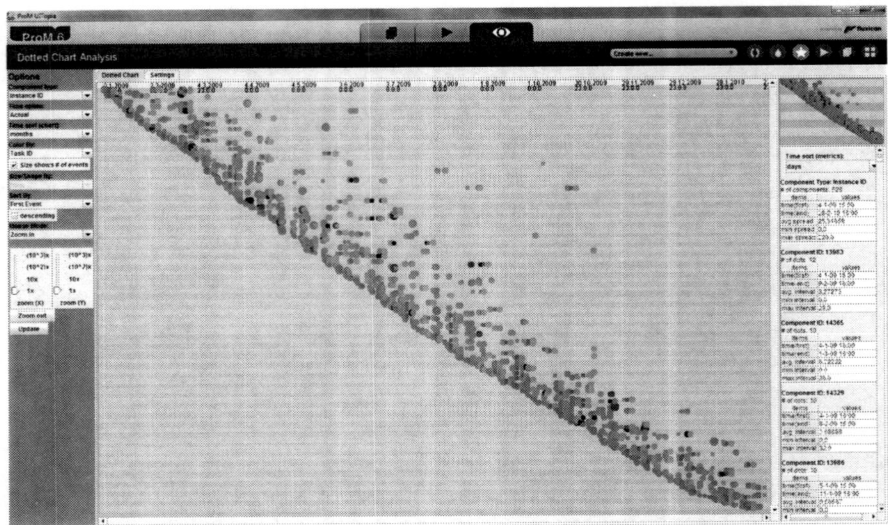

Fig. 11.1 Screenshot of ProM 6 showing a dotted chart for a WMO process of a Dutch municipality. *Each line* corresponds to one of the 528 requests that were handled in the period from 4-1-2009 until 28-2-2010. In total there are 5498 events represented as *dots*. The mean time needed to handled a case is approximately 25 days

experience, intuition, trail-and-error, rules-of-thumb, and vague qualitative information.

Let us consider an example of a Lasagna process. Figure 11.1 shows a dotted chart for one of the so-called WMO processes of a Dutch municipality. WMO (Wet Maatschappelijke Ondersteuning) refers to the social support act that came into force in The Netherlands on January 1st, 2007. The aim of this act is to assist people with disabilities and impairments. Under the act, local authorities are required to give support to those who need it, e.g., household help, providing wheelchairs and scootmobiles, and adaptations to homes. There are different processes for the different kinds of help. The dotted chart in Fig. 11.1 is based on the process for handling requests for household help. In a period of about one year, 528 requests for household WMO support were received. These 528 requests generated 5498 events each represented as a colored dot in Fig. 11.1. The color of the dot refers to the activity executed for the request, e.g., a red dot refers to activity "10 Process registratie" (register request) and a blue dot refers to activity "40 toetsen en beslissen" (evaluate and decide). The diagonal line of initial events shows that there is a steady flow of new requests. The dots also show that the time to completely handle requests is typically short (about one month).

Although no process model is shown in Fig. 11.1, the dotted chart already suggests that the process is a Lasagna process (regular arrival pattern, most cases are handled within one month, and clearly noticeable recurring patterns). Figure 11.2 demonstrates that this is indeed the case. The process model discovered by the heuristic miner shows that the process is highly structured and rather sequential.

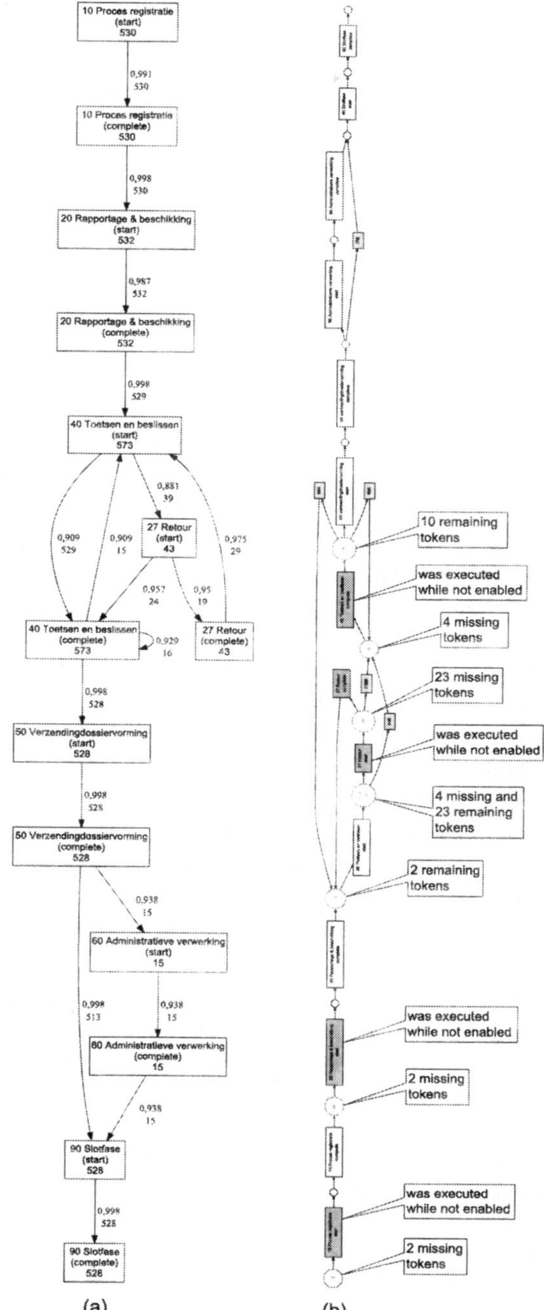

Fig. 11.2 The C-net discovered using the heuristic miner (**a**) and the corresponding Petri net with missing and remaining tokens after replay (**b**). The numbers generated by the heuristic miner show the flow of tokens. The C-net was translated into an equivalent Petri net with silent transitions. The fitness was analyzed using the ProM's conformance checker (cf. Sect. 7.2). The fitness of the discovered process is 0.99521667. Of the 528 cases, 496 cases fit perfectly whereas for 32 cases there are missing or remaining tokens. The missing and remaining tokens show where the model and log deviate. For example, for two cases the activity "40 toetsen en beslissen" (evaluate and decide) was not started although it should have. Activity "20 Rapportage & beschikking" (report and intermediate decision) was started twice while this was not possible according to the model

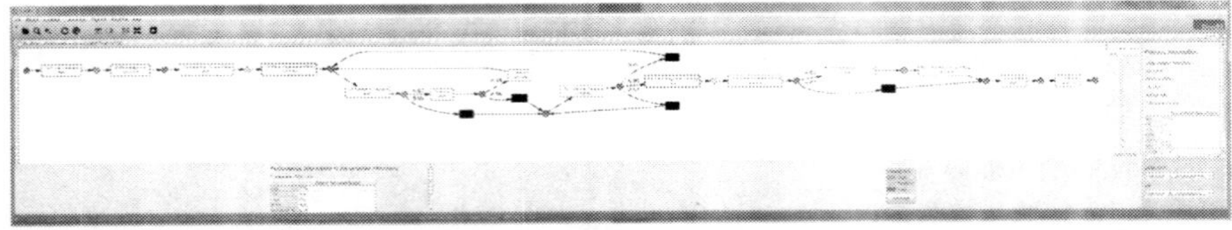

Fig. 11.3 Screenshot of ProM 5.2 while analyzing the bottlenecks in the process. The mean flow time of fitting cases is 24.66 days. Most time is spent on the activities "10 Process registratie", "40 Toetsen en beslissen", and "60 Administratieve verwerking". The average time in-between the completion of activity "10 Rapportage & beschikking" and "50 Verzending/dossiervorming" is 2.24 days

The figure does not show the logic of splits and joins, e.g., one cannot see the difference between AND/OR/XOR-splits/joins.[1] ProM's heuristic miner does not allow for the visualization of bindings used in Sect. 6.2. However, the logic of splits and joins is also discovered and can be shown if desired. When converting a C-net into a Petri net, EPC model, of BPMN model this information is taken into account. The discovered C-net in Fig. 11.2(a) is annotated with frequencies. The frequency of a node indicates how often the corresponding activity appeared in the event log. For instance, activity "20 Rapportage & beschikking" (report and intermediate decision) occurred 532 times. Arcs have a frequency indicating how often a token was passed along the arc when replaying the log. Figure 11.2(b) shows a WF-net obtained by using the corresponding conversion plug-in in ProM. The conformance checker of ProM shows that the fitness of model and log is 0.99521667. This shows that there are hardly any missing or remaining tokens when replaying all 528 cases. Figure 11.2(b) also shows some of the detailed diagnostics. The discovered process model and the high fitness value show that the WMO process is definitely a Lasagna process. This implies that, in principle, *all process mining techniques described in this book are applicable to this process* (assuming sufficient event data). Figure 11.3 shows one of many process mining techniques that can be applied. As explained in Sect. 8.4, delays can be analyzed by replaying the event log while taking timestamps into account. Figure 11.3 illustrates that it is possible to discover bottlenecks for a Lasagna process like the WMO process. Note that the plug-in used in Fig. 11.3 exploits the coupling between the event log and the discovered model (cf. Fig. 11.2).

In Sect. 11.4, we provide more examples of Lasagna processes. However, first we discuss typical use cases for process mining and present a life-cycle model for process mining projects.

---

[1] In the remainder, we will never show the set of input and output bindings for C-nets discovered by the heuristic miner. The heuristic miner can visualize the logic of splits and joins, but this typically impairs the readability of the diagram.

11.2 Use Cases

The goal of process mining is to *improve* operational processes. In order to judge whether process mining efforts are successful, we need to define *Key Performance Indicators* (KPIs). In Sect. 2.3.2, we identified three classes of KPIs: KPIs related to *time* (e.g., lead time, service time, waiting time, and synchronization time), KPIs related to *costs*, and KPIs related to *quality*. Note that quality may refer to compliance, customer satisfaction, number of defects, etc. To evaluate suggested improvements, the effectiveness and efficiency of the *as-is* and *to-be* processes need to be quantified in terms of KPIs.

For Lasagna processes, process mining can result in one or more of the following *improvement actions*:

- *Redesign.* Insights obtained using process mining can trigger changes to the process, e.g., sequential activities no longer need to be executed in a fixed order, checks may be skipped for easy cases, decisions can be delegated if more than 50 cases are queueing, etc. Fraud detected using process mining may result in additional compliance regulations, e.g., introducing the 4-eyes principle for critical activities.
- *Adjust.* Similarly, process mining can result in (temporary) adjustments. For example, insights obtained using process mining can be used to temporarily allocate more resources to the process and to lower the threshold for delegation.
- *Intervene.* Process mining may also reveal problems related to particular cases or resources. This may trigger interventions such as aborting a case that has been queuing for more than 3 months or disciplinary measures for a worker that repeatedly violated compliance regulations.
- *Support.* Process mining can be used for operational support, e.g., based on historic information a process mining tool can predict the remaining flow time or recommend the action with the lowest expected costs.

Figure 1.3 in Chap. 1 illustrates the difference between a *redesign* (a permanent change requiring alterations to software or model) and an *adjustment* (a temporary change realized without modifying the underlying software or model).

As shown in Fig. 11.4, *use cases for process mining refer to a combination of KPIs and improvement actions.* Given a Lasagna process, some typical use cases for process mining are:

- Identification of bottlenecks to trigger a process redesign that reduces the overall flow time with 30%.
- Identification of compliance problems using conformance checking. Some of the compliance problems result in ad-hoc interventions whereas others lead to adjustments of the parameters used for work distribution.
- Harmonization of two processes after a merger based on a comparison of the actual processes. The goal of such a harmonization is to reduce costs.
- Predicting the remaining flow time of delayed cases to improve customer service.
- Providing recommendations for resource allocation aiming at a more balanced utilization of workers.

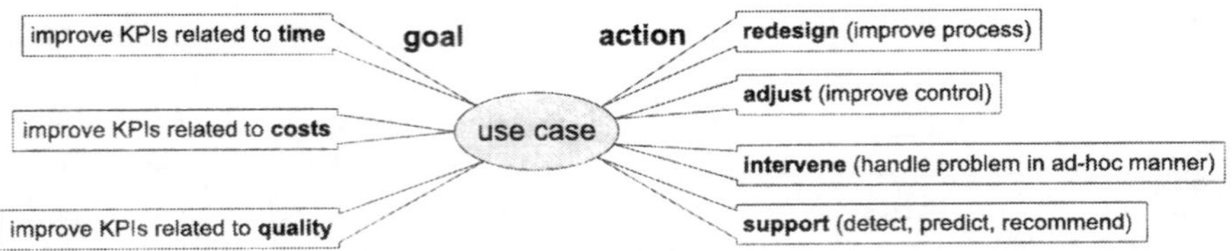

Fig. 11.4 Use cases for process mining combine goals (expressed in KPIs) and improvement actions, e.g., process mining can be used to shorten the flow time by providing insights that lead to a process redesign

- Identification of exceptional cases that generate too much additional work. By learning the profile of such cases, they can be handled separately to reduce the overall flow time.
- Visualization of the 10 most complicated or time consuming cases to identify potential risks.

These use cases illustrate the potential of process mining. It is easy to imagine the application of these use cases to the WMO process described earlier. For instance, results such as shown in Fig. 11.3 can be used to discover bottlenecks and to generate ideas for flow time reduction. The results of conformance analysis as depicted in Fig. 11.2(b) can be used to identify compliance problems, e.g., for the 32 cases having missing or remaining tokens one could analyze the social network of the people involved.

11.3 Approach

In Chap. 9, we described ten process mining related activities using the framework shown in Fig. 11.5. These ten activities are grouped into three categories: cartography (activities *discover*, *enhance*, and *diagnose*), auditing (activities *detect*, *check*, *compare*, and *promote*), and navigation (activities *explore*, *predict*, and *recommend*). Although the framework helps to understand the relations between the various process mining activities, it does not guide the user in conducting a process mining project. Therefore, this section introduces the *L^* life-cycle model for mining Lasagna processes*.

Several reference models describing the life-cycle of a typical data mining/BI project have been proposed by academics and consortia of vendors and users. For example, the *CRISP-DM* (CRoss-Industry Standard Process for Data Mining) methodology identifies a life-cycle consisting of six phases: (a) business understanding, (b) data understanding, (c) data preparation, (d) modeling, (e) evaluation, and (f) deployment [19]. CRISP-DM was developed in the late nineties by a consortium driven by SPSS. Around the same period SAS proposed the *SEMMA* methodology consisting of five phases: (a) sample, (b) explore, (c) modify, (d) model, and (e) assess. Both methodologies are very high-level and provide little support. Moreover, existing methodologies are not tailored toward process mining projects. Therefore, we propose the L^* life-cycle model shown in Fig. 11.6. This five-stage model

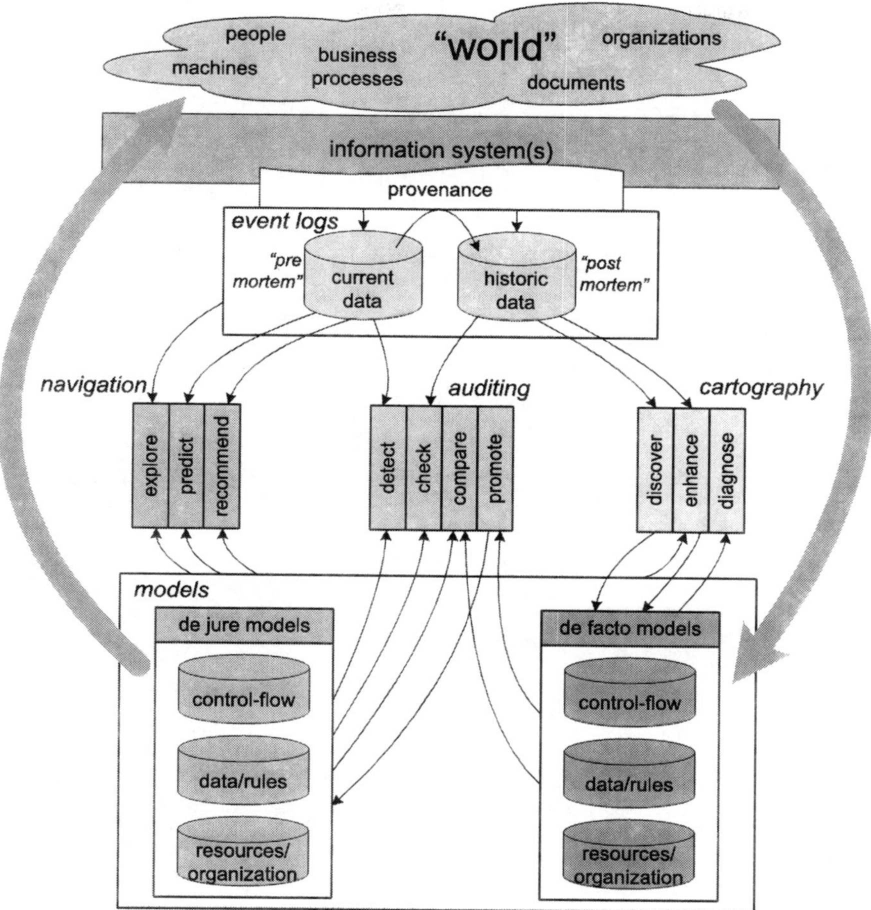

Fig. 11.5 The process mining framework introduced in Chap. 9. The framework identifies ten process mining activities (discover, check, enhance, etc.)

describes the life-cycle of a typical process mining project aiming to improve a Lasagna process.

In the remainder, we discuss each of the five stages. As shown in Fig. 11.6, the L^* life-cycle model refers to the ten process mining related activities (explore, discover, check, etc.) and the four improvement actions (redesign, adjust, intervene, and support) mentioned earlier.

11.3.1 Stage 0: Plan and Justify

Any process mining project starts with a planning and a justification of the planned activities. Before spending efforts on process mining activities, one should antic-

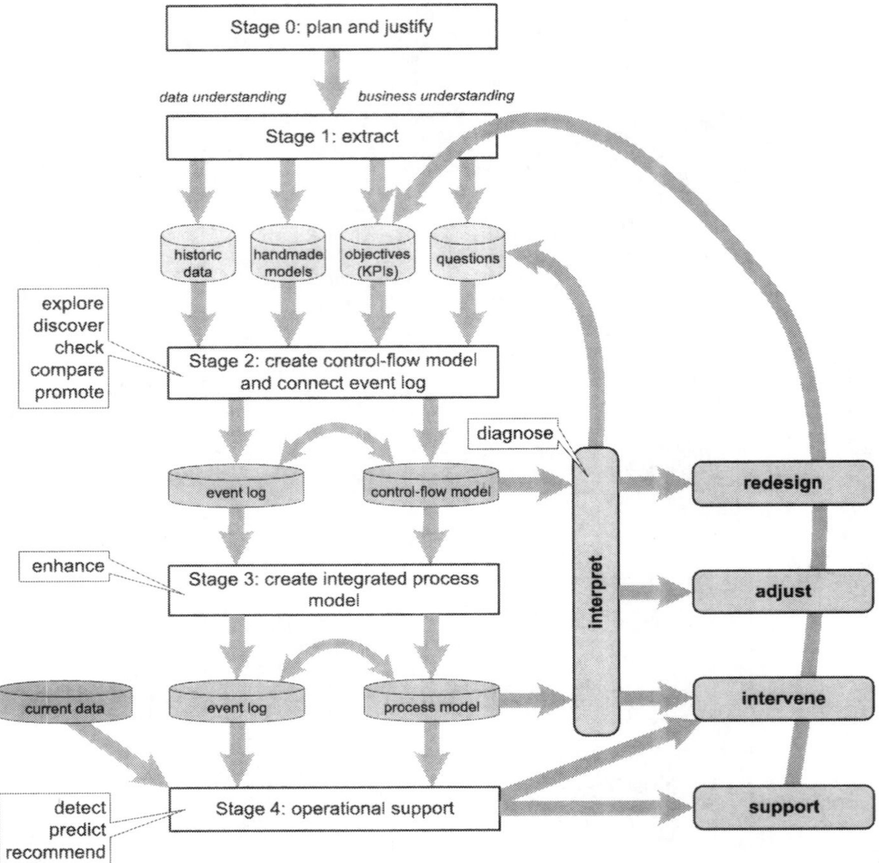

Fig. 11.6 The L^* life-cycle model describing a process mining project consisting of five stages: *plan and justify* (Stage 0), *extract* (Stage 1), *create control-flow model and connect event log* (Stage 2), *create integrated process model* (Stage 3), and *operational support* (Stage 4)

ipate benefits that may result from the project. There are basically three types of process mining projects:

- A *data-driven* (also referred to as "curiosity driven") process mining project is powered by the availability of event data. There is no concrete question or goal, however, some of the stakeholders expect that valuable insights will emerge by analyzing event data. Such a project has an explorative character.
- A *question-driven* process mining project aims to answer specific questions, e.g., "Why do cases handled by team X take longer than cases handled by team Y?" or "Why are there more deviations in weekends?".
- A *goal-driven* process mining project aspires to improve a process with respect to particular KPIs, e.g., cost reduction or improved response times.

For an organization without much process mining experience, it is best to start with a question-driven project. Concrete questions help to scope the project and guide data extraction efforts.

Like any project, a process mining project needs to be planned carefully. For instance, activities need to be scheduled before starting the project, resources need to be allocated, milestones need to be defined, and progress needs to be monitored continuously.

11.3.2 Stage 1: Extract

After initiating the project, event data, models, objectives, and questions need to be extracted from systems, domain experts, and management.

In Chap. 4, we elaborated on data extraction. For example, Fig. 4.1 describes the process of getting from raw data to suitable event logs. Recall that event logs have two main requirements: (a) events need to be ordered in time and (b) events need to be correlated (i.e., each event needs to refer to a particular case).

As Fig. 11.6 shows, it is possible that there are already handmade (process) models. These models may be of low quality and have little to do with reality. Nevertheless, it is good to collect all models present and exploit existing knowledge as much as possible. For example, existing models can help in scoping the process and judging the completeness of event logs.

In a goal-driven process mining project, the objectives are also formulated in Stage 1 of the L^* life-cycle. These objectives are expressed in terms of KPIs. In a question-driven process mining project, questions need to be generated in Stage 1. Both questions and objectives are gathered through interviews with stakeholders (e.g., domain experts, end users, customers, and management).

11.3.3 Stage 2: Create Control-Flow Model and Connect Event Log

Control-flow forms the backbone of any process model. Therefore, Stage 2 of the L^* life-cycle aims to determine the de facto control-flow model of the process that is analyzed. The process model may be discovered using the process discovery techniques presented in Part II of this book (activity *discover* in Fig. 11.6). However, if there is a good process model present, it may be verified using conformance checking (activity *check*) or judged against the discovered model (activity *compare*). It is even possible to merge the handmade model and the discovered model (activity *promote*). After completing Stage 2 there is a control-flow model tightly connected to the event log, i.e., events in the event log refer to activities in the model. As discussed in Sect. 7.4.3, this connection is crucial for subsequent steps. If the fitness of the model and log is low (say below 0.8), then it is difficult to move to Stage 3. However, by definition, this should not be a problem for a Lasagna process.

The output of Stage 2 may be used to answer questions, take actions, or to move to Stage 3. As Fig. 11.6 shows, the output (control-flow model connected to an event log) needs to be interpreted before it can be used to answer questions or trigger a redesign, an adjustment, or an intervention.

11.3.4 Stage 3: Create Integrated Process Model

In Stage 3, the model is enhanced by adding additional perspectives to the control-flow model (e.g., the organizational perspective, the case perspective, and the time perspective). Chapter 8 shows how these perspectives can be discovered and integrated, e.g., Fig. 8.16 describes the process of merging the different perspectives. The result is an integrated process model that can be used for various purposes. The model can be inspected directly to better understand the as-is process or to identify bottlenecks. Moreover, a complete process model can also be simulated as discussed in Sect. 8.6.

The output of Stage 3 can also be used to answer selected questions and take appropriate actions (redesign, adjust, or intervene). Moreover, the integrated process model is also input for Stage 4.

11.3.5 Stage 4: Operational Support

Stage 4 of the L^* life-cycle is concerned with the three operational support activities described in Chap. 9: *detect*, *predict*, and *recommend*. For instance, using short-term simulation (Sect. 8.6) or annotated transition systems (Sect. 9.4) it is possible to predict the remaining flow time for running cases. As shown in Fig. 11.6, Stage 4 requires current data ("pre mortem" data on running cases) as input. Moreover, the output does not need to be interpreted by the process mining analyst and can be directly offered to end users. For example, a deviation may result in an automatically generated e-mail sent to the responsible manager. Recommendations and predictions are presented to the persons working on the corresponding cases.

Note that operational support is the *most ambitious* form of process mining. This is only possible for Lasagna processes. Moreover, there needs to be an advanced IT infrastructure that provides high-quality event logs and allows for the embedding of an operational support system as described in Chap. 9.

11.4 Applications

In the last decade, we have applied process mining in over 100 organizations. Examples are municipalities (e.g., Alkmaar, Heusden, and Harderwijk), government

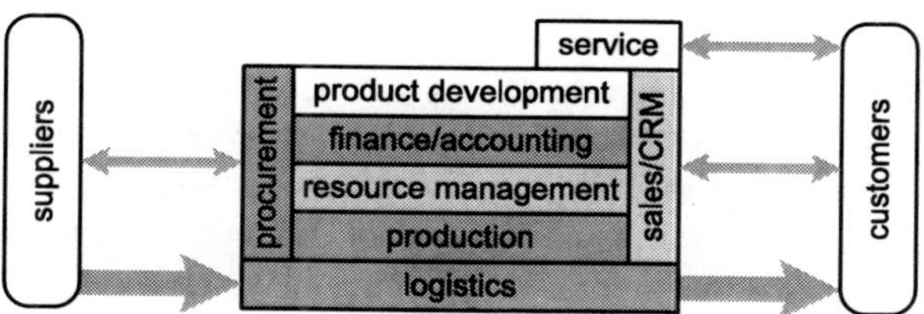

Fig. 11.7 Overview of the different functional areas in a typical organization. Lasagna processes are typically encountered in production, finance/accounting, procurement, logistics, resource management, and sales/CRM. Spaghetti processes are typically encountered in product development, service, resource management, and sales/CRM

agencies (e.g., Rijkswaterstaat, Centraal Justitieel Incasso Bureau, and Justice department), insurance related agencies (e.g., UWV), banks (e.g., ING Bank), hospitals (e.g., AMC hospital and Catharina hospital), multinationals (e.g., DSM and Deloitte), high-tech system manufacturers and their customers (e.g., Philips Healthcare, ASML, Ricoh, and Thales), and media companies (e.g., Winkwaves). This illustrates the broad spectrum of situations in which process mining can be applied. In remainder of this section, we identify process mining opportunities in different functional areas and in different sectors and industries. Moreover, we briefly discuss two case studies involving Lasagna processes.

11.4.1 Process Mining Opportunities per Functional Area

Figure 11.7 shows the main *functional areas* that can be found in most organizations:

- *Product development* is concerned with all the preparations and engineering work needed to start producing a particular product. Products do not need to be physical objects (e.g., a car or copier); the product may also be a piece of information or a service (e.g., a new kind of insurance). Product development processes are typically Spaghetti-like because they have a lower frequency and depend on problem solving, expertise, and creativity rather than repetition, routine, and efficiency.
- *Production* is the functional area where the products are actually produced. Processes may range from classical manufacturing (assembling a car) to information creation (opening a back account). Most production processes are Lasagna processes because they need to be reproducible and efficient.
- *Procurement* entails all activities to get the materials needed for production. Note that the input for the production process may also be information from other parties. The input materials need to be purchased, stocks need to be monitored, deliveries need to be checked, etc. Processes in this functional area are typically Lasagna processes.
- The functional area *Sales/CRM* is concerned with all activities related to "lead-to-order" and "order-to-cash". Besides the actual sales function, most organizations

need to market their products and manage long-term relationships with their customers (CRM). Both Lasagna processes and Spaghetti processes can be found in this functional area. The handling of sales activities can be very structured whereas marketing-related activities may be rather unstructured.

- *Logistics* is concerned with the movements of products and materials, e.g., shipping the product to the customer and managing the storage space. Most processes in logistics are Lasagna processes.
- The functional area *Finance/accounting* deals with all financial aspects of an organization, e.g., billing customers, checking invoices, financial reporting, and auditing. Processes in this functional area are also typically Lasagna processes.
- *Resource management* is the functional area that makes sure there are sufficient resources to perform all other functions. HRM (Human Resource Management) is concerned with human resources and similar functions exist for machines, buildings, etc. Both Lasagna processes and Spaghetti processes can be found in this functional area, e.g., the handling of job applications may be very structured whereas the handling of a problematic employee may be rather ad-hoc.
- The functional area *Service* deals with all activities after the product has been shipped and paid for, e.g., activities related to product support, maintenance, repairing defective products, and help-desk operations. Service related processes are typically Spaghetti-like. Customers will use products in many different ways and repair processes are rather unpredictable for most products, e.g., no faults are found in the product returned by the customer or the wrong component is replaced and the product still malfunctions intermittently.

The characterization of the different functional areas in terms of Lasagna processes and Spaghetti processes is only intended as an indication. Both types of processes can be found in all of the functional areas. However, as shown in Fig. 11.7, it is possible to pinpoint typical functional areas for both types. For example, in most organizations product development processes are rather unstructured compared to production processes. This implies that most of the techniques presented in this book can be applied to production processes. However, for product development processes it is unlikely that all stages of the L^* life-cycle model (Fig. 11.6) can be executed. (Stages 3 and 4 are typically not possible for Spaghetti-like processes.)

11.4.2 Process Mining Opportunities per Sector

After contemplating on the presence of Lasagna and Spaghetti processes in the functional areas in one organization (Fig. 11.7), we now look at different sectors and industries.

The *primary sector* of the economy is concerned with transforming natural resources into primary products (e.g., agriculture, agribusiness, fishing, forestry and all mining and quarrying industries). Information technology tends to play a minor role in these industries. Hence, the application potential of process mining is limited. Of course there are exceptions. Consider for instance the tracking and tracing of food. In some countries, meat and dairy products need to be tracked from source to sink. For example, meat products in supermarkets need to be linked to particular animals and farms. This requires the recording of events starting in the primary sector.

The *secondary sector* of the economy refers to the manufacturing of tangible products and includes the automotive industry, chemical industry, aerospace manufacturing, consumer electronics, etc. Organizations in the secondary sector typically have an organizational structure covering all functional areas depicted in Fig. 11.7. Hence, both Lasagna processes and Spaghetti processes can be encountered. An interesting observation across the different industries is that most manufacturers have become interested in monitoring their products after they have been sold. For example, Philips Healthcare is monitoring their medical equipment while being deployed in the field, e.g., their X-ray machines are connected to the Internet and the resulting logs are analyzed using ProM. The event logs of these X-ray machines provide vital information for marketing (What kind of features do customer use?), maintenance (When to service the machine?), development (Why do machines fail?), and testing (How to test machines under realistic circumstances?). In the future, more and more (consumer) products will be monitored remotely thus providing valuable information for the manufacturer.

The *tertiary sector* of the economy consists of all organizations that produce "intangible goods" such as services, regulations, and information. The term "services" should be interpreted in the broadest sense including transportation, insurance, wholesaling, retailing, entertainment, etc. Note that goods may be transformed in the process of providing the service (cf. preparing food in a restaurant). However, the focus is on serving the customer rather than transforming physical goods. In many industries in the tertiary sector, information plays a dominant role and many events are being recorded. This is the sector where the digital universe and the physical universe are aligned most. For example, an electronic bookstore can only sell a book if the information system indicates that the book is present. The bookstore would not be able to sell a particular book if the information system would indicate that it is out-of-stock; even if the book would be physically present in the warehouse.

Process mining can be used to improve a variety of Lasagna and Spaghetti processes encountered in the tertiary sector. Below we sketch some of the most interesting industries.

- The *healthcare* industry includes hospitals and other care organizations. Most events are being recorded (blood tests, MRI scans, appointments, etc.) and correlation is easy because each event refers to a particular patient. The closer processes get to the medical profession, the less structured they become. For instance, most diagnosis and treatment processes tend to be rather Spaghetti-like (see Fig. 12.1). Medical guidelines typically have little to do with the actual processes. On the one hand, this suggests that these processes can be improved by structuring them. On the other hand, the variability of medical processes is caused by the different characteristics of patients, their problems, and unanticipated complications. Patients are saved by doctors deviating from standard procedures. However, some deviations also cost lives. Clearly, hospitals need to get a better understanding of care processes to be able to improve them. Process mining can help as event data is readily available [64].

- *Governments* range from small municipalities to large organizations operating at the national level, e.g., institutions managing processes related to unemployment, customs, taxes, and traffic offences. Both local and national government agencies can be seen as "administrative factories" as they execute regulations and the "products" are mainly informational or financial. Processes in larger government agencies are characterized by a high degree of automation. Consider, for example, tax departments that need to deal with millions of tax declarations. Processes in smaller government agencies (e.g., small municipalities) are typically not automated and managed by office workers rather than BPM systems. However, due to the legal requirements, all main events are recorded in a systematic manner. Consider, for example, the WMO process shown in Fig. 11.2; any municipality in The Netherlands is obliged to record the formal steps in such processes. Typical use cases for process mining in governments (local or non-local) are flow time reduction (e.g., shorten the time to get a building permit), improved efficiency, and compliance. Given the role of governments in society, compliance is of the utmost importance.
- *Banking* and *insurance* are two industries where BPM technology has been most effective. Processes are often automated and all events are recorded in a systematic and secure manner. Examples are the processing of loans, claims management, handling insurance applications, credit card payments, and mortgage payments. Most processes in banking and insurance are Lasagna processes, i.e., highly structured. Hence, all of the techniques presented in this book can be applied. Process discovery is less relevant for these organizations as most processes are known and documented. Typical uses cases in these industries involve conformance checking, performance analysis, and operational support.
- Organizations involved in *education* (e.g., high-schools and universities) are recording more and more information related to the study behavior of individuals. For instance, at TU/e we are applying process mining to analyze study behavior using a database containing detailed information about exam results of all students that ever studied computer science. Moreover, this database also contains information about high-school exam grades, etc. Some of these educational processes are structured, others are very unstructured. For example, it is very difficult to predict the remaining study time of students at a university because the curriculum often changes and students tend to have very different study patterns. Nevertheless, valuable insights can be obtained. By visualizing that few students follow the courses in the order intended, one can show that the design of a curriculum should not only focus on the "ideal student" (that passes all courses the first time), but also anticipate problems encountered by other students.
- The products manufactured by organizations in the secondary sector are distributed through various *retail* organizations. Here it is interesting to see that more and more information about products and customers is being recorded. Customers are tracked using loyalty cards or through online profiles. Products are tagged and the shop has real-time information about the number of items still available.

A product that has an RFID tag has a unique identifier, i.e., two identical products can still be distinguished. This allows for the correlation of events and thus facilitates process mining.

- The *transportation* industry is also recording more and more information about the movement of people and products. Through tracking and tracing functionality the whereabouts of a particular parcel can be monitored by both sender and receiver. Although controversial, smartcards providing access to buildings and transportation systems can be used to monitor the movement of people. For example, the Dutch "ov-chipkaart" can be used to travel by train, subway, and bus. The traveler pays based on the distance between the entry point and exit point. The recorded information can be used to analyze traveling behavior. The booking of a flight via the Internet also generates lots of event data. In fact, the booking process involves only electronic activities. Note that the traveler interacts with one organization that contacts all kinds of other organizations in the background (airlines, insurance companies, car rental agencies, etc.). All of these events are being recorded, thus enabling process mining. The whole spectrum ranging from Lasagna processes to Spaghetti processes can be found in this industry.
- New technologies such as *cloud computing* and *Software-as-a-Service* (SaaS) have created a new industry that offers computing as a utility (like water and electricity). Google Apps. Salesforce.com, and Amazon EC2/S3 are examples of companies providing such utilities. The idea is not new: already in 1961 John McCarthy stated "If computers of the kind I have advocated become the computers of the future, then computing may someday be organized as a public utility just as the telephone system is a public utility. The computer utility could become the basis of a new and important industry". A well-known example of a SaaS provider that is using a cloud infrastructure is Salesforce.com. This company allows organizations to outsource the IT support of standard activities related to sales and CRM without worrying about scalability and maintenance. Users pay for using the software rather than owning it. Another example is the conference management system EasyChair that is currently probably the most commonly used system to host conferences and to manage the reviewing of scientific papers. To organize a conference, there is no need to install any software as everything is hosted and managed centrally. Organizations such as Salesforce.com and EasyChair have access to valuable event data. These data can be used to improve their software and to give advice to individual organizations. One of the challenges SaaS providers are facing is the need to deal with variability across organizations. Process mining can help analyzing differences between organizations using *cross-organizational process mining*, i.e., using process mining to compare similar processes within the same or in different organizations.
- The *capital goods* industry is also transforming from the situation in which customers purchase expensive machines to the situation in which customers only pay for the actual use of the machine. Note that this can be seen as a variant of the SaaS paradigm. The manufacturer of the machine remains being the owner and customers pay depending on usage and uptime of the machine. Clearly, such pricing models require the remote monitoring of capital goods. For instance, service provider and consumer need to agree on the actual use (e.g., hours of use

or number of production cycles). Moreover, there may be Service Level Agreements (SLAs) specifying a fine if the machine is down for an extended period. Event data can be used as a basis for billing and checking SLAs. Moreover, the manufacturer gets insights into the way that machines are used, when they malfunction, and when they require maintenance.

These examples show that there are opportunities for process mining in all three economic sectors.

11.4.3 Two Lasagna Processes

To conclude this chapter, we briefly discuss two case studies analyzing Lasagna processes.

11.4.3.1 RWS Process

The Dutch national public works department, called "Rijkswaterstaat" (RWS), has twelve provincial offices. We analyzed the handling of invoices in one of these offices [106]. The office employs about 1000 civil servants and is primarily responsible for the construction and maintenance of the road and water infrastructure in its province. To perform its functions, the RWS office subcontracts various parties such as road construction companies, cleaning companies, and environmental bureaus. Also, it purchases services and products to support its construction, maintenance, and administrative activities. The reason to employ process mining within RWS was twofold. First of all, RWS was involved in our longitudinal study into the effectiveness of WFM systems [76]. In the context of this study, RWS was interested to see the effects of WFM technology on flow times, response times, service levels, utilization, etc. Second, RWS was interested in better meeting deadlines with respect to the payment of invoices. Payment should take place within 31 days from the moment the invoice is received. After this period, the creditor is entitled (according to Dutch law) to receive interest over the outstanding sum. RWS would like to pay at least 90% of its invoices within 31 days. However, analysis of the event logs of RWS showed that initially only 70% of payments were paid in time.

Starting point for the analysis described in [106] was an event log containing information about 14,279 cases (i.e., invoices) generating 147,579 events. Figure 11.8 shows a C-net generated by the heuristic miner. This model shows that the RWS process is fairly structured, but not as structured as the WMO process depicted in Fig. 11.2(a). After some efforts (filtering the log and tuning the parameters of the mining algorithm), it is possible to create a model with a fitness of more than 0.9. The log can be replayed on this model to highlight bottlenecks. Such analysis shows that several activities had to be redone (as can be seen by the loops of length one or

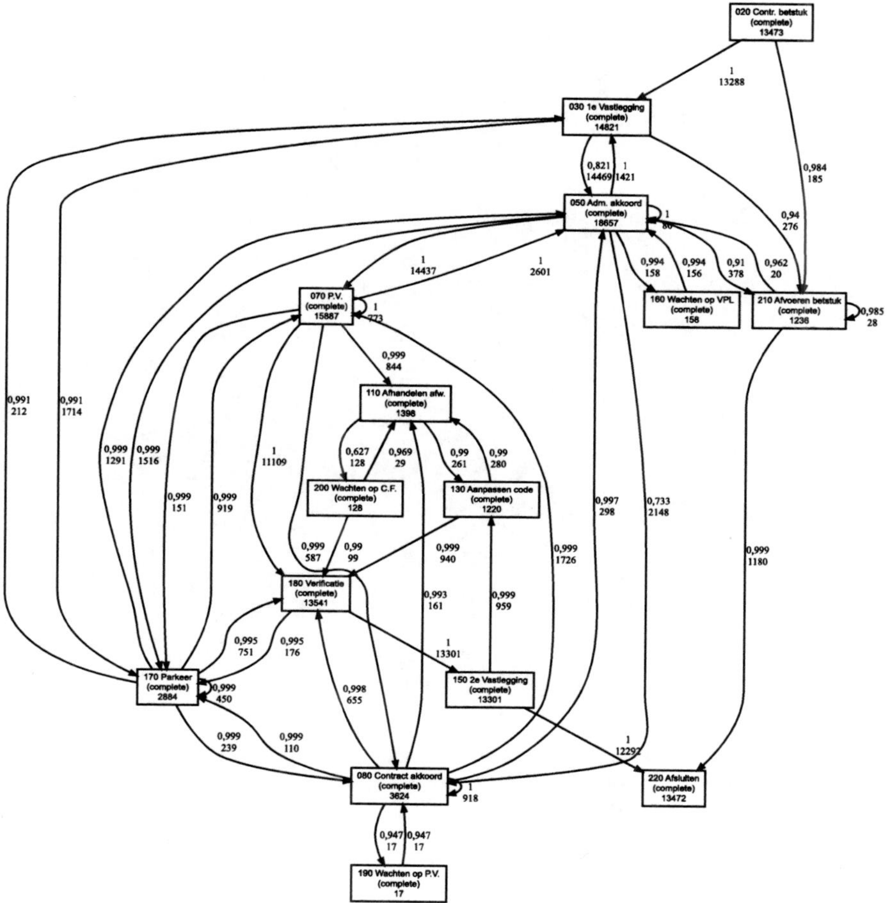

Fig. 11.8 Process model obtained using heuristic mining. The C-net describes the handling of invoices within one of the twelve provincial offices of RWS

two in Fig. 11.8), i.e., work was sent "back-and-forth" between different activities and people thus causing delays.

The event log contains information about 271 resources, i.e., civil servants involved in the handling invoices. Figure 11.9 shows the social network based on the frequency of handovers (cf. Sect. 8.3.1). Figure 11.10 shows the same social network, but now only for the 13 resources that executed most activities. RWS could use these social networks to better understand how work is flowing through the organization. This analysis showed that some project leaders considered invoice approval to be of low priority, not realizing that because of their slow reaction time many invoices took more than 31 days. They were not aware of the impact of their actions and agreed to give the invoice approval a higher priority thus speeding up the process. See [106] for more information.

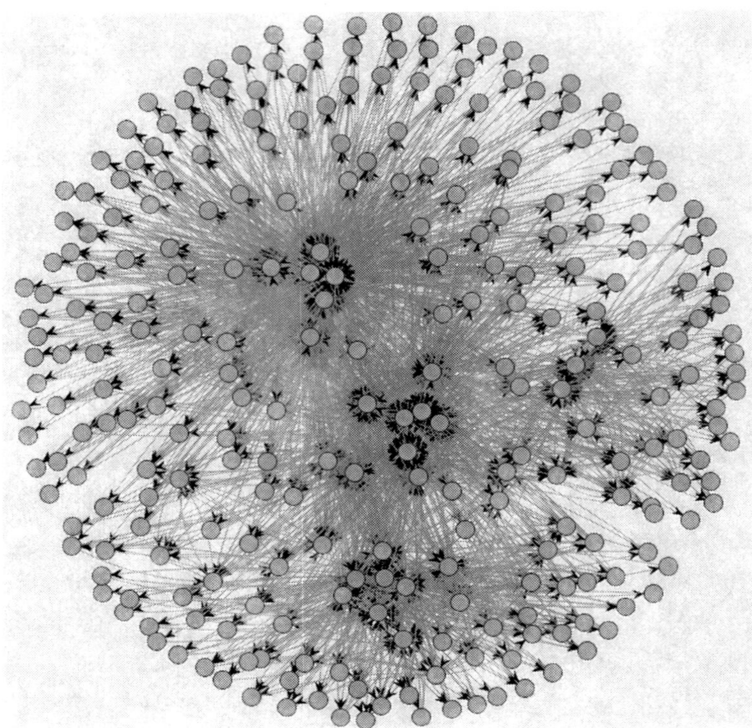

Fig. 11.9 Social network constructed based on handovers of work. *Each of the 271 nodes* corresponds to a civil servant. Two civil servants are connected if one executed an activity causally following an activity executed by the other civil servant

11.4.3.2 WOZ Process

In Sect. 11.1, we showed some analysis results for a WMO process of a municipality. To date, we have applied process mining in about a dozen municipalities. Moreover, we just started a new project (CoSeLoG) involving nine municipalities interested in cross-organizational process mining, i.e., analyzing differences between similar processes in different municipalities [24].

Processes in municipalities are typically Lasagna processes. To illustrate this, we present another example. Figure 11.11 shows a so-called "WOZ process" discovered for another municipality (i.e., different from the one for which we analyzed the WMO process). We applied the heuristic miner on an event log containing information about 745 objections against the so-called WOZ ("Waardering Onroerende Zaken") valuation. Dutch municipalities need to estimate the value of houses and apartments. The WOZ value is used as a basis for determining the real-estate property tax. The higher the WOZ value, the more tax the owner needs to pay. Therefore, Dutch municipalities need to handle many objections (i.e., appeals) of citizens that assert that the WOZ value is too high. For this municipality we analyzed four pro-

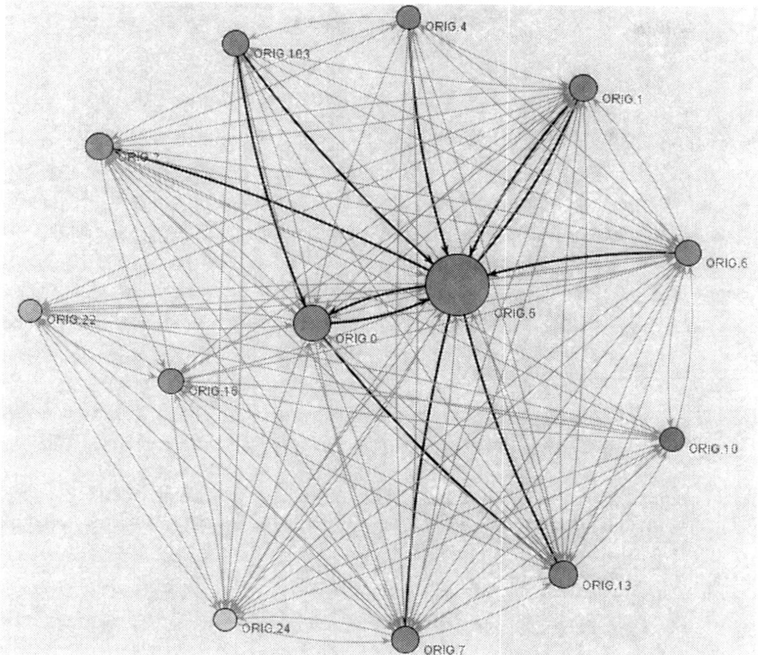

Fig. 11.10 (Color online) Social network consisting of civil servants that executed more than 2000 activities in a 9 month period. *The darker arcs* indicate the strongest relationships in the social network. *Nodes having the same color* belong to the same clique. Names of resources have been anonymized for privacy reasons

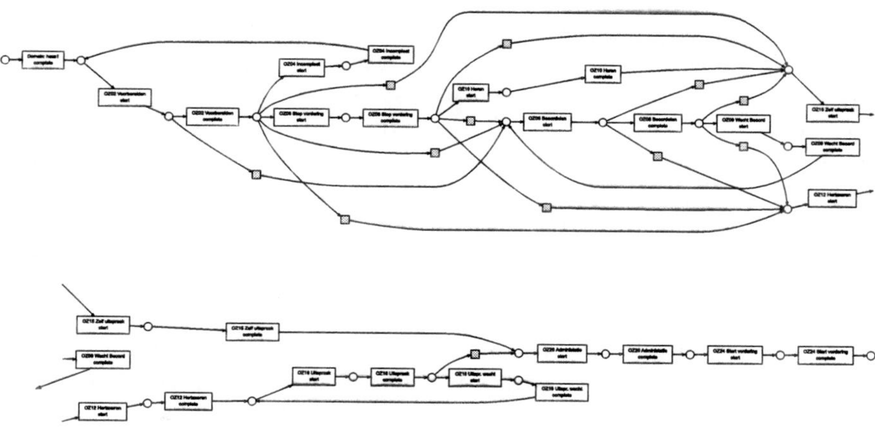

Fig. 11.11 WF-net discovered based on an event log of another municipality. The log contains events related to 745 objections against the so-called WOZ valuation. These 745 objections generated 9583 events. There are 13 activities. For 12 of these activities both start and complete events are recorded. Hence, the WF-net has 25 transitions

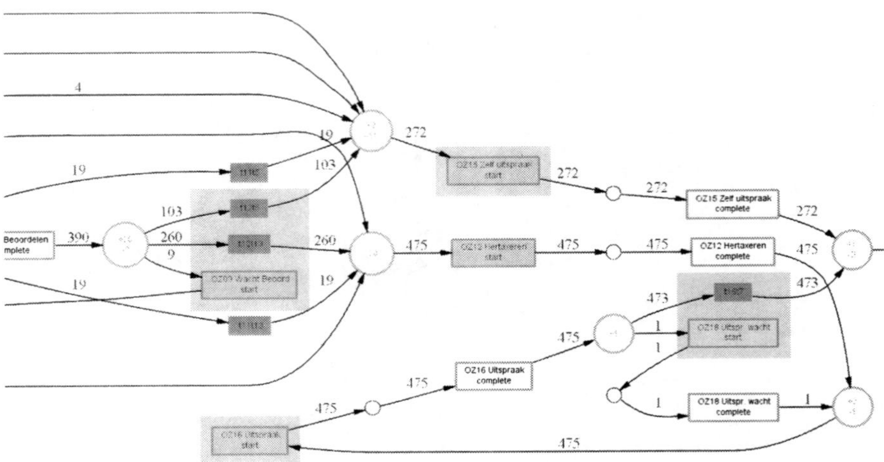

Fig. 11.12 Fragment of the WF-net annotated with diagnostics generated by ProM's conformance checker. The WF-net and event log fit well (fitness is 0.98876214). Nevertheless, several low-frequent deviations are discovered. For example. activity "OZ12 Hertaxeren" (re-evaluation of WOZ value) is started 23 times without being enabled according to the model

cesses related to objections and building permits. Here, we restrict ourselves to the WOZ process shown in Fig. 11.11.

The discovered WF-net has a good fitness: 628 of the 745 cases can be replayed without encountering any problems. The fitness of the model and log is 0.98876214 indicating that almost all recorded events are explained by the model. Hence, the WOZ process is clearly a Lasagna process. Nevertheless, it is interesting for the municipality to see the deviations highlighted in the model. Figure 11.12 shows a fragment of the diagnostics provided by the conformance checker (cf. Sect. 7.2).

The average flow time is approx. 178 days. Figure 11.13 shows some more performance-related diagnostics computed while replaying the event log containing timestamps. The standard deviation is approx. 53 days. ProM also visualizes the bottlenecks by coloring the places in the WF-net. Tokens tend to reside longest in the purple places. For example, the place in-between "OZ16 Uitspraak start" and "OZ16 Uitspraak complete" was visited 436 times. The average time spent in this place is 7.84 days. This indicates that activity "OZ16 Uitspraak" (final judgment) takes about a week. The place before "OZ16 Uitspraak start" is also colored purple; on average it takes 138 days to start this activity after enabling. As shown in Fig. 11.13, it is also possible to simply select two activities and measure the time that passes in-between these activities. On average 202.73 days pass in-between the completion of activity "OZ02 Voorbereiden" (preparation) and the completion of "OZ16 Uitspraak" (final judgment). Note that this is longer than the average overall flow time. This is explained by the observation that only 416 of the objections (approx. 56%) follow this route; the other cases follow the branch "OZ15 Zelf uitspraak" which, on average, takes less time.

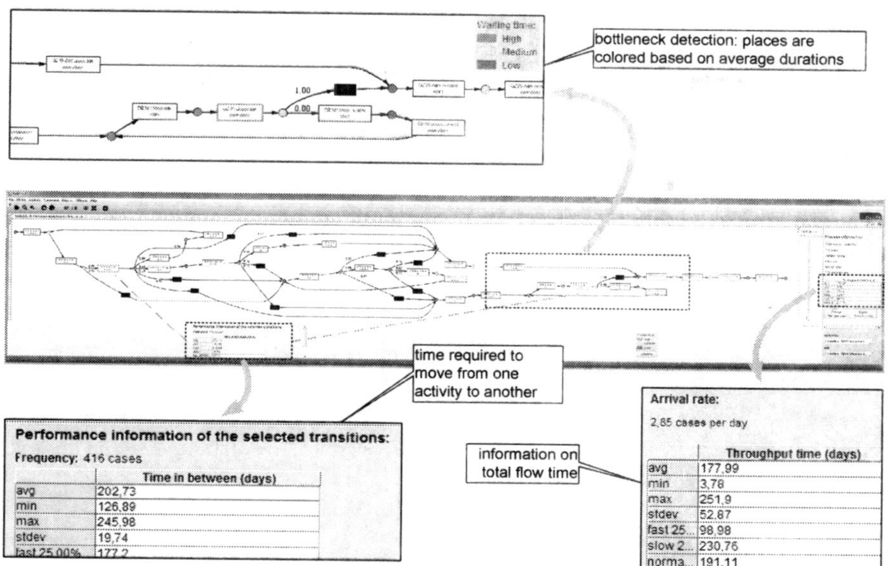

Fig. 11.13 Some diagnostics obtained by replaying the event log. These diagnostics explain why objections take on average approx. 178 days to be handled

The event log also contains information about resources. The 9583 events are executed by 20 resources. Most activity instances have a start and complete event. These are typically done by the same person. However, in exceptional situations an activity is started by one person and completed by another. Table 11.1 shows the resource-activity matrix introduced in Sect. 8.3. The table shows that some people executed many activities (e.g., user 8 generated 2621 events) whereas others executed just a few activities (e.g., users 13 and 14 generated only one event). Figure 11.14 shows a social network based on the user profiles shown in Table 11.1. Persons that have similar profiles are connected and the strength of a connection depends on the degree of similarity (here we used the correlation coefficient). This information can be used to group people. Figure 11.14 shows four cliques discovered by ProM's social network analyzer: *clique 1* consists of users 1, 2, 3, 8, 12, 13, 14, 16, and 17, *clique 2* consists of users 4, 5, 6, 9, 11, 18, and 19, *clique 3* consists of users 7 and 15, and *clique 4* consists of users 10 and 20. Consider, for example, *clique 4*. The two persons in this clique (users 10 and 20) only execute a_4 ("OZ06 Stop vordering") and a_{13} ("OZ24 Start vordering"). Hence, it makes perfect sense that they are grouped together. For organizations, it is interesting to see whether such clusters correspond to existing roles. Unexpected outcomes may trigger a redistribution of work.

The municipality for which we analyzed the WOZ process, provided us with several other event logs. For instance, event logs related to the handling of building permits. All of these processes can be classified as Lasagna processes and in principle all of the process mining techniques discussed in this book can be applied.

Table 11.1 Resource-activity matrix showing the number of times each user performed a particular activity: a_1 = "Domain: heus1", a_2 = "OZ02 Voorbereiden", a_3 = "OZ04 Incompleet", a_4 = "OZ06 Stop vordering", a_5 = "OZ08 Beoordelen", a_6 = "OZ09 Wacht Beoord", a_7 = "OZ10 Horen", a_8 = "OZ12 Hertaxeren", a_9 = "OZ15 Zelf uitspraak", a_{10} = "OZ16 Uitspraak", a_{11} = "OZ18 Uitspr. wacht", a_{12} = "OZ20 Administatie", a_{13} = "OZ24 Start vordering". The names of users have been anonymized for privacy reasons

User	a_1	a_2	a_3	a_4	a_5	a_6	a_7	a_8	a_9	a_{10}	a_{11}	a_{12}	a_{13}
User 1	0	0	51	0	0	0	0	0	0	0	0	0	0
User 2	1	2	0	0	2	0	0	0	0	38	0	69	0
User 3	0	9	0	0	0	0	0	0	0	0	0	0	0
User 4	2	0	0	0	0	0	0	0	0	0	0	0	0
User 5	117	0	4	0	3	0	0	0	0	1	0	20	6
User 6	172	6	14	0	7	3	0	0	1	2	0	48	53
User 7	1	41	8	14	275	8	8	865	55	180	0	128	5
User 8	2	868	7	6	105	0	0	79	266	441	0	844	3
User 9	90	0	2	0	1	2	0	0	1	2	0	27	28
User 10	0	0	0	899	0	0	0	0	0	0	0	0	1019
User 11	336	1	3	1	4	2	0	0	0	1	0	18	23
User 12	1	645	13	21	419	3	0	3	217	281	1	334	9
User 13	0	1	0	0	0	0	0	0	0	0	0	0	0
User 14	0	0	0	0	0	0	0	0	0	1	0	0	0
User 15	0	0	0	0	0	0	0	2	2	0	0	2	0
User 16	1	3	3	2	1	0	0	1	2	3	1	0	0
User 17	0	4	0	0	0	0	0	0	0	0	0	0	0
User 18	9	0	0	0	0	0	0	0	0	0	0	0	0
User 19	13	1	0	0	1	0	0	0	0	0	0	4	0
User 20	0	0	0	21	0	0	0	0	0	0	0	0	258

The application of conformance checking on the processes of this municipality is discussed in more detail in [80]. For example, there it is shown that, despite the presence of a WFM system, processes still deviate from the normative models. The municipality was using eiStream WFM system (formerly known as Eastman Software and today named Global 360), therefore, we did not expect any deviations. However, as discussed in [80], process mining could reveal misconfigurations of the WFM system. In [83], it is shown that, based on the event logs of this municipality, it is possible to discover simulation models covering all perspectives (control-flow, data dependencies, performance characteristics, and organizational characteristics). In Sect. 8.6, we showed how these perspectives can be merged into a single CPN model that can be simulated by CPN Tools. Although we did not conduct short-term simulations for this municipality, the validation of the models described in [83] shows that accurate simulations are possible for the selected process. Similarly, we showed in [113] that accurate time predictions are possible for the WOZ process of this municipality. In [113], various annotated transition systems are constructed

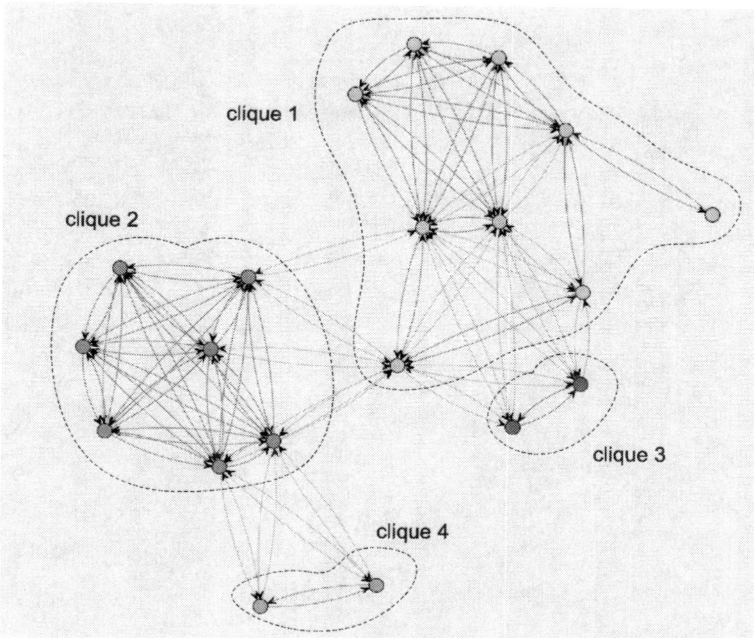

Fig. 11.14 Social network based on similarity of profiles. People that execute similar collections of activities are related and clustered in cliques

using the approach described in Sect. 9.4. Each of these annotated transition systems is learned using one half of the event log, and evaluated using the other half. This illustrates that operational support is indeed possible for Lasagna processes.

Chapter 12
Analyzing "Spaghetti Processes"

Spaghetti processes are the counterpart of Lasagna processes. Because Spaghetti processes are less structured, only a subset of the process mining techniques described in this book are applicable. For instance, it makes no sense to aim at operational support activities if there is too much variability. Nevertheless, process mining can help to realize dramatic process improvements by uncovering key problems.

12.1 Characterization of "Spaghetti Processes"

As explained in the previous chapter, there is a continuum of processes ranging from highly structured processes (Lasagna processes) to unstructured processes (Spaghetti processes). In this chapter, we focus on Spaghetti processes.

Figure 12.1 shows why unstructured processes are called Spaghetti processes. Only when zooming in one can see individual activities. Figure 12.2 shows a tiny fragment of the whole process. The fragment shows that activity "O_Bloedkweek 1" (a particular blood test) was scheduled 412 times and 230 times followed by "O_Bloedkweek 2" (another test). These activities are frequent. However, there are also several activities that are executed for only one of the 2765 patients.

The process model depicted in Fig. 12.1 was obtained using the heuristic miner with default settings. Hence, low frequent behavior has been filtered out. Nevertheless, the model is too difficult to comprehend. Note that this is not necessarily a problem of the discovery algorithm. Activities are only connected if they frequently followed one another in the event log (cf. Sect. 6.2). Hence, the complexity shown in Fig. 12.1 reflects reality and is not caused by the discovery algorithm!

Figure 12.1 is an extreme example used to explain the characteristics of a Spaghetti process. Given the data set, it is not surprising that the process is unstructured; the 2765 patients did not form a homogeneous group and included individuals with very different medical problems. The process model can be simplified dramatically by selecting a group of patients with similar problems. However, also for more homogeneous groups of patients (e.g., people that had heart surgery), the resulting process model is often Spaghetti-like.

W.M.P. van der Aalst, *Process Mining*,
DOI 10.1007/978-3-642-19345-3_12, © Springer-Verlag Berlin Heidelberg 2011

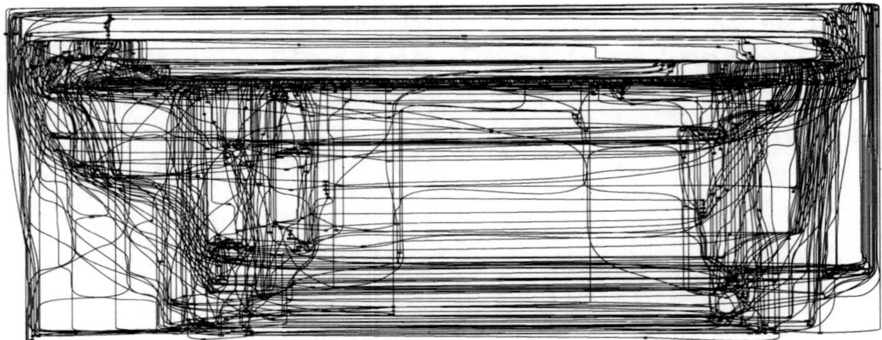

Fig. 12.1 Spaghetti process describing the diagnosis and treatment of 2765 patients in a Dutch hospital. The process model was constructed based on an event log containing 114,592 events. There are 619 different activities (taking event types into account) executed by 266 different individuals (doctors, nurses, etc.)

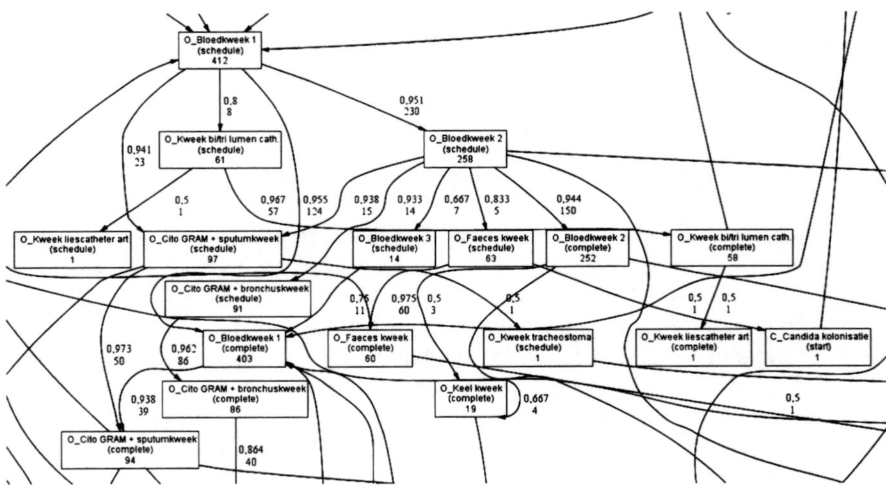

Fig. 12.2 Fragment of the Spaghetti process of Fig. 12.1 showing 18 activities of the 619 activities (2.9%)

Let us consider another, less extreme, example. Figure 12.3 shows the dotted chart for a process of one of the largest Dutch housing agencies (see also Figs. 8.3 and 8.4). Each case corresponds to a housing unit (accommodation such as a house or an apartment). The process starts when the tenant leasing the unit wants to stop renting it. The process ends when a new tenant moves into the unit after addressing all formalizaties. In between, activities such as "registering the new address", "first inspection", "final inspection", "finalize contract", "return deposit", "sign contract", "repair", and "update price" are executed. Figure 12.3 is based on an event log containing information about 208 units that changed tenant. There are 74 different ac-

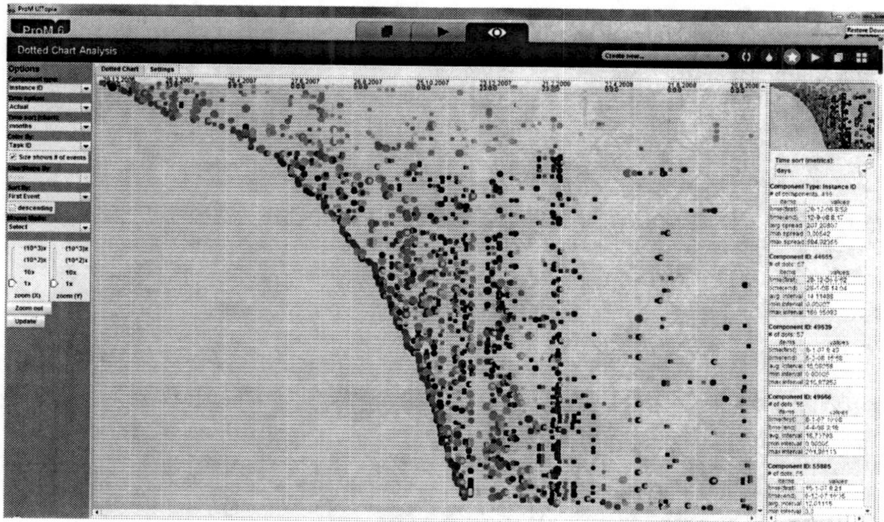

Fig. 12.3 Dotted chart created using an event log of a Dutch housing agency. *Each line* corresponds to a case (house or apartment). The event log contains 208 cases that generated 5987 events. There are 74 different activities

tivities. In total 5987 activities were executed for the 208 units. As Fig. 12.3 shows, there is a huge variance in flow time. For some units, it takes a very long time to change ownership (sometimes more than a year) for others this is matter of days. The initial events of the 208 cases do not form a straight line; the curve shows that the arrival rate of new cases is increasing during the period covered by the event log.

Figure 12.4 shows a process model discovered using the heuristic miner. Although the model does not look as Spaghetti-like as Fig. 12.1, it is rather complicated considering the fact that it is based on only 208 cases. The 208 cases generate 203 unique traces, i.e., almost all cases follow a path that is not followed by any of the other cases. This observation, combined with the complexity of the model suggests that the log is far from complete thus complicating analysis.

The processes of the Dutch hospital and housing agency illustrate the challenges one is facing when dealing with Spaghetti processes. Nevertheless, such processes are very interesting from the viewpoint of process mining as they often allow for various improvements. A highly-structured well-organized process is often less interesting in this respect; it is easy to apply process mining techniques but there is also little improvement potential. Therefore, one should not shy away from Spaghetti processes as these are often appealing from a process management perspective. *Turning Spaghetti processes into Lasagna processes can be very beneficial for an organization.*

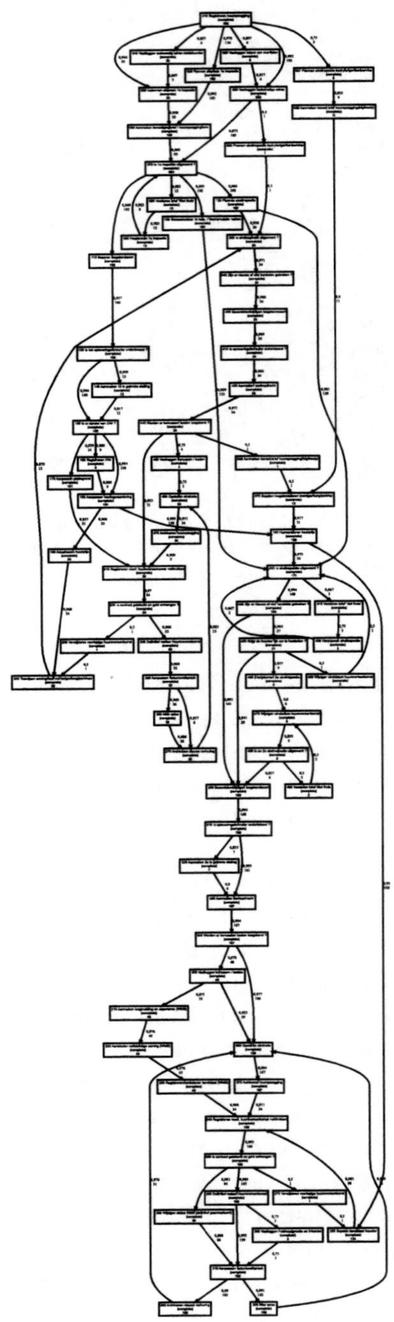

Fig. 12.4 C-net for the event log of the housing agency. The model was obtained using the heuristic miner (with default settings). The model was discovered based on an event log with 5987 events. All 208 cases start with activity "010 Registreren huuropzegging" (register request to end lease). Some of the activities are relatively infrequent, e.g., activity "020 Vastleggen datum van overlijden" occurred only 6 times (this activity is only executed if the tenant died)

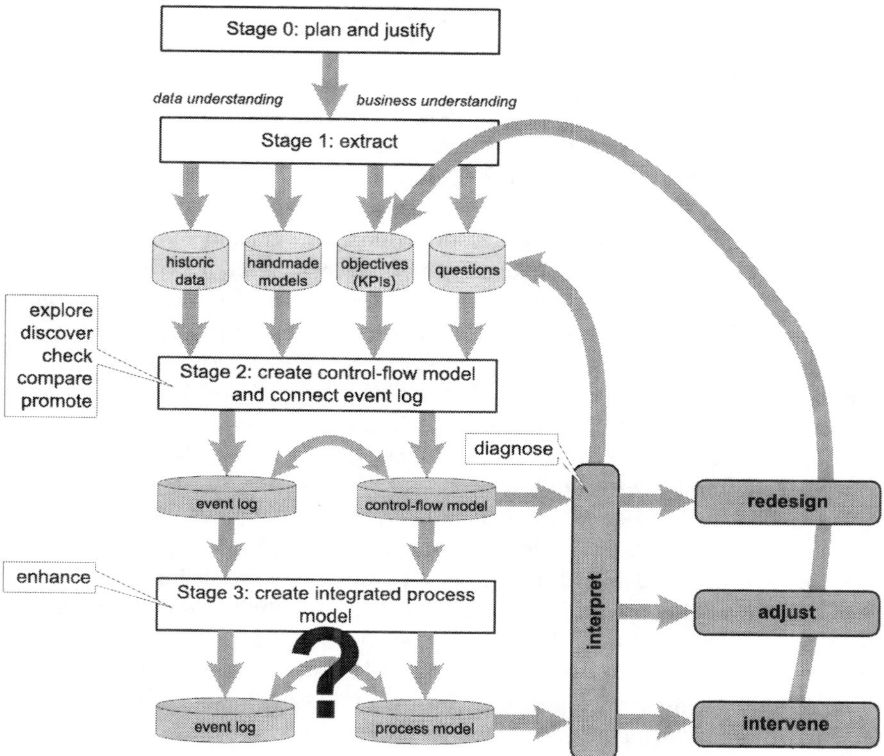

Fig. 12.5 The part of the L^* life-cycle model applicable to Spaghetti processes: Stages 0, 1 and 2 are also possible for unstructured processes. However, creating an integrated process model covering all perspectives (Stage 3) is often not possible. Instead separate models are generated for the other perspectives, e.g., a social network

12.2 Approach

In Sect. 11.3, we introduced the L^* life-cycle model describing an idealized process mining project aiming at improving a Lasagna process. Only the initial stages are applicable for Spaghetti processes. Figure 12.5 shows the most relevant part of the L^* life-cycle model. Note that Stage 4 has been removed because operational support is impossible for the processes just described. To enable history-based predictions and recommendations, it is essential to first make the "Spaghetti-like" process more "Lasagna-like". In fact, Stage 3 will also be too ambitious for most Spaghetti processes. It is always possible to generate process models as shown in Figs. 12.1 and 12.4 (Stage 2). Moreover, it is also possible to view dotted charts, create social networks, etc. However, it is very unlikely that all of these can be folded into a meaningful comprehensive process model as the basis (the control-flow discovered) is too weak.

In Sect. 5.4, we discussed the challenges related to process mining. They are of particular relevance when dealing with Spaghetti processes. Event logs do not contain negative examples, i.e., only positive example behavior is given. The fact that something does not happen in an event log does not mean that it cannot happen. For example, Fig. 12.4 is based on an event log in which almost all cases follow a unique path (the 208 cases generate 203 different traces). Therefore, the discovery algorithm needs to generalize. For more complex processes, i.e., processes that are large and that allow for many behaviors, the event log is typically far from complete (cf. Sect. 5.4.2). To further complicate matters, there may be noisy behavior, i.e., infrequent behavior that the user is not interested in. Because of these complications, a discovery algorithm needs to carefully balance the four quality dimensions introduced earlier: *fitness*, *simplicity*, *precision*, and *generalization* (see Fig. 5.22). The process models shown in Figs. 12.1 and 12.4 illustrate the relevance of these considerations. For the characteristics of the different process discovery algorithms, we refer to Part II of this book. Here, we only stress the importance of carefully *filtering* the event log before discovery.

Let us first consider the *filtering of activities* based on their characteristics, e.g., absolute or relative frequency. Figure 12.6(a) shows a filtering plug-in selecting all activities that occurred in at least 5% of all cases. This ProM 5.2 plug-in is applied to the event log used to construct Fig. 12.1, i.e., activities that do not appear frequently are removed from the event log. As a result, the process model will be simpler as fewer activities are included. Figure 12.6(b) shows a filtering plug-in in ProM 6 applied to the event log used to construct Fig. 12.4. In this case, the top 80% of activities are included; all other activities are removed from the log. The effect of filtering is shown in Fig. 12.6(c). This C-net was obtained by selecting all activities that occur in at least 50% of all cases handled by the housing agency. A comparison of the process model obtained using the original event log (Fig. 12.4) with the process model obtained using the filtered event log (Fig. 12.6(c)), demonstrates the effect of filtering. The discovered model shows only 28 of the 74 activities appearing in the event log of the housing agency.

In principle, any model *can be made as simple as desired* by simply abstracting from infrequent activities. In the extreme case, the model contains only the most frequent activity. Such a model is not very useful. However, it shows that filtering can be used to seamlessly simplify models. Interestingly, it is sometimes useful to also abstract from very frequent activities that are interleaved with other activities (e.g., some system action executed after every update). These clutter the diagram while being less relevant. Note that there may be multiple criteria for selecting/removing activities (e.g., average costs, duration, and risks).

Besides the simple activity-based filtering illustrated by Fig. 12.6, there are more advanced types of filtering that transform low-level patterns into activities [13]. Moreover, the cases in the log can be partitioned in homogeneous groups as shown in [12, 32, 46]. The basic idea is that one *does not try to make one large and complex model for all cases, but simpler models for selected groups of cases*. Here, one can use the classical clustering techniques described in Sect. 3.3 and adapt them for process mining. To apply these techniques, feature extraction is needed to describe

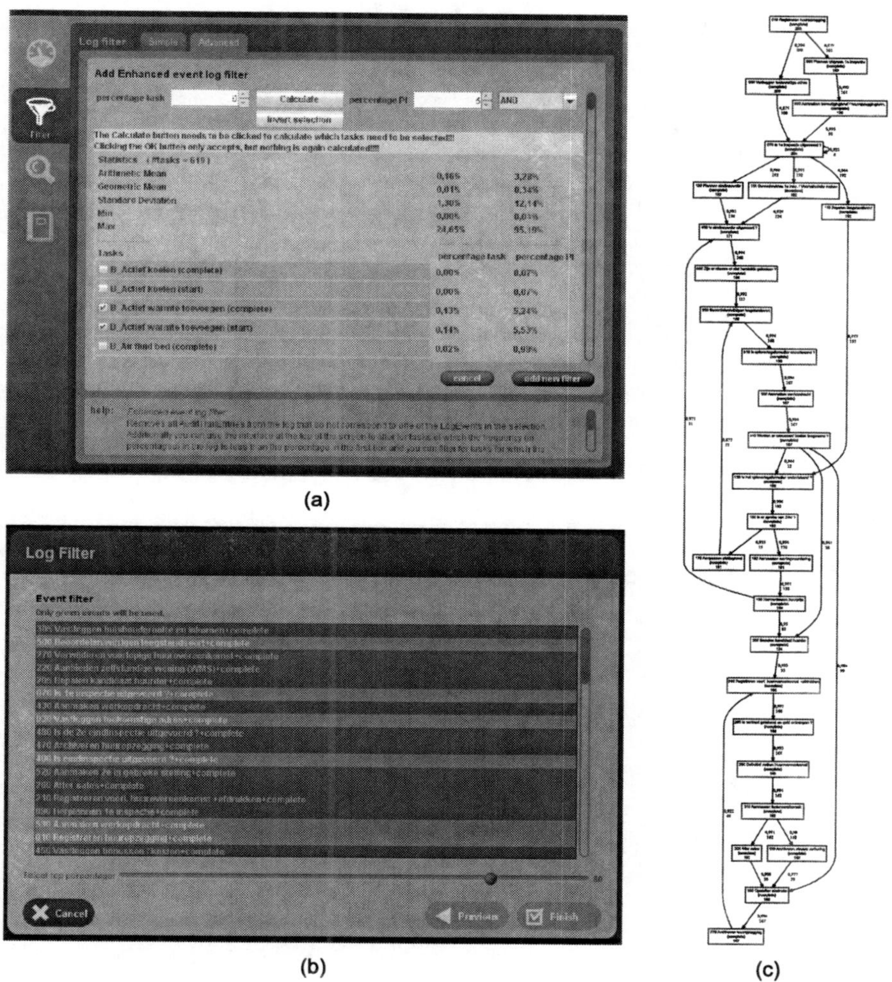

Fig. 12.6 Filtering the event log before process discovery: (**a**) selecting activities that occur for at least 5% of all 2765 patients, (**b**) selecting the top 80% of the 74 activities conducted by employees of the housing agency, (**c**) C-net discovered based on a filtered log (the event log of the housing agency after removing the activities occurring for less than 50% of the units)

cases in terms of a vector of variables (the features). By using a hierarchical clustering technique as shown in Fig. 12.7, one can view the same process at multiple levels. Cutting the dendrogram close to the root results in a few more complex models. Cutting the dendrogram closer to the leaves of the tree results in many simple models.

In the next chapter, we describe an alternative way to simplify process models. In contrast to filtering, simplification and abstraction techniques are directly applied to the process graph. This so-called *fuzzy mining* approach views process models

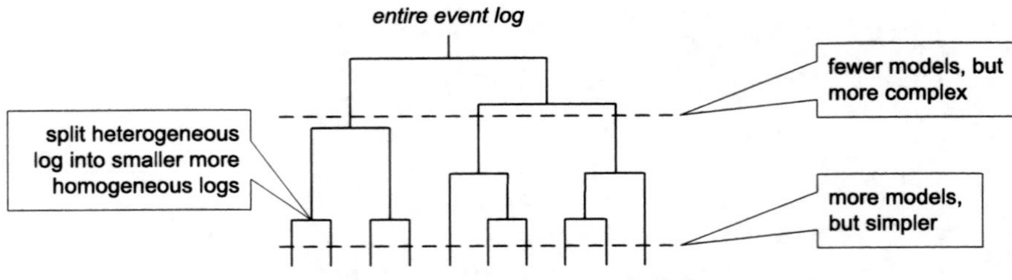

Fig. 12.7 Hierarchical clustering applied to heterogeneous event logs. The whole event log is partitioned into smaller, more homogeneous, event logs. This process is repeated until it is possible to create a "simple model" for each of the smaller logs. The resulting dendrogram can be cut closer to the root or closer to the leaves. This reflects the trade-off between the simplicity of models and the number of models

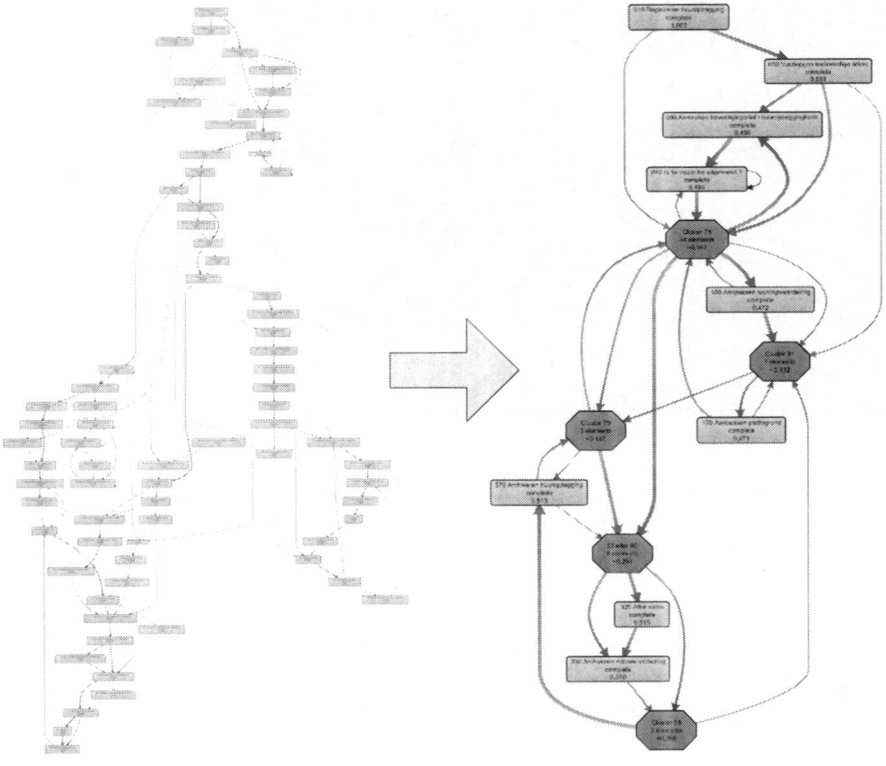

Fig. 12.8 Fuzzy mining applied to the event log of the housing agency. The cartography metaphor is used to support seamless abstraction and generalization. Both models provide a view on the same process. *In the right model* infrequent activities have been removed or amalgamated *into cluster nodes*. Moreover, *infrequent arcs* are removed based on the selected threshold

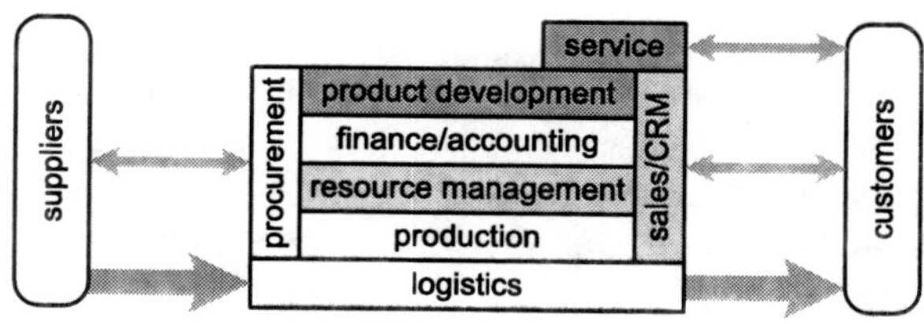

Fig. 12.9 Overview of the different functional areas in a typical organization. Spaghetti processes are typically encountered in product development, service, resource management, and sales/CRM

as if they are geographic maps (e.g., road maps or hiking maps). Depending on the map, insignificant roads and cities can be removed and streets and suburbs can be amalgamated into bigger structures. Figure 12.8 shows the effect this approach on the event log of the housing agency (i.e., the log used to construct the model in Fig. 12.4). Section 13.1.3 will elaborate further on the cartography metaphor used by the fuzzy mining approach.

12.3 Applications

In the previous chapter, we provided a systematic overview of the different sectors, industries, and functional areas where process mining can be used. In this section, we briefly revisit this overview for Spaghetti processes. Moreover, we give some pointers to case studies describing the analysis of highly unstructured processes.

12.3.1 Process Mining Opportunities for Spaghetti Processes

Many of the use cases presented in Sect. 11.2 also apply to Spaghetti processes. However, the "stakes are higher"; it will take more time to thoroughly analyze the process, but the potential gains are typically also more substantial.

Figure 12.9 highlights the functional areas where typically Spaghetti processes can be found.

Processes in *Product development* tend to be rather unstructured because they are low frequent (compared to production processes) and rely on creativity and problem-solving capabilities. For example, we have been mining event logs from Software Configuration Management (SCM) systems such as CVS and Subversion. In addition to managing the artifacts created by software engineers, these systems also collect and store information on the software development process to answer questions such as "Who created, accessed, or changed which documents?", "When was a particular task completed?", etc. Process discovery efforts using the event logs of SCM systems as input typically reveal Spaghetti-like processes as shown before.

Figure 12.9 indicates that one can also find Spaghetti processes in the functional area *Service*. An interesting development is that more and more products are monitored while being used in their natural habitat, e.g., modern high-end copiers, expensive medical devices, and critical production facilities collect event logs and can be observed remotely. Later, we will show that ASML and Philips Healthcare already monitor the systems they manufacture. In the future, manufacturers will start monitoring also less expensive goods, e.g., cars, consumer electronics, and heating systems will be connected to the Internet for a variety of reasons. Manufacturers would like to know how their products are used, when they malfunction, and how to repair them.

Resource management and *Sales/CRM* are two functional areas where a mixture of Spaghetti and Lasagna processes can be encountered (cf. Sect. 11.4.1).

One can come across Spaghetti processes in all sectors and industries mentioned in Sect. 11.4.2. However, processes in the tertiary sector tend to be less structured than processes in the other two sectors. For instance, as is illustrated by Fig. 12.1, the healthcare industry is notorious in this respect. In general, one can say that processes driven by humans that can operate in an autonomous manner are less structured. Situations, in which expertise, intuition, and creativity are important, stimulate self-government. Doctors in hospitals and engineers in large construction projects often need to deal with one-of-a-kind problems. Consumers that are using products also operate in an autonomous manner. Consider, for example, a television that can be monitored remotely to learn how it is used and when it malfunctions. Some users will watch television the whole day and constantly switch channels whereas other users only watch the news at 8 pm and then switch off the television. Self-directed behavior of consumers and professionals typically results in Spaghetti-like processes.

As mentioned earlier, *Spaghetti processes are interesting from the viewpoint of process mining*. First of all, it is interesting to learn from the amazing capabilities of humans to deal with complex unstructured problems. When automating parts of the process it is important to understand why processes are unstructured to avoid building counter-productive and inflexible information systems. Second, Spaghetti processes have the largest improvement potential. They are more difficult to analyze, but the prospective rewards are also higher.

12.3.2 Examples of Spaghetti Processes

We have encountered Spaghetti processes in a variety of organizations. In Chap. 11, we already mentioned several organizations where we applied process mining. In this section, we give three additional examples: ASML, Philips Healthcare, and AMC. The goal is not to describe the processes of these organizations in detail, but to provide pointers to applications of process mining in Spaghetti-like environments.

12.3.2.1 ASML

ASML is the world's leading manufacturer of chip-making equipment and a key supplier to the chip industry. ASML designs, develops, integrates and services advanced systems to produce semiconductors. Process mining has been used to analyze the test process of wafer scanners in ASML [82].

Wafer scanners are complex machines consisting of many building blocks. They use a photographic process to image nanometric circuit patterns onto a silicon wafer. Because of competition and fast innovation, the time-to-market is very important and every new generation of wafer scanners is balancing on the border of what is technologically possible. As a result, the testing of manufactured wafer scanners is an important, but also time-consuming, process. Every wafer scanner is tested in the factory of ASML. When it passes all tests, the wafer scanner is disassembled and shipped to the customer where the system is re-assembled. At the customer's site, the wafer scanner is tested again. Testing is time-consuming and takes several weeks on both sites. Since time-to-market is very important, ASML is constantly looking for ways to reduce the time needed to test wafer scanners.

Figure 12.10 shows that the testing of wafer scanners is indeed a Spaghetti process [82]. The model was discovered based on an event log containing 154,966 events. The event log contained information about 24 carefully chosen wafer scanners (same type, same circumstances, and having complete logs). The number of events per case (i.e., the length of the executed test sequence) in this event log ranges from 2820 to 16,250 events. There are 360 different activities, all identified by four-letter test codes. Each instance of these 360 activities has a start event and complete event. Figure 12.10 is based on just the complete events.

ASML also had a so-called reference model describing the way that machines should be tested. This reference model is at the level of job steps rather than test codes. However, ASML maintains a mapping from the lower level codes to these higher level activities. Comparing the reference model and our discovered model (both at the job step and test code level) revealed interesting differences. Moreover, using the ProM's conformance checker we could show that the average fitness was only $fitness(L, N) = 0.375$, i.e., less than half of the events can be explained by the model (Sect. 7.2). When replaying, we discovered many activities that had occurred but that should not have happened according to the reference model and activities that should have happened but did not.

Both the discovered process models and the results of conformance checking showed that process mining can provide new insights that can be used to improve the management of complex Spaghetti-like processes. We refer to [82] for more details.

12.3.2.2 Philips Healthcare

Philips Healthcare is one of the leading manufacturers of medical devices, offering diagnosing imaging systems, healthcare information technology solutions, patient monitoring systems, and cardiac devices. Like ASML, Philips Healthcare is developing complex high-tech machines that record massive amounts of events. Since 2007, there has been an ongoing effort to analyze the event logs of these machines using process mining.

Philips Remote Services (PRS) is a system for the active monitoring of systems via the Internet. PRS has been established to deliver remote technical support, monitoring, diagnostics, application assistance, and other added value services. Low level

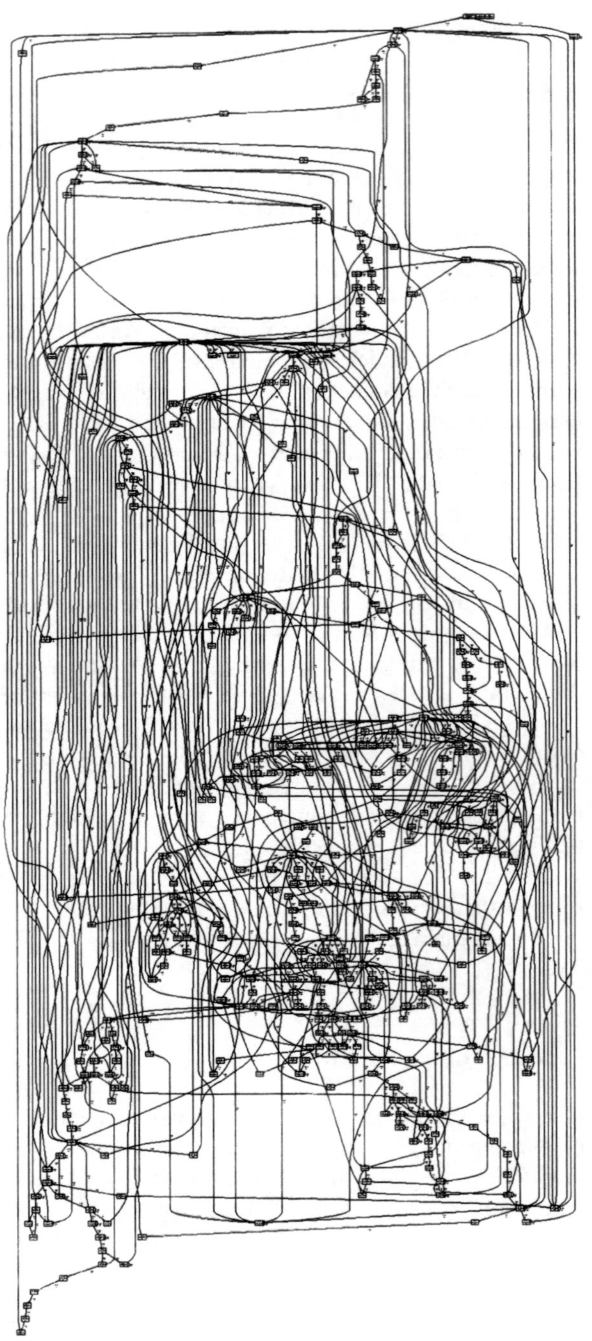

Fig. 12.10 Process model discovered for ASML's test process

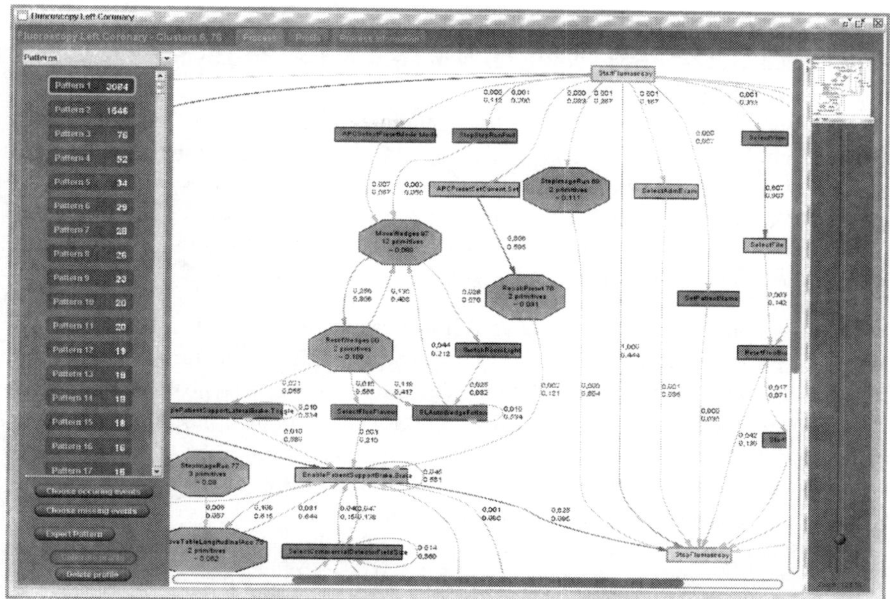

Fig. 12.11 Screenshot of a discovered process model for fluoroscopy runs in the context of the so-called "left coronary procedure" inside Allura Xper systems distributed all over the globe

events (e.g., pushing a button, changing the dosage) are recorded by the machine and subsequently sent to Philips via PRS. Using the Remote Analysis, Diagnostics And Reporting (RADAR) system, event logs are converted into an XML format and stored in the internal database of RADAR. Subsequently, the collected event data are translated into MXML files to enable process mining.

Process mining has been applied extensively to the event logs generated by Allura Xper systems. These are X-ray systems designed to diagnose and possibly assist in the treatment of all kinds of diseases, like heart or lung diseases, by generating images of the internal body. These systems record three types of events:

- *User messages.* When a message is shown to the user (e.g., "Geometry restarting"), this is recorded in the event log.
- *Commands.* Both users and system components can invoke commands. These are all recorded. Commands typically have various parameters (e.g., voltage values).
- *Warnings and errors.* Whenever a problem occurs (or is anticipated), an event is recorded.

Each event has a timestamp and contains information about the component that generated the event.

It is possible to analyze the processes in Allura Xper systems from various angles. The concept of a "case" (i.e., process instance) may refer to a machine, a machine day, the execution of a particular procedure, the repair of a machine, etc. Figure 12.11 shows an example taken from [51]. Processes discovered for these systems tend to be Spaghetti-like. To simplify diagnosis, the log is often preprocessed as discussed in [12–14]. Moreover, fuzzy mining, as illustrated by Fig. 12.8, is used to further simplify the model [51].

Mining processes from the event logs generated by Allura Xper systems is very challenging. The machines consist of many components and can be used in many different ways. Moreover, logging is rather low-level and changes with every new version. Nevertheless, there are various opportunities for process and system improvements using process mining. These are listed below. Note that opportunities also apply to other types of systems that are monitored remotely.

- Process mining provides *insight* into how systems are actually used. This is interesting from a *marketing* point of view. For example, if a feature is rarely used, then this may trigger additional after sales activities. It is also possible that, based on process mining results, the feature is removed or adapted in future systems.
- *Testing* can be improved by constructing test scenarios based on the actual use of the machines. For instance, for medical equipment it is essential to prove that the system was tested under realistic circumstances.
- Process mining can be used to improve the *reliability* of next generations of systems. Better systems can be designed by understanding why and when systems malfunction.
- Process mining can also be used for *fault diagnosis*. By learning from earlier problems, it is possible to find the root cause for new problems that emerge. For example, we have analyzed under which circumstances particular components are replaced. This resulted in a set of *signatures*. When a malfunctioning X-ray machine exhibits a particular "signature" behavior, the service engineer knows what component to replace.
- Historic information can also be used to *predict* future problems. For instance, it is possible to anticipate that an X-ray tube is about to fail. Hence, the tube can be replaced before the machine starts to malfunction.

These examples show the potential of remote diagnostics based on process mining.

12.3.2.3 AMC Hospital

Hospitals are particularly interesting from a process mining point of view. By law, hospitals need to record more and more data in a systematic manner and all event data are connected to patients. Therefore, it is relatively straightforward to correlate events. For example, by Dutch law all hospitals need to record the diagnostic and treatment steps at the level of individual patients in order to receive payments. This so-called "Diagnose Behandeling Combinatie" (DBC) forces Dutch hospitals to record all kinds of events. There is also consensus that processes in hospitals can be improved. Unlike most other domains, operational care processes are not tightly controlled by management. This, combined with the intrinsic variability of care processes, results in Spaghetti.

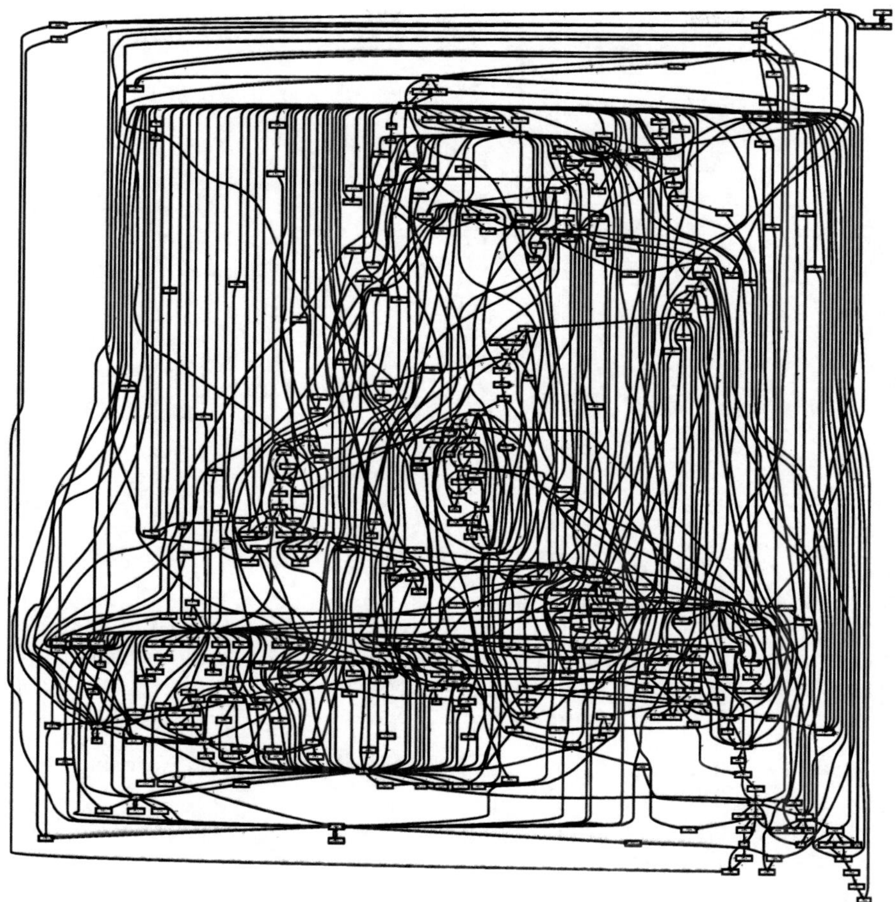

Fig. 12.12 Another Spaghetti process. The model is based on a group of 627 gynecological oncology patients. The event log contains 24,331 events referring to 376 different activities

Some think that care processes in hospitals can be improved by simple principles from operations management or by introducing workflow technology. Process models such as the one shown in Fig. 12.1 demonstrate that this is not case. One needs to better understand the variability, before suggesting solutions.

We conducted several process mining experiments based on event data of the AMC hospital in Amsterdam [64]. Together with people of the AMC, we have been investigating the introduction of workflow technology in this large academic hospital. This revealed many limitations of existing WFM/BPM systems when it comes to care processes. The variability in these processes is larger than in most other domains. This imposes unique requirements with respect to flexibility. Moreover, care processes combine flow oriented tasks with scheduled tasks [65]. As a result, con-

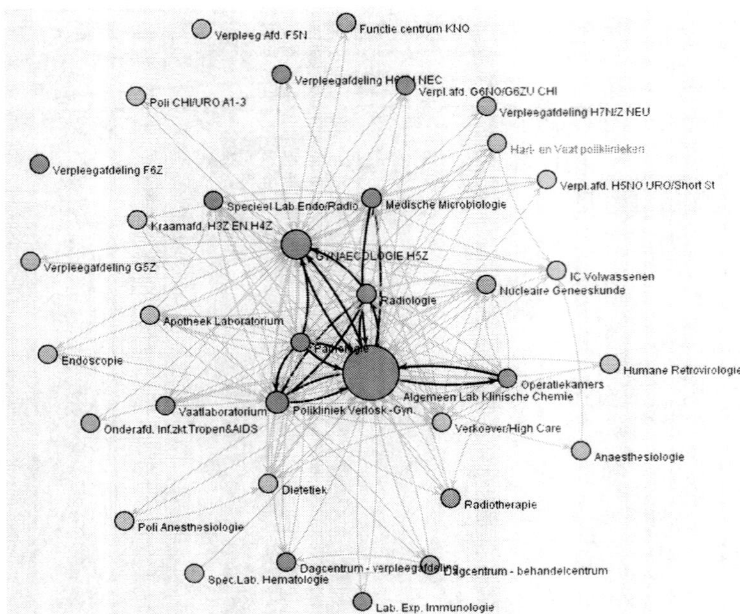

Fig. 12.13 Social network showing handovers between different organizational units of the AMC hospital

ventional workflow technology is not applicable and a better understanding of the processes is needed.

Figure 12.12 shows an example of a process model constructed for the AMC hospital. The model was discovered based on event data of a group of 627 gynecological oncology patients treated in 2005 and 2006. All diagnostic and treatment activities have been recorded for these patients. Clearly, this is a Spaghetti process. However, as shown in [64] it is possible to create simple models for homogeneous groups of patients using the hierarchical clustering technique illustrated by Fig. 12.7. The same event log also contained information about resources. For instance, Fig. 12.13 shows a social network based on this log. As in earlier examples, the social network is based on handovers of work. However, now we do not look at individuals but at the level of organizational units. Figure 12.13 can be used to analyze the flow of work between different departments of the AMC hospital. For example, the social network reveals that most handovers take place between the gynecology department and the general clinical lab.

Experiences with process mining in several hospitals revealed important challenges when applying this new technology. The databases of hospitals contain lots of event data. Since any event can be linked to a patient, correlation is easy. However, for many events only the date ("31-12-2010") is known and not the exact timestamp ("31-12-2010:11.52"). Therefore, it may be impossible to deduce the order in which events took place. Another problem is related to the trade-off illustrated by the dendrogram in Fig. 12.7. The process model for a large group of patients is typically Spaghetti-like as illustrated by Fig. 12.12. It is possible to create simpler models by looking at smaller homogeneous groups of patients. However, the drawback is that often the number of cases per group gets rather small. If there are only few cases in such a homogeneous group, the result is not very reliable. Only for homogeneous groups with more cases, the result is more trustworthy.

Despite these challenges, process mining provides a "mirror" for managers, doctors, and IT specialists in hospitals. To improve care-flows and to provide better IT support, it is essential to face the inherent complexity of these Spaghetti processes.

Part V
Reflection

Chapter 1
Introduction

Part I: Preliminaries

Chapter 2
Process Modeling and Analysis

Chapter 3
Data Mining

Part II: From Event Logs to Process Models

Chapter 4
Getting the Data

Chapter 5
Process Discovery: An Introduction

Chapter 6
Advanced Process Discovery Techniques

Part III: Beyond Process Discovery

Chapter 7
Conformance Checking

Chapter 8
Mining Additional Perspectives

Chapter 9
Operational Support

Part IV: Putting Process Mining to Work

Chapter 10
Tool Support

Chapter 11
Analyzing "Lasagna Processes"

Chapter 12
Analyzing "Spaghetti Processes"

Part V: Reflection

Chapter 13
Cartography and Navigation

Chapter 14
Epilogue

The final part of this book reflects on the relevance and positioning of process mining. Chapter 13 relates process mining to cartography and navigation. Limitations of traditional process models are revealed by studying the features of geographic maps. Many of these limitations can (and should) be addressed by process mining techniques. Moreover, navigation systems and mashups based on Google Maps illustrate how process maps can be actively used at run-time. Chapter 14 concludes this book by summarizing the benefits of process mining and listing challenges that need to be addressed to make process mining even more applicable.

Chapter 13
Cartography and Navigation

Process models can be seen as the "maps" describing the operational processes of organizations. Similarly, information systems can be looked at as "navigation systems" guiding the flow of work in organizations. Unfortunately, many organizations fail in creating and maintaining accurate business process maps. Often process models are outdated and have little to do with reality. Moreover, most information systems fail to provide the functionality offered by today's navigation systems. For instance, workers are not guided by the information system and need to work behind the system's back to get things done. Moreover, useful information such as the "estimated arrival time" of a running case is not provided. Process mining can help to overcome some of these problems.

13.1 Business Process Maps

The first geographical maps date back to the 7th Millennium BC. Since then cartographers have improved their skills and techniques to create maps thereby addressing problems such as clearly representing desired traits, eliminating irrelevant details, reducing complexity, and improving understandability. Today, most geographic maps are digital and of high quality. This has fueled innovative applications of cartography as is illustrated by modern car navigation systems (e.g., TomTom, Garmin, and Navigon), Google Maps, mashups using geo-tagging, etc. There are thousands of mashups using Google Maps, e.g., applications projecting information about traffic conditions, real estate, fastfood restaurants, or movie showtimes onto a selected map. People can seamlessly zoom in and out using such maps and interact with it, e.g., traffic jams are projected onto the map and the user can select a particular problem to see details.

Process models can be seen as the "*business process maps*" describing the operational processes of organizations [94]. Unfortunately, accurate business process maps are typically missing. Process models tend to be outdated and not aligned with reality. Moreover, unlike geographic maps, process models are typically not well understood by end users.

W.M.P. van der Aalst, *Process Mining*,
DOI 10.1007/978-3-642-19345-3_13, © Springer-Verlag Berlin Heidelberg 2011

As indicated in Sect. 9.1.1, we suggest *adopting ideas from cartography*. In the remainder of this section, we discuss ways of improving process models inspired by cartographic techniques. Some of these ideas are already supported by existing process mining techniques, others point to further innovations.

13.1.1 Map Quality

Geographical maps are typically of high quality compared to business process maps. For example, the maps used by navigation systems are very accurate, e.g., when driving from Amsterdam to Rome relatively few discrepancies between reality and the map will be encountered.

Process models tend to provide an idealized view on the business process that is modeled. Imagine that road maps would view the real highway system through similar rose-tinted glasses, e.g., showing a road that is not there but that should have been there. This would be unacceptable. However, these are the kind of business process maps used in many organizations. Such a "PowerPoint reality" limits the use and trustworthiness of process models.

In Chap. 7, we showed various conformance checking techniques that can be used as a "reality check" for business process maps. For instance, using replay the fitness of a process model and an event log can be determined. We encountered many real-life processes in which the fitness of the model and the log is less than 0.4. This implies that less than 40% of the behavior seen in reality fits into the model.

Some will argue that road maps are easier to maintain than process models, because a road system evolves at a much slower pace than a typical business process. This is indeed the case. However, this makes it even more important to have accurate up-to-date business process maps!

Besides differences in quality, there are also huge differences in understandability. Most people will intuitively understand geographical maps while having problems understanding process models. The dynamic nature of processes makes things more complicated (cf. workflow patterns [101, 130]). Therefore, the perceived complexity is partly unavoidable. Nevertheless, ideas from cartography can help to improve the understandability of process models.

13.1.2 Aggregation and Abstraction

Figure 13.1 shows a map. The map *abstracts* from less significant roads and cities. Roads that are less important are not shown. A cut-off criterion could be based on the average number of cars using the road per day. Similarly, the number of citizens could be used as a cut-off criterion for cities. For example, in Fig. 13.1 cities of less than 50,000 inhabitants are abstracted from. Maps also *aggregate* local roads and local districts (neighborhoods, suburbs, centers, etc.) into bigger entities.

Fig. 13.1 (Color online) Road map of The Netherlands. The map abstracts from smaller cities and less significant roads; only the bigger cities, highways, and other important roads are shown. Moreover, cities aggregate local roads and local districts

Figure 13.1, for instance, shows Eindhoven as a single dot while it consists of many roads, various districts (Strijp, Gestel, Woensel, Gestel, etc.), and neighboring cities (e.g., Veldhoven). People interested in Eindhoven can look at a city map to see more details.

Process models also need to abstract from less significant things. Activities can be removed if they are less frequent, e.g., activities that occur in less than 20% of completed cases are abstracted from. Also time and costs can be taken into account, e.g., activities that account for less than 8% of the total service time are removed unless the associated costs are more than € 50,000.

Aggregation is important for process mining because many event logs contain low-level events that need to be aggregated into more meaningful activities. In [13], it is shown how frequent low-level patterns can be identified and aggregated. Suppose that $x = \{\langle a,b,c\rangle, \langle a,b,b,c\rangle\}$, $y = \{\langle a,d,e,c\rangle, \langle a,e,d,c\rangle\}$, and $z = \{\langle d,d,d,a\rangle\}$ are frequent low-level patterns that represent meaningful activities,

d	d	d	a	a	b	b	c	a	d	e	c	a	b	c
z				x				y				x		

Fig. 13.2 A low-level trace is mapped onto a trace at a higher level of abstraction, e.g., the subsequence $\langle d, d, d, a\rangle$ is mapped onto z

e.g., the low-level subsequences a, b, c and a, b, b, c are possible manifestations of activity x. Now consider the low-level trace $\sigma = \langle d, d, d, a, a, b, b, c, a, d, e, c, a, b, c\rangle$. This trace can be rewritten into $\sigma' = \langle z, x, y, x\rangle$ showing the aggregated behavior (see Fig. 13.2). By preprocessing the event log in this way, it is possible to discover a simpler process model. Filtering, as described in Sect. 12.2, can be seen as another form of preprocessing. It is also possible to apply aggregation directly to the graph structure (see fuzzy mining [50] and Sects. 12.2 and 13.1.3).

Aggregation introduces multiple levels. For each aggregate node a kind of "city map" can be constructed showing the detailed low-level behavior. In principle there can be any number of levels, cf. country maps, state maps, city maps, district maps, etc.

13.1.3 Seamless Zoom

There may be different geographic maps of the same area using different scales. Moreover, using electronic maps it is possible to seamlessly zoom in and out. Note that, while zooming out, insignificant things are either left out or dynamically clustered into aggregate shapes (e.g., streets and suburbs amalgamate into cities). Navigation systems and applications such as Google Maps provide such a seamless zoom. Traditionally, process models are static, e.g., it is impossible to seamlessly zoom in to see part of the process in more detail. To deal with larger processes, typically a *static hierarchical decomposition* is used. In such a hierarchy, a process is composed of subprocesses, and in turn these subprocesses may be composed of smaller subprocesses.

Consider, for example, the WF-net shown in Fig. 13.3. The WF-net consists of atomic activities $(a, b, \dots, l)$ partitioned over three subprocesses x, y, and z. The overall process is composed of these three subprocesses. Figure 13.4 shows the top-level view of this composition. The semantics of such a hierarchical decomposition is the "flattened" model, i.e., subprocesses at the higher level are recursively replaced by their inside structure until one large flat process model remains (in our example there are only two levels).

Figures 13.3 and 13.4 show the limitations of hierarchical decomposition. At the highest level, one needs to be aware of all interactions at the lower levels. The reason is that higher levels in the decomposition need to be consistent with the lower levels, e.g., because there is a connection between activity l and activity b at the lower level, there also needs to be a connection between z and x at the higher level. This is not only the case for WF-nets, but holds for the hierarchy constructs in other

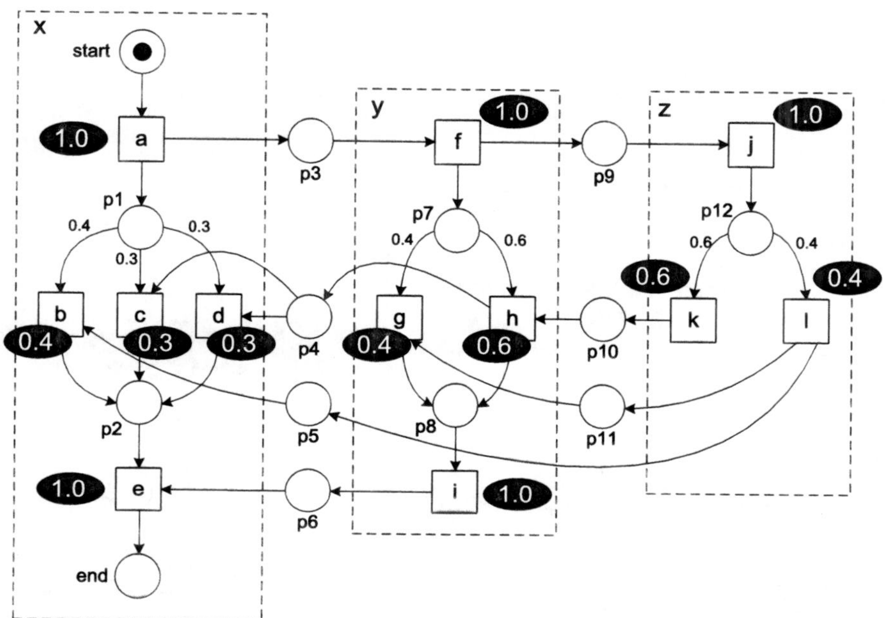

Fig. 13.3 A WF-net consisting of 12 atomic activities partitioned over three subprocesses x, y, and z. The average frequency of each activity is shown. For instance, activity h is executed for 60% of the cases

Fig. 13.4 Top-level view on the hierarchical WF-net shown in Fig. 13.3

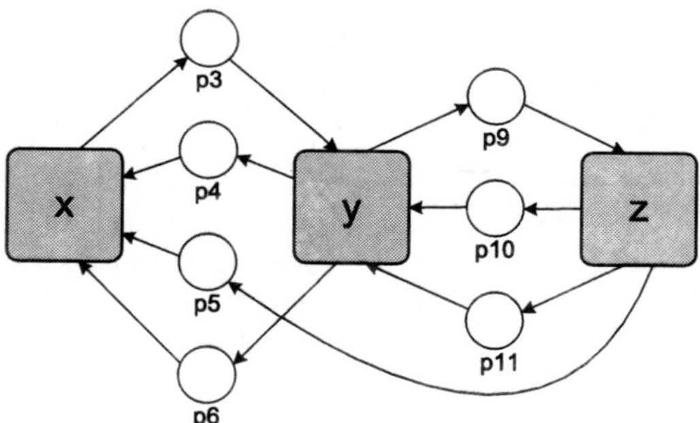

languages such as BPMN, YAWL and EPCs. From a design point of view, hierarchical decomposition makes perfect sense. When designing a system it is important to ensure consistency between different levels and the possibility to "flatten" models provides clear execution semantics.

However, when *viewing* a process model it is important to be able to zoom out to see fewer details and zoom in to see more details. This implies that the view is not static, i.e., activities should not be statically bound to a particular level chosen at design time. Moreover, when abstracting from infrequent low-level behavior the corresponding connections at higher levels should also be removed. For instance,

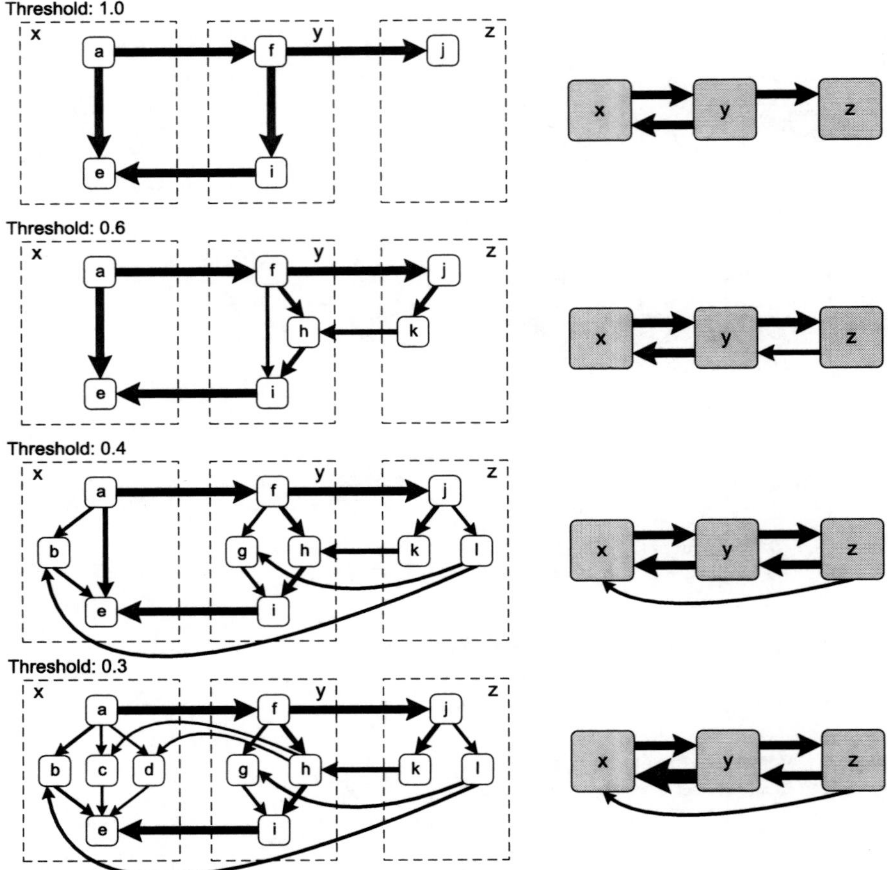

Fig. 13.5 The process specified by the WF-net of Fig. 13.3 viewed at different levels of abstraction. An activity and its corresponding connections are removed if the transition is less frequent than the threshold. Both the atomic view (*left*) and the aggregate view (*right*) are shown for four threshold values (0.3, 0.4, 0.6, and 1.0)

if activity l is very infrequent, it is not sufficient to hide it at a lower level: the connection between z and x (i.e., place $p5$) should also be removed.

Figure 13.5 illustrates how processes can be viewed while taking into account the frequencies of activities. As shown in Fig. 13.3, activities a, e, f, i, and j have a frequency of 1, i.e., they are executed once for each case. Activities h and k are executed for 60% of the cases, and activities b, g, and l are executed for 40% of the cases. Activities c and d are least frequent and are executed for only 30% of the cases. Assume that we would like to seamlessly simplify the model by progressively leaving out more activities based on their frequencies. Figure 13.5 shows four different levels. Here, we abstract from the detailed process logic and only show activities and their connections. Moreover, we show the intensity of connections by proportionally varying the width of the arcs. If the threshold is set to 0.3, then all activities are included. When the threshold is increased to 0.4, then activities c and d and their connections disappear. When the threshold is increased to 0.6, also activities b, g, and l and their connections disappear. If the threshold is set to 1, then only the most frequent activities are included. The left-hand side of Fig. 13.5 shows atomic activities and their relations. The right-hand side of the figure shows the connections if we assume that the activities are aggregated as shown in the original WF-net (cf. Fig. 13.3). It is important to note that the connection between z and x disappears when the threshold is higher than 0.4. If we abstract from the infrequent activities b and l, then we should also remove this connection. For the same reason the connection between z and y is not shown when the threshold is set to 1.

Figure 13.5 shows how one can seamlessly zoom in and zoom out to show more or less detail. This is very different from providing a static hierarchical decomposition and showing a particular level in the hierarchy as is done by the graphical editors of BPM systems, WFM systems, simulation tools, business process modeling tools, etc.

Thus far, we assumed a static partitioning of atomic activities over three subprocesses. Depending on the desired view this partitioning may change. To illustrate this, we use an example event log consisting of 100 cases and 3730 events. This event log contains events related to the reviewing process of journal papers. Each paper is sent to three different reviewers. The reviewers are invited to write a report. However, reviewers often do not respond. As a result, it is not always possible to make a decision after a first round of reviewing. If there are not enough reports, then additional reviewers are invited. This process is repeated until a final decision can be made (accept or reject). Figure 13.6 shows the process model discovered by the α-algorithm.

The α-algorithm does not allow for seamlessly zooming in and out. One would need to filter out infrequent activities from the log and subsequently apply the α-algorithm to different event logs. The *Fuzzy Miner* of ProM allows for seamlessly zooming in and out as is shown in Fig. 13.7 [49, 50]. The three fuzzy models shown in Fig. 13.7 are all based on the event log also used by the α-algorithm. Figure 13.7(a) shows the most detailed view. All activities are included. The color and width of the connections indicate their significance (like in Fig. 13.5). Figure 13.7(b) shows the most abstract view. The decision activity is typically executed multiple times per paper. Therefore, it is most frequent. The other 18 activities are partitioned over 4 so-called cluster nodes. Each cluster node aggregates multiple atomic activities. Using a threshold similar to the one used in Fig. 13.5, the Fuzzy Miner can seamlessly show more or less details. Figure 13.7(c) shows a model obtained using an intermediate threshold value. The top-level model shows the six most frequent activities. The other activities can be found in the three cluster nodes. Figure 13.7(d) shows the inner structure of an aggregate node consisting of 10 atomic activities. Note that the inner structure of an aggregate node shows the connections to nodes at the higher level.

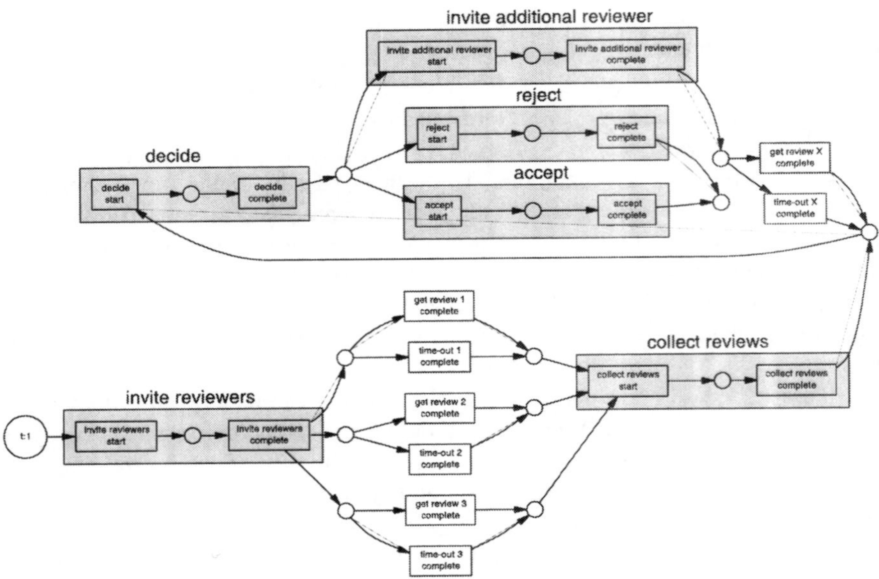

Fig. 13.6 WF-net discovered using the α-algorithm plug-in of ProM. An event log consisting of 100 cases and 3730 events was used to create the model. All activities are shown in the discovered model

When zooming out using Google maps, less significant elements are either left out or dynamically clustered into aggregate shapes. For example, streets and suburbs amalgamate into cities. This is similar to the zoom functionality provided by ProM's Fuzzy Miner as was demonstrated using Fig. 13.7. Note that in this particular example activities are aggregated and not removed. The Fuzzy Miner has many parameters that allow the user to influence the resulting model. Using different settings of these parameters it is also possible to abstract from activities (i.e., remove them) rather than aggregating them. Activities can also be removed by filtering the event log before applying a discovery algorithm (see Sect. 12.2).

13.1.4 Size, Color, and Layout

Cartographers not only eliminate irrelevant details, but also use colors to highlight important features. For instance, the map shown in Fig. 13.1 emphasizes the importance of highways using the color red. Moreover, graphical elements have a particular size to indicate their significance, e.g., the sizes of lines and dots may vary. For instance, in Fig. 13.1 the size of a city name is proportional to the number of citizens, e.g., Zaanstad is clearly smaller than Amsterdam. Geographical maps also have a clear interpretation of the x-axis and y-axis, i.e., the layout of a map is not arbitrary as the coordinates of elements have a meaning.

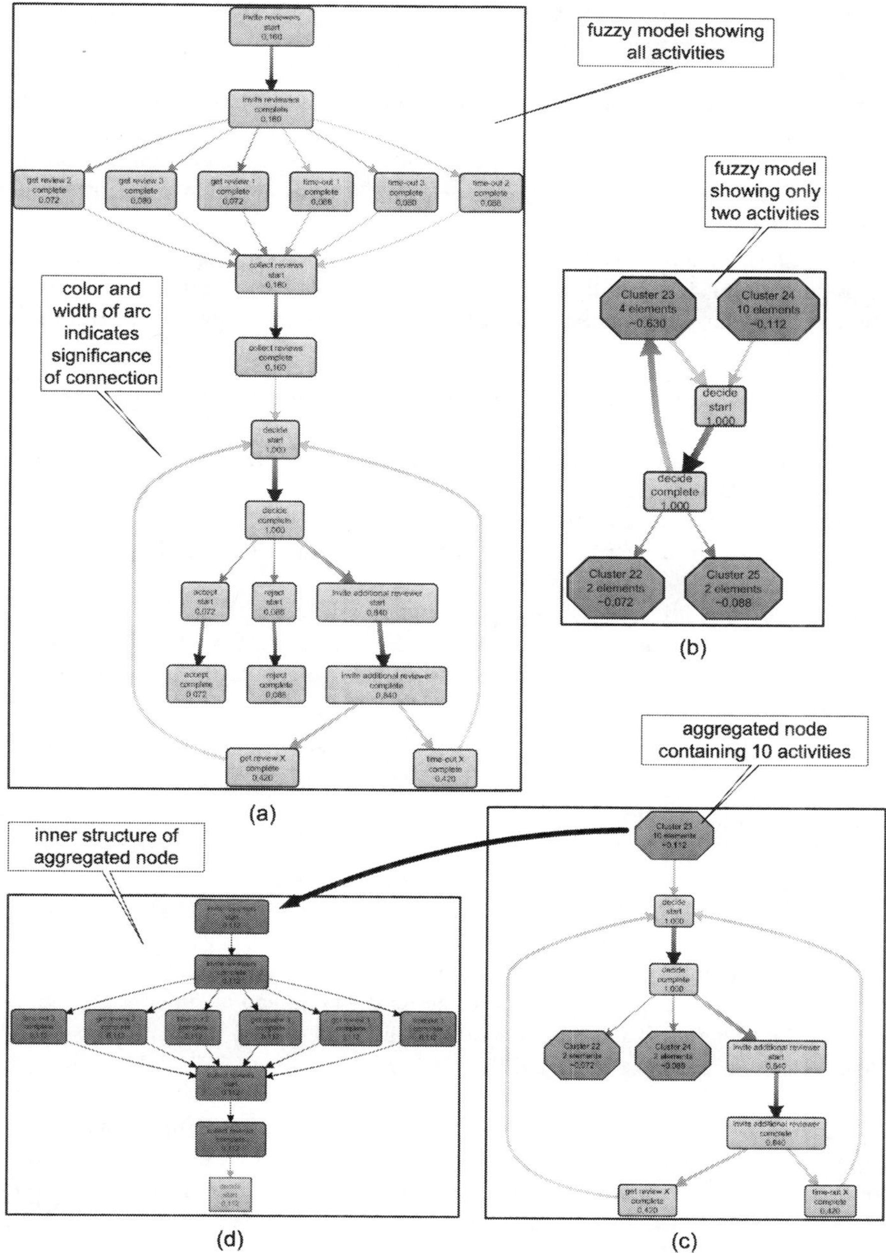

Fig. 13.7 Three business process maps obtained using ProM's Fuzzy Miner. The most detailed fuzzy model **(a)** shows all activities. The least detailed fuzzy model (**b**) shows only two activities; all other activities are aggregated into so-called "cluster nodes". The third fuzzy model (**c**) shows six activities. For one of the aggregate nodes, the inner structure is shown (**d**)

All of this is in stark contrast with mainstream process models. The x-axis and y-axis of a process model have no meaning, e.g., the layout of the WF-net shown in Fig. 13.6 was generated automatically without assigning any semantics to the positions of activities. Although modeling tools allow for using colors, the color typically has no semantics. The different types of model elements (e.g., activities, gateways, events, connectors, and places) typically have a default color. Moreover, the size of a model element also has no semantics. Typically all elements of a particular type have the same size.

Because size, color, and layout are not employed when creating business process maps, the result is less intuitive and less informative. However, ideas from cartography can easily be incorporated in the construction of business process maps. Some examples:

- The *size of an activity* can reflect its frequency or some other property indicating its significance (e.g., costs or resource use).
- The *color of an activity* can reflect the mean service time of the activity. For example, activities that take longer than average are colored red whereas short running activities are colored green.
- The *width of an arc* can reflect the importance of the corresponding causal dependency.
- The *coloring of arcs* can be used to highlight bottlenecks.
- The *positioning of activities* can have a well-defined meaning. Similar to swimlanes the y-axis could reflect the role associated to an activity. Similar to a Gantt chart, the x-axis could reflect some temporal aspect.

It is important to use these conventions in a consistent manner across different maps.

13.1.5 Customization

The same geographic area is typically covered by many different maps. There are different maps depending on the type of activity they intend to support, e.g., bicycle maps, hiking maps, and road maps. Obviously, these maps use different scales. However, there are more differences. For instance, a bicycle map shows bicycle paths that are not shown on motorists' map.

Figure 13.7 illustrates that multiple views can be created for the same reality captured in an event log. In earlier chapters, we already showed that there is no such thing as *the* process model describing a process. Depending on the questions, one seeks to answer, a customized process model needs to be created. In Sect. 5.4.4, we referred to this as taking a "2-D slice of a 3-D reality". The same process can be viewed from different angles and at different levels of granularity. For noisy event logs, one may prefer to focus on just the main behavior or also include less frequent behavior. For example, from an auditing point of view the low frequent behavior may be most interesting.

13.2 Process Mining: TomTom for Business Processes?

After comparing geographic maps with business process maps, we now explore the analogy between navigation systems and information systems. Section 9.1.3 already mentioned navigation activities in the context of the refined process mining framework (cf. Fig. 9.1) By establishing a close connection between business process maps and the actual behavior recorded in event logs, it is possible to realize TomTom-like functionality. Analogous to TomTom's navigation devices, process mining tools can help end users (a) by navigating through processes, (b) by projecting dynamic information on process maps (e.g., showing "traffic jams" in business processes), and (c) by providing predictions regarding running cases (e.g., estimating the "arrival time" of a case that is delayed) [94].

13.2.1 Projecting Dynamic Information on Business Process Maps

The navigation systems of TomTom can be equipped with so-called "LIVE services" (cf. www.tomtom.com) showing traffic jams, mobile speed cameras, weather conditions, etc. This information is projected onto the map using current data.

In Chap. 8, we showed that a tight coupling between an event log and a process model can be used to extend process models with additional perspectives, e.g., highlighting bottlenecks, showing decision rules, and relating the process model to organizational entities. The same coupling can also be used to visualize "pre mortem" event data. Information about the current state of running cases can be projected onto the process model.

The idea is analogous to mashups using geo-tagging (e.g., Panoramio, HousingMaps, Funda, and Flickr). Many of these mashups use Google Maps. Consider, for example, the map shown in Fig. 13.8. Prospective customers can visit the site of Funda to look for a house that meets particular criteria. Information about houses that are for sale are projected onto a map. Figure 13.8 shows the houses that are for sale in Hapert. Figure 13.9 shows another example. Now the map shows traffic jams. Both maps are dynamic, i.e., the information projected onto these maps changes continuously.

Both historic and current event data can be used to "breathe life" into otherwise static business process maps. Similar to the visualization of traffic jams in Fig. 13.9, "traffic" in business processes can be visualized. Besides process maps, one can also think of other maps to project information on. Consider, for example, the social networks shown in Figs. 8.6 and 8.7. Work items waiting to be handled can be projected onto these models, e.g., cases that are waiting for a decision by a manager are projected onto the manager role. Some work items also have a geographic component, e.g., a field service engineer could be provided with a map like the one in Fig. 13.8 showing the devices that need maintenance. It is also possible to project work items onto maps with a temporal dimension (Gantt charts, agendas, etc.). For instance, a surgeon could view scheduled operations in his agenda. Hence, a variety of maps covering different perspectives can be used to visualize event related data.

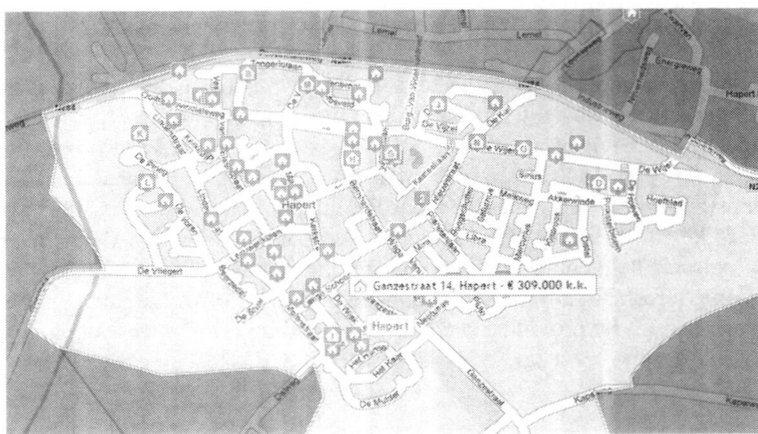

Fig. 13.8 Funda allows users to view maps with houses for sale that meet particular criteria, e.g., constraints related to size, volume, and pricing. The map shows the 53 houses for sale in the Dutch town Hapert

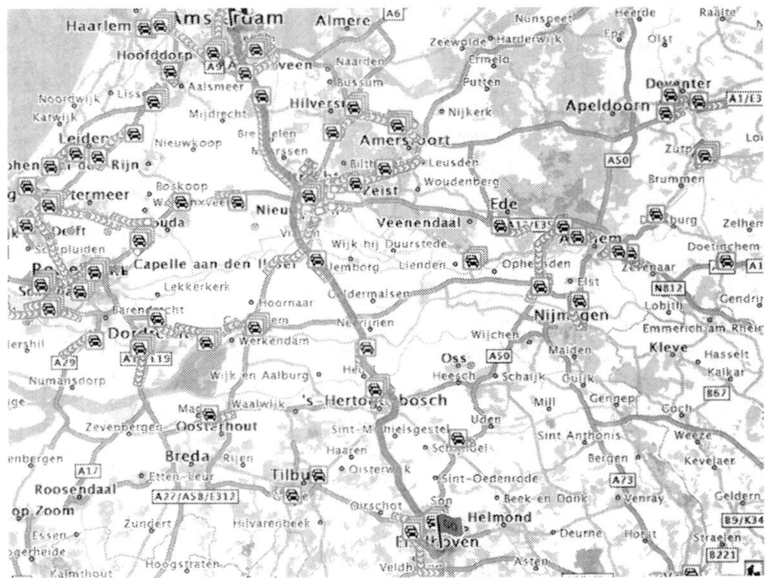

Fig. 13.9 Road map showing traffic jams: the car icons indicate problem spots and congested roads are highlighted. Modern navigation systems show such maps and, based on real-time traffic information, alternative routes are suggested to avoid bottlenecks

The YAWL system [28, 97] provides a visualization framework able to map pending work items and resources onto various maps, e.g., geographic maps, process maps, and organizational maps. YAWL also defines various distance notions based on these maps, for instance, a field service engineer can see the work items closest or most urgent.

From Business Process Maps to Business Process Movies
Once events in the log can be related to activities in the process model, it is possible to replay history on a case-by-case basis. This was used for conformance checking and model extension. Now we go one step further; we do not consider an individual case but all relevant cases at the same time. Assuming that events have a timestamp, all events in the log can be globally ordered, i.e., also events belonging to different cases can be sorted. After each event, the process is in a particular global state. One can think of this state as a *photograph* of the process. The state can be projected onto a business process map, a geographic map, or an organizational map. Since such a photograph is available after each event, it is also possible to create a *movie* by simply showing one photograph after another. Hence, it is possible to use event logs to create a "business process movie". Figure 13.10 shows an example using the ProM's Fuzzy Miner [49, 50]. The event log and the fuzzy model are converted into an animation. The dots visible in Fig. 13.10 are moving along the arcs and refer to real cases. Such a business process movie provides a very convincing means to show problems in the as-is process. Unlike simulation, the animation shows reality and people cannot dismiss the outcomes by questioning the model. Therefore, business process movies help to expose the real problems in an organization.

13.2.2 Arrival Time Prediction

Whereas a TomTom device is continuously showing the *expected arrival time*, users of today's information systems are often left clueless about likely outcomes of the cases they are working on. This is surprising as many information systems gather a lot of historic information, thus providing an excellent basis for all kinds of predictions (expected completion time, likelihood of some undesirable outcome, estimated costs, etc.). Fortunately, as shown in Sect. 9.4, event logs can be used build predictive models.

The annotated transition system [110, 113] described in Sect. 9.4 can be used to predict the remaining flow time of a running case. The transition system is constructed using an event log L and a state representation function $l^{state}()$ or obtained by computing the state-space of a (discovered) process model. By systematically replaying the event log, the states are annotated with historic measurements. The mean or median of these historic measurements can be used to make predictions for running cases in a particular state. Each time the state of a case changes, a new prediction is made for the remaining flow time. Clearly, this functionality is similar to

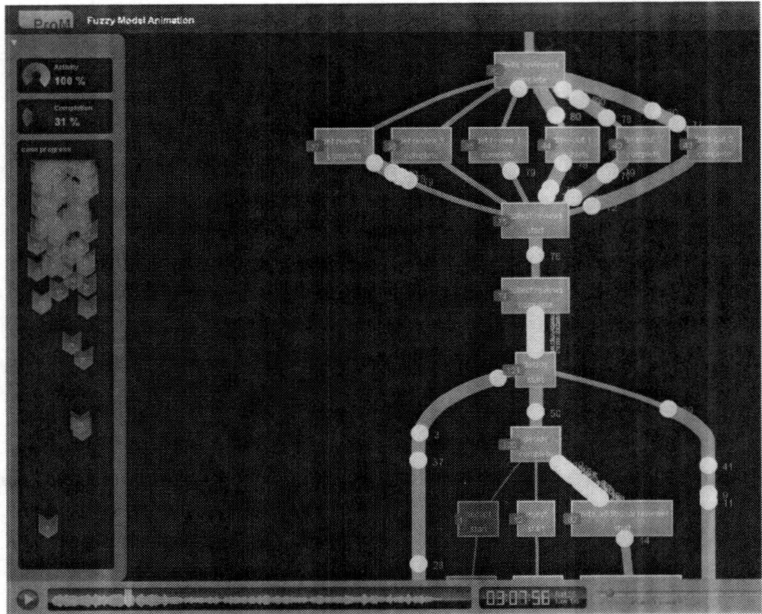

Fig. 13.10 The fuzzy model discovered earlier (cf. Fig. 13.7(a)) is used to replay the event log. The animation reveals the problem that many reviewers do not provide a report in time. As a result, the editor of the journal cannot make a final decision and needs to invite additional reviewers. There is long queue of work items waiting for a decision and many pending invitations

the prediction capabilities of a navigation device. Moreover, using different annotations, other kinds of predictions can be made. For instance, the transition system can be annotated with cost information to predict the total or remaining costs. Similarly, the outcome of a process or occurrence of an activity can be predicted.

Alternative approaches based on regression analysis, short-term simulation, or decision tree learning can be used to predict properties such as the remaining flow time of a running case. This illustrates that process mining can be used to extend information systems with predictive analytics.

13.2.3 Guidance Rather than Control

Car navigation systems provide *directions* and *guidance without controlling* the driver. The driver is still in control, but, given a goal (e.g., to get from A to B as fast as possible), the navigation system recommends the next action to be taken. In Sect. 9.5, we showed that predictions can be turned into recommendations. Recommendations are given with respect to a goal, e.g., to minimize costs, to minimize the remaining flow time, or to maximize the likelihood of success. Such a goal is operationalized by defining a performance indicator that needs to be minimized or maximized. For every possible next action, the value of the performance indicator is predicted. This information is used to rank the possible actions and thus recommend the next step to be taken (cf. Fig. 9.12).

Recommendations based on process mining allow for systems that are flexible but also supporting operational decision making. Today's information systems typically do not provide a good balance between flexibility and support. The system is either restricting people in their actions or not providing any guidance. BPM systems offering more flexibility (e.g., case handling systems like BPM|one or declarative workflow systems like Declare), can be extended with a recommendation service based on process mining techniques [110].

The TomTom metaphor illustrates that many information systems lack functionality present in today's navigation devices [94]. However, high-quality process models tightly coupled to event logs enable TomTom-like functionalities such as predicting the "arrival time" of a process instance, recommending the next activity to be executed, and visualizing "traffic jams" in business processes.

Chapter 14
Epilogue

To conclude this book, we summarize the main reasons for using process mining. Process mining can be seen as the "missing link" between data mining and traditional model-driven BPM. Although mature process mining techniques and tools are available, several challenges remain to further improve the applicability of the techniques presented in the preceding chapters. Therefore, we list the most important challenges. Finally, we encourage the reader to start using process mining today. For organizations that store event data in some form, the threshold to get started is really low.

14.1 Process Mining: A Bridge Between Data Mining and Business Process Management

Process mining is an important tool for modern organizations that need to manage nontrivial operational processes. On the one hand, there is an incredible growth of event data. On the other hand, processes and information need to be aligned perfectly in order to meet requirements related to compliance, efficiency, and customer service. The digital universe and the physical universe are amalgamating into one universe where events are recorded as they happen and processes are guided and controlled based on event data.

In *Part* I, we presented the two main disciplines that process mining is building on: Business Process Management (BPM) and data mining. Chapter 2 introduced several process modeling techniques and discussed the role of process models in the context of BPM. In Chap. 3, we introduced some of the basic data mining techniques.

Classical BPM approaches use process models as static descriptions or to drive a BPM/WFM system. If process models are just descriptive, they tend to be informal and of low quality (i.e., not describing reality well). If models are used to configure a BPM/WFM system, they tend to force people to work in a particular manner. Data mining techniques aim to describe and understand reality based on historic data.

W.M.P. van der Aalst, *Process Mining*,
DOI 10.1007/978-3-642-19345-3_14, © Springer-Verlag Berlin Heidelberg 2011

However, most data mining techniques are *not* process-centric. Fortunately, process mining provides a link between both disciplines. Like other BPM approaches, process mining is process-centric. However, unlike most BPM approaches, it is driven by factual event data rather than hand-made models. Hence, process mining can be seen as a bridge between the preliminaries presented in Chaps. 2 and 3.

In *Part* II, we focused on the most challenging process mining task: *process discovery*. First, we discussed the input needed for process mining (Chap. 4). Then, we presented a very basic algorithm (Chap. 5) followed by an overview of more powerful process discovery techniques (Chap. 6). Unlike basic data mining techniques such as decision tree and association rule learning, process discovery problems are characterized by a complex search space as is illustrated by the many workflow patterns. Whereas the aim of many data mining techniques is to be able to deal with many records or many variables, the main challenge of process discovery is to adequately capture behavioral aspects.

Process mining is not limited to process discovery. In fact, process discovery is just one of many process mining tasks. Therefore, *Part* III expanded the scope of process mining into several directions. These expansions have in common that the event log and the process model are tightly coupled, thus allowing for new forms of analysis and support. Chapter 7 presented various conformance checking techniques. As shown in Chap. 8, the organizational perspective, the case perspective, and the time perspective can be added to discovered process models or used to create complementary models. Recommendations and predictions (based on a combination of historic event data and partial traces of running cases) are examples of the operational support functionalities described in Chap. 9. Chapters 7, 8, and 9 illustrate the breadth of the process mining spectrum.

Part IV aimed to provide useful hints when applying process mining in practice. Chapter 10 discussed tool support for process mining. In Chaps. 11 and 12, we described two types of processes ("Lasagna processes" and "Spaghetti processes") that need to be handled differently.

In this last part (*Part* V), we take a step back and reflect on the material presented in the preceding parts. For example, Chap. 13 compared business process models, business process analysis, and business process support with geographic maps and navigation systems. This comparison revealed limitations of current BPM practices and confirmed the potential of process mining to "breathe life" into process models.

Process mining provides not only a bridge between data mining and BPM; it also helps to address the classical divide between "business" and "IT". IT people tend to have a technology-oriented focus with little consideration for the actual business processes that need to be supported. People focusing on the "business-side" of BPM are typically not interested in technological advances and the precise functionality of information systems. The empirical nature of process mining can bring both groups of people together. Evidence-based BPM based on process mining helps to create a common ground for business process improvement and information systems development.

14.2 Challenges

Existing process mining techniques and tools such as ProM are mature and can be applied to both Lasagna and Spaghetti processes. We have applied ProM in more than 100 organizations ranging from municipalities and hospitals to financial institutions and manufacturers of high-tech systems. Despite the applicability of process mining there are many interesting challenges; these illustrate that process mining is a young discipline.

Process discovery is probably the most important and most visible intellectual challenge related to process mining. As shown, it is far from trivial to construct a process model based on *event logs that are incomplete and noisy*. Unfortunately, there are still researchers and tool vendors that assume logs to be complete and free of noise. Although heuristic mining, genetic mining, and fuzzy mining (cf. Chap. 6) provide case-hardened process discovery techniques, many improvements are possible to construct more intuitive 80/20 *models*, i.e., simple models that are able to explain the most likely/common behavior.

New process mining approaches should reconsider the *representational bias* to be used. Almost all existing approaches use a graph-based notation that can represent models that do not make much sense. WF-nets, BPMN models, EPCs, etc. can represent processes that are not sound, e.g., a process having a deadlock or an activity that can never be activated. The search space of a technique using such a representational bias is too large. For instance, the α-algorithm can discover WF-nets that are not sound and the heuristic miner and the genetic miner can discover C-nets that deadlock. Therefore, the representational bias of discovery techniques should be refined to only allow for sensible process models. Clearly, this is a challenging problem requiring new approaches and representations.

Another challenge is the notion of *concept drift*, i.e., processes change while being observed. Existing process discovery approaches do not take such changes into account. It is interesting to detect when processes change and to visualize such changes.

Process mining heavily depends to the ability to extract suitable event logs. The scope and granularity of an event log should match the questions one would like to answer. Unfortunately, in some information systems event data are just a byproduct for debugging or scattered over many tables. Some systems also "forget" events, e.g., when a record is updated, the old values are simply overwritten. Earlier we used the term *business process provenance* to stress the importance of recording events in such a way that history is recorded correctly and cannot be tampered with. Event logs should be "first-class citizens" rather than some byproduct. Data elements in events logs should have clear *semantics*. Therefore, developers should not simply insert write statements without a reference to a commonly agreed-upon *ontology*. We encountered systems where parts of the logging depend on the language setting. For example, depending on the language setting of the system, an event attribute may have value "Off" in English, "Uit" in Dutch, or "Aus" in German. Semantically, these are all the same. However, such ad-hoc logging is making analysis more complex. Attributes of events and cases should refer to one or more ontologies that clearly define concepts and possible attribute values. Logging formats such as XES and SA-MXML (cf. Chap. 4) can relate event data to ontologies. However, the challenge is to make sure that organizations actually start using semantically annotated event logs.

Another challenge is produce process models that have a quality and understandability comparable to geographic maps. As shown in Chap. 13, we can learn many lessons from cartography.

Process mining can be used off-line and online. For off-line process mining, only historic ("post mortem") data is needed and no tight coupling between the process mining software and existing enterprise information systems is needed. For online process mining (e.g., providing predictions and recommendations), operational support capabilities need to be embedded in enterprise information systems. From a technological point of view this may be challenging. It is difficult to embed such advanced functionality in legacy systems. Moreover, online process mining typically requires additional computing power. It is important to overcome these challenges as the value of operational support based on process mining is evident (cf. Chap. 9). For example, a process model showing the current status of running cases is much more interesting than a static process model not showing any "live data".

14.3 Start Today!

As demonstrated in this book, process mining can be brought into play for many different purposes. Process mining can be used to diagnose the actual processes. This is valuable because in many organizations most stakeholders lack a correct, objective, and accurate view on important operational processes. Process mining can subsequently be used to improve such processes. Conformance checking can be used for auditing and compliance. By replaying the event log on a process model, it is possible to quantify and visualize deviations. Similar techniques can be used to detect bottlenecks and build predictive models. Given the applicability of process mining, we hope that this book encourages the reader to start using process mining *today*.

The threshold to start an off-line process mining project is really low. Most organizations have event data hidden in their systems. Once the data is located, conversion is typically easy. For instance, software tools such as ProMimport, Nitro, XESame, and OpenXES support the conversion of different sources to MXML or XES. The freely available open-source process mining tool ProM can be downloaded from www.processmining.org. ProM can be applied to any MXML or XES file and supports all of the process mining techniques mentioned in the preceding chapters. After reading this book, installing the software, and extracting the event data, the reader is able experience the "magic" of process mining, i.e., discovering and improving processes based on facts rather than fiction.

References

1. ACSI. Artifact-Centric Service Interoperation (ACSI) Project Home Page. www.acsi-project.eu.
2. A. Adriansyah, B.F. van Dongen, and W.M.P. van der Aalst. Towards Robust Conformance Checking. In J. Su and M. zur Muehlen, editors, *BPM 2010 Workshops, Proceedings of the 6th Workshop on Business Process Intelligence (BPI2010), Lecture Notes in Business Information Processing*. Springer, Berlin, 2011.
3. R. Agrawal and R. Srikant. Fast Algorithms for Mining Association Rules in Large Databases. In *Proceedings of the 20th International Conference on Very Large Data Bases (VLDB)*, pages 487–499, Santiago de Chile, Chile, 1994. Morgan Kaufmann, San Mateo, CA, 1994.
4. R. Agrawal, D. Gunopulos, and F. Leymann. Mining Process Models from Workflow Logs. In *6th International Conference on Extending Database Technology*, volume 1377 of *Lecture Notes in Computer Science*, pages 469–483. Springer, Berlin, 1998.
5. E. Alpaydin. *Introduction to Machine Learning*. MIT Press, Cambridge, MA, 2010.
6. D. Angluin and C.H. Smith. Inductive Inference: Theory and Methods. *Computing Surveys*, 15(3):237–269, 1983.
7. E. Badouel and P. Darondeau. Theory of Regions. In W. Reisig and G. Rozenberg, editors, *Lectures on Petri Nets I: Basic Models*, volume 1491 of *Lecture Notes in Computer Science*, pages 529–586. Springer, Berlin, 1998.
8. R. Bergenthum, J. Desel, R. Lorenz, and S. Mauser. Process Mining Based on Regions of Languages. In G. Alonso, P. Dadam, and M. Rosemann, editors, *International Conference on Business Process Management (BPM 2007)*, volume 4714 of *Lecture Notes in Computer Science*, pages 375–383. Springer, Berlin, 2007.
9. A.W. Biermann. On the Inference of Turing Machines from Sample Computations. *Artificial Intelligence*, 3:181–198, 1972.
10. A.W. Biermann and J.A. Feldman. On the Synthesis of Finite-State Machines from Samples of Their Behavior. *IEEE Transaction on Computers*, 21:592–597, 1972.
11. T. Blickle, H. Hess, J. Klueckmann, M. Lees, and B. Williams. *Process Intelligence for Dummies*. Wiley, New York, NY, 2010.
12. R.P.J.C. Bose and W.M.P. van der Aalst. Context Aware Trace Clustering: Towards Improving Process Mining Results. In H. Liu and Z. Obradovic, editors, *Proceedings of the SIAM International Conference on Data Mining (SDM 2009)*, pages 401–412. Society for Industrial and Applied Mathematics, Philadelphia, PA, 2009.
13. R.P.J.C. Bose and W.M.P. van der Aalst. Abstractions in Process Mining: A Taxonomy of Patterns. In U. Dayal, J. Eder, J. Koehler, and H. Reijers, editors, *Business Process Management (BPM 2009)*, volume 5701 of *Lecture Notes in Computer Science*, pages 159–175. Springer, Berlin, 2009.

W.M.P. van der Aalst, *Process Mining*,
DOI 10.1007/978-3-642-19345-3, © Springer-Verlag Berlin Heidelberg 2011

14. R.P.J.C. Bose and W.M.P. van der Aalst. Trace Alignment in Process Mining: Opportunities for Process Diagnostics. In R. Hull, J. Mendling, and S. Tai, editors, *Business Process Management (BPM 2010)*, volume 6336 of *Lecture Notes in Computer Science*, pages 227–242. Springer, Berlin, 2010.
15. M. Bramer. *Principles of Data Mining*. Springer, Berlin, 2007.
16. C. Bratosin, N. Sidorova, and W.M.P. van der Aalst. Distributed Genetic Process Mining. In H. Ishibuchi, editor, *IEEE World Congress on Computational Intelligence (WCCI 2010)*, pages 1951–1958, Barcelona, Spain, July 2010. IEEE Press, New York, NY, 2010.
17. A. Burattin and A. Sperduti. PLG: A Framework for the Generation of Business Process Models and Their Execution Logs. In J. Su and M. zur Muehlen, editors, *BPM 2010 Workshops, Proceedings of the 6th Workshop on Business Process Intelligence (BPI2010), Lecture Notes in Business Information Processing*. Springer, Berlin, 2011.
18. J. Carmona and J. Cortadella. Process Mining Meets Abstract Interpretation. In J.L. Balcazar, editor, *ECML/PKDD 2010*, volume 6321 of *Lecture Notes in Artificial Intelligence*, pages 184–199. Springer, Berlin, 2010.
19. P. Chapman, J. Clinton, R. Kerber, T. Khabaza, T. Reinartz, C. Shearer, and R. Wirth. CRISP-DM 1.0: Step-by-Step Data Mining Guide. www.crisp-dm.org, 2000.
20. E.M. Clarke, O. Grumberg, and D.A. Peled. *Model Checking*. MIT Press, Cambridge, MA, 1999.
21. B.D. Clinton and A. van der Merwe. Management Accounting: Approaches, Techniques, and Management Processes. *Cost Management*, 20(3):14–22, 2006.
22. J.E. Cook and A.L. Wolf. Discovering Models of Software Processes from Event-Based Data. *ACM Transactions on Software Engineering and Methodology*, 7(3):215–249, 1998.
23. J. Cortadella, M. Kishinevsky, L. Lavagno, and A. Yakovlev. Deriving Petri Nets from Finite Transition Systems. *IEEE Transactions on Computers*, 47(8):859–882, 1998.
24. CoSeLoG. Configurable Services for Local Governments (CoSeLoG) Project Home Page. www.win.tue.nl/coselog.
25. T. Curran and G. Keller. *SAP R/3 Business Blueprint: Understanding the Business Process Reference Model*. Prentice-Hall, Upper Saddle River, NJ, 1997.
26. A. Datta. Automating the Discovery of As-Is Business Process Models: Probabilistic and Algorithmic Approaches. *Information Systems Research*, 9(3):275–301, 1998.
27. S. Davidson, S. Cohen-Boulakia, A. Eyal, B. Ludaescher, T. McPhillips, S. Bowers, M. Anand, and J. Freire. Provenance in Scientific Workflow Systems. *Data Engineering Bulletin*, 30(4):44–50, 2007.
28. M. de Leoni, W.M.P. van der Aalst, and A.H.M. ter Hofstede. Visual Support for Work Assignment in Process-Aware Information Systems. In M. Dumas, M. Reichert, and M.C. Shan, editors, *International Conference on Business Process Management (BPM 2008)*, volume 5240 of *Lecture Notes in Computer Science*, pages 67–83. Springer, Berlin, 2008.
29. A.K.A de Medeiros. *Genetic Process Mining*. PhD Thesis, Eindhoven University of Technology, 2006.
30. A.K.A. de Medeiros, W.M.P. van der Aalst, and A.J.M.M. Weijters. Workflow Mining: Current Status and Future Directions. In R. Meersman, Z. Tari, and D.C. Schmidt, editors, *On the Move to Meaningful Internet Systems 2003: CoopIS, DOA, and ODBASE*, volume 2888 of *Lecture Notes in Computer Science*, pages 389–406. Springer, Berlin, 2003.
31. A.K.A de Medeiros, A.J.M.M. Weijters, and W.M.P. van der Aalst. Genetic Process Mining: An Experimental Evaluation. *Data Mining and Knowledge Discovery*, 14(2):245–304, 2007.
32. A.K.A de Medeiros, A. Guzzo, G. Greco, W.M.P. van der Aalst, A.J.M.M. Weijters, B. van Dongen, and D. Sacca. Process Mining Based on Clustering: A Quest for Precision. In A. ter Hofstede, B. Benatallah, and H.Y. Paik, editors, *BPM 2007 International Workshops (BPI, BPD, CBP, ProHealth, RefMod, Semantics4ws)*, volume 4928 of *Lecture Notes in Computer Science*, pages 17–29. Springer, Berlin, 2008.
33. A.K.A. de Medeiros, W.M.P. van der Aalst, and A.J.M.M. Weijters. Quantifying Process Equivalence Based on Observed Behavior. *Data and Knowledge Engineering*, 64(1):55–74, 2008.

34. J. Desel and J. Esparza. *Free Choice Petri Nets*, volume 40 of *Cambridge Tracts in Theoretical Computer Science*. Cambridge University Press, Cambridge, 1995.
35. J. Desel, W. Reisig, and G. Rozenberg, editors. *Lectures on Concurrency and Petri Nets*, volume 3098 of *Lecture Notes in Computer Science*. Springer, Berlin, 2004.
36. P.C. Diniz and D.R. Ferreira. Automatic Extraction of Process Control Flow from I/O Operations. In M. Dumas, M. Reichert, and M.C. Shan, editors, *Business Process Management (BPM 2008)*, volume 5240 of *Lecture Notes in Computer Science*, pages 342–357. Springer, Berlin, 2008.
37. M. Dumas, W.M.P. van der Aalst, and A.H.M. ter Hofstede. *Process-Aware Information Systems: Bridging People and Software through Process Technology*. Wiley, New York, NY, 2005.
38. A. Ehrenfeucht and G. Rozenberg. Partial (Set) 2-Structures—Part 1 and Part 2. *Acta Informatica*, 27(4):315–368, 1989.
39. D.R. Ferreira and D. Gillblad. Discovering Process Models from Unlabelled Event Logs. In U. Dayal, J. Eder, J. Koehler, and H. Reijers, editors, *Business Process Management (BPM 2009)*, volume 5701 of *Lecture Notes in Computer Science*, pages 143–158. Springer, Berlin, 2009.
40. Forrester. The Forrester Wave: Enterprise Business Intelligence Platforms (Q4 2010). www.forrester.com, 2010.
41. Gartner. Magic Quadrant for Business Intelligence Platforms. www.gartner.com, 2010.
42. Gartner. Magic Quadrant for Business Process Management Suites. www.gartner.com, 2010.
43. S. Goedertier, D. Martens, B. Baesens, R. Haesen, and J. Vanthienen. Process Mining as First-Order Classification Learning on Logs with Negative Events. In A. ter Hofstede, B. Benatallah, and H.Y. Paik, editors, *BPM 2007 International Workshops (BPI, BPD, CBP, ProHealth, RefMod, Semantics4ws)*, volume 4928 of *Lecture Notes in Computer Science*, pages 42–53. Springer, Berlin, 2008.
44. S. Goedertier, D. Martens, J. Vanthienen, and B. Baesens. Robust Process Discovery with Artificial Negative Events. *Journal of Machine Learning Research*, 10:1305–1340, 2009.
45. E.M. Gold. Language Identification in the Limit. *Information and Control*, 10(5):447–474, 1967.
46. G. Greco, A. Guzzo, L. Pontieri, and D. Saccà. Discovering Expressive Process Models by Clustering Log Traces. *IEEE Transaction on Knowledge and Data Engineering*, 18(8):1010–1027, 2006.
47. P.D. Grünwald. *Minimum Description Length Principle*. MIT Press, Cambridge, MA, 2007.
48. C.W. Günther. XES Standard Definition. www.xes-standard.org, 2009.
49. C.W. Günther. *Process Mining in Flexible Environments*. PhD Thesis, Eindhoven University of Technology, September 2009.
50. C.W. Günther and W.M.P. van der Aalst. Fuzzy Mining: Adaptive Process Simplification Based on Multi-Perspective Metrics. In G. Alonso, P. Dadam, and M. Rosemann, editors, *International Conference on Business Process Management (BPM 2007)*, volume 4714 of *Lecture Notes in Computer Science*, pages 328–343. Springer, Berlin, 2007.
51. C.W. Günther, A. Rozinat, W.M.P. van der Aalst, and K. van Uden. Monitoring Deployed Application Usage with Process Mining. BPM Center Report BPM-08-11, BPMcenter.org, 2008.
52. D. Hand, H. Mannila, and P. Smyth. *Principles of Data Mining*. MIT Press, Cambridge, MA, 2001.
53. D. Harel and R. Marelly. *Come, Let's Play: Scenario-Based Programming Using LSCs and the Play-Engine*. Springer, Berlin, 2003.
54. J. Herbst. A Machine Learning Approach to Workflow Management. In *Proceedings 11th European Conference on Machine Learning*, volume 1810 of *Lecture Notes in Computer Science*, pages 183–194. Springer, Berlin, 2000.
55. J. Herbst. *Ein induktiver Ansatz zur Akquisition und Adaption von Workflow-Modellen*. PhD Thesis, Universität Ulm, November 2001.
56. IDC iView. *The Digital Universe Decade—Are You Ready?* International Data Corporation, Framingham, MA, 2010. http://www.emc.com/digital_universe.

57. S. Jablonski and C. Bussler. *Workflow Management: Modeling Concepts, Architecture, and Implementation*. International Thomson Computer Press, London, 1996.
58. K. Jensen and L.M. Kristensen. *Coloured Petri Nets*. Springer, Berlin, 2009.
59. S.C. Kleene. Representation of Events in Nerve Nets and Finite Automata. In C.E. Shannon and J. McCarthy, editors, *Automata Studies*, pages 3–41. Princeton University Press, Princeton, NJ, 1956.
60. E. Lamma, P. Mello, M. Montali, F. Riguzzi, and S. Storari. Inducing Declarative Logic-Based Models from Labeled Traces. In G. Alonso, P. Dadam, and M. Rosemann, editors, *International Conference on Business Process Management (BPM 2007)*, volume 4714 of *Lecture Notes in Computer Science*, pages 344–359. Springer, Berlin, 2007.
61. F. Leymann and D. Roller. *Production Workflow: Concepts and Techniques*. Prentice-Hall, Upper Saddle River, NJ, 1999.
62. Z. Manna and A. Pnueli. *The Temporal Logic of Reactive and Concurrent Systems: Specification*. Springer, New York, NY, 1991.
63. H. Mannila, H. Toivonen, and A.I. Verkamo. Discovery of Frequent Episodes in Event Sequences. *Data Mining and Knowledge Discovery*, 1(3):259–289, 1997.
64. R.S. Mans, M.H. Schonenberg, M. Song, W.M.P. van der Aalst, and P.J.M. Bakker. Application of Process Mining in Healthcare: A Case Study in a Dutch Hospital. In *Biomedical Engineering Systems and Technologies*, volume 25 of *Communications in Computer and Information Science*, pages 425–438. Springer, Berlin, 2009.
65. R.S. Mans, N.C. Russell, W.M.P. van der Aalst, A.J. Moleman, and P.J.M. Bakker. Schedule-Aware Workflow Management Systems. In K. Jensen, S. Donatelli, and M. Koutny, editors, *Transactions on Petri Nets and Other Models of Concurrency IV*, volume 6550 of *Lecture Notes in Computer Science*, pages 121–143. Springer, Berlin, 2010.
66. J. Mendling, G. Neumann, and W.M.P. van der Aalst. Understanding the Occurrence of Errors in Process Models Based on Metrics. In F. Curbera, F. Leymann, and M. Weske, editors, *Proceedings of the OTM Conference on Cooperative Information Systems (CoopIS 2007)*, volume 4803 of *Lecture Notes in Computer Science*, pages 113–130. Springer, Berlin, 2007.
67. T.M. Mitchell. *Machine Learning*. McGraw-Hill, New York, NY, 1997.
68. M. Montali, M. Pesic, W.M.P. van der Aalst, F. Chesani, P. Mello, and S. Storari. Declarative Specification and Verification of Service Choreographies. *ACM Transactions on the Web*, 4(1):1–62, 2010.
69. H.R. Motahari-Nezhad, R. Saint-Paul, B. Benatallah, and F. Casati. Deriving Protocol Models from Imperfect Service Conversation Logs. *IEEE Transactions on Knowledge and Data Engineering*, 20(12):1683–1698, 2008.
70. J. Munoz-Gama and J. Carmona. A Fresh Look at Precision in Process Conformance. In R. Hull, J. Mendling, and S. Tai, editors, *Business Process Management (BPM 2010)*, volume 6336 of *Lecture Notes in Computer Science*, pages 211–226. Springer, Berlin, 2010.
71. A. Nerode. Linear Automaton Transformations. *Proceedings of the American Mathematical Society*, 9(4):541–544, 1958.
72. OMG. Business Process Model and Notation (BPMN). Object Management Group, dtc/2010-06-05, 2010.
73. C.A. Petri. *Kommunikation mit Automaten*. PhD Thesis, Institut für instrumentelle Mathematik, Bonn, 1962.
74. PoSecCo. Policy and Security Configuration Management (PoSecCo) Project Home Page. www.posecco.eu.
75. T. Pyzdek. *The Six Sigma Handbook: A Complete Guide for Green Belts, Black Belts, and Managers at All Levels*. McGraw Hill, New York, NY, 2003.
76. H.A. Reijers and W.M.P. van der Aalst. The Effectiveness of Workflow Management Systems: Predictions and Lessons Learned. *International Journal of Information Management*, 25(5):458–472, 2005.
77. W. Reisig and G. Rozenberg, editors. *Lectures on Petri Nets I: Basic Models*, volume 1491 of *Lecture Notes in Computer Science*. Springer, Berlin, 1998.
78. A. Rozinat. *Process Mining: Conformance and Extension*. PhD Thesis, Eindhoven University of Technology, November 2010.

79. A. Rozinat and W.M.P. van der Aalst. Decision Mining in ProM. In S. Dustdar, J.L. Fiadeiro, and A. Sheth, editors, *International Conference on Business Process Management (BPM 2006)*, volume 4102 of *Lecture Notes in Computer Science*, pages 420–425. Springer, Berlin, 2006.
80. A. Rozinat and W.M.P. van der Aalst. Conformance Checking of Processes Based on Monitoring Real Behavior. *Information Systems*, 33(1):64–95, 2008.
81. A. Rozinat, A.K.A. de Medeiros, C.W. Günther, A.J.M.M. Weijters, and W.M.P. van der Aalst. The Need for a Process Mining Evaluation Framework in Research and Practice. In A. ter Hofstede, B. Benatallah, and H.Y. Paik, editors, *BPM 2007 International Workshops (BPI, BPD, CBP, ProHealth, RefMod, Semantics4ws)*, volume 4928 of *Lecture Notes in Computer Science*, pages 84–89. Springer, Berlin, 2008.
82. A. Rozinat, I.S.M. de Jong, C.W. Günther, and W.M.P. van der Aalst. Process Mining Applied to the Test Process of Wafer Scanners in ASML. *IEEE Transactions on Systems, Man and Cybernetics. Part C*, 39(4):474–479, 2009.
83. A. Rozinat, R.S. Mans, M. Song, and W.M.P. van der Aalst. Discovering Simulation Models. *Information Systems*, 34(3):305–327, 2009.
84. A. Rozinat, M. Wynn, W.M.P. van der Aalst, A.H.M. ter Hofstede, and C. Fidge. Workflow Simulation for Operational Decision Support. *Data and Knowledge Engineering*, 68(9):834–850, 2009.
85. A.W. Scheer. *Business Process Engineering, Reference Models for Industrial Enterprises*. Springer, Berlin, 1994.
86. M. Sole and J. Carmona. Process Mining from a Basis of Regions. In J. Lilius and W. Penczek, editors, *Applications and Theory of Petri Nets 2010*, volume 6128 of *Lecture Notes in Computer Science*, pages 226–245. Springer, Berlin, 2010.
87. M. Song and W.M.P. van der Aalst. Supporting Process Mining by Showing Events at a Glance. In K. Chari and A. Kumar, editors, *Proceedings of 17th Annual Workshop on Information Technologies and Systems (WITS 2007)*, pages 139–145, Montreal, Canada, 2007.
88. M. Song and W.M.P. van der Aalst. Towards Comprehensive Support for Organizational Mining. *Decision Support Systems*, 46(1):300–317, 2008.
89. R. Srikant and R. Agrawal. Mining Sequential Patterns: Generalization and Performance Improvements. In *Proceedings of the 5th International Conference on Extending Database Technology (EDBT '96)*, pages 3–17, 1996.
90. A.H.M. ter Hofstede, W.M.P. van der Aalst, M. Adams, and N. Russell. *Modern Business Process Automation: YAWL and Its Support Environment*. Springer, Berlin, 2010.
91. A. Valmari. The State Explosion Problem. In W. Reisig and G. Rozenberg, editors, *Lectures on Petri Nets I: Basic Models*, volume 1491 of *Lecture Notes in Computer Science*, pages 429–528. Springer, Berlin, 1998.
92. W.M.P. van der Aalst. The Application of Petri Nets to Workflow Management. *The Journal of Circuits, Systems and Computers*, 8(1):21–66, 1998.
93. W.M.P. van der Aalst. Business Process Management Demystified: A Tutorial on Models, Systems and Standards for Workflow Management. In J. Desel, W. Reisig, and G. Rozenberg, editors, *Lectures on Concurrency and Petri Nets*, volume 3098 of *Lecture Notes in Computer Science*, pages 1–65. Springer, Berlin, 2004.
94. W.M.P. van der Aalst. Using Process Mining to Generate Accurate and Interactive Business Process Maps. In A. Abramowicz and D. Flejter, editors, *Business Information Systems (BIS 2009) Workshops*, volume 37 of *Lecture Notes in Business Information Processing*, pages 1–14. Springer, Berlin, 2009.
95. W.M.P. van der Aalst. Business Process Simulation Revisited. In J. Barjis, editor, *Enterprise and Organizational Modeling and Simulation*, volume 63 of *Lecture Notes in Business Information Processing*, pages 1–14. Springer, Berlin, 2010.
96. W.M.P. van der Aalst and C. Stahl. *Modeling Business Processes: A Petri Net Oriented Approach*. MIT Press, Cambridge, MA, 2011.
97. W.M.P. van der Aalst and A.H.M. ter Hofstede. YAWL: Yet Another Workflow Language. *Information Systems*, 30(4):245–275, 2005.

98. W.M.P. van der Aalst and K.M. van Hee. *Workflow Management: Models, Methods, and Systems*. MIT Press, Cambridge, MA, 2004.
99. W.M.P. van der Aalst, P. Barthelmess, C.A. Ellis, and J. Wainer. Proclets: A Framework for Lightweight Interacting Workflow Processes. *International Journal of Cooperative Information Systems*, 10(4):443–482, 2001.
100. W.M.P. van der Aalst, J. Desel, and E. Kindler. On the Semantics of EPCs: A Vicious Circle. In M. Nüttgens and F.J. Rump, editors, *Proceedings of the EPK 2002: Business Process Management Using EPCs*, pages 71–80, Trier, Germany, November 2002. Gesellschaft für Informatik, Bonn, 2002.
101. W.M.P. van der Aalst, A.H.M. ter Hofstede, B. Kiepuszewski, and A.P. Barros. Workflow Patterns. *Distributed and Parallel Databases*, 14(1):5–51, 2003.
102. W.M.P. van der Aalst, B.F. van Dongen, J. Herbst, L. Maruster, G. Schimm, and A.J.M.M. Weijters. Workflow Mining: A Survey of Issues and Approaches. *Data and Knowledge Engineering*, 47(2):237–267, 2003.
103. W.M.P. van der Aalst, A.J.M.M. Weijters, and L. Maruster. Workflow Mining: Discovering Process Models from Event Logs. *IEEE Transactions on Knowledge and Data Engineering*, 16(9):1128–1142, 2004.
104. W.M.P. van der Aalst, H.A. Reijers, and M. Song. Discovering Social Networks from Event Logs. *Computer Supported Cooperative Work*, 14(6):549–593, 2005.
105. W.M.P. van der Aalst, H.T. de Beer, and B.F. van Dongen. Process Mining and Verification of Properties: An Approach Based on Temporal Logic. In R. Meersman and Z. Tari et al., editors, *On the Move to Meaningful Internet Systems 2005: CoopIS, DOA, and ODBASE: OTM Confederated International Conferences, CoopIS, DOA, and ODBASE 2005*, volume 3760 of *Lecture Notes in Computer Science*, pages 130–147. Springer, Berlin, 2005.
106. W.M.P. van der Aalst, H.A. Reijers, A.J.M.M. Weijters, B.F. van Dongen, A.K.A. de Medeiros, M. Song, and H.M.W. Verbeek. Business Process Mining: An Industrial Application. *Information Systems*, 32(5):713–732, 2007.
107. W.M.P. van der Aalst, M. Dumas, C. Ouyang, A. Rozinat, and H.M.W. Verbeek. Conformance Checking of Service Behavior. *ACM Transactions on Internet Technology*, 8(3):29–59, 2008.
108. W.M.P. van der Aalst, M. Pesic, and H. Schonenberg. Declarative Workflows: Balancing Between Flexibility and Support. *Computer Science—Research and Development*, 23(2):99–113, 2009.
109. W.M.P. van der Aalst, J. Nakatumba, A. Rozinat, and N. Russell. Business Process Simulation. In J. vom Brocke and M. Rosemann, editors, *Handbook on Business Process Management, International Handbooks on Information Systems*, pages 313–338. Springer, Berlin, 2010.
110. W.M.P. van der Aalst, M. Pesic, and M. Song. Beyond Process Mining: From the Past to Present and Future. In B. Pernici, editor, *Advanced Information Systems Engineering, Proceedings of the 22nd International Conference on Advanced Information Systems Engineering (CAiSE'10)*, volume 6051 of *Lecture Notes in Computer Science*, pages 38–52. Springer, Berlin, 2010.
111. W.M.P. van der Aalst, V. Rubin, H.M.W. Verbeek, B.F. van Dongen, E. Kindler, and C.W. Günther. Process Mining: A Two-Step Approach to Balance Between Underfitting and Overfitting. *Software and Systems Modeling*, 9(1):87–111, 2010.
112. W.M.P. van der Aalst, K.M. van Hee, J.M. van der Werf, and M. Verdonk. Auditing 2.0: Using Process Mining to Support Tomorrow's Auditor. *IEEE Computer*, 43(3):90–93, 2010.
113. W.M.P. van der Aalst, M.H. Schonenberg, and M. Song. Time Prediction Based on Process Mining. *Information Systems*, 36(2):450–475, 2011.
114. W.M.P. van der Aalst, K.M. van Hee, A.H.M. ter Hofstede, N. Sidorova, H.M.W. Verbeek, M. Voorhoeve, and M.T. Wynn. Soundness of Workflow Nets: Classification, Decidability, and Analysis. *Formal Aspects of Computing*, 2011. 10.1007/s00165-010-0161-4.
115. J.M.E.M. van der Werf, B.F. van Dongen, C.A.J. Hurkens, and A. Serebrenik. Process Discovery Using Integer Linear Programming. *Fundamenta Informaticae*, 94:387–412, 2010.

116. B.F. van Dongen. *Process Mining and Verification*. PhD Thesis, Eindhoven University of Technology, 2007.
117. B.F. van Dongen and W.M.P. van der Aalst. Multi-Phase Process Mining: Building Instance Graphs. In P. Atzeni, W. Chu, H. Lu, S. Zhou, and T.W. Ling, editors, *International Conference on Conceptual Modeling (ER 2004)*, volume 3288 of *Lecture Notes in Computer Science*, pages 362–376. Springer, Berlin, 2004.
118. B.F. van Dongen, N. Busi, G.M. Pinna, and W.M.P. van der Aalst. An Iterative Algorithm for Applying the Theory of Regions in Process Mining. In W. Reisig, K. van Hee, and K. Wolf, editors, *Proceedings of the Workshop on Formal Approaches to Business Processes and Web Services (FABPWS'07)*, pages 36–55. Publishing House of University of Podlasie, Siedlce, 2007.
119. B.F. van Dongen, A.K.A. de Medeiros, and L. Wenn. Process Mining: Overview and Outlook of Petri Net Discovery Algorithms. In K. Jensen and W.M.P. van der Aalst, editors, *Transactions on Petri Nets and Other Models of Concurrency II*, volume 5460 of *Lecture Notes in Computer Science*, pages 225–242. Springer, Berlin, 2009.
120. R.J. van Glabbeek and W.P. Weijland. Branching Time and Abstraction in Bisimulation Semantics. *Journal of the ACM*, 43(3):555–600, 1996.
121. H.M.W. Verbeek, T. Basten, and W.M.P. van der Aalst. Diagnosing Workflow Processes Using Woflan. *Computer Journal*, 44(4):246–279, 2001.
122. S. Wasserman and K. Faust. *Social Network Analysis: Methods and Applications*. Cambridge University Press, Cambridge, 1994.
123. A.J.M.M. Weijters and J.T.S. Ribeiro. Flexible Heuristics Miner (FHM). BETA Working Paper Series, WP 334, Eindhoven University of Technology, Eindhoven, 2010.
124. A.J.M.M. Weijters and W.M.P. van der Aalst. Rediscovering Workflow Models from Event-Based Data Using Little Thumb. *Integrated Computer-Aided Engineering*, 10(2):151–162, 2003.
125. L. Wen, W.M.P. van der Aalst, J. Wang, and J. Sun. Mining Process Models with Non-free-Choice Constructs. *Data Mining and Knowledge Discovery*, 15(2):145–180, 2007.
126. L. Wen, J. Wang, W.M.P. van der Aalst, B. Huang, and J. Sun. A Novel Approach for Process Mining Based on Event Types. *Journal of Intelligent Information Systems*, 32(2):163–190, 2009.
127. M. Weske. *Business Process Management: Concepts, Languages, Architectures*. Springer, Berlin, 2007.
128. Wikipedia. Observable Universe. http://en.wikipedia.org/wiki/Observable_universe, 2011.
129. I.H. Witten and E. Frank. *Data Mining: Practical Machine Learning Tools and Techniques* (Second Edition). Morgan Kaufmann, San Mateo, CA, 2005.
130. Workflow Patterns Home Page. http://www.workflowpatterns.com.
131. M. Zur Muehlen and J. Recker. How Much Language Is Enough? Theoretical and Practical Use of the Business Process Modeling Notation. In Z. Bellahsene and M. Léonard, editors, *Proceedings of the 20th International Conference on Advanced Information Systems Engineering (CAiSE'08)*, volume 5074 of *Lecture Notes in Computer Science*, pages 465–479. Springer, Berlin, 2008.

Index

W.M.P. van der Aalst, *Process Mining*,
DOI 10.1007/978-3-642-19345-3,

CPSIA information can be obtained at www.ICGtesting.com
Printed in the USA
LVOW10*0854231114

415184LV00002B/14/P

9 783642 193446